CHINA
and Security
(Pakistan and Central Asia)

Attention A

Manas Publications is
the world that India can w
by the bullet but also by p
fighters into writers. Th
intellectuals in our cou
knowledge is confined to
effort has been made by
channelise their knowled
talent of every intellectu
author always presents t
shape of a manuscript a
publisher to convert it
Manas has been con
intellectuals and publis
for more than two deca
publish your manuscri
colleagues have a m
publication or are wo
with a detailed synops
Manas will also sugges
writing related to your
is known for its publ
utmost care in publish
publicity to the book
our national and int
network.

US-CHINA
Economy and Security

(Including Afghanistan, Pakistan and Central Asia)

US-China Economic and Security
Review Commission

Manas Publications
(We Convert Fighters into Writers)
New Delhi-110002 (INDIA)

MANAS PUBLICATIONS
(Publishers, Distributors, Importers & Exporters)
4402/5-A, Ansari Road
(Opp. HDFC Bank)
Darya Ganj, New Delhi-110 002 (INDIA)
Off. ✆ 23260783, 23265523, Res. ✆ 23842660
Fax: 011-23272766
E-mail: manaspublications@vsnl.com
www.manaspublications.in

ISBN 978-81-7049-378-5
Rs. 995/-

Typeset at
Manas Publications

Printed in India at
R.K. Offset Works, Delhi
and published by Mrs Suman Lata for
Manas Publications, 4402/5-A, Ansari Road
(Opp. HDFC Bank),
Darya Ganj, New Delhi-110 002 (INDIA)

Contents

CHAPTER 4

PREFACE

This is the major Report presented to Congress by the US-China Economic and Security Review Commission. The Report, which is current includes detailed treatment of investigations of the areas identified by Congress for examination and recommendation. These areas are:

(*a*) **Proliferation Practices:** The role of the People's Republic of China in the proliferation of weapons of mass destruction and other weapons (including dual use technologies), including actions the United States might take to encourage the People's Republic of China to cease such practices;

(*b*) **Economic Transfers:** The qualitative and quantitative nature of the transfer of United States production activities to the People's Republic of China, including the relocation of high technology, manufacturing, and research and development facilities, the impact of such transfers on United States national security, the adequacy of United States export control laws, and the effect of such transfers on United States economic security and employment;

(*c*) **Energy:** The effect of the large and growing economy of the People's Republic of China on world energy supplies and the role the United States can play (including joint research and development efforts and technological assistance), in influencing the energy policy of the People's Republic of China;

(*d*) **United States Capital Markets:**The extent of access to and use of United States capital markets by the People's Republic of China, including whether or not existing disclosure and transparency rules are adequate to identify People's Republic of China companies engaged in harmful activities;

(*e*) **Regional Economic and Security Impacts:** The triangular economic and security relationship among the United States, [Taiwan] and the People's Republic of China (including the military modernization and force deployments of the People's Republic of China aimed at [Taiwan]), the national budget of the People's Republic of China, and the fiscal strength of the People's Republic of China in relation to internal instability in the People's Republic of China and the likelihood of the externalization of problems arising from such internal instability;

(*f*) **United States–China Bilateral Programmes**:Science and technology programmes, the degree of noncompliance by the People's Republic of China with agreements between the United States and the People's Republic of China on prison labour imports and intellectual property rights, and United States enforcement policies with respect to such agreements;

(*g*) **World Trade Organization Compliance:**The compliance of the People's Republic of China with its accession agreement to the World Trade Organization (WTO); and

(*h*) **Freedom of Expression:** The implications of restrictions on speech and access to information in the People's Republic of China for its relations with the United States in the areas of economic and security policy.

Executive Summary

The 2009 Annual Report to Congress of the US-China Economic and Security Review Commission sets forth the Commission's analysis of the US-China relationship in the topical areas designated by the Commission's Congressional mandate. These areas are China's proliferation practices, the qualitative and quantitative nature of economic transfers of US production activities to China, the effect of China's development on world energy supplies, the access to and use of US capital markets by China, China's regional economic and security impacts, US-China bilateral programmes and agreements, China's compliance with its accession agreement to the World Trade Organization (WTO), and the implications of China's restrictions on freedom of expression. The Commission's analysis, along with recommendations to the Congress for addressing identified concerns, is chronicled in the Report and summarized herein.

Commission Assessment of US-China Economic and Security Relations

Congress gave the Commission the mission of evaluating "the national security implications of the bilateral trade and economic relationship between the United States and the People's Republic of China" and reporting its evaluation to Congress annually together with its findings. The Commission adopts a broad interpretation of "national security" in evaluating how the US-China relationship affects the economic health and industrial base of the United States and the state of US economic and security interests and influence in Asia.

As in its previous six Annual Reports, the Commission sees progress on some issues but the continuation of a number of troubling trends. The Commission also notes that it continues to stand behind both its conclusions as enunciated in the previous Reports to Congress and its recommendations to Congress contained in those Reports, and it does not routinely repeat either its conclusions or recommendations contained in prior Reports.

Commission Conclusions

The Report presents its conclusions, analyses, and recommendations to Congress in 13 segments organized in four chapters. However, the Commission has attempted to take an integrated approach to its assessments, believing that economic, security, and other issues are interrelated. The intersections of US geopolitical, economic, security, diplomatic, and cultural interests form a complex web of concerns that are connected to the overall relationship between the United States of America and the People's Republic of China.

The Commission's conclusions are included in this Executive Summary. At the end of this summary, the Commission's 10 key recommendations are listed. The Commission makes a total of 42 recommendations to the Congress in this Report. Those pertaining to each of the four Report chapters appear at the conclusion of the chapter.

The US-China Trade and Economic Relationship: The current global economic crisis poses unique challenges for the United States and China. Starting in 2008 and continuing into 2009, global trade and investment flows have been severely impacted, and China, whose economy is very dependent on exports, seemed particularly vulnerable. However, in November 2008, China launched an ambitious stimulus package, 4 trillion renminbi (RMB) ($586 billion) over two years, to help its economy.

The Chinese government is using the money to pursue specific policy initiatives, including infrastructure investment, strengthening of the social safety net, and increasing domestic consumption. The international community has welcomed China's swift response, but doubts remain about the eventual effect that China's stimulus will have. The fact that the government in Beijing is still pursuing an export-led strategy based on a wide variety of subsidies to export industries, including an RMB that remains substantially undervalued, is a cause for concern. If China continues to pursue huge trade and investment surpluses and to accumulate vast financial claims, it will hinder the necessary global economic adjustment, create excess manufacturing capacity, and lay the groundwork for the next crisis. Despite international calls for more market reforms and greater market access, China continues to employ an industrial policy that risks expanding the trade imbalance. China encourages foreign manufacturing to relocate to China and uses strict capital controls to keep the value of the RMB artificially low. China's industrial policy is also aimed at promoting the manufacture of higher-technology products, replacing lower valued-added and labour-intensive products. Indeed, Beijing's industrial policy was a contributing factor to the imbalances that led to the global financial crisis that affected the economies of rich and poor nations alike. Pursuit of export-promoting policies has contributed to China's massive trade surplus and its accumulation of more than $2.27 trillion in foreign exchange reserves by September 2009, the world's largest cache, most of which is in dollar-denominated bonds.

The United States today no longer is the world's biggest creditor; it is the world's biggest debtor, with China as the largest overseas holder of US debt instruments.

Conclusion

The US-China Trade and Economic Relationship's Current Status and Significant changes during 2009:

1. China's trade surplus with the United States remains near record levels, despite the global economic slowdown that has reduced imports from other nations. While the US trade deficit in goods with China through August 2009 was $143.7 billion, representing a decline of 17.6 percent over the same period in 2008, China now accounts for an increasing share of the US global deficit in goods. By September 2009, China had accumulated more than $2.27 trillion in foreign currency reserves.
2. China's currency has strengthened against the US dollar by about 21 percent since the government announced in July 2005 it was transitioning from a hard

peg to the dollar to a "managed float" against a basket of currencies. Starting in July 2008, however, the RMB's appreciation was halted by Chinese government policy as Beijing reimposed strict controls in order to support China's export industries. China's RMB remains significantly undervalued.

3. China's growing cache of dollar reserves, a consequence of a deliberate Chinese government policy, is a continuing source of tension between the two countries. Chinese leaders profess alarm that the value of their dollar cache depends on the health of the US economy and the willingness of the US Federal Reserve system to hold down inflation. On the other hand, the size of China's dollar reserves makes it unlikely that China could divest its dollars without reducing the value of its dollar holdings.
4. The Chinese leadership has become critical of the reserve currency status of the dollar, recommending a greater role for the International Monetary Fund's (IMF) accounting unit, special drawing rights, and perhaps even preparing the RMB for internationalization. For now, the RMB remains nonconvertible. China is also seeking more influence within the IMF.
5. China continues to use trade-distorting measures in violation of its WTO commitments. The WTO found that China failed to comply with its obligations in terms of enforcement of intellectual property rights laws and to provide sufficient market access to intellectual property rights-related products.

China's Role in the Origins of the Global Financial Crisis and China's Response.

6. The current economic crisis, which started in the United States but has now shifted to encompass the entire world, has its roots in the massive global economic imbalances. The responsibility for these imbalances can be placed partially on the United States as the world's biggest spender and borrower and partially on China as the world's biggest saver and lender.
7. China pursues policies that have the effect of increasing Chinese savings, restraining consumption, and keeping the RMB undervalued. These actions boost investment in manufacturing capacity and help to promote Chinese exports. Combined with other export incentives and subsidies, the boom in China's exports helped China accumulate the world's largest foreign exchange reserves, valued at more than $2.27 trillion by the end of September 2009, most of which is invested in US Treasury bonds and other dollar-denominated assets.
8. The policies that China adopted generated a huge flow of liquidity —or money that can be easily lent to borrowers—into US markets. This excess liquidity created perverse incentives in the United States that encouraged banks to make risky loans to US households, which in turn grew ever more indebted. High US demand for imports allowed China to save even more, creating a vicious cycle and laying the foundation for the current crisis.
9. In response to the crisis, China introduced a fiscal stimulus package, raised rebates to exporters, and introduced other measures supporting the manufacturers in the export sector. This will only exacerbate overcapacity, aggravating the overall problem. China has also taken some steps to increase domestic consumption, but they are far outweighed by measures supporting exports. China's

Industrial Policy and its Impact on US Companies, Workers, and the American Economy.

10. China's economic reforms were not based on traditional free market principles. China's policy during the past 30 years has instead relied on a government-directed industrial policy to promote certain segments of the economy over others and to bolster export-led growth.
11. China's more recent Five-Year Plans have shifted the emphasis away from labour-intensive operations and toward increasing the production of high-technology goods. China has matured as a manufacturer and assembler of advanced technology products and as a consumer of electronics and information technology products. The low cost of labour along with government investment in high-tech industrial parks—and a variety of direct and indirect subsidies—created an attractive environment for foreign companies to invest in China, particularly after China joined the WTO in 2001.
12. China provides subsidized land, energy, and water to many foreign manufacturers who relocate their operations in China. By providing these benefits, along with a cheap labour force without the ability to bargain collectively or join independent unions, the Chinese government has created a low-cost haven for foreign manufacturers. China's subsidies have grown over the years and now include tax incentives and preferential loans, which further reduce the cost of investing in China.
13. China has consistently used a 17 percent value added tax (VAT) as an instrument of industrial policy. China selectively rebates the VAT when a domestic manufacturer exports but imposes it on imports. The United States, on the other hand, does not use the VAT and is not allowed by WTO rules to rebate income taxes on exports. China's VAT policy therefore places US exports at a distinct disadvantage.
14. The US government has filed a variety of WTO cases against China's barriers to trade. These WTO cases, while important, are very industry specific, time consuming, and fail to have an impact on the trade-distorting aspects of China's industrial policy or to deal with the underlying causes of the US-China trade deficit. Tackling the systemic trade imbalances between China and the United States through WTO mechanisms will not address broader issues such as environmental pollution, or workers' rights abuses. The US government will have to find alternative venues in which to address such matters. China's Industrial Policy and its Impact on Upstate New York.
15. China's industrial policy targets and supports strategic industries identified as important to its economy in the 11th Five-Year Plan. This industrial policy promotes and subsidizes many of the same industries that comprise the industrial cluster of upstate New York. These industries include auto parts, machine tools, information technology, optics, photonics, and, more recently, clean renewable energy.
16. China's industrial policy has contributed to the loss of manufacturing in the region and presents a challenge to New York as it seeks to become a global leader in the renewable energy field.

17. The relocation of manufacturing from upstate New York has weakened the industrial cluster, which in turn has greatly impacted the ability of remaining firms to be innovative. Advanced technology companies in the region that have been moving their manufacturing operations to China are now relocating their research, development, and innovation operations there as well.

China's Activities Directly Affecting US Security Interests

As China's economy continues to grow, its military is also experiencing dramatic modernization and changes in its approach to national security. Beijing has mandated the People's Liberation Army (PLA) to change from a territorially focused military that counters traditional military threats to a more globally focused force that, in addition to maintaining its traditional competencies, can handle non-traditional security threats. In order to support the PLA's expanded activities abroad, China has rapidly modernized its naval forces. Since the mid-1990s, China has embarked on its largest naval modernization since the People's Republic of China (PRC) was founded in 1949, quantitatively and qualitatively improving its modern naval platforms. In addition to giving the PLA a greater reach, these improved naval forces have bolstered China's ability successfully to conduct a more diverse set of naval missions. These improvements could impede the US military's access to the region in the event of a crisis. As a means of enhancing its military modernization and economic development, China has been heavily involved in conducting human and cyber espionage against the United States. The US counterintelligence officials have concluded that Chinese intelligence collection efforts are growing in scale, intensity, and sophistication. In addition, there has been a marked increase in cyber intrusions originating in China and targeting the US government and defence related computer systems. This malicious activity has the potential to destroy critical infrastructure, disrupt commerce and banking systems, and compromise sensitive defence and military data.

Conclusion

China's Military and Security Activities Abroad

- Beijing has begun to broaden its national security concerns beyond a potential contingency across the Taiwan Strait and issues around its immediate periphery.
- Chinese leaders place a growing emphasis on militarily safeguarding China's expanding national interests. Hu Jintao codified this trend in 2004 when he declared a new set of guiding principles for the armed forces called the Historic Missions.
- China's leadership has a growing appreciation for the seriousness of overseas, non-traditional threats that could adversely affect China's economic and other interests, as evidenced by the military's increasing allocation of resources toward missions such as peacekeeping, counterpiracy, and disaster relief.
- These geographical and functional changes in China's military missions correlate with an increase in China's military, security, and economic activities abroad.
- China's expanded claim over freedom of navigation in what it considers to be its exclusive economic zone could lead to further incidents involving the US military.

- At the same time, however, the expansion of China's military and security activities abroad are more evolutionary than revolutionary in nature. Although the PLA is operating more frequently abroad, it should not yet be considered a global military or a military with a global reach.
- PLA activities abroad will improve the PLA's military capabilities —such as command, control, communications, and logistics— in ways that will contribute to PLA competence in a broad range of operations.
- The Chinese military's more international orientation is not a fundamentally negative development. A more activist PLA could in some circumstances provide a "public good" by contributing more to global stability. Other nations, including the United States, may benefit from Chinese peacekeeping operations and counterpiracy efforts.
- The Chinese military's more international orientation—combined with its improved military capacity—could, however, adversely affect US national security. Of particular import will be whether a militarily confident China will take a more confrontational stance toward the United States or its allies.

China's Naval Modernization

- Since the mid-1990s, China, enabled by its growing economy, has embarked on its largest naval modernization effort since the founding of the PRC in 1949. This modernization process includes foreign purchases and indigenous production of naval platforms, weapons, and equipment. In addition, institutional changes such as organizational, personnel, and logistics reforms have improved the PLA Navy's capacity to conduct operations.
- Deterring Taiwan from declaring independence is the near-term goal of this modernization process. A key component is the necessity to impede other nations—including the United States—from intervening on Taiwan's behalf.
- Other reasons driving China's naval modernization include the need to protect China's economic-intense coastal regions from maritime attacks, assert its maritime sovereignty and regional economic interests, safeguard its access to international sea lanes, provide a credible at-sea nuclear deterrent, and satisfy a national desire for a powerful navy.
- As China's naval modernization efforts progress, China increasingly will be able to project power in East Asia and interfere with US freedom of access to the region. China's anti-access strategy hinges upon deploying a powerful navy on, above, and below the surface, supported by its air and missile forces.
- Concern about China's naval modernization is beginning to fuel a maritime arms race in the region. Several nations, including close US allies, have recently officially questioned PLA Navy modernization efforts. Already a few nations have even begun to augment their own navies by purchasing naval platforms and weapons.

China's Human Espionage Activities that Target the United States, and the Resulting Impacts on US National Security.

- The intelligence services of the Chinese government are actively involved in operations directed against the United States and against US interests. China is the most aggressive country conducting espionage against the United States, focusing on obtaining US information and technologies beneficial to China's military modernization and economic development.

- Some of the espionage carried out on behalf of China is conducted by nonprofessional collectors. These nonprofessional collectors may be motivated by profit, patriotism, feelings of ethnic kinship, or coercion. Even in many cases where there is no obvious direct state involvement in the theft or illegal export of controlled technology, the Chinese government encourages such efforts and has benefited from them.
- Recent cases of espionage involving China show evidence of more focused efforts at information collection employing sources outside of the Chinese-American community.
- Chinese operatives and consular officials are actively engaged in the surveillance and harassment of Chinese dissident groups on US soil.

China's Cyber Activities that Target the United States, and the Resulting Impacts on US Security Interests

- The quantity of malicious computer activities against the United States increased in 2008 and is rising sharply in 2009; much of this activity appears to originate in China.
- The direct attribution of such activities targeting the United States presents challenges due to hackers' ability to conceal their locations. Nonetheless, a significant and increasing body of circumstantial and forensic evidence strongly indicates the involvement of Chinese state or state-supported entities.
- The Chinese government has institutionalized many of its capabilities for computer network operations within elements of the People's Liberation Army. The PRC is also recruiting from its growing population of technically skilled people, including those from the private sector, to increase its cyber capabilities. It is recruiting skilled cyber operators from information technology firms and computer science programmes into the ranks of numerous Information Warfare Militia units.
- China's peacetime computer exploitation efforts are primarily focused on intelligence collection against US targets and Chinese dissident groups abroad.
- In the early stages of a conflict, the PLA would employ computer network operations against opposition government and military information systems.
- Critical infrastructure in the United States is vulnerable to malicious cyber activity. Chinese military doctrine calls for exploiting these vulnerabilities in the case of a conflict.

China in Asia

In recent years, Beijing has enhanced its political, security, and economic relationships with Afghanistan, Pakistan, and Central Asia. The object has been to bolster stability in China's Xinjiang Province and to promote China's economic growth through greater trade and access to natural resources in the region. China has been reluctant to intercede directly in Afghanistan and Pakistan; rather, it depends on US and North Atlantic Treaty Organization (NATO) military forces and influence in the two countries to help secure China's investments.

Beijing's engagement in Taiwan also has increased significantly. Beijing and Taipei have taken numerous steps in the past year to increase political and economic cooperation, notably easing cross- Strait tensions. However, despite the warming of ties, Beijing's military modernization continues to pose a threat to the island, and China has offered no indication that it plans to downsize its military buildup vis-a`-vis Taiwan. During the Commission's May 2009 fact-finding trip to Hong Kong, meetings with Hong Kong government officials, US government officials, and private business leaders revealed that Beijing's political and economic influence over Hong Kong is growing. Because of the effects of the global financial crisis on the island and Hong Kong's increasing economic dependence on the mainland, Beijing has gained leverage over Hong Kong's much smaller economy.

Conclusion

China in Afghanistan, Pakistan, and Central Asia

- Beijing's primary interests in Afghanistan, Pakistan, and Central Asia concern isolating Chinese Muslim separatist groups from fundamentalist influences in Central Asia, maintaining stability along China's borders, diversifying its energy supplies, and increasing economic investments in the region.
- China continues to exercise a great deal of influence over Pakistan, stemming from the historic military and political ties between the two countries and their mutual desire to balance India's power.
- In Afghanistan, China also is increasing its influence due to its ability to offer economic aid and invest in large-scale infrastructure projects. However, China's influence in Afghanistan is still less than that of the United States.
- While China has not provided any direct military support to US and coalition forces in Afghanistan, Chinese investments in Afghanistan and Pakistan are contributing to those countries' economic development. China contributes no forces of its own, relying on US and NATO forces to protect these investments.
- China is increasing its economic, security, and political influence in Central Asia, possibly to the detriment of the United States. However, China's influence over the region is still limited because of historical mistrust, cultural barriers, and traditional Russian influence.
- The Shanghai Cooperation Organization has provided a forum for China to negotiate bilateral trade and energy deals with Central Asian states. It is not yet a genuine security alliance.
- In the wake of the June 2009 riots in Xinjiang, China will likely devote even more attention to developing political, security, and economic ties with Central Asia in order to ensure the security of its border and bolster stability in Xinjiang Province.
- China's energy investments in Central Asia are large. As Beijing seeks a means of importing oil and gas over land to ensure its energy security, Chinese investments in the Central Asian energy sector will continue to expand.

Taiwan

- Since the May 2008 inauguration of President Ma Ying-jeou, cross-Strait relations between China and Taiwan have improved on some fronts. Although noticeable political and economic improvements in the relationship have occurred, these improvements are not matched in the military arena. Instead, the PLA's capabilities continue to grow, increasing the military threat confronting Taiwan.

- One area of improvement entails the resumption of semi-regular, high-level meetings between the two sides. In particular, the cross-Strait dialogue between Taiwan's Straits Exchange Foundation and mainland China's Association for Relations Across the Taiwan Strait has occurred three times, with a fourth tentatively scheduled for late in 2009.
- As a result of improving cross-Strait relations, a growing number of agreements have been signed between Taiwan and China since May 2008. These agreements include the resumption of the Three Direct Links, the signing of a financial cooperation agreement, the commencement of cooperation on combating cross-Strait crime, and the establishment of a food safety agreement. In addition, there has been substantial progress toward the establishment of a free trade agreement.

Hong Kong

- The influence of China's central government in Hong Kong is increasing, including in the political and economic spheres.
- As a very export-dependent economy, Hong Kong has been severely impacted by the current economic crisis, both in its own right and as result of a fall in demand for Chinese exports.
- Beijing has been very active in offering economic support to Hong Kong, but democratic activists are worried about Hong Kong's growing economic dependence on the mainland, which they see as undermining Hong Kong's autonomy and international competitive edge.
- Beijing appears to be increasing its influence over the Hong Kong Special Administrative Region (SAR) government by strengthening the position of its official representative organization, the Central Government Liaison Office, and promoting pro-Beijing political parties within the Hong Kong Legislative Committee.
- A crucial component of Beijing's strategy of reining in Hong Kong appears to be its policy of chipping away incrementally at the legal support for Hong Kong's autonomy in domestic affairs. Evidence exists that Beijing already may be interfering in Hong Kong's domestic issues.
- Due to its geographic convenience as a trans-shipment point, as well as the long-standing presence of Chinese government-affiliated intelligence and commercial interests, Hong Kong could emerge as a significant trans-shipment point for transfers of export- controlled technologies into China in violation of US law.

China's Media and Information Controls—The Impact in China and the United States

China's propaganda and information control apparatus continue to support the authoritarian rule of the Chinese Communist Party (CCP). Journalists reporting on sensitive subjects or loosely defined "state secrets" are routinely harassed, intimidated, and/or imprisoned. Although the Internet has provided a freer venue for discussion of sensitive issues than traditional news media, the Chinese government has employed new techniques for controlling or "guiding" flows of publicly available information over the Internet. The Chinese government also has taken steps to improve its ability to shape international perceptions of China through the extensive use of propaganda and the dissemination of selective information. Motivated by a belief that western governments manipulate the press unfairly to portray China in a negative light, the Chinese government is increasing resources devoted to China's state-sponsored foreign language media outlets. Beijing has also employed western public relations and lobbying firms to help improve its international image, as well as to advocate for its preferred policies. Additionally, the Chinese government seeks to shape opinion in elite policy-making circles by influencing the commentary about China and US-China relations that emerges from US academics and think tanks.

Conclusion

Freedom of Expression in China.

- The January 2007 media reforms instituted in response to international pressure leading up to the Summer Olympics Games in Beijing and extended indefinitely in October 2008 have resulted in modest improvements in the working conditions for foreign journalists in China, but their effect has been limited because of the Chinese government's selective implementation and adoption of new strategies for restricting the flow of information.
- The January 2007 reforms have not improved working conditions for Chinese journalists, who remain subject to intimidation, harassment, violence, and imprisonment, often on vaguely defined "state secrets" charges.
- The Chinese government is employing a diverse array of strategies for silencing or guiding discussion about issues it considers politically sensitive.
- The Internet has emerged as a contested space in China. It provides a venue for discussion that is more open than traditional media but is also subject to the world's most sophisticated Web filtering system. The Chinese government's insecurity about Internet-enabled protests and the increased scrutiny of government officials on the Web has prompted the government to add additional elements to its already advanced Internet control system.
- The case of Green Dam demonstrates that even if the Chinese government had the technological capability to assert complete control over the Internet, it would not necessarily have the political clout to achieve this end. Furthermore, the case of Green Dam demonstrates that the Chinese government is not immune to pressure on information control issues from the international community.

China's External Propaganda and Influence Operations, and the Resulting Impacts on the United States

- The Chinese government is directly engaged in promoting its preferred propaganda narratives to foreign audiences and has an extensive bureaucracy dedicated to work in this area. The international propaganda messages of the government are similar in most respects to those for a Chinese audience—emphasizing China's economic growth, China's desire for a peaceful international system, and China's "stability" under CCP leadership.

- To its domestic audience, the Chinese government promotes the message that China is under attack from hostile forces abroad. Many figures within both the Chinese government and the public express a sense of frustration that the western media presents unfair portrayals of China and state that China therefore needs more effective international communication tools to counter such "attacks."
- The Chinese government views effective foreign propaganda as an essential tool of state power and is significantly increasing the level of effort and resources devoted to China's state-sponsored foreign language media outlets. Some of these efforts may also assume the form of nominally "independent" news outlets in which the Chinese government or Chinese state-owned firms exercise considerable influence behind the scenes.
- The Chinese government actively seeks to influence the commentary about China and US-China relations that comes from US academics and think tanks. This takes the form of providing both positive rewards to "friendly" scholars—such as preferred access to interviews and documents—as well as taking punitive actions such as denying visas for academics who anger Beijing. These rewards and punishments offer the Chinese government leverage over the careers of foreign scholars and thereby encourage a culture of academic self-censorship.
- In recent years, US public relations and lobbying firms have played a more prominent role in Beijing's efforts to improve its image and advocate for its preferred policies. The advice of western public relations firms has helped to shape the messages that the Chinese government presents to international audiences. However, China's use of direct lobbying in the United States is still limited in scale compared to the efforts of many other countries.

The Commission's Key Recommendations

The Commission believes that 10 of its 42 recommendations to Congress are of particular significance. These are presented below in the order in which they appear in the Report. The complete list of 42 recommendations appears at the Report's conclusion on page 325.

- Employing World Trade Organization trade remedies more aggressively. The Commission recommends that Congress urge the administration to employ more aggressively all trade remedies authorized by World Trade Organization rules to counteract the Chinese government's practices. The Commission further recommends that Congress urge the administration to ensure that US trade remedy laws are preserved and effectively implemented to respond to China's unfair or predatory trade activities.
- Responding effectively to China's currency manipulation. The Commission recommends that Congress urge the administration to press China to allow the RMB to become flexible and responsive to market forces, thereby contributing to the correction of global economic imbalances. The Commission further

recommends that Congress consider legislation that has the effect of offsetting the impact on the US economy of China's currency manipulation.

- Evaluating the impact of China's value added tax. The Commission recommends that Congress urge the United States Trade Representative to evaluate the use of selective value added tax rebates by China and their trade-distorting effect and determine what steps, if any, should be taken to address the issue.
- Reporting on the implications of Chinese subsidies to the US clean energy sector. The Commission recommends that Congress urge the Department of Energy, in consultation with other appropriate agencies, to report to Congress on the impact of Chinese subsidies and other elements of China's industrial policy on US-based companies manufacturing clean energy products.
- Ensuring adequate funding to limit China's anti-access capabilities. The Commission recommends that Congress assess the adequacy of planning and resourcing of Department of Defence programmes that would limit China's anti-access capabilities. In particular, Congress should focus on anti-submarine warfare and ballistic missile defence programmes. Congress should also assess the adequacy of funding and resources for the Department of Defence's Pacific Command.
- Meeting the rising challenge of Chinese espionage. The Commission recommends that Congress assess the adequacy of resources available for intelligence, counterintelligence, and export control enforcement programmes to ensure that US government agencies are able to meet the rising challenge of Chinese human intelligence and illicit technology collection.
- Ensuring adequate funding to respond to computer exploitation and computer attacks. The Commission recommends that Congress assess the effectiveness of and resourcing for law enforcement, defence, and intelligence community initiatives that aim to develop effective and reliable attribution techniques for computer exploitation and computer attacks.
- Encouraging China to draw down the number of forces opposite Taiwan. The Commission recommends that Congress urge the administration to take additional steps to encourage the People's Republic of China to demonstrate the sincerity of its desire for improved cross-Strait relations by drawing down the number of forces, including missiles, opposite Taiwan.
- Assessing the adequacy of US export control policy in Hong Kong. The Commission recommends that Congress examine and assess the adequacy of US export control policy for dual-use technology as it relates to the treatment of Hong Kong and the PRC as separate customs entities. The Commission further recommends that Congress urge the administration to consider ways to collaborate more closely with the authorities in Hong Kong in order to prevent the trans-shipment of controlled technologies from Hong Kong into the PRC.
- Monitoring the role of US companies in Internet censorship. The Commission recommends that Congress continue to monitor and assess the development and progress of industry and other efforts to create and implement an effective code of ethics and best practices related to the operations of US high tech firms in China and other authoritarian countries where Internet content and activity are controlled and monitored by the government.

INTRODUCTION

Early indicators suggest China is quickly emerging from the global recession and resuming its recent economic growth path. While many countries have been struggling with falling income and employment throughout the year, China's gross domestic product is on track to achieve an 8.5 percent gain, according to the International Monetary Fund (IMF).* This relatively rapid recovery, combined with comprehensive industrial policies, also has helped China capture market share from its competitors and add to its foreign currency reserves. China is now the world's largest exporter as well as the largest exporter to the United States. As a result, China's leaders are now proclaiming that their economic model— a blend of subsidies, government control of the market, export-led growth, and selective privatization—is superior.

Buoyed by its continued economic success, China also has grown more confident on the world stage and is seeking to expand its influence. Its leaders have sought a larger voice in international organizations ranging from the International Monetary Fund and the G–20 group of industrialized nations to the United Nations. To its credit, China has also begun to expand its international peacekeeping efforts, most notably by sending several warships to join an international effort to reduce piracy along the east African coast.

This year's report reflects the Commission's concern that despite its accomplishments and growing sense of confidence, China may be moving in the wrong direction and that this affects the US- China relationship. China has yet to embrace the challenge first issued in 2005 by the United States that it become a "responsible stakeholder" in world affairs.† Many of its recent global efforts appear more focused on enhancing China's access to raw materials than on promoting economic or political development, and China has not demonstrated leadership in working to solve difficult problems such as the civil war in Sudan or halting Iran's nuclear weapons programme.

Regarding China's economy, the Commission notes a disturbing trend away from the evolution toward a full market system and instead sees steps backward to greater government control. China continues to employ a wide range of subsidies to favoured companies and industries within China and to control the value of its currency and provide massive loans from state-owned banks to industries producing over-capacity. This approach gives Chinese exporters a substantial price advantage in international markets and disadvantages US companies hoping to export to China. China also continues to lag in enforcing international laws protecting intellectual property and continues to be identified by the US government and private organizations as the world's largest source of such thefts.

---

* The IMF predicted in October that the US economy would decline by 2.75 percent for the year.

† Robert B. Zoellick, "Whither China: From Membership to Responsibility" (remarks to the National Committee on US-China Relations, New York, NY, September 21, 2005).

In addition, China's role as the largest purchaser of US government securities has altered the economic relationship between the two countries. China's central bankers have joined a chorus of other officials in Beijing who point to the declining value of the American dollar against internationally traded currencies and suggest that it be replaced as the world's unofficial reserve currency. China's holdings have aroused fears in the United States of increased economic vulnerability to Chinese government decisions.

The Commission has been given the responsibility by Congress to advise it on economic and security policy toward China. The Commission's findings are contained in its seventh major Report to Congress. To complete its work, the Commission held seven hearings in Washington, DC, and one field hearing in Rochester, New York. Commissioners attended six classified briefings with five intelligence agencies. Commissioners visited the Chinese cities of Beijing, Xiamen, Nanjing, and Hong Kong. The Commission also contracted for independent research on topics the Commissioners viewed as important to US policy toward China.

China's growing assertiveness is also reflected in its naval modernization. China added two nuclear-powered ballistic missile submarines to its fleet. Even more significant is the navy's adoption of a "show the flag" strategy that includes support for China's acquisition of assets and resources from abroad. China also used its growing naval capabilities to assert a controversial theory of a 200- mile exclusive economic zone where foreign military vessels might be excluded. In March 2009, five Chinese vessels surrounded and stopped the USNS Impeccable, an intelligence and surveillance ship operating about 75 miles from Hainan Island, site of a large Chinese submarine base under construction. One other US naval surveillance ship was similarly confronted in 2009 amid demands from China that the United States cease air and sea surveillance inside the 200-mile exclusive economic zone.

China also continues to expand its capability to wage cyber warfare against other nations, to employ more sophisticated methods of espionage, and to increase its ability to obtain military technology surreptitiously from Europe and the United States. China's espionage activities in 2009 continued to evolve into a more targeted collection effort for specific information, much of it directed at obtaining specific western technologies useful in developing advanced weapons.

Cyber intrusions, including the exfiltration of large amounts of information, particularly data from America's largest defence contractors, were on the rise in 2009. Anecdotal and forensic evidence strongly implicates the Chinese government in many of the activities, either directly or through third-party surrogates sponsored by Beijing. Malicious activities directed against Defence Department computers in 2009 were running at a rate of 240 every day, costing as much as $200 million to repair the damage.

Managing these rapid changes and China's increased expectations will be a continuing challenge for Beijing and Washington. Despite China's success in emerging from the recession, China cannot continue to build its export sector and to direct investment into strategic industries that are already at overcapacity—without doing grave harm to its trading partners, particularly the United States. Unfortunately, the same imbalances among China, the United States, and Europe that caused so much trouble in the global financial sector are continuing to threaten the global economy. This will lead to further tensions.

CHAPTER 1

The US–China Trade and Economic Relationship

SECTION 1

The US–China Trade and Economic Relationship's Current Status and Significant Changes during 2009

The legislation passed by Congress in 2000 to establish the Commission sets forth specific topical areas of concern with respect to the People's Republic of China and associated issues, and requires the Commission to investigate and report to Congress on those topics. Congress has modified those topical areas in the intervening years. Today there are eight mandated topics. (They can be found at 22 U.S.C. 7002 and at the Commission's Web site—www.uscc.gov. They are also printed in full in appendix I of this Report, beginning on page 335.) At the beginning of each section of this Report, the mandated topical area (or areas) that section addresses is identified.

"The Commission shall investigate and report exclusively on—

"Economic Transfers: The qualitative and quantitative nature of the transfer of United States production activities to the People's Republic of China, including the relocation of high technology, manufacturing, and research and development facilities, the impact of such transfers on United States national security, the adequacy of United States export control laws, and the effect of such transfers on United States economic security and employment.

"World Trade Organization Compliance: The compliance of the People's Republic of China with its accession agreement to the World Trade Organization. . . ."

Introduction

During a momentous 12 months, with the world experiencing a deep recession, the economic relationship between the People's Republic of China (PRC) and the United States changed in ways large and small. Few aspects of the relationship remained untouched. Trade disputes over such sectoral issues as tyres, chicken, autoparts, and intellectual property rights occurred alongside major shifts: China has floated the idea that the world find a new reserve currency to replace the dollar that China hitherto had been only too happy to accumulate in record amounts. The US Government responded by promising to avoid the inflation that would harm Chinese investments in the US Treasury securities. China blamed the United States, its model of free market capitalism, and its lack of effective regulatory oversight for precipitating the credit crisis of September 2008 that threatened global trade. And the US Government reassured China and other global borrowers that their large investments in dollar-denominated bonds issued by the ailing mortgage giants Fannie Mae and Freddie Mac would be guaranteed by the US Government.

The United States and China approached the crisis in different ways. The United States experienced a sharp reduction in economic activity in the final quarter of 2008 (the gross domestic product [GDP] fell by 5.4 percent) and the first half of 2009 (down 6.4 percent). Meanwhile, according to Chinese government sources, China's economy grew 6.1 percent in the first quarter of 2009, 7.9 percent in the second, and is expected to grow even faster in the final two quarters, allowing Beijing to reach at least its target of 8 percent GDP growth for 2009.[1] American consumers reduced retail spending by 11 percent in the first half of 2009, year over year, as unemployment rose.[2] By contrast, retail sales in China were up by 17 percent in the 12 months ending in June 2009.[3] China's outbound foreign investment is set to exceed inbound investment for the first time.[4] The International Monetary Fund's (IMF) World Economic Outlook update in July 2009 forecast that China and India will be the engines of global growth, as they were the only major economies projected actually to grow in 2009.[5]

China's fast pace of growth, exceeding World Bank forecasts, is driven by the government's $586 billion in proposed stimulus spending, loose fiscal and monetary policies, record lending by state banks, and export-led growth policies. But the enviable statistics hide a darker side.* Economists in China and across the world have warned that the flood of bank lending in China may generate dangerous bubbles in the property and stock markets, squander financial resources, cause a rise in non performing bank loans, and further exacerbate the economic imbalances that have led to the present crisis. China's commitment to global rebalancing appears half-

* Considerable skepticism exists in regard to China's statistical reporting. China compiles its gross domestic product growth figures even faster than the United States despite having more than four times the population, far fewer computers, and less sophisticated sampling methodology. In addition, Beijing relies on provincial government officials to supply many of the details—the same officials who are assigned production quotas by the central government. For example, *see* Derek Scissors, "The Truth about China's Growth," The Heritage Foundation *WebMemo #2238*, January 22, 2009. *http://www.heritage.org/Research/AsiaandthePacific/ wm2238.cfm*; Michael F. Martin, "What's the Difference?—Comparing US and Chinese Trade Data," Congressional Research Service (CRS) Report to Congress RS22640 (Washington, DC: March 27, 2009); and "The Art of Chinese Massage," *Economist*, May 21, 2009. *http:// www.economist.com/businessfinance/displayStory.cfm?storyId=13692907*.

hearted, with aggressive efforts aimed at boosting exports and maintaining robust growth.

Indeed, a newly assertive China has used the global slowdown as an opportunity to seize the center stage and proclaim the superiority of its economic system over that of the United States. While Chinese Prime Minister Wen Jiabao never named the United States directly, his criticism at the January 2009 World Economic Forum in Davos of the "unsustainable model of development characterized by prolonged low savings and high consumption" was clearly aimed at the United States. [6] Chinese Central Bank Governor Zhou Xiaochuan, stressing the superiority of China's economic model, noted at the G–20 meeting in March 2009 that China "demonstrat[ed] its superior system advantage when it comes to making vital policy decisions." [7]

China has initiated two new World Trade Organization (WTO) cases against the United States and has sought a larger role in the affairs of the IMF and the World Bank. China has also introduced some programmes, such as currency swaps with some of its smaller trading partners, that may eventually lead to the internationalization of China's currency.

The US-China Trade Relationship

Despite the global economic crisis, China seems on track to achieve at least 8 percent growth this year, after reaching 7.9 percent growth in the second quarter of 2009.[8] Aggressive stimulus measures, including massive expansion of bank lending, export rebates, subsidies for consumption, and continuing manipulation of its currency have helped the Chinese economy to continue expanding throughout the global downturn (see chap. 1, sec. 2, for a detailed discussion of China's role in and response to the global economic crisis). The US GDP, by contrast, decreased at an annual rate of 1.0 percent in the second quarter of 2009.[9]

Despite the economic downturn and dramatic drop-off in US consumption in the last quarter of 2008, China's exports to the United States were almost five times the amount of its imports: China exported $337.8 billion worth of goods to the United States and imported just $69.73 billion in goods from the United States, which left the United States with a bilateral trade deficit of $268.04 billion. There are some signs that the size of the US trade deficit with China may grow at a slower pace due to the US economic slowdown and higher transportation costs, among other factors. For the first eight months of 2009, China's goods exports to the United States were $184.9 billion, while US exports to China were $41.2 billion, with China's trade surplus standing at $143.7 billion, a decrease of 17.8 percent over the same period last year ($169.2 billion).

Fig.1: US-China Trade in Goods ($ billion), 2000–2008

	2000	2001	2002	2003	2004	2005	2006	2007	2008
US Exports	$16.3	$19.2	$22.1	$28.4	$34.7	$41.8	$55.2	$65.2	$69.73
US Imports	100.0	102.3	125.2	152.4	196.7	243.5	287.8	321.5	337.8
Balance	-83.7	-83.1	-103.1	-124.1	-162.1	-201.6	-232.5	-256.3	-268.04

Source: US Department of Commerce, Bureau of Economic Analysis, 2009.

The US exports to China were down 16.7 percent in the first eight months of 2009 compared with the same period in 2008, while imports from China were down about 17.5 percent.

As the global recession reduced US demand for imports, the US trade deficit with the world and with China started to decline in late 2008. But the US's relative trade deficit with China, compared with the rest of the world, grew. The US manufacturing trade balance with China continued to deteriorate and is far larger than that with any country or region. In 2008, the US deficit with China accounted for 68.6 percent ($267.5 billion) of the total $389.8 billion US trade deficit in manufactured goods, compared with 56.7 percent ($255.6 billion) of the total $450.8 billion in 2007.[10] The US trade balance with China in advanced technology products is also deteriorating: the US deficit has soared from $6.1 billion in 2001 to $72.7 billion in 2008.[11] In the first half of 2009, the United States exported $7.6 billion in advanced technology products to China and imported $38.1 billion, for a six-month deficit of $30.5 billion.[12]

The issue of the US-China bilateral trade imbalance is one of the major points of contention between the two countries. The United States continues to push for improved access for US manufacturers and service providers to the Chinese market and for better intellectual property protection for US business software and entertainment products. China, however, prefers that the United States reduce its restrictions on exporting dual-use high-technology products to China.[13] (High-technology civilian goods that could also serve a military purpose are under a broad array of US government export restrictions. Europe also maintains restrictions.) During the Commission's May 2009 trip to China, such arguments cropped up repeatedly in conversations with senior Chinese policymakers and academics. Assistant Minister of Finance Zhu Guangyao recommended liberalizing the US' high-tech goods export policy to correct the trade imbalance, while Zheng Xinli, deputy director of the Policy Research Office of the Chinese Communist Party's (CCP) Central Committee and permanent vice president of the China Centre for International Economic Exchanges, also suggested relaxing restrictions on nuclear power technology.

Washington has restricted sales of some dual-use technologies with possible military applications and crime-control items. Though the July 27–28 Strategic and Economic Dialogue produced an agreement to "accelerate" the easing of restrictions, critics in the United States have objected to such a move, pointing to numerous instances of Chinese violations of current rules against weapons-related proliferation activities.[14] In 2008, US exports to China of advanced technology goods such as semiconductors and electronics amounted to $18.7 billion, or 26 percent of all US sales to China, despite the restrictions.[15] China maintains that the relaxation in US export controls will help reduce the US's trade deficit, but this is a spurious argument. In 2008, the US Bureau of Industry and Security approved exports to China valued at around $2.7 billion, while the total value of denied license applications was only $142.6 million.[16] (This figure does not account for license requests that are never made, so it does not represent fully the magnitude of possible sales of controlled exports.)

China's Exchange Rate Regime and Investment in the US Government Assets

The current economic crisis has brought into stark relief many contributing factors, such as the global saving and spending imbalances,which are addressed in chapter 1, section 2, of this Annual Report. The issue of currency valuation—specifically the undervaluation of the renminbi (RMB)—attracts attention whenever the US-China trade imbalance is discussed, and the Commission has addressed this topic in detail in previous Reports. China's deliberately undervalued RMB has unfairly conferred substantial economic advantages on China, to the detriment of major trading partners, including the United States and Europe, by making China's exports cheaper and imports more expensive and encouraging foreign direct investment into China. The refusal by China to allow its currency to be traded on international markets has contributed to China's massive trade surplus and its accumulation of more than $2.27 trillion in foreign exchange reserves by September 2009, the world's largest cache of foreign currency and other foreign liquid assets.[17]

The Chinese Central Bank has maintained its strict control of the value of the RMB by buying dollars entering the country through export earnings or investment and swapping them for newly printed RMB. Consequently, the exchange rate between the RMB and the dollar stayed within a narrow trading band determined by Beijing despite an announcement in July 2005 that the RMB's value would become "adjustable, based on market supply and demand with reference to exchange rate movements of currencies in a basket" of currencies. The composition of this basket still has not been revealed.[18] Between 2005 and the summer of 2008, the RMB appreciated by about 21 percent, at which point Beijing set its value at around 6.8 to the dollar. The RMB remains undervalued. The extent of the RMB's undervaluation is hard to estimate, because it has never been freely traded, but economists suggest anything from 12 percent to 40 percent.[19]

China's foreign exchange reserves, accumulated as a partial result of China's manipulation of the value of the RMB, are largely invested in US dollar-denominated assets. As of July 2009, China owned $800.5 billion of US Treasury bonds and is the biggest holder of US Treasuries in the world.[20] Although much has been made in China's state-run media over the $25 billion sell-off ofTreasury securities from May to June 2009, the message appears aimed at domestic critics of China's economic dependence on the United States. When the US sub-prime mortgage market collapsed, China responded by selling some dollar-denominated assets, in particular debt issued by mortgage giants Fannie Mae and Freddie Mac, but its purchases of US Treasury debt continued while stock and commodity markets were fluctuating wildly.[21] As a result, total Chinese holdings of US Treasury debt grew by more than 45 percent between July 2008 and July 2009.

The perceived dependence of the United States on China's lending has overshadowed the debate about China's trade practices in general and China's manipulation of its currency in particular. When US and Chinese officials met for the revamped Strategic and Economic Dialogue on July 27–28, 2009, the American negotiators did not raise the issue of China's currency manipulation, instead relegating the issue to a subset of its push for broader economic reforms in China.[22] Beijing has taken to lecturing Washington on the need to safeguard its $2.27 trillion in reserves, the bulk of which are parked in US dollar-denominated assets. "The [United States] has for now given up on pushing China on currency issues, partly because Washington has less leverage over Beijing than at any other point in recent history," said Eswar Prasad of The Brookings Institution.[23] Premier Wen Jiabao said in March 2009 that he was "worried" the dollar would weaken as US President Barack Obama sells record amounts of debt to fund his $787 billion economic stimulus plan. Yet since June 2008, the RMB has been strictly pegged to the dollar in order to help support exports during the global recession.[24]

For all the concern that the dollar's role is waning and that it may be a risky investment, China has continued to lead in the purchase of US government assets. (China does not disclose the currency composition of its reserves, but the dollar is thought to make up around 65 percent of the portfolio).[25] The reason that China continues to buy dollars is simple: China's policy of strictly controlling the value of the RMB depends upon it. China's commitment to a pegged currency means that under its current approach China must swap the dollars flowing into the country for RMB.[26] Analysts, including David Pilling, the Asia editor of the *Financial Times,* and Brad Setser, an economist formerly at the Council on Foreign Relations and now at the National Economic Council, argue that far from a sign of strength, "Beijing's accumulation of vast foreign reserves is the side-effect of an economic model too reliant on exports." [27] Writes Pilling:

> *The enormous trade surplus is the product of an under-valued [RMB] that has allowed others to consume Chinese goods at the expense of the Chinese people themselves. Beijing cannot dream of selling down its Treasury holdings without triggering the very dollar collapse it purports to dread. Nor are its shrill calls for the US to close its twin deficits—which would inevitably involve buying fewer Chinese goods—entirely convincing. Rather than exposing the superiority of China's state-led model, the global financial crisis has laid bare the compromising embrace in which the US and China find themselves.*[28]

Dr. Setser further suggests that although China still matters for financing the US's external and fiscal deficit (it controls a $1.5 trillion portfolio), US reliance on borrowing to support the trade deficit has diminished as the US's trade deficit has shrunk.[29] The latest official US statistics show that while US government borrowing to support the federal budget deficit has been growing rapidly, US hous holds have purchased 86 percent of all new Treasury issues in the first quarter of 2009. American households held about $643.9 billion by the end of the same period, while the Federal Reserve held about $704 billion by the end of July 2009.[30] The diminished role of foreign financing is only natural, since US borrowing to finance imports is down, with the US's current account deficit actually halved—from $829 billion in 2005 to an annualized $409.5 billion in the first quarter of 2009.[31]

China's exchange rate regime appears to have created a policy dilemma for the Chinese government. An undervalued RMB subsidizes China's exports, but it also compels China to keep buying up US dollars. Chinese officials have expressed concern that the growing US debt will eventually spark inflation in the United

States and a depreciation of the dollar, which would reduce the value of China's holdings of US securities. But if China stopped purchasing US dollars, it would seriously impact the RMB's peg to the dollar. As Michael Pettis, professor at Peking University's Guanghua School of Management, writes, as long as China remains dependent on boosting the value of the dollar to support its own export- driven growth, it "will have to recycle the surplus into the dollar pool that ultimately funds the US fiscal deficit." [32] There is an irreconcilable conflict between China's words and actions: Despite high-level criticism of the growing US debt, China continues to buy Treasury bonds and to buy up dollars flowing into the Chinese economy. As economist Paul Krugman notes, China remains captive in a "dollar trap" of its own making.[33]

China's Criticism of the US Dollar's Reserve Currency Status

During the July 26–27 Strategic and Economic Dialogue in Washington, Chinese Vice Premier Wang Qishan said at an event with Treasury Secretary Tim Geithner that "[a]s a major reserve currency-issuing country, the US should properly balance and properly handle the impact of the dollar supply on the domestic economy and the world economy as a whole." He later pronounced himself content with Washington's assurances that the United States would meet its financial commitments.[34] Chinese concerns over China's large dollar holdings also have been reflected in a paper issued by the governor of the People's Bank of China, Zhou Xiaochuan, on March 24, 2009. The paper called for replacing the US dollar as the international reserve currency with a new global system based on special drawing rights, an international reserve asset developed by the IMF, whose exchange rate is calculated by a mix of dollars, euros, pound sterling, and yen.[35]

The Dollar as a Reserve Currency and Special Drawing Rights

A reserve currency is held by governments, businesses, and individuals as an asset whose value is market based and, when in the form of bonds issued in the reserve currency, an investment that will pay interest. Parties hold reserves for a variety of reasons: as a medium of exchange to pay for imports, as a hedge against inflation, and as a guard against the effects of a run on a country's own currency. Central banks hold a reserve currency in lieu of gold or other precious metal deposits.

The US dollar became the world's official reserve currency following World War II and was used to establish a fixed rate of exchange among currencies. The dollar assumed an even larger, though unofficial, role in 1971 after the United States and most nations abandoned the gold standard, and currencies of industrialized countries came to be freely traded on international markets. Dollars make up about two-thirds of the world's currency reserves, followed by the euro and the Japanese yen. The dollar has been favoured as a reserve currency because the United States has the world's largest economy and is its largest trading country, the global market for dollars is large and highly liquid, and the US economy and its political system have proved to be stable. The choice of the dollar constitutes a vote of confidence in the US political system and the US economy.

The International Monetary Fund, which was founded after World War II to oversee the international payments system, created in 1969 a unit of account and a partial substitute for gold and the dollar called "special drawing rights."[36] This essentially established a medium of exchange whose value is linked to the dollar, as gold once was, but is not freely traded. The IMF determines the value of the special drawing rights daily by calculating the worth, in dollars, of four currencies traded on the London exchange (a trade-weighted dollar, euro, yen, and pound sterling). The special drawing rights can be exchanged for currencies of some IMF member countries, and holders of special drawing rights receive interest payments from the IMF. In March 2009, Zhou Xiaochuan, a governor of the People's Bank of China, proposed substituting special drawing rights as the reserve currency in place of the dollar.[37] However, only 204 billion special drawing rights are in existence, worth about $317 billion, far too few to constitute a reserve currency.[38] China alone is thought to have some 65 percent of its $2.27 trillion in foreign currency reserves in dollar-denominated investments, or a total of some $1.5 trillion.

The United States derives several advantages from the world's acceptance of the dollar as the reserve currency. The United States can issue bonds denominated in dollars, allowing it to borrow without fear that a fall in the dollar's value will increase its debt. Conversely, the United States can choose to inflate its currency and reduce the burden of its debt—a practice known as monetizing the debt. Also, US currency held by foreigners constitutes an interest-free loan to the US government, known as seigniorage. (There is $870 billion in currency outstanding. Of that, $646 billion is in $100 bills, most of which are thought to be held by foreigners).[39]

China's growing focus on the special drawing rights has coincided with China's reconciliation with the IMF. For the past three years, China has blocked IMF reviews of its economy, called an Article IV 27. Consultation, because it objected to public criticism of its controlled exchange-rate regime.[40] In the latest report issued in July 2009, the IMF board concluded that the RMB "remains substantially undervalued." This change is a step-down from previous statements and reports labeling China's exchange rate as "fundamentally misaligned." [41] Speaking at the opening of the World Bank and IMF annual meetings in October 2009, Dominique Strauss-Kahn, the head of the IMF, reiterated his criticism of the Chinese currency, saying that the IMF "view still is the [RMB] is undervalued." [42].

As its activism on the special drawing rights issue shows, China is becoming more engaged with the IMF and other international organizationsas it tries to boost its global influence. China is the world's third largest economy and wants greater recognition but has fewer IMF votes in proportion to the size of its economy (its share is roughly the same as Belgium and the Netherlands combined). [43] Instead of making a direct contribution, China signed an agreement to purchase $50 billion in special drawing rights-denominated bonds issued by the IMF.[44] China is hoping that buying bonds from the IMF will help increase China's say in the organization's governance, even though IMF allocations are determined by each country's financial contribution to the IMF—not the country's economic size or population.[45]

During the Commission's May 2009 Asia trip, the Commissioners met with Zhu Guangyao, China's assistant minister of Finance, who said that as the IMF is undergoing changes as a consequence of the global crisis, China's role in the IMF is changing, too. Echoing comments made by other prominent Chinese policymakers and scholars, he called for a more balanced representation in the IMF, with a bigger role for other developing countries. (China claims that it is a developing country.) Mr. Zhu said the goal was not to overthrow the system but rather to bring it into accordance with the global economy—for example, since the United States accounts for more than 15 percent of the global economy, its quota should reflect a similar allocation. (The United States currently holds 16.77 percent).[46] Mr. Zhu has also said that China would like to see the voting shares split equally between the developed and the developing countries.[47] In the joint communique´ from the G–20 Summit in Pittsburgh in September 2009, the leaders called for a shift in IMF voting by at least 5 percentage points from developed to underrepresented developing countries, which is certain to affect China's voting power.[48] In a statement to the IMF's steering committee in October 2009, Yi Gang, vice governor of the People's Bank of China, said Beijing wanted the IMF to "establish a system to automatically adjust [voting] quotas and to reflect changes in countries' economic status." [49]

Lending weight to its call for an alternative to the US dollar, Beijing is trying to diversify its investments by investing in commodities and overseas companies and gradually atttempting to internationalize the RMB by allowing it to be used for some regional trade transactions.[50] For example, in the 10 months after Lehman Brothers collapsed in September 2008, Chinese bidders announced 50 outbound offers worth over $50 billion, with more than two-thirds of the offers in buying mining or energy assets.[51] Chinese Premier Wen Jiabao announced in July 2009 that Beijing will use its massive foreign exchange reserves to "hasten the implementation of [the] 'going out' strategy," which translates into supporting the overseas expansion of and acquisitions by Chinese companies. [52] Taking advantage of falling commodity prices, China's State Reserve Bureau and other importers went on a buying spree to replenish China's strategic reserves, to insulate domestic producers of these goods from falling global prices, and to reallocate a portion of its foreign exchange reserves away from the dollar.[53] China has been stockpiling oil, iron, copper, and other metals, and canola and soybeans since the end of last year.[54] Despite its spending on such initiatives, China's reserves continue to accumulate.[55]

In its annual report on financial stability, issued in June 2009, the People's Bank of China formalized the call for a new reserve currency, saying that China will push reform of the international currency system to make it more diversified and will aim to reduce reliance on the current reserve currencies.[56] Though the report does not explicitly mention the US dollar, the dollar is the dominant reserve currency in the world. The People's Bank of China said in the report that under the proposal, the IMF "should manage part of the reserves of its members" and be reformed to increase the rights of emerging markets and developing countries.[57] That would be a significant change, since China currently does not even disclose to the IMF the composition of its reserves, let alone allow the IMF to manage them.[58] China also urged stronger monitoring of countries that issue reserve currencies.[59]

Many economists in China believe that the economic crisis has laid bare defects in the dollar-led global economy, and developments this year indicate that China is laying the groundwork for a long-term strategy to increase the international role for the RMB, perhaps even as a reserve currency. For example, Li Lianzhong, an academic at a key think tank under the Communist Party, said China's RMB should become the fifth currency in the special drawing rights basket, with an equal weighting of 20 percent according to each currency.[60]

But as Swaminathan Aiyar of the Cato Institute and Arvind Subramanian of the Peterson Institute for International Economics argue, political considerations may be as important as economic self-interest in the formulation of China's strategy. By calling for a greater role for special drawing rights, China may be seeking to reduce the political and financial power of the United States: China's move has been backed by Russia, Brazil, India, and other developing countries that "have long chafed at the de facto dollar standard." [61]

RMB Swaps and Cross-border Trade Settlement Agreements

In addition to calling for special drawing rights to replace the dollar as the world's reserve currency, China has signed currency swap agreements totaling 650 billion RMB (or about $95 billion) with Hong Kong, Argentina, Indonesia, South Korea, Malaysia, and Belarus, which would allow those partners to settle accounts with China using the RMB rather than the dollar in order to facilitate bilateral trade and investment.[62]

Limited use of the RMB has been allowed since 2003 in border trade with Vietnam and Laos to the south and Mongolia and Russia in the north, according to a book published by the State Administration of Foreign Exchange.[63] But now trade settlement is moving from border zones to China's largest financial centers, including Shanghai, Guangzhou, and Hong Kong. Starting in July 2009, the central bank extended settlement by offering companies in Shanghai and four southern cities—Shenzhen, Guangzhou, Dongguan, and Zhuhai—tax breaks to start conducting trade in the currency with Hong Kong and Macao and allowing certain banks in Hong Kong to issue bonds denominated in RMB.[64] (See chap. 3, sec. 3, for more details on China's currency swap and trade settlement agreements with Hong Kong.) The State Council has also specified that the pilot programme will apply to cross-border trade transactions with the 10 members of the Association of Southeast Asian Nations countries on a tentative basis, though details remain forthcoming.[65] There have also been some indications that trade-settlement deals are in the works with other countries, including reports that Brazilian President Luiz Ina´cio Lula da Silva and his Chinese counterpart Hu Jintao discussed the plan to settle trade in local currency during Lula's three-day state visit to China in May 2009.[66]

The Chinese government has ambitions to give its currency a wider regional and international presence, though the currency now is almost impossible to use outside of China's borders. Chinese firms are unlikely to convince their foreign business partners to settle transactions in RMB—not least because there are very limited opportunities for using the RMB.

HSBC, one of the world's largest banks, suggested that China's plans to internationalize the RMB, if successful, could lead to nearly $2 trillion in annual trade flows (as much as 50 percent of China's total) being settled in RMB as early as 2012. Many analysts, however, remain very skeptical.[67] Philip Bowring, Asia columnist for the *International Herald Tribune* and former editor of the *Far Eastern Economic Review*, wrote on the obstacles to internationalizing the RMB.

> *China's expressions of desire to reduce the role of the dollar are ... contradicted by its actual policy of maintaining a de facto peg to the US currency, meanwhile continuing to accumulate dollars in reserves now totaling $2 trillion. The modest [RMB] appreciation after 2005 came to a halt more than a year ago as China has sought to sustain exports in the face of the global slump. There is conflict between macro-economic stabilization goals and pressures from industries and employment creation not to put more pressure on exporters. China is still wedded to high growth and a cheap currency. . . . Nor has there been any significant move towards full convertibility as the financial crisis has, with good reason, made the authorities nervous of liberalization.*[68]

While Arthur Kroeber, managing director of Dragonomics Research & Advisory, an independent research firm based in Beijing, wrote that for the RMB to become a reserve currency,

> *foreigners must be able to invest freely in onshore [RMB] financial assets (stocks, bonds, and bank deposits) and freely repatriate both their earnings and their capital. For foreign investors to want to hold [RMB] assets on a large scale, they must be convinced that China's financial markets are trustworthy and not rigged. For the [RMB] to become even a secondary reserve currency, it must therefore fully liberalize its capital account and set up reliable financial markets that are reasonably free of government interference. Technical difficulties aside, this will require a significant retreat from the current state- dominated model of credit allocation—and this cannot happen quickly.*[69]

Even Chinese officials seem to have equivocated on the idea of moving to the special drawing rights. China's Vice Foreign Minister He Yafei said that the creation of a supranational reserve currency has been discussed "among academic circles" but that any proposal outlined "is not the position of the Chinese government," according to China's state-run Xinhua news agency.[70] Li Yang, a former adviser to the People's Bank of China and a prominent academic, said at the July 2009 Global Think Tank Summit in Beijing that the transition to a multi-reserve currency system could take 20–30 years or longer.[71] Making the RMB a reserve currency would also carry some dangers. Chancellor Lawrence Lau of the Chinese University of Hong Kong said that if the RMB becomes "a reserve currency held by multiple countries," then shifts in confidence in the RMB could destabilize the exchange rate, which in turn "may trigger an economic crisis in China."[72]

Still, China's proposals for changes in the international financial architecture have to be taken seriously. China's leaders plan ahead. For example, China's recently announced goal to turn Shanghai into an international financial center by 2020 may suggest that China wants a fully convertible RMB by then.[73] Chinese regulators have taken steps to broaden the international appeal of China's capital markets and establish an offshore bond market for the RMB. Plans have been announced to allow qualified foreign-invested firms to list on the Shanghai exchange next year, to approve foreign banks' issuance of RMB-denominated corporate bonds, and to raise individual quotas for foreign investment in stocks from $800 million to $1 billion.[74] The Ministry of Finance also announced in September that in order to "improve the international status of the [RMB] [and] promote development of the [RMB] bond market," 6 billion RMB ($879 million) of government bonds will be sold in Hong Kong to foreign and retail investors—the first time RMB sovereign debt will be sold outside mainland China.[75] According to a report in the official *China Securities Journal,* in July 2009 China's State Council put Hu Xiaolian, the current head of the State Administration of Foreign Exchange, which administers China's foreign exchange reserves, in charge of a soon-to-be-formed special monetary policy office under the People's Bank of China to promote internationalization of the RMB.[76] This new office will be responsible for drafting RMB exchange rate policy and execution, monitoring foreign currency supply and demand, and developing an RMB offshore market.[77]

US-China Bilateral Dialogues

In 2009, the Obama Administration adopted the basics of the Bush Administration's bi-annual Strategic Economic Dialogue and gave it a slightly new name: the Strategic and Economic Dialogue. Instead of twice a year, the group will meet once a year. Leadership on the US side is now shared by Treasury Secretary Timothy Geithner and Secretary of State Hillary Clinton. The new Strategic and Economic Dialogue's broader agenda will include broader foreign policy issues such as climate change and North Korea. Assistant Minister of Finance Zhu Guangyao, with whom the Commission met during its May 2009 trip to China, said the Strategic Economic Dialogue process was particularly helpful in cultivating strategic trust. While both sides hailed the importance of consulting with each other, the July 27–28 Strategic and Economic Dialogue failed to produce any new agreements. In fact, much of the final communique′ was repeated verbatim from the previous Strategic Economic Dialogue statements, including China's commitment to open its financial services market to foreign investors and to treat foreign investment the same as domestic investment when granting government contracts.[78] The latter item has long been a point of contention between the two countries, since China is not a signatory to the World Trade Organization's Government Procurement Agreement despite a 2001 promise by Beijing to do so "as soon as possible." Instead, the two sides compromised by agreeing that by October 2009 China will submit a report to the Government Procurement Committee "that sets out the improvements that China will make in its revised offer." [79] In October 2009, China submitted to WTO members a promise to deliver an improved offer for joining the Government Procurement Agreement some time in 2010 but indicated that the new offer may exempt state-owned enterprises and sub central government entities.[80]

The discussion of the Strategic and Economic Dialogue focused on the 2008–09 economic crisis and US-China trade in the global economy. As the biggest holder of US Treasury bonds, China expressed concern over the US budget deficit and the safety of China'sinvestment in billions of dollars. China expressed fears that the accumulating American budget deficit could weaken the dollar and put at risk China's vast holdings of Treasury securities andother dollar-denominated assets. (A fall in the value of the dollar relative to the RMB also would make China's exports more expensive.) China holds an estimated $1.5 trillion such securities, makingit the US's largest foreign creditor.[81] China's Finance Minister Xie Xuren said the delegation wished to "express the view that credible steps should be taken to prevent fiscal risks and to ensures ustainability" and that "high attention should be given to fiscal deficits."[82]

Many commentators saw the exchange of rebukes on the Chinese side and assurances on the American side as a sign of a power shift between the two countries, in which an assertive China seeks to protect its investment while the United States mutes its criticism because it depends on China's purchases of the Treasuries to finance the economic recovery.[83] And indeed, during the Strategic and Economic Dialogue, the US side was "quiet on human rights and muted on the [RMB]," according to news accounts.[84]

Now that the Strategic and Economic Dialogue will convene only once a year, discussion of sectoral US-China trade issues will depend on the US-China Joint Commission on Commerce and Trade, which will hold its next meeting on October 28–29, 2009, in Hangzhou, China. The United States promised to "earnestly consider China's concerns" and work through the joint commission "toward China's Market Economy Status in an expeditious manner" (the United States made similar pronouncements in the past, but there has been no change in China's status as a non-market economy).[85]

This issue has long been a sore point for China: 97 members of the WTO officially recognize China as a market economy, but its biggest trading partners—the United States, the European Union, and India—do not.[86] Under its WTO accession agreement, China will automatically attain market economy status by 2016, but for now, the US Department of Commerce treats China as a non-market economy when determining anti-dumping penalties, which can frequently result in higher fees. The United States has a statutory test for determining whether an economy can be classified as a market economy.[87] The factors to be considered under US law in granting market economy status include the extent to which the country's currency is convertible, the extent to which wage rates are freely determined by negotiations between labour and management, and the extent to which the government owns or controls the means and decisions of production.[88]

In what could prove to be a significant development in the imposition of trade remedies on Chinese imports, in September 2009 the US Court of International Trade ordered the US Department of Commerce to develop methodologies to prevent double-counting of subsidies if it applies anti-dumping and countervailing duties simultaneously on imports of the same product from non-market economies. If the Commerce Department cannot develop such methodologies, then it must refrain from imposing simultaneous anti-dumping and countervailing duties.[89] China initiated a WTO case against the United States on its concurrent use of anti-dumping and countervailing measures against certain Chinese-made products, which is currently pending.

The WTO Cases

Cases brought by the United States against China Export Restrictions

The United States and the European Union have cited China's export restrictions (such as export quotas and taxes) on raw materials (bauxite, coke, fluorspar, magnesium, manganese, silicon metal, silicon carbide, yellow phosphorus, and zinc) in their June 2009 request to convene a dispute settlement panel. The United States charged that such policies are intended to discriminate against foreign firms by lowering prices for Chinese companies in the steel, aluminium, and chemical sectors. China ranks as either the top or a dominant producer of all the restricted materials. US Trade Representative (USTR) Ron Kirk called China's export restraints a "conscious policy to create unfair advantages."[90]

This problem had been first raised six years ago as part of China's WTO transition review, and the formal complaint came after more than two years of unsuccessful talks between China and the United States to resolve this issue.[91] Beijing responded that its export restrictions are legitimate under WTO regulations and insisted that the "main purpose of certain export measures is to protect the environment and precious resources . . . .in line with WTO rules."[92] Perhaps not coincidentally, on the same day the United States filed its complaint, China asked the WTO to investigate a US ban on imports of Chinese poultry.

Export Subsidies

In December 2008, the US Trade Representative requestedWTO dispute settlement consultations with China over China's support for "Famous Brands" programmes, charging that such programmes use export subsidies (including cash grant rewards, preferential loans, research and development funding to develop new products, and payments to lower the cost of export credit insurance) at the central and local government level to promote the recognition and sale of Chinese brand products overseas, unfairly disadvantaging foreign competition as part of a "protectionist industrial policy."[93] China's use of preferential policies and standards to promote domestic industries over foreign competitors has a long history. The "Famous Brands" programme is just one of the many ways in which China tries to give its indigenous businesses a legup in domestic and international markets.[94] (For China's use of technological standards as a tool for supporting domestic producers, see chap. 1, sec. 3, of this Report.)

Resolved US Cases against China

China's government has long tolerated rampant violations of intellectual property rights. China also has imposed stringent censorship and performance and distribution restrictions on imported movies, books, and other intellectual content, often arguing that its regulation of such materials was intended to foster "a high level of protection of public morals." [95] In April 2007, the USTR filed two related cases against China: The first case charged that China failed to comply with the WTO agreement on intellectual property protection, and the second case charged that China failed to provide sufficient market access to intellectual property rights-related products, in terms of trading rights and distribution services. The United States initiated these cases after China failed to comply with five separate memoranda of understanding it had signed with the United States. Both of these cases have now been resolved, with the panel ruling largely in favour of the US position, although China is appealing the latter case.

Intellectual Property Rights

In the first case, on "Measures Affecting the Protection and Enforcement of Intellectual Property Rights," the United States argued that the thresholds for criminal prosecutions of intellectual property rights violations in China were too high, creating a loophole for smaller producers or violators. In addition, China's copyright laws fail to protect imported works (such as movies) that are under review by Chinese censorship authorities (and must be approved before the works can be distributed in China). As a result, pirated copies of the works can be widely distributed without violating copyright law and thus do not face prosecution. Finally, the US side also argued that China often allowed seized pirated goods to re-enter the market rather than destroying them, after removing the infringing label or trademark. In January 2009, the WTO ruled that many of China's intellectual property rights enforcement policies did not comply with WTO obligations, finding that China failed to protect intellectual property rights works under review by the government for content and mishandled the disposal of seized, pirated products. However, the panel determined that it needed more evidence on the issue of thresholds for criminal prosecutions of intellectual property rights piracy. The USTR, while admitting disappointment on the WTO findings on thresholds, noted that, right before it filed the WTO case on China's intellectual property rights enforcement, China lowered its criminal copyright threshold from 1,000 to 5000 infringing copies.[96] China said in June 2009 that it will implement the recommendations and rulings of the dispute settlement body by May 20, 2010.[97]

Market Access

In the second case, on "Measures Affecting Trading Rights and Distribution Services for Certain Publications and Audiovisual Entertainment Products," the United States sought to address three significant market access concerns. The United States claimed that the measures violated China's WTO obligations. First, the WTO panel examined prohibitions on the rights of foreign companies and individuals to import products, including reading material, audiovisual home entertainment products, sound recordings, and films for theatrical release into China. Second, the WTO panel addressed prohibitions and restrictions on the rights of foreign suppliers to distribute most of these products in China. Third, the WTO panel reviewed discriminatory treatment of imports of most of these products in China's market.[98] Like the ruling on the intellectual property rights protection case, the panel's decision, handed down in August 2009, was not an unqualified success for the United States, though the panel largely backed US claims. For example, the panel found that China was breaking WTO rules by forcing US- made magazines and video games and other media to be sold through government-owned monopolies but that the United States had failed to prove that China's distribution of US films (which made US films go through one of two designated distributors) violated China's WTO obligations. The WTO also ruled that it was illegal to give one government-owned company the monopoly to import films and books and that China must let foreign companies sell music over the Internet. China appealed the panel's decision on September 22, 2009, citing the need to protect "public morals" as a justification for restricting access for US products.[99] On October 6, the United States issued a cross appeal, seeking review by the Appellate Body of the panel's conclusion that the Chinese state plan mandating the number, structure, and geographic distribution of importers could efficiently allow imports while maintaining China's stated objective of protecting public morals.[100]

It is too early to tell what effect these two rulings will have on copyright protection and piracy in China. China announced its intention to appeal the ruling in the second case. Even if the appeal is lost, it is unlikely that better distribution of copyrighted US media will guarantee better treatment for US businesses as long as there is money to be made in China by manufacturing and selling counterfeit movies, CDs, and videogames.[101] In what may prove to be a first promising step toward better intellectual property protection, four men were imprisoned and heavily fined by a district court in Suzhou for distributing a counterfeit version of Microsoft Windows XP and other computer programmes over the Internet.[102]

Trading Rights Authorization

In March 2008, the USTR requested WTO dispute resolution consultations with China regarding its discriminatory treatment of US suppliers of financial information services in China. The United States claimed that China violates global trade rules by giving the Xinhua news agency the right to issue annual licenses for overseas media organizations, barring them from directly distributing information and soliciting subscribers in China. Xinhua was given sole power in September 2006 to regulate news services that distribute financial information in China, such as Bloomberg and Reuters—while it also is a direct competitor of such services. In response to the US complaint, in November 2008 the USTR announced that China had agreed to eliminate discriminatory restrictions on how US and other foreign suppliers of financial information services do business in China. The two sides signed a contract in which China agreed to have the State Council Information Office serve as a regulator. However, in April 2009 China raised the possibility of renewed information controls when the government said financial information providers must not engage in news-gathering in China.[103] The State Council Information Office published the regulations that formalized the agreement but also said in Article XIX that "foreign financial information providers set up in China . . . must not undertake news-gathering activities."[104] At the time of this Report's writing, it is unclear whether there will be any follow-up or requests for clarification from the US side.

Chinese WTO Cases against the United States

In July 2009, China brought a WTO case against the United States over a provision in the Omnibus Appropriations Act of 2009 that in effect prohibits the establishment or implementation of any measures that would allow poultry products to be imported from China. At the center of the case is the 2006 rule issued by US Department of Agriculture (USDA) that allowed China to export cooked poultry products to the United States as long as the raw poultry meat originated in the United States or Canada. In 2007, however, the US Congress stopped the USDA from implementing the rule by inserting a provision in the 2008 fiscal year spending bill that prohibited the USDA from allowing chicken processed in China to be imported.[105] The same prohibition was included in the spending bill in the next two fiscal years. The Omnibus Appropriations Act of 2009, signed into law on March 11, 2009, includes a section that bans any funding from being used to "establish or implement a rule" allowing the import of poultry products from China. China's Ministry of Commerce said that US restrictions on Chinese chicken imports were "totally unfair and of a bad nature" and in violation of WTO's most-favoured-nation principle.[106]

In response to China's second request, after the first had been blocked by the United States, the WTO dispute settlement body established a panel. USDA and the USTR announced on September 25 that House and Senate lawmakers have agreed to a provision in the fiscal year 2010 agriculture appropriations bill that would allow imports of processed poultry or poultry products from China if certain conditions are met. The agreement mandates US inspections of Chinese facilities before any cooked chickens could be imported, and more port-of-entry reinspections. The proposal also requires the Agriculture Department to report frequently to Congress on the implementation of any rule authorizing China to export poultry products to the United States.[107] The law that created the ban lacks health or safety rationale language that might justify it. US poultry and other meat industries also argue that the law prevents the United States from using science-based arguments to effectively open markets overseas for US meat exports.[108]

China has another case pending against the United States. In September 2008, China initiated a WTO case against the United States on its concurrent use of antidumping and countervailing measures against certain Chinese-made steel pipes, tyres, and laminated woven sacks. As of the date of this Report, no panel has been convened for the first case, while a panel was established but no report issued for the second case.

The Chinese Tyre Case

When China joined the WTO, it agreed to the so-called "China-specific safeguard" that permits China's trading partners to impose tariffs on surges of Chinese imports if these imports harm domestic producers. This provision was codified in US law in Section 421 of the 1974 Trade Act. On September 11, 2009, the White House announced its decision to impose remedies under Section 421 to stop a surge of imports into the United States of Chinese tyres for passenger cars and light trucks.[109] Imports of Chinese tyres have grown from 4.7 percent of the US market in 2004 to 16.7 percent in 2008. The International Trade Commission determined that the surge of imports of Chinese tyres has disrupted the US market.[110] The duty will be

35 percent in the first year, 30 percent in the second, and 25 percent in the third (the International Trade Commission recommended 55 percent in the first year, 45 percent in the second year, and 35 percent in the third year). This "safeguard" provision was made part of China's accession agreement to the WTO in 2001 and allows American companies or workers to ask the government for protection simply by demonstrating a surge of Chinese imports.

Within hours of President Obama's announcement, the Chinese Ministry of Commerce accused the United States of protectionism and violation of international trade laws. Commerce Minister Chen Deming, for example, called the imposition of tariffs a "serious protectionist act" that has "seriously damaged" the US-China economic relationship.[111] This was followed by an announcement on September 14 that China's Ministry of Commerce has launched an investigation into whether "certain imported automotive products and certain imported chicken meat products originating from the United States" were being subsidized or "dumped" in the Chinese markets, although the Chinese government made no announcements linking the investigations to US tyre tariffs.[112] China has also requested formal consultation at the WTO regarding US tariffs, a first step toward launching a dispute settlement.[113] On September 15, the Ministry of Commerce also announced that it was drafting measures to support the tyre industry and related sectors to offset the impact of US tariffs.[114]

Conclusion

- China's trade surplus with the United States remains near record levels, despite the global economic slowdown that has reduced imports from other nations. While the US trade deficit in goods with China through August 2009 was $143.7 billion, representing a decline of 17.6 percent over the same period in 2008, China now accounts for an increasing share of the US global deficit in goods. By September 2009, China had accumulated more than $2.27 trillion in foreign currency reserves.
- China's currency has strengthened against the US dollar by about 21 percent since the government announced in July 2005 it was transitioning from a hard peg to the dollar to a "managed float" against a basket of currencies. Starting in July 2008, however, the RMB's appreciation was stymied by Chinese government policy as Beijing reimposed strict controls in order to support China's export industries. China's RMB remains significantly undervalued.
- China's growing cache of dollar reserves, a consequence of a deliberate Chinese government policy, is a continuing source of tension between the two countries. Chinese leaders profess alarm that the value of their dollar cache depends on the health of the US economy and the willingness of the US Federal Reserve system to hold down inflation. On the other hand, the size of China's dollar reserves makes it unlikely that China could divest its dollars without reducing the value of its dollar holdings.
- The Chinese leadership has become critical of the reserve currency status of the dollar, recommending a greater role for the IMF accounting unit, special drawing rights, and perhaps even preparing the RMB for internationalization. For now, the RMB remains nonconvertible. China is also seeking more influence within the IMF.

- China continues to use trade-distorting measures in violation of its WTO commitments. The WTO found that China failed to comply with its obligations in terms of enforcement of intellectual property rights laws and to provide sufficient market access to intellectual property rights-related products.

SECTION 2

China's Role in the Origins of the Global Financial Crisis and China's Response

"The Commission shall investigate and report exclusively on . . .

"Economic Transfers: The qualitative and quantitative nature of the transfer of United States production activities to the People's Republic of China, including the relocation of high technology, manufacturing, and research and development facilities, the impact of such transfers on United States national security, the adequacy of United States export control laws, and the effect of such transfers on United States economic security and employment.

"United States Capital Markets: The extent of access to and use of United States capital markets by the People's Republic of China, including whether or not existing disclosure and transparency rules are adequate to identify People's Republic of China companies engaged in harmful activities. . . ."

Introduction

The global financial crisis of 2008 that affected the economies of rich and poor nations alike has been blamed on a confluence of factors, including, but not limited to, the collapse of real estate values; lax regulation of financial services; historically low interest rates managed by central banks; and speculation in commodities and fixed assets. While informed opinions differ on the relative weight of the many contributing factors, much attention has also focused on the role of the unbalanced trade relationship between the United States and China. While this relationship does not tell the whole story, it does provide a guide to understanding how the many economic threads of the crisis converge in these two global powers.

Both nations have responded to the global economic crisis with large-scale spending programmes, tailored to address each nation's individual problems. The United States in late 2008 addressed the crisis in the financial services industries by recapitalizing companies whose failure would create a systemic risk to the overall economy. Most of the government's initial response focused on the financial services sector, which included mortgage giants Fannie Mae and Freddie Mac. Later, in early 2009, Congress passed a $786 billion economic stimulus programme designed to boost government and consumer spending.

China's response to the global recession emphasized quick spending on infrastructure projects such as highways, railroads, and ports, rather than on the financial services industry. Chinese banks had avoided many of the risky investments in financial derivatives that threatened American banks, money market funds, securities firms, and mortgage lenders. China was first, in November 2008, to announce its economic stimulus package—$586 billion over two years—chiefly intended to realize China's goal of an 8 percent annual growth rate. This is supplemented by bank lending, export promotion policies, and some consumption-boosting measures. As the details of China's recovery plan have emerged, problems have also surfaced. Beijing claims its yearly growth rate is on track to reach 8 percent yet admits that unemployment has skyrocketed and that disaffected workers have been migrating back to the rural areas. China's labour minister, Yin Weimin, said in September that although there has been a modest increase in the number of jobs in the second quarter of 2009, the unemployment situation remained "grave."[115]

In addition to the stimulus package, the Chinese government has directed its state-owned banks to drastically loosen credit—some 8.7 trillion RMB ($1.3 trillion) has been lent out in the first nine months of 2009. This lending risks creating unwanted financial imbalances and strains on bank balance sheets.[116] Much of the stimulus lending has also apparently wound up in the hands of inefficient state-owned and state-controlled enterprises rather than in the private economy or in the hands of consumers.[117] Some of the bank lending has fuelled stock speculation, which drove up the Shanghai stock index by 70 percent in the first half of 2009, making it the best-performing market in the world.[118] Realizing this, regulatory authorities in China urged the state-owned banks to rein in lending to large, state-owned companies that might have been investing the funds in the stock market.[119] The market quickly sold off 20 percent, and volatility has remained high.

Governments in both countries have claimed some success for their responses to the 2008 financial downturn. In the United States, the housing industry shows signs of stabilizing, and the equity market has begun to revive, but unemployment remains perilously high. In China, officials point to gross domestic product (GDP) growth that has returned to historic norms and to rising asset values. The International Monetary Fund (IMF) predicted in October that China's real GDP will grow at an annual rate of 8.5 percent for 2009, compared to a GDP decline of 2.7 percent in the United States.

But underlying problems in the economic relationship between the two countries remain. The stimulus plans of neither country have managed to address the bilateral imbalance that many economists identify as one of the principal factors for the precarious position of the global economy. China produces far more than its consumers buy, and the United States consumes far in excess of its production. (Personal savings in the United States is showing some improvement, however. The personal savings rate as a percentage of disposable personal income, which dipped below zero during the housing boom, was 4.2 percent in July 2009).[120] Even with the increase in private savings, US government debt is expected to rise from 41 percent of GDP in fiscal 2009 to 60 percent of GDP by the end of fiscal 2010.[121] Rather than address these fundamental problems, Washington's economic stimulus programme still depends on federal deficit spending and high levels of consumption by American households to eventually float the US economy off the rocks. Beijing still depends on an export and investment-led growth model to keep its factories humming and its workers employed. China's central government continues to serve as America's largest creditor. While the overall American trade deficit has declined from its record levels of 2008 ($216.9 billion in the first half of 2009 versus $406.2 over the same period in 2008), the goods trade deficit with China remains abnormally high ($143.7 billion in the first eight months of 2009 versus $169.2 billion during the same period in 2008) and represents an increasing percentage of the US's global trade imbalance.[122] By continuing to consume more than is produced, the United States must continue to borrow. Meanwhile, China continues to add manufacturing capacity, producing more than it can consume domestically.

Global Financial and Trade Imbalances

The February 2009 hearing before the Commission on the origins of the financial crisis and the response of the United States and China mirrored the disagreements among a larger group of analysts and economists in both capitals seeking to apportion blame for the crisis to each country's economic policies. Experts also differ in assessing the likely success of China's and America's responses to the crisis. The debate over which government policies created which problems and which remedies will ultimately prove effective will take years to resolve. But while history takes its own time to reach a conclusion, the Commission has considered much evidence and identified some common theories that have emerged from the discussion. The Commission's February hearing on "China's Role in the Origins of and Response to the Global Recession" provides a useful framework for the debate.

In his testimony at the February hearing, Michael Pettis, a finance professor at Peking University and a former Wall Street trader, connected several of the disparate economic elements to fashion a unified theory of how China contributed to the imbalances and how those imbalances helped to sink the world's economy. The key, said Mr. Pettis, is to follow the money.

As America's largest supplier of imported goods, China has accumulated an enormous amount of dollars. China has run record-setting trade surpluses during the past decade with the United States by exporting five to six times as much in dollar terms as it takes in imports from the United States. In addition, US-based corporations have invested large sums in China. The Chinese government then gathers up the accumulated dollars and buys US Treasury bonds, which pay interest to China's central bank, the People's Bank of China. The government might have chosen to allow those dollars to remain in the hands of the Chinese people and companies that earned them, but in order to control the value of the renminbi (RMB) relative to the dollar, China chooses to keep dollars out of the private economy by requiring Chinese citizens to exchange them at the state-owned banks.

This "recycling process" put the dollars back into the hands of the US government and, indirectly, into the hands of US consumers, who were thus able to purchase even more Chinese goods at very low interest rates. The process, said Mr. Pettis, became "self-reinforcing": Americans went on a buying spree.

> *In the [United States], the torrent of inward-bound liquidity boosted real estate and stock market prices. As they surged, substantially raising the wealth of US households, these [households] became increasingly willing to divert a rising share of their income to consumption. At the same time, rising liquidity always forces financial institutions to adjust their balance sheets to accommodate money growth, and the most common way is to increase outstanding loans. With banks eager to lend, and households eager to monetize their assets in order to fund consumption, it was only a question of time before household borrowing ballooned.*

> *Meanwhile, in China, as foreign currency poured into the country via its trade surplus, the [People's Bank of China] had to create local money with which to purchase the inflow [of dollars]. In China, most new money creation ends up in banks, and banks primarily fund investment (consumer lending is a negligible part of bank lending). With investment surging, industrial production grew faster than consumption. A country's trade surplus is the gap between its production and its consumption, and as this gap grew, so did China's trade surplus, which resulted in even more foreign currency pouring into the country, thus reinforcing the cycle.*[123]

Mr. Pettis's analysis supports a generally accepted explanation for the dramatic decline in the overall US savings rate: Consumers watching their stock holdings and home values soar felt wealthy enough to stop saving entirely, a phenomenon known as "the wealth effect." Meanwhile, voters gave up demanding that the federal government stop deficit spending. While economic theory holds that government borrowing crowds out private investment and makes interest rates rise, this did not occur. The economy continued to grow as American consumers emptied their savings accounts and even borrowed from the equity in their homes. Meanwhile, interest rates fell rather than rose, thanks to Beijing's willingness to buy US government bonds, thereby driving down interest rates even as government borrowing increased. The ultimate result: an asset bubble driven by overspending in personal and commercial real estate and the stock market, aided by increasingly risky loans offered by commercial banks and investments in derivatives made by investment banks.

Other witnesses at the Commission's hearing agreed that China's trade surpluses were part of the problem, but they placed more of the blame on the US government and American consumers for the ensuing economic troubles. Nicholas Lardy, a senior fellow at the Peterson Institute for International Economics, insisted that American consumers borrowed too much, and US regulators lacked the foresight to recognize the dangers of the new financial instruments, such as securitized subprime mortgages, that facilitated the borrowing and the overspending. In contrast, home equity loans, which allowed Americans to withdraw equity from their homes and use it for consumer purchases, do not even exist in China, Dr. Lardy noted.[124] Chinese regulators did not approve of investments in collateralized debt obligations—the practice of bundling thousands of mortgages together and marketing the result as a bond secured by the underlying mortgages. In addition, Dr. Lardy said, China's "regulators have not allowed the introduction of complex derivative products of any kind, and the result is the central government has not had to inject capital into any financial institution, bank or otherwise, as a result of the crisis, nor have they had to guarantee the liabilities of any bank or other kind of financial institution."

Dr. Lardy praised China's efforts to rescue its own economy as "the gold standard" when compared to stimulus programmes in Japan, Europe, and the United States. China was first among nations, in September 2008, to ease lending standards at its state-owned banks and to slash interest rates. China's government followed this action in November 2008 with the announcement of plans for a massive public works spending plan and in December announced plans for greatly expanded government-provided health care, with a goal of attaining universal coverage by 2011.[125]

Stephen Roach, chairman of Morgan Stanley's Asia branch, was no less critical of the role that US indebtedness has played in setting up the world economy for a fall. "No one forced the American consumers to lever all their assets up to their eyeballs and squander the appreciation of those assets on current consumption," Dr. Roach told the Commission. However, he also believed that China has adopted policies that have led to massive trade imbalances and in turn have contributed to the destabilization of global finances. For example, China adopted a successful, export-dependent growth strategy that resulted in China's exports as a share of GDP to almost double in just seven years, from 20 percent in 2001 to 37 percent in 2008. Meanwhile, China's GDP grew at an average 10.4 percent rate in the seven years ending in 2007.[126]

Dr. Roach chastised America for its "reliance on China's funding of its external deficit—a reliance that can only grow in an era of open-ended, trillion-dollar budget deficits." But Dr. Roach was also critical of China's policy of undervaluing its currency to make its exports cheaper in the United States and its selective subsidies to boost exports. China, he said, should not "be tempted to use the currency lever or other subsidies to boost its export sector" but rather "shift its growth model from one that has been overly reliant on exports to one that draws increased support from private consumption." [127]

Nevertheless, Dr. Roach warned against any effort to "portray American consumers as innocent victims of Asia or Chinese mercantilist policies." Rather, Dr. Roach said, "We made dumb mistakes that were reinforced by, I think, poor policies and poor behaviour across our economy, from politicians to central banks to regulators to Wall Street to Main Street, and I think it is really incorrect to even think that the Chinese are responsible for those poor decisions." [128] One of the most detrimental consequences of runaway consumption in the United States was the drastic fall in its domestic savings rate. Between 2002 and 2007, the US net national savings rate—the sum of household, business, and government saving after adjustment for depreciation—plunged to a record low of 1.8 percent of national income, and then actually turned negative in 2008.[129]

Robert B. Cassidy, an international trade and services professional at Kelley Drye & Warren LLP, had a different view from Drs. Lardy and Roach and was more critical of China's policies as a cause for the financial crisis. Mr. Cassidy conducted the final negotiations with China over the terms of its 2001 entry into the World Trade Organization, a highly detailed process that stretched out over 13 years. The deal overseen by Mr. Cassidy required China to make many promises to empty its policy toolbox of central planning and state ownership and to adopt western free-market mechanisms. The problem, according to Mr. Cassidy, is that China has purposefully nullified one of the most powerful forces in any free market—the price factor. By artificially pegging the value of its currency at a rate that most economists agree is significantly undervalued, China is effectively "subsidiz[ing] its exports, subsidiz[ing] foreign direct investment, and [taxing] China's imports."[130]

At the same time, China has attracted the world's largest manufacturers by offering discounted land, energy, and taxes to relocate in China and to use China as a global export platform. More than half of China's exports originate from foreign-invested manufacturing enterprises located in China.* "The main driver of exports out of China has been foreign-invested enterprises," both wholly foreign owned and joint ventures with Chinese companies, which together account for roughly 55 percent ($790 billion) of the total exports in 2008, Terence P. Stewart, a Washington attorney and trade expert, told the Commission.[131] (For further information on the role of foreign invested enterprises in China's industrial policy, see chap. 1, sec. 3.)

The undervalued currency, which also attracts foreign investors by discounting land and manufacturing inputs, is the cornerstone of China's export-led growth strategy, said Mr. Cassidy. In effect, China simply "exports its savings to the United States rather than using those funds for domestic investment" or consumption, said Mr. Cassidy. "If China is unprepared to [allow its currency to appreciate in value as the market dictates], then the United States and other countries should consider initiating, in a progressive manner, strong actions against China's beggar-thy-neighbour policies," he suggested.[132]

Eswar S. Prasad, a professor of trade policy at Cornell University and former chief economist of the China division at the International Monetary Fund, offered a warning to the Commission that China's currency peg to the dollar will likely do even more harm to the world's economy by limiting the ability of the People's Bank of China to manage the fast-growing economy and to even out the business cycles by controlling inflation. "Flexibility of the currency is an essential prerequisite . . . rather than an objective in itself," he said. "Giving the Chinese central bank room to raise or lower interest rates by freeing it from having to target a particular exchange rate would help rein in credit growth and deter reckless investment, reducing the risk of boom-bust cycles; an important point here is that an independent monetary policy requires a flexible exchange rate," he said.

The Global Savings Glut

The speed and ferocity of the 2008 global financial crisis may have taken investors by surprise, but at the beginning of the millennium there were warnings that the world economy had entered a new and potentially destabilizing phase. Those warnings specifically focused on the financial and trade relationship between China and the United States and more broadly between the developed world and the emerging nations of Asia. Witnesses at the Commission's February 17 hearing referred to these early warnings, which went unheeded during the early and mid-2000s.

* In China, foreign equity capital inflows are classified as foreign direct investment only if they lead to a foreign equity stake at or above 25 percent, and most foreign direct investment inflows into China finance foreign equity stakes in joint ventures, usually with only two investors in a joint venture. This is different from countries in the Organization for Economic Cooperation and Development (OECD), including the United States, where a 10 percent threshold is a common definition for foreign direct investment, and shareholding of a publicly traded company is diffuse. For more information, see Yasheng Huang, *Selling China: Foreign Direct Investment during the Reform Era* (New York: Cambridge University Press: 2003), pp. 4–6.

For example, Federal Reserve Board Chairman Ben Bernanke, while an economics professor at Princeton, helped originate the idea that a "global savings glut" had reversed the historic financial relationship between rich and poor nations. Ordinarily, poor nations borrow from rich nations. Poor nations put these loans to work by improving the low productivity of their labour force— through education, better health care, and especially through the automation of manufacturing processes and the application of more efficient energy sources. Poor nations historically ran trade deficits with rich nations as the poor nations borrowed to automate assembly lines and add electrical generating capacity.

Dr. Bernanke recognized in 2005 that "a combination of diverse forces has created a significant increase in the global supply of saving —a global saving glut— which helps to explain both the increase in the US current account deficit and the relatively low level of long-term real interest rates in the world today." [133] Asian countries, led by China, had responded to the 1997 Asian financial crisis by adopting industrial and trade policies aimed at encouraging production and exports while suppressing domestic consumption. Rather than spend their income, Chinese citizens reacted to a variety of government actions or inactions by saving it in low-interest-bearing bank accounts. These savings became available to the government through its state-owned banks to build enormous manufacturing capacity, much of it also state owned, in effect providing low-cost capital.

In particular, the Chinese government chose not to rebuild a safety net to replace the "iron rice bowl" that was dismantled when Deng Xiaoping instituted market reforms and started selling off the government-owned industries that had been providing health care, education, and housing to the workers and their families. This situation forced Chinese citizens to save much of their income to meet medical, educational, and retirement needs and inhibited the development of a consumer culture. State-owned banks did their part by limiting consumer lending, refusing to issue credit cards, and requiring large downpayments for mortgages. Chinese citizens were prohibited from investing abroad for higher returns and could only expect low returns at home. As a result, the consumption share of Chinese GDP fell to a record low of 36 percent in 2007 (see figure 1), "underscoring the dark side of China's macro imbalances that is now so problematic in this global crisis," according to Dr. Roach.[134]

Fig. 1: Chinese Personal Consumption as a Percent of GDP, 1952–2006

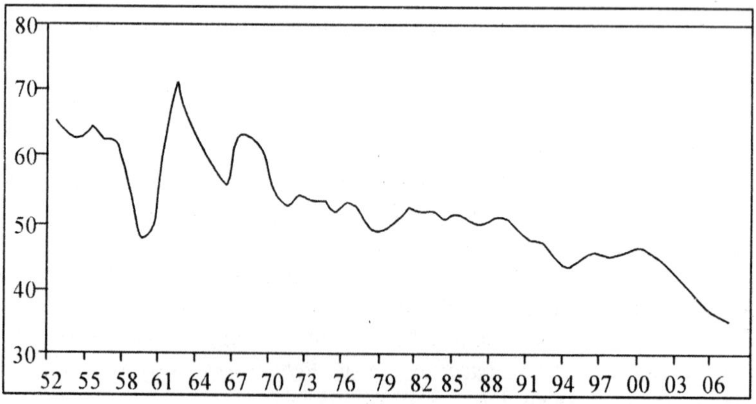

Sources: China National Bureau of Statistics and Morgan Stanley Research.

The resulting sharp rise in savings created a financial counterweight that made it easy for trading partners, such as the United States and Europe, to run deficits. China's high national savings rate and its policy of tightly managing the value of the RMB "abetted US profligacy by providing cheap goods and cheap financing for those goods," setting the stage for a crisis, said Dr. Prasad.[136] The political economist Robert Skidelsky explained how China's loans to the US government wound up in the checking accounts of Americans:

> *With Chinese savings available, the US government could run a deficit without crowding out private spending. This allowed the Fed to establish a much lower funds rate—the rate at which banks borrow from the Fed and one another —than it would otherwise have been able to do, helped in this by the downward pressure on prices exerted by the import of cheap Chinese goods produced by cheap Chinese labour. Cheap money in turn enabled banks to expand their deposits and their loans to customers more than they could otherwise have done. In short, it was via their impact on the financing of the federal deficit that Chinese savings made it possible for the US consumers to go on a spending spree.*[137]

Dr. Skidelsky also noted that this

> *has left much too large a part of our own economic activity dependent on foreign loans. It is one thing to borrow from abroad for investment, a different matter to borrow for consumption, since this does not create assets which can service the debt. The global imbalances helped pump up the inverted debt pyramid that brought the system crashing down.*[138]

Speaking at a conference on Asia and the financial crisis in October 2009, Dr. Bernanke returned to the theme of unsustainable imbalances in trade in capital flows, saying that the United States "must increase its national savings rate," while most Asian economies "must act to narrow the gap between saving and investment and to raise domestic demand." He also cautioned against "trade surpluses achieved through policies that artificially enhance incentives for domestic saving and the production of export goods," because they "distort the mix of domestic industries and the allocation of resources." [139] However, as Dr. Bernanke pointed out, following the 1997 Asian financial crisis Asian economies' "commitment to export-led growth" only strengthened.

Before the 1997 Asian crisis, the normal range of the US trade deficit was one percent of GDP; afterward, it soared to 7 percent of GDP.[140] It is clear that the currency is under pressure from China's rising trade surplus which, in a market economy, would cause the RMB to increase in value. As Derek Scissors, an economist at The Heritage Foundation and a witness at the Commission's February hearing, pointed out, from the end of 2004 to the end of 2008 the RMB appreciated at most by 21 percent against the dollar. At the same time, China's aggregate trade surplus with the world increased by 800 percent.[141] Since June 2008, the RMB has been held by Beijing at around 6.8 RMB to the dollar in order to help support exports during the global recession.[142]

China's government and its export industries benefited greatly from these imbalances when the times were good. Between 2001 and 2006, the export share of Chinese GDP nearly doubled, from 20 percent to 36 percent (see figure 2).[143] China was exporting its products and providing US consumers with the wherewithal to buy them.[144]

Fig. 2: China's Exports as a Percent of GDP, 1952–2006

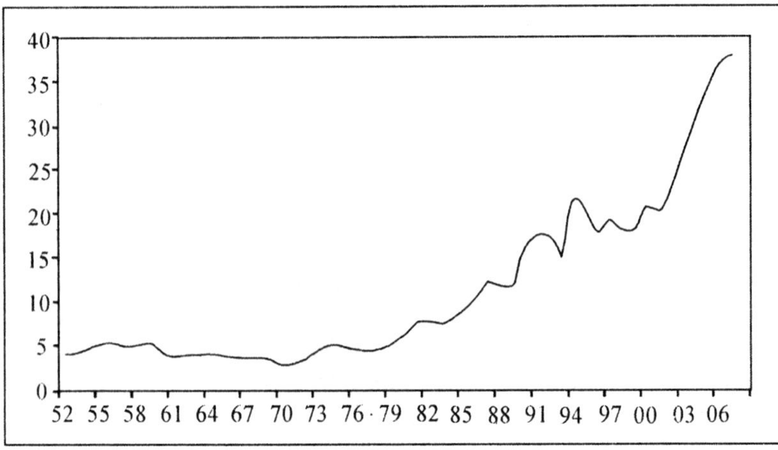

Sources: China National Bureau of Statistics and Morgan Stanley Research.

China's tightly managed exchange rate regime, rising overall trade surplus, and rapid accumulation of foreign exchange reserves have relied on the manipulation of the value of its currency to aid its exporters. In addition, other, more subtle practices remain pervasive. Through its business-oriented but consumer-unfriendly financial system, which is dominated by state-owned banks, China provides cheap capital to many of its enterprises. Land and energy subsidies have also held down the effective cost of production.[146] (See chap. 1, sec. 3, for a detailed discussion of China's industrial policy.) While personal consumption in China moved the opposite way, from 45 percent of GDP in the 1990s to 35 percent of GDP currently, excessive consumption in the United States inevitably led to trade deficits.[147]

China Denies Responsibility

The Chinese leadership has rejected the notion that Beijing shares responsibility for the financial crisis. Chinese policymakers believe that only US overconsumption is to blame for the creation of the global imbalances and "are aghast at any mention of China's contributory role . . . consider[ing] Chinese overproduction to be nothing more than a response to US demand," noted Mr. Pettis.[148] Premier Wen Jiabao told leaders at the World Economic Forum in Davos in January 2009 that the global economic collapse was caused by US policies that included "an excessive expansion of financial institutions in blind pursuit of profit" and an "unsustainable model of development characterized by prolonged low savings and high consumption" as well as lax regulation of the financial sector.[149] In a February 2009 interview with the *Financial Times* in London, Premier Wen expanded on his theory that the meltdown was caused by US borrowing rather than Chinese saving. "It is completely confusing right and wrong when some countries that have been overspending then blame those that lend them money for their spending." Premier Wen insisted that the written statement by Treasury Secretary Tim Geithner to the Senate Finance

Committee during his confirmation hearings that China is manipulating its currency to gain a trade advantage was "completely unfounded." [150] White House Press Secretary Robert Gibbs later clarified that Mr. Geithner's statement "was restating what [President Obama] had said during the [election] campaign" rather than presenting a determination by the administration. [151] In its October 2009 semiannual report to Congress, the US Department of the Treasury said that while it "remains of the view that the [RMB] is undervalued," and that "the recent lack of flexibility of the [RMB] exchange rate and China's renewed accumulation of foreign exchange reserves risk unwinding some of the progress made in reducing" global imbalances, no country "met the standards" for illegal currency manipulation.[152]

But few economists outside China think the global meltdown can be blamed on just one party. Wynne Godley, Dimitri Papadimitriou, and Genaaro Zezza, economists at the Levy Economics Institute of Bard College, wrote:

> *Some economists have gone so far as to suggest that the growing imbalance problem was entirely the consequence of the saving glut in Asian and other surplus countries. In our view, there was an interdependent process in which all parties played an active role. The United States could not have maintained growth unless it had been happy to sponsor, or at least permit, private sector [particularly personal sector] borrowing on such an unprecedented scale.*[153]

China's Response to the Crisis

Two years ago, Premier Wen Jiabao warned that the Chinese economy was "unstable, unbalanced, uncoordinated, and unsustainable." The 11th Five-Year Plan, currently in effect, essentially acknowledges this statement and stresses China's need to embark on a major structural transformation from export- to consumer-led growth.[154] However, that reform, welcomed at the time by China's major trading partners, including the United States, has been put on the back burner by Beijing policymakers in favour of stimulating the economy and maintaining a growth rate of around 8 percent.

The stimulus programme, detailed below, is not channeling the stimulus money to household consumers and service industries, whose rising demand could absorb a greater share of Chinese production. [155] Instead, the fiscal stimulus is still based on raising production and investment in the manufacturing sector, especially the large, state-owned enterprises that dominate the economy, because exports are still considered a key source of job growth. China's overall trade surplus has continued to grow from just under $17 billion in the first half of 2008 to nearly $33 billion in the second half. In 2009, the increase in China's global surplus continued, despite a decline in exports: for example, the monthly trade surplus grew from $8.25 billion in June to $10.6 billion in July to 15.7 billion in August 2009.[156] Moreover, Chinese household savings are likely to increase due to the economic uncertainty, putting further constraints on consumption. Thus, the fiscal stimulus could end up actually worsening the global imbalances by boosting investment and exports rather than private consumption.[157]

The major risk to the United States and to China's other trading partners comes from several unique aspects of China's stimulus plan. China's plan has increased manufacturing capacity in areas that are already producing excess goods, which has resulted in more export sales at even lower prices. A series of tax rebates and cuts aimed at export industries has been performing the same function, leading to greater trade imbalances. Implementation of plans to create a better health care system and to extend free public education to rural areas has been long overdue, while too little attention has been given to consumer banking reform or an easing of strict capital controls that might encourage Chinese consumers to spend more on imported goods.

China's reliance on US Treasury bonds to park its accumulation of foreign exchange reserves is also unlikely to diminish. First, Beijing continues to effectively peg the RMB to the dollar as a matter of national policy, so China will need to continue to employ capital controls and buy dollars. Second, given the turmoil in world financial markets and the dearth of safe and liquid financial instruments, US Treasuries remain one of the most secure assets for investing China's foreign currency reserves.[158] Between September 2008 and July 2009, Chinese purchases of US Treasury bills amounted to more than $182.3 billion, further consolidating China's position as the biggest holder of US Treasuries.[159]

China's Economic Stimulus Package

In response to the economic crisis, on November 9, 2008, China's State Council announced a plan to increase domestic demand and stimulate economic growth by investing 4 trillion RMB ($586 billion) by the end of 2010 in 10 major areas. By most accounts, the stimulus has reversed China's economic slide, boosting GDP and setting off a domestic construction spree. But the plans also stoked speculation in the Shanghai and Hong Kong stock exchanges and produced warnings that the runaway inflation of the 1990s could return. A heavy reliance on bank lending (some $1.3 trillion in loans in the first nine months of 2009) has also caused the government to instruct banks to reimpose some lending restraint.

China's stimulus has been criticized on a number of grounds. The stimulus includes existing programmes, such as earthquake reconstruction, that had already been announced. It requires the provinces and local governments to come up with one-third to nearly three-quarters of the funding—raising doubts as to whether these funds will actually be forthcoming. In addition, the plan will further stimulate export industries at the expense of domestic consumption, contrary to Beijing's stated goal of switching to a more homegrown expansion.[160] Dr. Scissors of the Heritage Foundation wrote that China's stimulus package is "largely a repackaging of previous measures designed to immediately bolster domestic confidence" [161] and that the stimulus is "not intended as a permanent solution, but instead as a mechanism to buy time until foreign demand recovers." [162]

The business and investment-friendly policies announced last November would also cut the value added tax (VAT) on purchases of fixed assets such as machinery, which would lower business costs by 120 billion RMB ($17.6 billion). Additionally, commercial banks' credit ceilings were abolished to channel more lending to priority projects, rural areas, smaller enterprises, and "industrial rationalization through mergers and acquisitions."[163] The government said it would give priority to "maintaining steady and relatively fast growth" in 2009, with "positive" fiscal and "moderately relaxed" monetary policies, translating to support for the export sectors. Meanwhile, easier credit terms reversed a 2007 policy of cutting back lending to fight economic overheating and inflation.[164]

In November 2008, Premier Wen Jiabao announced 10 areas that will receive investment: (1) low-income housing; (2) rural infrastructure; (3) major infrastructure, including railways, highways, and airports; (4) health, culture, and education; (5) ecological environment; (6) science and technology innovation and industrial structure adjustment; (7) post-earthquake rebuilding; (8) income increases for urban and rural residents; (9) value-added tax reform and other methods to reduce the burden on enterprises by 120 billion RMB (about $17.6 billion); and (10) improvement of financial systems in support of economic growth.[165]

Details revealed later that the central government will pay only a third of the total 4 trillion RMB ($586 billion). Government-owned banks, state-owned enterprises, and local governments are expected to provide the remaining 2.28 trillion RMB ($413.3 billion).

Typically, stimulus projects get fast approval and a partial financial contribution from the central government, while local authorities are left to come up with the majority of the funds. But local authorities do not have much money, as China's tax system channels most revenue to Beijing.[166] According to a recent report by China's National Audit Office, many infrastructure projects are being delayed because local governments cannot match the funds provided by the central government, coming up with only 48 percent of their matching funds.[167] Some local governments were so strapped for cash that they used stimulus money from Beijing to retire some of their older debts, the auditor said.[168]

Much of the stimulus spending is long term, designed not only to create jobs quickly but also to strengthen competitiveness in key areas. The loosening of monetary policy, easing of regulations on lending, and extension of tax breaks for exporters will provide quick relief. Some affected social groups, such as the urban poor, farmers, and migrant workers, will receive direct transfer payments, but otherwise the stimulus contains major infrastructure projects that will take years to produce tangible economic effects. And since it is relying on new government bonds and bank lending, the plan is debt driven. China, it appears, is using the global recession to launch long-anticipated reforms in underdeveloped regions, as well as a broad strategic development plan.[169] National Development and Reform Commission Deputy Secretary Ma Liqiang said that many of the projects "were previously on our agenda," but the crisis accelerated implementation plans, with some long-term projects moved up.[170]

China has experienced intense growth in the past decade by relying on manufactured exports. The central government plans to stimulate export-promoting programmes by increasing the export tax rebates for a variety of industries including textile, steel, and machinery; upgrading petrochemical refineries; encouraging manufacturing of domestic goods; and eliminating export tariffs.[171]

Rebates of the VAT on goods produced for export were raised seven times between August 2008 and June 2009, in amounts ranging from 5 percent to 17 percent on products including textiles, ethanol, toys, and sewing machines.[172] The government also has extended more than 6 trillion RMB ($878 billion) in loans in the first half of 2009 to help small- and medium-sized companies expand into the international markets and establish distribution channels in emerging markets.[173] Credit lending programmes favouring farmers and low-income groups have also been introduced, but urban consumers are not expected to get the income tax rebates that could spur consumption.[174] The government is also launching specific campaigns aimed at boosting exports. For example, in June 2009, China's Ministry of Commerce initiated a "421 project," the goal of which is to secure $42.1 billion of machinery and electronics orders within three months by mobilizing the resources of the state, including China's powerful, state-owned banks.[175]

Shifting to consumption-driven growth is a complex process that cannot happen overnight, but Beijing has shown reluctance to move away from export-oriented growth, despite warnings from economists not to rely on exports to fuel China's recovery and instead to initiate structural economic reforms. Li Yining, a noted economist and deputy director of the Chinese People's Political Consultative Committee's economic committee, argued that China "must not delay economic reform," cautioning that there will be "no true economic recovery without economic transformation." [176]

Later announcements, however, focused on boosting internal consumption. For example, the government announced a three-year, $850 billion RMB ($124.5 billion) plan to improve health care and a 13 percent rebate for rural dwellers on purchases of appliances such as refrigerators and washing machines.[177] The government cut consumption taxes on small cars. Interest rates have been cut five times since September 2008, and controls on bank lending have been eased. In addition, banks have been ordered to reduce required downpayments for mortgages from 40 percent to 20 percent. [178] In June 2009, China also approved a pilot pension programme that aims to cover 10 percent of rural counties this year.[179] The Chinese government hopes the programme will encourage farmers to spend more and help narrow the wealth gap between cities and the countryside.

For a government long focused on what it termed "social stability," a short fall in GDP growth is a worrisome development, and a rough official calculation estimates that 1 percentage point of Chinese GDP growth creates about one million jobs.[180] In fact, the Chinese government maintains that a growth rate of at least 8 percent is necessary to avoid massive unemployment. The toll on Chinese employment has already been serious.* Researchers at the Chinese Academy of Social Sciences said that 41 million Chinese workers have lost their jobs as a result

* China's National Bureau of Statistics reported that in 2007 (the latest figures available), the total number of employed persons was 769.9 million. Chinese employment statistics, however, are notoriously unreliable, with the government consistently understating the rate of unemployment; it is also unclear how the migrant worker population is estimated and whether they are made part of the total employment statistics. These data should be viewed with caution. "Table 4–1 Employment," China Statistical Yearbook 2008 (Beijing: National Bureau of Statistics of China, September 2008). http://www.stats.gov.cn/tjsj/ndsj/2008/indexeh.htm.

of the crisis and that about 23 million of those still remained out of work.[181] The government also acknowledged that by the start of the Chinese New Year festival on January 25, 2009, 20 million, or 15.3 percent, of China's 130 million migrant workers had lost their jobs and had left coastal manufacturing centers to return home.[182]

"Buy American" and "Buy Chinese" in the Economic Stimulus Packages

China is not a signatory of the World Trade Organization's (WTO) Government Procurement Agreement, which leaves it free to favour domestic suppliers in government procurement and allows the United States to exclude Chinese companies from US government procurement programmes. Although China criticized a proposed "Buy American" clause in the US economic stimulus package (requiring that construction funds approved by the act be spent only on iron, steel, and manufactured goods produced by companies in countries that are signatories of the WTO's Government Procurement Agreement),[183] that did not stop China from implementing its own policy to keep stimulus money at home. On June 4, 2009, the Chinese central government introduced a comprehensive "Buy Chinese" policy, saying that government procurement with money from the stimulus programme must use only Chinese products or services instead of foreign counterparts, unless a domestic equivalent was not commercially or legally available.[184] The edict—issued jointly by the legislative office of the State Council; the National Development and Reform Commission; and the ministries of Industry and Information, Supervision, Housing, Transport, Railways, Water Resources, and Commerce—also accused local governments of favouring foreign suppliers. Foreign companies with a presence in China responded that they have never had much access to government procurement.

Lending Surge by Chinese Banks

Chinese banks are currently under pressure to provide financing for the stimulus. Because the central government will supply only about one quarter to one third of the stimulus, and the local governments that need to finance the remaining three quarters are perpetually strapped for cash, banks will have to finance much of the remainder of the package. They have no option to refuse, because most senior bankers are appointed by the Communist Party.[185] With so much money to push out, there is concern that transparent risk management will take a back seat and nonperforming loans will rise.

The flood of bank credit also raises the specter of inflation and the crucial question of whether borrowers will be able to cover interest costs. Chinese bank lending increased to 8.7 trillion RMB ($1.3 trillion) between January and September 2009—a 149 percent increase over the credit level reported during the same period last year.[186] The central bank reported that new bank lending in June alone has surged by 1.53 trillion RMB ($224 billion).[187] *Caijing,* China's well-respected independent economic magazine, estimated that this year's total is on track to exceed all loans issued over the previous two years combined.[188]

Wei Jianing, deputy director at the macroeconomics department of the Development and Research Center under China's State Council, worries about stimulus lending being wasted on stock and real estate speculation. Wei Jianing, citing China Business News, a Shanghai-based newspaper, reported that an estimated 1.16 trillion RMB ($170 billion) was invested in the stock market in the first five months of this year—that is 20 percent of the 5.8 trillion RMB ($849 billion) loans that banks extended in the period.[189]

The Chinese leadership appears to be aware of the concerns over potential bubbles in stock markets, real estate, and commodities, as well as nonperforming bank loans, as a result of the nation's lending spree. New lending in July 2009 fell to 355.9 billion RMB ($52 billion), from 1.53 trillion RMB ($224 billion) in June.[190] Chinese banks habitually "frontload" lending in the first half of each year, but a drop of more than 75 percent is extreme. *The Financial Times* reported that China's central bank had told the heads of the largest state-owned banks to slow the pace of lending, although bank loans again picked up—410.4 billion RMB ($60 billion) in August 2009 and 517 billion RMB ($76 billion) in September 2009.[191] The plunge in lending is unlikely, however, to signal that the Chinese government will start winding down the stimulus measures. In a speech at the World Economic Forum in Dalian on September 10, 2009, China's Premier Wen Jiabao said that China "cannot and will not" pull back from its expansionary policies.[192] Liu Yuhui, an economist at the Chinese Academy of Social Science, said that Chinese policymakers are aware of the harm expansionary policies can do, "but they are unwilling to sacrifice short-term growth and wean the economy from addiction to the stimulus policies," especially with the 60th anniversary of the founding of the People's Republic of China on October 1, 2009.[193]

Most large credit flows are going to state-owned enterprises. In its report on monetary policy, the People's Bank of China said that of the 7.4 trillion RMB ($1.1 trillion) loaned out for the first six months of 2009, 6.3 trillion RMB ($993 billion) went to "non-financial companies and other sectors"—the large state-owned enterprises and infrastructure projects that the government has lined up as part of its stimulus.[194] Data from China's National Association of Industry and Commerce indicate that between December 2008 and January 2009, short-term lending extended to private firms dropped by 700 million RMB ($102.5 million), to 421 billion RMB ($61.7 billion), despite the surge in total lending.[195] The biggest borrower in the first quarter of 2009 was China Aviation Industry Corp, or AVIC, a Chinese aerospace state-owned enterprise, which reportedly received around 336 billion RMB ($49.2 billion) in credit lines.[196] In fact, AVIC received excessive amounts of money and is looking for places to allocate borrowing to increase returns, ranging from resorts and watch manufacturers to makers of airplanes, cars, and electronics.[197] "There are a lot of companies that borrowed not for the need of business expansion, but rather were talked into borrowing by banks," said Ma Jun, chief China economist at Deutsche Bank AG in Hong Kong.[198] Some of those companies in turn lend proceeds to firms that do not qualify for financing from banks, increasing the risk of defaults spreading through the economy, Mr. Ma said. In other cases, corporate loans are being used to cover operating expenses rather than investments.[199] As the banking sector is still dominated by state-owned enterprises, a big rise in nonperforming loans would probably require a further state bailout of the banks.[200]

The government is also trying to extend lending to a broader range of sectors. The China Banking Regulatory Commission, for example, has required banks to open up lending departments to target small and medium-sized enterprises. However, such steps have had limited effect, because banks are reluctant to shift lending toward firms that are not effectively backed by the government and also because of weaker demand for borrowing amid the economic downturn.[201]

One Chinese economist pointed out that the loose lending encouraged by the stimulus comes with an implicit government guarantee against any losses, which poses a dangerous scenario. He Fan, an assistant director and professor at the Chinese Academy of Social Sciences who frequently advises top leaders, said that as much as two-thirds of Beijing's 4 trillion RMB stimulus programme will be spent by local governments, financed mainly by state-owned banks: "Some local governments will virtually go bankrupt. . . . Previously, local governments got all their money from selling land. This is not sustainable. Some areas have already sold quotas from the next 30 years." This risk is exacerbated by a slump in real estate sales. Professor He is also concerned that easy money has poured into asset markets as well as into questionable projects that the National Development and Reform Commission previously rejected. "Banks have strong incentives to lend to National Development and Reform Commission-approved projects, because if they end up as a fiasco, there is no political risk," professor He said. "They can say 'it is not my fault, the [National Development and Reform Commission] told us to lend.'" [202]

Chinese banks are lending at a pace so rapid it will almost certainly lead to a future increase in nonperforming loans, and they are channeling the money into the manufacturing and infrastructure sector. The employment effect of this lending will "naturally contribute to global demand if it takes workers off the unemployment line." [203] However, the consequent increase in production may raise overcapacity, so that China will try to continue to export into a world struggling with collapsing demand.[204]

Conclusion

- The current economic crisis, which started in the United States but has now shifted to encompass the entire world, has its roots in the massive global economic imbalances. The responsibility for these imbalances can be placed partially on the United States as the world's biggest spender and borrower and partially on China as the world's biggest saver and lender.
- China pursues policies that have the effect of increasing Chinese savings, restraining consumption, and keeping the RMB undervalued. These actions boost investment in manufacturing capacity and help to promote Chinese exports. Combined with other export incentives and subsidies, the boom in China's exports helped China accumulate the world's largest foreign exchange

reserves, valued at more than $2.27 trillion by the end of September 2009, most of which is invested in US Treasury bonds and other dollar-denominated assets.

- The policies that China adopted generated a huge flow of liquidity —or money that can be easily lent to borrowers—into US markets. This excess liquidity created perverse incentives in the United States that encouraged banks to make risky loans to US households, which in turn grew ever more indebted. High US demand for imports allowed China to save even more, creating a vicious cycle and laying the foundation for the current crisis.
- In response to the crisis, China introduced a fiscal stimulus package, raised rebates to exporters, and introduced other measures supporting the manufacturers in the export sector. This will only exacerbate overcapacity, aggravating the overall problem. China has also taken some steps to increase domestic consumption, but they are far outweighed by measures supporting exports.

SECTION 3

China's Industrial Policy and its Impact on US Companies, Workers, and the American Economy

"The Commission shall investigate and report exclusively on—

"**Economic Transfers:** The qualitative and quantitative nature of the transfer of United States production activities to the People's Republic of China, including the relocation of high technology, manufacturing, and research and development facilities, the impact of such transfers on United States national security, the adequacy of United States export control laws, and the effect of such transfers on United States economic security and employment.

"**United States Capital Markets**: The extent of access to and use of United States capital markets by the People's Republic of China, including whether or not existing disclosure and transparency rules are adequate to identify People's Republic of China companies engaged in harmful activities.

"**World Trade Organization Compliance**: The compliance of the People's Republic of China with its accession agreement to the World Trade Organization (WTO). . . ."

Introduction

China's rapid industrialization and economic growth during the past 30 years has often been attributed to the economic reforms implemented in 1978 by Deng Xiaoping. These reforms were not based on traditional "free market" principles. China's economic policy during this period has instead relied on a government-directed industrial policy to promote certain segments of the economy over others and to promote export-led growth. China has a process to develop and implement Five-Year Plans that identify broad goals—such as attracting foreign investment. The process then develops tools to accomplish those objectives—such as providing subsidies to companies to spur investment in plants, equipment, and technology.

While China prefers to be considered a market-oriented economy, it continues to engage in comprehensive economic planning, direction, support, and control from the central government. This reality undermines China's claim that its economy is market driven rather than directed by government policy.

A widely shared goal in China is to make the country rich and powerful and to regain the nation's former status as a great power that controls its own fate.[205] China's overall industrial policy for realizing this goal is characterized by three main parts: (1) the creation of an export-led and foreign investment-led manufacturing sector; (2) an emphasis on fostering the growth of industries suchas high technology products that add maximum value to the Chinese economy; and (3) the creation of jobs sufficient to reliably employthe Chinese workforce, thereby allowing the Chinese

Communist Party to maintain control. China adopts, modifies, and abandons other economic policies in order to meet these primary goals.

China's industrial policy is promulgated through a top-to-bottom process that has been outlined in 11 successive Five-Year Plans adopted by the State Council and implemented by the central and provincial governments at the direction of officials of the Communist Party. China has designated certain industries that are to remain government owned and others that are to remain government controlled. Both are to be favoured with direct and indirect subsidies.[206] (For more information on China's strategic industries, see chap. 1, sec. 2, of the Commission's 2007 Annual Report to Congress.)

China's goal of attracting foreign companies to invest in China has been combined successfully with its goal of nurturing state-owned enterprises, most notably in the manufacturing of automobiles. China transformed itself in just two decades from a nation of bicycles to the largest producer and consumer of cars in the world.[207] Over the years, China has used subsidies and tax incentives both to attract foreign investment and to facilitate growth among favoured industries. At the same time, China has instituted a variety of barriers to trade in order to protect domestic industry from foreign competition. Finally, China's currency, labour, and environmental practices and laws as well as other policies provide further support to domestic industries.

Governments at all levels in China are required to follow the State Council's Five-Year Plan creating an actual advantage for Chinese goods in the global market place.[208] This collection of government tools—industrial policy—can bestow a large advantage on favoured industries and the economy as a whole. While some of these tools are World Trade Organization (WTO)-compliant in the hands of government, other tools advocated by the Five-Year Plans fall outside the boundaries of the international trade rules and agreements to which China is a party. A close examination of China's evolving industrial policy, its effect on America, and the use of possible remedies to counter unfair or illegal actions is essential to understanding the overall health of the US economy.

China Promotes Domestic Industries

China's policies for promoting domestic industries have evolved over the years from providing simple land and energy subsidies to offering sophisticated tax-reduction measures and technology transfer incentives, as well as a variety of other measures. The primary objective of these policies has been to attract foreign investment and to promote its economic capability, which has paid off handsomely for China. China's total foreign direct investment grew from a yearly trickle of a few billion dollars in the 1980s to more than $80 billion annually by 2008, of which $15 billion came from the United States in 2008 alone.[209] In 2003, China overtook the United States as the destination for the largest amount of foreign direct investment in the world.[210] Although foreign direct investment to China has been declining and was down nearly 18 percent in the first half of 2009, China retained its lead among favoured destinations. [211]

China uses foreign direct investment to achieve greater domestic growth through exports but also for access to foreign technology. The main driver of exports out of China has been foreign-invested enterprises (both foreign owned and joint ventures), which accounted for roughly 55 percent of the total exports in 2008 (or $790 billion), according to Terence Stewart, a Washington trade attorney who studies China's industrial policy and export promotion.[212] For example, two-thirds of the growth in exports of electronic information products from China in 2007 originated from foreign-owned companies, and one-sixth was from joint ventures.[213]

But it is also clear from China's industrial policy that promoting joint ventures and foreign investment is not Beijing's ultimate goal. A large and/or globally dominant state-owned and-controlled sector is the actual goal.[214] Recent policy initiatives by the Chinese government, such as the new corporate income tax that is discussed later in this section, have focused more on shielding national champions[215] from foreign competition than on attracting further investment from overseas, according to Clyde Prestowitz, president of the Economic Strategy Institute, a Washington economic think tank, who testified before the Commission in March. Joint ventures between Chinese and foreign companies have in some cases seen their subsidies reduced.[216]

Subsidies

China has long provided subsidized energy and water to many manufacturers, despite the fact that China must import large quantities of oil and gas and already has very limited supplies of water for agricultural purposes. Also, many manufacturers have been offered free or discounted land, particularly in the vast, government-run industrial parks.[217] Today, China's subsidies still include free land and discounted electricity, but support for business is also growing more subtle and harder to detect. This support includes tax incentives for investment, funding for research and development, refunds of value added taxes (VAT) on exports, and the construction of strategically planned industrial parks in favoured locations. Commissioners visited one such park near Nanjing, where the government has set aside a vast stretch of land; constructed roads and other infrastructure, including a scenic lake; and set out a welcome mat for foreign investors. The principal intent remains the same: to attract foreign investors to locate research, manufacturing, and service centers to China. Although many of America's Fortune 500 companies might have moved to China regardless of subsidies in order to have better access to China's 1.3 billion consumers, [218] the extensive web of subsidies certainly helped make the investments more attractive.

A study conducted by Capital Trade Inc. for the Commission found that China's subsidies to strategic and heavyweight industries played a role in facilitating the relocation of US operations to China. According to this study,* China's desire to

* For more information about Capital Trade's Study, An Assessment of China's Subsidies to Strategic and Heavyweight Industries, visit the Commission's Web site: http://ww.uscc.gov/researchpapers / 2009 CAP%20 TRADE% 20 China% 27s% 20Subsidies %20to%20Strategic%20%20 Heavyweight %20 Industries%20l%20 FINAL%20 Report% 20 23March2009.pdf.

control and guide the development of key industries is singular, but the goals of this support vary substantially from industry to industry.[219] In some cases, the Chinese government is seeking to upgrade the industry's technological sophistication, while in others it is trying to ensure that its companies have the financial means to secure needed resources for China.[220] The study concludes that the Chinese government has the necessary leverage to compel firms to act, because usually the majority or primary owner of each firm is a state-owned enterprise.[221]

Industries Identified by the People's Republic of China as "Strategic" and "Heavyweight" [222]

Strategic Industries:	**Heavyweight Industries:**
(1) Armaments	(1) Machinery
(2) Power Generation and Distribution	(2) Automobiles
(3) Oil and Petrochemicals	(3) Information Technology
(4) Telecommunications	(4) Construction
(5) Coal	(5) Iron, Steel, and Non-Ferrous Metals
(6) Civil Aviation	
(7) Shipping	

Some subsidies are exclusive to domestic companies. For example, China's state-owned banking sector is directed by the Chinese government and by Chinese Communist Party officials to make loans directly to Chinese companies.[223] These loans are offered at below-market interest rates and are issued without expectation of repayment. China's banks built up a vast portfolio of nonperforming loans during the 1990s as a result of this practice. China subsequently has managed to recapitalize many of the banks that had devoted so much of their capital to unsecured and risky loans, but that free money has contributed to China's favoured industries and made some of them even more formidable competitors.[224] The Chinese government's new stimulus plan is directing state banks once again to make questionable loans to state-owned companies.[225]

China's export subsidies and the special treatment for Chinese-owned companies violate China's obligations as a member of theWorld Trade Organization.[226] The US government has tried todeal with the distorting effect of Chinese subsidies, with some limited success. In December 2008, the United States, along with Guatemala and Mexico, initiated a WTO case concerning measures offering grants, loans, and other incentives in support of China's "Famous Brands" programmes. The purpose of the "Famous Brands" programme is to promote the recognition and sale of Chinese brand products overseas. The US government charged that these programme sutilize various export subsidies, including cash grant awards, preferential loans, research and development funding to develop newproducts, and payments to lower the cost of export credit insurance.[227] At the time of the writing of this Report, the decision was still pending.

Starting in 2007, representatives of the US paper, steel, tyres, furniture, and chemical industries alleged injury from Chinese subsidies and petitioned the administration for relief in the form of countervailing duties.[228] The US Department of Commerce determined that certain Chinese subsidies[229] violated US countervailing duty laws, and by August of 2009, it initiated 19 investigations and issued 11 countervailing duty orders concerning China, with eight other investigations currently pending.[230*]

Income Tax Preferences

China has also used income tax breaks both to attract foreign direct investment and to encourage exports from domestic manufacturers. For years, foreign investors in China have benefited from investment incentives such as tax holidays and grace periods. 231 For example, if a foreign company relocated to an industrial park in China, the company's income tax rate for the first two years would be zero, and then the company would be taxed at only half the normal rate for the next three years. If the company were located in certain high-technology areas, the tax might never exceed 15 percent.[232] For years, the Chinese government has made income tax preferences available to foreign-invested firms in connection with their purchase of domestically manufactured equipment. A similar measure has made an income tax refund available to domestic firms for purchases of domestically manufactured equipment for technology upgrading.[233] These measures have encouraged foreign investment and promoted the purchase of domestic goods over foreign imports.

In February 2007, the United States and Mexico requested consultations with China concerning measures granting refunds, reductions, or exemptions from taxes and other payments owed to the Chinese government by enterprises in China.[234] The US government argued that these Chinese government tax regulations constituted illegal (WTO inconsistent) import and export subsidies to various industries in China (such as steel, wood, and paper) that distort trade and discriminate against imports.[235] This WTO dispute was settled with the signing of a memorandum of understanding in which China agreed to end all of these preferential tax incentives by January 1, 2008. [236] At the time of the writing of this Report, there have been no complaints that China has not been fulfilling its obligations under this memorandum of understanding. (For more details about this case, see chap. 1, sec. 1, of this Report.)

In March 2007, China passed a new corporate income tax law to comply with the conditions of the memorandum of understanding. This law is also structured to steer the economy away from low-skilled, labour-intensive manufacturing. [237] The new law went into effect on January 1, 2008, imposing a unified, 25 percent corporate tax rate that applies to both foreign and domestic corporations. The uniform tax code will be phased in over a five-year period, raising the tax rate for foreign-invested enterprises from 15 percent in 2007 to 25 percent by 2012.[238] However, the law includes exceptions in the application of the new rate on qualified, high-technology companies registered in special economic zones, or companies investing in agriculture, or public infrastructure projects, or environmental protection, or

* In September 2008, the Chinese government brought a WTO case of its own to challenge the legality of the US's application of countervailing duties on imports from China, which is still pending.

energy/water conservation projects.[239] For those types of companies, the tax rate will still be 15 percent. According to the US Trade Representative's (USTR) 2009 report on foreign trade barriers, domestic enterprises have long objected to rebates and other tax benefits enjoyed by foreign-invested firms.[240] Therefore, the current arrangement will be more equitable for Chinese firms. It will likely result in narrowing profit margins for foreign-invested enterprises in China.

The Value Added Tax

China has consistently used the value added tax as an instrument of industrial policy, applying the VAT selectively to penalize imports and to encourage exports. The VAT, which has been adopted by 140 countries, including most industrialized countries other than the United States, is applied to manufactured goods at each stage of production. China levies a 17 percent VAT on the value of most goods. However, this 17 percent rate is rebated selectively on exports and applied to all imports.

Two other uses of the VAT by China appear to violate the WTO rules to treat domestic and imported goods within a country equally, a concept known as "national treatment." China in some cases rebates part of the VAT for domestic producers selling in China but applies the full VAT to similar imports. This differential treatment has continued even after China's accession to the WTO. [241] Furthermore, the VAT disadvantage is compounded when China applies the VAT on all costs associated with imports, such as freight, insurance, and tariff costs, in addition to the actual value of all imported items.[242]

Based on the most recent data compiled by the Trade Lawyers Advisory Group, the VAT disadvantage to US producers and exporters as a result of China's discriminatory application of the VAT is estimated at $55 billion in 2008.[243]

China applies different rules for rebating its VAT in order to promote select industries. Following are examples of other VAT rebate programmes provided by the Chinese government with that intent, as they have been identified by the US Department of Commerce in the course of subsidies investigations:

- The government of China refunds the VAT on purchases by foreign-invested enterprises of certain domestically produced equipment. Producers are only required to present documents showing foreign-invested enterprise status in order to receive the rebates.[244]
- The Chinese government exempts both foreign-invested enterprises and certain domestic enterprises from the VAT and from tariffs on imported equipment used in their production facilities. The objective of the programme is to encourage foreign investment and to introduce foreign advanced technology equipment and industry technology upgrades.[245]
- High-technology or labour-intensive enterprises in select Economic Development Zones with investment over 3 billion renminbi (RMB) ($438 million) and more than 1,000 local employees may be refunded 25 percent of

the VAT paid on domestic sales (the percentage of the tax received by the local government) starting in the first year the company has production and sales. The VAT refund can continue for five years.[246]

Starting in 2007, the Chinese government has been reducing the VAT rebate on exports of labour-intensive goods in an effort to direct the economy away from low-end production and more toward high value added exports. However, this policy was reversed late in 2008 as part of China's stimulus programme, to increase Chinese exports and to preserve jobs in low-end manufacturing, such as textiles and apparel. In particular, in December 2008 the Chinese government raised VAT rebates to 27.9 percent on 3,770 types of exported goods.[247] Value-added taxes for businesses subsequently were cut 120 billion RMB ($17.5 billion), and rebates have been expanded to cover up to 30 percent of Chinese exported goods. Some excise taxes have also been reduced.[248] (For more details on China's stimulus plan, see chap. 1, sec. 2, of this Report.)

China's Policies to Protect Domestic Industries

China has been protecting and nurturing its domestic industries while it has been attracting foreign investment to further promote its industrial development. Most of the methods detailed below are illegal under the WTO agreements as prohibited barriers to trade, and the United States has responded by bringing WTO cases against China to correct such trade-distorting measures. However, the WTO's trade remedy provisions, as well as its dispute settlement procedures, are specifically designed to address narrow issues and may be limited in their ability to address the negative impact of China's broad, industrial policy.[249]

Export Restrictions

Export restrictions or export quotas, especially on energy and raw materials, have two general effects: First, they suppress prices in the domestic market for these goods, which lowers production costs for industries that use the export-restricted materials; and second, these restrictions increase the world price for the raw materials that are affected by limiting the world supply, thereby raising production costs in competing countries.[250]

According to the USTR, "despite China's commitment since its accession to the WTO to eliminate all taxes and charges on exports, including export duties . . . China has continued to impose restrictions on exports of certain raw materials,[251] including quotas, related licensing requirements, and duties, as China's state planners have continued to guide the development of downstream industries." [252] The USTR's 2009 report on foreign trade barriers concludes that "China's export restrictions affect US and other foreign producers on a wide range of downstream products such as steel, chemicals, ceramics, semiconductor chips, refrigerants, medical imagery, aircraft, refined petroleum products, fiber optic cables, and catalytic converters, among many others." [253]

In June 2009, the Obama Administration initiated a WTO case against China over export restraints on numerous important raw materials. US officials have been concerned for years about export restraints on raw materials from China and, in cooperation with European and Japanese officials, have held regular bilateral and multilateral discussions with Chinese officials since China joined the WTO, before the WTO's Import Licensing Committee.[254] The USTR reports that these efforts had no effect and that China in fact increased export restraints on raw materials over time.[255] According to the USTR, "China's measures appear to be part of a troubling industrial policy aimed at providing a substantial competitive advantage for the Chinese industries using these inputs." [256] Others have reported concerns that China's export restrictions are part of a larger effort to stockpile resources in order to insulate China from sudden fluctuations in global commodities markets and to increase China's ability to influence those markets. [257]

China's Restrictions on Exports of Rare Earth Minerals

China appears to be tightening its control over the supply of rare earth elements, valuable minerals that are used prominently in the production of such high-technology goods as flat panel screens and cell phones, and crucial green technologies such as hybrid car batteries and the special magnets used in wind turbines.[258] Rare earth minerals are also critical for many military technologies, including the magnets used in the guidance systems of US military smart bombs like Joint Direct Attack Munitions, and super-alloys (used to make parts for jet aircraft engines).

China accounts for the vast majority—93 percent—of the world's production of rare earth minerals, and for the last three years it has been reducing the amount that can be exported.[259] After a draft policy outlining the tightening of exports for rare earth minerals was issued in August 2009 by the Ministry of Industry and Information Technology, Zhao Shuanglian, deputy chief of the Inner Mongolia autonomous region, spoke out to quell global concerns. According to Mr. Zhao, rare earth elements are "the most important resource for Inner Mongolia," which contains 75 percent of China's deposits, and by cutting exports and controlling production, the government wants to "attract users of rare earths to set up in Inner Mongolia" to develop manufacturing. [260] China also is taking steps to consolidate its rare earths industry, with the aim of creating a consortium of miners and processors in Inner Mongolia.[261]

China's Ministry of Industry and Information Technology says it is limiting production in some mines and closing others completely because some of the rare earths are extracted under dire environmental conditions, but tighter limits on exports of rare earths place foreign manufacturers at a disadvantage compared to the domestic producers, whose access will not be so restricted. There has been no official US government response so far, but a spokeswoman for the US embassy in Beijing questioned the WTO-legality of such restrictions, noting that "[w]e would be concerned by any WTO member's policies that appear to be inconsistent with its WTO obligations." [262]

Trading Rights Authorization

Prior to its WTO accession, China restricted the types and numbers of commercial enterprises that were allowed to import and export. Only those domestic and foreign firms with trading rights could import goods into, or export goods out of China. This internal control measure, intended to nurture and promote domestic industries, remained in place until 2004, when China finally had to liberalize its trading rights regime as part of its WTO accession. However, China has retained some restrictions on trading rights, thereby putting foreign firms at a disadvantage.

Granting trading rights selectively has been one way in which the Chinese government implements its ambitious industrial policy. Industries that have been affected by China's use of licensing regulations include autos, telecommunications, pharmaceuticals, and the scrap recycling industry. In the case of scrap recycling, which is also affected by China's licensing regulations and constitutes one of the largest US exports to China by value (more than $7.56 billion dollars in 2008), China limited imports by justifying restrictions under the rubric of health and safety.[263] Starting in 2003, reportedly due to frequent receipt of dangerous waste and illegal material in past overseas shipments, the Chinese government established a registration programme as well as a pre-shipment inspection requirement to be conducted by Chinese-authorized inspectors at the shipment's origin point.[264] Currently, according to the USTR, US scrap suppliers continue to report unexplained delays in application approvals and to face problems with new requirements imposed with little or no notice.

Although China has greatly liberalized its trading rights regime since its WTO accession (within the limits of its accession protocol, which still allows for restrictions in certain categories, such as petroleum, sugar, grains, and fertilizers), it has not yet given licensees trading rights for the import of copyright-intensive products such as theatrical films, DVDs, music, books, and journals.[265] The Bush Administration filed two WTO cases in response to China's trading rights restrictions. (For more details about these cases, see chap. 1, sec. 1, of this Report.)

Local Content Rules ("Buy Chinese")

Local content rules, or "buy domestic" practices, are one of the most effective ways in which a government can promote and protect its domestic industries. China regularly follows internal rules that "direct central and sub-central government entities to give priority to local goods and services, with limited exceptions."[266] Recently, China introduced "buy Chinese" regulations as part of its stimulus plan. China is not a signatory to the WTO Government Procurement Agreement and therefore is not subject to its limitations, although it did commit in its Protocol of Accession to the WTO to join the agreement "as soon as possible." Similarly, because China is not part of the Government Procurement Agreement, the United States does not have to extend equal treatment to China. The US government still hopes that China will join the WTO's Government Procurement Agreement, but in the Strategic and Economic Dialogue in July, the United States was once again unable to secure a commitment from China that Beijing would sign the document by the end of this year.[267] (For more information on China's accession to the WTO's

Government Procurement Agreement and China's recent "buy Chinese" regulation, see chap.1, sec.1, of this Report.)

One industry that has clearly benefited from China's local content rules is telecommunications equipment. Since 1998, the Ministry of Information has had in force an internal circular "instructing telecommunications companies to buy components and equipment from domestic sources." [268] More recently, China has been using local content rules to shield its clean energy sector. China has built the world's largest solar panel manufacturing industry and exports more than 95 percent of its output to the United States and Europe. However, when China authorized the construction of its first solar power plant this spring, it required that at least 80 percent of the equipment be made in China.[269] Furthermore, when the Chinese government requested proposals this spring for 25 large contracts to supply wind turbines, every contract was won by one of seven domestic companies. All six multinationals that submitted bids were disqualified on various technical grounds, such as allegedly not providing sufficiently detailed data.[270]

The biggest beneficiaries of China's local content rules are China's auto and auto parts manufacturers. In May 2004, the Chinese government issued a new automobile industrial policy that included provisions discouraging imports of automobile parts and encouraging the use of domestic technology in new vehicles assembled in China.[271] As part of this industrial policy, Beijing levied a new 25 percent import tariff on cars if they were made predominantly of imported parts. The Chinese auto industry has been growing quickly in recent years; by the end of 2009, China was expected to become the world's biggest vehicle producer.[272] In the first nine months of 2009, a total of 9.66 million passenger cars were sold in China, compared to 7.8 million cars and light trucks sold in the United States during the same time.[273]

In March 2008, the United States, along with Canada and the European Union, initiated a WTO case against China for China's use of these discriminatory regulations as applied to imported auto parts. The United States won both the cases and the subsequent appeal filed by China. In January 2009, China promised that it would comply with the recommendations and rulings of the WTO.[274] On August 28, 2009, the Chinese government announced the reduction of its steep tax on imported auto parts for cars that do not meet certain local content standards. But this action may have come too late for US domestic auto parts manufacturers. China's remedial action was delayed by lengthy negotiations, during which time many automakers moved their production to China. These automakers stopped using imported auto parts for the cars they assembled in China.[275]

National Standards

China has used the standards-setting process to advance its domestic industries and to protect them from foreign competition. The Chinese government dominates the process by drafting most national standards without any foreign or public input or only letting foreign representatives "be observers without voting rights." [276] For example, China gives its wireless telecommunications equipment manufacturers and operators a competitive advantage by developing a domestic standard and then forcing foreign companies to adopt it for their Chinese products and operations.

Furthermore, the Chinese government is supporting the development of a domestic cell phone battery standard that may force US manufacturers to redesign their products, at a considerable cost.[277] (For more on the use of standards by the Chinese government, see the portion entitled "Using Standards to Strengthen Domestic Firms" later in this section.)

Technology Transfers

The development of new and advanced technologies is paramount for staying competitive in manufacturing. China has been particularly successful in utilizing joint manufacturing ventures and joint research efforts to achieve technology transfers. Since the early 1990s, when China began aggressively to promote domestic technological innovation, it has developed policies to encourage technology transfers.[278] Some of the early approaches that China used included setting requirements for foreign companies to donate equipment and to establish research labs.[279] The United States recognized the danger of such transfers when it negotiated with China in the late 1990s on the terms of China's eventual 2001 entry into the WTO. In its WTO accession agreement, China was required expressly to forgo any forced technology transfer arrangements with foreign companies. (For more on the transfer of research labs by US companies to China, see chap.1, sec. 4.)

Despite such commitments, China has insisted that portions of commercial passenger jets be manufactured and assembled in China as a condition for purchasing them, a practice known as "offsets." A key objective for China is acquiring technology from American and European aerospace companies so that it can independently manufacture its own aerospace products. (For further discussion of this issue, see the Commission's 2008 Report to Congress.) As a result of these efforts, in June 2009 Airbus delivered its first commercial jet fully made in China. Airbus is expecting that China will need more than 3,200 passenger planes in the next 20 years, valued at almost $400 billion, an order book that Airbus certainly took into account when deciding to shift final assembly to China.[280] In addition, AVIC, the state-owned Chinese aerospace company, has produced a regional jet for commercial sale that was developed with the benefit of technology and other assistance from western companies. In May 2008, Premier Wen Jiabao was reported to have said, "This is the dream of several generations, and we will finally realize it. We should rely on ourselves to build the large planes' main technologies, materials, and engines."[281]

General Market Conditions that Favour Relocation to China

This section describes three elements of China's industrial policy: (1) low wages and unfair labour standards, (2) lax enforcement of environmental protection laws, and (3) the manipulation of its exchange rate regime. China has made it profitable for companies from around the world to move production facilities to China and more recently to expand research and development there as well.[282] "In particular," said Ralph E. Gomory, a research professor at New York University's Sloan School of Business, "China is wisely exploiting the fact that the capabilities of today's global corporations are available to the bidder who offers the highest profit." The result has been to create jobs in China, particularly in export industries.

China's Low Wages and Unfair Labour Standards

Unions and worker rights organizations have complained that Chinese companies do not pay their employees even the Chinese minimum wage levels. Employers also withhold promised health benefits from employees and subject employees to forced labour.[283] Last year, however, the Chinese government implemented a new labour law intended to combat forced labour, withholding of pay, and other abuses by providing for formal contracts and severance pay.[284]

Although the text of the new labour law seems to address the persistent injustices, the law's implementation and enforcement have been spotty.[285] The major deficiency of the new labour law is the continued restriction on union organizing and collective bargaining. According to the Congressional-Executive Commission on China, the labour contract law does not include provisions to guarantee equal bargaining power between workers and employers. Because there is only one legal trade union in China (the All-China Federation of Trade Unions), which is required to "uphold the leadership of the Communist Party," all the trade unions remain under the control of management.[286]

This new labour law provoked an outcry from some business organizations representing foreign-invested enterprises. They claimed that the legislation would drive up costs and make doing business in China more difficult.[287] The American Chamber of Commerce in Shanghai complained that the law "could have a negative impact on the investment environment in China," while the European Union Chamber of Commerce argued that "the rigid provisions of the draft law will restrict employer flexibility, and ultimately will increase costs for Chinese producers." [288]

China's Lax Enforcement of Environmental Protection Laws

China is rapidly becoming one of the most polluted countries in the world.[289] Although China has some strict environmental laws on the books, the fines that can be levied to enforce the regulations are so insignificant that they are seen merely as a cost of doing business rather than a true deterrent.[290] Furthermore, the Chinese state environmental protection agency is critically understaffed; it has 300 employees compared to the US Environmental Protection Agency's 20,000 employees.[291]

China's weak enforcement provides a variety of cost advantages to both domestic and foreign industries. Companies operating in China can save money by not providing protective equipment for workers, by not investing in expensive pollution control technologies, and by not properly disposing of their waste.[292] Furthermore, some of China's pollution also reaches the United States, as the Commission heard during its 2008 hearing on China's energy policies and their environmental effects. The US scientists on the West Coast have used a variety of tools to trace the flow of air pollution from Asia (including China) and have found that air pollutants such as ozone and mercury do reach the United States and degrade air quality. (For further information, see the Commission's 2008 Report.)

The Chinese government acknowledges its environmental problem and has adopted the related goals of protecting the environment and shifting to cleaner energy sources. However, China's industrial policy continues to promote investment in energy-consuming production activities.[293] For example, Beijing has spent lavishly on nuclear, gas, and wind power in an attempt to diversify the country's energy sources and move away from coal, and it has tried to close small coal mines.[294] Despite those efforts, coal production jumped from 525 million tons in 2002 to 1.26 billion tons in 2008, and China increased its coal burning by 7 percent in 2008. China accounted for 43 percent of global coal use in 2008.[295] The need for greater industrial production always seems to take precedence over environmental protection, especially now that China is struggling with declining exports.[296]

China's Exchange Rate Regime

Through strict capital controls and the coordinated efforts of the central bank and the Ministry of Finance, the government of China has frozen the value of the RMB at about 6.8 to the dollar since June 2008. If the RMB were allowed to float and to be traded on international markets, as is the case with most major trading nations, the RMB would climb in value.[297] By keeping the value of the RMB artificially low, China provides an incentive to foreign corporations to shift production there, because it reduces the price of investing in China and makes their exports from China cheaper. China's currency manipulation has been addressed in previous Annual Reports and is also described in section 1 of this chapter.

Derek Scissors, an economist at the Heritage Foundation, suggests that encouraging Beijing to liberalize its capital account will allow money to move freely in and out of China, which was once one of the goals for China's admission to the WTO.[298] "It was once assumed that the difficult process of liberalizing China's capital account would occur naturally as the country started complying with the conditions for its accession to the WTO," said Dr. Scissors.[299] So far there has been no progress, and the Chinese government has shown little interest in allowing multinationals, much less Chinese citizens, to freely send earnings or savings out of the country. [300]

Capital account liberalization would allow for easier repatriation of profits by foreign firms operating in China. It would reduce state intervention in the Chinese economy. It would allow Chinese citizens and businesses to purchase goods directly from other countries and even to invest abroad, reducing trade and capital imbalances. Chinese banks would lose some of the guaranteed deposits they now enjoy. That, in turn, would inhibit the type of state-directed lending that has effectively blocked privatization and hindered competition.[301] Dr. Scissors concluded that although such liberalization is still far in the future, it is a goal worth pursuing now. He noted, however, that even if China were compelled to revalue the RMB against the dollar, the Chinese government's most obvious countermeasure would be to raise the export tax rebate, as it has already done several times since the global financial crisis reduced global demand.[302]

The Impact of the WTO on China's Industrial Policy

The primary objective of China's accession to the WTO, both for the United States and the rest of the world, was to expand access to the Chinese market by lowering tariffs, quotas, and regulatory barriers and to facilitate foreign investment in China.[303]

While in the past some progress had been achieved, 2009 was marked by a reversal in market access. While foreign direct investment in China has grown dramatically since China joined the WTO, market access has been hampered, and domestic industries still enjoy preferential treatment. Since China's accession to the WTO, the United States has initiated eight cases against China, three of which were decided by a dispute panel, three of which were settled by a memorandum of understanding, and two of which are still pending. Of the six cases that have been completed, the United States views the resolution of all as marginally favourable. (For more details on US WTO cases against China, see chap. 1, sec. 1, of this Report.) The United States prevailed in its challenge of China's discriminatory corporate tax policy, yet China has not stopped subsidizing and helping its domestic industries. The United States had to bring a second WTO case challenging China's grants, loans and other incentives.

The United States also prevailed in its challenge of China's VAT rebates, but that decision was limited to the integrated circuits industry. China still rebates the VAT in a way that benefits other domestic industries and distorts trade. The United States prevailed in its challenge of China's trading rights restrictions; however, once again, all China had to do was amend its laws, as they relate only to the two industries that were the subject of the two challenges—financial information service suppliers and audiovisual entertainment products suppliers. The WTO might be a forum for addressing industry-specific issues but not for dealing with the more systemic imbalances caused by China's industrial policy.

Part of the problem, according to Mr. Prestowitz, is that the WTO rules, largely carried over from the General Agreement on Tariffs and Trade (GATT) and eight rounds of global trade negotiations dating back more than 40 years, assume free, perfectly competitive markets; no economies of scale; and fixed exchange rates.[304] Because the GATT and its successor, the WTO, were initially a collection of countries with capitalist systems and relatively low, nonmarket trade barriers, the WTO does not adequately address problems arising from industrial policies. It also does not deal with other factors such as lax environmental laws or workers' rights abuses. Furthermore, the Chinese leadership sees nothing inconsistent between the current WTO rules and China's brand of capitalism. "There has not been a vision about China's future that has not included a central role for the state as the ultimate source of guidance and control, even allowing for all of the reforms and the introduction of market mechanisms throughout the last 30 years," said Denis Simon, professor at Penn State's School of International Affairs. [305] The pursuit by the United States of a global market economy and China's state-controlled, export-led growth model "is like one team playing football and one team playing baseball," Mr. Prestowitz noted.[306]

The Obama Administration is continuing the Bush Administration's Strategic Economic Dialogue as the Strategic and Economic Dialogue, reflecting the larger role in the talks that the State Department is having. The long-running Joint Committee on Commerce and Trade, led by the Commerce Department and the USTR, will continue. The United States and China are also negotiating a Bilateral Investment Treaty, which could be used to address investment, labour, and environmental practices.

Incentives offered by China to attract High-Technology Investment

The Chinese government's initial efforts in industrial development were focused on developing manufacturing, from such heavy industries as steel to assembly lines for basic household items. With the more recent Five-Year Plans, the emphasis has been shifting away from labour-intensive operations to more capital-intensive production.[307] The Chinese government has been trying to develop its manufacturing and design capabilities in the computing, telecommunications, and software development sectors, but it was not until the collapse of the high-tech bubble of 2001–2002 that the conditions were right for foreign companies to relocate their operations to the Chinese mainland.[308] US companies suffered heavy losses during that period, so they went looking for ways to cut their operating costs. China's gradual maturation, both as a manufacturer of advanced technology products and as a consumer of electronics and information technology products, coincided with the US collapse. Since then, American, Japanese, and Taiwanese manufacturers and researchers have relocated aggressively to China. The low cost of labour along with government investment in high-tech industrial parks and a variety of direct and indirect subsidies created an attractive environment for foreign companies hit hard by the tech-bubble collapse.[309] China's global exports of information technology products (which include computers, semiconductors, telecommunications, and photonics products) during 2000–2004 grew nearly fourfold, from $54 billion to $201 billion. China's trade surplus with the United States in information technology products also experienced its largest growth during 2000-2004, increasing more than six times, from $5 billion to $35 billion. [310]

To accelerate the growth of the information technology sector, the Chinese government has used direct and indirect subsidies, including low- or no-cost loans, tax concessions, grants of land and infrastructure, and government support for graduate education and for research and development.[311] At the same time, the Chinese government has fostered the development of Chinese manufacturers through requirements that foreign suppliers establish joint ventures with Chinese partners, build manufacturing plants in China, transfer technology, and offset their imports of component parts through domestic purchases.[312] China also seeks to speed up its scientific and technological development by sending students and scholars abroad for advanced training, purchasing vast amounts of foreign technology, developing a foreign investment regime to attract foreign high-tech companies, and signing a large number of agreements with other governments for scientific and technological cooperation.

China is primarily a re-export platform for electronics. Foreign firms dominate China's information technology hardware market. Telecommunications and information technology are very knowledge intensive, and holders of patents and standards guide the entire industry. Almost all internationally important standards that generate revenue (through licensing) are held by western companies. Foreign standards are viewed as a constraint on China's technological development because of the need to pay license fees. If China develops its own innovative, internationally recognized standards for its market, foreign companies that want to do business in China either will have to pay licensing fees to enter the market, or they will have to withdraw from the market. By denying foreigners access to its market through the use of standards, China will effectively protect its domestic industries.

Using Standards to Strengthen Domestic Firms

Proprietary technology and domestic standards are seen in China as a potential means of strengthening the market position of domestic firms while diminishing that of foreign competitors. The Chinese government largely views standards not as mechanisms for encouraging innovation but as a matter of national prestige, security, and revenue creation through generating royalty in come that benefits domestic firms.[313] Therefore, through administrative action, legal innovation, and increased support for research and development, China actively has been developing a new technology policy based on the promotion of its own technical standards.[314]

Chinese efforts to develop domestic standards and use them for national advantage span many areas of information technology— its own microprocessor, a successor to DVD, a new digital audio standard, a new Internet Protocol, and a different standard for radio frequency identification tagging.[315] However, so far, China's efforts to achieve technological independence through setting indigenous standards have largely been unsuccessful. The onlystandard that may emerge as a viable contender in the international market is China's third generation (3G) wireless standard, called TD–SCDMA.[316]

In 2003, China's Ministry of Industry Information announced that all wireless devices sold in China (such as laptops) would have to conform to a domestically developed wireless application protocol interface standard (called WAPI).[317] This technology was only available to Chinese vendors, forcing foreign firms to license the technology and reveal key elements of their technology to the Chinese authorities in order to get it to work properly with their systems.[318] The mandatory adoption of the Chinese-developed wireless application protocol interface standard provoked strong protests from foreign firms, and the International Standards Organization rejected it in 2006 because it was scarcely innovative. Since then, the Chinese authorities decided to make the protocol optional in China, and although it never gained wide acceptance, it is once gain being resubmitted to the International Standards Organization for consideration as a global standard.[319]

Unlike the Chinese-developed wireless application protocol interface standard, its 3G wireless standard has been accepted by the international telecommunications standards body, but even Chinese mobile operators are not particularly eager to adopt it. China's 3G wireless standard has a limited selection of equipment and almost no international support, and there is some concern that it will actually hamper the Chinese industry's progress.[320] While China's 3G wireless standard struggles to gain a foothold in the telecommunications industry, a global race is on to develop the next generation standard, or 4G.[321]

Telecommunications, a Chinese Strategic Industry

China has one of the world's fastest-growing telecommunications markets and operates the world's largest fixed and wireless telecommunications networks. In 2008, there were nearly 600,000,000 mobile subscribers and 360,000,000 fixed-line customers, providing $244 billion in revenue to the Chinese telecommunications companies.[322] The development of a telecommunications infrastructure has proceeded unevenly throughout the country. Nearly one-half of China's telecommunications users reside in the provinces on the east coast, while the western provinces are still greatly underserved. This situation contributes to the government's efforts to foster telecommunications development in those areas.[323] In that sense, argues Richard Suttmeier, professor emeritus at the University of Oregon, Chinese government subsidies directed at the expansion of telecommunications services to western China is a national development issue, no different from the US government's efforts to bring electricity and broadband Internet service to rural areas.[324]

The telecommunications industry is considered a strategic sector of the economy, right along with energy, aviation, and steel. Severe restrictions are in place on foreign ownership and market share for foreign providers and producers. The government has control and majority ownership of these telecommunications companies, as envisioned in the 11th Five-Year Plan. In 2008, the government consolidated China's telecommunications industry. Initially, the market included six providers, which were merged by the government into three, each spanning mobile, fixed, and broadband services.[325] One of the reorganization's goals is to create "managed competition," but it will also allow the Chinese government to grant licenses for third generation (3G) mobile services.[326] This restructuring also appears to be an effort by the Chinese government to test and refine the domestic standard so that it may eventually come to dominate the domestic market.

Information Technology

Choices about technological standards, domestic preferences, and business rules shape the future of China's information technology industry.[327] One factor significantly aiding the emergence of China's telecommunications industry is the success of indigenous telecommunications equipment makers, who constitute an important subset of China's information technology industry and develop technology at far lower costs than foreign competitors. This success, while a substantial achievement, does not reflect significant Chinese innovation, however.[328]

The low value of China's information technology product assembly is a source of intense concern for the government, which views an innovative and successful information technology sector as a key indicator of both national security and economic pride.[329] Thus, a crucial goal for the government is to reduce China's dependence on imported electronics products, such as semiconductor chips and other hardware, and to increase the domestic value added of electronics exports.[330] During the initial reforms of the 1990s, China's prime objective was to create indigenous substitutes for foreign technologies, such as Red Flag Linux to replace the Windows operating system, or the Dragon processor chip to replace Intel, but this effort has been largely unsuccessful. This failure is due to a variety of reasons, including the lack of fully trained and educated professionals and the absence of a culture of collabourative innovation, such as exists in California's Silicon Valley.[331] Nonetheless, China considers development of standards as a key to its efforts to strengthen technological independence. Special research and development programmes for standards have been initiated, and direct research and development support and tax and procurement policies are being used to help Chinese enterprises develop indigenous intellectual property and standards.[332]

According to the Organization for Economic Cooperation and Development in Paris, China surpassed Japan, the United States, and the European Union in 2004 to become the biggest exporter of information technology goods.[333] The range of China's information technology manufacturing is broad, with substantial exports of computers, consumer audio-video equipment, telecommunications equipment, and components. This production, however, is mostly focused in last-stage, low-value-added assembly, while the core technologies (and most of the value of the final product) belong to designers in the United States, Europe, and Japan.[334] Because of China's assembly operations, electronic parts and components are the largest categories of China's information technology imports, accounting for 70 percent of all information technology goods imported into China in 2006.[335] There is evidence of movement up the production value ladder, as more value-added processing is transferred to China from Taiwan, although this transfer might have been slowed down by the current global financial crisis. Two of China's more successful information technology companies that are moving up the production value ladder are Huawei and Lenovo.

China's Information Technology Giants: Huawei and Lenovo

The biggest, most influential, and most recognizable of China's domestic telecom equipment manufacturers is Huawei, which claims to be a private firm. It was established in 1988 by several former members of the logistics operation of the People's Liberation Army. Huawei got its start, like many Chinese information technology companies, in commoditizing technologies developed by foreign companies, often reverse-engineering the patented designs first.[336] Cisco sued Huawei for illegally copying its Internetwork Operating System software and infringing on numerous Cisco patents in order to develop a lineup of routers and switches. The suit was settled out of court for an undisclosed amount.[337] Today, Huawei's technology is internationally competitive. Huawei now competes with Lucent, Nortel Networks, and Motorola and has established six regional headquarters and 32 subsidiaries in the Middle East, the Asia-Pacific region, South America, and Europe.

Huawei's counterpart in the information technology sector is Lenovo, a successful computer manufacturer and a spin-off from the government's Chinese Academy of Sciences' Institute of Computing Technology, which still retains partial ownership. Lenovo started out primarily as a reseller of foreign computers, gradually moving into assembly. Eventually, Lenovo developed a strong domestic brand and good design, distribution, and supply networks, with some government help.[338] After becoming the top retailer in the Chinese market, in 2005 Lenovo became a more global company by buying IBM's personal computer and laptop division, based in the United States.

Optoelectronics

Optoelectronics is another example of an advanced technology industry that might have stayed in the United States but is now almost completely relocated overseas.

Optoelectronics are used in photovoltaic panels; in new solid-state lighting systems that reduce electricity consumption by a factor of five; in a new generation of television and telecommunication networks; and in sensors that will be deployed to monitor thousands of mechanical and industry systems, roadways, electrical grids, and manufacturing production lines.[339]

China's government has successfully supported the shift of some manufacturing of optoelectronics to China and is now intent on attracting the highest value-added portion of the industry—the research and design work. China's Ministry of Science and Technology has created five national laboratories and is sponsoring academic-industry collaborations around the country in an effort to leapfrog the United States and Europe.[340] China has focused on liquid crystal displays, plasma screens, light-emitting diodes, and solar technology, among others. Other advanced technologies that originally moved from the United States to Taiwan are now relocating across the Strait to the mainland.[341]

China is aided in this effort by one of the peculiarities of optoelectronics itself. Many of the advanced applications of optoelectronics rely on bundling simpler components, or "enabling" technologies—lasers, light-emitting diode lights, infrared sensors, semiconductors, photovoltaic cells, fiber-optic cables, liquid crystal displays, transistors, and so on, with new technologies coming out of the most sophisticated research labs—such as quantum dots, nanowires, nanocrystals, and the like. To do this efficiently and successfully, scientists and engineers may need to be on-site to brainstorm about new applications and solutions and to solve manufacturing problems that may come up in the adaptation phase.[342]

Optoelectronic companies suffered the same fate as most information technology producers, which, after the burst of the 2001– 2002 tech bubble, went looking for cheaper production facilities to recover their losses. China, with its government-funded, high-tech parks and low labour costs, presented a very attractive destination. According to Michael Lebby, president of the Optoelectronics Industry Development Association, US companies in search of a low- labour-cost solution relocated to Asia "like a herd mentality."[343] This, despite the fact that labour accounts for only 10 to 15 percent of component production and most optoelectronics companies would rather stay in the United States. Mr. Lebby polled the members of his association and concluded that "optoelectronics companies want help from US government agencies in designing and innovating the next generation of products.[344] They understand that they cannot bring back the old manufacturing operations, but with help from government agencies they are confident they can establish new manufacturing platforms for new, next-generation products."[345]

Impact of China's Industrial Policy on the US Economy: One of the principal strengths of the US economy has always been the ingenuity of its inventors, scientists, and engineers and the vigour of its entrepreneurs. As American ideas and inventions became commonplace around the world, new US innovators came up with new ideas. Rather than depend on protecting national technologies from competition, the United States has instead relied on constant innovation. China's industrial policy has had a profound effect on international trade and the US economy. The explosive growth of exports out of China since the Deng Xiaoping reforms and the outsourcing of production by US companies to China have been well documented by this

Commission. China's trade balance with the United States went from a deficit of $2.7 billion in 1980 to a surplus of $268 billion in 2008. Since 1980, the United States has run a cumulative trade deficit with China of approximately $1.9 trillion.[346] The effectiveness of China's industrial policy in creating an actual advantage for Chinese exporters while protecting China's import-sensitive industries can be seen, in part, by the growth of China's exports to the United States over the past 30 years and particularly since 2001. In a study conducted for the Commission by Charles McMillion of MBG Information Services, looking into total bilateral goods trade between the United States and China, US producers enjoyed surpluses with China in only 27 industries in 2001 while suffering a deficit in 70. By 2008, US surpluses existed in only 20 industries and deficits in 77.*

Fig.1: China's Growing Share of the Overall US Trade Deficit 2000 to May 2009 (non-oil goods)[347]

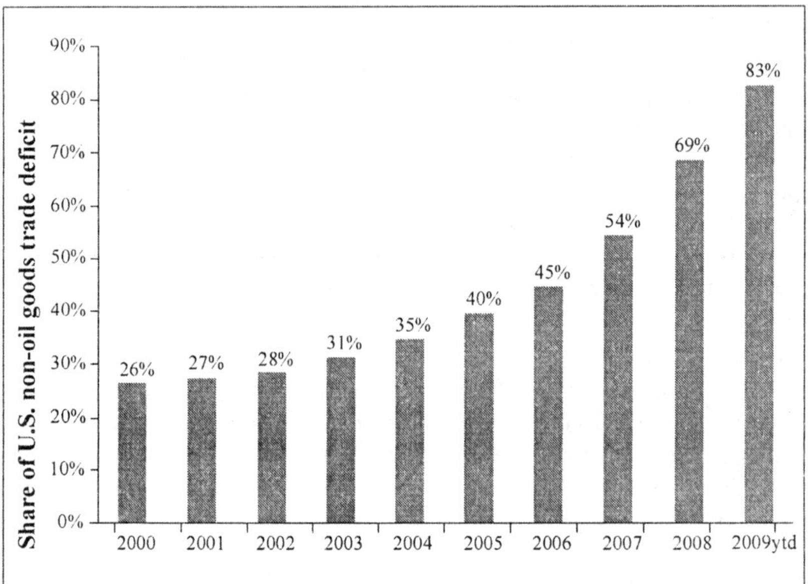

Source: U.S. International Trade Commission and the Economic Policy Institute.

The impact of trade and competition with China has been devastating to specific industries and local communities throughout the United States. The Commission has held numerous hearings around the country on the impact of trade with China on local economies. For example, Chinese exports of textiles, clothing, and furniture to the United States have severely damaged North Carolina's three signature manufacturing industries. By 2003, China's share of the US market for bedroom furniture was 53 percent, despite the great distance involved and the lack in Asia of the maple and oak that Americans prefer in their furniture. The Chinese advantage,

* For more details, see MBG's study, "China' Soaring Commercial and Financial Power: How it is affecting the US and the orld," posted on the Commission's *Website at http://ww. uscc.gov/researchpapers/2009/MBG%20Info%20Svs%20US China % 20Trade%20 Report%201%20 FINAL%20June%202009.pdf.*

however, was due largely to predatory pricing. (For further discussion of the impact of trade with China on North Carolina, see the Commission's 2007 Report to Congress.)

Another example is the fishing industry, where China has become the world's largest exporter of seafood and the largest volume supplier of seafood to the US market, due to China's adoption of industrial fish farming and Chinese government policies that support the industry and encourage fish exports. China's support of fish farmers and processors, through local and national government aid, low-interest loans, and lax environmental and health controls, has provided China's industry with considerable cost advantages over the American fishing fleet. (For further discussion of the impact of trade with China on the US's Gulf Coast, see the Commission's 2008 Report to Congress.)

This year, the Commission traveled to upstate New York and examined the erosion of the advanced technology cluster of Rochester as well as efforts by China to attract both production and research and development facilities of advanced technology companies. (For more information on upstate New York, see chap. 1, sec. 4, of this Report.)

China's High-tech Priorities

China's industrial policy clearly aims to promote the manufacturing of higher-technology products, replacing lower valued-added and labour-intensive products. China's advanced technology product exports to the United States rose in the past eight years, with exports of communications equipment rising from 10th in 2000 ($2.9 billion) to third by 2008 ($26.6 billion) and exports of computer equipment rising from third in 2000 ($8.2 billion) to the number one export to the United States in 2008 ($45.8 billion). Following are the major US exports to and imports from China, starting with the year before China's accession to the WTO:

Fig. 2: Major US Exports to China, 2000–2008 (in millions of US $)

	2000	**2004**	**2008**	**2000–2008 % Change**
Waste & Scrap	$744	$2,508	$7,562	916%
Semiconductors & other Electronic Components	$1,317	$3,565	$7,475	467%
Oilseeds & Grains	$1,048	$2,829	$7,316	598%
Aerospace Products & Parts	$1,770	$2,111	$5,470	209%
Resin, Synthetic Rubber, & Artificial & Synthetic Fibers & Filament	$660	$1,630	$3,523	433%
Total US Exports	**$16,253**	**$34,721**	**$71,457**	**339%**

Source: US International Trade Commission, Interactive Tariff and Trade DataWeb (Washington, DC).

Fig. 3: Major US Imports from China, 2000–2008 (in millions of US $)

	2000	2004	2008	2000–2008 % Change
Computer Equipment	$8,256	$29,486	$45,820	454%
Miscellaneous Manufacturing Commodities	$16,296	$23,712	$35,834	119%
Communications Equipment	$2,957	$9,015	$26,618	800%
Apparel	$6,972	$10,530	$22,582	223%
Audio & Video Equipment	$6,264	$12,421	$19,715	214%
Total US Imports	**$100,062**	**$196,698**	**$337,789**	**237%**

Source: US International Trade Commission, Interactive Tariff and Trade DataWeb (Washington, DC).

One measure of China's successful industrial policy and economic modernization can be demonstrated by China's trade with the United States in advanced technology products.[348] Throughout the1980s and 1990s, it was hoped that a national surplus in advanced technology products would eventually pay for a significant share of the US's net imports of oil, apparel, autos, and other products of mature manufacturing industries.[349] However, according to Dr. McMillion, the United States began suffering deficits in advanced technology products trade with China in 1995 and with the rest of the world in 2002. Currently, China accounts for 28 percent of the US's advanced technology products imports and only 7 percent of its exports.[350] Some of the reasons for the narrowing of the US's historic lead in high-technology products are attributable to economic factors—lower wage costs overseas, faster and more efficient global transportation, and the spread of higher education. But some of America's edge has been lost as a result of careful economic planning by other governments, in particular the Chinese government.

In 2008, China's exports comprised 36.5 percent of its gross domestic product (GDP), while only 13 percent of the US's GDP came from exports.[351] Export-led growth policies pursued by China and other industrializing nations have inevitably led to excess capacity in many products, notably steel and automobiles, which has contributed to declining manufacturing jobs and production in many market-oriented countries, including the United States. Problems arise for China's trading partners as China exports its excess capacity at prices that the rest of the world cannot match. For example, in 2008, China accounted for 38 percent of the world's crude steel production (about 500 million tons), compared to only 7 percent for the United States, and China's excess capacity of steel isgreater then Japan's entire yearly output.[352] Such exports also exacerbate the global economic downturn, as China essentially exports unemployment to countries unable or unwilling to compete onthe basis of subsidies provided to favoured industries."This imbalance underlies the current economic crisis that we are suffering," said Mr. Prestowitz at the Commission's March hearing on China's industrial policy.[353] Nevertheless, China sees the global financial crisis as an affirmation that "China holds thephilosophical high ground, reinforcing its long-held position at home and abroad that unbridled capitalism and a weak state are a sure recipe for serious sociopolitical and economic problems," according to Dr. Simon, who testified at the March hearing.[354] China is now authorizing even more subsidies, increasing the rebating of its VAT, erecting new barriers to trade, and implementing a "buy Chinese" policy. (For more details on China's response to the global financial crisis, see chap. 1, sec. 2, of this Report.)

Conclusion

- China's economic reforms were not based on traditional free market principles. China's policy during the past 30 years has instead relied on a government-directed industrial policy to promote certain segments of the economy over others and to promote export-led growth.
- China's more recent Five-Year Plans have shifted the emphasis away from labour-intensive operations and toward increasing the production of high-technology goods. China has matured as a manufacturer and assembler of advanced technology products and as a consumer of electronics and information technology products. The low cost of labour along with government investment in high-tech industrial parks—and a variety of direct and indirect subsidies—created an attractive environment for foreign companies to invest in China, particularly after China joined the WTO in 2001.
- China provides subsidized land, energy, and water to many foreign manufacturers who relocate their operations in China. By providing these benefits, along with a cheap labour force without the ability to bargain collectively or join independent unions, the Chinese government has created a low-cost haven for foreign manufacturers. China's subsidies have grown over the years and now include tax incentives and preferential loans, which further reduce the cost of investing in China.
- China has consistently used a 17 percent value added tax (VAT) as an instrument of industrial policy. China selectively rebates the VAT when a domestic manufacturer exports but imposes it on imports. The United States, on the other hand, does not use the VAT and is not allowed by WTO rules to rebate income taxes on exports. China's VAT policy therefore places US exports at a distinct disadvantage.
- The US government has filed a variety of WTO cases against China's barriers to trade. These WTO cases, while important, are very industry specific, time consuming, and fail to have an impact on the trade-distorting aspects of China's industrial policyor to deal with the underlying causes of the US-China trade deficit.Tackling the systemic trade imbalances between China and the United States through WTO mechanisms will not address broader issues such as environmental pollution or workers' rights abuses. The US government will have to find alternative venues in which to address such matters.

SECTION 4

China's Industrial Policy and Its Impact on Upstate New York

"The Commission shall investigate and report exclusively on—

"ECONOMIC TRANSFERS—The qualitative and quantitative nature of the transfer of United States production activities to the People's Republic of China, including the relocation of high technology, manufacturing, and research and development facilities, the impact of such transfers on United States national security, the adequacy of United States export control laws, and the effect of such transfers on United States economic security and employment.

"WORLD TRADE ORGANIZATION COMPLIANCE—The compliance of the People's Republic of China with its accession agreement to the World Trade Organization (WTO). . . ."

Introduction

In March 2009, the Commission held a hearing in Washington, DC, on China's industrial policy, receiving testimony from experts on China's efforts to promote its information technology, telecommunications, and other advanced technology industries such asoptoelectronics. Following up on that hearing, the Commission traveled to Rochester, New York, in July 2009 to assess the impact of China's industrial policy on some of the industries of the region. Of particular interest to the Commission was evaluating the growing concern that research and development, essential to high-technology innovation, is following manufacturing abroad.

Currently, upstate New York is home to numerous small-and medium-sized companies ranging from auto parts and solar panel suppliers to biotech and optoelectronics producers. Although the region is rich in technical talent and has advanced research universities with curricula oriented to science and technology, it has not yet been able to replicate the success of the industrial clusters in Silicon Valley or along Boston's Route 128.[355] The New York State government is trying to invest in the clean energy sector and other sunrise technologies and industries, but funding is fragmented and difficult to obtain, and small entrepreneurs and parts suppliers remain almost entirely dependent upon the individual decisions of larger producers and assemblers who outsource much of their operations overseas.

Loss of Industries Impacts Communities: The three main cities in central and western New York State—Buffalo, Syracuse, and Rochester—have developed different industrial bases. Buffalo and Syracuse were home to major industries such as appliance, dinner ware, furniture, and air conditioner manufacturers, as well as many auto parts and machine tool companies that were suppliers to bigger companies. The outsourcing of manufacturing from Buffalo and Syracuse has left big employment gaps that the growing services industries at universities and hospitals have partially filled, but at significantly lower wages. Meanwhile, the national trend by major manufacturers to outsource their production has compounded job losses by the many autoparts and machinetool suppliers in the region.

Rochester, on the other hand, was a city of engineers and scientists. Rochester was home to Eastman Kodak, Xerox, and Bausch & Lomb, companies that were technology innovators throughout the 20th century. With the downsizing of Eastman Kodak and Xerox in the 1980s and 1990s, many former employees took their expertise and started niche companies, some of which are doing well.[356] Former employees of Eastman Kodak, in particular, purchased its equipment, labs, or entire divisions and started their own companies.

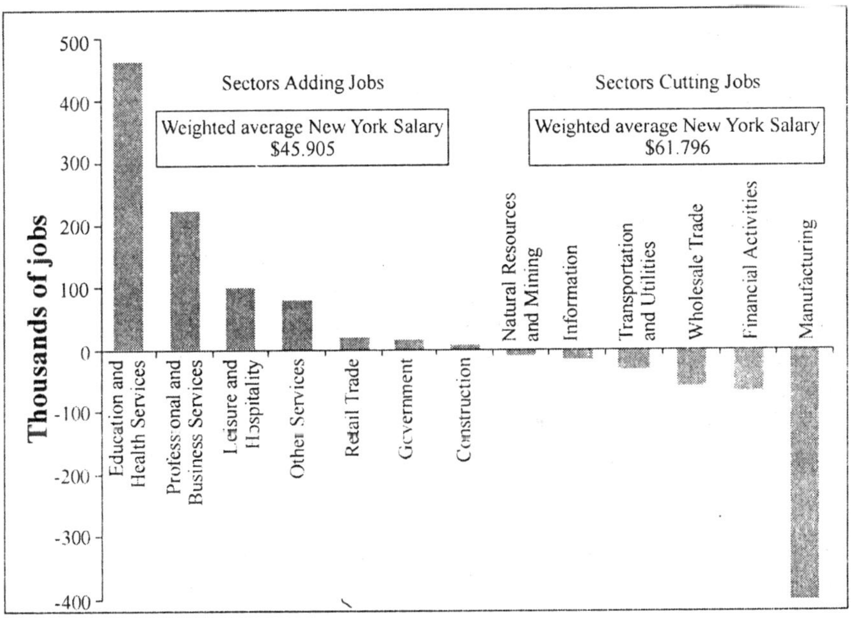

Note: "Sector" refers to Bureau of Labour Statistics "super-sectors." All super-sectors are included in the analysis above, collectively accounting for the entire New York State economy.

Source: A.T. Kearney analysis of Bureau of Labour Statistics. A.T. Kearney, "Delivering on the Promise of New York State: A Strategy for Economic Growth & Revitalization," prepared for Empire State Development Agency (New York, NY: July 2007), p.7.

Employment has shifted during the past 20 years from higher paying manufacturing jobs to lower-paying service jobs in industries such as education and health care.[357] From 1990 to 2005, manufacturing in the region declined by almost 400,000 jobs, while education and health services gained 450,000 jobs. The average salary in the state of New York for manufacturing jobs was $62,000in 2008, while the average for jobs in education and health serviceswas only $46,000.[358]

This shift from manufacturing to services has been particularlypronounced in upstate New York. William Johnson, former mayor of Rochester and current distinguished professor of public and urban studies at the Rochester Institute of Technology, testified at the Commission's hearing on this shift and on the impact of downsizing on the local communities. He testified that in 1981, Kodak was the top employer in Rochester, with 59,582 employees. By 2007, Kodak's employment had dropped to 12,500 jobs; the Universityof Rochester/Strong Health was the top employer (17,802),with Wegmans grocery stores in second place (13,642). Universities are the top employers in Buffalo and Syracuse as well. In 1983, Kodak accounted for 11.63 percent of the property tax valuation in Rochester. By 2008, Kodak accounted for only 1.95 percent.[359] In his written testimony to the Commission, Mr. Johnson said,

> *When a company like Kodak shrinks its presence in its hometown, there are significant side effects: the loss ofjobs leads to a decline in the quality of life for the families who were dependent on that income. Many people are unable to maintain their middle-class life styles, and neighbourhoods suffer as these families either move on or cut back. Kodak was recognized for its civic leadership. Not only were its top managers involved in a host of important community initiatives, but it encouraged its work force to also be good citizens through volunteerism and generous financial support. Kodak's philanthropic activities supported a host of worthwhile community endeavours.*[360]

Key Industries in Upstate New York

The following industries are examples of the past, present, and potential future of industrial activity in upstate New York. In the past, machine tools companies were vital suppliers to original equipment manufacturers. At present, optoelectronics companies have been evolving and now comprise many of the small- and medium-sized employers in the region. In addition, healthcare and education providers make up the top employers in Rochester, Buffalo,and Syracuse. Clean energy companies could represent the futurefor innovation and development in the region.

Machine Tools

Machine tools are metalworking machines that have sophisticated, computer-based motion control systems, which allow the machine to perform a range of tasks with high productivity while achieving high precision. Machine tools are the engine of manufacturing, and advances in machine tool technology have been a vital part of the remarkable strides made in manufacturing productivity in past decades.[361] As recently as the 1980s, the United States was the global leader in technological innovation and the production of machine tools. Today, with the general decline of domestic manufacturing, the United States barely makes the top 10 list of countries producing machine tools.[362] Historically, the United States had been the largest global consumer of machine tools, because the United States was a far larger manufacturer.[363] However, after Japan's industrial policy targeted manufacturing, the US machinetools sector lost this advantage. Now China seeks to dominate manufacturing through its own industrial policy.

In Japan and Germany, the machine tools sector is considered vital to the countries' long-term economic prosperity; accordingly, both countries have emerged as the technology leaders in this field. China and Taiwan are also top producers of machine tools, but their products are typically less technologically advanced.[364]

China considers machine tools to be a strategic industry and is making vigorous efforts to advance the growth of the industry domestically. In the past two years, China has purchased 25 percent of all the machine tools produced in the world, more than two times the amount of machine tools purchased by the next highest consuming country, Germany.[365] Nabil Nasr, director of the Center for Integrated Manufacturing Studies at the Rochester Institute of Technology, testified to the Commission that Chinese officials and companies have bought state-of-the-art machine-tool manufacturing companies in Germany that are in financial trouble. After acquiring the companies, China sent all the companies' equipment, as well as their German experts, to China to facilitate the transfer of this technology.

There are some machine tool success stories for upstate New York. The Gleason Corp., a local machine tool manufacturer with production facilities both in New York and overseas, exports 70 percent of its Rochester-made products to China.[366] John Perrotti, chief executive officer of the Gleason Corp., testified at the Commission's hearing about competing with China's machine tool industry. According to Mr. Perrotti, Chinese machine tool companies that are state owned have access to capital and subsidies that are not available in the United States.[367] As a result of Chinese government policies, many of the basic expenses of doing business, including health care, energy, and acquisition of certain raw materials and regulatory costs, are subsidized.[368] Said Mr. Perrotti: "Certain of these companies would not survive based on their own financial performance."

Optoelectronics

Optoelectronics or photonics applies the science of using light to a number of products such as light-emitting diodes (LEDs), sensors, infrared remote controls, liquid crystal display TVs, and laserprinters. According to the Washington, DC-based Optoelectronics Industry Development Association, the global optoelectronics market in 2008 amounted to $356 billion. Edward Patton, director of sales and marketing for Rochester Precision Optics, who testified at the Commission's Rochester hearing, noted that "if it were not for the progress in ultraviolet lasers and optics, the dramatic, exponential growth of the digital chip could not have occurred." [369]

The New York optoelectronics cluster is among the largest and most active photonics clusters in the country and, according to Mr. Patton, it is a vital resource for the economic growth of the region.[370] There are more than 60 leading opto electronics companies in Rochester alone, many of which are spin-offs of former Eastman Kodak divisions. One such example is Rochester Precision Optics, which acquired the assets of one Eastman Kodak precision glass manufacturing operation, Kodak Optical Imaging Systems. In addition to the 60 companies, there are outstanding university centers conducting opto electronic research, such as the Rochester Institute of Technology and the University of Rochester's Institute of Optics. Since its creation in 1929, the Rochester Institute of Optics has awarded approximately half of all the degrees in optics in the United States.[371]

However, as noted in section 3 of this chapter, the optoelectronics industry has moved much of its manufacturing operations to Asia over the past 10 years. For the optoelectronics industry in particular, the main reason for relocating to China is the proximity to the customers and the supply chain, rather than China's low labour costs, which, in the optoelectronics industry, account for only 10 to15 percent of the production cost.[372]

Mr. Patton noted that if it were not for the defence industry, there would be very little of the optoelectronics industry left in the United States. To accelerate the development of its own domestic optoelectronics industry, China has successfully attracted foreign investment in manufacturing and research and development. The outsourcing of optoelectronics manufacturing by US firms is a national security concern for the United States, according to Mr. Patton:"There are a lot of today's weapons systems that have optics on them, that are driven by developments in optics, and as more of the jobs in the optics industry get displaced to China, and moreof the businesses go away, the US defence industry could be seriously disadvantaged."[373]

One of the success stories in optoelectronics is Corning Incorporated, a leader in high-technology applications, primarily due to its investment in research and development. Corning's management has focused on a long-term strategy of innovation and investment, and the company has accordingly invested for the longterm.[374] Corning, once best known for its line of tableware and cookware, has transformed itself over the years into a high-technology company, allocating a significant amount of its resources to research and development. Corning employs more than 23,000 people worldwide, 4,900 of whom work in upstate New York. Corning's revenues for 2008 were $5.9 billion. Annually, 10 percent of Corning's total revenues go to research and development, which has allowed Corning to retain its competitive edge.[375] Moreover, in 2000, Corning consolidated its labs in New York State to better coordinateits research, development, and innovation needs.

Life Sciences and Education

During the past 20 years, as manufacturing has declined in upstate New York, the service sector, in particular hospitals and universities, has grown and absorbed some of the former factory workers. New York has the second-largest public university system in the United States. The state has more than 250 colleges and universities in total and one of the highest densities of institutions of higher learning in the world. With 138,000 students, the Rochester region has the highest concentration of undergraduate and graduate students in the nation.[376]

Education and health care are fields that can create opportunities for the development of a thriving, innovation-based economy. To this end, the New York State government has established Centers of Excellence throughout the state to better facilitate innovation and assist in the cooperation between academia and the private sector, and the commercialization of new technologies. At present, about $2 billion in annual research and development activity is underway at research institutions in the region.[377]

The New York State Foundation for Science, Technology and Innovationis one of the economic development agencies that provide funding for research and development projects. It has established 15 programmes across the state to help start up companies take advantage of technological developments. During the Commission's hearing in Rochester, Marnie LaVigne, the director of Business Development for the University of Buffalo's Center for Advanced Biomedical and Bioengineering Technology, testified on the center's mission in bioinformatics and life sciences. Created from a $200 million public-private sponsorship, the Buffalo

Life Sciences Complex is the type of center where a combination of business development talent and investment capital for companies, supported at least in part with public dollars, may accelerate high-tech industry growth.[378] A dozen private sector firms are currently benefiting from transnational research, startup company activity, and support resources offered at the Buffalo Complex.[379]

Clean Energy

Both the Obama Administration and the current New York State government have placed a priority on developing a strong, domestic, clean energy industry as a key element of America's economic future.[380] Many view the development of a vibrant clean energy industry that promotes investments in batteries, fuel cells, and renewable energy as a job-creating alternative to the industrial sectors that have been lost to outsourcing and overseas competition.[381]

New York has achieved some modest success in nurturing its own clean energy industry. For example, in upstate New York, the growth in clean energy jobs in 2008 was double that of the traditional manufacturing sectors: 9.1 percent, versus 3.7 percent in overall job market growth.[382] Opportunities for growth exist in upstate New York, where there are several business incubators focused primarily on clean technology.[383]

Fuel Cells and Batteries

In the area of alternative fuels, Dr. Nasr sees significant growth potential as compared to other traditional job opportunities. Upstate New York also has significant infrastructure and capabilitiesin fuel cell technology, led by such companies as General Motors, General Electric, and the Delphi Corporation. The Delphi Corporation, for example, in cooperation with the Rochester Institute of Technology, has fuel cell technology in the advanced phase of development that should be ready for production locally by 2012.[384] China currently enjoys an innovation advantage in a very important renewable energy technology: batteries.[385] The lithiumion battery is the highest-value component of the Chevy Volt and is sourced from China and South Korea.[386] According to testimony provided at the hearing by Willy Shih, professor of management practice at the Harvard Business School,

> *Most innovation in batteries in recent decades has been driven by the demands of consumer electronics products for portable power in small packages. So when US companies largely abandoned the 'mature' consumer electronics business, the locus of R&D [research and development] and manufacturing—not just for the laptops, cell phones, and such but also for the batteries that power them—shifted to Asia. The Chinese company BYD is now the second largest manufacturer of lithium ion batteries in the world.*

Electric cars depend on the same battery technology used in laptops and cell phones. BYD, which is also an automobile manufacturer, has announced its intention to produce electric cars and market them in the United States by 2010.[387] Dr. Shih believes that the Chinese government is strategically using the global transition to hybrid and electric vehicles as an opportunity to assert global leadership in the next generation of automobiles, unburdened by a gasoline-powered vehicle manufacturing infrastructure.[388]

Solar Panels

Ed Kowalewski, director of International Trade and Development for the Empire State Development Agency, and Sam Natapoff, senior advisor to the governor of New York for International Trade, maintain that upstate New York has a natural resource that gives it an advantage in the development of a green economy: the Niagara Falls hydro electric generators that supply relatively in expensive electricity. Silicon, the major raw material used in the manufacture of solar panels, requires an energy-intensive process to turn it into solar-grade silicon. Because global demand for silicon is growing, silicon could become more expensive.[389] The New York government is counting on Niagara Falls to provide the area with a comparative advantage in competing with foreign producers.[390] Recently, Global Specialty Metals reopened old silicon plants in the Niagara Falls region that it acquired in 2006 and is expanding production of metallurgical-grade silicon meant for solar panels.[391] These two developments give upstate New York potential for growth in the solar power sectors. There are more than 400 small solar power firms in the region, providing more than 10,000 jobs in the solar power sector. The growth rate for this industry is 50 percent higher than for other comparable sectors.[392] Currently, however, no large-scale production facilities for solar panels existin upstate New York.

Paul Vargovich, president of National Solar Technologies, a small producer of solar technology products in the Rochester region, testified that merely being able to meet domestic demand should be enough to facilitate growth and the creation of many high-paying jobs in upstate New York and nationally as well. Upstate New York companies and government agencies are already facing tough competition from China, a leader in the development of the clean energy sector. China is home to a burgeoning solar industry, due to generous government subsidies for electricity, export incentives, and tariff protections from foreign competition.[393] Recently, China has been using local content rules to help build its clean energy sector.

However, China already has the world's largest solar panel manufacturing industry and exports more than 95 percent of its output to the United States and Europe. In contrast, Linda DickersonHartsock, director of the Syracuse Center for Clean Tech Entrepreneurship, who worked with some of the largest solar and wind equipment manufacturers, said that US companies first look for planned government projects rather than to state subsidies when determining where to build manufacturing capacity.[394] In part becauseof China's actions, the United States ran a $9.6 billion trade deficit for 2008 in green economy products with the whole of Asia.[395]

Erosion of Capacity to Innovate

Dr. Shih suggests that an "industrial commons"—the collective research and development, engineering, and manufacturing capabilities in a region—is required to sustain innovation. Such resources exist in the clusters of companies, universities, and suppliers in the value network. The capabilities in an industrial commons sustain all the companies that access it, and they form the foundation of capabilities upon which those companies can build.[396] However, if the specialized resources or customers that originally attracted firms to a region decline or shift their focus away from those firms, the result can be disastrous for the region.

New York's competitive advantage historically has included research, development, and innovation combined with manufacturing. As manufacturing was outsourced, there is strong evidence that research, development, and innovation are following.[397] "Innovation and manufacturing are inextricably linked," said Ron Hira, associate professor of public policy at the Rochester Institute of Technology. "Lose manufacturing and you're going to lose innovation," he added. [398] Examples include Eastman Kodak, which established a Product Development Center in Shanghai in 1998 to develop software for local and worldwide markets and which is now part of Kodak's Engineering and Design Center; Dow Corning, which operates a China Application Center in Shanghai that doubled in size in 2003; [399] General Electric, whose 1,000-person technology center in Shanghai conducts research on clean coal and advanced environmental technologies;[400] and IBM, which opened a new researchand development center in Shanghai in October 2008 to complement its China Research Laboratory in Beijing.[401]

By relocating their research, development, and innovation functions overseas, New York manufacturers have retained fewer talented employees and have reduced high-paying jobs in NewYork.[402] In the short term, this may increase profits. While on an individual basis these decisions may be rational and entirely appropriate ways to maximize profits and enhance shareholder value, the cumulative effect of these individual decisions has been to diminish considerably the industrial commons in upstate New York, there by making this region a less attractive place for future investment. Large original equipment manufacturers such as Eastman Kodak, the Carrier Corporation, Corning Incorporated, IBM, and General Electric have restructured their upstate New York operations and shifted manufacturing abroad. The flow of revenues, world-class technology, and best practices has diminished considerably in these formerly original equipment manufacturing-centered communities. This trend has exacerbated a steady and troubling erosion of financial and technical resources among smaller regional manufacturers.[403]

Despite the advantages that upstate New York has to offer, with its many universities and highly educated workforce, it has one of the highest-cost environments for doing business. This fact, according to many of the Commission's witnesses, is a major contributor to the decline of manufacturing in the region. According to a study by the Center for Integrated Manufacturing, healthcare, energy, and taxes have significantly contributed to New York's high-cost business environment. Another factor complicating efforts to improve the business environment in upstate New York is that the economic development strategies in New York State are generally set independently at the municipal, county, regional, and state levels,with only limited coordination. This often leads to duplicating or conflicting investments that reduce return rates.[404]

Adopt a National Strategy for the Future

Witnesses testifying at the Commission's Rochester hearingmade a number of suggestions about how to improve the local economy.* Many witnesses highlighted

---

* For a full transcript of the hearing, visit the Commission's Web site, at http://www.uscc.gov/hearings/2009hearings/transcripts/09l06l11ltrans/09l06l11ltrans.pdf.

the need for a national strategy to deal with the effects of competition with and outsourcing to China. Although representatives from the various industry sectors that testified differed on the direction of this national strategy, they were all unanimous on one subject: China already has a national strategy to advance its industries and to become a leading technology and innovation economy. They insisted that US policy makers should be aware of China's industrial strategy when formulating national policies and of the difficulties that state governments face in countering China's policies and activities.

Some of the witnesses at the Commission's Rochester hearing recommended a national strategy to focus industrial activity and to provide down stream opportunities.[405] Dr. Nasr argued that the state of New York does try to fill in the gaps where it can, but only a national effort by the federal government can make a difference. Although several federal agencies provide grants and money for local projects, Dr. Nasr believes that "we need to tie all the research and development money to some tangible economic goal that advances our competitiveness." [406] Ms. Hartsock testified that "this is only going to happen if there is a true public policy infrastructure plan that provides regulatory policy and incentives to really jump-start at a large, national scale the kind of innovation effort that put a man on the moon 40 years ago."[407]

Innovation requires critical mass, lab support, the right equipment and instrumentation, and peer review. It takes open communication among peers and other subtle, but critical, cultural factors. It takes a tolerance for risk and a tolerance for failure as well as a willingness to think and apply innovation laterally, as many of the big break throughs were originally aimed at other targets.[408]And it takes a culture that attracts, encourages, and rewards the best minds.[409] Although China is developing quickly, both commercially and technologically, witnesses testifying at the Commission's hearings in Washington and in Rochester identified innovation as America's main competitive advantage over China. Upstate New York could be, but is not yet, a market that attracts the level of investment that Silicon Valley or Boston's high-tech corridor do, and therefore there is far less early-stage technology development in the greater Rochester area than might be expected, given the area's history and technological strengths.[410]

Conclusion

- China's industrial policy targets and supports strategic industries identified as important to its economy in the 11th Five-Year Plan. This industrial policy promotes and subsidizes many of the same industries that comprise the industrial cluster of upstate New York. These industries include auto parts, machine tools, information technology, optics, photonics, and, more recently, clean renewable energy.
- China's industrial policy has contributed to the loss of manufacturing in the region and presents a challenge to New York as it seeks to become a global leader in the renewable energy field.
- The relocation of manufacturing from upstate New York has weakened the industrial cluster, which in turn has greatly impacted the ability of remaining firms to be innovative. Advanced technology companies in the region that have been moving their manufacturing operations to China are now relocating their research, development, and innovation operations there as well.

RECOMMENDATIONS

The US-China Trade and Economic Relationship's Current Status and Significant Changes During 2009

- The Commission recommends that Congress urge the administration to employ more aggressively all trade remedies authorized by World Trade Organization (WTO) rules to counteract the Chinese government's practices. The Commission further recommends that Congress urge the administration to ensure that US trade remedy laws are preserved and effectively implemented to respond to China's unfair or predatory trade activities.
- The Commission recommends that Congress urge the United States Trade Representative (USTR) to strengthen its oversight of China's compliance with the rulings of the WTO's dispute settlement panels.
- The Commission recommends that Congress urge the USTR, as part of its annual National Trade Estimates report, to identify and prioritize for elimination barriers in China limiting the exportof US goods and services.
- The Commission recommends that Congress undertake oversight of the Strategic and Economic Dialogue to ensure that the talks benefit American farmers, workers, and businesses.
- The Commission recommends that Congress direct the US Department of the Treasury to report annually on the status of the US dollar as the world's reserve currency. This report should highlight actions, if any, taken during the reporting period by China and other nations that may contribute to the erosion of this status.

China's Role in the Origins of the Global Financial Crisis and China's Response

- The Commission recommends that Congress urge the administration to press China to allow the renminbi (RMB) to become flexible and responsive to market forces, thereby contributing to the correction of global economic imbalances. The Commission further recommends that Congress consider legislation that has the effect of offsetting the impact on the US economy of China'scurrency manipulation.
- The Commission recommends that Congress pass legislation urging the administration to report specifically on information regarding Chinese-sourced products and services used in US federally funded stimulus programmes and make this information available to the public on a periodic basis.

China's Industrial Policy and its Impact on US Companies, Workers, and the American Economy

- The Commission recommends that Congress urge the administration to employ more aggressively trade remedies to counteract the Chinese government's subsidies to favoured industries. The Commission further recommends that Congress assess the adequacy of the resources of the US Department of Commerce to investigate such subsidies.
- The Commission recommends that Congress urge the National Science Foundation to study and recommend to Congress ways to enhance the effectiveness of basic and applied research programmes in the United States,

with particular emphasis on advancing the competitiveness of key domestic production sectors.

- The Commission recommends that Congress urge the US Department of Commerce to prepare an annual report on productive capacity in China in major industrial sectors. The report should identify what steps, if any, China has taken to develop, expand, retract, or change the utilization of capacity in these sectors over the previous years.
- The Commission recommends that Congress urge the US Department of Commerce to develop rules and procedures for the collection and evaluation of information on the activities of US companies in terms of their sourcing arrangements with producers (whether independent, joint venture, subsidiary, or other relationship) in China, to the extend authorized by law. The US Department of Commerce shall prepare an annual report, based on this information, identifying changing sourcing patterns and key areas of interest and concern. This information should be subject to business proprietary confidentiality and only utilized in the report, to the extent practicable, on an aggregate basis.
- The Commission recommends that Congress urge the USTR to evaluate the use of selective value added tax rebates by China and their trade-distorting effect and determine what steps, if any, should be taken to address the issue. China's Industrial Policy and its Impact on Upstate New York.
- The Commission recommends that Congress explore the economic benefits to local communities of a national innovation strategy to meet the challenges of China's industrial policy.
- The Commission recommends that Congress request the National Academy of Sciences to conduct a study on the impact of outsourcing of manufacturing on US domestic research, development, and innovation.
- The Commission recommends that Congress urge the US Departmentof Energy, in consultation with other appropriate agencies, to report to Congress on the impact of Chinese subsidies and other elements of China's industrial policy on US-based companies that manufacture clean energy products.

ENDNOTES

1. Bureau of Economic Analysis, "Table 1.1.1. Percent Change From Preceding Period in Real Gross Domestic Product" (Washington, DC: US Department of Commerce, August 27, 2009). *http://www.bea.gov/national/nipaweb/TableView.asp?Selected Table=1& FirstYear=2008 & LastYear=2009& Freq =Qtr.*
2. Bureau of Economic Analysis, National Income and Products Accounts, Personal Income and its Disposition (Washington, DC: US Department of Commerce, September 30, 2009). *http://www.bea.gov/national/nipaweb/TableView.asp? Selected Table=58 & Freq=Qtr&FirstYear=2007&LastYear=2009.*
3. "The Spend is Nigh," *Economist*, July 30, 2009.
4. Jerry Lou, "A Speculation Bubble in China," China Daily, August 10, 2009. *http:/ www.chinadaily.com.cn/bw/2009–08/10/content_8547378.htm; People's Daily,* "China's Outbound Investment to Exceed FDI [foreign direct investment] for First Time in 2009," August 25, 2009. *http://english.people.com.cn/90001/90778/90857 908 61/6738845.html.*
5. International Monetary Fund, "World Economic Outlook Update: Contractionary Forces Receding But Weak Recovery Ahead" (Washington, DC: July 8, 2009). *http:/ /www.imf.org/external/pubs/ft/weo/2009/update/02/index.htm.*
6. Marc Champion and Andrew Batson, "Russia, China Blame Woes on Capitalism," *Wall Street Journal*, January 29, 2009. *http://online.wsj.com/article/SB123 315961511224575.html.*
7. Li Yanping and Kevin Hamlin, "China Chastises West in Leadership Bid Before G–20," Bloomberg, March 27, 2009. *http://www.bloomberg.com/apps/news? pid=20601009&sid=a1UC7pF1qNbw.*
8. Richard McGregor, "China GDP Growth Accelerates to 7.9%," *Financial Times*, July 16, 2009.
9. Bureau of Economic Analysis, "National Income and Product Accounts: Gross Domestic Product: Second Quarter 2009 (advance estimate)" (Washington, DC: US Department of Commerce, July 31, 2009). *http://www.bea.gov/newsreleases/national/ gdp/gdpnewsrelease.htm.*
10. Charles W. McMillion, "China's Soaring Commercial and Financial Power: How It Is Affecting the US and the World" (prepared under contract for the US-China Economic and Security Review Commission, Washington, DC: June 2009), pp. 14–15. *http://www.uscc.gov/researchpapers/2009 MBG %20 Info % 20Svs % 20US–China %20 Trade%20Report%20_%20FINAL%20June%202009.pdf.*
11. Charles W. McMillion, "China's Soaring Commercial and Financial Power: How It Is Affecting the US and the World" (prepared under contract for the US- China Economic and Security Review Commission, Washington, DC: June 2009), pp. 30–31. *http:/ www.uscc.gov/researchpapers/2009/MBG% 20Info %20Sv s%20US–China %20Trade%20Report%20_%20FINAL%20June%202009.pdf.*
12. US Census Bureau, "US Trade with China in Advanced Technology Products" (Washington, DC. US Department of Commerce, August 12, 2009). *http:// www.census.gov/foreign-trade/statistics/product/atp/2009/06/ctryatp/atp5700.html.*
13. *Kang Juan, "US Economic Remedy Questioned,"* Global Times, *July 28, 2009. http://english.sina.com/world/2009/0727/258712.html.*

14. Michael Levyveld, "Eased Exports for China Unlikely," Radio Free Asia, August 10, 2009; also see the Commission's Reports for previous reporting cycles for analyses of China's proliferation activities.
15. Michael Levyveld, "Eased Exports for China Unlikely," Radio Free Asia, August 10, 2009.
16. US Bureau of Industry and Security, *Annual Report to the Congress for Fiscal Year 2008* (Washington, DC: US Department of Commerce, 2009). *http://www. bis.doc.gov/news/2009/bis_annual_report_08.pdf.*
17. Andrew Batson, "Rise in China's Forex Reserves Highlights Continued Flow of Capital," *Wall Street Journal,* October 14, 2009.
18. Wayne M. Morrison and Marc Labonte, "China's Currency: A Summary of the Economic Issues," Congressional Research Service (CRS) Report to Congress RS21625 (Washington, DC: June 17, 2009), p. 1.
19. Morris Goldstein and Nicholas R. Lardy, "The Future of China's Exchange Rate Policy" (Washington, DC: Peterson Institute for International Economics, July 2009), p.86; Wayne M. Morrison and Marc Labonte, "China's Currency: A Summary of the Economic Issues," Congressional Research Service Report to Congress RS21625 (Washington, DC: June 17, 2009), p.3.
20. Federal Reserve Board, "Major Foreign Holders of Treasury Securities" (Washington, DC: US Department of the Treasury, September 16, 2009). *http:// www.ustreas.gov/tic/mfh.txt.*
21. See US-China Economic and Security Review Commission, *2008 Report to Congress* (Washington, DC: November 2008), pp. 30–31. *http://www.uscc.gov/annual_report/2008/annual_report_full_08.pdf.*
22. Richard McGregor and Daniel Dombey, "Beijing in Uneasy Embrace of the Greenback," *Financial Times,* July 26, 2009.
23. Richard McGregor and Daniel Dombey, "Beijing in Uneasy Embrace of the Greenback," *Financial Times,* July 26, 2009.
24. Bloomberg, "Yuan Deposes Dollar on China Border in Sign of Future," July 8, 2009.
25. Rachel Ziemba, "Chinese Reserves: Boiling Over Again?" *Follow the Money blog,* July 15, 2009. *http://blogs.cfr.org/setser/2009/07/15/chinese-reserves-boiling-over-again/.*
26. Richard McGregor and Daniel Dombey, "Beijing in Uneasy Embrace of the Greenback," *Financial Times,* July 26, 2009.
27. David Pilling, "Washington Risks Taking China Too Seriously," *Financial Times,* July 29, 2009.
28. David Pilling, "Washington Risks Taking China Too Seriously," *Financial Times,* July 29, 2009.
29. Brad Setser, "Doesn't a Smaller (External) Deficit Mean Less Dependence on (External) Creditors, Including China?" *Follow the Money blog,* July 28, 2009. *http://blogs.cfr.org/setser/2009/07/28/doesnt-a-smaller-external-deficit-mean-less-dependence-on-external-creditors-including-china/.*
30. Andrew Batson, "Households Start to Rival the Chinese in Treasury Market," *Wall Street Journal,* August 17, 2009.
31. Andrew Batson, "Households Start to Rival the Chinese in Treasury Market," *Wall Street Journal,* August 17, 2009.
32. Michael Pettis, "The USG Doesn't Need Foreigners to Finance the US Fiscal Deficit? Who Knew?" *China Financial Markets blog,* August 17, 2009. *http:// mpettis.com/*

2009/08/the-usg-doesn%E2%80%99t-need-foreigners-to-finance-the-us-fiscal-deficit-who-knew/.

33. Paul Krugman, "China's Dollar Trap," *New York Times*, April 3, 2009. *http://www.nytimes.com/2009/04/03/opinion/03krugman.html.*

34. Daniel Dombey and Sarah O'Connor, "US and China Display United Economic Stance," *Financial Times*, July 29, 2009.

35. For a copy of the proposal, see the Chinese People's Bank of China's Web site at *http://www.pbc.gov.cn/english/detail.asp?col=6500&id=178.*

36. Reuters, "Replacing the Dollar as Reserve Currency," July 8, 2009. *http://www.reuters.com/article/usDollarRpt/idUSN0627861320090708?sp=.*

37. Due to the dollar's status as a global reserve currency, most commodities, including oil, are currently priced in dollars. *The Independent,* a U.K. newspaper, reported in October 2009 that Gulf oil producers and nations including China, Japan, Russia, and Brazil had held secret talks on a nine-year plan to phase out the dollar in oil trade in favour of a basket of currencies plus gold. Saudi Arabia's central bank chief denied holding any such talks. See Robert Fisk, "The Demise of the Dollar," Independent, October 6, 2009. *http://www.independent.co.uk/news/business/ news/the-demise-of-the-dollar-1798175.html;* Camilla Hall, "Saudi Central Bank Chief Backs Dollar, Cites Its 'Convenience,'" Bloomberg, October 7, 2009. *http:// www.bloomberg.com/apps/news?pid=20601068&sid=apt5We30uqlA.*

38. International Monetary Fund, *Factsheet: Special Drawing Rights (SDRs)* (Washington, DC: August 27, 2009). *https://www.imf.org/external/np/exr/facts/sdr.htm.*

39. US Department of the Treasury, *US Currency and Coin Outstanding and in Circulation* (Washington, DC: June 30, 2009). *http://www.fms.treas.gov/bulletin/ b2009–3uscc.doc.*

40. Andrew Batson, "China to Boost Ties with IMF," *Wall Street Journal,* July 2, 2009. *http://online.wsj.com/article/SB124652084497984885.html.*

41. The report has not yet been made available to the public, although the IMF provided a summary. See IMF, "IMF Executive Board Concludes 2009 Article IV Consultation with the People's Republic of China," Public Information Notice No. 09/ 87 (Washington, DC: July 22, 2009). *http://www.imf.org/external/np/sec/pn/2009/pn0987.htm#P26_395.*

42. Chris Giles, Krishna Guha, and Delphine Strauss, "Strauss-Kahn Renews Attack on Renminbi," *Financial Times*, October 3, 2009.

43. Andrew Batson, "China to Boost Ties with IMF," *Wall Street Journal*, July 2, 2009. *http://online.wsj.com/article/SB124652084497984885.html.*

44. Meena Thiruvengadam, "China Set to Buy $50 Billion in IMF Notes," *Wall Street Journal,* September 3, 2009.

45. Timothy R. Homan, "IMF Board Authorizes Debut Bond Issuance to Fund Aid," Bloomberg, July 1, 2009. *http://www.bloomberg.com/apps/news?pid=20601087&sid=ankFTAhAUk68.*

46. IMF, "IMF Members' Quotas and Voting Power, and IMF Board of Governors" (Washington, DC: September 11, 2009). *http://www.imf.org/external/np/sec/ memdir/members.htm#u.*

47. Andrew Batson, "China Seeks an End to US Trade Spat," *Wall Street Journal,* September 16, 2009. *http://online.wsj.com/article/SB125298715993811161.html.*

48. "Leaders' Statement: The Pittsburgh Summit" (Pittsburgh, PA: Pittsburgh G–20 Summit, September 24–25, 2009). *http://www.pittsburghsummit.gov/media-center/129639.htm.*

49. Simon Rabinovitch, "China Calls for Automatic IMF Voting Adjustments," Reuters, October 4, 2009.
50. Richard McGregor and Daniel Dombey, "Beijing in Uneasy Embrace of the Greenback," *Financial Times*, July 26, 2009.
51. Lex, "China's Buying Spree," *Financial Times*, July 26, 2009.
52. The "Going Out" strategy is a Chinese government campaign introduced at the 2002 Communist Party Congress to raise China's global economic profile by investing overseas and acquiring foreign assets. Jamil Anderlini, "China to Deploy Forex Reserves," *Financial Times*, July 21, 2009.
53. Kevin Hamlin, "China's Stockpiles are New Sovereign Wealth Strategy, RBC Says," Bloomberg, May 18, 2009; Keith Bradsher, "China's Commodity Buying Spree," *New York Times*, June 11, 2009; D'Arcy Doran, "China-Driven Commodities Rally Nearing End," Agence France-Presse, June 20, 2009.
54. Keith Bradsher, "China's Commodity Buying Spree," *New York Times*, June 11, 2009; D'Arcy Doran, "China-Driven Commodities Rally Nearing End," Agence France-Presse, June 20, 2009.
55. Richard McGregor and Daniel Dombey, "Beijing in Uneasy Embrace of the Greenback," *Financial Times*, July 26, 2009.
56. Liu Li, Joan R. Magee, and Riva Froymovich, "Beijing Formalizes Call for New Reserve Currency," *Wall Street Journal*, June 29, 2009.
57. Liu Li, Joan R. Magee, and Riva Froymovich, "Beijing Formalizes Call for New Reserve Currency," *Wall Street Journal*, June 29, 2009.
58. Brad Setser, "The PBoC's [People's Bank of China] Call for a New Global Currency, the SDR [special drawing rights], the US and the IMF," *Follow the Money blog, March 29, 2009. http://blogs.cfr.org/setser/2009/03/29/the-pbocs-call-for-a- new-global-currency-the-sdr-the-us-and-the-imf/.*
59. Andrew Batson, "China Seeks More Involvement—and More Clout," *Wall Street Journal*, March 31, 2009.
60. Liu Li, Joan R. Magee, and Riva Froymovich, "Beijing Formalizes Call for New Reserve Currency," *Wall Street Journal*, June 29, 2009.
61. Swaminathan Aiyar and Arvind Subramanian, "China's Dollar Delusion," *Guardian* (London), July 8, 2009.
62. Under a currency swap arrangement, two parties exchange currencies for a certain length of time and agree to reverse the transaction at a later date. See the Federal Reserve Bank of New York, *The Basics of Foreign Trade and Exchange. http://www.ny.frb.org/education/fx/foreign.html.*
63. Bloomberg, "Yuan Deposes Dollar on China Border in Sign of Future," July 8, 2009.
64. Keith Bradsher, "China Begins Pilot Programme to Settle Trade in Renminbi," *New York Times*, July 6, 2009. *http://www.nytimes.com/2009/07/07/business/global/07yuan.html.*
65. The People's Bank of China, "Responsible Person from the PBC Answers Questions on the Administrative Rules on Pilot Programme of Renminbi Settlement of Cross-border Trade Transactions" (Beijing: July 2, 2009). *http://www.pbc.gov.cn/ english//detail.asp?col=6400&ID=1394.*
66. *Market Watch*, "China, Brazil Plan Currency Trade Deal: Reports," June 28, 2009. *http://www.marketwatch.com/story/china-brazil-plan-currency-trade-deal-reports; Fabiola Moura, "Brazil, China Plan to Drop Dollar Is 'Idle Talk,' " Bloomberg, May 21, 2009.*

67. Peter Garnham, "China Plans Global Role for Renminbi," *Financial Times,* July 14, 2009.
68. Phillip Bowring, "It's Not Easy to Internationalize China's Yuan," *Korea Times,* July 19, 2009.
69. Arthur Kroeber, "Time to Stop Talking of Renminbi as Reserve Currency," *Financial Times Dragonbeat blog,* May 26, 2009. *http://blogs.ft.com/dragonbeat/2009/ 05/ 26/time-to-stop-talking-of-renminbi-as-reserve-currency/.*
70. *"He Yafei: Chuang Chao Zhuquan Guoji Chubei Huobi Bushi Zhongguo Zhengfu Lichang"* (He Yafei: A Super-Sovereign International Reserve Currency is Not the Position of the Chinese Government), Xinhua, July 6, 2009. *http://www. gov.cn/ jrzg/2009 07/06/content_1358042.htm*
71. Liu Li, "Smart Money in China Knows Limits of Yuan," *Wall Street Journal China Journal blog,* July 6, 2009. *http://blogs.wsj.com/chinajournal/2009/07/06/smart - money-in-china-knows-limits-of-yuan/.*
72. "PRC Experts Support RMB as One of Diversified Reserve Currencies," *Beijing Zhongguo Xinwen She,* July 4, 2009. OSC ID: CPP20090705136001. *www. opensource.gov.*
73. Keith Bradsher, "In Step to Enhance Currency, China Allows Its Use in Some Foreign Payments," *New York Times,* July 7, 2009.
74. Friedrich Wu, "How China's Yuan Can Become a Global Currency," *Business Week,* September 15, 2009.
75. Bob Chen, "China to Sell 6 Billion Yuan of Bonds in Hong Kong," Bloomberg, September 8, 2009; Wang Ming et al., "China to Sell Yuan Government Bonds in Hong Kong," *Wall Street Journal,* September 8, 2009.
76. Justine Lau and John Burton, "China Names New Forex Chief," *Financial Times,* July 17, 2009.
77. Wen Xiu, Zhang Man, and Wang Ziwu, "Mapping Out a Global Path for the Yuan," *Caijing,* July 10, 2009; Wen Xiu, "China Appoints Chief for Yuan's Global Push," *Caijing,* July 10, 2009.
78. Dan Neumann, "Loevinger Highlights Long Term Nature of S&ED [Strategic and Economic Dialogue] Economic Agenda," *Inside US–China Trade,* August 5, 2009.
79. US Department of the Treasury, "The First US-China Strategic and Economic Dialogue Economic Track Joint Fact Sheet" (Washington, DC: July 28, 2009). *http:/ /www.ustreas.gov/press/releases/tg240.htm.*
80. Dan Neumann, "China to Focus on Improved Procurement Offer on Central Entities, not SOEs," *Inside US-China Trade,* October 14, 2009.
81. Mark Landler and David E. Sanger, "China Seeks Assurances that US Will Cut Its Deficit," *New York Times,* July 29, 2009.
82. Tom Barkley and Deborah Solomon, "Chinese Convey Concern on Growing US Debt," *Wall Street Journal,* July 29, 2009.
83. See, for example, Mark Landler and David E. Sanger, "China Seeks Assurances that US Will Cut Its Deficit," *New York Times,* July 29, 2009; and Tom Barkley and Deborah Solomon, "Chinese Convey Concern on Growing US Debt," Wall Street Journal, July 29, 2009.
84. David Pilling, "Washington Risks Taking China Too Seriously," *Financial Times,* July 29, 2009.
85. US Department of the Treasury, "The First US-China Strategic and Economic Dialogue Economic Track Joint Fact Sheet" (Washington, DC: July 28, 2009). *http:/ /www.ustreas.gov/press/releases/tg240.htm.*

86. Lex, "China Trade Spat," *Financial Times,* June 24, 2009.

87. In the most basic sense, a market economy is an economic system in which decisions about the allocation of resources and production are made on the basis of prices generated by voluntary exchanges between producers, consumers, workers, and owners of factors of production. This is often contrasted with a planned economy, which is an economy where crucial economic processes are determined to a large extent not by market forces but by an economic planning body that implements society's major economic goals.

88. According to 19 USC. § 1677(18). *http://frwebgate6.access.gpo.gov/cgi-bin/PDFgate.cgi?WAISdocID=024730349214+0+2+0&WAISaction=retrieve.*

89. Sidley Austin LLP, "Court Challenges Commerce Department To Develop Methodologies To Apply the AD/CVD Laws to Imports from Non-Market Economy Countries: International Trade and Arbitration Update," *International Trade Update,* September 4, 2009. *http://www.sidley.com/files/News/bf39e1b7-ab03–48f0-b4e6–65ba9b203bd5/Presentation/NewsAttachment/765deae0–7b53–4751-abc6–6785b9b8 3b18/International_Trade_Update_092309.pdf;* Ryan Davis, "CIT Rules Commerce Can't Double up Duties on China," *Law 360, September 21, 2009. http://internationaltrade.law360.com/articles/123477.* For more details of the case, see GPX *International Tire Corporation and Hebei Starbright Tire Co., Ltd. v. United States,* US Court of International Trade Consol. Court No. 08–00285 (September 18, 2009). *http://www.cit.uscourts.gov/slip_op/Slip_op09/Slip%20Op.%2009–103.pdf.*

90. US Trade Representative press release, "United States Files WTO Case against China over Export Restraints on Raw Material" (Washington, DC: June 23, 2009). *http://www.ustr.gov/about-us/press-office/press-releases/2009/june/united-states-files-wto-case-against-china-over-expor.*

91. Jack Healy, "China Accused of Trade Restrictions," *New York Times,* June 24, 2009; Tom Braithwaite, Joshua Chaffin, and Kathrin Hille, "US Lodges WTO Case against China," *Financial Times,* June 23, 2009.

92. Ding Qingfen, "US, EU Charges on Export Curbs Rejected," *China Daily,* June 25, 2009. *http://www.chinadaily.com.cn/china/2009–06/25/contentl8320078 .htm.*

93. US Trade Representative press release, "United States Files WTO Case against China over Illegal Support for Chinese 'Famous Brands' " (Washington, DC: December 19, 2008). *http://www.ustr.gov/about-us/press-office/press-releases/archives/ 2008/december/united-states-files-wto-case-against-chi.*

94. The "Famous Brands" programme is a means to promote the recognition and sale of Chinese brand products. See *People's Daily,* "China to Promote Famous Brands on World Market," April 28, 2000. *http://english.peopledaily.com.cn/english/ 200004/2/eng20000428l39920.html.*

95. Daniel Dombrey and Andrew Edgecliffe-Johnson, "China 'Regrets' WTO Ruling on Media Imports," *Financial Times,* August 12, 2009.

96. US Trade Representative press release, "United States Wins WTO Dispute over Deficiencies in China's Intellectual Property Rights Laws" (Washington, DC: January 26, 2009). *http://www.ustr.gov/about-us/press-office/press-releases/2009/january/united-states-wins-wto-dispute-over-deficiencies-c.*

97. World Trade Organization, "China—Measures Affecting the Protection and Enforcement of Intellectual Property Rights—Communication from China and the United States Concerning Article 21.3(b) of the DSU," WT/DS362/13 (Geneva, Switzerla..d: July 3, 2009).

98. US Trade Representative press release, "World Trade Organization Report Upholds US Trade Claims against China" (Washington, DC: August 12, 2009). *http://www.ustr.gov/about-us/press-office/press-releases/2009/august/world-trade-organization- report-upholds-us-trade-cl.*

99. John W. Miller, "China Cites 'Morals' in Its WTO Appeal," *Wall Street Journal*, September 23, 2009.

100. Dan Neumann, "US Cross Appeal on Article XX Defence Aims to Block Chinese Gains," *Inside US-China Trade*, October 14, 2009; 101. Associated Press, "China to Appeal Trade Ruling on Media Products," August 18, 2009.

102. Justine Lau, "Software Groups Hail China Piracy Verdict," *Financial Times*, August 21, 2009.

103. Kathrin Hille, "China Bans Foreign Financial News Operations," *Financial Times*, May 1, 2009.

104. State Council Information Office of the People's Republic of China, *"Waiguo Jigou zai Zhongguo Jingnei Tigong Jinrong Xinxi Fuwu Guanli Guiding"* (Regulations for Provision of Financial Information by Foreign Organizations in China), April 30, 2009. *http://www.scio.gov.cn/zcfg/zcfg/200906/t341501.htm.*

105. Richard Dobson and William Bi, "China to File WTO Complaint on US Chicken Imports," Bloomberg, March 11, 2009; Lauren Etter and Stephen Power, "China is Expected to Block Imports of Chicken from US," *Wall Street Journal*, July 2, 2009.

106. Deng Shasha, "China Protests US Measure Blocking Poultry Imports," Xinhua, March 11, 2009. *http://news.xinhuanet.com/english/2009–03/11/content_10993935.htm.*

107. "Move to Allow Poultry Imports from China Could Head Off New Trade Dispute," *WorldTrade/INERACTIVE*, September 29, 2009. *http://www.strtrade.com/wti/wti.asp?pub=0&story=32042&date=9%2F29%2F2009&company=;* "Lifting the China Poultry Import Ban," *Washington Trade Daily*, September 28, 2009.

108. "Senate Looks to Remove Poultry Ban Challenged at the WTO," *Inside US- China Trade*, July 8, 2009.

109. *US Trade Representative press release, "Kirk: White House Fulfilling Trade Enforcement Pledge with Announcement of Remedies in Chinese Tyre Case" (Washington, DC: September 11, 2009).* http://www.ustr.gov/about-us/press-office/press-releases/2009/september/kirk-white-house-fulfilling-trade-enforcement-pl.

110. *Edmund L Andrews, "US Adds Tariffs on Chinese Tires,"* New York Times, *September 12, 2009; International Trade Commission, "Certain Passenger Vehicle and Light Truck Tyres from China," Inv. No. TA–421–7 (Washington, DC: June 29, 2009).* http://www.usitc.gov/trade_remedy/731_ad/701_cvd/investigations/2009/421_tires/safeguard.htm.

111. *"PRC Commerce Minister: US Tyre Special Safeguard Measures 'Bridge of Commitments,'" Xinhua, September 12, 2009. OSC ID: CPP20090912066004.* www.opensource.gov.

112. Keith Bradsher, "China Moves to Retaliate Against US Tyre Tariff," *New York Times*, September 14, 2009.

113. Alan Beattie and Geoff Dyer, "China Turns to WTO in Trade Dispute," *Financial Times*, September 14, 2009; Andrew Batson, "China Seeks an End to US Trade Spat," *Wall Street Journal*, September 16, 2009.

114. Yu Hairong and Huokan, "China Making Policy to Support Tire Industry," *Caijing*, September 16, 2009. *http://english.caijing.com.cn/2009–09–16/110251832 .html.*

115. Geoff Dyer, "China's Economic Rebound Boosts Jobs," *Financial Times*, September 9, 2009.

116. Associated Press, "Stimulus-Stoked Market Alarms Beijing," in *China Daily*, August 10, 2009.

117. "China Is Spending to Recover," *Economist*, June 1, 2009.

118. Jerry Lou, "A Speculation Bubble in China," *China Daily*, August 10, 2009. *http://www.chinadaily.com.cn/bw/2009–08/10/content_8547378.htm.*

119. Jack Healy and Bettina Wassener, "Key Index in China Falls on Fear of a Bubble," *New York Times*, August 20, 2009, p. B1.

120. Bureau of Economic Analysis, "Personal Income and Outlays: July 2009" (Washington: DC, National Economic Accounts, August 28, 2009). *http://www.bea.gov/newsreleases/national/pi/pinewsrelease.htm.*

121. Greg Ip, "We're Borrowing Like Mad. Can the US Pay it Back?" *Washington Post*, July 11, 2009.

122. US Census Bureau, "US Trade in Goods (Imports, Exports and Balance) by Country" (Washington, DC: October 9, 2009). *http://www.census.gov/foreign-trade/ balance/index.html.*

123. US-China Economic and Security Review Commission, *Hearing on China's Role in the Origins of and Response to the Global Recession*, written testimony of Michael Pettis, February 17, 2009.

124. U.S–China Economic and Security Review Commission, *Hearing on China's Role in the Origins of and Response to the Global Recession*, testimony of Nicholas R. Lardy, February 17, 2009.

125. U.S–China Economic and Security Review Commission, *Hearing on China's Role in the Origins of and Response to the Global Recession*, testimony of Nicholas R. Lardy, February 17, 2009.

127. US-China Economic and Security Review Commission, *Hearing on China's Role in the Origins of and Response to the Global Recession*, written testimony of Stephen S. Roach, February 17, 2009.

128. US-China Economic and Security Review Commission, *Hearing on China's Role in the Origins of and Response to the Global Recession*, testimony of Stephen S. Roach, February 17, 2009.

129. US-China Economic and Security Review Commission, *Hearing on China's Role in the Origins of and Response to the Global Recession*, written testimony of Stephen S. Roach, February 17, 2009.

130. US-China Economic and Security Review Commission, *Hearing on China's Role in the Origins of and Response to the Global Recession*, written testimony of Robert B. Cassidy, February 17, 2009.

131. US-China Economic and Security Review Commission, *Hearing on China's Industrial Policy and its Impact on US Companies, Workers, and the American Economy*, testimony of Terence P. Stewart, March 24, 2009.

132. US-China Economic and Security Review Commission, *Hearing on China's Role in the Origins of and Response to the Global Recession*, written testimony of Robert B. Cassidy, February 17, 2009.

133. Ben Bernanke, "The Global Saving Glut and the US Current Account Deficit" (Sandridge lecture, Virginia Association of Economics, Richmond, VA: March 10, 2005). *http://www.federalreserve.gov/boarddocs/speeches/2005/200503102.*

134. US-China Economic and Security Review Commission, *Hearing on China's Role in the Origins of and Response to the Global Recession*, written testimony of Stephen S. Roach, February 17, 2009.

135. US-China Economic and Security Review Commission, *Hearing on China's Role in the Origins of and Response to the Global Recession*, written testimony of Stephen S. Roach, February 17, 2009.

136. US-China Economic and Security Review Commission, *Hearing on China's Role in the Origins of and Response to the Global Recession*, written testimony of Eswar S. Prasad, February 17, 2009.

137. Robert Skidelsky, "The World Finance Crisis & the American Mission," *New York Review of Books*, July 16, 2009.

138. Robert Skidelsky, "Keynesian Reforms Could Stop Us Falling into More Economic Foxholes," *Daily Telegraph*, August 30, 2009, *http://www.skidelskyr.com/site/ article/ keynesian-reforms-could-stop-us-falling-into-more-economic-foxholes/*.

139. Ben Bernanke, "Asia and the Global Financial Crisis" (Federal Reserve Bank of San Francisco's Conference on Asia and the Global Financial Crisis, Santa Barbara, CA: October 19, 2009). *http://www.federalreserve.gov/newsevents/speech/ bernanke20091019a.htm*.

140. Michael Pettis, "The G20 Meetings: No Common Framework, No Consensus," *Carnegie Policy Brief* 79 (May 2009): 4.

141. US-China Economic and Security Review Commission, *Hearing on China's Role in the Origins of and Response to the Global Recession*, testimony of Derek Scissors, February 17, 2009.

142. Bloomberg, "Yuan Deposes Dollar on China Border in Sign of Future," July 8, 2009.

143. US-China Economic and Security Review Commission, *Hearing on China's Role in the Origins of and Response to the Global Recession*, written testimony of Stephen S. Roach, February 17, 2009.

144. US-China Economic and Security Review Commission, *Hearing on China's Role in the Origins of and Response to the Global Recession*, written testimony of Michael Pettis, February 17, 2009.

145. US-China Economic and Security Review Commission, *Hearing on China's Role in the Origins of and Response to the Global Recession*, written testimony of Stephen S. Roach, February 17, 2009.

146. US-China Economic and Security Review Commission, *Hearing on China's Role in the Origins of and Response to the Global Recession*, written testimony of Eswar S. Prasad, February 17, 2009.

147. David Pilling, "China Should Raise Wages to Stimulate Demand," *Financial Times*, February 5, 2009.

148. Michael Pettis, "The G20 Meetings: No Common Framework, No Consensus," *Carnegie Policy Brief* 79 (May 2009): 6.

149. Lionel Barber et al., "Interview: Message from Wen," *Financial Times*, February 1, 2009.

150. Lionel Barber et al., "Interview: Message from Wen," *Financial Times*, February 1, 2009.

151. "Wen to Defend China's Role in Battling Economic Crisis," Agence France-Presse, January 28, 2009. *http://www.google.com/hostednews/afp/article/ALeqM5g fpcLKZrAosM5YgK9w458K1IpP7Q*.

152. US Department of the Treasury, *Report to Congress on International Economic and Exchange Rate Policies* (Washington, DC: October 15, 2009), pp. 2–3. *http://www.treasury.gov/offices/international-affairs/economic-exchange-rates/pdf/FX%20Report%20FINAL%20October%2015%202009.pdf.*

153. Wynne Godley, Dimitri Papadimitriou, and Genaaro Zezza, "Prospects for the US. and the World: A Crisis that Conventional Remedies Cannot Resolve," *Strategic Analysis* (Annandale-on-Hudson, NY: Bard College, The Levy Economics Institute, December 2008), p.2. *http://www.levy.org/pubs/sa_dec_08.pdf.*

154. US-China Economic and Security Review Commission, *Hearing on China's Role in the Origins of and Response to the Global Recession*, written testimony of Stephen S. Roach, February 17, 2009.

155. Michael Pettis, "The G20 Meetings: No Common Framework, No Consensus," *Carnegie Policy Brief 79* (May 2009): 9.

156. Bloomberg, "China's Exports Fall by Record after Global Demand Dries Up," June 10, 2009; Reuters, "Update 2–China Imports Fall in June, Trade Surplus Shrinks," July 10, 2009; Geoff Dyer and Justine Lau, "China's Economic Recovery Gains Pace," *Financial Times*, September 11, 2009.

157. Michael Pettis, "The G20 Meetings: No Common Framework, No Consensus," *Carnegie Policy Brief 79* (May 2009): 9. 158. Andrew Batson, "Rise in China's Forex Reserves Highlights Continued Flow of Capital," *Wall Street Journal*, October 14, 2009.

159. US Department of the Treasury, "Major Foreign Holders of Treasury Securities" (Washington, DC: September 16, 2009). *http://www.ustreas.gov/tic/mfh.txt.*

160. See, for example, a *People's Daily* article in which Premier Wen Jiabao "stressed the importance of promoting domestic consumption." Xinhua, "Premier Wen Stresses Expansion of Domestic Consumption," June 15, 2009. *http://english.peopledaily.com.cn/90001/90776/90785/6677996.html.*

161. Derek Scissors, "China's Stimulus Plan: Repackaged and Misdirected," The Heritage Foundation, WebMemo No. 2128 (Washington, DC: November 10, 2008). *http://www.heritage.org/research/asiaandthepacific/upload/wm_2128.pdf.*

162. Derek Scissors, "China's Stimulus: More of the Same, and Not That Much More" (Washington, DC: The Heritage Foundation, April 20, 2009. *http://www. heritage.org/Press/Commentary/ed042009a.cfm.*

163. Xinhua, "China's 4 Trillion Yuan Stimulus to Boost Economy, Domestic Demand," November 10, 2008. *http://news.xinhuanet.com/english/2008–11/09/content _10331324.htm.*

164. Wang Changyong and Zhang Hunyu, "Devil's in Details for China's Stimulus Plan," *Caijing*, December 24, 2008.

165. Xinhua, "*Wen Jiabao Zhuchi Guowuyan Changwu Hui Jueding Kuoda Neixu Shi Xiang Cuoshi"* (Premier Wen Jiabao Presides over State Council Executive Meeting, Decides on Ten Measures to Increase Domestic Demand), November 19, 2008. *http://news.xinhuanet.com/newscenter/2008–11/09/content _10331258_1.htm.*

166. Andrew Batson, "Concerns about Cost of China's Stimulus Grow," *Wall Street Journal*, June 10, 2009.

167. Jamil Anderlini, "Beijing's Stimulus Measures Questioned," *Financial Times*, May 18, 2009.

168. Andrew Batson, "Concerns about Cost of China's Stimulus Grow," *Wall Street Journal*, June 10, 2009.

169. *Stratfor Today*, "China: Emerging Details of the 'Radical Stimulus Package' " (Austin, TX: November 14, 2008).

170. Wang Changyong and Zhang Hunyu, "Devil's in Details for China's Stimulus Plan," *Caijing*, December 24, 2008.

171. Wang Xu, "Exporters Get Sops to Fight Crisis," *China Daily*, June 9, 2009.

172. Wang Xu, "Exporters Get Sops to Fight Crisis," *China Daily*, June 9, 2009.

173. Wang Xu, "Exporters Get Sops to Fight Crisis," *China Daily*, June 9, 2009.

174. Wang Changyong and Zhang Hunyu, "Devil's in Details for China's Stimulus Plan," *Caijing*, December 24, 2008.

175. Jamil Anderlini, " '421 Project' to Boost China Exports," *Financial Times*, June 23, 2009.

176. *People's Daily*, "PRC: Interview with Economist Li Yining on Transforming PRC Economy," May 28, 2009. OSC ID: CPP20090529412001. *www.opensource.gov*.

177. Gordon Fairclough, "China Aims to Improve Health Care," *Wall Street Journal*, April 7, 2009; *Economist*, "Strong as an Ox?" January 22, 2009.

178. "Strong as an Ox?" *Economist*, January 22, 2009. It is difficult to estimate the extent of home ownership in China. The Chinese government reports that roughly 80 percent of China's urban households own their homes—an astonishing number for a country that only began housing privatization in 1998; their figure is even higher for rural areas—100 percent. *See* Hao Zhou, "Owning a Home 'the Most Important,' " *China Daily*, June 28, 2007. *http://www.chinadaily.com.cn/bizchina/ 2007–06/28/ content_905025.htm;* Rosealea Yao and Tom Miller, "What's Behind China's Skyrocketing Residential Property Market? Subsidies . . . Subsidies . . . Subsidies," *Dragonbeat blog*, September 22, 2009. *http://blogs.ft.com/dragonbeat/2009/09/22/ whats-behind-chinas-skyrocketing-residential-property-market-subsidies-subsidies-subsidies/*.

179. Kevin Hamlin and Dune Lawrence, "China to Start Trial Rural Pension System to Boost Consumption," Bloomberg, June 24, 2009.

180. Jamil Anderlini and Geoff Dyer, "Downturn Causes 20m Job Losses in China," *Financial Times*, February 2, 2009.

181. Geoff Dyer, "China's Economic Rebound Boosts Jobs," *Financial Times*, September 9, 2009.

182. Jamil Anderlini and Geoff Dyer, "Downturn Causes 20m Job Losses in China," *Financial Times*, February 2, 2009.

183. For a list of parties and observers of the WTO Government Procurement Agreement, see "Parties and Observers to the GPA" (Geneva, Switzerland: World Trade Organization). *http://www.wto.org/english/tratop_e/gproc_e/memobs_e.htm*.

184. Jamil Anderlini, " 'Buy China' Policy Set to Raise Tensions," *Financial Times*, June 16, 2009.

185. Victor Shih, "Chinese Banks' Great Leap Backward," *Wall Street Journal*, December 19, 2008.

186. Geoff Dyer, "China Bank Lending Still on Rise," *Financial Times*, October 14, 2009.

187. Kevin Hamlin, "China's New Lending Surges, Fuelling Bad-Loan Concerns," Bloomberg, July 8, 2009.

188. Lu Lei, "No End in Sight for Loose Monetary Policy," *Caijing*, June 4, 2009. *http://english.caijing.com.cn/2009–06–04/110178076.html*.

189. Bloomberg, "China Bank Lending Funneled into Stocks, News Says," June 29, 2009.
190. Bloomberg, "China's July New Lending Cools, Easing Risk of Asset Bubbles," August 11, 2009.
191. Jamil Anderlini, "Beijing Orders State Banks to Slow New Loans," *Financial Times*, August 8, 2009; Geoff Dyer and Justine Lau, "China's Economic Recovery Gains Pace," *Financial Times*, September 11, 2009; Geoff Dyer, "China Bank Lending Still on Rise," *Financial Times*, October 14, 2009.
192. Bloomberg, "Wen says China 'Cannot' Yet Pull Back on Stimulus," September 10, 2009.
193. Bloomberg, "Bank of China's Zhu Sees 'Bubbles' in Asset Markets," September 10, 2009.
194. People's Bank of China, "China Monetary Policy Report Quarter Two, 2009," August 5, 2009. *http://www.pbc.gov.cn/english/detail.asp?col=6400&id=1420.*
195. *Economist*, "China is Spending to Recover," June 1, 2009.
196. Philip Lagerkranser, "China Bank Surge to World's Biggest May Be Too Good to Be True," Bloomberg, April 29, 2009.
197. Philip Lagerkranser, "China Bank Surge to World's Biggest May Be Too Good to Be True," Bloomberg, April 29, 2009.
198. Philip Lagerkranser, "China Bank Surge to World's Biggest May Be Too Good to Be True," Bloomberg, April 29, 2009.
199. Philip Lagerkranser, "China Bank Surge to World's Biggest May Be Too Good to Be True," Bloomberg, April 29, 2009.
200. *Economist*, "China is Spending to Recover," June 1, 2009.
201. *Economist*, "China is Spending to Recover," June 1, 2009.
202. John Garnaut, "China's Cities on the Brink," *The Age* (Melbourne, Australia), May 19, 2009.
203. US-China Economic and Security Review Commission, *Hearing on China's Role in the Origins of and Response to the Global Recession*, written testimony of Michael Pettis, February 17, 2009.
204. US-China Economic and Security Review Commission, *Hearing on China's Role in the Origins of and Response to the Global Recession*, written testimony of Michael Pettis, February 17, 2009.
205. David Lampton, *The Three Faces of Chinese Power* (Berkeley and Los Angeles, CA: University of California Press, Ltd., 2008), p. 25.
206. US-China Economic and Security Review Commission, *Hearing on China's Industrial Policy and its Impact on US Companies, Workers, and the American Economy*, testimony of George Haley, March 24, 2009.
207. China accomplished this feat by mid-2009. Elaine Kurtenbach, "China auto sales jump 78 percent in September," *Associated Press,* October 14, 2009.
208. As opposed to the theory of *comparative advantage*, which holds that every country has an advantage in some specific production capacity, if it is able to specialize and therefore trade with the world on the basis of that comparative advantage. Also see *US-China Economic and Security Review Commission, 2006 Report to Congress* (Washington, DC: November 2006), p. 29.
209. Based on statistics available at the UN Conference on Trade and Investment, Division of Investment and Enterprise. *http://stats.unctad.org/FDI/TableViewer/*

tableView.aspx?ReportId=3084; and US Department of Commerce, Bureau of Economic Analysis. *http://www.bea.gov/international/index.htm#iip.*

210. Consulate General of the People's Republic of China in New York, "China Overtakes US as Top Investment Destination." *http: www.nyconsulate. prchina.org/ eng/xw/ t160511.htm.* See also UN Conference on Trade and Development, "World Investment Report 2005" (Geneva, Switzerland: September 9, 2005).

211. Terence Poon, "Foreign Direct Investment in China Continues to Slide," Dow Jones Newswire, *http://online.wsj.com/article/SB125047781996935959.html.*

212. US-China Economic and Security Review Commission, *Hearing on China's Industrial Policy and its Impact on US Companies, Workers, and the American Economy,* testimony of Terence Stewart, March 24, 2009.

China's Trade by Type of Enterprise

Millions of US $	2006	2007	2008
		TRADE BALANCE	
State-owned enterprise	$–33,898	$–44,301	$–96,274
Sino-foreign contractual joint venture	7,782	9,237	9,518
Millions of US $	2006	2007	2008
Sino-foreign equity joint venture	28,107	43,950	45,084
Foreign-invested enterprise	55,345	81,783	115,999
Collective enterprise	21,148	23,700	25,971
Private enterprise	97,940	147,238	199,223
Private firm	1,827	1,815	1,686
Other, including foreign embassy, foreign company's office in China, etc.	–722	–1,529	–3,807
TOTAL	**177,530**	**261,894**	**297,401**
		EXPORTS	
State-owned enterprise	191,382	225,376	257,229
Sino-foreign contractual joint venture	17,714	18,116	18,349
Sino-foreign equity joint venture	163,801	198,972	227,006
Foreign-invested enterprise	382,497	478,834	545,477
Collective enterprise	41,098	46,920	54,679
Private enterprise	170,764	247,551	323,985
Private firm	1,878	1,913	1,860
Other, including foreign embassy, foreign company's office in China, etc.	190	473	284
TOTAL	**969,324**	**1,218,155**	**1,428,869**
		IMPORTS	
State-owned enterprise	225,281	269,677	353,503
Sino-foreign contractual joint venture	9,932	8,879	8,831

Sino-foreign equity joint venture	135,693	155,021	181,922
Foreign-invested enterprise	327,152	397,051	429,478
Collective enterprise	19,949	23,220	28,709
Private enterprise	72,824	100,313	124,762
Private firm	51	98	174
Other, including foreign embassy, foreign company's office in China, etc.	912	2,002	4,091
TOTAL	**791,794**	**956,261**	**1,131,469**

Source: China Customs.

213. Alan William Wolff, "Innovation Policies in the United States, China and India" (New Delhi, India: December 18, 2007).

214. Geoff Dyer and Richard McGregor, "China's champions: Why state ownership is no longer proving a dead hand," *Financial Times* (March 16, 2008).

215. "China began to experiment with industrial policies in the 1980s, with policies that were designed to strengthen larger firms and to grow 'national champions'that could reap economies of scale." US-China Economic and Security Review Commission, *"Hearing on the Control of China's Economy by its Government and the Effect on the United States,"* testimony of Barry Naughton, May 24, 2007.

216. US-China Economic and Security Review Commission, *Hearing on China's Industrial Policy and its Impact on US Companies, Workers, and the American Economy*, testimony of Clyde Prestowitz, March 24, 2009.

217. Peter Navarro, "Benchmarking the Advantages Foreign Nations Provide their Manufacturers," in Richard McCormack, ed., *Manufacturing a Better Future for America* (Washington, DC: The Alliance for American Manufacturing, 2009), p. 124.

218. The American Chamber of Commerce in Shanghai, *2009 White Paper: American Business in China* (Shanghai, China: April 2009), Part 1, p. 14.

219. Capital Trade Inc., *An Assessment of China's Subsidies to Strategic and Heavy weight Industries* (Washington, DC: March 2009), p. 85.

220. Capital Trade Inc., *An Assessment of China's Subsidies to Strategic and Heavyweight Industries* (Washington, DC: March 2009), p. 86.

221. Capital Trade Inc., *An Assessment of China's Subsidies to Strategic and Heavy weight Industries* (Washington, DC: March 2009), p. 86.

222. The Chinese government seeks to maintain absolute control of the seven strategic industries (meaning over 50 percent ownership) and to maintain a dominant presence in the six heavyweight industries through regulation and government control. See US-China Economic and Security Review Commission, *Hearing on the Extent of the Government's Control of China's Economy, and Implications for the United States*, written testimony of Barry Naughton and George Haley, March 24–25, 2007.

223. US-China Economic and Security Review Commission, *Hearing on China's Industrial Policy and its Impact on US Companies, Workers, and the American Economy*, testimony of George Haley, March 24, 2009.

224. David Barboza, "China Faces Delicate Task of Reining in Bank Lending," *New York Times*, August 6, 2009.

225. US-China Economic and Security Review Commission, *Hearing on China's Industrial Policy and its Impact on US Companies, Workers, and the American Economy*, testimony of George Haley, March 24, 2009.

226. US Trade Representative press release, "United States Files WTO Case Against China Over Illegal Support for Chinese 'Famous Brands' " (Washington DC: April 26, 2009).

227. Congressional Research Service, *China-US Trade Issues* (Washington, DC: March 4, 2009), p. 17.

228. US statute and regulations establish standards for determining when an unfair subsidy has been conferred by a foreign government on an exporting producer. The amount of subsidy the foreign producer receives from the government is the basis for the rate by which the subsidy is offset, or "countervailed," through higher import duties.

229. Including the following types of subsidies: Government Policy Lending, VAT Rebates, VAT and Tariff Exemptions, Preferential Tax Policies (reduced tax or exemption from tax), Provisions of Goods or Services for Less than Adequate Remuneration, Provision of Land for Less than Adequate Remuneration, Debt Forgiveness, Grants, and Export Assistance.

230. US Department of Commerce, *Highlights and News Items* (Washington, DC: International Trade Administration, Import Administration, September 2009). *http://ia.ita.doc.gov/ia-highlights-and-news.html.*

231. US Trade Representative, *2009 National Trade Estimate Report on Foreign Trade Barriers* (Washington, DC: March 29, 2009), p. 84.

232. US-China Economic and Security Review Commission, *Hearing on China's Industrial Policy and its Impact on US Companies, Workers, and the American Economy*, testimony of Alan Wolff, March 24, 2009.

233. US Trade Representative, *2009 National Trade Estimate Report on Foreign Trade Barriers* (Washington, DC. March 29, 2009), p. 77.

234. US Trade Representative, *2009 National Trade Estimate Report on Foreign Trade Barriers* (Washington, DC: March 29, 2009), p. 77.

235. Congressional Research Service, *China-US Trade Issues* (Washington, DC: March 4, 2009), p. 17.

236. US Trade Representative, *2009 National Trade Estimate Report on Foreign Trade Barriers* (Washington, DC: March 29, 2009), p. 77.

237. "Enterprise Income Tax Law of the People's Republic of China," Order of the President of the People's Republic of China, No. 63 (Beijing: People's Republic of China, March 16, 2007).

238. US Trade Representative, *2009 National Trade Estimate Report on Foreign Trade Barriers* (Washington, DC: March 29, 2009), pp. 84–85.

239. US Trade Representative, *2009 National Trade Estimate Report on Foreign Trade Barriers* (Washington, DC: March 29, 2009), pp. 84–85; and Steven Go, "Tax Preferences and Transitional Measures on China's New Tax Law" (Taiwan: Price Waterhouse Cooper, April 25, 2008). *http://www.pwc.com/TW/en/challenges/taxation/indissue0425.jhtml.*

240. US Trade Representative, *2009 National Trade Estimate Report on Foreign Trade Barriers* (Washington, DC: March 29, 2009), p. 85.

241. US Trade Representative, *2009 National Trade Estimate Report on Foreign Trade Barriers* (Washington, DC: March 29, 2009), p. 85.

242. Terence P. Stewart, Eric P. Salonen, and Patrick J. McDonough, "More than 50 Years of Trade Rule Discrimination on Taxation: How Trade with China is Affected" (Washington DC: Trade Lawyers Advisory Group, August 2007), pp. 142–145.

243. US-China Economic and Security Review Commission, *Hearing on China's Industrial Policy and its Impact on US Companies, Workers, and the American Economy*, written testimony of Terence Stewart, March 24, 2009.

244. US Department of Commerce, "US DOC IA, Electronic Subsidies Enforcement Library, Subsidies Programmes Investigated by DOC" (Washington, DC: International Trade Administration, Import Administration, February 2009). *http:// ia.ita.doc.gov /esel/eselframes.html.*

245. US Department of Commerce, "US DOC IA, Electronic Subsidies Enforcement Library, Subsidies Programmes Investigated by DOC" (Washington, DC: International Trade Administration, Import Administration, February 2009).*http:// ia.ita.doc.gov/ esel/eselframes.html.*

246. US Department of Commerce, "US DOC IA, Electronic Subsidies Enforcement Library, Subsidies Programmes Investigated by DOC" (Washington, DC: International Trade Administration, Import Administration, February 2009). *http:// ia.ita.doc.gov/ esel/eselframes.html.*

247. Dickie Mure, "Tax rebates raised for Chinese exporters," *Financial Times*, November 12, 2008.

248. *Stratfor Today*, "China: Emerging Details of the 'Radical Stimulus Package'" (Austin, TX: November 14, 2008.

249. US-China Economic and Security Review Commission, *Hearing on China's Industrial Policy and its Impact on US Companies, Workers, and the American Economy*, testimony of Alan Wolff, March 24, 2009.

250. Peter Navarro, "Benchmarking the Advantages Foreign Nations Provide their Manufacturers," in Richard McCormack, ed., *Manufacturing a Better Future for America* (Washington, DC: The Alliance for American Manufacturing, 2009), p. 113.

251. China maintains export quotas and, at times, export duties on antimony, bauxite, coke, fluorspar, indium, magnesium carbonate, molybdenum, rare earths, silicon, talc, tin, tungsten, and zinc.

252. US Trade Representative, *2009 National Trade Estimate Report on Foreign Trade Barriers* (Washington, DC: March 29, 2009), p. 97.

253. US Trade Representative, *2009 National Trade Estimate Report on Foreign Trade Barriers* (Washington, DC: March 29, 2009), p. 97.

254. US Trade Representative, *2008 Report to Congress on China's WTO Compliance* (Washington, DC: December 2008), pp. 29–30.

255. US Trade Representative, *2008 Report to Congress on China's WT Compliance* (Washington, DC: December 2008), pp. 5–6.

256. *USTR News*, "United States Files WTO Case Against China Over Export Restraints on Raw Materials" (Washington, DC: US Trade Representative, June 23, 2009).

257. STRATFOR, "China: Alleged WTO Violations and Commodity Prices" (Austin, TX: June 24, 2009).

258. The rare earth elements group is comprised of 17 minerals—scandium, yttrium, and the 15 lanthanoids—and they play a crucial role in many advanced technological devices. For more information, see, for example, Gordon B. Haxel, James B. Hedrick, and Greta J. Orris, "Rare Earth Elements—Critical Resources for High Technology,"

US Geological Survey Fact Sheet 087–02 (Reston, VA: 2002). *http://pubs.usgs.gov/fs/2002/fs087–02/fs087–02.pdf.*

259. Keith Bradsher, "China Tightens Grip on Rare Minerals," *New York Times*, September 1, 2009.

260. Xiao Yu and Eugene Tang, "China Considers Rare-Earth Reserve in Inner Mongolia," Bloomberg, September 2, 2009.

261. Chuin-Wei Yap, "China Plays Down Rare Earth Fears," *Wall Street Journal*, September 2, 2009.

262. Keith Bradsher, "Backpedaling, China Eases Proposal to Ban Exports of Some Vital Minerals," *New York Times*, September 3, 2009. *http://www.nytimes.com/ 2009/09/04/business/global/04minerals.html.*

263. Congressional Research Service, *China-US Trade Issues* (Washington, DC: March 4, 2009), p. 3.

264. US Trade Representative, *2009 National Trade Estimate Report on Foreign Trade Barriers* (Washington, DC: March 29, 2009), p. 92.

265. US Trade Representative, *2009 National Trade Estimate Report on Foreign Trade Barriers* (Washington, DC: March 29, 2009), pp. 76–77.

266. Peter Navarro, "Benchmarking the Advantages Foreign Nations Provide their Manufacturers," in Richard McCormack, ed., *Manufacturing a Better Future for America* (Washington, DC: The Alliance for American Manufacturing, 2009), p. 118.

267. *Inside US–China Trade*, "China Agrees to Timely Report on Revised Procurement Offer in S&ED," July 29, 2009.

268. Peter Navarro, "Benchmarking the Advantages Foreign Nations Provide their Manufacturers," in Richard McCormack, ed., *Manufacturing a Better Future for America* (Washington, DC: The Alliance for American Manufacturing, 2009), p.119.

269. Keith Bradsher, "China Builds High Wall to Guard Energy Industry," *New York Times*, July 14, 2009.

270. Keith Bradsher, "China Builds High Wall to Guard Energy Industry," *New York Times*, July 14, 2009.

271. US Trade Representative, *2009 National Trade Estimate Report on Foreign Trade Barriers* (Washington, DC: March 29, 2009), p. 78.

272. Fang Yan and Jacqueline Wong, "China August car sales surge, set 2009 record," Reuters, September 8, 2009.

273. Elaine Kurtenbach, "China auto sales jump 78 percent in September," Associated Press, October 14, 2009.

274. Congressional Research Service, *China-US Trade Issues* (Washington, DC: March 4, 2009), p. 17.

275. Keith Bradsher, "Despite Trade Rulings, Beijing Gains From Delay Tactics," *New York Times*, August 31, 2009.

276. Robert Atkinson and Julie Hadlund, "The Rise of the New Mercantilists: Unfair Trade Practices in the Innovation Economy" (Washington, DC: The Information Technology and Innovation Foundation, June 2007), p. 25.

277. Robert Atkinson and Julie Hadlund, "The Rise of the New Mercantilists: Unfair Trade Practices in the Innovation Economy" (Washington, DC: The Information Technology and Innovation Foundation, June 2007), p. 26.

278. Robert Atkinson and Julie Hadlund, "The Rise of the New Mercantilists: Unfair Trade Practices in the Innovation Economy" (Washington, DC: The Information Technology and Innovation Foundation, June 2007), p. 22.

279. Ron Hira, "The Offshoring of Innovation—US Innovation System Morphs as Investments in R&D Increasingly Go to Low Cost Countries," EPI (Economic Policy Institute) Briefing Paper (Washington, DC: December 1, 2008), pp. 14–15.

280. *China Daily*, "Airbus delivers 1st China-made plane; to raise output," June 23, 2009.

281. Irene Shen, "China Sets Up Planemaker to Challenge Airbus, Boeing," Bloomberg, May 11, 2008.

282. US-China Economic and Security Review Commission, *Hearing on China's Industrial Policy and its Impact on US Companies, Workers, and the American Economy*, testimony of Ralph E. Gomory, March 24, 2009.

283. Congressional-Executive Commission on China, *2008 Annual Report* (Washington, DC: October 31, 2008), p. 41.

284. PRC (People's Republic of China) Labour Contract Law; Articles 10, 46, and 47 (Beijing: January 1, 2008).

285. Congressional-Executive Commission on China, *2008 Annual Report* (Washington, DC: October 31, 2008), p. 42.

286. Congressional-Executive Commission on China, *2008 Annual Report* (Washington, DC: October 31, 2008), p. 42.

287. China Labour Bulletin, *Going it Alone: The Workers' Movement in China (2007–2008)* (Hong Kong, China: July 9, 2009), p. 10.

288. China Labour Bulletin, *Going it Alone: The Workers' Movement in China (2007–2008)* (Hong Kong, China: July 9, 2009), p. 10.

289. Elizabeth C. Economy, "The Great Leap Backward?" *Foreign Affairs* (September 7, 2007).

290. Senate Committee on Foreign Relations, *Challenges and Opportunities for US-China Cooperation on Climate Change*, written testimony of Elizabeth Economy, 111th Cong., 1st sess., June 4, 2009.

291. Peter Navarro, "Benchmarking the Advantages Foreign Nations Provide their Manufacturers," in Richard McCormack, ed., *Manufacturing a Better Future for America* (Washington, DC: The Alliance for American Manufacturing, 2009), p.134.

292. Peter Navarro, "Benchmarking the Advantages Foreign Nations Provide their Manufacturers," in Richard McCormack, ed., *Manufacturing a Better Future for America* (Washington, DC: The Alliance for American Manufacturing, 2009), p. 134.

293. Derek Scissors, "Liberalization in Reverse" (Washington, DC: The Heritage Foundation, May 4, 2009).

294. Derek Scissors, "Liberalization in Reverse" (Washington, DC: The Heritage Foundation, May 4, 2009).

295. Terry Macalister, "China leads escalation of coal consumption," *Guardian*, June 10, 2009.

296. Derek Scissors, "Liberalization in Reverse" (Washington, DC: The Heritage Foundation, May 4, 2009).

297. Economists differ on their predictions, and their estimates range from 12 to 25 to 40 percent. Morris Goldstein and Nicholas R. Lardy, "The Future of China's Exchange Rate Policy" (Washington, DC: Peterson Institute for International Economics, July 2009), p. 86; Wayne M. Morrison and Marc Labonte, "China's Currency: A Summary of the Economic Issues," Congressional Research Service Report to Congress RS21625 (Washington, DC: June 17, 2009), p. 3.

298. Together with the current account—the balance of exports and imports of goods and services—the capital account makes up most of a country's balance of payments. See Derek Scissors, "Liberalization in Reverse" (Washington, DC: The Heritage Foundation, May 4, 2009).

299. Derek Scissors, "Liberalization in Reverse" (Washington, DC: The Heritage Foundation, May 4, 2009).

300. Derek Scissors, "Liberalization in Reverse" (Washington, DC: The Heritage Foundation, May 4, 2009).

301. Derek Scissors, "Liberalization in Reverse" (Washington, DC: The Heritage Foundation, May 4, 2009).

302. Derek Scissors, "US-China Trade: Do's and Don'ts for Congress" (Washington, DC: The Heritage Foundation, July 20, 2009), p. 5.

303. Charles W. Freeman III, deputy assistant US-Trade Representative, statement to the Congressional-Executive Commission on China, Washington, DC, September 24, 2003.

304. US-China Economic and Security Review Commission, *Hearing on China's Industrial Policy and its Impact on US Companies, Workers, and the American Economy*, testimony of Clyde Prestowitz, March 24, 2009.

305. US-China Economic and Security Review Commission, *Hearing on China's Industrial Policy and its Impact on US Companies, Workers, and the American Economy*, testimony of Denis Simon, March 24, 2009.

306. US-China Economic and Security Review Commission, *Hearing on China's Industrial Policy and its Impact on US Companies, Workers, and the American Economy*, testimony of Clyde Prestowitz, March 24, 2009.

307. Ma Kai, "The 11th Five-Year Plan: Targets, Paths and Policy Orientation" (Beijing: March 19, 2006). Mr. Ma is the minister, National Development and Reform Commission.

308. *Manufacturing and Technology News*, "The Promise of Optoelectronics is Headed to Asia," January 16, 2009; and U.S, Department of Commerce, "Digital Economy 2003" (Washington, DC: December 2003), p. 30.

309. US-China Economic and Security Review Commission, *Hearing on China's Industrial Policy and its Impact on US Companies, Workers, and the American Economy*, testimony of Michael Lebby, March 24, 2009.

310. US-China Economic and Security Review Commission, *Hearing on China's Industrial Policy and its Impact on US Companies, Workers, and the American Economy*, written testimony of Terence Stewart, March 24, 2009.

US-China Bilateral Trade in Information Technology Products
(in millions of US $)

		1996	2000	2004	2008
IT Products (Total)	China Exports	$4,799	$12,393	$45,765	$87,114
	China Imports	2,661	7,056	10,710	16,731
	US Deficit in IT Prod	**–2,137**	**–5,337**	**–35,055**	**–70,383**
Consumer Electronics	China Exports	1,393	2,754	7,109	19,082
	China Imports	67	199	294	96
	US Deficit in IT Prod.	**–1,326**	**–2,555**	**–6,815**	**–18,986**
Communications Equipment	China Exports	847	2,142	10,184	17,267
	China Imports	715	1,980	953	1,448
	US Deficit in IT Prod.	**–132**	**–162**	**–9,230**	**–15,819**
Computer & Office Equipment	China Exports	1,570	4,897	23,781	39,429
	China Imports	745	1,835	1,876	2,054
	US Deficit in IT Prod.	**–825**	**–3,062**	**–21,904**	**–37,375**
Semiconductors	China Exports	91	488	1,018	1,565
	China Imports	277	1,338	3,813	7,706
	US Deficit in IT Prod.	**186**	**850**	**2,794**	**6,141**
Electrical Components	China Exports	541	1,173	1,949	4,154
	China Imports	87	350	603	858
	US Deficit in IT Prod.	**–454**	**–823**	**–1,346**	**–3,297**
Industrial Electronics	China Exports	180	404	1,091	3,899
	China Imports	709	1,137	2,805	4,035
	US Deficit in IT Prod.	**529**	**733**	**1,713**	**136**
Photonics	China Exports	177	535	633	1,718
	China Imports	61	217	366	535
	US Deficit in IT Prod.	**–116**	**–318**	**–267**	**–1,183**

Source: GITS World Trade Atlas, China Edition.

China's Exports of Information Technology Products
(in millions of US $)

		1996	2000	2004	2008
IT Products (Total)	China Total Exports	$21,867	$54,353	$201,314	$463,652
	China US Exports	4,799	12,393	45,765	87,114
	US Share of Total Exp.	21.9%	22.8%	22.7%	18.8%
Consumer Electronics	China Total Exports	6,077	10,758	27,190	63,844
	China Imports	4,799	2,754	7,109	19,082
	US Share of Total Exp.	21.9%	25.6%	26.1%	29.9%
Communications Equipment	China Total Exports	3,147	9,293	42,475	114,924
	China US Exports	847	2,142	10,184	17,267
	US Share of Total Exp.	26.9%	23.1%	24.0%	15.0%
Computer & Office Equipment	China Total Exports	6,019	17,501	86,094	160,081
	China US Exports	1,570	4,897	23,781	39,429
	US Share of Total Exp.	26.1%	28.0%	27.6%	24.6%
Semiconductors	China Total Exports	1,065	4,490	14,493	41,807
	China US Exports	91	488	1,018	1,565
	US Share of Total Exp.	8.6%	10.9%	7.0%	3.7%

Electrical Components	China Total Exports	3,732	8,297	17,177	39,295
	China US Exports	541	1,173	1,949	4,154
	US Share of Total Exp.	14.5%	14.1%	11.3%	10.6%
Industrial Electronics	China Total Exports	789	1,402	3,853	16,063
	China US Exports	180	404	1,091	3,899
	US Share of Total Exp.	22.8%	28.8%	28.3%	24.3%
Photonics	China Total Exports	1,039	2,613	10,032	27,637
	China US Exports	177	535	633	1,718
	US Share of Total Exp.	17.1%	20.5%	6.3%	6.2%

Source: GITS World Trade Atlas, China Edition.

311. James A. Lewis, "Building an Information Technology Industry in China: National Strategy, Global Markets," Center for Strategic and International Studies Report (Washington, DC: May 2007), pp. 2–4.

312. US Department of Commerce, *ExportIT China: Telecommunications and Information Technology Market Opportunities for Small and Medium-Sized Enterprises* (Washington, DC: April 2003), p. vii.

313. Arthur Kroeber, "China's Push to Innovate in Information Technology," in *Innovation with Chinese Characteristics: High-Tech Research in China,* ed. Linda Jakobson (New York: Palgrave Macmillan, 2007), p. 61.

314. Richard P. Suttmeier and Yao Xiangkui, "China's Post-WTO Technological Policy: Standards, Software, and the Changing Nature of Techno-Nationalism," The National Bureau of Economic Research Special Report 7 (May 2004): 3.

315. Richard P. Suttmeier and Yao Xiangkui, "China's Post-WTO Technological Policy: Standards, Software, and the Changing Nature of Techno-Nationalism," The National Bureau of Economic Research Special Report 7 (May 2004): 8.

316. The International Telecommunication Union defines 3G (or 3rd Generation/International Mobile Telecommunications-2000) as a family of standards for mobile telecommunications. Services include wide-area wireless voice telephone, video calls, and wireless data in a mobile environment. 3G also allows simultaneous speech and data service use. TD–SCDMA stands for Time Division Synchronous Code Division Multiple Access, which is an approved standard by the International Telecommunications Union.

317. Richard P. Suttmeier and Yao Xiangkui, "China's Post-WTO Technological Policy: Standards, Software, and the Changing Nature of Techno-Nationalism," The National Bureau of Economic Research Special Report 7 (May 2004): 8.

318. Arthur Kroeber, "China's Push to Innovate in Information Technology," in *Innovation with Chinese Characteristics: High-Tech Research in China,* ed. Linda Jakobson (New York: Palgrave Macmillan, 2007), pp. 63–64.

319. John Walko, "Watch Out: WAPI is back on the Wi-Fi agenda," *EE (Electronic Engineering) Times*, June 19, 2009.

320. *The Economist*, "Rewired," May 29, 2008.

321. 4G is the next generation (or an evolution of the 3rd Generation) of wireless networks that will replace 3G networks sometime in the future. The major requirements driving its architecture are converged data and Voice Over Internet Protocol. 4G networks will have higher speeds and higher bandwidths, with an all-digital switching design basis.

322. *The Economist*, "Rewired," May 29, 2008.

323. US Department of Commerce, "Telecom Market Summary: China" (Washington, DC: International Trade Administration, Office of Technology and Commerce, November 1, 2006).

324. US-China Economic and Security Review Commission, *Hearing on China's Industrial Policy and its Impact on US Companies, Workers, and the American Economy*, testimony of Richard Suttmeier, March 24, 2009.

325. *The Economist*, "Rewired," May 29, 2008.

326. In January 2009, the Ministry of Industry and Information Technology in China assigned licenses for three different third-generation mobile phone standards to three carriers. The Chinese-developed standard, TD–SCDMA, was assigned to China Mobile. Licenses for two existing 3G standards, WCDMA and CDMA–2000, were assigned to China Unicom and China Telecom, respectively. See "China Issues 3G Licenses to Main Carriers," Reuters, January 7, 2009. *http://uk.reuters.com/article/idUKTRE5061KP20090107?sp=true*.

327. Dieter Ernst and Barry Naughton, "China's Emerging Industrial Economy: Insights from the IT Industry," in *China's Emergent Political Economy: Capitalism in the Dragon's Lair*, ed. Christopher A. McNally (New York: Routledge, 2008), p.44.

328. Arthur Kroeber, "China's Push to Innovate in Information Technology," in *Innovation with Chinese Characteristics: High-Tech Research in China,* ed. Linda Jakobson (New York: Palgrave Macmillan, 2007), pp. 38–39.

329. "China on weaponry's cutting edge," Xinhua Net, April 13, 2009.

330. Richard Suttmeier, Xiangkui Yao, and Alex Zixiang Tan, "Standards of Power? Technology, Institutions, and Politics in the Development of China's National Standards Strategy" (Washington, DC: The National Bureau of Asian Research, June 2006), pp. 1–3.

331. US-China Economic and Security Review Commission, *Hearing on China's Industrial Policy and its Impact on US Companies, Workers, and the American Economy*, testimony of Denis Simon, March 24, 2009.

332. Ming Shuliang and Ouyang Changzheng, "Wiring China for the Next Telecom Era," *Caijing*, February 25, 2008. *http://english.caijing.com.cn/2008–02–25/100049440.html*.

333. Organization for Economic Cooperation and Development (OECD), "OECD Finds that China is the Biggest Exporter of Information Technology Goods in 2004, Surpassing US and EU" (Paris, France: December 12, 2005). *http://www.oecd.org/document/8/0,3343,en_2649_33757_35833096_1_1_1_1,00.html*. As of 2007 (the latest numbers available), China remains the leading exporter of information technology goods.

334. Arthur Kroeber, "China's Push to Innovate in Information Technology," in *Innovation with Chinese Characteristics: High-Tech Research in China,* ed. Linda Jakobson (New York: Palgrave Macmillan, 2007), p. 37.

335. Organization for Economic Cooperation and Development (OECD), *OECD Information Technology Outlook 2008* (Paris, France: December 2008), pp. 77–78. *http://browse.oecdbookshop.org/oecd/pdfs/browseit/9308041E.PDF*.

336. "Commoditizing" means producing at low cost in large volumes. Arthur Kroeber, "China's Push to Innovate in Information Technology," in *Innovation with Chinese Characteristics: High-Tech Research in China,* ed. Linda Jakobson (New York: Palgrave Macmillian, 2007), p. 55.

337. Cisco press release, "Cisco Files Lawsuit Against Huawei Technologies," January 23, 2003. *http://newsroom.cisco.com/dlls/corp_012303.html.*

338. Dieter Ernst and Barry Naughton, "China's Emerging Industrial Economy: Insights from the IT Industry," in *China's Emergent Political Economy: Capitalism in the Dragon's Lair*, ed. Christopher A. McNally (New York: Routledge, 2008), p.46.

339. *Manufacturing and Technology News*, "The Promise of Optoelectronics is Headed to Asia," January 16, 2009.

340. US-China Economic and Security Review Commission, *Hearing on China's Industrial Policy and its Impact on US Companies, Workers, and the American Economy* written testimony of Michael Lebby, March 24, 2009.

341. *Manufacturing and Technology News*, "The Promise of Optoelectronics is Headed to Asia," January 16, 2009.

342. US-China Economic and Security Review Commission, *Hearing on China's Industrial Policy and its Impact on US Companies, Workers, and the American Economy*, testimony of Michael Lebby, March 24, 2009.

343. US-China Economic and Security Review Commission, *Hearing on China's Industrial Policy and its Impact on US Companies, Workers, and the American Economy*, testimony of Michael Lebby, March 24, 2009.

344. US-China Economic and Security Review Commission, *Hearing on China's Industrial Policy and its Impact on US Companies, Workers, and the American Economy*, testimony of Michael Lebby, March 24, 2009.

345. US-China Economic and Security Review Commission, *Hearing on China's Industrial Policy and its Impact on US Companies, Workers, and the American Economy*, testimony of Michael Lebby, March 24, 2009.

346. Figure compiled from *China Business Review* (March-April 1985); and US Census Bureau. *http://www.census.gov/foreign-trade/balance/c5700.html.*

347. Robert Scott, "China dominates US non-oil trade deficit in 2009" (Washington, DC: Economic Policy Institute, July 23, 2009).

348. The US Department of Commerce maintains and updates a list of advanced technology products, which is currently comprised of 533 products.

349. Charles W. McMillion, *China's Soaring Commercial and Financial Power: How it is affecting the US and the World* (Washington, DC: MBG Information Services, June 2009), p. 30.

350. Charles W. McMillion, *China's Soaring Commercial and Financial Power: How it is affecting the US and the World* (Washington, DC: MBG Information Services, June 2009), p. 30.

351. Marcus Walker, "Germany Can Change to Confront Export Slump—but Will it?" *Wall Street Journal*, June 29, 2009.

352. Loren Thompson, "Reversing Industrial Decline—A Role for the Defence Budget" (Arlington, VA: Lexington Institute, August 18, 2009), p. 2.

353. US-China Economic and Security Review Commission, *Hearing on China's Industrial Policy and its Impact on US Companies, Workers, and the American Economy*, testimony of Clyde Prestowitz, March 24, 2009.

354. US-China Economic and Security Review Commission, *Hearing on China's Industrial Policy and its Impact on US Companies, Workers, and the American Economy*, testimony of Denis Simon, March 24, 2009.

355. Gary Pisano and Willy Shih, "Restoring American Competitiveness," *Harvard Business Review* 87:7 (July-August 2009).

356. US-China Economic and Security Review Commission, *Hearing on the Impact of Trade with China on New York State and Opportunities for Economic Growth*, testimony of Willy Shih and John Perrotti, July 23, 2009.

357. A.T. Kearney, "Delivering on the Promise of New York State: A Strategy for Economic Growth & Revitalization," prepared for Empire State Development Agency (New York, NY: July 2007), p. 6.

358. Bureau of Labour Statistics, "Databases, Tables, and Calculators: State and County Wages" (Washington, DC: US Department of Labour). *http://www.bls.gov/ data/ #wages.*

359. US-China Economic and Security Review Commission, *Hearing on the Impact of Trade with China on New York State and Opportunities for Economic Growth*, written testimony of William Johnson, July 23, 2009.

360. US-China Economic and Security Review Commission, *Hearing on the Impact of Trade with China on New York State and Opportunities for Economic Growth*, written testimony of William Johnson, July 23, 2009.

361. US-China Economic and Security Review Commission, *Hearing on the Impact of Trade with China on New York State and Opportunities for Economic Growth*, written testimony of John Perrotti, July 23, 2009.

362. *2009 World Machine Tool Output & Consumption Survey* (Cincinnati, OH: Gardner Publications, Inc.). *http://www.gardnerweb.com/consump/survey.html.*

363. US-China Economic and Security Review Commission, *Hearing on the Impact of Trade with China on New York State and Opportunities for Economic Growth*, written testimony of John Perrotti, July 23, 2009.

364. US-China Economic and Security Review Commission, *Hearing on the Impact of Trade with China on New York State and Opportunities for Economic Growth*, written testimony of John Perrotti, July 23, 2009.

365. *2009 World Machine Tool Output & Consumption Survey* (Cincinnati, OH: Gardner Publications, Inc.). *http://www.gardnerweb.com/consump/survey.html.*

366. US-China Economic and Security Review Commission, *Hearing on the Impact of Trade with China on New York State and Opportunities for Economic Growth*, written testimony of John Perrotti, July 23, 2009.

367. US-China Economic and Security Review Commission, *Hearing on the Impact of Trade with China on New York State and Opportunities for Economic Growth*, written testimony of John Perrotti, July 23, 2009.

368. US-China Economic and Security Review Commission, *Hearing on the Impact of Trade with China on New York State and Opportunities for Economic Growth*, written testimony of Ed Kowalewski, July 23, 2009.

369. US-China Economic and Security Review Commission, *Hearing on the Impact of Trade with China on New York State and Opportunities for Economic Growth*, written testimony of Edward Patton, July 23, 2009.

370. US-China Economic and Security Review Commission, *Hearing on the Impact of Trade with China on New York State and Opportunities for Economic Growth*, testimony of Edward Patton, July 23, 2009.

371. US-China Economic and Security Review Commission, *Hearing on the Impact of Trade with China on New York State and Opportunities for Economic Growth*, testimony of Edward Patton, July 23, 2009.

372. Mike Morris (chief executive officer, Apollo Optic Systems), interview with Commission staff, July 9, 2009.

373. US-China Economic and Security Review Commission, *Hearing on the Impact of Trade with China on New York State and Opportunities for Economic Growth*, testimony of Edward Patton, July 23, 2009.

374. US-China Economic and Security Review Commission, *Hearing on the Impact of Trade with China on New York State and Opportunities for Economic Growth*, written testimony of Willy Shih, July 23, 2009.

375. Corning Incorporated, "Our Innovation Recipe." *http://www.corning.com/rd/ culture of innovation/innovation_recipe.aspx*.

376. US-China Economic and Security Review Commission, *Hearing on the Impact of Trade with China on New York State and Opportunities for Economic Growth*, testimony of Linda Dickerson Hartsock, July 23, 2009.

377. US-China Economic and Security Review Commission, *Hearing on the Impact of Trade with China on New York State and Opportunities for Economic Growth*, testimony of Linda Dickerson Hartsock, July 23, 2009.

378. US-China Economic and Security Review Commission, *Hearing on the Impact of Trade with China on New York State and Opportunities for Economic Growth*, testimony of Marnie La Vigne, July 23, 2009.

379. US-China Economic and Security Review Commission, *Hearing on the Impact of Trade with China on New York State and Opportunities for Economic-Growth*, written testimony of Marnie LaVigne, July 23, 2009.

380. The American Recovery and Reinvestment Act included more than $80 billion in clean energy investments, intended to jump-start the economy and build the clean energy jobs of the future. *http://www.whitehouse.gov/issues/energy_and_environment/*. US-China Economic and Security Review Commission, *Hearing on the Impact of Trade with China on New York State and Opportunities for Economic Growth*, written testimony of Sam Natapoff and Ed Kowalewski, July 23, 2009.

381. US-China Economic and Security Review Commission, *Hearing on the Impact of Trade with China on New York State and Opportunities for Economic Growth*, testimony of Nabil Nasr and Linda Dickerson Hartsock, July 23, 2009.

382. US-China Economic and Security Review Commission, *Hearing on the Impact of Trade with China on New York State and Opportunities for Economic Growth*, testimony of Nabil Nasr, July 23, 2009.

383. US-China Economic and Security Review Commission, *Hearing on the Impact of Trade with China on New York State and Opportunities for Economic Growth*, testimony of Nabil Nasr, July 23, 2009.

384. Delphi Corporation press release, "For Second Consecutive Year, Delphi and Rochester Institute of Technology Receive $2 Million + in Federal Fuel Cell Funding—Continued Commitment Advancing Solid Oxide Fuel Cell Technology Production,"March 13, 2009. *http://delphi.com/news/press Releases/pr_2009_03_13_001/*.

385. US-China Economic and Security Review Commission, *Hearing on the Impact of Trade with China on New York State and Opportunities for Economic Growth*, written testimony of Willy Shih, July 23, 2009.

386. A123 Systems, "GM and A123Systems to Co-Develop Lithium-Ion Battery Cell for Chevrolet Volt," August 9, 2007. *http://ir.a123systems.com releasedetail.cfm? ReleaseID=403105.*

387. Norihiko Shirouzu, "BYD to Sell Electric Car in US Market Next Year," *Wall Street Journal*, August 22, 2009.

388. US-China Economic and Security Review Commission, *Hearing on the Impact of Trade with China on New York State and Opportunities for Economic Growth*, written testimony of Willy Shih, July 23, 2009.

389. Metallurgical silicon could become a rare commodity, according to *Photon International* (February 2009). *http://www.photon-magazine.com/news_archiv details.aspx?cat =News _ PI&sub = world wide & pub = 4 & parent =1555.*

390. Governor David A. Paterson press release, "Governor Paterson Announces New Solar Cell Manufacturer to Move to Dutchess County," New York, NY, April7, 2009.

391. "Green Corridor Emerging?" *SITE Selection online*, November 2008. *http://www.site selection.com/features/2008/nov/Upstate-New-York/.*

392. Based on a study by the Battelle Institute, commissioned by the Syracuse Center of Excellence on Environmental and Energy Systems. US-China Economic and Security Review Commission, *Hearing on the Impact of Trade with China on New York State and Opportunities for Economic Growth*, testimony of Linda Dickerson Hartsock, July 23, 2009.

393. Todd Woody, "US Company and China Plan Solar Project," *New York Times*, September 9, 2009.

394. US-China Economic and Security Review Commission, *Hearing on the Impact of Trade with China on New York State and Opportunities for Economic Growth*, testimony of Linda Dickerson Hartsock, July 23, 2009.

395. Samuel Sherraden, "Green Trade Balance" (Washington, DC: New America Foundation, June 22, 2009).

396. US-China Economic and Security Review Commission, *Hearing on the Impact of Trade with China on New York State, and Opportunities for Economic Growth*, written testimony of Willy Shih, July 23, 2009.

397. Center for Integrated Manufacturing Studies, "Roadmap for the Revitalization of Upstate New York Manufacturing" (Henrietta, NY: Rochester Institute of Technology), p. 7.

398. US-China Economic and Security Review Commission, *Hearing on the Impact of Trade with China on New York State and Opportunities for Economic Growth*, testimony of Ron Hira, July 23, 2009.

399. Dow Corning press release, "Dow Corning Expands China Application Center to Double Capacity for Customer Innovation" (Midland, MI: October 28, 2003).

400. China recently signed a memorandum of understanding that explicitly allows General Electric to provide certain advanced technologies to China. *Business Wire*, "GE, People's Republic of China Sign Memorandum of Understanding on Environmental Technology," May 29, 2006.

401. IBM press release, "IBM China Research Lab Expands into Shanghai to Promote Collaboration and Scientific Exploration," October 14, 2008. *http://www-03.ibm.com/ press/pressrelease/25486.wss.*

402. Center for Integrated Manufacturing Studies, "Roadmap for the Revitalization of Upstate New York Manufacturing" (Henrietta, NY: Rochester Institute of Technology), p. 7.

403. Center for Integrated Manufacturing Studies, "Roadmap for the Revitalization of Upstate New York Manufacturing" (Henrietta, NY: Rochester Institute of Technology), p 11.

404. Center for Integrated Manufacturing Studies, "Roadmap for the Revitalization of Upstate New York Manufacturing" (Henrietta, NY: Rochester Institute of Technology), p. 24.

405. US-China Economic and Security Review Commission, *Hearing on the Impact of Trade with China on New York State and Opportunities for Economic Growth*, testimony of Nabil Nasr, Linda Dickerson Hartsock, Paul Vargovich, and Edward Patton, July 23, 2009.

406. US-China Economic and Security Review Commission, *Hearing on the Impact of Trade with China on New York State and Opportunities for Economic Growth*, testimony of Nabil Nasr, July 23, 2009.

407. US-China Economic and Security Review Commission, *Hearing on the Impact of Trade with China on New York State and Opportunities for Economic Growth*, testimony of Linda Dickerson Hartsock, July 23, 2009.

408. Andrian Slywotzky, "Where have you gone, Bell labs?" *Business Week*, August 27, 2009.

409. Andrian Slywotzky, "Where have you gone, Bell labs?" *Business Week*, August 27, 2009.

410. US-China Economic and Security Review Commission, *Hearing on the Impact of Trade With China on New York State and Opportunities for Economic Growth*, testimony of Peter Robinson, July 23, 2009.

Chapter 2

China's Activities Directly Affecting US Security Interests

SECTION 1

China's Military and Security Activities Abroad

> "... the United States-China Economic and Security Review Commission... shall investigate and report exclusively on—
>
> "Regional Economic And Security Impacts—The triangular economic and security relationship among the United States, Taipei and the People's Republic of China (including the military modernization and force deployments of the People's Republic of China aimed at Taipei), the national budget of the People's Republic of China, and the fiscal strength of the People's Republic of China in relation to internal instability in the People's Republic of China and the likelihood of the externalization of problems arising from such internal instability. ..."

Introduction

The growing strength of China's economy has permitted it to expend more resources on its military development. Over the past several years, the Chinese military, or People's Liberation Army (PLA), has experienced a sea change in its approach to national security.* This change follows from Beijing's interest in ensuring China's continued economic development: The PLA needs the military capacity to secure China's expanding overseas interests and respond to non traditional security issues, such as disaster relief and transnational crime. Therefore, Beijing has mandated the PLA to transition from a territorially focused military that counters traditional military threats, such as invasion or separatism, to a more globally focused military that, in addition to traditional competencies, can handle nontraditional security threats. As a result, the PLA has gradually increased its operational ranges, expanded

* Although this section addresses the overseas role of China's military and security forces, the term "military," or "People's Liberation Army," will be used throughout, since the PLA conducts the vast majority of China's overseas military and security activities. In those instances where it is necessary to point out the role of other security forces, this Report will do so.

its participation in international security operations, augmented its global military-to-military relationships, and improved its abilities to conduct noncombat operations. A case in point is the on-going deployment —now in its third rotation—of PLA Navy vessels to the Gulf of Aden, off the east coast of Africa, to assist a multinational effort to defend from local pirates international sea lanes upon which China is increasingly reliant for economic growth.

The PLA's new capabilities and reach can both positively and negatively affect US, regional, and international security. The Chinese military can contribute to global stability if it increasingly supports peace keeping and humanitarian operations. This effort could lead to greater cooperation between the US military and the PLA when the interests of their respective nations coincide. However, a more capable PLA could also potentially act as a destabilizing force should Beijing seek to employ it to further its regional or global interests to the detriment of the United States or other regional actors.

This section of the Report addresses some of the factors behind China's decision to have its military undertake a more active role on the global stage, identifies examples of the Chinese military and security forces' increased activity around the globe, and examines possible implications for the United States as a result of this outward expansion.

An Expansion of Chinese Views on National Security

China is now a global player, with global interests. According to China's official news agency, Xinhua, when China was less developed, its national interests were confined to concerns within its borders. However, globalization has caused China's national interests to expand, particularly into the maritime, space, and cybers pace (electromagnetic spectrum) environments.[1] The maritime environment is vital to China because of China's increasing reliance upon seaborne trade; overseas oil imports; and maritime resources, such as hydrocarbons, minerals, and fishing.[2] Expansion into space benefits economic, social, and military development.[3] Similarly, China maintains that cyberspace is critical to its future economic and military development.[4]

As China's national interests have expanded into these new areas, Beijing has realized that its interests are increasingly susceptible to new and emerging threats.[5] Also, as China's overseas economic footprint grows, locals in countries with Chinese investments may perceive the Chinese as neo-imperialists—resulting in greater hostility toward China and its interests. For example, in April 2007, the Ogaden National Liberation Front, Muslim separatists in the Ogaden region of Ethiopia, killed nine and kidnapped several more Chinese workers of the Chinese oil company Sinopec.[6] A few months later, Pakistani fundamentalists in Islamabad kidnapped seven Chinese workers, three of whom were subsequently killed.* In August 2009, angry locals in Algiers, Algeria, attacked Chinese migrant workers, injuring 10 and

* Some observers attribute Pakistan's July 2007 decision to raid an influential mosque in Islamabad that was believed to be responsible for the kidnappings and killings of the Chinese workers to pressure from Beijing. See Howard French, "Letter from China: Mosque Siege Reveals the Chinese Connection," *New York Times*, July 12, 2007. *http://www.nytimes.com/2007/07/ 12/world/asia/12iht-letter.1.6629789. html?_r=1.*

looting five Chinese shops, over resentment toward the migrants' economic success.[7] In that same month, a Uighur independence group, the Turkic Independence Party, called upon Muslims around the globe to attack Chinese interests as retaliation for Beijing's crackdown on Uighur violence in Xinjiang in July.[8]

In addition, as the Commission frequently heard during its May 2009 trip to China, Chinese security analysts are deeply concerned about sea lane security.[9] Beijing's growing reliance on overseas trade and foreign oil imports, both of which predominantly rely upon maritime trade routes, makes the nation susceptible to disruptions in its sea lanes. A reported four-fifths of China's oil imports traverse the Strait of Malacca in Southeast Asia,[10] yet China has at best a minimal ability to patrol and defend this vital maritime life line.[11]

Finally, Beijing understands the importance of actively countering international, nontraditional security threats, such as transnational crime, natural disasters, and global pandemics, which can hinder China's economic development.* China's 2008 defence white paper, for example, points out how overseas, nontraditional security problems could impact China domestically.[12] Susan L. Craig, author of the monograph Chinese Perceptions of Traditional and Non-Traditional Threats, told the Commission that China "perceives nontraditional security threats as more challenging than traditional threats." Said Ms. Craig,

> *China's elite believe the likelihood of traditional military conflict has decreased through deterrence and diplomatic skill. It is nontraditional threats—those that are unpredictable, nonmilitary in nature, transcend national boundaries, and have both internal and external ramifications—that are more worrisome.*[13]

Representatives from the PLA's National Defence University told the Commission in May 2009 that China has a strong desire to increase its capabilities to deal with international, nontraditional security issues.[14]

In December 2004, China's president and Communist Party leader, Hu Jintao, provided the Chinese military with what he characterized as a new set of missions that changed the military's roles and responsibilities to better handle these new threats.[15] These missions, entitled the "Historic Missions of our Military in the New Period of the New Century" (hereafter, the Historic Missions), contain four tasks:

1. *"To provide an important force for guaranteeing the Party'sruling position;*
2. *To provide a strong security guarantee for safeguarding the important strategic opportunity period for national development;*
3. *To provide a powerful strategic support for safeguarding national interests;*
4. *To play a role in upholding world peace and promoting mutual development."*[16]

---

* The PLA has historically played a role in handling nontraditional security threats within China. For example, China's 2008 defence white paper states that "[i]n the past two years the [armed forces] have dispatched a total of 600,000 troops/time; employed 630,000 vehicles (or machines)/time of various types; flown over 6,500 sorties/time (including the use of helicopters); mobilized 1.39 million militiamen and reservists/time; participated in over 130 disaster relief operations in cases of floods, earthquakes, snowstorms, typhoons and fires; and rescued or evacuated a total of 10 million people." Information Office of the State Council, China's National Defence in 2008 (Beijing: January 2009).

Each of these tasks will be addressed in turn below. The first task of the Historic Missions calls on the PLA to ensure its support for the Chinese Communist Party's (CCP) rule in China in the event of a crisis. It is important to note that this task is not new, since CCP "control over the gun" has been a mantra since the Mao Zedong era. Instead, it seeks to reaffirm the policy of having the Chinese armed forces remain loyal to the CCP, and not necessarily to the state, as in western democracies. Therefore, in the event of another Tiananmen-like incident, the CCP fully expects the PLA to come to its aid again as a means of last resort, according to Daniel M. Hartnett, then a China analyst with the non profit research organization CNA.[17] As President Hu stated in his Historic Missions speech, "[s]o long as [the CCP] firmly controls the military, there will be no large disturbances in China, and we will be able to face with confidence any dangers that might arise."[18]

Like the first task, the second task reaffirms traditional PLA responsibilities, this time requiring the PLA to continue its focus on defending China from what Beijing feels are its traditional threats. President Hu identified five specific concerns during his Historic Missions speech: 1) land and maritime border issues, 2) Taiwan separatism, 3) ethnic separatism in Xinjiang and Tibet, 4) terrorism, and 5) domestic social stability.[19]

Unlike the previous two tasks, the third task posits a new requirement for the armed forces, calling on them to protect China's expanding national interests. This task singles out three areas in particular where the PLA and security forces need to focus: the maritime, space, and cyberspace environments. During his Historic Missions speech, President Hu stated that

> *[t]he progress of the period and China's development have caused our national security interests to gradually go beyond the scope of our territorial land, seas, and airspace, and continually expand and stretch into the oceans, space, and [cyberspace]. Maritime, space, and [cyberspace] security have already become important areas of [China's] national security.*[20]

The final task of the Historic Missions requires the Chinese military to play a larger role in international peacekeeping and humanitarian operations. The impetus behind this requirement is China's growing integration with the rest of the world, as reflected in astatement from China's 2008 defence white paper, claiming that "China cannot develop in isolation from the rest of the world, nor can global prosperity and stability do without China." [21] Because of this inter dependency, the PLA should help handle problems abroad before they can adversely affect China's economic development.[22] One crucial way for the PLA to do this is to participate more actively in peacekeeping and humanitarian operations around the world.[23]

The effect of the Historic Missions speech on the PLA has already translated into observable changes in China's military and security activities abroad. As then Deputy Assistant Secretary of Defence for East Asia David S. Sedney stated, the PLA "has embarked on a transformation from a force that focused principally on domestic response and preparing for what it considers local contingencies, into a more expanded set of roles that encompass a wide range of missions and activities."[24]

The next part of this section addresses several of these activities in detail—in particular, peacekeeping, counterpiracy, humanitarian operations, combined exercises, military diplomacy, port calls, and maritime patrols.

Peacekeeping Operations

Since its first personnel contribution in 1990, China has become an increasingly active participant in international peacekeeping operations. China's 2008 defence white paper states that over the past 20 years, China has contributed more than 11,000 individual peacekeepers to 18 United Nations (UN) operations.[25] For the month of June 2009, China had 2,153 peacekeepers deployed to UN missions in Haiti, the Democratic Republic of the Congo, Sudan, Lebanon, Liberia, Timor-Leste, Co^te d'Ivoire, the Western Sahara, and the Middle East.[26] Of note, many of the countries and regions in which China is contributing peacekeepers are also places where China has economic interests.

China's Participation in UN Peacekeeping Operations (June 2009)

UN Mission	Troops		Police		Mil. Observers		Total	
	China	Total	China	Total	China	Total	China	Total
UNTSO—Middle East	0	0	0	0	4	151	4	151
MINURSO—W. Sahara	0	20	0	6	13	201	13	227
MONUC—DR Congo	218	16,921	0	1,078	16	692	234	18,691
UNMIL—Liberia	564	10,065	16	1,205	2	136	582	11,406
UNOCI—Co^te d'Ivoire	0	7,662	0	1,174	7	190	7	9,026
MINUSTAH—Haiti	0	7,030	143	2,050	0	0	143	9,080
UNMIS—Sudan	444	8,479	18	647	12	517	474	9,643
UNIFIL—Lebanon	343	12,030	0	0	0	0	343	12,030
UNMIT—Timor-Leste	0	0	27	1,559	2	33	29	1,592
UNAMID—Darfur	324	13,300	0	2,959	0	176	324	16,435
TOTAL	**1,893**	**75,507**	**204**	**10,678**	**56**	**2,096**	**2,153**	**88,281**

Sources: UN Peacekeeping Operations, "Background Note" (New York: June 30, 2009). *http://www.un.org/Depts/dpko/dpko/bnote.htm;* and The United Nations, "UN Mission's Summary Detailedby Country" (New York: June 30, 2009), pp. 7–8. *http://www.un.org/Depts/dpko/dpko/contributors/2009/june09_3.pdf.*

This heightened level of commitment to peacekeeping operations likely follows from several policy considerations. First, the substantial increases in personnel contributions to UN peacekeeping operations demonstrate that China's military has endeavored to meet the objectives Hu Jintao promulgated in the fourth task of the Historic Missions, namely to play a larger role in international peacekeeping and humanitarian operations.[27] As figure 1 below shows, since 2004, the year when the Historic Missions were first articulated, China has doubled the number of peacekeepers committed to UN missions.

Fig. 1: Chinese Personnel Contributions to UN Peacekeeping Operations, 1990–2008

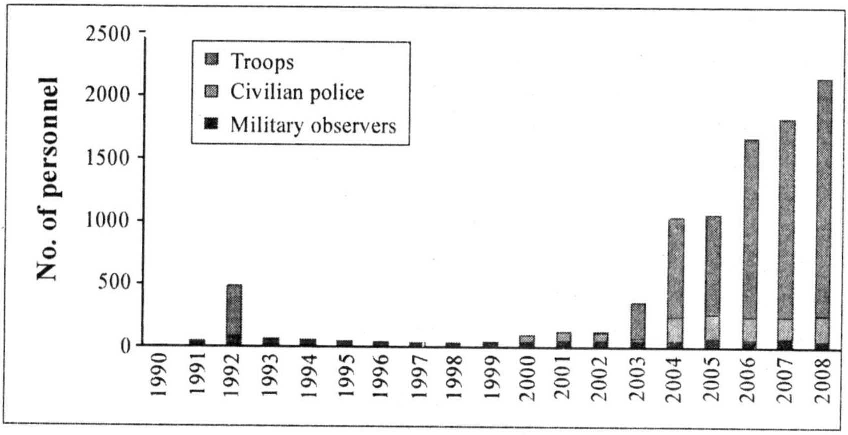

Source: Bates Gill and Chin-hao Huang, "China's Expanding Peacekeeping Role: Its significance and the policy implications," Stockholm International Peace Research Institute (SIPRI), February 2009. *http://books.sipri.org/files/misc/SIPRIPB0902.pdf.*

Second, China's greater involvement in peacekeeping operations is a component of a comprehensive, decades-long effort from Beijing to present China as a responsible international player, thus expanding its international influence. According to Chin-hao Huang, a researcher at the Stockholm International Peace Research Institute, China's leadership believes that "positive engagement with the outside world helps China to project a more benign and 'harmonious' image beyond its borders" and reassures its neighbours that China has peaceful intentions—analysis repeated in the testimony to the Commission by two other expert witnesses.[28]

In recent years, China's military has taken several steps to institutionalize its commitment to peacekeeping operations. China has established at least three facilities to provide specialized training to Chinese troops, police officers, and observers prior to participating in peacekeeping operations.[29] One of these facilities is in Nanjing, Jiangsu Province; another is in Langfang, Hebei Province; and a third, which became fully operational in mid-2009, is in Beijing. This third facility will help the PLA to "centralize and better coordinate Chinese peacekeeping activities" in anticipation of additional UN peacekeeping commitments.[30]

Activities Supporting Counterpiracy Operations in the Gulf of Aden

On December 26, 2008, following the fourth UN Security Council resolution that year concerning Somali pirates operating in the Gulf of Aden, China deployed a naval task group to participate alongside a multinational counterpiracy effort in that region. The decision to dispatch PLA Navy vessels was in response to the repeated hijacking attempts that Chinese vessels faced while transiting past the Horn of Africa. According to official Chinese statements, of the 1,265 Chinese commercial vessels or vessels carrying Chinese goods that traversed the region from January to November 2008,[31] pirates attacked 20 percent of them, successfully capturing seven.[32]

China's task group, currently in its third rotation, is composed of three PLA Navy vessels and crew and about 70 special operations forces. From December 2008 to April 2009, the task group included two guided-missile destroyers (Haikou and Wuhan) and a replenishment ship (Weishanhu). Bernard D. Cole, a professor at the US National War College, called these destroyers "two of China's newest, most capable surface combatants." [33] In April 2009, the destroyers were relieved by another destroyer (Shenzhen) and a frigate (Huangshan), while the replenishment ship remained.[34] All three vessels were replaced in July 2009 with the third deployment, consisting of two frigates (Zhoushan and Xuzhou) and another replenishment ship (Qiandaohu). Although the Chinese task groups are participating in international counterpiracy efforts in the region, they are not official members of the multinational counter piracy coalition, Combined Task Force 151, established on January 8, 2009.[35] The PLA Navy's mission is to escort Chinese ships sailing through the region, as well as non-Chinese ships carrying humanitarian goods, such as items for the UN World Food Programme. This mission differs from the Combined Task Force 151's mission, which is to conduct broad counter piracy operations.[36]

China's dispatch of naval vessels to the region is significant in several ways. Dr. Cole stated that it is the first time that the PLA Navy is

- conducting combat operations outside of China's territorial waters;
- operating "for an extended period of time at great distance from home port" (more than 3,400 miles from Hainan Island);
- relying on "foreign sources... for logistics support for an extended period of time";
- operating "in an environment of international naval forces, other than for a brief naval review"; and
- coordinating with US warships on nonexercise operations.[37]

Although this is a major step for the PLA, it should be understood that the dispatch of three PLA Navy task groups does not automatically mean the PLA Navy is a "blue water" navy capable of operating around the globe. Each deployment is small in size, consisting of only three vessels. In addition, this is currently China's sole naval deployment. As the Pentagon reports, "China's ability to sustain military power at a distance remains limited."[38]

Humanitarian Operations

Historically, the PLA has always participated in humanitarian operations (including disaster relief operations) within China, such as after the 2008 earthquake in Sichuan Province. Abroad, the PLA has contributed to 10 such operations since 2002.[39] International agreements and new military platforms intended for such non combat operations indicate that the PLA will likely participate in more international humanitarian operations in the future.

China has worked to establish channels for international cooperation on humanitarian operations. For example, the Chinese government proposed and drafted the General Guidelines for Disaster Relief Cooperation for the Association of

Southeast Asian Nations'(ASEAN) Regional Forum,* which adopted the protocol at aministerial meeting in 2007.[40] In 2008, China hosted a regional workshop with several Southeast Asian nations on military disaster relief.[41] China's focus on international disaster relief coordination led then Deputy Assistant Secretary of Defence for EastAsia Sedney to state that this sort of cooperation represents much of the recent increase in military engagement between China and Southeast Asia.[42]

China also has developed military platforms to bolster its effectiveness in conducting humanitarian operations. After the 2004 Indian Ocean tsunami, the PLA was unable to participate effectively in relief efforts throughout South east Asia, demonstrating to China's leadership the need to develop improved hospital ship capabilities[43]—especially in light of the goodwill the United States received during that crisis from its deployment of USNS Mercy to the region.[44] As a result, in 2008 the PLA Navy built a new hospitalship, the 10,000-ton Heping Fangzhou.[45] While not China's first hospital ship,[46] it is its most capable and, in addition to its primary role of providing combat support, will allow the PLA Navy to better carry out international humanitarian operations.[47]

Combined Exercises †

In recent years, the Chinese military has placed a greater emphasis on military exercises with foreign countries, or "combined exercises." The Chinese military's first bilateral military exercise occurred with Kyrgyzstan in 2002. "Exercise 01," as it was called, took place on the border between the two nations and reportedly involved hundreds of troops from both sides. It focused on counterterrorism operations and was the first bilateral military exercise between member-states of the Shanghai Cooperation Organization.[48]

Since then, China has participated in at least 33 combined exercises of various kinds. Significantly, more than half of these exercises have occurred outside of Chinese territory.[49] The Chinese military has increased the number of countries with which it has participated in combined exercises. As of the writing of this Report, the Chinese military has conducted combined exercises with atleast 20 different countries.[50] So far this year, China has conducted exercises with Russia (twice), the Shanghai Cooperation Organization, Mongolia, Singapore, and Gabon.[51] The combined exercise with Gabon was the first time that China carried out an exercise with an African nation.[52]

Participating in combined exercises provides the Chinese military with the opportunity to improve its operational capability by learning from other militaries—sometimes even from militaries that have had actual combat experience. For example, several recent Chinese articles on "Peace Mission 2009," a combined

* Current members of the Association of Southeast Asian Nations' Regional Forum include Australia, Bangladesh, Brunei, Cambodia, Canada, China, the European Union, India, Indonesia, Japan, the Democratic People's Republic of Korea, the Republic of Korea, Laos, Malaysia, Myanmar, Mongolia, New Zealand, Pakistan, Papua New Guinea, the Philippines, Russia, Singapore, Sri Lanka, Thailand, Timor-Leste, the United States, and Vietnam.

† Throughout this Report, the Commission will use the term "combined exercise" to signify amilitary exercise between two or more nations.

counter terrorism exercise between China and Russia, discuss lessons the PLA learned from the Russian military. Examples of lessons learned include counter terrorism tactics, urban combat, helicopter operations, combined and joint operations, command and control, special forces operations, and readiness.[53] Even participation in peace keeping operations yields significant operational benefits for the PLA, such as improving its engineering experience, responsiveness, and command and control capabilities.[54]

As with other PLA activities abroad, however, it should be recognized that there are limits to the extent of China's participation in combined exercises. For example, the PLA participated in an average of six combined exercises annually from 2007 to 2009 (to date), a comparable number for the Brazilian and Indian militaries.[55] In contrast, the US Navy's Seventh Fleet alone conducts three times as many combined exercises every year.[56] In addition, the size of the PLA combined exercises generally remains small, averaging about 1,000 personnel in total.* Further more, although the PLA has participated in more combined exercises over the years, these exercises remain very limited in nature. Most combined maritime exercises have been modeled on search and rescue missions, and almost all combined land exercises have been counterterrorism oriented.[57] Recent exceptions include the China-Gabon combined exercise and the 2009 China-Mongolia combined exercise, a humanitarian medical rescue and a peace keeping exercise, respectively.[58] Finally, despite the greater diversity of these exercises, many of them have been conducted with the same countries. For example, more than a third of China's combined exercises have been held with Pakistan (five), India (four), and the Shanghai Cooperation Organization countries (four).[59]

Military Diplomacy

In recent years—and especially since 2002—China's military diplomacy with other countries has become more robust. Demonstrating the importance of military exchanges, the PLA Navy commander wrote in an influential CCP journal that

> *[In order] to build a powerful navy adapted to the needs for carrying out the [Historic Missions], we must stress the expansion of exchanges with foreign militaries, open up our world view, and expand our strategic field of vision. In the new environment of reform and opening up, we must strengthen the navy's foreign affairs functions.*[60]

To this extent, the PLA's foreign activities have "increased in frequency and scope" as China "seeks to enhance its national power by improving foreign relationships, bolstering its international image, and assuaging concerns among other countries about China's rise."[61] China has developed stronger military ties with other nations, particularly throughout the developing world. In the Middle East, Africa, South America, and throughout Asia, China's military relationships are slowly, yet steadily, growing.[62]

---

* An exception to this was the first Peace Mission 2005, held between China and Russia in 2005. According to Chinese sources, about 10,000 troops in total participated in this combined exercise, China's largest to date.

In contrast, the US-China military relationship experienced a setback in October 2008, when Beijing abruptly suspended military contacts after a US notification of impending arms sales to Taiwan. In practice, however, some interaction has occurred. For example, US naval forces conducting counter piracy operations in the Gulf of Aden have coordinated with their Chinese counter parts,[63] while US defence officials met with high level Chinese officials for the Defence Policy Coordination Talks in February 2009.[64] In April, the chief of Naval Operations, Admiral Gary Roughead, traveled to China to observe the fleet review held for the PLA Navy's 60th anniversary, during which he met with the PLA Navy commander, Admiral Wu Shengli.[65] Further military-to-military contact occurred during the 10th US-China Defence Consultative Talks in June. These talks reportedly resulted in an agreement to hold a Military Maritime Consultative Agreement session in late summer or fall of 2009, which, from China's perspective, would mark the full resumption of military-to-military relations with the United States.[66] Since then, Under Secretary of Defence for Policy Michele Flournoy and Admiral Timothy Keating, then commander of the US Pacific Command, met with a PLA Navy rear admiral on the sidelines of the Strategic and Economic Dialogue in July 2009.[67]

With the notable exception of the Shanghai Cooperation Organization, China's military engagement typically takes place on a bilateral basis.[68] Chinese military forces send and receive high-level delegations, defence attaches, and students to study in foreign professional military education exchanges. In these efforts, China focuses on South America [69] and Africa,[70] in particular.

International exchanges are not confined to the PLA. According to China's 2008 defence white paper, China's paramilitary security force responsible for domestic security, the People's Armed Police

> *has sent delegations to over 30 countries for bilateral or multilateral counter terrorism exchanges, including France, Germany, Spain, Italy, Australia, Israel, Brazil, Cuba, South Africa, Russia and Pakistan, and hosted delegations from 17 countries, such as Russia, Romania, France, Italy, Hungary, South Africa, Egypt, Australia and Belarus.*[71]

China has a range of motivations to increase its military's contacts. The US Department of Defence's 2009 Military Power of the People's Republic of China report states that these military exchanges

> *provide China with opportunities to increase military officers' international exposure, communicate China's positions to foreign audiences, better understand alternative world views, and advance foreign relations through inter personal contacts and military assistance programmes.*[72]

Furthermore, familiarity with foreign militaries gives Chinese military personnel a better understanding of alternative forms of operational doctrine.[73]

Though China's military engagement with other nations is increasing, this activity typically does not drive China's overall bilateral relationships. According to then Deputy Assistant Secretary of Defence for East Asia Sedney, all of China's military ties are secondary to its economic relationships and generally are used as a means to further its economic interests.[74]

Port Calls

PLA Navy port calls serve as a visible reminder of China's growing diplomatic and military presence abroad. Over the past few years, both the frequency and range of PLA Navy port calls have increased. For example, the PLA Navy conducted more port calls in 2007 than in the preceding three years combined.[75] Although 2008 saw a decrease in the number of Chinese port calls to foreign countries (likely due to the PLA's focus on hosting the Beijing Olympics and to supporting disaster relief efforts after the Sichuan earthquake), 2009 port calls to date have already reached 2007's level.[76]

The range of PLA Navy port calls has also expanded. According to testimony by Michael R. Auslin, a resident scholar at the American Enterprise Institute, PLA naval vessels "now make port calls throughout the world, not just in Asia," demonstrating the PLA Navy's "ability to undertake extended, transoceanic voyages." [77] In 2007, for example, after visiting St. Petersburg, Russia, for the launch of the "Year of China" public relations event in Russia, two Chinese vessels then made port calls to England, Spain, and France before returning to China.[78] In 2009, PLA Navy vessels supporting counter piracy operations in the Gulf of Aden visited Yemen (Port of Aden), three times and Oman (Port Salalah) once.[79]

Although China's port calls have increased in range and number, they are still limited. First, the overall number of PLA Navy portcalls is small—only 21 in 2007, 2008, and 2009 combined.[80] By comparison, the US Seventh Fleet (Western Pacific and Indian Ocean) on average conducts "more than 250 port visits every year."[81] Second, China's port calls generally involve at most two vessels. For example, of the 21 port calls made in the past three years, only one, the June 2009 visit to Oman, involved three vessels; the rest were either made by one or two vessels.[82] Finally, the PLA Navy does not truly have a global presence, as there appears to be no record of any port calls to either Latin America or Africa since 2002.*

Maritime Patrols

According to testimony submitted to the Commission by Senator Jim Webb, China's maritime forces have demonstrated a "growing assertiveness" in enforcing Beijing's maritime claims. For example, in early March 2009, five Chinese vessels harassed an unarmed US ocean surveillance vessel, USNS Impeccable, while it was conducting operations in international waters about 75 miles south of Hainan Island in the South China Sea.[83] At approximately the same time, another Chinese government vessel used a high-intensity spotlight to illuminate the bridge of the US surveillance ship Victorious in the Yellow Sea, endangering the ship by potentially blinding her operators.[84] In addition, Chinese aircraft conducted

* The last apparent visit to either Latin America or Africa was during China's first-ever circumnavigation of the globe, in 2002, when the PLA Navy visited Brazil, Ecuador, Peru, and Egypt, among other nations. *People's Daily*, "PLA Fleet Starts First Round-the-World Voyage," May 16, 2002. *http://english.people.com.cn/200205/15/eng 20020515_95767.shtml;* Information Office of the State Council, *China's National Defence in 2004* (Beijing: December 2004); Information Office of the State Council, *China's National Defence in 2006* (Beijing: December 2006); and Information Office of the State Council, *China's National Defence in 2008* (Beijing: January 2009).

numerous provocative fly-bys during both incidents.[85] According to former Senator John W. Warner's testimony to the Commission, the various activities of the Chinese vessels were quite dangerous and could have resulted in a collision had the US vessels not reacted quickly.[86]

These incidents displayed a high level of coordination between military and civilian entities involved on the Chinese side, likely demonstrating that they were planned and supported by Beijing. For example, five Chinese vessels from various entities took part in the USNS Impeccable incident: a PLA Navy intelligence collection vessel; a Bureau of Maritime Fisheries patrol vessel; a State Oceanic Administration patrol vessel; and two small, Chinese-flagged fishing vessels.[87] Furthermore, six months earlier, China held a large, high-profile inter agency training event that presaged the Impeccable incident. During the training event, observed by two members of China's supreme military body, the Central Military Commission, more than 30 ships, airplanes, and helicopters participated. These vessels and aircraft belonged to four different organizations: the PLA Navy and naval reserve; the State Oceanic Administration's China Marine Surveillance Force; the Ministry of Commerce's Rescue and Salvage Bureau; and the maritime militia.[88] During this interagency training exercise, one of the training tasks was to "jointly control a maritime area."[89] Therefore, as Senator Webb pointed out, the Impeccable and Victorious incidents should be interpreted "not as singular, tactical events, but as a concerted, calculated effort" of the Chinese government." [90]

Maritime incidents between the United States and China arise in part from Beijing's unique perspective on rights associated with the exclusive economic zone—an area that extends 200 nautical miles from a nation's coastal baseline. The Chinese government asserts a level of control over this area that is in consistent with generally accepted interpretations of the international laws that govern the issue.[91] This divergence of views about what constitutes acceptable behavior in the zone and, crucially, China's sometimes belligerent practices, has led to serious naval standoffs. Aside from freedom of navigation rights, China's exclusive economic zone disputes involve exploitation rights for hydrocarbons and under sea minerals, as well as fishing rights, with several of China's maritime neighbours.

Implications for the United States

As then Deputy Assistant Secretary of Defence for East Asia Sedney told the Commission, the "expansion of [the PLA's] military and security activities abroad poses both challenges and opportunities" for the United States.[92] The Chinese armed forces' increasingly outward orientation could allow the military to contribute more to multinational operations aimed at ensuring global stability, such as peacekeeping operations, humanitarian assistance, disaster relief, and counterpiracy operations—areas where Washington and Beijing's interests align.[93] Deputy Assistant Secretary of State for East Asian and Pacific Affairs John J. Norris Jr. identified additional areas where China's growing military influence could help the United States, such as addressing the North Korean and Iranian nuclear issues.[94] In addition, the US and Chinese militaries could possibly cooperate on counter terrorism efforts.[95]

As the PLA increases its overseas presence, there will be more opportunities for the US military to interact and hold dialogues with the Chinese military on a variety of issues, thus furthering the overall bilateral relationship. Rear Admiral

Eric A. McVadon, US Navy (Ret.), told the Commission that frequent setbacks in the US military-PLA relationship make "it difficult for either side to develop trust and confidence in the other and to play a positive role in influencing the other in mutually desirable ways." [96] However, opportunities to maintain and improve the dialogue would help to build trust and understanding between the two, thus minimizing the potential for in advertent crises.[97] Through increased dialogues and contacts, it also might be possible to "identify additional areas of common under standing and interest." [98]

However, as the PLA acquires experience from its overseas activities, it will further improve its military capacity to conduct avariety of operations, some of which are contrary to US interests. Many military capabilities are fungible and are suited to both peacetime and wartime usage. For example, while pointing out the global benefits that the PLA's increased capabilities could provide, the Department of Defence also stated that "some of these capabilities... could allow China to project power to ensure access to resources or enforce claims to disputed territories."[99] Frederic Vellucci Jr., a China analyst at CNA, testified to the Commission that the same capabilities used to conduct counter piracy operations around the Gulf of Aden could also be used to "interfere with the lawful activities of foreign vessels in China's exclusive economic zones." [100] Supporting this statement, Dr. Cole indicated how China's counter piracy operations in the Gulf of Aden provide the PLA Navy with "increased expertise and experience in operations, logistics, command and control, and interagency cooperation."[101]

Historical Note: Incidents at Sea with Soviet Vessels

China is not the first nation with which the US Navy has had maritime run-ins. In June 2009, former Senator John W. Warner, who served as under secretary of the Navy (1969–1972) and secretary of the Navy (1972–1974), testified to the Commission that the harassment of USNS *Impeccable* is reminiscent of similar incidents between US and Soviet vessels in the late 1960s and early 1970s. According to Senator Warner, both the United States and the Soviet Union realized they needed to "determine a common basis by which [they] could recognize a nation's right over international waters to operate on the surface and in the air, but at the same time to do so in a way that does not bring about physical or property damage to the other."[102] Eventual negotiations between a US delegation, led by Senator Warner, and a Soviet delegation resulted in the Agreement between the Government of the United States of America and the Government of the Union of Soviet Socialist Republics on the prevention of incidents on and over the High Seas, in 1972.[103]

At its core, this agreement is a rules-based approach to safety on the high seas. According to one expert on this accord, the agreement "served to moderate the behaviour of the naval surface and air forces of the two sides through the end of the Cold War," despite other problems in the relationship.[104] In his testimony, Senator Warner stated that

> *[the agreement] almost totally was successful in avoiding any incidents of a magnitude of seriousness that could have been a*

tripwire to starting a more serious confrontation between the Soviet Union and the United States.[105]

Currently the United States has a mechanism for discussing maritime issues with China, the Military Maritime Consultative Agreement. Unlike the high seas agreement, however, the Military Maritime Consultative Agreement did not contain an "agreement on communication during crises or rules of engagement."[106] As Senator Warner described to the Commission, the Military Maritime Consultative Agreement lacks the strength necessary to avoid incidents at sea that the high seas agreement contained.[107] A more robust agreement, or a reinforced Military Maritime Consultative Agreement, particularly one which—like the high seas agreement—included "formal rules of interaction," could "reduce both the likelihood of inadvertent clashes, as well as promote understanding and reduce the long-term likelihood of conflict" on the sea.[108]

Finally, a more active PLA will likely increase China's security influence around the globe. China's recent global security activities strengthen China's diplomatic relationships, enhance its global image and influence, and promote its economic development.[109] Some of China's increased influence could come at the expense of the United States. For example, when Uzbekistan demanded in July 2005 that the United States close its Karshi-Khanabad airbase—a crucial supply base for US operations in Afghanistan—General Richard Myers, then chairman of the Joint Chiefs of Staff, stated that the demand was partially due to China's influence.[110] Similarly, China's increased participation in peace keeping operations could adversely impact the United States by "gradually counter balanc[ing] US influence and more actively shap[ing]—in ways consistent with Chinese foreign policy principles and national interests—the norms guiding UN peace keeping operations."[111] In addition, Deputy Assistant Secretary of State for East Asian and Pacific Affairs Norris told the Commission that China's continued military support for states that pursue policies contrary to global norms, such as Burma, Sudan, and Zimbabwe, is also troubling.[112]

Conclusion

- Beijing has begun to broaden its national security concerns beyond a potential contingency across the Taiwan Strait and around its immediate periphery.
- Chinese leaders place a growing emphasis on militarilysafe guarding China's expanding national interests. Hu Jintao codified this trend in 2004 when he declared a new set of guiding principles for the armed forces called the Historic Missions.
- China's leadership has a growing appreciation for the seriousness of overseas, nontraditional threats that could adversely affect China's economic and other interests, as evidenced by the military's increasing allocation of resources toward missions such as peacekeeping, counter piracy, and disaster relief.
- These geographical and functional changes in China's military missions correlate with an increase in China's military, security, and economic activities abroad.
- China's expanded claim over freedom of navigation in what it considers to be its exclusive economic zone could lead to further incidents involving the US military.

- At the same time, however, the expansion of China's military and security activities abroad are more evolutionary than revolutionary in nature. Although the PLA is operating more frequently abroad, it should not yet be considered a global military or a military with a global reach.
- PLA activities abroad will improve the PLA's military capabilities—such as command, control, communications, and logistics—in ways that will contribute to PLA competence in a broad range of operations.
- The Chinese military's more international orientation is not a fundamentally negative development. A more activist PLA could in some circumstances provide a "public good" by contributing more to global stability. Other nations, including the United States, may benefit from Chinese peacekeeping operations and counter piracy efforts.
- The Chinese military's more international orientation—combined with its improved military capacity—could, however, adversely affect US national security. Of particular import will be whether a militarily confident China will take a more confrontational stance toward the United States or its allies.

SECTION 2

China's Naval Modernization

> "... the United States-China Economic and Security Review Commission ... shall investigate and report exclusively on—
>
> "Regional Economic and Security Impacts—The Triangular economic and security relationship among the United States, Taipei and the People's Republic of China (including the military modernization and force deployments of the People's Republic of China aimed at Taipei), the national budget of the People's Republic of China, and the fiscal strength of the People's Republic of China in relation to internal instability in the People's Republic of China and the likelihood of the externalization of problems arising from such internal instability. ..."

Introduction

On April 30, 2009, the Chinese military conducted a large fleet review in the port city of Qingdao, China, commemorating the 60th anniversary of the People's Liberation Army Navy, or PLA Navy. On display were many of the navy's newest vessels and aircraft, including its little-seen nuclear-powered ballistic missile submarines. In total, the review included 25 Chinese vessels, as well as 21 foreign navy vessels that Beijing invited.* For China, the Qingdao fleet review was an opportunity to demonstrate to domestic and international audiences the tremendous progress the PLA Navy has made in modernizing its forces over the years.

Since the mid-1990s, China has embarked on its largest naval modernization since the People's Republic of China (PRC) was founded in 1949. In recent years, China has quantitatively and qualitatively improved its modern naval platforms, purchasing or indigenously producing 38 submarines, 13 destroyers, 16 frigates, at least 40 fast-attack craft, and dozens of naval aircraft. In addition to these more modern platforms, the PLA Navy has also developed advanced offensive and defensive weapons, such as antiship cruise missiles, land-attack cruise missiles, and sea mines. Advances in the navy's command and control systems permit the new platforms and weapons to exchange data and to coordinate with each other. In order to better use these new weapons, platforms, and equipment, the navy has also carried out a series of organizational, personnel, training, and logistics reforms. With the introduction of these various reforms and modernization programmess, the Chinese navy also appears to have adjusted its methods of conducting operations to better match its new capabilities.

* On the Chinese side, only domestically produced vessels participated in the fleet review; Chinese vessels procured from foreign suppliers, such as the *Kilo*-class submarines bought from Russia, did not participate.

Figure 1: Comparison of Modern* and Legacy PLA Navy Combatants (2000 vs. 2009)

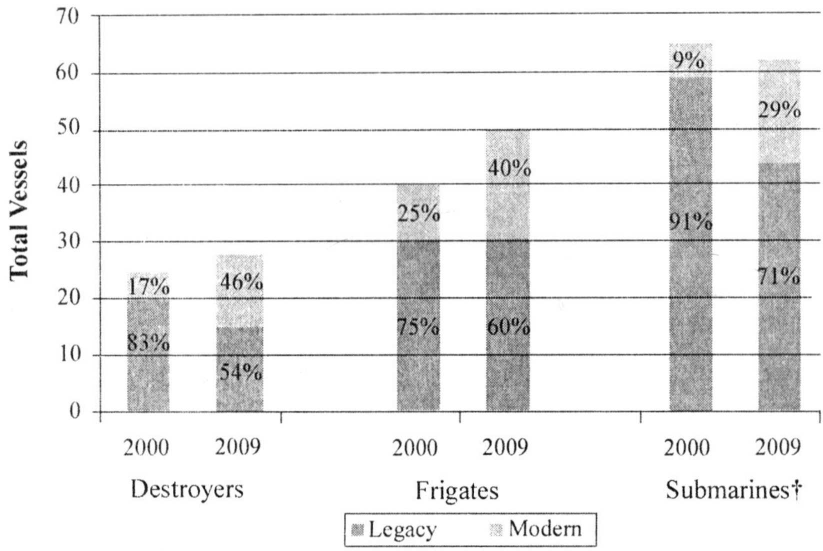

Sources: International Institute for Strategic Studies, *The Military Balance 2000–2001* (Oxford: Oxford University Press, 2000), p. 195; and International Institute for Strategic Studies, *The Military Balance 2009* (London: Routledge, 2009), p. 383–84.

The Chinese government presents several reasons for its large-scale naval modernization. First, China seeks to prevent Taiwan from declaring independence. This includes deterring, denying, or delaying any nation from coming to Taiwan's aid in the event of a crisis with the mainland. Second, in order to safeguard China's continued economic development, the PLA Navy needs to be able to defend China's coast from any maritime assaults. A third reason, also tied to China's economy, is that the navy must be able to defend China's disputed maritime territorial claims. Fourth, the navy is increasingly being called upon to protect international sea lanes used by China's merchant fleet, a task that, until recently, the navy was incapable of performing. Fifth, part of China's naval modernization is to improve China's nuclear deterrent capabilities by creating a credible, at-sea nuclear deterrent force. A final factor is nationalistic pride and the desire for China to have a modern navy that befits a global power.

---

* This Report categorizes the following Chinese classes as modern vessels. Destroyers: *Luhai, Luhu, Luyang (I & II), Luzhou, and Sovremenny;* frigates: *Jiangkai* (I&II), and *Jiangwei (I & II);* and submarines: *Jin, Kilo. Shang, Song,* and Yuan.

† This graph aggregates both ballistic missile submarines and attack submarines for purposes of determining final numbers.

The importance of China's Naval Modernization to Beijing

Demonstrating the importance that Beijing attaches to modernizing its navy, Vice Admiral Su Shiliang, chief of staff of the PLA Navy, wrote in June 2009 that

> *[p]resently, while [China's] national economic development still faces many difficulties, the Party Central Committee and the Central Military Commission regard the navy as a priority service for force building, and continually increase naval investments. This fully reflects the importance and aspirations they have for the navy, and raises new, even higher requirements for us to scientifically plan naval military work.*[113]

China's naval modernization impacts US interests in the region. A more powerful and capable PLA Navy will increasingly have the ability to inhibit US military access to the region. Dubbed an "antiaccess strategy" by western observers, this strategy rests on the ability to exert control over China's coastal seas in order to deny an opponent the ability to operate safely in those areas in the event of a conflict. As the PLA Navy improves its reach, surveillance, and antiaccess capabilities, the area over which it can exert control will likely expand outward. And as Chinese naval capabilities improve, other actors, including US friends and allies, may feel threatened. This in turn could provoke a naval arms race— signs of which are already beginning to appear.

This section of the Annual Report identifies some of the factors behind China's naval modernization, describes examples of how Beijing is modernizing the PLA Navy, and examines the possible implications for the United States.

Reasons for China's Naval Modernization

This section will discuss six reasons for China's naval modernization that are most commonly referred to in Chinese statements and documents: 1) deter Taiwan's independence; 2) defend China's maritime security; 3) defend China's maritime sovereignty and maritime economic interests; 4) ensure China's access to increasingly important sea lanes; 5) develop China's at-sea nuclear deterrent capabilities; and 6) satisfy a national desire for a modern navy. Each reason will be discussed in turn.

Deter Taiwan's Independence

Since the mid 1990s, the central focus of China's naval modernization efforts has been to deter Taiwanese independence.[114] For China, deterring Taiwan's independence has political, military, and economic significance. Taiwan independence ultimately challenges the Chinese Communist Party's (CCP) continued rule in Beijing,because the CCP has partially staked its legitimacy on reunification with Taiwan.[115] In addition, Taiwan's continued defacto independence hinders "China's emergence as a regional power since it would limit the [People's Liberation Army's] strategic space."[116] Describing the economic costs of formally losing

Taiwan, the PLA Academy of Military Science—China's premier military think tank—wrote that

> *Taiwan is the strategic key for mainland China's passage to the ocean, and is extremely critical to the development of our maritime economy and ensuring our maritime safety. If Taiwan successfully separates, then China's gateway to the Pacific Ocean will close.*[117]

For Beijing, a key component of ensuring that Taiwan does not declare independence requires deterring, denying, or delaying the United States from intervening on Taiwan's behalf. Rear Admiral Michael McDevitt (US Navy, Ret.), vice president of the not-for-profit research corporation CNA and director of its Strategic Studies division, testified to the Commission that China aims to keep "an approaching force from closing to within striking range of the Chinese mainland and the Taiwan Strait"—a sentiment echoed by several experts who testified to the Commission on this topic.[118] Cortez A. Cooper, a senior international policy analyst at the RAND Corporation, stated that a goal of China's naval modernizationis to "vastly improv[e] the capability to hold US naval formations at risk in the Western Pacific, and to delay or deny their entry into a Taiwan theater of operations."[119] Paul S. Giarra, president of the defence analysis company Global Strategies and Transformation, directly attributed China's attempts to develop an antiship ballistic missile (discussed further below) to the need to prevent US naval surface vessels—"the centerpiece of American naval power and the basis for US deterrence strategy"— from nearing China's coastline.[120]

Although cross-Strait relations have improved since the election of Ma Ying-jeou to Taiwan's presidency in March 2008, Beijing still watches Taiwan warily (see chap. 3, sec. 2, for more on cross-Strait relations). For example, in May 2008, then Lieutenant General MaXiaotian, deputy chief of the PLA general staff, stated that while the cross-Strait relationship had taken a positive turn, pro-Taiwan independence advocates on the island remain a problem.[121] More recently, this wariness was repeated in China's authoritative 2008 defence white paper, which stated that "separatist forces working for 'Taiwan independence' pose threats to China's unity and security."[122]

Defend China's Maritime Security

A core task of any navy is to prevent and resist maritime assaults and, as China's defence white papers over the years demonstrate, the PLA Navy is no exception.[123] During Chinese President Hu Jintao's *Historic Missions* speech (see sec. 1 of this chapter for more on the *Historic Missions*), he stated that the military should "firmly resist foreign invasions."[124] Demonstrating the navy's role in this task, the PLA Academy of Military Science wrote that the navy should "independently or along with ground or air force operations, effectively resist enemy assaults coming from the seas."[125] In 2008, President Hu again pointed out the importance of maritime security, stating, "currently, the main threats to our national security. . .come from the sea."[126] Writing earlier this year, the PLA Navy chief of staff stated that although a major maritime invasion was unlikely, the navy still needs to improve its capabilities to defend China's maritime security because of possible regional crises.[127]

A key reason for the focus on protecting China's maritime approach is the need to shield the heart of China's economy—its eastern sea board.[128] According to China's official 2008 statistical yearbook, the gross domestic product (GDP) of the eastern coastal provinces made up at least 65 percent of China's total GDP in 2007.[129] Furthermore, 18 of the top 20 Chinese cities with the highest GDP per capita are all located in coastal provinces.[130] Any military conflict involving China's coastal areas would likely severely hurt China's continued economic development. For this reason, Rear Admiral Yao Wenhuai, deputy director of the navy's Political Department, wrote in 2007 that "China's economic center of gravity is increasingly concentrated in the coastal areas. If these areas are not secure, then there can be no talk of China's economic security."[131]

Defend China's Maritime Sovereignty and Maritime Economic Interests

The PLA's naval modernization also aims to support and defend China's disputed maritime territorial claims and their associated maritime economic interests. Besides Taiwan, China is currently involved in several maritime territorial disputes. As President Hu stated in 2004,

> *[m]ore than half of the three million square kilometers of maritime surface area over which China has sovereignty and jurisdiction is involved in territorial water or maritime rights and interest disputes with neighbouring states.*[132]

The most important maritime territorial disputes are with Japan and Taiwan over the Senkaku (Diaoyu) Islands in the East China Sea; with Vietnam and Taiwan over the Paracel (Xisha) Islands in the South China Sea; and with Brunei, Malaysia, the Philippines, Taiwan, and Vietnam over the Spratly (Nansha) Islands also in the South China Sea. While some of these disputed islands are little more than rock out croppings with limited intrinsic value, the presence of nearby natural resources, such as oil, natural gas, minerals, and fisheries; significantly increases their strategic value.[133]

The leadership in Beijing increasingly feels that maritime resources are an important fuel for China's continued economic growth. For example, during his *Historic Missions* speech in 2004, President Hu stated that China's economic progress had caused China's interests to expand out into the ocean.[134] Four years later, he again pointed out that "China has enormous strategic maritime interests."[135] In February 2009, Vice Premier Li Keqiang starkly emphasized the importance of the maritime environment to China's future, stating that

> *[e]very day the oceans are becoming an increasingly important area and resource treasure trove for mankind's economy and society, and competition among nations to develop their maritime interests is intensifying. Looking into the future, whoever doesn't value the oceans will lose their room for development. Therefore, maritime enterprises concern the overall situation of China's economic and social development, and concern the fundamental interests of the Chinese people.*[136]

Because of the importance of maritime economic resources for China, its leaders believe its maritime interests need to be defended. When President Hu stated in 2004 that China's interests had expanded into the oceans, he also called upon the military to defend these newly expanded interests.[137] He repeated this statement in

2008, when he called on China "to strongly emphasize defending[its] maritime rights and interests." [138] According to China's 2008 defence white paper, defending these maritime interestsis a key responsibility of the PLA Navy.[139] As Frederic Vellucci Jr, a China analyst with the research institute CNA, testified to the Commission, the naval forces and capabilities that China is currently developing to counter a Taiwan crisis could just as easily beused to enforce China's various territorial claims.[140]

Protect China's Access to International Energy and Trade Sea Lanes

As emphasized by Chinese security analysts during the Commission's May 2009 trip to China, Beijing is deeply concerned about China's access to international sea lanes.[141] China's economy is increasingly dependent upon energy imports and overseas trade, both of which predominantly rely upon maritime routes. Lu Zhongwei, then president of the influential Chinese think tank China Institutes of Contemporary International Relations (CICIR), wrote in the foreword to a 2005 book dedicated entirely to sea lane security that

> *[a] long with persistent and rapid increase of China's GDPand the development of the 'Go Out' strategy, China's dependency on overseas natural resources, energy, and commodity markets will continue to grow. ...Sea lanes will increasingly become the main artery of [China's] economy.*[142]

Beijing appears to be particularly concerned about China's energy imports. As President Hu Jintao stated in 2005 at a Central Political Department conference, "Energy resources are a major strategic issue concerning China's overall economic and social development."[143] This was not President Hu's first mention of energy security: In late December 2003, he told attendees at an Economic Work Conference of the CCP Central Committee that although more than 80 percent of China's oil imports traversed the Malacca Strait, China was incapable of responding should a foreign power decide to sever this sea lane—a situation he reportedly referred to as the "Malacca Dilemma."[144] In 2007, the deputy director of the navy's Political Department, Yao Wenhaui, echoed these sentiments, writing that

> *(e)nsuring the security of strategic sea lanes is extremely important, especially key imported strategic materials, such as petroleum, which are highly dependent upon sea lanes for transportation.*[145]

The Chinese security community is also aware of the constraints placed on both Japan and the United Kingdom during the Second World War due to blockades of their respective sea borne energy supplies.[146]

Some western analysts believe that during a time of conflict China would likely be incapable of successfully defending those sealanes upon which it relies. Mr. Giarra testified to the Commission that "China has very limited ability to respond to large-scale threats to Chinese shipping in the Strait of Malacca and distant reaches of the South China Sea." [147] Gabriel B. Collins, a research fellow at the US Naval War College's China Maritime Studies Institute and William S. Murray, a professor at the same institute, list the PLA Navy's lack of access to regional ports for supplies and repair, lack of at-sea replenishment vessels, and lack of long-distance training as hindrances to its ability to defend those sealanes that China is reliant upon.[148]

Not all western analysts believe that sealane security is a valid worry for China's leadership. According to the research of Mr. Collinsand Mr. Murray, it is unlikely that any military—including the US military—would or could impose an energy blockade on China. They believe that any attempted blockade would likely fail and possibly result in negative global economic and political ramifications.[149] However, regardless of the chance of a successful blockade, Beijing's "perceived dependence and vulnerability ... are bound to have real psychological effects on strategic planning." [150] The ongoing PLA Navy counterpiracy escort mission off the Horn of Africa demonstrates that Beijing and its navy are serious about being capable of defending their international sea lanes (for moreon China's counter piracy mission, see sec. 1 of this chapter).

Develop China's Sea-based Nuclear Deterrence Capability

A less-discussed but still key reason for China's naval modernization is Beijing's desire to have an operational, submarine-based, nuclear deterrent force. According to Mr. Cooper, the goal is to "improve the deterrent impact of Beijing's nuclear counter strike strategy."[151] China has clearly articulated this goal in each of its biennially published defence white papers released since 2004. Each paper states that the PLA Navy is attempting to enhance its nuclear deterrent capability.[152] The first defence white paper to mention this, in 2004, was also the year that China launched the first of its new, nuclear-powered ballistic missile submarines (discussed in further detail below).

Properly Represent China on the International Stage

A final reason for China's naval modernization is the desire within China for a modern navy. As Rear Admiral McDevitt told the Commission, Beijing wants to "field a military establishment worthy of a great power." Similarly, Peter A. Dutton, an associate professor at the US Naval War College, testified that there is a sense of pride and nationalism within China regarding its naval modernization. Mr. Dutton specifically referred to the PLA Navy's likely aircraft carrier programmes as partially driven by China's growing naval pride.[153] National pride or prestige also is a potential reason for China's desire to develop an at-sea nuclear deterrent force.[154] An example of China's naval pride was evident in the PLA Navy commander's May 2009 speech describing the success of the navy's first task group dispatched to conduct counter piracy escort missions off the Horn of Africa. In this speech, Admiral Wu Sheng listated that

> *(t)his (escort mission) fully demonstrated the fine behavior of our country as a responsible large country, demonstrated the fine image of our armed forces as a mighty and civilized force for peace; demonstrated the perfect military and political quality of the People's Navy, the brilliant achievements of its development and building, and its firm determination to safeguard our national development interests; and demonstrated the navy's brand-new achievements in its Military Combat Preparations and Army Building in recenty ears.*[155]

The Three Pillars of China's Naval Modernization

In order to fulfill the above requirements, Beijing has been seeking to develop and reform all facets of the PLA Navy in order to make it into a modern, capable force. This modernization process can best be understood using the "Three Pillars" method. According to David M. Finkelstein, vice president of CNA and director of its China Studies division, China's military modernization rests upon three crucial aspects, which he terms the "Three Pillars:"

- Material modernization, including the development and procurement of new weapons, equipment, platforms, and systems;
- Institutional modernization, including systemic changes, suchas organizational, personnel, and training reforms (among other things);
- Doctrinal modernization, including the development of new operational concepts and combat techniques.[156]

This Report will use this paradigm to assess China's various naval modernization efforts.

The Material Pillar

China has substantially modernized its naval fleet and related equipment through a combination of indigenous production and foreign procurement. Since 2001, the PLA Navy has acquired diversetypes of capable surface vessels, submarines, and naval aircraft.*All indications are that China is developing an aircraft carrier programme. In preparation for supporting these new platforms, China has also acquired or developed new offensive and defensive weapons systems, such as antiship, land-attack, and supersonic cruise missiles; sea mines; and advanced torpedoes. The Chinese navy has also procured several significant naval-related systems, including command, control, communications, computers, intelligence, surveillance, and reconnaissance (C4ISR) assets as well as early warning systems. In addition, China is also developing a nascent antiship ballistic missile programme, which, although ostensibly controlled by the PLA's Second Artillery (Strategic Rocket) forces, could have significant naval implications if successfully developed. China's large-scale naval modernization shows no signs of ebbing, either, as the PLA Navy commander recently laid out ambitious goals concerning the navy's development over the next 10 years:

> *We are going to strengthen the development of key weapons and equipment, develop large surface combat vessels, newtypes of submarines with good under water endurance and stealthy characteristics, combat aircraft that cruise at supersonic speeds, powerful long-range missiles with precision penetration capabilities, very deep and high-speedsmart torpedoes, electronic warfare equipment with good general-purpose and compatibility features, and other such new generation weapons and*

* The year 2001 was selected as the starting point for Chinese naval modernization, since this is when China's 10th Five-Year Plan (2001–2005) began. For China, Five-Year Plans represent plans where the CCP maps strategies for national development in various areas, including military development. Selecting this year also allows the reader to better understand the breadth of China's naval modernization, since these efforts take years to reach fruition.

equipment, enabling the quality and performance of the new generation of weapons and equipment to ascend to new heights.[157]

Submarines: According to Rear Admiral Mc Devitt, China's submarine forces are a "pocket of excellence" within the PLA Navy.[158] Chinese submarine development is of two types: attack and nuclear-powered ballistic missile. Attack submarines account for the bulk of new submarines in China's fleet. Mr. Cooper testified that China primarily relies upon its growing attack submarine fleet"[f] or sea denial and control operations in and just beyond [China's] littoral waters." [159] As the table below shows, China has acquired at least 22 modern attack submarines since 2001.* Eight of these are diesel Kilo-class attack submarines purchased from Russia. Two other submarines, both Shang-class, are nuclear powered, which allows for longer patrol ranges and much higher speeds.[160] In addition, China has developed the Yuan and Song-class, two comparatively quiet diesel submarines. China's attack submarines are variously armed with antiship, land-attack, and supersonic cruise missiles; wake-homing torpedoes, and sea mines.[161] Besides the obvious danger that the greater number of Chinese submarines poses to opposing navies, their improved quality increases the difficulty for an opposing force to detect and track them.[162]

New PLA Navy Submarines since 2001	
Attack Submarines	
Shang (nuclear powered)	2
Kilo (diesel, Russian-made)	8
Yuan (diesel)	2
Song (diesel)	10
Ballistic Missile Capable Submarines	
Jin (nuclear powered)	2

Source: Ronald O'Rourke, "China's Naval Modernization: Implications for US Navy Capabilities—Background Issues for Congress" (Washington, D.C.: Congressional Research Service, July 17, 2009), p.7.

The second type of submarine that the PLA Navy has developed since 2001 is a nuclear-powered ballistic missile submarine, the *Jin*-class. Currently, China has built two such submarines, both of which have yet to be commissioned.* The US Department of Defence estimates that the PLA Navy will eventually produce up to five such submarines, which, when fully deployed, will give Beijing its first "credible sea-based nuclear strike capability."[163] As discussed more fully below, the submarine-launched ballistic missile intended for the *Jin*-class submarine has yet to be successfully tested.

* In addition to these 24, the PLA Navy also acquired one *Song*-class submarine and two older *Ming*-class submarines. However, all three were likely planned and developed prior to the tenth Five-Year Plan, since they were officially launched in 2001 or 2002. Therefore, they are not counted for the purposes of this Report.

* China also has an older ballistic missile submarine, the *Xia*-class. However, this submarine, of which only one was ever built, has reportedly never completed an actual deterrent patrol due to technical problems. See Andrew Erickson and Michael Chase, "China's SSBN Forces: Transitioning to the Next Generation," *China Brief* 9, no.12 (June 12, 2009): 10.

Surface combatants: After submarines, large surface combatants, such as destroyers and frigates, are the second key component of the PLA Navy's antiaccess strategy.[164] As the table below demonstrates, since 2001 the navy has acquired eight new destroyers spread over four classes: three classes are indigenously produced, and one—the *Sovremenny*-class—was purchased from Russia. The Chinese-made destroyers are "substantially more modern in terms of their hull designs, propulsion systems, sensors, weapons, and electronics" than previous domestically produced destroyers.[165] These vessels were designed to greatly improve previous PLA Navy weaknesses in air defence and are armed with highly capable, antiship cruise missiles.[166]

New PLA Navy Surface Combatants since 2001	
Destroyers	
Luyang I	2
Luyang II	2
Luzhou	2
Sovremenny II (Russian-built)	2
Frigates	
Jiangwei II	5
Jiangkai I	2
Jiangkai II	4
Fast-attack Craft	
Houbei	40+

Sources: Ronald O'Rourke, "China's Naval Modernization: Implications for US Navy Capabilities—Background Issues for Congress" (Washington, D.C.: Congressional Research Service, July 17, 2009), pp. 11–13.

Since 2001, the PLA Navy has also approved production of three new frigate classes (including one variant), building 11 frigates so far. These new frigates have improved air defences, while the most recent two classes, the Jiangkai I and II class, also employ stealth design technology.[167] The Jiangkai II-class frigate likely will be built in sufficient numbers to become a key vessel of the navy.[168]

In addition to producing large surface combatants, China has also emphasized production of small, fast-attack craft. In 2004, China introduced a new type of fast-attack craft, the Houbei-class and has since built at least 40. These fast-attack craft have a stealthy, catamaran hull design and are armed with highly capable antiship cruise missiles.[169] According to Mr. Cooper's testimony to the Commission,

> *(T)he Houbei-class fast attack craft is an excellent example of an asset that supports a range of missions: it is a highly capable littoral warfare platform with missiles that can support combat operations in a Taiwan theater or a South China Sea conflict, as well as antiaccess or area denial operations against US or allied forces.*[170]

Amphibious ships: As the table below shows, the PLA Navy has built a large number of amphibious ships and landing craft since 2001. The largest, a Yuzhao-class amphibious ship, is the first of a possible six ships of this class. In addition to being employed in a cross-Strait scenario, these vessels could also be used to conduct amphibious landings, humanitarian or disaster relief activities, evacuation operations, and maritime security operations far from China's shores.[171] Finally, in August 2009, the Russian press reported that Ukraine has agreed to sell China four Zubr-class heavy assault hovercraft, providing China with additional amphibious capacity. Two of the four vessels are to be built in China, possibly providing the technological know-how for a much larger fleet in the future.[172]

New PLA Navy Amphibious Ships since 2001	
Amphibious Ships	
Yuzhao	1
Yuting II	10
Yunshu	10
Yubei	10

Sources: Ronald O'Rourke, "China's Naval Modernization: Implications for US Navy Capabilities—Background Issues for Congress" (Washington, D.C.: Congressional Research Service, July 17, 2009), p. 13; US-China Economic and Security Review Commission, Hearing on the Implications of China's Naval Modernization for the United States, written testimony of Richard D. Fischer Jr., June 11, 2009; and Stephen Saunders, ed., Jane's Fighting Ships 2008–2009 (Alexandria, VA: Jane's Information Group, 2008).

Mine warfare ships: In recent years, the PLA Navy has also increased its mine warfare capabilities by building several new mine warfare ships.* These new vessels are paralleled by an active mine warfare research programme in China. Recently, three professors from the China Maritime Studies Institute, US Naval War College, concluded their research on Chinese mine warfare by stating that

> *[I]t now seems that China is engaged in a significant effort to upgrade its mine warfare prowess . . . Relying heavily on sea mines, the [PLA Navy] is already fully capable of blockading Taiwan and other crucial [sea lanes] in the Western Pacific.*[173]

New PLA Navy Mine Warfare Ships since 2001	
Mine Warfare Ships	
Wozang	1
Wochi	5

Source: Stephen Saunders, ed., *Jane's Fighting Ships 2008–2009* (Alexandria, VA: Jane's Information Group, 2008), pp. 147–48.

Auxiliaries

In 2002 and 2003, the PLA Navy built two Fuchi class modern underway replenishment ships, improving its at-sea replenishment capabilities. These ships accompanied Chinese combatants on port calls to Europe and Asia and supported China's anti-piracy escort operations in the Gulf of Aden. A smaller supply ship, the Danyao-class, was completed in 2006 and is likely intended for supplying Chinese outposts

* In addition to these specific mine-laying vessels, the Chinese military can use "surface warships, submarines, aircraft, and civilian merchant and fishing vessels" to deliver its vast arsenal of sea mines. Andrew S. Rickson, Lyle J. Goldstein, and William S. Murray, "Chinese Mine Warfare: A PLA Navy 'Assassin's Mace' Capability," *China Maritime Studies* 3 (June 2009): 25.

in the South China Sea.[174] Further increases to China's logistics support fleet can be expected, as the PLA Navy commander's statement of April 2009 suggests:

> *[Over the next 10 years] we will...further improve our mobile support capabilities at sea, and strengthen the transport and supply forces at sea, with the priority being on large auxiliary vessels.*[175]

New PLA Navy Auxiliaries since 2001	
Replenishment Ships	
Fuchi	2
Danyao	1
Hospital Ships	
Anwei	1

Source: Stephen Saunders, ed., Jane's Fighting Ships 2008–2009 Alexandria, VA: Jane's Information Group, 2008), pp.152–55.

At the end of 2008, China launched a new hospital ship. According to the US Department of Defence, this vessel will provide the PLA Navy with improved at-sea medical response capabilities. In addition, it may also improve China's ability to support humanitarian and disaster relief efforts throughout the region.[176]

Aircraft carriers

Although the PLA Navy currently does not have an operational aircraft carrier, recent Chinese public statements regarding the navy's desire to build one suggest that China is moving toward building an aircraft carrier in the near future.[177] In March 2009, for example, Chinese Defence Minister General Liang Guanglie stated during a meeting with Japan's Minister of Defence that China cannot remain "without an aircraft carrier indefinitely."[178] That same month, in a National People's Congress session, Vice Admiral Xu Hongmeng, commander of China's East Sea Fleet, stated that China would have its own aircraft carrier "very soon."[179] In April 2009, the PLA Navy commander also said that China is going to "develop large surface combat vessels" in the near future, a possible oblique reference to future Chinese aircraft carriers.[180]

Most western observers of the PLA Navy anticipate that China's potential carrier fleet will be small in number. In March 2009, the Commission received testimony from Michael R. Auslin, a resident scholar in foreign and defence policy studies at the American Enterprise Institute, that China was likely looking to build a three-carrier navy for the near future.[181] Richard D. Fisher Jr., a senior fellow for Asian Military Affairs at the International Assessment and Strategy Center, presented a higher number, possibly four to five carriers by 2020.[182] Similarly, Mr. Cooper testified that China is unlikely to transition to a full, carrier-based navy in the near term due to the prohibitive costs. More likely, he said, China will seek to create a "hybrid" navy composed of a limited number of carriers "designed to provide force projection for regional contingencies or a show of presence in distant sea lanes."[183]

Naval aviation

Unlike other areas of naval modernization, PLA naval aviation forces have received but a slight increase in resources since 2001, making them the navy's "least capable warfare community."[184] In 2004, the PLA Navy received 24 Su-30 Mkk2, a capable Russian-made fighter bomber. Although additional orders were anticipated, as of yet they have failed to materialize.[185] Some reports indicate that the Chinese military may instead purchase the Russian SU–33 carrier-based fighters to be used on a future aircraft carrier.[186] However, to date there has been no public announcement of a contract between Beijing and Moscow to purchase these aircraft. In addition to foreign procurement, China indigenously produced 18 JH–7A fighter bombers for its navy in 2004.[187] While both the Su-30 Mkk2 and the JH–7A are the most modern of China's naval fighters, their overall numbers are still small (13 percent) compared to the total number of PLA Navy fighters (322).[188] According to Mr. Fisher, the navy may also have recently acquired an unknown number of H–6M bombers, a newer version of China's indigenous bomber based on an older Soviet design.[189] The PLA Navy has also begun to reinforce its early warning capabilities by developing upgraded variants of Chinese airborne early warning systems, such as the KJ–2000 early warning and control aircraft.[190]

New PLA Naval Aircraft Since 2001	
Aircraft	
Su-30 MKK2 fighter bomber	24
JH–7A fighter bomber	18
H–6M bomber unknown	
KJ–2000 airborne early warning and control aircraft	2

Sources: US-China Economic and Security Review Commission, *Hearing on the Implications of China's Naval Modernization for the United States, testimony* of Richard D. Fischer Jr., June 11, 2009; Richard D. Fisher Jr. (senior fellow for Asian Military Affairs at the International Assessment and Strategy Center), e-mail communication with Commission staff, August 27, 2009; and Stephen Saunders, ed., *Jane's Fighting Ships 2008–2009* (Alexandria, VA: Jane's Information Group, 2008), pp.139–140.

Naval missiles

The PLA Navy currently has a well-developed arsenal of missiles. This section will discuss the Chinese navy's antiship and land-attack cruise missiles and submarine-launched ballistic missiles. This section will also discuss the PLA's antiship ballistic missile programme—ostensibly controlled by the PLA's Second Artillery (Strategic Rocket) Forces, because of its clear naval implications.[191]

- *Antiship cruise missiles:* China has a substantial quantity of antiship cruise missiles that can be launched from a variety of platforms—including aircraft, surface combatants, submarines, and possibly even land-based launchers.[192] While China's most capable cruise missiles—the supersonic "Sizzler" and "Sunburn" —are of Russian origin, Chinese defence industries have become "sufficiently self-reliant" at producing moderately advanced cruise missiles.[193] China's antiship cruise missile capability allows it to conduct a more efficient antiaccess strategy.[194]
- *Land-attack cruise missiles:* The Chinese also possess a variant of a short-range cruise missile that can be launched from land, air, or sea—including possibly from submarines.[195] The US Department of Defence reported that these missiles could be used to "threaten regional bases, logistics, and support infrastructure." [196]

- *Submarine-launched ballistic missiles:* The PLA Navy is currently developing the JL–2, a submarine-launched ballistic missile, to be deployed on the navy's newest nuclear-powered ballistic missile submarines, the *Jin*-class. Although this missile has not yet been successfully tested, the US Department of Defence anticipates that it will have a range of at least 7,200 kilometers.[197] When operational, this missile will allow Chinese submarines for the first time to target the continental United States from operating areas located near the Chinese coast.[198]
- *Antiship ballistic missiles:* The PLA is developing a conventionally armed antiship ballistic missile. According to the US Department of Defence, this missile will have a likely range of 1,500 kilometers, be armed with manoeuvreable warheads, and is intended to deny regional access to surface ships of the opposing side.[199] When combined with appropriate surveillance and targeting sensor systems, this missile could have the potential to destroy or disable aircraft carriers and their associated battle groups while in transit.[200] Mr. Giarra testified to the Commission that the US Navy currently lacks adequate defence mechanisms, making this weapon what he called a potential "game changer" for naval warfare in the region.[201]

Maritime Military Systems

PLA Navy top officials have strongly emphasized the need to enhance elements of its C4ISR systems. In April 2009, the PLA Navy commander stated that the navy's first modernization priority is to develop its early warning systems. Commander We also stated that the navy must establish a joint command model that will integrate "shore, sea, and air [components], and achieve digital linkage between command information systems and equipment platforms." [202] The following month, the PLA Navy chief of staff wrote how naval reconnaissance, early warning, and command and control capabilities must be improved. [203]

Over the past few years, the PLA Navy has taken concrete steps to improve its C4ISR systems. Ronald O'Rourke, a naval expert at the Congressional Research Service, testified to the Commission in June that "China reportedly is developing or deploying maritime surveillance and targeting systems" based on a variety of advanced technologies.[204] In addition, Mr. Cooper stated that China's "[e]ssential C4ISR capabilities such as joint command and control, long-range surveillance and reconnaissance, maritime area air defences, and a joint targeting architecture probably will be in place between 2015 and 2020." [205]

An improved C4ISR system will greatly bolster China's naval capabilities, since early warning and command and control are continuing weaknesses of the PLA Navy.[206] Correcting this weakness—particularly in the maritime domain—will allow Beijing to carry out operations against approaching maritime forces, using a myriad of capabilities.[207] The US Department of Defence maintains that improvements in "China's space-based reconnaissance and positioning, navigation, and timing, as well as survivable terrestrial over-the-horizon targeting" will enhance the PLA's ability to conduct precision strikes.[208] Mr. Cooper told the Commission that such capabilities also will provide the navy with the ability to conduct operations farther out at sea, possibly in the Malacca Strait, the Indian Ocean, and perhaps even the Persian Gulf.[209]

The Institutional Pillar

Although harder to quantify and evaluate than more easily observed material developments, reforms on the soft side of China's navy are equally important. In order to properly operationalize its growing collection of modern platforms, weapons, and equipment, China also needs to improve the way in which this new hardware is operated.[210] To this extent, over the past few years, the PLA Navy has implemented several institutional reforms, which can be divided into four areas: personnel, organizational, training, and logistics. Each of these will be discussed in turn.

Personnel reforms: According to Rear Admiral McDevitt,

> *The leadership of the PLA recognizes that to achieve their vision of ... a high-tech military that's able to operate modern and sophisticated weapon systems, they need to have a professional military that is more carefully balanced toward professionalism while not losing sight of Party loyalty and fealty.*[211]

To that end, the PLA Navy has implemented a series of personnel reforms, including increasing the minimum criteria for officer and enlisted entry, creating a noncommissioned officer corps, improving the education levels of the sailors and officers, and raising pay in order to retain more of its qualified personnel.[212] According to Mr. Vellucci, the PLA Navy is changing how it recruits its officers in order to acquire people who are more technologically proficient, better educated, loyal to the Communist Party, and who have diverse practical experiences. One way the navy is accomplishing this goal, said Mr. Vellucci, is by increasing the number of officers directly recruited from civilian colleges, thus raising the educational level of incoming officers.[213] In addition to recruitment reforms, the navy has also been reforming the way it conducts professional military education for its commanding officers in order to better prepare them for modern warfare, Senior Captain Yan Juejin, commandant of the PLA Navy Branches Command Academy, stated in an April 2009 article.[214]

Military Training Reforms

According to both China's 2006 and 2008 defence white papers, reforming military training is a priority for the PLA Navy.[215] Rear Admiral McDevitt stated that in order to do this, the navy has increased the rigour of its operational training, strengthened its methods for evaluating training, and bolstered the realistic nature of its training.[216] Additional goals include standardizing training throughout the navy and increasingly relying on specialized training facilities, thus further improving training results.[217] In an April 2009 interview, the PLA Navy commander listed three accomplishments of the navy's training reform since 2001: 1) an increase in the realism of naval training, 2) an improvement in combat techniques, and 3) a routinization of training far out at sea.[218]

Organizational Reforms

As stated in China's 2004 and 2006 defence white papers, the PLA has implemented several organizational reforms in an attempt to streamline the navy and improve its capabilities to conduct modern combat operations.* For example, the 2004 defence white paper mentioned how the PLA Navy "compressed its chain of command and reorganized its combat forces in a more scientific way while giving prominence to the building of maritime combat forces—especially amphibious combat forces."[219] The 2006 defence white paper listed organizational reforms aimed at improving the command structure of naval aviation units and naval bases.[220]

Logistics and supply reforms: Closely related to its organizational reform, the PLA Navy has sought to reform its logistics system in order to improve its capabilities to conduct maritime operations, as stated in China's 2004, 2006, and 2008 defence white papers.[221] Demonstrating the progress made to date, the 2008 version states that

> *[the PLA Navy] is in the first stages of constructing a logistics support system with shore bases as the foundation and maritime logistics as the focal point, meshing the two into one. It has stepped up the building of ship bases, berthing supply points, docks, and airfields; thus basically forming a shore-based support system that is coordinated with the development of weaponry and equipment, and suited to war-time support tasks.*[222]

Over the past few years, the PLA Navy has been constructing or expanding five naval bases, including an underground submarine base on the southern side of Hainan Island, in the South China Sea. When completed, these bases will increase the navy's logistics capabilities.[223] According to an April 2009 article in the China Daily, China's official English-language newspaper, "This network of naval bases, airports and ammunition supply systems have enabled the navy to conduct missions further offshore [sic]." [224] Mr. Cooper testified that the high costs of these endeavors "indicate the importance that China's leaders place on providing a solid logistical foundation for growing mission[s]." [225] Some analysts have pointed out that, in addition to developing these domestic naval bases, China has bolstered its commercial investments in, and development of, foreign ports in the Indian Ocean region as possible logistical hubs for future PLA Navy operations.[226] These parts include Chittagong, Bangladesh; Gwadar, Pakistan; Hambantota, Sri Lanka; and Sittwe, Burma.

The Doctrinal Pillar

Outside access to official PLA Navy (and PLA) doctrinal writing is very rare through open sources, thus limiting western analysts' understanding of this important guide post to China's military modernization. However, one trend that continually appears is that the navy is likely to expand its operational range. As early as 2004, President Hu explicitly called upon the navy to defend China's interests farther out at sea, not just along its littoral areas as before.[227] China's 2006 defence white paper maintained that the navy "aims at the gradual extension of the strategic depth for off shore

* Organizational restructuring was not mentioned in the 2008 defence white paper.

defensive operations."[228] The 2008 version similarly claimed an expanded range for the navy, stating that it "has been striving... to gradually develop its capabilities of conducting cooperation in distant waters"—a reference to China's ongoing antipiracy escort operations in the Gulf of Aden, Africa.[229] The PLA Academy of Military Science illustrated how this naval expansion is tied to China's growing economy:

> *Along with the continued growth of our economic power and our scientific and technical level, [our] naval forces will further expand, and our operational sea area will gradually expand out into the northern part of the Pacific until the second island chain.*[230]

Implications for the United States

China's naval modernization will likely have serious implications for the United States. First, as the PLA Navy continues to increase its maritime capabilities, Beijing will improve its capacity to inhibit US access to the region in the event of a crisis. As Admiral Michael Mullen, chairman of the Joint Chiefs of Staff, stated in May 2009, China is "developing capabilities that are very maritime-focused . . .and, in many ways, very much focused on [the United States]." [231] According to Rear Admiral McDevitt, "China has adopted a military concept of operations aimed at keeping an approaching force from closing to within striking range of the Chinese mainland and the Taiwan Strait." [232] In addition to targeting at-sea forces, China's antiaccess strategy also threatens regional land bases, such as the US forward-deployed bases on Okinawa and Guam.[233] The maritime portion of this antiaccess strategy can be summarized as follows:

- Endanger large surface ships, including aircraft carriers.
- Deny an opponent the use of regional bases.
- Threaten an opponent's airborne aircraft.[234]

As China strengthens its antiaccess capabilities, it may hinder the US military's ability to operate in the region.[235] Mr. Cooper testified to the Commission that "[Chinese] threats to US freedom of movement and action in Asia include conventional, long-range strike threats to US bases and maritime formations, and counter-C4ISR threats to US forces' 'eyes and ears'." [236] The Science Applications International Corporation's report drafted for the Commission further demonstrated China's growing antiaccess capability, stating that Chinese cruise missiles fired from forward-deployed air or sea platforms could potentially hit targets as far away as Guam. Such a capability would "effectively limit US military operations from mainland Japan, Okinawa, the Philippines, and all of the Senkaku islands... [and] potentially force US aircraft carriers to adopt 'safe operating zones' out to as much as 1,000 miles off the Chinese mainland."[237] (see map overleaf).

Figure 2: China's Conventional Antiaccess Capabilities

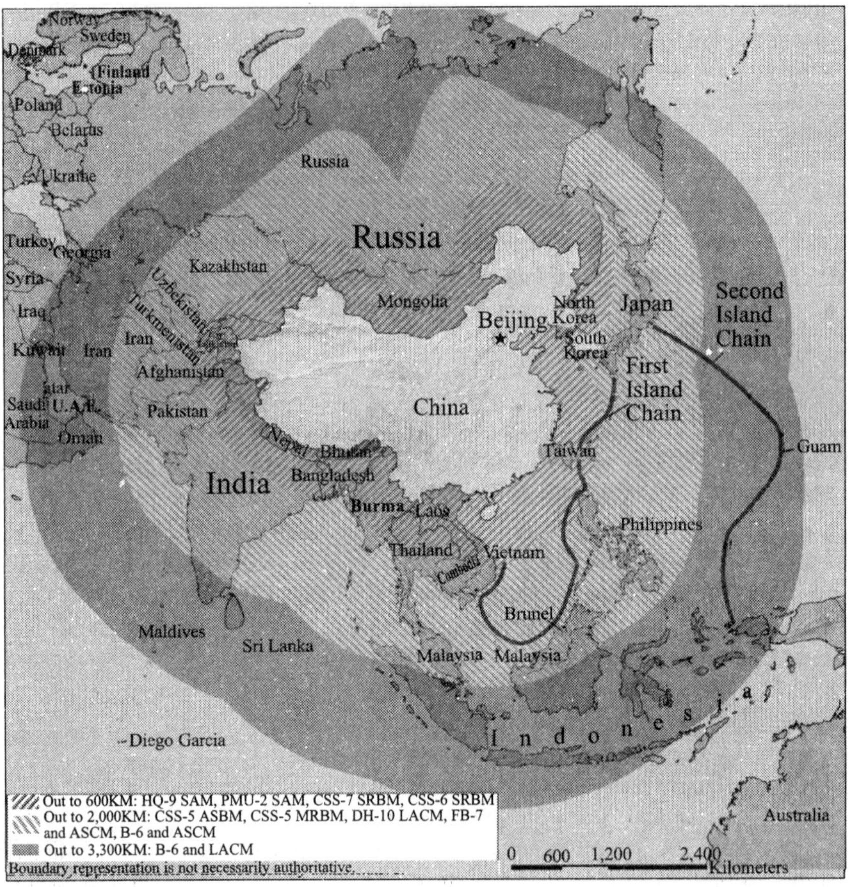

Source: Office of the Secretary of Defence, Annual Report to Congress: Military Power of the People's Republic of China, 2009 (Washington, D.C.: US Department of Defence, 2009), p. 23.The "first island chain" represents a line of islands running from Japan, the Senkaku (Diaoyu) Islands, Taiwan, and the west coast of Borneo to Vietnam. The "second island chain" denotes the set of islands that run in a north-south line from Japan, the Bonin (Osaga wara) Islands, the Mariana Islands, and Indonesia.

It is important, however, to distinguish intent from capability. Although Beijing may desire the ability to prevent the United States from intervening on behalf of Taiwan (or any other nation) in the event of a conflict with China, it is not clear whether the PLA is capable of such an endeavour. Instead, according to Rear Admiral McDevitt, as China's antiaccess capabilities increase, US military capabilities will likely grow apace, allowing the United States to maintain the "delta of advantage" it currently enjoys for "the next four to five years."[238]

A second implication for the United States is that China's new naval capabilities could impact other Asian states, including key US allies and friends, and possibly provoke a naval arms race in the region. Rear Admiral McDevitt told the Commission that China'smilitary modernization, ostensibly defensive in nature, "is creating a dynamic that, as its security situation improves, it is making the security environment for many of its neighbours worse."[239] Recent official government publications and statements from states in the region demonstrate the growing apprehension with which they view China's naval modernization. For example, in May 2009, Australia released a defence white paper that stated that China'smilitary modernization was of potential concern to regional states due to the PLA's lack of transparency.[240] Two months later, Japan's Ministry of Defence also released a defence white paper that went even further, identifying China's military modernization as aprimary factor for Japan to increase its military investment.[241] At a March 2009 conference on South China Sea issues, a foreign policy research institute within the Vietnamese Foreign Affairs Ministry cited China's military modernization as a key factor for modernizing Vietnam's military.[242] Finally, in its 2008 annual report, India's Ministry of Defence pointed to the Chinese goal of improving the PLA Navy's strategic depth, articulated in China's 2006 defence white paper, as affecting India's security environment.[243]

Signs of a naval arms race within the region can already be seen. Australia, for example, seeks to double its submarine fleet from six to 12; modernize its surface combatants; acquire a satellite to improve its intelligence, surveillance, and reconnaissance capabilities; and purchase approximately 100 F–35A Joint Strike Fighters by 2030.[244] Vietnam in early 2009 contracted with Russia to purchase six Kilo-class attack submarines and 12 Russian Su-30MK2 fighter jets.[245] India has also begun a large-scale naval modernization programme that includes constructing a new aircraft carrier, purchasing three new stealth frigates from Russia and six long-range maritime surveillance aircraft from the United States, and launching a new surveillance satellite intended for costal defence and naval applications.[246] The Indian Navy also has made a concerted effort to modernize its submarine fleet; for example, in the past several years, India has built six attack submarines; leased two Russian nuclear submarines; and in July 2009, launched its first Russian designed and indigenously constructed ballistic missile nuclear submarine.[247] Other Asian maritime nations seeking to increase their submarine forces include Indonesia, Malaysia, Singapore, and South Korea.[248]

Conclusion

- Since the mid-1990s, China, enabled by its growing economy, has embarked on its largest naval modernization effort since the founding of the PRC in 1949. This modernization process includes foreign purchases and indigenous production of naval platforms,weapons, and equipment. In addition, institutional changes such as organizational, personnel, and logistics reforms have improved the PLA Navy's capacity to conduct operations.
- Deterring Taiwan from declaring independence is the near-term goal of this modernization process. A key component is the necessity to impede other nations—including the United States—from intervening on Taiwan's behalf.
- Other reasons driving China's naval modernization include the need to protect China's economic-intense coastal regions from maritime attacks, assert its maritime sovereignty and regional economic interests, safeguard its access to international sealanes, provide a credible at-sea nuclear deterrent, and satisfy a national desire for a powerful navy.

- As China's naval modernization efforts progress, China increasingly will be able to project power in East Asia and interfere with US freedom of access to the region. China's antiaccess strategy hinges upon deploying a powerful navy on, above, and below the surface, supported by air and missile forces.
- Concern about China's naval modernization is beginning to fuel a maritime arms race in the region. Several nations, including close US allies, have recently officially questioned PLA and PLANavy modernization efforts. Already a few nations have even begun to augment their own navies by purchasing naval platforms and weapons.

SECTION 3

China's Human Espionage Activities that target the United States, and the Resulting Impacts on US National Security

> "The Commission shall investigate and report exclusively on
>
> "Regional Economic and Security Impacts—The triangular economic and security relationship among the United States, Taipei and the People's Republic of China (including the military modernization and force deployments of the People's Republic of China aimed at Taipei), the national budget of the People's Republic of China, and the fiscal strength of the People's Republic of China in relation to internal instability in the People's Republic of China and the likelihood of the externalization of problems arising from such internal instability...."

Introduction

In recent years, the Department of Justice has filed an increasing number of cases concerning espionage or illegal technology acquisition involving the People's Republic of China (PRC). While these filings include some colourful spy cases that grab media headlines, the majority of them involve violations of export control laws or instances of industrial espionage. These cases attract far less public attention but are no less significant to US economic and national security.

David Szady, a former assistant director of the Federal Bureau of Investigation's (FBI) counter intelligence division, has referred to China as "the biggest [espionage] threat to the US today." [249] FBI Director Robert Mueller has warned that "China is stealing our secrets in an effort to leap ahead in terms of its military technology, but also the economic capability of China. It is a substantial threat."[250] Joel Brenner, a former senior counter intelligence official in the office of the Director of National Intelligence, has characterized China's intelligence services as the most aggressive out of 140 such entities trying to penetrate US targets.[251]

Other statements from government counter intelligence officials suggest a Chinese intelligence collection effort that is growing in scale, intensity, and sophistication. "The Counter Intelligence Community considers the People's Republic of China to be one of the most aggressive countries targeting US military, political, and economic secrets as well as sensitive US trade secrets and technologies," according to a May 2009 statement from the Office of the Director of National Intelligence. "For a number of reasons, we believe China poses a significantly greater foreign intelligence threat today than it did during most of the cold war era."[252]

Most of the law enforcement cases that have China at the nexus involve the illegal acquisition of US controlled technologies. While some of these cases have ties to China's intelligence services, the vast majority are linked to other state organizations, particularly the factories and research institutes of China's military-industrial complex. Data released by the US Department of Justice have indicated that, in cases resulting in federal prosecutions during fiscal years 2007 and 2008, China was ranked second only to Iran as the leading destination for illegal exports of restricted US technology. The specific technologies illegally exported to China in these cases included rocket launch data, space shuttle technology, missile technology, naval warship data, unmanned aerial vehicle technology, thermal imaging systems, and military night vision systems.[253]

This year the Commission examined the extent of Chinese espionage directed against the United States as well as the impacts of such espionage on both US national security and future US economic competitiveness. Multiple Chinese state entities are engaged in an active effort to acquire restricted US technologies; the Chinese government also encourages and rewards the actions of private individuals to obtain technology on its behalf. Agents of the Chinese government are also displaying an increasing willingness to offer financial inducements to US government officials in order to encourage them to compromise classified information. Finally, Chinese government officials are engaged in the surveillance and harassment of Chinese dissident organizations within the United States.

Additional analysis will be included in the classified annex of the Commission's 2009 Report to Congress. China's extensive and growing cyber espionage activities will be addressed in chapter 2, section 4, of this Report, "China's Cyber Activities that Target the United States, and the Resulting Impacts on US National Security."

China's Traditional Intelligence Methodologies

Traditional Chinese approaches to espionage differ significantly from those of the "classical" approach to espionage that has been encountered by the United States in the past.[254] Generally, where foreign sources are concerned, China has not "normally [paid] an agent for information, request[ed] that the person provide classified documents, [or] use[d] intelligence officers to elicit information from the agent or engage[d] in clandestine activity like 'dead drops.'... China prefers to obtain its information a little bit at a time."[255] The means used to accomplish this have included inviting foreign scientific experts to conferences in China; flattering them; subjecting them to grueling schedules intended to wear them down mentally; and peppering them with incessant, coordinated elicitation intended to produce in discreet disclosures rather than consciouses pionage.[256]

Unlike Russian intelligence officers looking to exploit ego, greed, or other personal weaknesses, Chinese intelligence personnel are more inclined to make use of sympathetic people willing to act asa "friend of China."[257] While this most clearly has been seen in PRC-targeted recruitment of Chinese-Americans, PRC agents also have used as sources US citizens of other ethnic backgrounds.

A Shift in Traditional Practices of Source Recruitment

Many historical cases of PRC-directed espionage against the United States have involved US citizens of Chinese ethnic heritage. The issue is not that Chinese-Americans are less trustworthy than US citizens of other ethnic backgrounds; instead, as former FBI analyst Paul Moore once noted, "the reason that it is always ethnic Chinese who seem to be involved in Chinese intelligence matters is that they typically are the only ones China asks for assistance."[258]

One US government handbook on counter intelligence has explained that

> *the selling point in a normal PRC recruitment operation is not an appeal to ethnicity per se, but to whatever feelings of obligation the targeted individual may have towards China, family members in China, old friends in China, etc.The crux of the PRC approach is not to try to exploit a perceived vulnerability but to appeal to an individual's desire to help China out in some way . . . ethnic targeting to arouse feelings of obligation is the single most distinctive feature of PRC intelligence operations.*[259]

However, in a shift from these historical practices, the Commission has noted that at least two prominent cases of Chinese affiliated espionage within the United States over the past year have displayed an increased willingness by Chinese intelligence to reach beyond the confines of the Chinese-American community to seek sources as well as a greater willingness to offer financial inducements in exchange for information. (See "The Bergersen and Fondren Cases" later in this section.)

China's Intelligence and Technology Collectors

The Ministry of State Security

The Ministry of State Security is China's leading civilian intelligence agency, with responsibility for both foreign intelligence and domestic security operations.[260] Similar to the intelligence services of other Communist states, China's Ministry of State Security is best understood as an arm of the ruling Chinese Communist Party (CCP), entrusted with a primary mission of preserving the CCP in power.[261] The Ministry of State Security collects foreign intelligence but also has a leading role in counter intelligence, broadly defined in political terms—*i.e.*, to include the surveillance and suppression of groups viewed as oppositional to the CCP, such as political dissidents and ethnic separatists.[262] This role of acting against internal "opposition elements" has also been directed abroad. LiFengzhi, a reported former Ministry of State Security officer who has since resettled in the United States, stated in early 2009 that a major emphasis of Ministry of State Security activities abroad is targeting Chinese dissident and prodemocracy groups.[263]

The foreign intelligence operations of the Ministry of State Security are centered in its Second Bureau, which operates agents abroad under a range of covers, including both official diplomatic covers and unofficial covers such as students and businessmen. The Ministry of State Security also makes extensive use of news media covers, sending agents abroad as correspondents for the state newsagency Xinhua and as reporters for newspapers such as the *People's Daily* and *China Youth Daily*.[264]

The Ministry of State Security also maintains a public face in the form of its affiliated think tank, the China Institutes for Contemporary International Relations (CICIR), located in north western Beijing. Aside from its public role, CICIR is fully incorporated as the Eighth Bureau of the Ministry of State Security and provides research and analysis for the Chinese leadership.[265] CICIR also publishes its own journal, "*Xiandai Guoji Guanxi*" (Contemporary International Relations) and frequently hosts US visitors to China.[266] Members of this Commission have met on multiple occasions with representatives of CICIR during annual Commission fact finding trips to China. (For further discussion of CICIR and the relationships between Chinese think tanks and US institutions, see chap. 4, sec. 2, of this Report, "China's External Propaganda and Influence Operations, and the Resulting Impacts on US National Security.")

The Military Intelligence Department of the People's Liberation Army (PLA)

China's military intelligence agency is the Second Department of the People's Liberation Army General Staff Department, also known as the Military Intelligence Department. As a military organization, the Military Intelligence Department primarily collects intelligence on foreign military orders of battle, military doctrine, and weapons systems.[267] The Military Intelligence Department conducts overt collection of information through its military attaches in Chinese embassies but also has run covert collection operations through agents operating under cover.[268]

According to sources dating from the 1990s, the Military Intelligence Department has been the most active of China's intelligence services in acquiring foreign technology, particularly technology with potential military applications.[269] The Military Intelligence Department has operated multiple front companies in Hong Kong to facilitate technology transfers and other intelligence operations.[270]

Like the Ministry of State Security, the Military Intelligence Departmental so maintains affiliated think tank institutions. The foreign policy and national security affairs think tank of the Military Intelligence Department is the China Institute of International Strategic Studies, or CIISS.[271] Although CIISS does not publicly acknowledge its ties to the Military Intelligence Department, most of its researchers are current or former PLA officers, and the active-duty military officers assigned there divide work responsibilities between the institute and the Military Intelligence Department.[272] The current chairman of the institute is General (Ret.) Xiong Guangkai, a former director of the Military Intelligence Department.[273] Members of this Commission have held discussions with representatives of the China Institute of International Strategic Studies in the course of fact-finding visits to China. The Military Intelligence Department is also directly affiliated with the PLA Institute of International Relations in Nanjing, which functions as a training center for officers of the Military Intelligence Department.[274]

PRC Security, Foreign Intelligence & Technology Collection Agencies	Institutional Subordination	Primary Missions
Civilian Entities		
Ministry of State Security	PRC State Council/ CCP Politburo Politics and Law Committee [275]	• Foreign intelligence collection • Intelligence analysis • Counter intelligence • Suppression of dissident groups
Ministry of Public Security	PRC State Council/ CCP Politburo Politics and Law Committee [276]	• Domestic security operations/ law enforcement • Counter intelligence
CCP International Liaison Department	CCP Central Committee[277]	• Liaison with foreign political parties • Influence operations • Intelligence collection
CCP United Front Work Department	CCP Central Committee[278]	• Liaison with non Communist Chinese groups • Influence operations • Intelligence collection
Various Civilian Scientific Research & Development Institutions	Chinese Academy of Sciences (primary)[279]	• Technology acquisition
Military Entities		
Second Department, PLA General Staff Department (Military Intelligence)	PLA General Staff Department	• Foreign intelligence collection (especially military data) • Intelligence analysis • Technology acquisition
Third Department, PLA General Staff Department (Signals intelligence)	PLA General Staff Department	• Signals intelligence collection and analysis • Cyber intelligence collection and analysis
Fourth Department, PLA General Staff Department (Electronic Warfare)	PLA General Staff Department	• Electronic warfare (jamming, etc.) • Computer network attacks
International Liaison Department, PLA General Political Department	PLA General Political Department	• Foreign intelligence collection • Political/psychological warfare
Various Defence Industrial Firms	11 different stateowned defence enterprise group companies [280]	• Technology acquisition

Source: Compiled by Commission staff from multiple sources.

This chart, although not comprehensive, shows some of the most prominent PRC agencies involved in security, and counterintelligence and the collection of foreign intelligence and/or restricted technology, along with their primary areas of responsibility.

Other Intelligence Entities

The Chinese government also has a number of other institutional entities involved in foreign intelligence collection operations. The Third Department of the People's Liberation Army General Staff Department is China's leading signals intelligence agency and is also reportedly the largest of all of China's intelligence services, although no authoritative open-source figure is available for its total number of personnel.[281] The Third Department may also have a complementary relationship with the Fourth Department of the People's Liberation Army General Staff Department, which is responsible for electronic warfare.[282] (Further discussion of the activities of the Third and Fourth Departments may be found in chap. 2, sec. 4, of this Report.)

Alongside the Ministry of State Security and the Military Intelligence Department, the International Liaison Department of the PLA General Political Department has been identified by a US government counter intelligence handbook as one of three Chinese agencies that conduct covert intelligence collection against the United States.[283] Bearing responsibility for propaganda and psychological warfare, the International Liaison Department has in past years been active in targeting Taiwan military officers.[284] Although the organization has been described as both smaller and less effective than either the Ministry of State Security or the Military Intelligence Department in its US Operations,[285] there is little publicly available information about the agency's operations within the United States.[286] However, a statement from the US Office of the Director of National Intelligence in May 2009 listed the International Liaison Department as an active collector against US interests.[287]

Other entities of the Chinese party-state also maintain a role in gathering foreign intelligence and spreading propaganda on behalf of the government. These include the United Front Work Department of the CCP and the Foreign Liaison Department of the CCP.[288] China's official Xinhua state news agency also serves some of the functions of an intelligence agency, gathering information and producing classified reports for the Chinese leadership on both domestic and international events.[289]

Chinese Intelligence and Technology Collection within the United States

Information from recent criminal indictments indicates that Chinese intelligence and technology collection operations within the United States are more varied and complex than previously understood. A wide range of actors are at work collecting information and technology on behalf of the Chinese government, ranging from agents of the professional intelligence services described above to individuals seeking out technology and data that they might be able to sell to Chinese agencies. These efforts fall into four broad categories: 1) "actuarial" intelligence cobbled together from multiple sources; 2) "professional" intelligence-gathering conducted or directly sponsored by PRC intelligence agents; 3) "enterprise-directed" acquisition of controlled technology driven by entities within the Chinese state scientific research and development and military-industrial sectors; and 4) "entrepreneurial" industrial espionage and illegal technology exports carried out by private actors seeking rewards from the Chinese government.

"Actuarial Intelligence"

One distinctive element of Chinese espionage is the "grains of sand" or "actuarial" approach to intelligence-gathering. Rather than going after a narrowly targeted set of restricted information, Chinese intelligence efforts often focus on gathering immense quantities of raw information—most of which may not be classified or otherwise restricted, and much of which could be completely extraneous— and seeking to combine the vast number of puzzle pieces into a revealing "mosaic."[290] As former FBI special agent I.C. Smith told the Commission, this traditional approach has been one of "just get the information to us, and we will sort it out later."[291]

PRC intelligence operatives have also displayed a past preference for gathering information from many agents or sources rather than from any one, well-placed *source:* "The entire process is sometimes referred to as 'actuarial intelligence,' because its basis is not unlike the principles that insurance company actuaries apply to determine the profitability of insuring large groups of people."[292] This approach allows cross-checking of information from multiple sources while also increasing deniability in any particular instance and reducing the risk to any single source of exposure.

This traditional Chinese intelligence collection methodology is less likely than the "classical" model[293] to produce unambiguous evidence of espionage that can be prosecuted in a US courtroom. As characterized in a Central Intelligence Agency (CIA) and FBI report to Congress, Chinese spying activities "are usually low-key and singular in nature, thus creating a significant counter intelligence dilemma for the FBI."[294] And while this Chinese approach may appear unwieldy, it can produce significant results over time; in the memorable phrase of a US government counter intelligence handbook, the traditional Chinese approach to espionage is "inefficient but not ineffective."[295]

A declassified joint CIA and FBI report from 2000 indicated that the widespread collection of "grains of sand" could be explained in part by China's relatively low level of technological development compared to western countries:

> *Because the Chinese consider themselves to be in a developmental 'catch-up' situation, their collection programme tends to have a comparatively broad scope. Chinese collectors target information and technology on anything of value to China, which leads them to seek to collect open-source information as well as restricted/proprietary and classified information.*[296]

However, the rapid and dramatic advancement of science and technology in China in recent years is likely to produce gradually diminishing returns on such a scattershot method of collection. As China's scientific research and development and industrial sectors become more advanced, their identified areas of short fall— and therefore their collection requirements—are likely to become more focused and specific. Many of the recent cases of Chinese state-or enterprise-directed information and technology acquisition that are cited in the examples to follow show signs of a more specific collection focus than that observed in the "actuarial" practices of past years.

"Professional" Chinese Government-directed Espionage

In contrast to the looser "actuarial" method of collection described above, agents working for the PRC's professional intelligence services also seek out technological and intelligence information of a more specific nature. Three prominent cases of PRC affiliated espionage that came into public view in recent years displayed this pattern, in which collectors operating on behalf of the Chinese government pursued specific technologies or information requirements tasked to them by higher authority.

The Chi Mak Case

Chi Mak was the central figure in an espionage investigation that culminated with his arrest in October 2005 and his sentencing in March 2008 to 24 years in prison. Born in China's Guangzhou Province, Mr. Mak emigrated to southern California in the early 1980s and was naturalized as a US citizen in 1985. By 1996, he was employed as an engineer with Power Paragon in Anaheim, California, a subsidiary of L–3/SPD Technologies/Power Systems Group, and had been granted a "Secret" level security clearance. At the time of his arrest, Mr. Mak was working as the lead project engineer on the "Quiet Electric Propulsion" project meant for future US Navy warships.[297]

Mr. Mak took information about the Quiet Electric Propulsion project, as well as other Power Paragon projects, back to his residence and copied the information to compact discs that he then gave to his brother, Tai Mak, for encryption. Tai Mak operated as a courier for Chi Mak, relaying material to an unidentified PRC official in Guangzhou, China. Tai Mak intended to deliver a set of discs containing data on the Quiet Electric Propulsion project and other projects to this individual in Guangzhou at the end of October 2005 but was arrested while en route by FBI agents at Los Angeles International Airport.[298]

Prior to the arrests of Chi Mak and Tai Mak, FBI agents had retrieved shredded documents from the trash of Chi Mak's residence that provided instructions and collections tasking to Chi Mak from his handler in China. These included instructions to Chi Mak to perform more networking through professional associations and conferences. The documents also laid out an extensive and specific list of 17 different categories of naval and space-based military technology on which Chi Mak was to seek out further information. In May 2007, Chi Mak was convicted in the US Court for the Central District of California on charges of conspiracy, two counts of attempted violation of export control laws, failing to register as an agent of a foreign government, and making false statements to federal investigators. In March 2008, he was sentenced to 24 years in prison. Statements from federal officials indicated that Chi Mak had admitted to moving to the United States more than two decades earlier with the intention of gradually working his way into the US defence industrial complex to steal military technology on behalf of the Chinese government.[299]

The Chi Mak case clearly reveals strong interest on the part of China's military research and development sector in gaining surreptitious access to specific US military technologies under development. The information compromised by Chi Mak may prove to be of significant benefit to the PRC's naval systems modernization programmes and may also improve the ability of PRC engineers to identify vulnerabilities in US systems currently under development. (For more on China's naval modernization and increasing naval capabilities, see chap. 2, sec. 2, of this Report, "China's Naval Modernization and Strategy.")

The Bergersen and Fondren Cases

Two linked Chinese espionage cases in 2008–2009 displayed a hybrid amateur-professional espionage model, in which an apparently amateur agent or asset took directions from a Chinese government official to seek out classified and restricted distribution information from US government officials. The first of these cases emerged into public view in February 2008 with a trio of arrests—that of Tai Shen Kuo, a naturalized US citizen born in Taiwan; Yu Xin Kang ("Katie"), a PRC citizen and legal resident alien of the United States, who worked as an assistant to Kuo; and Gregg William Bergersen, a weapon systems policy analyst with the Defence Security Cooperation Agency, a Department of Defence (DoD) agency that implements foreign military sales.[300]

Tai Shen Kuo operated a furniture business in New Orleans and also maintained, through family connections, high-level contacts with defence officials in Taiwan.* By an undisclosed series of events, he became affiliated with a PRC official in Guangzhou, China, who is not identified by name in the affidavit. This individual both provided funding for Mr. Kuo and assigned specific items of information that Mr. Kuo was to obtain from his contacts within the US government.

Mr. Kuo deceived Mr. Bergersen by making him believe that he (Kuo) was using his contacts in Taiwan to lay the foundation for lucrative future defence contracting deals and that he was seeking information related to Taiwan military systems and future weapons sales in order to facilitate his business arrangements. Plying Mr. Bergersen with cash and gifts, and stringing him along with the hope of becoming a business partner for the expected future military contracting deals, Mr. Kuo was able to obtain from Mr. Bergersen information on the "Po Sheng" (Broad Victory) project,[301] a command-and-control upgrade programme for the Taiwanese armed forces developed with US assistance; publications on the "Global Information Grid" communications network of the DoD; and data from the "Javits Report" (classified "Secret"), a 2007 Defence Security Cooperation Agency spreadsheet on the planned US sales of military equipment to foreign nations for the next five years.

In at least some instances—such as the information on the Global Information Grid and on future military sales to Taiwan—Mr. Bergersen was responding to specific requests from Mr. Kuo, who was in turn relaying taskings from the unnamed PRC official in Guangzhou. Throughout the time that he was handling over documents and information to Mr. Kuo, Mr. Bergersen apparently believed that this information was bound for officials in Taiwan and not the PRC. He was therefore

* Tai Shen Kuo is a son-in-law of Hsueh Yeh, a former Republic of China Navy admiral who served the Guomindang during World War II and the Chinese Civil War of 1945–1949. See Peter Enav, "Taiwan Reviews Impact of New US Spy Charges," *Taipei Times*, February 14, 2008. *http://www.taipeitimes.com/News/taiwan/archives/2008/02/14/2003401185.*

deceived in a classic "false flag" operation, in which a source is misinformed regarding the identity of the end-user of the information.[302]

The other source exploited by Tai Shen Kuo was James Fondren, a retired US Air Force lieutenant colonel who served from August 2001 through February 2008 as the deputy director of the United States Pacific Command Washington Liaison Office, located inside the Pentagon. Ties between the two men dated back to at least 1998, when Mr. Kuo allegedly became the sole client for a consulting service, "Strategy, Incorporated" that Mr. Fondren operated from his home. Mr. Kuo was in fact staying as a guest in Mr. Fondren's home at the time of Mr. Kuo's arrest in February 2008.[303]

Through Mr. Fondren's consulting service, Mr Kuo requested from Mr. Fondren "opinion papers" on topics related to military-to-military ties between the United States and China. The subjects of these papers included a description of the visit to the United States of a senior PRC military official, an overview of defence talks between DoD and PLA officials, and an assessment of a US Navy- PLA Navy joint exercise. A review of Mr. Fondren's "opinion papers" by investigators alleged that Mr. Fondren incorporated information from documents classified "Confidential" and "Secret," including some passages copied nearly verbatim.

The affidavit in the Fondren case also indicates that Mr. Kuo's PRC handler provided topics of interest that Mr. Kuo was to pass to Mr Fondren and also suggested to Mr. Kuo that Mr. Fondren be misled into believing that his "opinion papers" were bound for senior military officials in Taiwan. If true, then Mr. Fondren, like Mr. Bergersen, was also duped by Mr. Kuo under a "false flag." Mr. Fondren had also maintained some direct contacts with Mr. Kuo's handler, reportedly exchanging 40 e-mail messages with him in 1999 and 2000.[304]

The actions of Gregg Bergersen and James Fondren could indicate a significant shift in the traditional character of Chinese state supported espionage against the United States. There are significant differences between these cases and the traditional Chinese model: both men were US government officials with access to classified information; neither man is Chinese-American; both were given specific taskings of documentation and information to hand over; and both were paid for their services. This indicates a set of practices verging closer to a more "classical" model of espionage[305] and shows a growing willingness on the part of PRC intelligence operatives to seek out individuals in the United States who have access to specific, required information.

Gregg Bergersen pled guilty on March 31, 2008, in the US Court for the Eastern District of Virginia to a single count of conspiracy to disclose national defence secrets and was sentenced on July 11, 2008, to 57 months in prison.[306] Tai Shen Kuo pled guilty on May 13, 2008, in the US Court for the Eastern District of Virginia to a one-count criminal charge of conspiracy to deliver national defence information to a foreign government and was sentenced on August 8, 2008, to 188 months in prison and a fine of $40,000.[307] On September 25, 2009, James Fondren was convicted by a federal jury on one count of unlawfully communicating classified information to an agent of a foreign government and two counts of making false statements to the FBI. He is scheduled for sentencing on January 22, 2010.[308]

"Enterprise-directed" Espionage Conducted by Chinese State controlled Research Institutes and Commercial Entities

While a significant part of Chinese espionage against the United States may be conducted at the behest of professional PRC intelligence agents, much of it—particularly in terms of economic and industrial espionage—is driven by the state-owned research institutes and factories of China's military-industrial complex and/or by subsidiary companies spun off from these state institutions. As described by the CIA and FBI, "China's commercial entities play a significant role in the pursuit of proprietary/trade secret US technology. The vast majority of Chinese commercial entities in the United States are legitimate companies; however, some are a platform for intelligence collection activities."[309] While many individual instances of collection may be conducted piecemeal, there is a central, national-level PRC programme for technological acquisition and modernization dating back to the 1980s—the "863 Programme"—that underlies this broader effort to obtain advanced technology.[310]

"Enterprise-directed" espionage may also be growing in importance and taking on a less random and more targeted form. The 2008 unclassified report of the Defence Security Service cited a rise in efforts undertaken by commercial entities to target restricted technologies, speculating that this likely represents "a purposeful attempt to make the contacts seem more innocuous by using nongovernmental entities as surrogate collectors for interested government or government-affiliated entities."[311] Although it does not provide specific country breakdowns, the same report also asserts that the East Asia and Pacific region is the origin of the most active efforts illegally to acquire US defence technologies.[312]

However, if there is an increasingly organized and coordinated effort to target specific technologies by state-affiliated commercial and research entities, the collection prioritization and tasking process by which this is handled has not heretofore been well documented or understood. James Mulvenon, director of the Center for Intelligence Research and Analysis, Defence Group, Inc., described to the Commission a complex process that is by turns both state directed and driven by private initiative:

> *I think it's both bottom up and top down . . . we know from open sources that there is a high-level state coordination on [science & technology] procurement that goes on at the Beijing level, whether it's in the Ministry of Science and Technology, whether it's . . . under the Ministry of Industry and Information, whether it is derivative of the 863 Programme, which itself was the result of high-level state coordination to identify key future technology gaps that China needed to push. . . . At the same time, there is innovation going on at the bottom level where people are for their own materialist interests trying to acquire things that they know would be valuable and then going to find customers for it . . . and so I think both of those processes are working at the same time.*[313]

Expanding on the matter of "enterprise-driven" collection, Dr. Mulvenon described a prominent role in technology acquisition undertaken by profit-driven commercial companies spun off from Chinese government-controlled defence industrial research institutes in the course of defence reforms in the late 1990s. He also described a decentralized, free-market system for the pursuit of technology acquisitions:

> *[it's] often as mundane as simply receiving a fax saying, 'Here is the shopping list of things that we're interested in,' with no clear direction as to where they're going to find them, and then relying on the natural entrepreneurship and aggressiveness of the people that they've contacted... often they're not the only people within the network that are being given this similar tasking... this is a distributed network in which there is redundant multiple tasking, and often it's [a question of who gets there first].*[314]

The Dongfan "Greg" Chung Case

An example of "enterprise-directed" industrial espionage that was recently made public is the case of Dongfan "Greg" Chung, a naturalized US citizen of Chinese heritage. Mr. Chung worked in the US aviation industry from 1973 to 2006, holding positions with both the Boeing Company and Rockwell International. He held a "Secret" level clearance and worked as an engineer on various aerospace projects, including doing stress test analysis on space shuttle fuselages and developing a phased-array antenna for space shuttle communications.[315]

Mr. Chung was arrested in February 2008, in Orange, California. According to the indictment in his case, sometime around 1979 he established contact with a professor at the Harbin Institute of Technology and offered his services to "contribute to the [scientific modernizations] of China." In succeeding years, Mr. Chung further communicated with officials at the China National Aero Technology Import and Export Corporation, the Nan Chang Aircraft Company, and the China Aviation Industry Corporation, receiving very specific questions regarding aircraft development and specific taskings for technical information. In response, Mr. Chung took multiple unreported trips to the PRC to deliver lectures. He also handed over—either via mail delivery or by passing them to an individual at the PRC consulate in San Francisco—a large number of proprietary Boeing and Rockwell technical manuals. These materials included, among many other items, a shipment in 1985 that contained 27 manuals related to airframe stress analysis and 24 manuals related to the B–1 bomber programme.

On July 16, 2009, Mr. Chung was convicted in the US Court for the Central District of California of conspiracy to commit economic espionage; six counts of economic espionage to benefit a foreign country; one count of acting as an agent of the People's Republic of China; and one count of making false statements to the FBI. Mr. Chung was scheduled for sentencing on November 9, 2009.[316]

"Entrepreneurial Espionage" on Behalf of China

Another distinctive feature of Chinese intelligence collection— and one that is highly significant in terms of US security—is the extent to which spying is also practised by private individuals acting either independently or on behalf of the Chinese government. The Office of the Director of National Intelligence has reported the following:

Nonprofessional intelligence collectors—including government and commercial researchers, students, academics, scientists, business people, delegations, and visitors—also provide China with a significant amount of sensitive US technologies and trade secrets. Some members of this group knowingly or unknowingly collect on behalf of [PRC intelligence agencies] or Chinese defence industries, presenting a significant intelligence threat. But in many cases, the collection efforts of these private-sector players are driven entirely by the opportunity for commercial or professional gain and have no affiliation with [PRC intelligence].[317]

Such reliance on amateur efforts to collect science and technology has led to a vast amount of "entrepreneurial" economic and industrial espionage conducted by Chinese students, trade delegations, businessmen, and educational and research institutions. The range of motivations for such espionage on private initiative can be varied and complex. Former FBI special agent I.C. Smith testified that the Ministry of State Security sometimes places pressure on Chinese citizens going abroad for educational or business purposes and may make pursuit of foreign technology a quid pro quo for permission to travel abroad.[318] However, this phenomenon of "entrepreneurial espionage" appears to be particularly common among businessmen who have direct commercial ties with Chinese companies and who seek to skirt US export control and economic espionage laws in order to export controlled technologies to the PRC. In such instances, profit appears to be a primary motive, although the desire to "help China" can intersect in many cases with the expectation of personal financial gain.

The nature of such privately organized and implemented espionage efforts raises a number of thorny issues for US counterintelligence and law enforcement officials. As special agent Smith asked, "Is it truly an intelligence operation in the absence of the presence of an intelligence service?"[319] Even in instances where there is no direct state involvement, however, the Chinese government has been a major beneficiary of technology acquired through industrial espionage.[320]

"Espionage entrepreneurs" are not focused solely on obtaining state-of-the-art, high-tech data and equipment. Dr. Mulvenon testified to the Commission that many older technologies are still of considerable value to China's military modernization:

I would also submit to you that our export control system is overly focused on the state-of -the-art and doesn't apply a means-ends test to why the Chinese are requiring a specific piece of technology. There are pieces of technology . . . that the Chinese are trying to acquire that are 20, 25 years old, [and] that are mainstays of existing US defence systems but come nowhere close to being considered state-of-the-art, and yet a means-ends test would correctly identify those as critical gaps in the Chinese system.[321]

Expanding on this point, Dr. Mulvenon described to the Commission the existence of numerous entrepreneurial "mom-and-pop" companies—many of them nothing more than a titular business registered at a residential address—that legally purchase older military technology from US manufacturers or through a secondary market of defence industrial equipment auctions, or even from the Internet, and then look for customer institutions back in China.[322]

Two Cases of Industrial Espionage to Benefit China's Space Industry

Two illustrative cases of industrial espionage occurred within the United States during the Commission's 2009 reporting period, both of which involved the intended illegal export to China of US controlled technology and materials that would benefit China's rapidly developing space industry. This is far from an exhaustive list—even within the narrow field of aerospace-related technologies other examples could be cited from 2009.

The first case is that of Quan-Sheng Shu, the owner of the firm AMAC International Inc., in Newport News, Virginia. Born in Shanghai in 1940, Dr. Shu was naturalized as a US citizen in 1998.[323] He holds a PhD in physics and is the author of six books and more than 100 papers on the subjects of cryogenics and superconductivity.[324] Dr. Shu and his firm had worked on several research and development contracts on behalf of the US Department of Energy and the National Aeronautics and Space Administration. [325]

In November 2008, Dr. Shu pled guilty in the US Court for the Eastern District of Virginia to two violations of the Arms Export Control Act and one count of bribing Chinese officials in violation of the Foreign Corrupt Practices Act. Dr. Shu was sentenced to 51 months in prison and a fine of $386,740.[326] As of summer 2009, AMAC International had divested itself of many of its past projects and proprietary technologies and had shut down its office in Beijing. [327]

The export control law violations pertained to Dr. Shu's export to the PRC of a cryogenic fueling system for space launch vehicles and technical data for a liquid hydrogen tank and cryogenic equipment. The items exported by Dr. Shu were intended to assist in the design and development of a cryogenic fueling system for space launch vehicles to be used at a heavy payload launch facility located on the southern island province of Hainan, PRC. According to the US Department of Justice, the space launch facility at Hainan is affiliated with the PLA and the China Academy of Launch Vehicle Technology and is expected to be a launch site for space stations and satellites, manned space flights, and future lunar missions.[328]

A second case of alleged export violation in support of China's space programme was revealed on October 28, 2008, when a grand jury in the US District Court for Minnesota indicted Jian Wei Ding and Kok Tong Lim, both officials of FirmSpace Limited, an import/export company in Singapore; and Ping Cheng, a New York resident and reportedly the sole shareholder of Firm Space. The three men were allegedly involved in a plan to sell carbon fiber material, with applications in aircraft, rockets, spacecraft, and uranium enrichment, to the China Academy of Space Technology.[329] Mr. Ding and Mr. Lim allegedly purchased the carbon fiber materials from an undisclosed firm in Minnesota via remote wire transfer, with the materials shipped to Mr. Cheng's address in New York. Mr. Cheng was allegedly then to inspect and store them and prepare them for shipment onwards to the China Academy of Space Technology.[330] Two other individuals, Firm Space company directors, Hou Xinlu and Gao Xiang, are mentioned in conjunction with the case but have not been charged. Both men are believed to reside in China.[331]

Local media in Singapore have remarked that Firm Space Limited seemed to have little else in the way of business activity. Despite the lack of the company's observable business, one local news outlet noted that the firm had not laid off any employees and had continued to pay them regularly. The firm's receptionist was quoted as saying, "I found it quite strange but I never thought of asking the bosses, as long as I still got my salary." [332]

How Well Is This Information Processed?

With such a large intake of data and material, there remains a question as to how effective the Chinese system might actually be in separating the wheat of useful information from the mass quantities of chaff. The nature of the Chinese government bureaucracy, in which officials may be inclined to exaggerate successes to their superiors for purposes of career advancement, may facilitate waste within the system. For example, retired FBI agent I.C. Smith has described interviewing a former Ministry of State Security officer about that individual's responsibilities to obtain military technology inside the United States and being told of time wasted gathering useless US military surplus items simply for the sake of bureaucratic appearances.[333]

However, amid the vast quantities of equipment and information collected by the Chinese system there emerge nuggets of genuinely useful material. One report from the late 1990s indicated that PLA-affiliated enterprises were actively involved in buying surplus and cast-off equipment from US military bases and may have been able in this way to acquire models of US military systems for reverse engineering, possibly including the radar digital guidance system for the Pershing II intermediate-range ballistic missile system.[334]

Targeting Chinese Dissident Groups Abroad

Another highly significant aspect of Chinese intelligence activities within the United States and one with disturbing implications for many citizens and foreign residents of the United States— is the intensive effort put forward by Chinese government operatives to monitor, harass, and disrupt the activities of Chinese dissident groups operating abroad. There is ample evidence of such activity by Chinese officials within the United States, extending back for many years. In testimony presented before the House Foreign Affairs Committee in June 1990, Lin Xu, a former PRC consular official who had sought asylum within the United States, testified that Ministry of State Security officials had visited the Chinese embassy in Washington, DC, in the wake of the Tiananmen Square massacre to consult with educational services consular officials. These officials were subsequently assigned to monitor and harass Chinese students within the United States who were perceived to have reformist or prodemocracy sympathies.[335]

There have also been very similar and even more detailed accounts by PRC defectors in recent years. Chen Yonglin, a former PRC first secretary and consul in Sydney, Australia, defected in May 2005 and sought asylum in Australia. Mr. Chen provided a detailed account of efforts by Chinese government officials to monitor, harass, and disrupt the activities of "hostile elements." Mr. Chen stated that the same model of PRC intelligence activities applies in both Australia and the United States.[336]

Mr. Chen produced an internal PRC government document that referred to the "Five Poisonous Groups" of Falun Gong members, Tibetan separatists, Uighur separatists, Taiwan pro-independence activists, and pro-democracy activists. The document further described the "Consulate's main counter-strategy in the battle" against such groups, with consular officials directed to "strengthen monitoring" of the activists on a list of names; to "conduct propaganda work through multiple channels," with a particular focus on local Chinese language media; and to "try to work on local government officials."[337] In regard to the latter effort, Mr. Chen described specific efforts to levy quid pro quo economic pressure on Australian officials and lobbying pressure placed on Sydney-area education officials to deny public funding to a school whose principal was a Falun Gong member. In such efforts driven by PRC government officials, a central point of emphasis is "mobilizing the force of the [local] Chinese community" to act on behalf of PRC interests.[338]

Falun Gong activists in the United States have alleged activities by PRC consular officials of a similar nature to those described by Chen Yonglin. A Falun Gong-affiliated newspaper, Epoch Times, has alleged that officials from the PRC's New York consulate organized a series of assaults in 2008 against Falun Gong demonstrators in the New York neighborhood of Flushing, Queens.[339]

Two expert witnesses who spoke before the Commission this year, neither of whom has any affiliation with Falun Gong, both testified that PRC embassy and consular officials take an active role in organizing and mobilizing Chinese-American civic groups to act on behalf of the Chinese government.[340]

Other recent examples of PRC consular officials mobilizing ethnic Chinese groups were observed during the worldwide running of the Olympic Torch in spring 2008. As the torch relay made its way toward Beijing, scuffles took place in a number of cities between protesters made up of pro-Tibetan, pro-human rights, and other activists critical of the Chinese government, and counter demonstrators made up of Chinese students or local ethnic Chinese residents. In some of these locations, particularly in Paris and Seoul, these confrontations turned violent. One such example within the United States occurred on April 8, 2008, at a protest and large counterprotest on the campus of Duke University in Durham, North Carolina. This incident attracted significant media attention after a Chinese student attempting to mediate between the two opposing groups was vilified on the Internet by nationalist activists and the home of her parents in China subsequently vandalized.[341] In the incident at Duke, a group of approximately 15 students from a campus human rights group organized a pro-Tibet rally timed to coincide with the date of the torch relay, only to find themselves surrounded and drowned out by a crowd of approximately 400 counterdemonstrators. As described in an account provided to the Commission by a Duke student who witnessed the event,

> *[t]he most striking characteristic of the gathering was the organization of the China supporters. In addition to gathering hundreds of supporters, which is no small feat on such a relatively small campus, most had large, pre-designed posters, printed leaflets, full-size Chinese flags, large US flags, and were chanting and singing in unison. The Chinese supporters were not gathered in pell-mell like you'd expect from a gathering of 400 people. The organization and size of the pro-China crowd could be attributed to the fact that a large portion of those gathered ... were not even Duke students.*[342]

In many such instances, the groups of ethnic Chinese counterprotesters showed clear signs of being encouraged and organized by officials from PRC embassies or consulates. As stated in a report issued by the analytical firm Strategic Forecasting, Inc., about the April 9, 2008, passage of the torch relay through San Francisco,

> *[b]y 8 a.m. April 9, the pro-China demonstrators were taking up positions along the planned torch relay route, pulling in groups carrying Chinese, US and Olympic flags, and equipped with cases of food and water. However, these were not spontaneous gatherings of overseas Chinese supporting the motherland, as Beijing media have portrayed them. Rather, there was a coordinated effort between local Chinese business and social associations and the consulate to attract, equip, deploy and coordinate the large pro-China turnout. . . . By some estimates, as many as 50 busloads of Chinese from other parts of California were brought to San Francisco.*

This account also alleges the use of prank calls, text messages, and even low-level, localized jamming against the cell phones of the anti-PRC demonstrators—demonstrating, if true, prior knowledge of the phone numbers of the activists organizing the protests. Also described are possible efforts to incite confrontations in such a way as to make the anti-PRC demonstrators appear violent:

> *On numerous occasions, individuals or small groups carrying cameras would seek to incite the anti-China demonstrators to acts of confrontation or violence, frequently by parading through the middle of a group of Free Tibet or Save Darfur demonstrators with a large Chinese flag, walking back and forth through the group. In some cases, small scuffles broke out—and pictures were snapped— though the anti-China demonstrators soon deployed individuals to try to keep the two opposing sides separated. The same day, Chinese media ran photos of pro-Tibet demonstrators shoving pro-China demonstrators, 'proving' their point that the Tibet supporters are violent.*[343]

Such activities directed at, by turns, either mobilizing or monitoring Chinese-Americans may be explained in part by a pervasive attitude among PRC officials that ethnic Chinese everywhere naturally owe loyalty to Beijing.[344]

Such examples also paint the Chinese government as highly fearful of dissident or ethnic minority activity organized abroad and willing to devote considerable attention and resources to thwarting activist groups backing these causes. They also reinforce Chen Yonglin's description of PRC government officials seeking to hide their hand by coopting and mobilizing local ethnic Chinese business and community groups to undertake work on their behalf. This pattern of activity is best understood within the context of the CCP's political imperative to present its domestic audience with a narrative of Chinese people around the world united in support of the Chinese government. It also fits in with a long-standing CCP pattern of "united front" activity intended to subvert and turn non-Communist Chinese groups into tools for advancing the goals of the CCP.

Conclusion

- The intelligence services of the Chinese government are actively involved in operations directed against the United States and against US interests. China is the most aggressive country conducting espionage against the United States, focusing on obtaining US information and technologies beneficial to China's military modernization and economic development.

- Some of the espionage carried out on behalf of China is conducted by non-professional collectors. These nonprofessional collectors may be motivated by profit, patriotism, feelings of ethnic kinship, or coercion. Even in many cases where there is no obvious direct state involvement in the theft or illegal export of controlled technology, the Chinese government encourages such efforts and has benefited from them.
- Recent cases of espionage involving China show evidence of more focused efforts at information collection employing sources outside of the Chinese-American community.
- Chinese operatives and consular officials are actively engaged in the surveillance and harassment of Chinese dissident groups on US soil.

SECTION 4

China's Cyber Activities that Target the United States, and the Resulting Impacts onUS National Security

"The Commission shall investigate and report exclusively on—

"Regional Economic and Security Impacts—The triangular economic and security relationship among the United States, Taipei and the People's Republic of China (including the military modernization and force deployments of the People's Republic of China aimed at Taipei), the national budget of the People's Republic of China, and the fiscal strength of the People's Republic of China in relation to internal instability in the People's Republic of China and the likelihood of the externalization of problems arising from such internal instability. . . ."

Introduction

In May 2009, President Obama labeled cyber attacks "one of the most serious economic and national security challenges" that the country faces.[345] Joel Brenner, former director of the Office of the National Counter Intelligence Executive, has identified China as the origin point of extensive malicious cyber activities that target the United States.[346] Anecdotal evidence suggests that Chinese attacks targeting US government and defence-related information have been damaging. For example, in June 2007, the Office of the Secretary of Defence took its information systems off line for more than a week to defend against a serious in filtration that investigators attributed to China.[347] In April 2009, reports surfaced that attacks on defence contractor information systems in 2007 and 2008 allowed intruders—probably operating from China—to successfully exfiltrate "several terabytes of data related to design and electronics systems" of the F35 Lightning II, one of the United States' most advanced fighter planes.[348] A large body of both circumstantial and forensic evidence strongly indicates Chinese state involvement in such activities, whether through the direct actions of state entities or through the actions of third-party groups sponsored by the state.

Malicious cyber activity has the potential to destroy critical infrastructure, disrupt commerce and banking systems, and compromise sensitive defence and military data. Malicious cyber incidents are on the rise, and attacks against US government computer systems illustrate the severity of the problem. In testimony to the Commission in May 2008, Colonel Gary McAlum, then chief of staff for the US Strategic Command's Joint Task Force for Global Network Operations, stated that the reported incidents of malicious cyber activity against the Department of Defence reached 43,880 throughout 2007.[349] For 2008, that figure increased almost

20 percent, to 54,640 incidents. The numbers from the first half of 2009 foretell a steep increase for this year as well: 43,785 incidents occurred from January 1to June 30.[350] If these trends continue through the end of 2009, there would be a 60 percent increase in malicious cyber activity compared to 2008. The cost of such attacks is significant. Army Brigadier General John Davis, deputy commander of the Joint Task Force-Global Network Operations, stated in April 2009 that, in just the preceding six months, the US military alone had spent more than $100 million on "manpower, time, contractors, tools, technology and procedures" to remediate attacks on its networks. [351]

Figure 1: DoD Reported Incidents of Malicious Cyber Activity, 2000–2008, With Projection for 2009

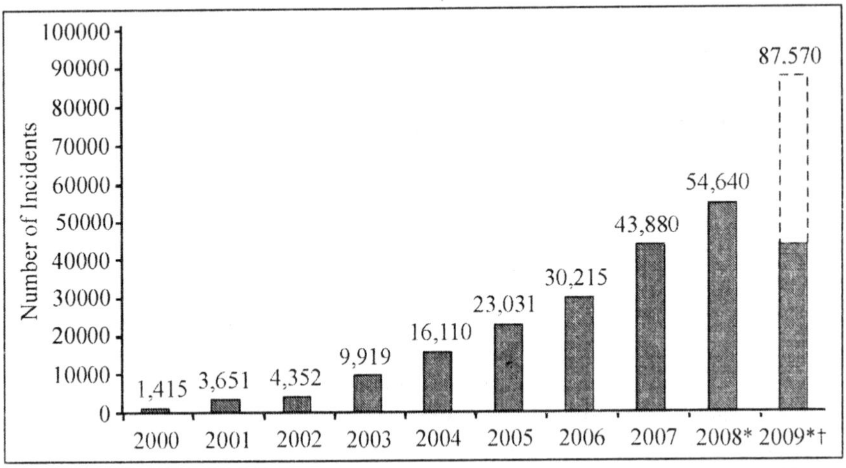

Source: US-China Economic and Security Review Commission, *Hearing on China's Proliferation Practices, and the Development of its Cyber and Space Warfare Capabilities*, testimony of Gary McAlum, May 20, 2008.

In 2009, the executive branch of the US government took several measures in order to address cyber threats to national security. In April, the White House announced the creation of a position called the "Cyber Security Coordinator" (known colloquially as the "Cyber Czar"), who will manage a more centralized and "top-down" approach to the US government's interagency cybersecurity process and make recommendations for the nation's cyber policies and standards.[352] The coordinator will have some budgetary control over new and existing initiatives through the Office of Management and Budget,[353] and he or she would report to both the National Security Council and the National Economic Council.[354] In June 2009, Secretary of Defence Robert Gates directed the Department of Defence to

* *Source:* Name withheld (staff member, US Strategic Command), telephone interview with Commission staff. August 28, 2009.

† Solid portion accounts for reported malicious incidents from January 1 to June 30, 2009, as provided by the US Strategic Command. Dotted portion estimates malicious incidents from July 1 to December 31, 2009, assuming a constant rate of attacks throughout the year.

form a unified Cyber Command in order to "develop a comprehensive approach to [Department of Defence] cyberspace operations." [355] The new command, which will include the National Security Agency and at least initially be subordinate to the US Strategic Command, reportedly will integrate the Department of Defence's offensive and defensive cyber capabilities. The extent to which the Cyber Command will work to secure nondefence or intelligence related government networks and civilian network infrastructure remains unclear; the Department of Homeland Security may retain the majority of that responsibility.[356]

Attribution of Responsibility for Cyber Attacks

Cyber attacks that originate in China can defy easy classification; some malicious activity appears to originate from private hacking groups, while other activity is almost certainly state sponsored. The latter, which will be the primary focus of this section, can be recognized to a certain extent by two important factors. First, cyber incidents leave behind signatures that can, with forensic analysis, sometimes reveal the affiliation of the responsible actors to a reasonable degree of certainty. This sometimes allows investigators to implicate the Chinese government directly, or sometimes even specific parts of the Chinese government, such as the People's Liberation Army (PLA).[357] Although this section draws on the conclusions of investigators involved in conducting forensic analysis of cyber intrusions, a thorough description of the techniques used is not publicly available.

Second, the nature of the malicious activity—including the type of information targeted—helps supplement the understanding of the attackers and their affiliations. One can infer state involvement in some instances based on the specific targeting of government and defence networks. According to a study for the Commission by Northrop Grumman that implicates the Chinese government in extensive malicious cyber activities against the United States,

> *China is likely using its maturing computer network exploitation capability to support intelligence collection against the US government and US defence industries by conducting a long-term, sophisticated, computer network exploitation campaign.... The depth of resources necessary to sustain the scope of computer network exploitation targeting the US and many countries around the world coupled with the extremely focused targeting of defence engineering data, US military operational information, and China-related policy information is beyond the capabilities or profile of virtually all organized cybercriminal enterprises and is difficult at best without some type of state sponsorship. ... The type of information often targeted for exfiltration has no inherent monetary value to cybercriminals like credit card numbers or bank account information.*[358]

On whether attackers are in the employ of the Chinese government or just selling information the attackers have stolen after the fact, the study suggests that "[i]f the stolen information is being brokered to interested countries by a third party, the activity can still technically be considered 'state-sponsored,' regardless of the affiliation of the actual operators at the keyboard." [359]

Department of Defence Definitions for Cyber Activity

This section uses the following definitions to describe the tactics used in cyber activities:

Computer Network Operations: "Comprised of computer network attack, computer network defence, and related computer network exploitation enabling operations." [360]

Computer Network Exploitation: "Enabling operations and intelligence collection capabilities conducted through the use of computer networks to gather data from target or adversary automated information systems or networks." [361]

Computer Network Attack: "Actions taken through the use of computer networks to disrupt, deny, degrade, or destroy information resident in computers and computer networks, or the computers and networks themselves." [362]

Computer Network Defence: "Actions taken to protect, monitor, analyze, detect and respond to unauthorized activity within Department of Defence information systems and computer networks." [363]

The Development of Doctrine in China for Computer Network Operations

The Chinese government's lack of transparency in the field of computer network operations makes analysis of the involvement of Chinese state actors challenging at the unclassified level. However, while much about China's government-backed computer network warfare programmes remains opaque, military newspapers and professional military journals in China have long expressed professional admiration for perceived US network and electronic warfare capabilities in conflicts such as the 1999 Kosovo campaign and the 2003 invasion of Iraq and have discussed the need to catch up.[364] These journals have engaged in a surprisingly open discussion of the need to develop greater capabilities for computer network operations and have even provided a number of details as to what form these capabilities should assume.[365]

The Chinese government has not publicly issued a strategy or governing concepts for computer network operations [366] such as those contained within *Joint Publication 3–13: Information Operations*, released in 2006 by the US Department of Defence.[367] However, some determined western open-source researchers have been able to gain insights into the institutional developments of China's cyber capabilities through studying the debates in these journals.

Chinese Terms for Computer Network Operations

Researchers with the Center for Naval Analyses have identified and translated the major doctrinal terms employed by Chinese military authors as follows: [368]

"*Computer network warfare*": equivalent meaning to the US doctrinal term "computer network operations"; "*Computer network attack*": same as the US doctrinal term "computer network attack";

"*Computer network defence*": same as the US doctrinal term "computer network defence"; "*Computer network reconnaissance*": equivalent meaning to the US doctrinal term "computer network exploitation."

When the preceding terms are discussed in this chapter within a Chinese context, they will be used interchangeably with their US counterparts.

Researchers such as Timothy Thomas of the Foreign Military Studies Institute at Fort Leavenworth, Kansas, have been able to assemble detailed histories of the development of PLA network warfare thought over the past decade.[369] The PLA views computer network warfare as both a key enabler of modern warfare and a critical new spectrum of conflict in its own right. These professional journal writings describe actions against an enemy's command, control, computers, communications, intelligence, surveillance, and reconnaissance nodes, and the defence of one's own, as the critical foci of modern warfare—thereby raising even further the importance of computer network operations. Chinese analysts also describe computer network warfare as a critical tool that can be exploited by a weaker military force to level the playing field against a stronger opponent.[370]

"Integrated Network Electronic Warfare"

Analysis of writings from authoritative PLA publications also has revealed the existence of a guiding PLA operational concept titled "Integrated Network Electronic Warfare." Integrated Network Electronic Warfare incorporates elements of computer network operations in tandem with elements of traditional electronic warfare.[371]

Integrated Network Electronic Warfare advocates the employment of traditional electronic warfare operations—such as the jamming of radars and communications systems—in coordination with computer network attack operations. The goal is to create a multispectrum attack on enemy command, control, communications, computers, intelligence, surveillance, and reconnaissance systems in the early stages of conflict, thereby denying the opposing force access to information and communications necessary to move forces and fight in a modern battlespace. As summarized in a 2009 publication, Integrated Network Electronic Warfare would use

> *techniques such as electronic jamming, electronic deception and suppression to disrupt information acquisition and information transfer, launching a virus attack or hacking to sabotage information processing and information utilization, and using anti-radiation and other weapons based on new mechanisms to destroy enemy information platforms and information facilities.*[372]

While some aspects of Integrated Network Electronic Warfare may remain aspirational for the Chinese military, the PLA takes the concept seriously and views cyberspace, in tandem with the electromagnetic spectrum, as critical arenas of conflict in full spectrum modern warfare. (For further discussion of China's military modernization, see chap. 2, sec. 1, of this Report, "China's Military and Security Activities Abroad.") The 2007 revised Outline for Military Training and Evaluation training guidance issued by the PLA General Staff Department directed all branches of the PLA to make training "under complex electromagnetic environments" the core of campaign and tactical training.[373]

In one recent example of such training, in early January 2008 approximately 100 senior-ranking PLA officers from multiple service branches reportedly observed an Integrated Network Electronic Warfare exercise hosted by elements of a group army of the Shenyang Military Region. In the exercise, troops of the defending PLA forces had to fend off attacks from mock aggressor forces* employing simulated cyber and electronic attacks. These attacks included a computer virus that sowed confusion by changing logistics requirements, using electrical pulse attacks that destroyed computer motherboards, and jamming communications and radar systems.[374]

Chinese Government Entities Involved in Computer Network Operations

The Third and Fourth Departments of the PLA General Staff Department

The Third Department of the PLA General Staff Department, which has traditionally engaged in signals intelligence collection, bears primary responsibility within the PLA for computer network exploitation. For these purposes, the organization likely maintains "technical reconnaissance bureaus" within each of China's seven military regions. The Fourth Department of the PLA General Staff Department, which has traditionally engaged in electronic warfare, plays the leading role in computer network attack.[375]

In 2009, the Commission contracted with the Northrop Grumman Corporation to perform a detailed, unclassified study on the development of Chinese capabilities for conducting cyber warfare and cyber espionage. This report, titled "Capability of the People's Republic of China to Conduct Cyber Warfare and Computer Network Exploitation," contains significant additional detail on PLA entities involved in cyber warfare. The full report is now available on the Commission's Web site.[376]

The Role of "Information Warfare Militia" Units of the PLA

The efforts of the PLA regarding computer network warfare are not limited solely to its active duty forces. The PLA has been forming cyber militia units since the late 1990s, "comprised of personnel from the commercial information technology sector and academia . . . represent[ing] an operational nexus between PLA [computer network operations] and Chinese civilian information security professionals."[377] The first such unit formed may be one created on an experimental basis in Datong City, Shanxi Province, in early 1998.[378] According to Chinese press reports, at the time of its creation the Datong unit contained 40 personnel[379] and was located within "a certain Datong City state-owned enterprise."[380] The unit relies upon "the resources of the local area's scientific talent, information technology, and facilities,"

* In US military exercises, the friendly (i.e., US) forces are identified as "blue," and the opposing aggressor forces are "red" forces. In PLA exercises, this convention is reversed: The Chinese forces are "red," and the units acting the role of the enemy are the "blue" forces.

with personnel drawn from "all over the city's 20 scientific research institutes, universities, and information occupations." [381] In 2006, the authoritative Chinese Academy of Military Science published an article that explicitly endorsed the information warfare militia concept and directed the PLA to make the creation of such units a priority.[382]

A 2008 study by the Internet security research firm iDefence identified 33 probable such militia units, mostly located within government research institutes, information technology firms, or university computer science departments. Personnel recruited for these units tend to be young (under 45 years of age); many are professors or graduate students and/or have experience with information technology gained through work with civilian information technology firms and may also have foreign language skills useful for intelligence collection.[383] PLA commanders reportedly have been directed to relax standard age and physical fitness requirements for the members of information warfare militia units in order to ensure that individuals with valuable skills not be turned away or attrited from the ranks.[384]

Other sources indicate that political reliability is also a factor in the selection of personnel: An article from an authoritative military journal about the process of forming a particular information warfare militia unit described the importance of a "thorough analysis of the degree of ideological awareness"of each recruit and further indicated that 94 percent of the selected personnel were members either of the Chinese Communist Party or its Communist Youth League.[385]

A Profile of a Chinese Information Warfare Militia Unit

In March 2008, the PLA established an information warfare militia unit in Yongning County, in Ningxia Province. The establishment ceremony for the unit was publicized by the local government and included a number of prominent local figures, including the local PLA garrison commander and chief of staff as well as leading officials of the county government.[386]

According to a concurrent Web posting made by the county government, the duties of an information warfare militia unit include "[s]trengthening research and exercises related to network warfare, and continuously improving methods for network attacks. ... In peacetime, extensively collect information from adversary networks and establish databases of adversary network data. . . . In wartime, attack adversary network systems, and resist enemy network attacks." [387]

According to a press release about the establishment ceremony for the unit, the Yongning Militia Information Warfare Unit will have approximately 80 personnel divided into three detachments, focused on network warfare, information collection and processing, and network defence. The unit was constructed according to "standardized requirements," with facilities including an operations center, a generator room, the commander's office, an activities room, and a set of charts and other necessary materials.

The same source indicated that individual unit personnel would undergo 10 days of foundational military training, including basic military skills and general knowledge of network warfare. A "Three-Year Development Plan" for the training of the unit was also mentioned, but no further details were provided. Finally, the local government announcement also underscored concern for the loyalty and political reliability of unit members, stating that their efforts would build "a unit that is steadfast in political belief, that has pure ideology and morals, that has a superior quality of professionalism . . . that performs propaganda for the Party, that benefits the people, and that can provide effective strength to the military for winning future wars under informationized conditions." [388]

The Role of "Patriotic Hackers"

Another category of actors involved in cyber activities directed against the United States consists of privately organized groups of Chinese computer hackers, sometimes referred to as "patriotic hackers" or "red hackers." [389] Motivated both by a desire to test their hacking skills as well as an anti-western sense of Chinese nationalism, such groups have been involved in many high-profile "hacktivist" defacements or distributed denial of service attacks directed against US Web sites. These have most frequently occurred during times of strained Sino-American relations, such as in the aftermath of the accidental May 1999 bombing of a People's Republic of China (PRC) embassy annex in Serbia by US forces, or following the April 2001 collision between a US Navy EP–3 surveillance aircraft and a PLA Navy F–8 fighter aircraft over the South China Sea.[390] Many Chinese hacker organizations operate quite openly on the Internet, maintaining their own Web pages, recruiting new members, and boasting of their hacking exploits. In the past, these groups have generally been tolerated by the Chinese government, as long as their hacking activities were directed abroad.[391]

It remains unclear as to the extent these "red hackers" receive support or sanction from the Chinese government. Some experts on Chinese hacker groups have tended to emphasize that they are indeed privately organized and that they operate largely independent of the government.[392] These arguments also emphasize that, from the point of view of the PRC authorities, "several factors argue against formal PLA plans to include 'hacktivism' as part of a [computer network operations] campaign." [393] One such factor could be concerns about reliance upon personalities assessed to be unsuited for disciplined government service, [394] a concern that may be further revealed in the strong emphasis placed on political reliability in the selection of personnel for information warfare militia units (see above). Other factors could include the unpredictable nature of red hacker activity in the midst of a crisis in which the government might wish to control both escalatory measures and international public opinion,[395] as well as the need to control the list of targets selected for computer exploitation or attack.[396] The Chinese government has recently signaled its intent to rein in privately initiated, unsanctioned hacker activity, publishing antihacker editorials in the state media,[397] passing the February 2009 antihacking law by the National People's Congress,[398] and arresting members of some hacker groups.[399]

However, these factors aside, there are clear signs of relationships between Chinese government agencies and some individual hackers or red hacker groups.

Reservations that might apply to a wartime computer network operations campaign do not necessarily apply to peacetime computer exploitation and cyber harassment, and the PRC appears willing to make use of its "patriotic hackers" for certain of these tasks.[400] For example, the Chinese government has encouraged efforts to counter "foreign forces subverting China via the Internet," and red hackers have duly directed distributed denial of service attacks, malicious code, and computer exploitation activity against the Web sites and affiliated users of pro-Tibet, pro-Xinjiang, Falun Gong, and Chinese prodemocracy organizations.[401] Additionally, at least one prominent Chinese hacker is known to have been recruited into the ranks of an information warfare militia unit,[402] and in 2007–2008 the Ministry of Public Security (one of China's primary domestic security agencies) placed job recruitment postings on *EvilOctal.com* and *XFocus.net*, two of China's foremost hacker forum Web sites.[403]

These latter examples may be part of a broader recent trend— the Chinese government's effort to draw from the talent available in its hacker community while also curbing some freelance hacker activities and seeking to bring them under state control. One aspect of this activity is the conversion of formerly state-tolerated, private hacker groups into information security firms that maintain extensive government ties and contracts.[404] The PRC authorities also have made high-profile arrests of selected hackers, intended to send a clear message that their activities could come under state supervision if they were to continue. One such example was seen in Henan Province in February 2006, when

> *[the] authorities shut down The Patriot Hackers—Black Eagle Base Website and arrested its members.... The group, however, was operational again six months later.... At that time its members released a statement that the group vowed to focus its efforts on training people for the state and working to improve the state's security network.... The Black Eagle leadership also expressed appreciation to the State Security Bureau ... for the educational guidance they provided to members while in custody.*[405]

Profiles of Alleged Chinese Cyber Espionage

Cases of cyber espionage that leave trails leading back to China are observable across the spectra of business, politics, and technological research. These include instances of computer exploitation directed against Chinese ethnic and political dissident groups abroad, Members and offices of the US Congress, and US infrastructure targets. An examination of the particulars of these cases highlights the extensive and persistent character of probable state sponsored Chinese computer exploitation activity, as well as the serious potential threat that this activity poses to US interests.

The "GhostNet"

In March 2009, researchers of the Information Warfare Monitor— a collaborative initiative of the The SecDev Group, a think tank based in Ottawa, Canada, and the Citizen Lab, an interdisciplinary information technology and social science research institute based at the University of Toronto [406]—released a highly detailed report on their research into a wide-ranging cyber espionage network. Their forensic investigation revealed that the network, which they came to call "GhostNet," had infected 1,295 host computers in 103 different countries around the world, many of them belonging to embassies, ministries of foreign affairs, and other high-profile government targets.[407] While Information Warfare Monitor could not conclusively identify GhostNet's operators, the circumstantial evidence surrounding GhostNet's pattern of activity strongly suggested Chinese state involvement.

The Information Warfare Monitor forensic investigation started in the summer and autumn of 2008 with examinations of computers used by the personal office of the Dalai Lama; the Tibetan government-in-exile in Dharamsala, India; and Tibetan government in-exile offices in New York, Brussels, and London. The researchers found multiple computers that had been infected with malicious software (malware) implanted by e-mails masquerading as legitimate messages sent either by professional contacts or by persons politically sympathetic to the intended victim. The e-mails contained either attached documents or Internet links that, when activated, installed malware. This malware would later connect to an external control server and download additional malware, including a remote administration tool (RAT) titled "ghost RAT." "ghost RAT" is a Trojan horse* that allows an attacker to remotely take full, real-time control of the computer. Once ghost RAT was installed, the attacker could exfiltrate files, log keystrokes, and activate Webcams, among many other functions, all without the knowledge of the computer's legitimate operator.[408]

By intentionally infecting a computer with the GhostNet malware, the Information Warfare Monitor researchers were able to observe the network's activities and there by identify the external servers issuing instructions to infected computers. They identified 26 "command" and "control" servers for GhostNet, all of which were located in China.[409] The team also found that the control interface to the GhostNet network used the Chinese language.[410]

The report also provides at least one concrete example that directly links Chinese intelligence officials to Internet monitoring of Tibetan exile groups. It describes the case of a young woman who had worked two years in Dharamsala for a Tibetan nongovernmental organization named "Drewla," an online outreach initiative founded in 2005 that uses Tibetans with Chinese language skills to engage young Chinese in online discussions.[411] When attempting to enter Tibet from Nepal to visit her family, she was arrested and detained for two months. During this time, she was interrogated by PRC intelligence officials, who presented her with transcripts of her Internet chats. She was warned that her group was under surveillance and that its members were not welcome to return to Tibet.[412]

The report is cautious in ascribing responsibility for GhostNet and warns against a "rush to judgment in spite of circumstantial and other evidence." In its conclusion, however, the report does state that

* A "Trojan horse" is an "apparently useful programme containing hidden functions that can exploit the privileges of the user [running the programme], with a resulting security threat. A Trojan horse does things that the programme user did not intend." See Rita C. Summers, *Secure Computing Threats and Safeguards* (New York: McGraw-Hill, 1997), quoted in CERT, "Advisory CA– 1999–02 Trojan Horses" (Pittsburgh, PA: Carnegie Mellon University, February 5, 1999). *http:// www.cert.org/advisories/CA–1999–02.html.*

> *[the explanation] in which the circumstantial evidence tilts the strongest, would be that this set of high profile targets has been exploited by the Chinese state for military and strategic-intelligence purposes . . . many of the high confidence, high-value targets that we identified are clearly linked to Chinese foreign and defence policy, particularly in South and South East Asia. Like radar sweeping around the southern border of China, there is an arc of infected nodes from India, Bhutan, Bangladesh and Vietnam, through Laos, Brunei, Philippines, Hong Kong, and Taiwan. Many of the high profile targets reflect some of China's most vexing foreign and security policy issues, including Tibet and Taiwan.*[413]

One of the authors of the GhostNet report, Rafal A. Rohozinski, principal and chief executive officer of The Sec Dev Group and advisory board member of the Citizen Lab at the University of Toronto, testified before the Commission in April 2009 and assented to a follow-on interview with Commission staff in September 2009. Mr. Rohozinski was cautious in ascribing Ghost Net's activity to the Chinese government but stated that "all the circumstantial evidence does point to a network which, in effect, is Chinese operated." He also indicated that, based on analysis of Internet Protocol addresses, the team believed with "a high degree of confidence that the attackers were located in Hainan Island in China."[414]

Mr. Rohozinski also identified characteristics of Ghost Net that indicated state sponsorship rather than the work of cyber criminals. He noted that the network was directed toward the collection of political intelligence rather than financial or personal data of interest to cyber criminals and that the particular targets—such as Tibetan exile groups and government ministries—were unlikely targets for profitable financial fraud.[415] He also noted that while the collection methods of GhostNet were relatively low-tech,

> *[t]he requirements that would be needed to put in place to exploit the information gathered through [GhostNet] do require a scale larger than a small [nongovernmental organization]. Why? Linguistically, 103 different targets, including the Prime Minister's Office of Laos, the Israeli Consulate in Hong Kong, the Russian Embassy in Beijing, the Iranian Foreign Ministry, requires linguistic skills as well as domain expertise in terms of being able to know what to look for and what to make of it.*[416]

This analysis suggests that while the GhostNet's methods for the collection of information were available to semiskilled private hackers, effective exploitation and analysis of that material probably required state resources. Mr. Rohozinski suggested that the intelligence collection of GhostNet likely represented state-sponsored activity carried out by private actors working on behalf of the government. As he stated,

> *[O]ur suspicion is that this was an operation which was essentially outsourced to third parties, essentially third-party actors possessing the equivalent of a letter of marque, legal pirates of the state, which had either some contractual arrangements or had some assurance of financial remuneration or reward in return for maintaining a specific kind of network such as this.*

In support of this analysis, Mr. Rohozinski noted signs that GhostNet involved attackers from multiple vectors, with forensic analysis showing the affected computers to contain multiple infections of malware, "which means that it wasn't just one GhostNet, it was a multiple of GhostNets."[417] This analysis, which postulates private hacking groups undertaking intelligence collection under the sponsorship of the government, accords with the view of one of the leading western analysts of Chinese hacker organizations.[418] It also accords with activity discernible in human espionage and illegal technology acquisition conducted on behalf of the PRC, in which multiple private "entrepreneurial" actors are at work, and even in competition with one another, to procure information and technology on behalf of PRC institutions. (For more on this latter topic, see chap. 2, sec. 3, of this Report, "China's Human Espionage Activities that Target the United States, and the Resulting Impacts on US Security.")

Case Study of Probable Chinese Network Intrusion Directed Against a US- Firm

The Northrop Grumman report prepared for the Commission provides a detailed case study about the 2007 penetration of an unnamed US high-technology commercial firm's network. The penentration was carried out by hackers with probable ties to the Chinese government. A summary of this case study, below, describes the tradecraft commonly used in Chinese computer network operations.

In this instance, a first team of hackers, dubbed the "breach team," reconnoitered the firm's network for months. During this phase of the operation, the hackers gained critical information about computer accounts, employee names and passwords, and general network architecture. They mapped network directories to gain intimate knowledge of the contents of the compromised systems. The breach team then identified and exploited network vulnerabilities.

A second team of hackers, dubbed the "collection team," then used information gathered by the first team to collect sensitive information from the firm's network. Though linked to the first team through common attack vectors, the second team used different tools in unique ways, indicating distinct operators. The collection team quickly and efficiently navigated to precise directories and copied specific high-value files, often ignoring other similarly named and co-located files. This approach, given that the team opened none of the targeted files during the collection process, indicated precise knowledge of file contents as a result of the breach team's efforts and very specific tasking.

The collection team then copied the files and transferred them to high-speed "staging servers" within the firm's network. This decreased the attackers' operational footprint on machines known to the firm to contain high-value data, and it centralized activity on machines with high volumes of traffic, where the malicious activity would be more effectively disguised. The team then compressed and encrypted the files and assigned them innocuous names before exfiltrating the data from the firm's network.

The attackers demonstrated impressive professionalism and tradecraft. They discerned and attempted to secure only the most critical files. Throughout the process, the attackers consolidated attacks to one specific region—in the same time zone—in order to conduct activity after work hours in order better to avoid detection. The attackers set up redundant exfiltration channels so as to maximize the volume of data that they could simultaneously steal and to safeguard against errors and failures in the transfer process. Together, the teams accessed the firm's network on more than 150 occasions using dozens of legitimate but compromised accounts.

The attacks, at times, originated from a host with an Internet Protocol address located in China. The tools and techniques used in both the breach and collection phases of the attack were consistent with other attacks previously attributed to China. "The type and specificity of data stolen in this case also suggests that the end users were already identified and that they likely had deep science and technology resources at their disposal to make use of the stolen information," another factor that strongly indicates state or institutional sponsorship.[419]

Instances of Probable Chinese Computer Network Exploitation and Attack Directed Toward Critical Infrastructure

In written testimony to the Commission, Kevin Coleman, senior fellow with The Technolytics Institute, an information security consultancy, warned of China's computer exploitation activities and cited "reports of malicious code being found in the computer systems of oil and gas distributors, telecommunications companies, [and] financial services industries." He highlighted the possibility of computer attacks on US "water treatment and distribution systems." [420] These matters are of particular concern because, as the Department of Homeland Security's 2009 National Infrastructure Protection Plan states, "[t]he United States relies on cyber infrastructure for government operations, a vibrant economy, and the health and safety of its citizens." [421] All of these issues hinge to some extent on the operability of the US electrical grid, which has surfaced as a prime target for attacks. This is perhaps because of the enabling role it plays with other types of infrastructure: communications, financial, and water networks all require electrical inputs.

Malicious actors use these probes to gain information for more deliberate exploitation. In April 2009, the Wall Street Journal reported pervasive penetration of the US electric grid and other critical infrastructure nodes. According to the report, in some of these breaches intruders implanted software which, when remotely activated, could disrupt or destroy the system. Citing intelligence officials involved in the investigation, the Wall Street Journal report identified China as a primary actor in the intrusions.[422] The United States already may have suffered consequences from China's exploitation of infrastructure controls. In May 2008, the National Journal reported that Chinese cyber attacks may have been responsible for blackouts in 2003 and 2007 in New York and Florida, respectively.[423] Attacks on critical infrastructure could be used to gain an advantage in a time of crisis or war. [424] Specifically seeking such targets is consistent with authoritative PLA writings on computer network operations. According to James Mulvenon, an expert in China's cyber warfare practices, Chinese analysts state that "computer network attacks on non-military targets are designed to 'shake war resoluteness, destroy war potential and win the upper hand in war,' thus undermining the political will of the population for participation in military conflict." [425]

Instances of Probable Chinese Computer Network Exploitation Directed Toward the US Congress

In December 2008, reports surfaced about the 2006 penetration of computers in the US House of Representatives. Investigators found that the information systems of eight Congressmen and seven congressional committees had been compromised. After taking a roundabout route, the malware used in these attacks sought to establish connections to servers in China. While reports of the attacks stopped short of directly linking them to the Chinese government, compelling circumstantial information suggests government ties. Aside from forensic data, for example, the lawmakers targeted had information with little or no intrinsic criminal value but immense political value. Among those attacked were Representative Frank Wolf (R–VA.), a Member with long-standing ties to human rights groups and prodemocracy activists, and Representative Mark Kirk (R–IL), then cochair of the US-China Working Group, that, among other things, addresses bilateral trade issues.[426]

At least one Member of the Senate has also publicly complained of cyber intrusions into his office computer systems. On March 19, 2009 Senator Bill Nelson (D–FL) stated during a hearing of the Senate Armed Services Committee that "I have had my office computers invaded three times in the last month, and one of them we think is very serious." An aide to Senator Nelson indicated that the attacks were traced to China through analysis of Internet Protocol data.[427]

Conclusion

- The quantity of malicious computer activities against the United States increased in 2008 and is rising sharply in 2009; much of this activity appears to orginate in China.
- The direct attribution of such activities targeting the United States presents challenges due to hackers' ability to conceal their locations. Nonetheless, a significant and increasing body of circumstantial and forensic evidence strongly indicates the involvement of Chinese state and state-supported entities.
- The Chinese government has institutionalized many of its capabilities for computer network operations within elements of the People's Liberation Army. The PRC is also recruiting from its growing population of technically skilled people, including those from the private sector, to increase its cyber capabilities. It is recruiting skilled cyber operators from information technology firms and computer science programmes into the ranks of numerous Information Warfare Militia units.
- China's peacetime computer exploitation efforts are primarily focused on intelligence collection against US targets and Chinese dissident groups abroad.
- In the early stages of a conflict, the PLA would employ computer network operations against opposition government and military information systems.
- Critical US infrastructure is vulnerable to malicious cyber activity. Chinese military doctrine calls for exploiting these vulnerabilities in the case of a conflict.

RECOMMENDATIONS

China's Military and Security Activities Abroad

- The Commission recommends that Congress make freedom of navigation a priority issue in its US-China interparliamentary exchanges.
- The Commission recommends Congress urge the administration to encourage further People's Liberation Army (PLA) participation in United Nations (UN) multinational security operations.
- To emphasize continued US commitments to and interests in the region, the Commission recommends that Congress encourage the US Department of Defence to maintain and strengthen robust military diplomacy with nations throughout East Asia.

China's Naval Modernization

- The Commission recommends that Congress assess the adequacy of planning and resourcing of US Department of Defence programmes that would limit China's antiaccess capabilities. In particular, Congress should focus on antisubmarine warfare and ballistic missile defence programmes. Congress should also assess the adequacy of funding and resources for the US Department of Defence's Pacific Command.
- The Commission recommends that Members of Congress, in their inter parliamentary exchanges, encourage Beijing to increase the transparency of its naval modernization efforts. Of particular interest are China's aircraft carrier, antiship ballistic missile, and ballistic missile submarine programmes, as well as its naval expansion and modernization efforts.
- The Commission recommends that Congress urge the US Department of Defence to continue to interact actively with US allies and friends in Asia to reassure them of the US's commitment to the region.
- The Commission recommends that Congress encourage the administration to continue to push for more engagement between the US Navy and the PLA Navy as a confidence-building measure.
- The Commission recommends that Congress encourage the administration to consider establishing a formal mechanism for preventing and managing maritime incidents between the US and Chinese navies.

China's Human Espionage Activities that Target the United States, and the Resulting Impacts on US National Security

- The Commission recommends that Congress assess the adequacy of resources available for intelligence, counterintelligence, and export control enforcement programmes to ensure that US government agencies are able to meet the rising challenge of Chinese human intelligence and illicit technology collection.
- The Commission recommends that Congress assess the adequacy of resources available for China-oriented counterintelligence awareness and law enforcement programmes throughout the US government and contractor community.

- The Commission recommends that Members of Congress in their interparliamentary exchanges raise US concerns regarding the monitoring and harassment of US citizens and legal permanent residents by agents of the Chinese government.

China's Cyber Activities that Target the United States, and the Resulting Impacts on US National Security

- The Commission recommends that Congress assess the effectiveness of and resourcing for law enforcement, defence, and intelligence community initiatives that aim to develop effective and reliable attribution techniques for computer exploitation and computer attacks.
- The Commission recommends that Congress urge the administration to develop measures to deter malicious Chinese cyber activity directed at critical US infrastructure and US government information systems.

ENDNOTES

1. Xinhua, "*Renmin Jiefangjun wei Weihu Guojia Liyi Tigong Youli de Zhanlu¨ e Zhiyuan*" (PLA to Provide a Powerful Strategic Support for Safeguarding National Interests), October 20, 2005. *http://news.xinhuanet.com/mil/2005–10/20/content_3652447.htm.* Chinese texts interchangeably use the terms "cyberspace" and "electromagnetic spectrum." Hereafter, this report will use the term "cyberspace"throughout.
2. Sun Kejia et al., eds., *Zhongshi Luxing Xinshiji Xinjieduan Wojun Lishi Shiming* (Faithfully Carry Out Our Military's Historic Missions in the New Period of the New Century) (Beijing: Haichao Publishing, 2006), pp. 67–81.
3. Hu Jintao, "*Renqing Xinshiji Xinjieduan Wojun Lishi Shiming*" (See Clearly Our Military's Historic Missions in the New Period of the New Century) (speech given to China's Central Military Commission, Beijing, December 24, 2004). *http://gfjy.jiangxi.gov.cn/htmnew 11349.htm.*
4. US-China Economic and Security Review Commission, *Hearing on China's Military and Security Activities Abroad*, testimony of Daniel M. Hartnett, March 4, 2009. At the time of his testimony, Mr. Hartnett worked as a China analyst at CNA and has since joined the US-China Economic and Security Review Commission staff.
5. Theory Research Institute of the Guangzhou Military Region, "*Kexue Renshi he Chongshi Luxing Xinshiji Xinjieduan Wojun de Lishi Shiming*" (Scientifically Understand and Sincerely Implement Our Army's Historic Missions in the New Period of the New Century), *Zhongguo Junshi Kexue* 3 (2005): 88–95.
6. Tom Holland, "China's 'Go-Out' Policy Means Trouble," *South China Morning Post*, April 24, 2007.
7. Reuters, "Violence Flairs in Algeria's 'Chinatown,' " *Financial Times*, August 4, 2009. *http://www.ft.com/cms/s/0/a74efac2–8177–11de-92e7–00144feabdc0.html.* According to the article, it is estimated that Algeria has more than 35,000 Chinese migrant workers.
8. Inal Ersan, "Prepare to Fight China, Qaeda Figure Tells Uighurs," Reuters, October 7, 2009. *http://www.alertnet.org/thenews/newsdesk/L7516001.htm.*

9. Representatives from China's National Defence University, Beijing, China, meeting with US-China Economic and Security Review Commission, May 5, 2009.

10. *Economist*, "Chasing Ghosts," June 11, 2009. *http://www.economist.com/ world/ asia/PrinterFriendly.cfm?story_id=13825154.*

11. US-China Economic and Security Review Commission, *Hearing on China's Military and Security Activities Abroad*, testimony of Daniel M. Hartnett, March 4, 2009.

12. Information Office of the State Council, *China's National Defence in 2008* (Beijing: January 2009).

13. US-China Economic and Security Review Commission, *Hearing on China's Military and Security Activities Abroad*, testimony of Susan L. Craig, March 4, 2009.

14. US-China Economic and Security Review Commission meeting with representatives from the Chinese National Defence University, Beijing, China, May 5, 2009.

15. Hu Jintao is concurrently the president of China, general secretary of the Chinese Communist Party, and chairman of the Central Military Commission.

16. Hu Jintao, "*Renqing Xinshiji Xinjieduan Wojun Lishi Shiming*" (See Clearly Our Military's Historic Missions in the New Period of the New Century) (speech given to China's Central Military Commission, Beijing, December 24, 2004). *http:// gfjy.jiangxi.gov.cn/htmnew 11349.htm.*

17. US-China Economic and Security Review Commission, *Hearing on China's Military and Security Activities Abroad*, testimony of Daniel M. Hartnett, March 4, 2009.

18. Hu Jintao, "*Renqing Xinshiji Xinjieduan Wojun Lishi Shiming*" (See Clearly Our Military's Historic Missions in the New Period of the New Century) (speech given to China's Central Military Commission, Beijing, December 24, 2004). *http:// gfjy.jiangxi.gov.cn/htmnew/11349.htm.*

19. Hu Jintao, "*Renqing Xinshiji Xinjieduan Wojun Lishi Shiming*" (See Clearly Our Military's Historic Missions in the New Period of the New Century) (speech given to China's Central Military Commission, Beijing, December 24, 2004). *http:// gfjy.jiangxi.gov.cn/htmnew/11349.htm.* For examples of previous iterations of these concerns, see Sun Kejia et al., eds., *Zhongshi Luxing Xinshiji Xinjieduan Wojun Lishi Shiming* (Faithfully Carry Out Our Military's Historic Missions in the New Period of the New Century) (Beijing: Haichao Publishing, 2006), pp. 1–35.

20. Hu Jintao, "*Renqing Xinshiji Xinjieduan Wojun Lishi Shiming*" (See Clearly Our Military's Historic Missions in the New Period of the New Century) (speech given to China's Central Military Commission, Beijing, December 24, 2004). *http:// gfjy.jiangxi.gov.cn/htmnew/11349.htm.*

21. Information Office of the State Council, *China's National Defence in 2008* (Beijing: January 2009).

22. *PLA Daily* Editorial Board, "*Lun Xinshiji Xinjieduan Wojun de Lishi Shiming*" (On Our Military's New Historic Missions in the New Period of the New Century), *Jiefangjun Bao* (January 9, 2006): 1.

23. US-China Economic and Security Review Commission, *Hearing on China's Military and Security Activities Abroad*, testimony of Daniel M. Hartnett, March 4, 2009.

24. US-China Economic and Security Review Commission, *Hearing on China's Military and Security Activities Abroad*, testimony of David S. Sedney, March 4, 2009.

25. Information Office of the State Council, *China's National Defence in 2008* (Beijing: January 2009).

26. The United Nations, "Monthly Summary of Contributors" (New York: June 30, 2009). *http://www.un.org/Depts/dpko/dpko/contributors/2009/june09_1.pdf.*
27. US-China Economic and Security Review Commission, *Hearing on China's Military and Security Activities Abroad*, testimony of Chin-hao Huang, March 4, 2009.
28. US-China Economic and Security Review Commission, *Hearing on China's Military and Security Activities Abroad*, testimony of Chin-hao Huang, March 4, 2009; US-China Economic and Security Review Commission, *Hearing on China's Military and Security Activities Abroad*, testimony of Michael R. Auslin, March 4, 2009; and US-China Economic and Security Review Commission, *Hearing on China's Military and Security Activities Abroad*, testimony of Susan L. Craig, March 4, 2009.
29. Ian Taylor, "The Future of China's Overseas Peacekeeping Operations," *China Brief* 8:6 (March 14, 2008). *http://www.jamestown.org/programmes/chinabrief/single/?tx_ttnews% 5Btt_news%5D =4792& tx_ttnews %5Bback Pid%5 D= 168&no_cache=1.*
30. US-China Economic and Security Review Commission, *Hearing on China's Military and Security Activities Abroad*, testimony of Chin-hao Huang, March 4, 2009.
31. Mark McDonald, "China Confirms Naval Role in the Gulf of Aden," *New York Times*, December 18, 2008. *http://www.nytimes.com/2008/12/19/world/asia/19patrols.html?lr=1&ref=world.*
32. People's Republic of China (PRC) Foreign Ministry, "Foreign Ministry Spokesperson Liu Jianchao's Regular Press Conference on December 18, 2008," Chinese embassy in Poland, December 19, 2008. *http://pl.china-embassy.org/pol/fyrth/ t527087.htm.*
33. US-China Economic and Security Review Commission, *Hearing on China's Military and Security Activities Abroad*, testimony of Bernard D. Cole, March 4, 2009.
34. Zhang Ning, "Two China Navy Vessels Leave for Gulf of Aden," CCTV (China Central Television), April 3, 2009. *http://www.cctv.com/english/20090403/106951.shtml.*
35. Commander, Combined Maritime Forces Public Affairs, "New Counter-Piracy Task Force Established" (Bahrain: January 8, 2009). *http://www.navy.mil/search/display.asp?story_id=41687.*
36. Xinhua, "China decides to send navy vessels to fight pirates off Somali coast," December 20, 2008. *http://lr.china-embassy.org/eng/majorevents/t527395.htm.*
37. US-China Economic and Security Review Commission, *Hearing on China's Military and Security Activities Abroad*, testimony of Bernard D. Cole, March 4, 2009.
38. Office of the Secretary of Defence, *Annual Report to Congress: Military Power of the People's Republic of China, 2009* (Washington, D.C.: US Department of Defence, 2009), p. I.
39. Office of the Secretary of Defence, *Annual Report to Congress: Military Power of the People's Republic of China, 2009* (Washington, D.C.: US Department of Defence, 2009), p. 56.
40. Information Office of the State Council, *China's National Defence in 2008* (Beijing: January 2009).
41. Information Office of the State Council, *China's National Defence in 2008* (Beijing: January 2009). This workshop was "the Second ASEAN Plus Three Workshop on Disaster Relief by Armed Forces."
42. US-China Economic and Security Review Commission, *Hearing on China's Military and Security Activities Abroad*, testimony of David S. Sedney, March 4, 2009.

43. US-China Economic and Security Review Commission, *Hearing on China's Military and Security Activities Abroad*, testimony of Bernard D. Cole, March 4, 2009.

44. US-China Economic and Security Review Commission, *Hearing on China's Military and Security Activities Abroad*, testimony of Daniel M. Hartnett, March 4, 2009. For an example of the goodwill that the US hospital ship garnered, see Tamalia Alisjahbana, "From Indonesia, 'terima kasih,' " *Boston Globe*, March 4, 2005. *http://www.boston.com/news/globe/editorial_*opinion/*oped/articles/2005/05/04/from_indonesia_terima_kasih? pg =full.*

45. Wendell Minnick, "China's Navy Takes Delivery of Hospital Ship," *DefenceNews*, November 5, 2008. *http://www.defencenews.com/story.php?i=3805439.*

46. US-China Economic and Security Review Commission, *Hearing on China's Military and Security Activities Abroad*, testimony of Bernard D. Cole, March 4, 2009.

47. US-China Economic and Security Review Commission, *Hearing on China's Military and Security Activities Abroad*, testimony of Eric A. McVadon, March 4, 2009.

48. An Lu, "Backgrounder: Major PLA-related Joint Anti-Terror Military Trainings," Xinhua, December 21, 2007. *http://news.xinhuanet.com/english/2007–12/21/content_7290327.htm.*

49. Information Office of the State Council, *China's National Defence in 2004* (Beijing: December 2004); Information Office of the State Council, *China's National Defence in 2006* (Beijing: December 2006); and Information Office of the State Council, *China's National Defence in 2008* (Beijing: January 2009).

50. Information Office of the State Council, *China's National Defence in 2004* (Beijing: December 2004); Information Office of the State Council, *China's National Defence in 2006* (Beijing: December 2006); and Information Office of the State Council, *China's National Defence in 2008* (Beijing: January 2009).

51. Xinhua, "Backgrounder: Major PLA-related joint anti-terror military trainings," *PLA Daily*, December 22, 2007. *http://english.chinamil.com.cn/site2/special- reports/2007–12/22/content_1065727.htm;* and Zha Chunming, " 'Peace Mission 2009' Improves Anti-terror Response," Xinhua, July 24, 2009. *http://www.china.org.cn/international/2009–07/24/content_18197933.htm.*

52. Zhou Feng, " 'Peace Angel 2009' Wraps Up," *PLA Daily*, June 29, 2009. *http://english.chinamil.com.cn/site2/news-channels/2009–06/29/content1817105.htm.*

53. Dennis J. Blasko (LTC, US Army, Ret.), e-mail discussion with Commission staff, August 14, 2009; Zhao Feipeng et al., "PLA Officers Discuss Experiences of Sino-Russian 'Peace Mission 2009' Exercise," *Zhongguo Qingnian Bao*, July 31, 2009. OSC ID: CPP20090731710007; *Jiefangjun Bao,* "Coordination of PRC, Russian Forces in Exercise Peace Mission 2009," July 27, 2009, p. 2. OSC ID: CPP20090727710011; and Li Xuanliang and Wang Tiande, "PRC: Interpretation of New Concepts in Exercise 'Peace Mission 2009,' " Xinhua, July 26, 2009. OSC ID: CPP20090726005011. *http://www.opensource.gov.*

54. US-China Economic and Security Review Commission, *Hearing on China's Military and Security Activities Abroad*, testimony of Chin-hao Huang, March 4, 2009.

55. Indian Ministry of Defence, *2007–2008 Annual Report* (New Delhi: 2008), pp: 172–180; Robert Godoy, "US Aircraft Carrier Visits Rio," *O Estado de Sao Paulo*, April 21, 2008. OSC ID: LAP20080421032004. *http://opensource.gov;* Doordarshan DD News, "Indian Naval Ships Arrive in South Africa for Joint Exercises," April 27, 2008. OSC ID: SAP 20080427428008. *http://opensource.gov;* Greame Hosken, "Arrival of Sub Completes SA Navy's Order," *Independent*, May 23, 2008. OSC

ID: AFP20080523534012. *http://opensource.gov; La Republica*, "Uruguay, Argentina, Brazil to Participate in Naval Exercise," July 14, 2008. OSC ID: LAP20080714010002. *http://opensource.gov;* and Tania Monteiro and Roberto Godoy, "Exercise Mobilizes Two-Thousand Five-Hundred Troops in Rio Grande do Norte State," *O Estado de Sao Paulo*, November 15, 2008. OSC ID: LAP2008 1115032001. *http://opensource.gov.*

56. US Navy, "About the Seventh Fleet," Seventh Fleet official Web site. *http://www.c7f.navy.mil/about.htm.*

57. Information Office of the State Council, *China's National Defence in 2004* (Beijing: December 2004); Information Office of the State Council, *China's National Defence in 2006* (Beijing; December 2006); and Information Office of the State Council, *China's National Defence in 2008* (Beijing: January 2009).

58. Zhou Feng, " 'Peace Angel 2009' Wraps Up," *PLA Daily*, June 29, 2009. *http://english.chinamil.com.cn/site2/news-channels/2009–06/29/content_1817105.htm;* Xinhua, "China, Mongolia to Hold Joint Peacekeeping Exercise," June 25, 2009. *http://news.xinhuanet.com/english/2009–06/25/content_11601106.htm.*

59. Information Office of the State Council, *China's National Defence in 2004* (Beijing: December 2004); Information Office of the State Council, *China's National Defence in 2006* (Beijing; December 2006); and Information Office of the State Council, *China's National Defence in 2008* (Beijing: January 2009). Xinhua, "Backgrounder: Major PLA-related joint anti-terror military trainings," *PLA Daily*, December 22, 2007. *http://english.chinamil.com.cn/site2/special-reports/2007–12/22/content_1065727.htm.*

60. Wu Shengli and Liu Xiaojiang, "*Jianshe Yizhi yu Lu¨xing Xinshiji Xinjieduan Wojun Lishi Shiming Yaoqiu Xiang Sheying de Qiangda de Renmin Haijun*" (Build a Powerful Navy Suited to Fulfilling the Requirements of the New Historic Missions of our Armed Forces in the New Period of the New Century), *Qiushi* 9 (May 1, 2009).*http://www.qsjournal.com.cn/zxdk/2009/200909/200906/t2009 0609 _1846.htm.* Wu Shengli is the commander of the PLA Navy, and Liu Xiaojiang is the political commissar. The journal is the premier journal of the Chinese Communist Party's Central Committee.

61. Office of the Secretary of Defence, *Annual Report to Congress: Military Power of the People's Republic of China, 2009* (Washington, D.C.: US Department of Defence, 2009), p. 54.

62. US-China Economic and Security Review Commission, *Hearing on China's Military and Security Activities Abroad*, testimony of David S. Sedney, March 4, 2009.

63. US-China Economic and Security Review Commission, *Hearing on China's Military and Security Activities Abroad*, testimony of Bernard D. Cole, March 4, 2009; and Shirley A. Kan, *US-China Military Contacts: Issues for Congress* (Washington, D.C.: Congressional Research Service, April 2009), p. 53.

64. US-China Economic and Security Review Commission, *Hearing on China's Military and Security Activities Abroad*, testimony of David S. Sedney, March 4, 2009; and Shirley A. Kan, *US-China Military Contacts: Issues for Congress* (Washington, D.C.: Congressional Research Service, April 2009), p. 53.

65. Christopher Bodeen, "US Admiral Hails China Anti-Piracy Cooperation," ABC News online, April 19, 2009. *http://abcnews.go.com/International/WireStory?id=7372472&page=1;* and Shirley A. Kan, *US-China Military Contacts: Issues for Congress* (Washington, D.C.: Congressional Research Service, April 2009), p. 54.

66. Donna Miles, "Admiral Expects US-China Military Talks to Resume Soon," *Defencelink*, July 28, 2009. *http://www.defencelink.mil/news/newsarticle.aspx?id=55287.* The Military Maritime Consultative Agreement was signed between then US Secretary of Defence William Cohen and then Chinese Minister of Defence General Chi Haotian on January 19, 1998. The goal of this agreement was to establish a "forum for dialogue on maritime communication" between the United States and China. NuclearThreatInitiative.org, "Military Maritime Consultative Agreement (MMCA): Summary." *http://nuclearthreatinitiative.org/db/china/mmcaorg.htm.*

67. Shirley A. Kan, *US-China Military Contacts: Issues for Congress* (Washington, D.C.: Congressional Research Service, April 2009), p. 54.

68. US-China Economic and Security Review Commission, *Hearing on China's Military and Security Activities Abroad*, testimony of David Sedney, March 4, 2009.

69. US-China Economic and Security Review Commission, *Hearing on China's Military and Security Activities Abroad*, testimony of Eric A. McVadon, March 4, 2009.

70. US-China Economic and Security Review Commission, *Hearing on China's Military and Security Activities Abroad*, testimony of David S. Sedney, March 4, 2009.

71. Information Office of the State Council, *China's National Defence in 2008* (Beijing: January 2009). It is unclear from the white paper what time frame these events occurred within.

72. Office of the Secretary of Defence, *Annual Report to Congress: Military Power of the People's Republic of China, 2009* (Washington, D.C.: US Department of Defence, 2009), p. 54.

73. Office of the Secretary of Defence, *Annual Report to Congress: Military Power of the People's Republic of China, 2009* (Washington, D.C.. US Department of Defence, 2009), p. 54.

74. US-China Economic and Security Review Commission, *Hearing on China's Military and Security Activities Abroad*, testimony of David S. Sedney, March 4, 2009.

75. Information Office of the State Council, *China's National Defence in 2004* (Beijing: December 2004); Information Office of the State Council, *China's National Defence in 2006* (Beijing: December 2006); and Information Office of the State Council, *China's National Defence in 2008* (Beijing: January 2009).

76. Information Office of the State Council, *China's National Defence in 2008* (Beijing: January 2009); *PLA Daily, "Zhongguo Haijun 'Guangzhou' Chuan Dida Kelunpo Gang Buji"* (The Chinese Navy Vessel 'Guangzhou' Arrives at the Port of Colombo to Resupply), March 2, 2009. *http://www.chinamil.com.cn/site1/xwpdxw/ 2009-03/02/content_1670754.htm.* Xia Hongping and Hou Yaming, "Chinese Naval Ship Formation Visits Pakistan," *Jiefangjun Bao*, August 6, 2009. OSC ID: CPP20090806702015; Xinhua, "*Wo Haijun Huhang Junjian Shouci Tingkao Waigang Buji Shenghuo Yongpin"* (Our Navy Escort Vessels for the First Time Stopped in a Foreign Port to Supply up with Daily Use Items), CCTV, February 24, 2009. *http://news.cctv.com/china/20090224/111361.shtml; PLA Daily, "Zhongguo Haijun 'Weishanhu' Jian Yemen Yading Gang Kaogang Buji"* (The Chinese Naval Vessel 'Weishanhu' Makes a Port Call to the Port of Aden, Yemen, for Supplies), April 27, 2009. *http://www.chinanews.com.cn/gn/news/2009/04-27/1664503.shtml.*

77. US-China Economic and Security Review Commission, *Hearing on China's Military and Security Activities Abroad*, testimony of Michael R. Auslin, March 4, 2009.

78. Xinhua, "China's Naval Vessels Wrap up Four-Nation Goodwill Visit," September 25, 2007. *http://news.xinhuanet.com/english/2007–09/25/content_6791785 .htm.*

79. Xinhua, "*Wo Haijun Huhang Junjian Shouci Tingkao Waigang Buji Shenghuo Yongpin*" (Our Navy Escort Vessels for the First Time Stopped in a Foreign Port to Supply up with Daily Use Items), CCTV, February 24, 2009. *http:// news.cctv.com/china/20090224/111361.shtml;* and *PLA Daily*, "*Zhongguo Haijun 'Weishanhu' Jian Yemen Yading Gang Kaogang Buji*" (The Chinese Naval Vessel 'Weishanhu' Makes a Port Call to the Port of Aden, Yemen, for Supplies), April 27, 2009. *http://www.chinanews.com.cn/gn/news/2009 04–27/1664503.shtml.*

80. Information Office of the State Council, *China's National Defence in 2008* (Beijing: January 2009); *PLA Daily*, "*Zhongguo Haijun 'Guangzhou' Chuan Dida Kelunpo Gang Buji*" (The Chinese Navy Vessel 'Guangzhou' Arrived at the Port of Colombo to Resupply), March 2, 2009. *http://www.chinamil.com.cn/site1/xwpdxw/ 2009–03/02/content_1670754.htm;* Xia Hongping and Hou Yaming, "Chinese Naval Ship Formation Visits Pakistan," *Jiefangjun Bao*, August 6, 2009. OSC ID: CPP20090806702015; Xinhua, "*Wo Haijun Huhang Junjian Shouci Tingkao Waigang Buji Shenghuo Yongpin*" (Our Navy Escort Vessels for the First Time Stopped in a Foreign Port to Supply up with Daily Use Items), CCTV, February 24, 2009. *http://news.cctv.com/china/20090224/111361.shtml;* and *Jiefangjun Bao*, "*Zhongguo Haijun 'Weishanhu' Jian Yemen Yading Gang Kaogang Buji*" (The Chinese Naval Vessel 'Weishanhu' Makes a Port Call to the Port of Aden, Yemen, for Supplies). April 27, 2009. *http://www.chinanews.com.cn/gn/news/2009/04–27/1664503.shtml.*

81. US Navy, "About the Seventh Fleet," Seventh Fleet official Web site. *http://www.c7f.navy.mil/about.htm.*

82. See, for example, "Chinese Warship Makes Historic Visit to Japan," Associated Press, November 27, 2007. *http://www.msnbc.msn.com/id/21999001/;* Chinese embassy in Indonesia, "Chinese Navy Ships to Visit Indonesia." *http://www.mfa.gov.cn/ce/ceindo/eng/xwdt/t305880.htm;* Xinhua, "Two Chinese Naval Ships Leave for Russia, Britain, Spain, France," ed. Du Xiaodan, July 24, 2007. *http://www.cctv.com/english/20070724/110448.shtml;* Xinhua, "Chinese Navy Task Force Back from Visits to Australia, New Zealand," November 4, 2007. *http://english.people. com.cn/90001/90776/90883/6296081.html.* Xinhua, "Chinese Military Makes First Ever Visit to Cambodia," November 5, 2008. *http://news.xinhuanet.com/English/2008–11/05/content_10312833.htm.* Xinhua, "Chinese Navy Ship Makes First Visit to Thailand," November 11, 2008. *http://www.chinadaily.com.cn/china/2008- 11/11/content_7193310.htm;* Xinhua, "Chinese Naval Ship Visits Vietnam," November 19, 2008. *http://www.cctv.com/english/20081119/100866.shtml;* Xinhua, "Chinese Warships Visit Russian Port to Enhance Communication," *Chinaview*, October 15, 2008. *http://news.xinhuanet.com/english/2008–10/15/content_10200597. htm;* Xinhua, "*Wo Haijun Huhang Junjian Shouci Tingkao Waigang Buji Shenghuo Yongpin*" (Our Navy Escort Vessels for the First Time Stopped in a Foreign Port to Supply up with Daily Use Items), CCTV, February 24, 2009. *http://news.cctv.com/china/20090224/ 111361.shtml;* and *PLA Daily*, "*Zhongguo Haijun 'Weishanhu' Jian Yemen Yading Gang Kaogang Buji*" (The Chinese Naval Vessel 'Weishanhu' Makes a Port Call to the Port of Aden, Yemen, for Supplies), April 27, 2009. *http://www.chinanews. com.cn/gn/news/2009/04–27/1664503.shtml.*

83. BBC, "Chinese ships 'harass' US vessel," March 9, 2009. *http://news.bbc. co.uk/2/hi/asia-pacific/7933171.stm.*

84. Tony Capaccio, "US Destroyer Escorts Surveillance Ship in South China Sea," Bloomberg, March 13, 2009. *http://www.bloomberg.com/apps news? pid = 20601081&sid = amIroy SaKn 24 &refer=australia#.*

85. Jim Garamone, "Chinese Vessels Shadow, Harass Unarmed US Survey Ship," *American Forces Press Service*, March 9, 2009. *http://www.defencelink.mil/ news/ newsarticle.aspx?id=53401;* and BBC, "Chinese ships 'harass' US vessel," March 9, 2009. *http://news.bbc.co.uk/2/hi/asia-pacific/7933171.stm.* It is unclear from open source reporting whether the Chinese aircraft belonged to the PLA or civilian government agencies.

86. US-China Economic and Security Review Commission, *Hearing on the Implications of China's Naval Modernization for the United States*, written testimony of John W. Warner, June 11, 2009. Senator Warner also served as secretary of the Navy from 1972 to 1974.

87. Jim Garamone, "US Will Continue to Sail in International Waters, Official Says," *American Forces Press Service*, March 10, 2009. *http://www.defencelink.mil/ news/ newsarticle.aspx?id=53421.* It is likely that the fishing vessels in question were part of China's maritime militia. See Lyle Goldstein, "Strategic Implications of Chinese Fisheries Development," *China Brief* 9:16 (August 5, 2009): 12; and Hiroshi Yuasa, "Japan: China's Tactics, Intentions in South China Sea 'Skirmish' With US Navy," *Sankei Shimbun*, March 18, 2009. OSC ID: JPP20090318044001. *http:// www.opensource.gov.*

88. According to Lyle Goldstein, director of the US Naval War College's China Maritime Studies Institute, the Chinese fishing vessels can be considered part of the maritime militia. Lyle Goldstein, "Strategic Implications of Chinese Fisheries Development," *China Brief* 9:16 (August 5, 2009):12.

89. Li Yun, "*Daxing Haishang Lianhe Shibing Yanlian Zai Lu"shun Juxing*" (Large-scale, Joint, Live Training Exercise at Sea Held at Lushun), Xinhua, September 3, 2008. OSC ID: CPP20080903004006. *http://www.opensource.gov.s*

90. US-China Economic and Security Review Commission, *Hearing on the Implications of China's Naval Modernization for the United States*, written testimony of Jim Webb, June 11, 2009. Senator Webb served as secretary of the Navy from 1987 to 1988.

91. The US-China Economic and Security Review Commission, *2008 Annual Report to Congress* (Washington, DC: 2008), p. 267. *http://www.uscc.gov/annual_report/ 2008/ chapter4_section_2/part2.pdf.* For a more complete discussion, see chapter 2, section 2, "China's Views on Sovereignty and Methods of Controlling Access to its Territory," of the Commission's *2008 Annual Report to Congress.*

92. US-China Economic and Security Review Commission, *Hearing on China's Military and Security Activities Abroad*, written testimony of David S. Sedney, March 4, 2009.

93. Office of the Secretary of Defence, *Annual Report to Congress: Military Power of the People's Republic of China, 2009* (Washington, D.C.: US Department of Defence, 2009), p. I.

94. US-China Economic and Security Review Commission, *Hearing on China's Military and Security Activities Abroad*, testimony of John J. Norris Jr., March 4, 2009.

95. US-China Economic and Security Review Commission, *Hearing on China's Military and Security Activities Abroad*, written testimony of John J. Norris Jr., March 4, 2009.

96. US-China Economic and Security Review Commission. *Hearing on China's Military and Security Activities Abroad*, written testimony of Eric A. McVadon, March 4, 2009.

97. US-China Economic and Security Review Commission, *Hearing on China's Military and Security Activities Abroad*, testimony of John J. Norris Jr., March 4, 2009.

98. US-China Economic and Security Review Commission, *Hearing on China's Military and Security Activities Abroad*, written testimony of David S. Sedney, March 4, 2009.

99. Office of the Secretary of Defence, *Annual Report to Congress: Military Power of the People's Republic of China, 2009* (Washington, D.C.: US Department of Defence, 2009), p. I.

100. US-China Economic and Security Review Commission, *Hearing on the Implications of China's Naval Modernization for the United States*, testimony of Frederic Vellucci Jr., June 11, 2009

101. US-China Economic and Security Review Commission, *Hearing on China's Military and Security Activities Abroad*, testimony of Bernard D. Cole, March 4, 2009.

102. US-China Economic and Security Review Commission, *Hearing on the Implications of China's Naval Modernization for the United States*, testimony of John W. Warner, June 11, 2009.

103. David F. Winkler, *Cold War at Sea* (Annapolis, MD: Naval Institute Press, 2000), p. 7.

104. David F. Winkler, *Cold War at Sea* (Annapolis, MD: Naval Institute Press, 2000), pp. 172–73.

105. US-China Economic and Security Review Commission, *Hearing on the Implications of China's Naval Modernization for the United States*, testimony of John W. Warner, June 11, 2009.

106. Shirley A. Kan, *US-China Military Contacts: Issues for Congress* (Washington, D.C.: Congressional Research Service, April 6, 2009), p. 18.

107. US-China Economic and Security Review Commission, *Hearing on the Implications of China's Naval Modernization for the United States*, testimony of John W. Warner, June 11, 2009.

108. Julian Schofield, "The Prospects for a Sino-American Incidents at Sea Agreement," *The Korean Journal of Defence Analysis* XI: no. 1 (Summer 1999): 93. *http://www.kida.re.kr/data/2006/04/13/FF407021Y_004.pdf.*

109. US-China Economic and Security Review Commission, *Hearing on China's Military and Security Activities Abroad*, testimony of David S. Sedney, March 4, 2009.

110. Jim Nichol, *Uzbekistan's Closure of the Airbase at Karshi-Khanabad: Context and Implications* (Washington, D.C.: Congressional Research Service, October 7, 2005), p. 3. *https://www.policyarchive.org/bitstream/handle/10207/4245/RS22295_20051007.pdf? sequence=1.*

111. US-China Economic and Security Review Commission, *Hearing on China's Military and Security Activities Abroad*, testimony of Chin-hao Huang, March 4, 2009.

112. US-China Economic and Security Review Commission, *Hearing on China's Military and Security Activities Abroad*, testimony of John J. Norris Jr., March 4, 2009.

113. Su Shiliang, "Persistently Follow the Guidance of Chairman Hu's Important Thought on the Navy's Building, Greatly Push Forward Innovation and Development in the

Navy's Military Work," *Renmin Haijun*, June 6, 2009, p. 3. OSC ID: CPP2009 0716478009. *http://www.opensource.gov*.

114. Eric C. Anderson and Jeffrey G. Engstrom, *Capabilities of the Chinese People's Liberation Army to Carry out Military Action in the Event of a Regional Military Conflict* (McLean, VA: Science Applications International Corporation, March 2009), p. 30; and US-China Economic and Security Review Commission, *Hearing on the Implications of China's Naval Modernization for the United States*, testimony of Cortez A. Cooper, June 11, 2009.

115. Eric C. Anderson and Jeffrey G. Engstrom, *Capabilities of the Chinese People's Liberation Army to Carry out Military Action in the Event of a Regional Military Conflict* (McLean, VA: Science Applications International Corporation, March 2009), p. 30.

116. Nancy Bernkopf Tucker, "China's Relations with the West: The Role of Taiwan and Hong Kong" (Philadelphia, PA: Foreign Policy Research Institute, May 2008), cited in Eric C. Anderson and Jeffrey G. Engstrom, *Capabilities of the Chinese People's Liberation Army to Carry out Military Action in the Event of a Regional Military Conflict* (McLean, VA: Science Applications International Corporation, March 2009), p. 30.

117. War Theories and Strategic Studies Department, *"Guojia Anquan Zhanlue Lun"* (Theory of National Security Strategy), ed. Ge Dongsheng (Beijing: Military Science Publishing, 2006), p. 223. The War Theories and Strategic Studies Department is a department within the PLA's premier military think tank, the Academy of Military Science.

118. US-China Economic and Security Review Commission, *Hearing on the Implications of China's Naval Modernization for the United States*, testimony of Michael McDevitt, June 11, 2009; US-China Economic and Security Review Commission, *Hearing on the Implications of China's Naval Modernization for the United States*, testimony of Cortez A. Cooper, June 11, 2009; US-China Economic and Security Review Commission, *Hearing on the Implications of China's Naval Modernization for the United States*, testimony of Paul S. Giarra, June 11, 2009; .US- China Economic and Security Review Commission, *Hearing on the Implications of China's Naval Modernization for the United States*, testimony of Ronald O'Rourke June 11, 2009; and US-China Economic and Security Review Commission, *Hearing on the Implications of China's Naval Modernization for the United States*, testimony of Richard D. Fisher Jr., June 11, 2009.

119. US-China Economic and Security Review Commission, *Hearing on the Implications of China's Naval Modernization for the United States*, testimony of Cortez A. Cooper, June 11, 2009.

120. US-China Economic and Security Review Commission, *Hearing on the Implications of China's Naval Modernization for the United States*, testimony of Paul S. Giarra, June 11, 2009.

121. Eric C. Anderson and Jeffrey G. Engstrom, "Capabilities of the Chinese People's Liberation Army to Carry out Military Action in the Event of a Regional Military Conflict" (McLean, VA: Science Applications International Corporation, March 2009), p. 31. On July 20, 2009, Lieutenant General Ma was promoted to a full general. Cao Zhi, *"Zhongyang Jinsheng Ma Xiaotian, Liu Yuan, Zhang Haiyang wei Shangjiang"* (Central Military Commission Promotes Ma Xiaotian, Liu Yuan, and Zhang Haiyang to General), Xinhua, July 21, 2009. *http://news.163.com/09/0721/05/ 5ENK02SD0001124J.html*.

122. Information Office of the State Council, *China's National Defence in 2008* (Beijing: January 2009). Chinese defence white papers are officially published documents that express the Chinese government's view on matters related to China's national security. Since 1998, Beijing has published a defence white paper every two years.

123. According to the 2002, 2004, and 2008 defence white papers, China's maritime security is a key responsibility of the PLA Navy. Information Office of the State Council, *China's National Defence in 2002* (Beijing: December 2002) Information Office of the State Council, *China's National Defence in 2004* (Beijing: December 2004); and Information Office of the State Council, *China's National Defence in 2008* (Beijing: January 2009). Naval missions were not discussed in the 2006 defence white paper.

124. Hu Jintao, "*Renqing Xinshiji Xinjieduan Wojun Lishi Shiming*" (See Clearly Our Military's Historic Missions in the New Period of the New Century) (speech given to China's Central Military Commission, Beijing, December 24, 2004). *http://gfjy.jiangxi.gov.cn/htmnew/11349.htm.*

125. War Theories and Strategic Studies Department, *"Guojia Anquan Zhanlue Lun"* (Theory of National Security Strategy), ed. Ge Dongsheng (Beijing: Military Science Publishing, 2006), pp. 227–28.

126. Quoted in Wang Shicheng, "*Guanyu 'Dazao Shandong Bandao Lanse Jingji Qu'de Sikao*" (Reflections Concerning "Forging a Blue Economic Area on the Shandong Peninsula), Web site of the Weifang Coastal Economic Development Information Network, June 25, 2009. *http://www.wfyh.gov.cn/html/2009–7/20090714 162943.htm.*

127. Su Shiliang, "Persistently Follow the Guidance of Chairman Hu's Important Thought on the Navy's Building, Greatly Push Forward Innovation and Development in the Navy's Military Work," *Renmin Haijun,* June 6, 2009, p. 3. OSC ID: CPP20090716478009. *http://www.opensource.gov.* The author of this piece is the PLA Navy chief of staff and a vice admiral.

128. US-China Economic and Security Review Commission, *The Implications of China's Naval Modernization for the United States*, written testimony of Cortez A. Cooper, June 11, 2009.

129. National Bureau of Statistics of China, "2–15, Gross Regional Product (2007)," *China Statistical Yearbook: 2008* (Beijing: China Statistics Press, 2008). *http://www.stats.gov.cn/tjsj/ndsj/2008/indexeh.htm.* The provinces and provinciall evel municipalities used in this calculation include Beijing, Fujian, Guangdong, Hainan, Hebei, Jiangsu, Liaoning, Shandong, Shanghai, Tianjin, and Zhejiang. Beijing is included due to its proximity to the coast.

130. National Bureau of Statistics of China, "10–3, Main Social and Economic Indicators of Provincial Capitals and Cities Specially Designated in the State Plan (2007)," *China Statistical Yearbook: 2008* (Beijing: China Statistics Press, 2008). *http://www.stats.gov.cn/tjsj/ndsj/2008/indexeh.htm.* Beijing is included due to its proximity to the coast. The two noncoastal cities are Hohhut (Inner Mongolia Province) and Wuhan (Hubei Province).

131. Yao Wenhaui, "*Jianshe Qiangda Haijun, Weihu Woguo Haiyang Zhanlue Liyi*"(Build a Powerful Navy, Safeguard China's Maritime Strategic Interests), *Guofang* 7 (2007): 6. Rear Admiral Yao is the deputy director of the PLA Navy's Political Department.

132. Hu Jintao, "*Renqing Xinshiji Xinjieduan Wojun Lishi Shiming*" (See Clearly Our Military's Historic Missions in the New Period of the New Century) (speech given to China's Central Military Commission, Beijing, December 24, 2004). *http://gfjy.jiangxi.gov.cn/htmnew/11349.htm.* This area includes Beijing's definition of its exclusive economic zone.

133. Bernard D. Cole, *The Great Wall at Sea: China's Navy Enters the Twenty- First Century* (Annapolis. MD: Naval Institute Press, 2001), pp. 37–38. According to the United Nations (UN) Convention on the Law of the Sea, whoever has jurisdiction over islands such as these also enjoys exclusive economic rights of the surrounding area out to 200 nautical miles. United Nations, *Convention on the Law of the Sea*, part V, articles 56–57 (New York: December 10, 1982). *http://www.un.org/ Depts/ los/convention_*agreements/*texts/unclos/UNCLOS–TOC.htm.*

134. Hu Jintao, "*Renqing Xinshiji Xinjieduan Wojun Lishi Shiming*" (See Clearly Our Military's Historic Missions in the New Period of the New Century) (speech given to China's Central Military Commission. Beijing, December 24, 2004). *http:// gfjy.jiangxi.gov.cn/htmnew/11349.htm.*

135. Quoted in Wang Shicheng, "*Guanyu 'Dazao Shandong Bandao Lanse Jingji Qu'de Sikao*" (Reflections Concerning "Forging a Blue Economic Area on the Shandong Peninsula"), Web site of the Weifang Coastal Economic Development Information Network, June 25, 2009. *http://www.wfyh.gov.cn/html/2009–7/200907141 62943.htm.*

136. China Ministry of Land and Resources, "*Quanguo Haiyang Xitong Renzhen Xuexi Li Keqiang Fuzongli Zhongyao Zhishi Jingshen*" (The Entire Ocean System Seriously Studies Implementing the Spirit of Vice Premier Li Keqiang's Important Instructions), *Zhongguo Guotu Ziyuan Bao* (February 17, 2009). *http://www.mlr.gov.cn/xwdt/jrxw/ 200902/t20090217_114826.htm.*

137. Hu Jintao, "*Renqing Xinshiji Xinjieduan Wojun Lishi Shiming*" (See Clearly Our Military's Historic Missions in the New Period of the New Century) (speech given to China's Central Military Commission, Beijing, December 24, 2004). *http:// gfjy.jiangxi.gov.cn/htmnew/11349.htm.*

138. Quoted in Wang Shicheng, "*Guanyu 'Dazao Shandong Bandao Lanse Jingji Qu'de Sikao*" (Reflections Concerning "Forging a Blue Economic Area on the Shandong Peninsula"), Web site of the Weifang Coastal Economic Development Information Network, June 25, 2009. *http://www.wfyh.gov.cn/html/2009–7/200907141 62943.htm*

139. Information Office of the State Council, *China's National Defence in 2008* (Beijing: January 2009).

140. US-China Economic and Security Review Commission, *Hearing on the Implications of China's Naval Modernization for the United States*, testimony of Frederic Vellucci Jr., June 11, 2009.

141. Representatives from China's National Defence University, Beijing, China, meeting with US-China Economic and Security Review Commission, May 5, 2009.

142. Maritime Sea Lane Security Study Group, "*Haishang Tongdao Anquan yuGuoji Hezuo*" (Sea Lane Security and International Cooperation) (Beijing: Shishi Publishing, 2005), p. 7. The Maritime Sea Lane Security Study Group was a study group composed of senior leaders of the Chinese think tank China Institutes of Contemporary International Relations. Members of this group included Lu Zhongwei, then president of CICIR; Wang Zaiban, current vice president; Yang Mingjie, current vice president; and Fu Mengzhi, assistant vice president; among others. According to many western observers, CICIR is an influential think tank affiliated with the Ministry of State Security. See Michael D. Swaine, "The PLA in China's National Security Policy: Leadership, Structures, and Processes," in *China's Military in Transition*, eds. David Shambaugh and Richard H. Yang (New York: Oxford University Press, 1997), p. 123.

143. Huang Jikuan, "*Xuyou Kongji, Simian Chuqu: Zhongguo Xun You Qiandong Quanqiu Zhanlue Geju*" (Hitting out in all Directions in an Urgent Search for Oil: China's

Search for Oil is Affecting the Structure of its Global Strategy), *CNA News World* 37 (July 2006). *http://www.cnanews.gov.tw/service/magazine/cns/content_037/ 37-p62.htm;* and Pan Xiaomin, "*Jiceng Guanlizhe ye Yao you Guojihua da Shiyou Guan*" (Grassroot Managers also Desire to have an International Big-Oil Point of View), *Sinopec News*, October 14, 2005. *http://www.sinopecnews.com.cn/shzz/2005– 10/ 14/content_305396.htm.*

144. Wen Han, "Hu Jintao Urges Breakthrough in 'Malacca Dilemma,' " *Wei Wen Pao* (January 14, 2004). OSC ID: CPP20040114000049. *http://www.opensource.gov.*

145. Yao Wenhaui, "*Jianshe Qiangda Haijun, Weihu Woguo Haiyang Zhanlue Liyi*"(Build a Powerful Navy, Safeguard China's Maritime Strategic Interests), *Guofang* 7 (2007): 6.

146. Andrew Erickson and Lyle Goldstein, "Gunboats for China's new 'Grand Canals," *Naval War College Review* 62, no. 2 (2009): 55; and Maritime Sea Lane Security Study Group, "*Haishang Tongdao Anquan yu Guoji Hezuo*"(Sea Lane Security and International Cooperation) (Beijing: Shishi Publishing, 2005), p. 80.

147. US-China Economic and Security Review Commission *The Implications of China's Naval Modernization for the United States*, written testimony of Paul S. Giarra, June 11, 2009.

148. Gabriel B. Collins and William S. Murray, "No Oil for the Lamps of China?" *Naval War College Review* 61, no. 2 (2008): 80.

149. Gabriel B. Collins and William S. Murray, "No Oil for the Lamps of China?" *Naval War College Review* 61, no. 2 (2008): 79–95.

150. US-China Economic and Security Review Commission, *Hearing on the Implications of China's Naval Modernization for the United States*, written testimony of Paul S. Giarra, June 11, 2009.

151. US-China Economic and Security Review Commission, *Hearing on the Implications of China's Naval Modernization for the United States*, written testimony of Cortez A. Cooper, June 11, 2009.

152. Information Office of the State Council, *China's National Defence in 2004* (Beijing: December 2004); Information Office of the State Council, *China's National Defence in 2006* (Beijing: December, 2006); and Information Office of the State Council, *China's National Defence in 2008* (Beijing: January 2009).

153. US-China Economic and Security Review Commission, *Hearing on the Implications of China's Naval Modernization for the United States*, testimony of Peter A. Dutton, June 11, 2009.

154. Andrew Erickson and Michael Chase, "China's SSBN Forces: Transitioning to the Next Generation," *China Brief* 9, no. 12 (June 12, 2009): 10–11. Dr. Erickson is an associate professor at the China Maritime Studies Institute, US Naval War College; Dr. Chase is an assistant professor in the Strategy and Policy Department, US Naval War College.

155. Liu Xiang and Zhang Xinxin, "Calls for Raising the Capability of Performing Open Ocean Missions from a New Starting Point," *Renmin Haijun*, May 29, 2009, p. 1. OSC ID: CPP20090702318002. *http://www.opensource.gov.*

156. David M. Finkelstein, "China's National Military Strategy: An Overview of the Military Strategic Guidelines," in *Right-Sizing the People's Liberation Army: Exploring the Contours of China's Military*, eds. Roy Kamphausen and Andrew Scobell (Carlisle, PA: Strategic Studies Institute, 2007), pp. 70–73.

157. *Jiefangjun Bao*, "A New Voyage towards Scientific Development," April 18, 2009. OSC ID: CPP20090420701001. *http://www.opensource.gov*. This article is an interview with the commander of the PLA Navy, Admiral Wu Shengli.

158. US-China Economic and Security Review Commission, *Hearing on the Implications of China's Naval Modernization for the United States*, testimony of Michael McDevitt, June 11, 2009.

159. US-China Economic and Security Review Commission, *Hearing on the Implications of China's Naval Modernization for the United States*, testimony of Cortez A. Cooper, June 11, 2009.

160. William S. Murray, "An Overview of the PLAN Submarine Force," in *China's Future Nuclear Submarine Force*, eds. Andrew S. Erickson et al. (Annapolis, MD: Naval Institute Press, 2007), p. 65.

161. US-China Economic and Security Review Commission, *Hearing on the Implications of China's Naval Modernization for the United States*, testimony of Ronald O'Rourke, June 11, 2009.

162. US-China Economic and Security Review Commission, *Hearing on the Implications of China's Naval Modernization for the United States*, testimony of Michael McDevitt, June 11, 2009.

163. Office of the Secretary of Defence, *Annual Report to Congress: Military Report of the People's Republic of China, 2009* (Washington, D.C.: Department of Defence, 2009), p. 48.

164. US-China Economic and Security Review Commission, *Hearing on the Implications of China's Naval Modernization for the United States*, testimony of Cortez A. Cooper, June 11, 2009.

165. Ronald O'Rourke, "China's Naval Modernization: Implications for US Navy Capabilities—Background Issues for Congress" (Washington, DC: Congressional Research Service, July 17, 2009), p. 10.

166. US-China Economic and Security Review Commission, *Hearing on the Implications of China's Naval Modernization for the United States*, written testimony of Richard D. Fischer Jr., June 11, 2009.

167. Ronald O'Rourke, "China's Naval Modernization: Implications for US Navy Capabilities—Background Issues for Congress" (Washington, DC: Congressional Research Service, July 17, 2009), p 10; and US-China Economic and Security Review Commission, *Hearing on the Implications of China's Naval Modernization for the United States*, testimony of Richard D. Fischer Jr., June 11, 2009.

168. Ronald O'Rourke, "China's Naval Modernization: Implications for US Navy Capabilities—Background Issues for Congress" (Washington, DC: Congressional Research Service, July 17, 2009), p. 12.

169. US-China Economic and Security Review Commission, *Hearing on the Implications of China's Naval Modernization for the United States*, testimony of Richard D. Fischer Jr., June 11, 2009.

170. US-China Economic and Security Review Commission, *Hearing on the Implications of China's Naval Modernization for the United States*, testimony of Cortez A. Cooper, June 11, 2009.

171. US-China Economic and Security Review Commission, *Hearing on the Implications of China's Naval Modernization for the United States*, testimony of Ronald O'Rourke, June 11, 2009.

172. Trefor Moss, "China Plans to Buy Ukrainian Hovercraft," *Jane's Defence Weekly* 46, iss. 33 (August 19, 2009): 15. According to the article, China was originally in talks with Russia to purchase 10 such vessels back in 2007, but the talks ended without a deal. This hovercraft is a Russian-Ukrainian jointly developed hovercraft. No dates for the sale were mentioned in the article.

173. Andrew S. Erickson, Lyle J. Goldstein, and William S. Murray, "Chinese Mine Warfare: A PLA Navy 'Assassin's Mace' Capability," *China Maritime Studies* 3 (June 2009): 2.

174. US-China Economic and Security Review Commission, *Hearing on the Implication of China's Naval Modernization for the United States*, testimony of Richard D. Fischer Jr., June 11, 2009.

175. *Jiefangjun Bao*, "A New Voyage Toward Scientific Development," April 18, 2009. OSC ID: CPP20090420701001. *http://www.opensource.gov.* This article is an interview with the commander of the PLA Navy, Admiral Wu Shengli.

176. Office of the Secretary of Defence, *Annual Report to Congress: Military Power of the People's Republic of China, 2009* (Washington, D.C.: US Department of Defence, 2009), p. 49.

177. US-China Economic and Security Review Commission, *Hearing on the Implications of China's Naval Modernization for the United States*, testimony of Richard D. Fischer Jr., June 11, 2009; and US-China Economic and Security Review Commission, *Hearing on the Implications of China's Naval Modernization for the United States*, testimony of Ronald O'Rourke, June 11, 2009. China currently does have one decommissioned aircraft carrier, which it bought from Ukraine in 1998.

178. Government of Japan, Ministry of Defence, *Defence of Japan 2009* (tentative translation) (Tokyo: 2009), p. 31. *http://www.mod.go.jp/e/publ/w_paper/pdf/2009/Part1 -chap2.pdf.*

179. Associated Press, "PLA Close to Getting Aircraft Carrier," *Taipei Times*, April 22, 2009, p. 5. *http://www.taipeitimes.com/News/world/archives/2009/04/22/2003441668.*

180. *Jiefangjun Bao*, "A New Voyage towards Scientific Development," April 18, 2009. OSC ID: CPP20090420701001. *http://www.opensource.gov.* This article in the PLA's official newspaper is an interview with the commander of the PLA Navy, Admiral Wu Shengli.

181. US-China Economic and Security Review Commission, *Hearing on China's Military and Security Activities Abroad*, testimony of Michael R. Auslin, Mar 4, 2009.

182. US-China Economic and Security Review Commission, *Hearing on the Implications of China's Naval Modernization for the United States*, testimony of Richard D. Fischer Jr., June 11, 2009.

183. US-China Economic and Security Review Commission, *Hearing on the Implications of China's Naval Modernization for the United States*, testimony of Cortez A. Cooper, June 11, 2009.

184. Bernard D. Cole, "The PLA Navy's Developing Strategy," *China Brief* 6, no. 21 (October 25, 2006).

185. US-China Economic and Security Review Commission, *Hearing on the Implications of China's Naval Modernization for the United States*, testimony of Richard D. Fischer Jr., June 11, 2009.

186. US-China Economic and Security Review Commission, *Hearing on the Implications of China's Naval Modernization for the United States*, testimony of Cortez A. Cooper,

June 11, 2009; Ronald O'Rourke, "China's Naval Modernization: Implications for US Navy Capabilities—Background Issues for Congress" (Washington, DC: Congressional Research Service, July 17, 2009), p. 8; and Richard D. Fisher Jr., *China's Military Modernization: Building for Regional and Global Reach* (Westport, CT: Praeger, 2008).

187. Stephen Saunders, ed., *Jane's Fighting Ships 2008–2009* (Alexandria, VA: Jane's Information Group, 2008), p. 140.

188. Stephen Saunders, ed., *Jane's Fighting Ships 2008–2009* (Alexandria, VA:Jane's Information Group, 2008), pp. 140–41.

189. Richard D. Fisher Jr. (senior fellow for Asian Military Affairs at the International Assessment and Strategy Center), e-mail communication with Commission staff, August 27, 2009. Other sources are unclear regarding the number of H–6M. Stephen Saunders, ed., *Jane's Fighting Ships 2008–2009* (Alexandria, VA: Jane's Information Group, 2008), p. 140; and The International Institute for Strategic Studies, *The Military Balance: 2009* (London: Routledge, 2009), p. 385.

190. Eric C. Anderson and Jeffrey G. Engstrom, "Capabilities of the Chinese People's Liberation Army to Carry out Military Action in the Event of a Regional Military Conflict" (McLean, VA: Science Applications International Corporation, March 2009), p. 41.

191. According to testimony by Richard D. Fischer Jr., China's antiship ballistic missile programmes seem to operate through the Second Artillery Forces rather than the PLA Navy. The weapon is discussed here because of its potential implications for the US Navy. US-China Economic and Security Review Commission, *Hearing on the Implications of China's Naval Modernization for the United States*, testimony of Richard D. Fischer Jr., June 11, 2009.

192. Ronald O'Rourke, "China's Naval Modernization: Implications for US Navy Capabilities—Background Issues for Congress" (Washington, DC: Congressional Research Service, July 17, 2009), p. 5.

193. US-China Economic and Security Review Commission, *Hearing on the Implications of China's Naval Modernization for the United States*, testimony of Ronald O'Rourke, June 11, 2009.

194. US-China Economic and Security Review Commission, *Hearing on the Implications of China's Naval Modernization for the United States*, testimony of Cortez A. Cooper, June 11, 2009.

195. US-China Economic and Security Review Commission, *Hearing on the Implications of China's Naval Modernization for the United States*, testimony of Ronald O'Rourke, June 11, 2009.

196. Office of the Secretary of Defence, *Annual Report to Congress: Military Power of the People's Republic of China, 2009* (Washington, D.C.: US Department of Defence, 2009), p. 21.

197. Office of the Secretary of Defence, *Annual Report to Congress: Military Power of the People's Republic of China, 2009* (Washington, D.C.: US Department of Defence, 2009), p. 48. Some analysts posit that the range could actually be substantially higher, possibly reaching 12,000 kilometers. See US-China Economic and Security Review Commission, *Hearing on the Implications of China's Naval Modernization for the United States*, testimony of Cortez A. Cooper, June 11, 2009; and US-China Economic and Security Review Commission, *Hearing on the Implications of China's Naval*

Modernization for the United States, testimony of Richard D. Fisher Jr., June 11, 2009.

198. National Air and Space Intelligence Center, *Ballistic and Cruise Missile Threat* (Wright-Patterson Air Force Base, OH: April 2009), p. 23.

199. Office of the Secretary of Defence, *Annual Report to Congress: Military Power of the People's Republic of China, 2009* (Washington, D.C.: US Department of Defence, 2009), p. 48.

200. US-China Economic and Security Review Commission, *Hearing on the Implications of China's Naval Modernization for the United States*, testimony of Ronald O'Rourke, June 11, 2009.

201. US-China Economic and Security Review Commission, *Hearing on the Implications of China's Naval Modernization for the United States,* testimony of Paul S. Giarra, June 11, 2009. One possible defence against future Chinese antiship ballistic missiles may be directed energy weapons (lasers). According to a recent US Missile Defence Agency report, a prototype of this weapon, the airborne laser, is designed "to detect, track, target, and destroy ballistic missiles shortly after launch during the boost-phase." Currently, however, this missile is still in its test phase. Missile Defence Agency, "Factsheet: The Airborne Laser" (Washington, D.C.: September 16, 2009). *http://www.mda.mil/mdalink/pdf/laser.pdf.*

202. Chen Wanjun and Wu Dengfeng, "Wu Shengli Says Navy Will Gradually Create a Maritime Security Defence System," Xinhua, April 15, 2009. OSC ID: CPP20090415364004. *http://www.opensource.gov.*

203. Su Shiliang, "Persistently Follow the Guidance of Chairman Hu's Important Thought on the Navy's Building, Greatly Push Forward Innovation and Development in the Navy's Military Work," *Renmin Haijun*, June 6, 2009, p. 3. OSC ID: CPP20090716478009. *http://www.opensource.gov.*

204. US-China Economic and Security Review Commission, *Hearing on the Implications of China's Naval Modernization for the United States*, testimony of Ronald O'Rourke, June 11, 2009.

205. US-China Economic and Security Review Commission, *Hearing on the Implications of China's Naval Modernization for the United States*, written testimony of Cortez A. Cooper, June 11, 2009.

206. US-China Economic and Security Review Commission, *Hearing on the Implications of China's Naval Modernization for the United States*, written testimony of Ronald O'Rourke, June 11, 2009.

207. US-China Economic and Security Review Commission, *Hearing on the Implications of China's Naval Modernization for the United States*, written testimony of Michael McDevitt, June 11, 2009.

208. Office of the Secretary of Defence, *Annual Report to Congress: Military Power of the People's Republic of China, 2009* (Washington, D.C.: US Department of Defence, 2009), p. VII.

209. US-China Economic and Security Review Commission, *Hearing on the Implications of China's Naval Modernization for the United States*, written testimony of Cortez A. Cooper, June 11, 2009.

210. US-China Economic and Security Review Commission, *Hearing on the Implications of China's Naval Modernization for the United States*, testimony of Paul S. Giarra, June 11, 2009.

211. US-China Economic and Security Review Commission, *Hearing on the Implications of China's Naval Modernization for the United States*, testimony of Michael McDevitt, June 11, 2009.

212. Office of Naval Intelligence, *China's Navy 2007* (Suitland, MD: Office of Naval Intelligence, 2007), pp. 65–72, and 81–86.

213. US-China Economic and Security Review Commission, *Hearing on the Implications of China's Naval Modernization for the United States*, testimony of Frederic Vellucci Jr., June 11, 2009.

214. Yan Yuejin, "*Zuoqiang Renzhi Jiaoyu, Peiyang Lianhe Zuozhan Zhihui Rencai*" (Strengthening Professional Education and Developing Joint Combat Command Talent), *Renmin Haijun*, May 26, 2009, p. 4.

215. Information Office of the State Council, *China's National Defence in 2006* (Beijing: December 2006); and Information Office of the State Council, *China's National Defence in 2008* (Beijing: January 2009).

216. US-China Economic and Security Review Commission, *Hearing on the Implications of China's Naval Modernization for the United States*, testimony of Michael McDevitt, June 11, 2009.

217. Frederic Vellucci Jr., et al., *The Science of PLA Training: Analysis and Overview of PLA Training Theory* (Alexandria, VA: CNA, 2009), pp. 10–14.

218. Chen Wanjun and Wu Dengfeng, "Wu Shengli Says Naval Training Far Out At Sea Has Become the Norm," Xinhua, April 15, 2009. OSC ID: CPP200904150 74021. *http://www.opensource.gov*.

219. Information Office of the State Council, *China's National Defence in 2004* (Beijing: December 2004).

220. Information Office of the State Council, *China's National Defence in 2006* (Beijing: December 2006).

221. Information Office of the State Council, *China's National Defence in 2004* (Beijing: December 2004); Information Office of the State Council, *China's National Defence in 2006* (Beijing: December 2006); and Information Office of the State Council, *China's National Defence in 2008* (Beijing: January 2009).

222. Information Office of the State Council, *China's National Defence in 2008* (Beijing: January 2009).

223. US-China Economic and Security Review Commission, *Hearing on the Implications of China's Naval Modernization for the United States*, testimony of Richard D. Fisher Jr., June 11, 2009; and US-China Economic and Security Review Commission, *Hearing on the Implications of China's Naval Modernization for the United States*, testimony of Cortez A. Cooper, June 11, 2009.

224. Cui Xiaohuo and Peng Kuang, "Navy Chief lists Key Objectives," *China Daily*, April 16, 2009. OSC ID: CPP20090416968022. *http://opensource.gov*.

225. US-China Economic and Security Review Commission, *Hearing on the Implications of China's Naval Modernization for the United States*, testimony of Cortez A. Cooper, June 11, 2009.

226. US-China Economic and Security Review Commission, *Hearing on the Implications of China's Naval Modernization for the United States*, written testimony of Cortez A. Cooper, June 11, 2009; and US-China Economic and Security Review Commission, *Hearing on the Implications of China's Naval Modernization for the United States*, written testimony of Richard D. Fisher Jr., June 11, 2009.

227. For more information on these missions, see this Report's discussion of Hu Jintao's *Historic Missions* found in section 1 of this chapter.

228. Information Office of the State Council, *China's National Defence in 2006* (Beijing: December 2006).

229. Information Office of the State Council, *China's National Defence in 2008* (Beijing: January 2009).

230. The second island chain is a phrase to distinguish the set of islands that run in a north-south line from Japan, the Bonin (Osagawara) Islands, the Mariana Islands, and Indonesia. War Theories and Strategic Studies Department, *"Guojia Anquan Zhanlue Lun"* (Theory of National Security Strategy), ed. Ge Dongsheng (Beijing: Military Science Publishing, 2006), p. 227.

231. Michael Mullen (chairman of the Joint Chiefs of Staff), "Remarks and Q & A at the Navy League Sea-Air-Space Exposition" (National Harbor, MD, May 4, 2009). *http://www.jcs.mil/speech.aspx?ID=1178.*

232. US-China Economic and Security Review Commission, *Hearing on the Implications of China's Naval Modernization for the United States*, testimony of Michael McDevitt, June 11, 2009.

233. US-China Economic and Security Review Commission, *Hearing on the Implications of China's Naval Modernization for the United States*, testimony of Paul S. Giarra, June 11, 2009.

234. Office of the Secretary of Defence, *Annual Report to Congress: Military Power of the People's Republic of China, 2009* (Washington, D.C.: US Department of Defence, 2009), p. VII.

235. US-China Economic and Security Review Commission, *Hearing on the Implications of China's Naval Modernization for the United States*, testimony of Paul S. Giarra, June 11, 2009.

236. US-China Economic and Security Review Commission, *Hearing on the Implications of China's Naval Modernization for the United States*, written testimony of Cortez A. Cooper, June 11, 2009.

237. Eric C. Anderson and Jeffrey G. Engstrom, "Capabilities of the Chinese People's Liberation Army to Carry out Military Action in the Event of a Regional Military Conflict" (McLean, VA: Science Applications International Corporation, March 2009), pp. 48–49.

238. US-China Economic and Security Review Commission, *Hearing on the Implications of China's Naval Modernization for the United States*, testimony of Michael McDevitt, June 11, 2009.

239. US-China Economic and Security Review Commission, *Hearing on the Implications of China's Naval Modernization for the United States*, written testimony of Michael McDevitt, June 11, 2009.

240. Australian Department of Defence, *Defending Australia in the Asia Pacific Century: Force 2030* (Canberra: Commonwealth of Australia, 2009), p. 34. 241. Open Source Center, "OSC Report: Japanese Media Highlight White Paper's Concerns on China, DPRK," July 22, 2009. OSC ID: JPP20090722321002. *http:// opensource.gov.*

242. Open Source Center, "OSC Feature: Vietnam Conference on Islands Urges Action To Assert Sovereignty, Stop Possible Chinese Use of Force," March 30, 2009. OSC ID: FEA20090330839757. *http://www.opensource.gov.*

243. *The Pioneer Online*, "China Defence Modernisation Programme Alarms India," July 10, 2009. OSC ID: FEA20090710868502. *http://www.opensource.gov.*

244. Gregor Ferguson, "Australia Reveals Naval Expansion Plans," *Defence News*, May 4, 2009. *http://www.defencenews.com/story.php?i=4071788.*

245. *DefenceNews*, "Vietnam to Purchase 6 Russian Subs: Report," April 27, 2009. *http://www.defencenews.com/story.php?i=4059508&c=ASI&s=SEA;* and *Straits Times*, "Vietnam to Buy 12 Fighter Jets," May 14, 2009. *http://www.straitstimes.com/Breaking%2BNews/SE%2BAsia/Story/STIStory_376749.html.*

246. *Straits Times*, "India Builds Aircraft Carrier," February 27, 2009. *http://www.straitstimes.com/Breaking%2BNews/Asia/Story/STIStory_343449.html;* Vivek Raghuvanshi, "Russia Says Indian Frigates Will Arrive on Time," *DefenceNews*, June 29, 2009. *http://www.defencenews.com/story.php?i=4163005&c=ASI&s=SEA;* Vivek Raghuvanshi, "P–8s To Expand India's Networked Maritime Power," *DefenceNews*, January 7, 2009. *http://www.defencenews.com/story.php?i=3890225&c=ASI&s=SEA;* and Vivek Raghuvanshi, "India Launches Risat-2 Surveillance Sat," *DefenceNews*, April 20, 2009. *http://www.defencenews.com/story.php?i=4047490 &c=ASI&s=SEA.*

247. Vivek Raghuvanshi, "India's Scorpene Subs Delayed," *DefenceNews*, July 21, 2009. *http://www.defence news.com/story.php?i=4199352&c=ASI&s=SEA;* Vivek Raghuvanshi, "India Anticipates Russian Sub Delivery by Year-End," *DefenceNews*, July 10, 2009. *http://www.defencenews.com/story.php?i=4181134;* and *Defence News*, "With Launch, India Joins Nuclear Submarine World," July 26, 2009. *http://www.defence news.com/story.php?i=4205995&c=ASI&s=SEA.*

248. *Stratfor Today*, "China: The South China Sea and Submarine Warfare," June 15, 2009. *http://www.stratfor.com/analysis/20090615_china/south/sea/and_submarine_warfare.* Thomas Newdick, "South Korea Orders Six More Type 214 Submarines," *Defence News*, January 8, 2009. *http://www.defencenews.com/story.php?i=3892480&s+SEA;* and *Defence News* "Malaysia Takes Delivery of First Submarine," January 28, 2009. *http://www.defencenews.com/*story.php?i=3921838&c= ASI&s=SEA.

249. Jay Solomon, "FBI Sees Big Threat from Chinese Spies," *Wall Street Journal*, August 12, 2005.

250. House Committee on the Judiciary, *Oversight Hearing on the Federal Bureau of Investigation*, testimony of FBI Director Robert Mueller, 110th Cong., 1st sess., July 26, 2007.

251. Jeff Bliss, "China's Spying Overwhelms US Counterintelligence," Bloomberg, April 2, 2007. *http://www.bloomberg.com/apps/news?pid=20601087&sid=ab2 PiDl1q W9Q&refer=home.*

252. Office of the Director of National Intelligence (DNI), letter to the Senate Select Committee on Intelligence (SSCI), dated May 2, 2009. The letter provides responses to Member questions presented to DNI Dennis C. Blair in the course of the SSCI hearing, *Current and Projected National Security Threats to the United States*, February 5, 2009. *http://www.fas.org/irp/congress/2008_hr/020508threat-qfr.pdf.*

253. US Department of Justice press release, "More Than 145 Defendants Charged in National Export Enforcement Initiative During Past Fiscal Year," October 28, 2009. *http://www.usdoj.gov/opa/pr/2008/October/08-nsd-958.html.*

254. For a more detailed discussion of both the Russian "classical" model of espionage and the different approach traditionally employed by China, see: Interagency Operational Security [OPSEC] Support Staff, *Intelligence Threat Handbook* (2004), pp. 6–29. *http://www.fas.org/irp/threat/handbook/foreign.pdf.*

255. Paul Moore, "China's Subtle Spying," *New York Times*, September 2, 1999.

256. Paul Moore, "China's Subtle Spying," *New York Times*, September 2, 1999.

257. Paul Moore, "How China Plays the Ethnic Card," *Los Angeles Times*, June 24, 1999.

258. Paul Moore, "How China Plays the Ethnic Card," *Los Angeles Times*, June 24, 1999.

259. Interagency Operations Security (OPSEC) Support Staff, *Intelligence Threat Handbook* (2004), p. 21. *http://www.fas.org/irp/threat/handbook/front.pdf.*

260. Interagency OPSEC Support Staff, *Intelligence Threat Handbook* (2004), pp. 19–20. *http://www.fas.org/irp/threat/handbook/front.pdf*; also Howard DeVore, *China's Intelligence and Internal Security Forces* (Alexandria, VA: Jane's Information Group, 1999), p. 29.

261. US-China Economic and Security Review Commission, *Hearing on China's Propaganda and Influence Operations, Its Intelligence Activities that Target the United States, and the Resulting Impacts on US National Security*, testimony of I.C. Smith, April 30, 2009.

262. Open Source Center, "An Overview of PRC Internal Security Institutions," November 17, 2007. OSC ID: CPP20071114507001. *www.opensource.gov.*

263. Bill Gertz, "Chinese Spy Who Defected Tells All," *Washington Times*, March 19, 2009; Cable News Network (CNN), interview with Li Fengzhi, March 20, 2009, *http://www.youtube.com/watch?v=VAAL95dbORU;* and Australian Broadcasting Corporation, "China Has 'Vast, Dark, Spy Network': Defector," March 20, 2009, *http:// www.abc.net.au/news/stories/2009/03/20/2521919.htm.*

264. Howard DeVore, *China's Intelligence and Internal Security Forces* (Alexandria, VA: Jane's Information Group, 1999), p. 31.

265. Michael Pillsbury, "China's Research Institutes" (contracted research paper for the US-China Economic and Security Review Commission, October 2001). *http:// www.uscc.gov/researchpapers/2000_2003/pdfs/cri.pdf*; and Kan Chung-kuo, "Intelligence Agencies Exist in Great Numbers, Spies Are Present Everywhere; China's Major Intelligence Departments Fully Exposed," *Chien Shao* (Frontline), January 1, 2006. OSC ID: CPP20060110510011. *www.opensource.gov.*

266. Michael Pillsbury, "China's Research Institutes" (contracted research paper for the US-China Economic and Security Review Commission. October 2001). *http:// www.uscc.gov/researchpapers/2000_2003/pdfs/cri.pdf.*

267. InteragencyOPSECSupport Staff, *Intelligence Threat Handbook* (2004), p. 22. *http:/ /www.fas.org/irp/threat/handbook/front.pdf.*

268. Howard DeVore, *China's Intelligence and Internal Security Forces* (Alexandria, VA: Jane's Information Group, 1999), p. 42.

269. Nicholas Eftimiades, *Chinese Intelligence Operations* (Annapolis, MD: Naval Institute Press, 1994), p. 77; and Howard DeVore, *China's Intelligence and Internal Security Forces* (Alexandria, VA: Jane's Information Group, 1999), p. 42.

270. Nicholas Eftimiades, *Chinese Intelligence Operations* (Annapolis, MD: Naval Institute Press, 1994), pp. 30, 80; and Howard DeVore, *China's Intelligence and Internal Security Forces* (Alexandria, VA: Jane's Information Group, 1999), p. 43.

271. Michael Pillsbury, "China's Research Institutes" (contracted research paper for the US-China Economic and Security Review Commission, October 2001). *http:// www.uscc.gov/researchpapers/2000_2003/pdfs/cri.pdf.*

272. Nicholas Eftimiades, *Chinese Intelligence Operations* (Annapolis, MD: Naval Institute Press, 1994), p. 82; and Michael Pillsbury, "China's Research Institutes" (contracted research paper for the US-China Economic and Security Review Commission, October 2001). *http://www.uscc.gov/researchpapers/2000_2003/pdfs/cri.pdf.*

273. Michael Pillsbury, "China's Research Institutes" (contracted research paper for the US-China Economic and Security Review Commission, October 2001). *http://www.uscc.gov/researchpapers/2000_2003/pdfs/cri.pdf*; and Royal United Services Institute, "Commentary: General Xiong Guangkai's Address" (London, United Kingdom: May 9, 2008). *http://www.rusi.org/research/studies/asia/commentary/ref:C484FE18753415.*

274. Howard DeVore, *China's Intelligence and Internal Security Forces* (Alexandria, VA: Jane's Information Group, 1999), p. 46.

275. Although the Ministry of State Security is nominally subordinate to the PRC State Council, it is more properly viewed as an organ of the Communist Party. See US-China Economic and Security Review Commission, *Hearing on China's Propaganda and Influence Operations, Its Intelligence Activities that Target the United States, and the Resulting Impacts on US National Security*, testimony of I.C. Smith, April 30, 2009. Senior political control over the security apparatus (both the Ministry of State Security and the Ministry of Public Security) is exercised through the Politics and Law Committee of the CCP Politburo, headed since 2008 by Politburo Standing Committee Member Zhou Yongkang. See Alice Miller, "Xi Jinping and the Party Apparatus," *China Leadership Monitor* no. 25 (Summer 2008). *http://www.hoover.org/publications/clm/issues/20101829.html;* and Kenneth Lieberthal, *Governing China* (New York, NY: WW Norton & Company, 2004), p. 215.

276. Alice Miller, "Xi Jinping and the Party Apparatus," *China Leadership Monitor* no. 25 (Summer 2008), *http: // www.hoover.org/publications/clm/issues/ 20101829.html;* and Kenneth Lieberthal, *Governing China* (New York, NY: WW Norton & Company, 2004), p.215.

277. Alice Miller, "Xi Jinping and the Party Apparatus," *China Leadership Monitor* no. 25 (Summer 2008). *http://www.hoover.org/publications/clm/issues/20101829.html.*

278. Alice Miller, "Xi Jinping and the Party Apparatus," *China Leadership Monitor* no. 25 (Summer 2008). *http://www.hoover.org/publications/clm/issues/20101829.html.*

279. Chinese Academy of Sciences, "Mission Statement." *http://english.cas.cn/ eng2003/page/about.htm;* and Chinese Academy of Sciences, "CAS Institutes." *http://english.cas.cn/eng2003/dmk01a/institutes.asp.*

280. James Mulvenon and Rebecca Samm Tyroler-Cooper, "China's Defence Industry on the Path of Reform" (contracted research report performed for the US- China Economic & Security Review Commission, June 2009).

281. For two sources, see Howard DeVore, *China's Intelligence and Internal Security Forces* (Alexandria, VA: Jane's Information Group, 1999), p. 48; and Nicholas Eftimiades, *Chinese Intelligence Operations* (Annapolis, MD: Naval Institute Press, 1994), p. 46. A figure of 20,000 personnel is provided by Mr. DeVore. A figure of 130,000 is provided in Kan Chung-kuo, "Intelligence Agencies Exist in Great Numbers, Spies Are Present Everywhere; China's Major Intelligence Departments Fully Exposed," "*Chien Shao*" (Frontline), January 1, 2006. OSC ID: CPP20060110510011. *www.open source.gov.*

282. James Mulvenon, "PLA Computer Network Operations: Scenarios, Doctrine, Organizations, and Capability," in *Beyond the Strait: PLA Missions Other Than*

Taiwan, eds. Roy Kamphausen, David Lai, and Andrew Scobell (Carlisle, PA: US Army War College, 2009), pp. 272–274.

283. Interagency OPSEC Support Staff, *Intelligence Threat Handbook* (2004), p. 19. *http://www.fas.org/irp/threat/handbook/front.pdf.*

284. Howard DeVore, *China's Intelligence and Internal Security Forces* (Alexandria, VA: Jane's Information Group, 1999), p. 50; and Interagency OPSEC Support Staff. *Intelligence Threat Handbook* (2004), p. 23. *http://www.fas.org/irp/threat/handbook/front.pdf.*

285. Howard DeVore, *China's Intelligence and Internal Security Forces* (Alexandria, VA: Jane's Information Group, 1999), pp. 50–52.

286. Interagency OPSEC Support Staff, *Intelligence Threat Handbook* (2004), p. 23. *http://www.fas.org/irp/threat/handbook/front.pdf.*

287. Office of the Director of National Intelligence (DNI), letter to the Senate Select Committee on Intelligence (SSCI), dated May 2, 2009. The letter provides responses to Member questions presented to DNI Dennis C. Blair in the course of the SSCI hearing, *Current and Projected National Security Threats to the United States*, February 5, 2009. *http://www.fas.org/irp/congress/2008*_hr/*020508threat-qfr.pdf.*

288. See, respectively: Kan Chung-kuo, "Intelligence Agencies Exist in Great Numbers, Spies Are Present Everywhere; China's Major Intelligence Departments Fully Exposed," "*Chien Shao*" (Frontline), January 1, 2006. OSC ID: CPP2006 0110510011. *www.opensource.gov;* and David Shambaugh, "China's Quiet Diplomacy: The International Department of the Chinese Communist Party," *China: An International Journal* 5:1 (March 2007).

289. Anne-Marie Brady, *Marketing Dictatorship: Propaganda and Thought Work in Contemporary China* (Lanham, MD: Rowman & Littlefield, 2008), p. 36; and *The Tiananmen Papers*, eds. Andrew Nathan and Perry Link (Public Affairs Books, 2001), pp. 20, 453.

290. Strategic Forecasting, Inc. (STRATFOR), "China: Cybersecurity and Mosaic Intelligence" (Austin, TX: August 6, 2008).

291. US-China Economic and Security Review Commission, *Hearing on China's Propaganda and Influence Operations, Its Intelligence Activities that Target the United States, and the Resulting Impacts on US National Security*, testimony of I.C. Smith, April 30, 2009.

292. Interagency OPSEC Support Staff, *Intelligence Threat Handbook* (2004), p. 22. *http://www.fas.org/irp/threat/handbook/front.pdf.*

293. Interagency Operational Security [OPSEC] Support Staff, *Intelligence Threat Handbook* (2004), pp. 6–8. *http://www.fas.org/irp/threat/handbook/front.pdf; http:// www.fas.org/irp/threat/handbook/front.pdf;* and *http://www.fas.org/irp/threat/handbook/ supplement.pdf.*

294. Central Intelligence Agency and Federal Bureau of Investigation, *Report to Congress on Chinese Espionage Activities Against the United States* (Washington. DC: January 2000). Document declassified January 2006. *http://www.foia.cia.gov.*

295. Interagency OPSEC Support Staff, *Intelligence Threat Handbook* (2004), p. 22. *http://www.fas.org/irp/threat/handbook/front.pdf.*

296. Central Intelligence Agency and Federal Bureau of Investigation, *Report to Congress on Chinese Espionage Activities Against the United States* (Washington, DC: January 2000). Document declassified January 2006. *http://www.foia.cia.gov.*

297. Unless otherwise noted, all cited information about the Chi Mak case in this section was obtained from the affidavit for the criminal complaint against Chi Mak, filed in the US Court for the Central District of California, October 2005. *http:// cicentre.com/ Documents/Mak\Affidavit\Oct_2005.pdf.*

298. The Centre for Counterintelligence and Security Studies, "Counterintelligence/ Espionage/Spy Case: Chi Mak" (Alexandria, VA). *http://www.cicentre .com/ Documents/ DOC_Chi_Mak.html.*

299. Joby Warrick and Carrie Johnson, "Chinese Spy 'Slept' in US for 2 Decades," *Washington Post*, April 3, 2008.

300. Unless otherwise noted, cited information about the Kuo/Bergersen case in this section was obtained from the affidavit for the criminal complaint against Tai Shen Kuo, Gregg William Bergersen, and Yu Xin Kang filed in the US Court for the Eastern District of Virginia, February 6, 2008.

301. Members of a Commission delegation to Taiwan in August 2007 received a briefing on "*Po Sheng*" from officials of Taiwan's Ministry of Defence. For further information, see U.S–China Economic and Security Review Commission, *2007 Annual Report to Congress* (Washington, DC: November 2007), p. 219.

302. Bob Burton, *Top Secret: The Dictionary of Espionage and Intelligence* (Richmond, Australia: Citadel Press, 2005), pp. 71–72.

303. Unless otherwise noted, cited information about the Kuo/Fondren case in this section was obtained from the affidavit for the criminal complaint against James Fondren. filed in the US Court for the Eastern District of Virginia, May 11, 2009.

304. US Department of Justice press release, "Jury Convicts Defence Department Official of Unlawful Communication of Classified Information and Making False Statements," September 25, 2009. *http://washingtondc.fbi.gov/dojpressrel/press rel09/ wfo092509.htm.*

305. For discussion of the Russian "classical" model of espionage, see Interagency Operational Security [OPSEC] Support Staff, *Intelligence Threat Handbook* (2004), pp. 6–17. *http://www.fas.org/irp/threat/handbook/foreign.pd*

306. US Department of Justice press release, "Former Defence Department Official Sentenced to 57 Months in Prison for Espionage Violation," July 11, 2008. *http:// cicentre.com/spycase/pr/Bergersen\pr_11JUL08.htm.*

307. US Department of Justice press release, "New Orleans Man Sentenced to More Than 15 Years in Prison for Espionage Involving China," August 8, 2008. *http:// www.usdoj.gov/usao/vae/Pressreleases/08–AugustPDFArchive/08/20080808 kuonr.html.*

308. US Department of Justice press release, "Jury Convicts Defence Department Official of Unlawful Communication of Classified Information and Making False Statements," September 25, 2009. *http://washingtondc.fbi.gov/dojpressrel/ pressrel09/ wfo092509.htm.*

309. Central Intelligence Agency and Federal Bureau of Investigation, *Report to Congress on Chinese Espionage Activities Against the United States* (Washington, DC: January 2000). Document declassified January 2006. *http://www.foia.cia.gov.*

310. House Committee on the Judiciary, Subcommittee on Immigration, Border Security, and Claims, *Hearing on Sources and Methods of Foreign Nationals Engaged in Economic and Military Espionage*, testimony of Heritage Foundation Fellow Dr. Larry Wortzel, 109th Cong., 1st sess., September 15, 2005.

311. Defence Security Service, *Targeting US Technologies: A Trend Analysis of Reporting from Defence Industry* (Alexandria, VA: 2008), p. 4.

312. Defence Security Service, *Targeting US Technologies: A Trend Analysis of Reporting from Defence Industry* (Alexandria, VA: 2008), p. 5.

313. US-China Economic and Security Review Commission, *Hearing on China's Propaganda and Influence Operations, Its Intelligence Activities that Target the United States, and the Resulting Impacts on US National Security*, testimony of James Mulvenon, April 30, 2009.

314. US-China Economic and Security Review Commission, *Hearing on China's Propaganda and Influence Operations, Its Intelligence Activities that Target the United States, and the Resulting Impacts on US National Security*, testimony of James Mulvenon, April 30, 2009.

315. Unless otherwise noted, all information regarding the Chung case was obtained from the affidavit for the criminal complaint against Dongfan "Greg" Chung, filed in the US Court for the Central District of California, February 6, 2008; and The Centre for Counterintelligence and Security Studies, "Counterintelligence/Espionage/ Spy Case: Chung, Dongfan" (Alexandria, VA). *http://cicentre.com/Documents/chung_dongfan_greg_case.html.*

316. US department of Justice press release, "Former Boeing Engineer Dongfan 'Greg' Chung Convicted of Economic Espionage in Theft of Space Shuttle Secrets for China," July 16, 2009. *http://cicentre.com/spycase/courtdoc/CHUNG*l Dongfanl*DOJ* l*Conviction* l*PR*l*16Jul09.html.*

317. Office of the Director of National Intelligence (DNI), letter to the Senate Select Committee on Intelligence (SSCI), dated May 2, 2009. The letter provides responses to Member questions presented to DNI Dennis C. Blair in the course of the SSCI hearing, *Current and Projected National Security Threats to the United States*, February 5, 2009. *http://www.fas.org/irp/congress/2008_hr/020508threat-qfr.pdf.*

318. US-China Economic and Security Review Commission, *Hearing on China's Propaganda and Influence Operations, Its Intelligence Activities that Target the United States, and the Resulting Impacts on US National Security*, testimony of I.C. Smith, April 30, 2009.

319. US-China Economic and Security Review Commission, *Hearing on China's Propaganda and Influence Operations, Its Intelligence Activities that Target the United States, and the Resulting Impacts on US National Security*, testimony of I.C. Smith, April 30, 2009.

320. Office of the Director of National Intelligence (DNI), letter to the Senate Select Committee on Intelligence (SSCI), dated May 2, 2009. The letter provides responses to Member questions presented to DNI Dennis C. Blair in the course of the SSCI hearing, *Current and Projected National Security Threats to the United States*, February 5, 2009. *http://www.fas.org/irp/congress/2008_hr/020508threat-qfr.pdf.*

321. US-China Economic and Security Review Commission, *Hearing on China's Propaganda and Influence Operations, Its Intelligence Activities that Target the United States, and the Resulting Impacts on US National Security*, testimony of James Mulvenon, April 30, 2009.

322. US-China Economic and Security Review Commission, *Hearing on China's Propaganda and Influence Operations, Its Intelligence Activities that Target the United States, and the Resulting Impacts on US National Security*, testimony of I.C. Smith and James Mulvenon, April 30, 2009.

323. The Centre for Counterintelligence and Security Studies, "Economic/Industrial/ Corporate Espionage Case: SHU, Quan-Sheng" (Alexandria, VA). *http://www.cicentre.com/spycase/ecoesp/SHU\Quan-Sheng.html.*

324. AMAC International Inc., profile of company President Dr. Quan-Sheng Shu (Newport News, VA). *http://www.amacintl.com/AMAC.html.*

325. *Washington Post*, "Scientist Quan-Sheng Shu Sentenced in Rocket Technology Case," April 7, 2009.

326. US Department of Justice press release, "Shu Quan-Sheng Virginia Physicist Sentenced to 51 Months in Prison for Illegally Exporting Space Launch Data to China and Offering Bribes to Chinese Officials," April 7, 2009. *http://www.cicentre.com/spycase/courtdoc SHU_Quan_Sheng_ Sentencing/ DOJ_PR_7 apr09.html.*

327. AMAC International Inc., notices on company Web page (Newport News, VA). *http://www.amacintl.com.*

328. US Department of Justice press release, "Virginia Physicist Pleads Guilty to Illegally Exporting Space Launch Data to China and Offering Bribes to Chinese-Officials" (Washington, DC: November 17, 200). *http://www.cicentre.com/spycase/ courtdoc/ SHU_quan_sheng/pleads_guilty/press_release_17nov08.html.*

329. US Department of Justice press release, "Fact Sheet: Major US Export Enforcement Prosecutions During the Past Two Years" (Washington, DC: October 28, 2008). *http://www.usdoj.gov/opa/pr/2008/October/08-nsd-959.html.*

330. Teo Xuanwei, "Singapore Residents Indicted for Illegal Export in US," *Channelnewsasia.com*, October 30, 2008. *http://www.channelnewsasia.com/stories/singaporelocalnews/view/386445/1/.html.*

331. The Centre for Counterintelligence and Security Studies, "Economic/ Industrial/ Corporate Espionage Case: DING, Jian Wei and LIM, Kok Tong and CHENG, Ping" (Alexandria, VA). *http://www.cicentre.com/spycase/ecoesp/DING_ LIM_ CHENG.html.*

332. Teo Xuanwei, "Singapore Residents Indicted for Illegal Export in US," *Channelnewsasia.com*, October 30, 2008. *http://www.channelnewsasia.com/stories/singaporelocalnews/view/386445/1/.html.*

333. I.C. Smith, "The FBI and Chinese Espionage" (lecture presented at the Third Raleigh Spy Conference, Raleigh, NC, September 2, 2005), p. 18. *http://www.raleigh spyconference.com/news/The%20FBI%20and%20Chinese%20Espionage.pdf.*

334. Howard DeVore, *China's Intelligence and Internal Security Forces* (Alexandria, VA: Jane's Information Group, 1999), p. 130.

335. House Committee on Foreign Affairs, Subcommittee on Human Rights and Organizations, and Subcommittee on Asian and Pacific Affairs, *Hearing on Alleged Intimidation and Harassment of Chinese Citizens in the United States*, testimony of Lin Xu, 101st Cong., 2nd sess., June 19, 1990.

336. House Committee on International Relations, Subcommittee on Africa, Global Human Rights and International Operations, and Subcommittee on Oversight and Investigations, *Hearing on Falun Gong and China's Continuing War on Human Rights*, testimony of Chen Yonglin, 109th Cong., 2nd sess., July 21, 2005. *http://www.foreignaffairs.house.gov/archives/109/22579.pdf.*

337. "Reference Materials for Envoys Conference in Beijing: Overseas Battle on Falun Gong Issue," PRC Foreign Ministry document dated February 7, 2001. Document entered into the hearing record of the House Committee on International Relations,

Subcommittee on Africa, Global Human Rights and International Operations, and Subcommittee on Oversight and Investigations, *Hearing on Falun Gong and China's Continuing War on Human Rights*, testimony of Chen Yonglin, 109th Cong., 2nd sess., July 21, 2005. *http://www.foreignaffairs.house.gov/archives/109/22579.pdf.*

338. House Committee on International Relations, Subcommittee on Africa, Global Human Rights and International Operations, and Subcommittee on Oversight and Investigations, *Hearing on Falun Gong and China's Continuing War on Human Rights*, testimony of Chen Yonglin, 109th Cong., 2nd sess., July 21, 2005. *http://www.foreignaffairs.house.gov/archives/109/22579.pdf.*

339. Joshua Philipp, "Complaint Filed Against New York Chinese Consul General," *Epoch Times* (New York), August 15, 2008; Joshua Philipp, "Violence and Espionage in New York, Part 1," *Epoch Times* (New York), November 2, 2008.

340. US-China Economic and Security Review Commission, *Hearing on China's Propaganda and Influence Operations, Its Intelligence Activities that Target the United States, and the Resulting Impacts on US National Security*, testimonies of Anne-Marie Brady and Ross Terrill, April 30, 2009.

341. Grace Wang, "Caught in the Middle, Called a Traitor," *Washington Post*, April 20, 2008.

342. Duke University student (name withheld), statement to Commission staff, June 2009.

343. Rodger Baker, "Beijing's Obvious Hand at the US Olympic Torch Run," (Austin, TX: Strategic Forecasting, Inc., April 16, 2008).

344. US-China Economic and Security Review Commission, *Hearing on China's Propaganda and Influence Operations, Its Intelligence Activities that Target the United States, and the Resulting Impacts on US National Security*, testimony of I.C. Smith, April 30, 2009.

345. Speech by Barack Obama, "Remarks by the President on Securing Our Nation's Cyber Infrastructure" (Washington, DC:, May 29, 2009). *http://www. whitehouse. gov/the/press_office/Remarks-by-the-President-on-Securing-Our-Nations- Cyber-Infrastructure/.*

346. Shane Harris, "China's Cyber-Militia," *National Journal*, May 31, 2008. *http:/ www.nationaljournal.com/njmagazine/cs_20080531_6948.php.*

347. Demetri Sevastopulo, "Chinese hacked into Pentagon," *Financial Times*, September 3, 2007. *http://www.ft.com/cms/s/0/9dba9ba2–5a3b-11dc-9bcd-0000779fd2ac.html.*

348. The plane is sometimes referred to as the Joint Strike Fighter. See Siobhan Gorman, August Cole, and Yochi Dreazen, "Computer Spies Breach Fighter-Jet Project," *Wall Street Journal*, April 21, 2009. *http://online.wsj.com/article/SB124027491029837401.html.*

349. US-China Economic and Security Review Commission, *Hearing on China's Proliferation Practices, and the Development of its Cyber and Space Warfare Capabilities*, testimony of Gary McAlum, May 20, 2008.

350. Data for the years 2008 and 2009 have been updated. Name withheld (staff member, US Strategic Command), telephone interview with Commission staff, August 28, 2009.

351. Jim Garamone, "Officials say cyber defence costly," *AF.mil*, April 9, 2009. *http:// www.af.mil/news/story.asp?id=123143695.*

352. White House Executive Report, "Cyberspace Policy Review: Assuring a Trusted and Resilient Information and Communications Infrastructure," April 2009. *http:// www. whitehouse.gov/assets/documents/Cyberspace_Policy_Review/final.pdf.*

353. Melissa Hathaway ("Speech to the Center for International and Strategic Studies" (Washington, DC: June 12, 2009). *http://csis.org/multimedia/audio-cybersecurity-policy-review-melissa-hathaway-cybersecurity-chief-national-security-.*

354. Siobhan Gorman, "Security Cyber Czar Steps Down," *Wall Street Journal*, August 4, 2009. *http://online.wsj.com/article/SB124932480886002237.html.*

355. Robert Gates, "Establishment of a Subordinate Unified US Cyber Command Under US Strategic Command for Military Cyberspace Operations," memorandum for secretaries of the Military Departments, June 23, 2009. *http://www. wired.com/images_blogs/dangerroom/2009/06/cybercommand.pdf.*

356. Siobhan Gorman and Yochi J. Dreazen, "New Military Command to Focus on Cybersecurity," *Wall Street Journal*, April 22, 2009. *http://online.wsj.com/article/SB124035738674441033.html;* Ellen Nakashima, "Gates Creates Cyber-Defence Command," *Washington Post*, June 24, 2009. *http://www.washingtonpost.com/wpdyn/content/article/2009/06/23/AR2009062303492.html.*

357. For example, see Demetri Sevastopulo, "Beware: enemy attacks in cyberspace," *Financial Times*, September 3, 2007. *http://www.ft.com/cms/s/0/a89c1c88– 5a38–11dc-9bcd-0000779fd2ac.html.*

358. Northrop Grumman Corporation, "Capability of the People's Republic of China to Conduct Cyber Warfare and Computer Network Exploitation" (contracted research paper for the US-China Economic and Security Review Commission. June 2009), pp. 7–8. *http://www.uscc.gov/researchpapers/2009/Northrop Grumman_PRC_Cyber_Paper_ FINAL_ Approved % 20Report_16Oct 2009.pdf.*

359. Northrop Grumman Corporation, "Capability of the People's Republic of China to Conduct Cyber Warfare and Computer Network Exploitation" (contracted research paper for the US-China Economic and Security Review Commission, June 2009), p. 39. *http: // www.uscc.gov/researchpapers/2009/North rop Grumman_PRC_Cyber_Paper_FINAL_ Approved% 20 Report_16Oct2009.pdf.*

360. US Department of Defence (DoD), *DoD Dictionary of Military and Associated Terms*, "Computer Network Operations" (Washington, DC: Defence Technical Information Center, April 12, 2001, as amended through March 17, 2009). *http:// www.dtic.mil/doctrine/jel/doddict/data/c/18167.html.*

361. US Department of Defence, *DoD Dictionary of Military and Associated Terms*, "Computer Network Exploitation" (Washington, DC: Defence Technical Information Center, April 12, 2001, as amended through March 17, 2009). *http:// www.dtic.mil/doctrine/jel/doddict/data/c/18166.html.*

362. US Department of Defence, *DoD Dictionary of Military and Associated Terms*, "Computer Network Attack" (Washington, DC: Defence Technical Information Center, April 12, 2001, as amended through March 17, 2009). *http://www. dtic.mil/doctrine/jel/doddict/data/c/10082.html.*

363. US Department of Defence, *DoD Dictionary of Military and Associated Terms*, "Computer Network Defence," (Washington, DC: Defence Technical Information Center, April 12, 2001, as amended through March 17, 2009). *http://www. dtic.mil/doctrine/jel/doddict/data/c/10869.html.*

364. As one example of Chinese military references to US military performance in Kosovo and Iraq, see Ding Shaowu, "Some Thoughts About Organizing The Provincial Military District (Garrison) Setup To Conduct Training In A Complex Electromagnetic Environment," *Guofang* (National Defence) 6 (2008).

365. A partial, but by no means comprehensive, list of some of the more prominent and authoritative of these publications would include *Zhongguo Junshi Kexue* (China Military Science), *Guofang* (National Defence), *Zhongguo Guofang Bao* (*China National Defence News*), *Jiefangjun Bao* (*PLA Daily*), and the various official newspapers of China's seven military regions.

366. Northrop Grumman Corporation, "Capability of the People's Republic of China to Conduct Cyber Warfare and Computer Network Exploitation" (contracted research paper for the US-China Economic and Security Review Commission, June 2009), p. 7. *http: // www.uscc.gov / researchpapers /* 2009 */North ropGrumman/ PRC_Cyber_Paper_ FINAL_ Approved%20 Report_16 Oct 2009.pdf.*

367. US Department of Defence, *Joint Publication 3–13: Information Operations* (Washington, DC: February 2006). *http://www.fas.org/irp/doddir/dod/jp3_13.pdf.*

368. Daniel M. Hartnett and Frederic Velucci Jr., *PLA Doctrine: Emerging Concepts in Preparing for War* (Alexandria, VA: Center for Naval Analyses, 2009), p. 70. The report cites Chinese language terms obtained from "*Xinxihua Zuozhan Lilun Xuexi Zhinan: Xinxihua Zuozhan 400 Ti*" (Study Guidelines on Informatized Operations Theory: 400 Questions on Informatized Operations) (Beijing: Military Science Press, 2005), p. 97.

369. Timothy Thomas, *Dragon Bytes: Chinese Information Warfare Theory and Practice* (Fort Leavenworth, KS: Foreign Military Studies Office, 2004).

370. Timothy Thomas, "China's Electronic Long-Range Reconnaissance," *Military Review* (November/December 2008).

371. The Commission has not utilized the primary source. Analysis drawn from James Mulvenon, "PLA Computer Network Operations," in *Beyond the Strait: PLA Missions Other Than Taiwan*, eds. Roy Kamphausen, David Lai, and Andrew Scobell (Carlisle, PA: US Army War College Strategic Studies Institute, 2009); and Northrop Grumman Corporation, "Capability of the People's Republic of China to Conduct Cyber Warfare and Computer Network Exploitation" (contracted research paper for the US-China Economic and Security Review Commission, June 2009), pp. 9–11. *http: // www.uscc.gov / researchpapers / 2009 / Northrop Grumman_PRC_Cyber_Paper_FINAL_Approved%20Report_16Oct2009.pdf.*

372. "PRC S&T: Constructing PLA Information System Security Architecture," "*Jisuanji Anquan*" (Computer Security), February 1, 2009. OSC ID: CPP2009 0528670007. *http://www.opensource.gov.* Source is cited in Northrop Grumman Corporation, "Capability of the People's Republic of China to Conduct Cyber Warfare and Computer Network Exploitation" (contracted research paper for the US-China Economic and Security Review Commission, June 2009), pp. 9–11. *http:// www.uscc.gov / researchpapers / 2009 Northrop Grumman_PRC_ Cyber_ Paper_FINAL_Approved%20Report_16Oct2009.pdf.*

373. "Constructing New System of Military Training Under Informatized Conditions—Interpreting New Generation 'Outline of Military Training and Evaluation,' " *Jiefangjun Bao* (*PLA Daily Online*), August 1, 2008. Available as "PRC: JFJB on Implementing New Outline of Military Training, Evaluation," August 1, 2008. OSC ID: CPP20080801710005. *http://www.opensource.gov.*

374. " *'Kan bu Jian de Zhanxian' Kaoyan Zhuangbei Zhihuiguan*" (Commanders Test Equipment on the 'Invisible Battle Line'), *Jiefangjun Bao* (*PLA Daily Online*), January 14, 2008. Available as "JFJB: Military Commanders Take Part in Armament Support Training in Shenyang MR," January 14, 2008. OSC ID: CPP2008 01147100007.*http:/ /www.opensource.gov.*

375. James Mulvenon, "PLA Computer Network Operations," in *Beyond the Strait: PLA Missions Other Than Taiwan*, eds. Roy Kamphausen, David Lai, and Andrew Scobell (Carlisle, PA: US Army War College Strategic Studies Institute, 2009); Northrop Grumman Corporation, "Capability of the People's Republic of China to Conduct Cyber Warfare and Computer Network Exploitation" (contracted research paper for the US-China Economic and Security Review Commission, June 2009), p. 19. *http: // www.uscc.gov / researchpapers / 2009 Northrop Grumman_PRC_Cyber _Paper_FINAL_Approved%20Report_16Oct2009.pdf.*

376. Northrop Grumman Corporation, "Capability of the People's Republic of China to Conduct Cyber Warfare and Computer Network Exploitation" (contracted research paper for the US-China Economic and Security Review Commission, June 2009). *http://www.uscc.gov/research papers/2009/North ropGrumman/PRC_ Cyber_ Paper _ FINAL_Approved% 20Report_16Oct2009.pdf.*

377. Northrop Grumman Corporation "Capability of the People's Republic of China to Conduct Cyber Warfare and Computer Network Exploitation" (contracted research paper for the US-China Economic and Security Review Commission, June 2009), p. 19. *http: // www.uscc.gov / research papers / 2009 / North rop Grumman_ PRC_ Cyber_ Paper_ FINAL_Approved% 20Report_16 Oct 2009.pdf.*

378. iDefence (subsidiary of Verisign, Inc.), "Development, Capacity and Motivations of the Chinese Hacker Community" (Sterling, VA: October 2008), p. 11.

379. "*Zhongguo Minbing Kaishi Buru Xinxizhan Zhanchang*" (China's Militia Begins to Enter the Information Warfare Battlefield), *Zhong Xin She* (China News Service), April 26, 2000. Translation performed by Commission staff. *http://news. sina.com.cn/ china/2000–04–26/85005.html.*

380. "*Datong Junfenqu Minbing Wangluo Fendui Wangluo Fanghu Jishu Quebao Xinxi Anquan*" (Datong Military District Militia Network Unit, Network Defence Technology Ensure Information Security), *Jiefangjun Bao* (*PLA Daily*), July 21, 2003. Translation performed by Commission staff. *http://www.pladaily.com.cn/gb/ pladaily/2003/07/21/20030721001023_army.html.*

381. "*Datong Junfenqu Minbing Wangluo Fendui Wangluo Fanghu Jishu Quebao Xinxi Anquan*" (Datong Military District Militia Network Unit, Network Defence Technology Ensure Information Security), *Jiefangjun Bao* (*PLA Daily*), July 21, 2003. Translation performed by Commission staff. *http://www.pladaily.com.cn/gb/ pladaily/2003/07/21/20030721001023_army.html.*

382. Northrop Grumman Corporation, "Capability of the People's Republic of China to Conduct Cyber Warfare and Computer Network Exploitation" (contracted research paper for the US-China Economic and Security Review Commission, June 2009), p. 22. *http: // www.uscc.gov /researchpapers/2009 /Northrop Grumman/ PRC_Cyber_ Paper_ FINAL_ Approved% 20Report_16 Oct 2009.pdf.*

383. iDefence (subsidiary of Verisign, Inc.), "Development, Capacity and Motivations of the Chinese Hacker Community" (Sterling, VA: October 2008), pp. 9–17.

384. Northrop Grumman Corporation, "Capability of the People's Republic of China to Conduct Cyber Warfare and Computer Network Exploitation" (contracted research paper for the US-China Economic and Security Review Commission, June 2009), p. 23. *http: // www.uscc.gov / researchpapers / 2009 / NorthropGrumman_PRC_ Cyber_ Paper_ FINAL_ Approved% 20 Report_16 Oct2009.pdf.*

385. Ye Youcai and Zhou Wenrui, "*Jianshe Yi Zhi Gao Suzhi de Minbing Xinxi Jishu Fendui*" (Building a High Quality Militia Information Technology Unit), *Guofang* (National Defence), September 2003. Available as "Telecomm Experts in Guangzhou

Doubling as Militia Information Warfare Elements," September 15, 2003. OSC ID: CPP20031002000138. *http://www.opensource.gov.*

386. Yongning County Government Information Office, "*Yongning Xian Minbing Xinxi Zuozhan Fendui Jin Ri Chengli*" (Yongning County Militia Information Warfare Unit Established Today), March 18, 2008. Translation performed by Commission staff. *http://old.chinayn.gov.cn/info_www/news/detailnewsb.asp?infoNo=26428.*

387. Yongning County Government Information Office, "*Minbing Wangluo Zhan Fendui Zhize* "(Militia Network Warfare Unit Responsibilities), March 16, 2008. Translation performed by Commission staff. *http://old.chinayn.gov.cn/info_www/ news/detail news b.asp? info No=26366.*

388. Yongning County Government Information Office, "*Yongning Xian Minbing Xinxi Zuozhan Fendui Jin Ri Chengli*" (Yongning County Militia Information Warfare Unit Established Today), March 18, 2008. Translation performed by Commission staff. *http://old.chinayn.gov.cn/info_www/news/detailnewsb.asp?infoNo=26428.*

389. Scott Henderson, *The Dark Visitor* (Fort Leavenworth, KS: Foreign Military Studies Office, 2004), pp. 3–5.

390. Northrop Grumman Corporation, "Capability of the People's Republic of China to Conduct Cyber Warfare and Computer Network Exploitation" (contracted research paper for the US-China Economic and Security Review Commission, June 2009), p. 24. *http: // www.uscc.gov / research papers / 2009 / Northrop Grumman_ PRC_Cyber_Paper_F!NAL_Approved% 20 Report_16Oct 2009.pdf.*

391. Scott Henderson, *The Dark Visitor* (Fort Leavenworth, KS: Foreign Military Studies Office, 2004), p. 139; and Nathan Vardi, "Chinese Take-Out," *Forbes.com*, July 25, 2005. *http://www.forbes.com/forbes/2005/0725/054\print.html.*

392. As two such examples, see Scott Henderson, *The Dark Visitor* (Fort Leavenworth, KS: Foreign Military Studies Office, 2004); and James Mulvenon, "PLA Computer Network Operations," in *Beyond the Strait: PLA Missions Other Than Taiwan*, eds. Roy Kamphausen, David Lai, and Andrew Scobell (Carlisle, PA: US Army War College Strategic Studies Institute, 2009).

393. Northrop Grumman Corporation, "Capability of the People's Republic of China to Conduct Cyber Warfare and Computer Network Exploitation" (contracted research paper for the US-China Economic and Security Review Commission, June 2009), p. 26. *http: // www.uscc.gov/researchpapers/2009 Northrop Grumman_ PRC_Cyber_ Paper_FINAL_Approved% 20 Report_16Oct 2009. pdf.*

394. James Mulvenon, "PLA Computer Network Operations," in *Beyond the Strait: PLA Missions Other Than Taiwan*, eds. Roy Kamphausen, David Lai, and Andrew Scobell (Carlisle, PA: US Army War College Strategic Studies Institute, 2009).

395. James Mulvenon, "PLA Computer Network Operations," in *Beyond the Strait: PLA Missions Other Than Taiwan*, eds. Roy Kamphausen, David Lai, and Andrew Scobell (Carlisle, PA: US Army War College Strategic Studies Institute, 2009).

396. Northrop Grumman Corporation, "Capability of the People's Republic of China to Conduct Cyber Warfare and Computer Network Exploitation" (contracted research paper for the US-China Economic and Security Review Commission, June 2009), p. 27. *http: // www.uscc.gov/researchpapers / 2009 / Northrop Grumman_ PRC_Cyber_Paper_\ FINAL_Approved% 20 Report_16 Oct 2009.pdf.*

397. James Mulvenon, "PLA Computer Network Operations," in *Beyond the Strait: PLA Missions Other Than Taiwan*, eds. Roy Kamphausen, David Lai, and Andrew Scobell (Carlisle, PA: US Army War College Strategic Studies Institute, 2009).

398. "Analysis: PRC Media Tout Anti-Hacking Amendment: Hackers Appear Unaffected," March 30, 2009. OSC ID: FEA20090331840801. *http://www.opensource.gov.*

399. Northrop Grumman Corporation, "Capability of the People's Republic of China to Conduct Cyber Warfare and Computer Network Exploitation" (contracted research paper for the US-China Economic and Security Review Commission, June 2009), pp. 28–29. *http: // www.uscc.gov/researchpapers /2009/ Northrop Grumman_PRC_ Cyber_ Paper_ FINAL_Approved% 20 Report_16 Oct2009.pdf.*

400. James Mulvenon, "PLA Computer Network Operations," in *Beyond the Strait: PLA Missions Other Than Taiwan*, eds. Roy Kamphausen, David Lai, and Andrew Scobell (Carlisle, PA: US Army War College Strategic Studies Institute, 2009).

401. iDefence (subsidiary of Verisign, Inc.), "Development, Capacity and Motivations of the Chinese Hacker Community" (Sterling, VA: October 2008), p. 29.

402. The hacker in question was Tan Dailin, also known as "Wicked Rose." See iDefence (subsidiary of Verisign, Inc.), "Development, Capacity and Motivations of the Chinese Hacker Community" (Sterling, VA: October 2008), p. 11.

403. Northrop Grumman Corporation, "Capability of the People's Republic of China to Conduct Cyber Warfare and Computer Network Exploitation" (contracted research paper for the US-China Economic and Security Review Commission, June 2009), pp. 32–33. *http: // www.uscc.gov / researchpapers / 2009 / Northrop Grumman_PRC _Cyber_ Paper_FINAL_Approved% 20 Report_16 Oct 2009.pdf.*

404. Northrop Grumman Corporation, "Capability of the People's Republic of China to Conduct Cyber Warfare and Computer Network Exploitation" (contracted research paper for the US-China Economic and Security Review Commission, June 2009), p. 28. *http: // www.uscc.gov / researchpapers / 2009 / North ropGrumman_PRC_ Cyber_ Paper_ FINAL_ Approved% 20Report_16 Oct2009.pdf.*

405. Northrop Grumman Corporation, "Capability of the People's Republic of China to Conduct Cyber Warfare and Computer Network Exploitation" (contracted research paper for the US-China Economic and Security Review Commission, June 2009), p. 28–29. *http: // www.uscc.gov/research papers/2009/North ropGrumman_ PRC_Cyber_Paper_FINAL_Approved%20Report_16Oct2009.pdf.*

406. Information Warfare Monitor, "About" (Toronto, Canada: Undated). *http:// www.infowar-monitor.net/about/. http://www.uscc.gov/researchpapers/2009/.*

407. Information Warfare Monitor, "Tracking GhostNet: Investigating a Cyber Espionage Network" (Toronto, Canada: March 2008). *http://www.infowar-monitor.net. http:// www.uscc.gov/researchpapers/2009/.*

408. Information Warfare Monitor, "Tracking GhostNet: Investigating a Cyber Espionage Network" (Toronto, Canada: March 2008), p. 34. *http://www.infowar-monitor.net.*

409. Rafal A. Rohozinski (principal and chief executive officer of The SecDev Group), telephone interview with Commission staff, September 3, 2009. According to Mr. Rohozinski, a "control" server provides the immediate contact point for infected computers; a "command" server is the next echelon above a control server and issues commands to control servers.

410. US-China Economic and Security Review Commission, *Hearing on China's Propaganda and Influence Operations, Its Intelligence Activities that Target the United States, and the Resulting Impacts on US National Security*, testimony of Rafal A. Rohozinski, April 30, 2009.

411. Kajal Basu, "The Chinese Flu," *Businessworld*, April 3, 2009.

412. Information Warfare Monitor, "Tracking GhostNet: Investigating a Cyber Espionage Network" (Toronto, Canada: March 2008), p. 28. *http://www.infowar-monitor.net.*

413. Information Warfare Monitor, "Tracking GhostNet: Investigating a Cyber Espionage Network" (Toronto, Canada: March 2008), p. 58. *http://www.infowar-monitor. net.*

414. US-China Economic and Security Review Commission, *Hearing on China's Propaganda and Influence Operations, Its Intelligence Activities that Target the United States, and the Resulting Impacts on US National Security*, testimony of Rafal A. Rohozinski, April 30, 2009.

415. Rafal A. Rohozinski (principal and chief executive officer of The SecDev Group), telephone interview with Commission staff, September 3, 2007.

416. US-China Economic and Security Review Commission, *Hearing on China's Propaganda and Influence Operations, Its Intelligence Activities that Target the United States, and the Resulting Impacts on US National Security*, testimony of Rafal A. Rohozinski, April 30, 2009.

417. US-China Economic and Security Review Commission, *Hearing on China's Propaganda and Influence Operations, Its Intelligence Activities that Target the United States, and the Resulting Impacts on US National Security*, testimony of Rafal A. Rohozinski, April 30, 2009.

418. Scott Henderson, *The Dark Visitor* (Fort Leavenworth, KS: Foreign Military Studies Office, 2004). See in particular chapter four, "Government Affiliation: Black and White Do Not Exist."

419. Northrop Grumman Corporation, "Capability of the People's Republic of China to Conduct Cyber Warfare and Computer Network Exploitation" (contracted research paper for the US-China Economic and Security Review Commission, June 2009), p. 59–66. *http: // www.uscc.gov / research papers / 2009 / Northrop Grumman_PRC_Cyber_ Paper_FINAL_Approved% 20Report_16 Oct 2009.pdf.*

420. US-China Economic and Security Review Commission, *Hearing on China's Propaganda and Influence Operations, Its Intelligence Activities that Target the United States, and the Resulting Impacts on National Security*, testimony of Kevin Coleman, April 30, 2009.

421. Department of Homeland Security, "2009 National Infrastructure Protection Plan" (Washington, DC: 2009), p. 113. *http://www.dhs.gov/xlibrary/assets/NIPP_Plan.pdf.*

422. Siobhan Gorman, "Electricity Grid in US Penetrated By Spies," *Wall Street Journal*, April 8, 2009. *http://online.wsj.com/article SB12 39148 0520 40990 85.html.*

423. Shane Harris, "China's Cyber-Militia," *National Journal*, May 31, 2008. *http:// www.nationaljournal.com/njmagazine/cs_20080531_6948.php.*

424. Siobhan Gorman, "Electricity Grid in US Penetrated By Spies," *Wall Street Journal*, April 8, 2009. *http://online.wsj.com/article SB1239 14805 20409 9085. html.*

425. James Mulvenon, "PLA Computer Network Operations: Scenarios, Doctrine, Organizations, and Capability," in *Beyond the Strait: PLA Missions Other than Taiwan*, eds. Roy Kamphausen, David Lai, and Andrew Scobell (Carlisle, PA: Army WarCollege Strategic Studies Institute, 2009), p. 258. *http://www.strategicstudiesin stitute.army.mil/pubs/download.cfm?q=910.*

426. Shane Harris, "Hacking The Hill," *National Journal*, December 20, 2008. *http:// www.nationaljournal.com/njmagazine/cs_20081220_6787.php.*

427. *Josh Rogin, "Hackers Based in China Break into Florida Senator's Office Computers,* "Congressional Quarterly Today, *March 20, 2009.*

CHAPTER 3

China in Asia

SECTION 1

China in Afghanistan, Pakistan and Central Asia

> "The Commission shall investigate and report exclusively on—
>
> "Energy—The effect of the large and growing economy of the People's Republic of China on world energy supplies and the role the United States can play (including joint research and development efforts and technological assistance), in influencing the energy policy of the People's Republic of China. . . .
>
> "Regional Economic and Security Impacts—The triangular economic and security relationship among the United States, Taipei and the People's Republic of China (including the military modernization and force deployments of the People's Republic of China aimed at Taipei), the national budget of the People's Republic of China, and the fiscal strength of the People's Republic of China in relation to internal instability in the People's Republic of China and the likelihood of the externalization of problems arising from such internal instability. . . ."

Introduction

China has deep security, economic, political, and strategic interests throughout Afghanistan, Pakistan and Central Asia. As it strives to develop its economy and become a prominent actor on the world stage, China has taken steps to expand its relationships with the countries along its periphery. China's interests in the region include maintaining the security of its borders and preventing extremism from destabilizing China domestically; ensuring energy security; balancing traditional powers in the region, such as India, Russia, and the United States; and increasing trade and economic investments. Because of its strong historic military and politicalties to Pakistan and its growing economic investments in Afghanistan, China is a key player in both countries. Sharing a border with Afghanistan and Pakistan, China has a particular interest in ensuring stability and protecting its western border from being subjected to the destabilizing effects of terrorism. Increasingly, Chinese companies have made investments in the war-torn region that are contributing to China's economic growth through greater trade and access to natural resources. The United States and China share several interests in the two countries, including promoting regional stability, fighting terrorism, and fostering economic development. However, China has been reluctant to intercede directly in the two neighbouring countries; rather, it depends on US and North Atlantic Treaty Organization (NATO) military forces and influence in Afghanistan and Pakistan to help secure China's investments, while keeping a watchful eye on the level and duration of their presence.

Figure 1: Afghanistan, Pakistan and Central Asia

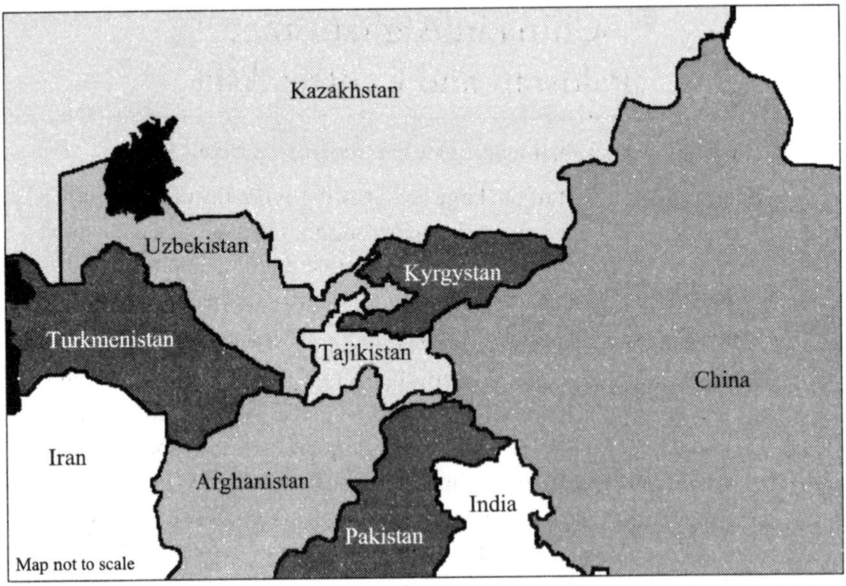

Source: Relief Web, ''Map of Central Asia.'' http://www.reliefweb.int/mapc/cis/reg centrlas.html.

In recent years, China also has developed stronger relationships with each of the countries in Central Asia. Through these ties, China has helped to promote regional security and to support the development of Central Asian economies, ultimately leading to stronger political and military relationships with China's western neighbours. Beijing has worked toward creating a strategy in the region that ensures its energy security and access to greater resources for the country's growing energy demands. This section of the Commission's Report will help explain China's interests in Afghanistan, Pakistan and Central Asia. It also will examine how China's interests in these countries may affect US interests in the region.

China's Interests in Pakistan and Afghanistan

Historical Perspectives

Historically, China's relationships with Pakistan and Afghanistan have been markedly different. While Beijing established diplomatic ties with both of the countries nearly six decades ago, China's ties with Pakistan have developed into a strategic relationship based upon mutually beneficial cooperation.[1] In February 2009, Pakistani President Asif Ali Zardari wrote, "No relationship between two sovereign states is as unique and durable as that between Pakistan and China. . . . It is a friendship that is rooted in the hearts and minds of the people of the two countries."[2] China's relations with Pakistan have been close since well before the end of the Cold War, with China supporting Pakistan's anti-Soviet stance.[3] During the Sino-Indian War in the early 1960s, the ties between China and Pakistan became more prominent. Even after the breakup of the Soviet Union, the Sino-Pakistani relationship matured based on a mutual desire to stymie India. According to Lisa Curtis, senior research fellow at the Heritage Foundation, "Chinese policy toward Pakistan is driven primarily by its interest in countering Indian power in the region and diverting Indian military force and strategic attention away from China." [4] As a result, China developed strong military ties with Pakistan, ultimately becoming Pakistan's largest defence supplier.[5] The strong relationship that Pakistan and China forged led to the settlement of border disputes between the nations, formal trade agreements, and privileged diplomatic ties.[6]

History of Sino-Pakistan Military Relations

While Beijing established diplomatic relations with Islamabad in 1951, the two countries first began cooperating militarily in 1962 with the start of the Sino-Indian border war. Since then, China has aligned itself with Islamabad and has made heavy military and economic investments in Pakistan to keep India under strategic pressure.[7] When the United States imposed an arms embargo on Pakistan as a result of the 1965 Indo-Pakistani War, Beijing filled the void by providing Islamabad with large quantities of arms and ammunition, including Chinese-produced F–6 fighters, T–59 tanks, and anti-aircraft guns.[8] According to Lisa Curtis of the Heritage Foundation, "The most significant development in China–Pakistan military cooperation occurred in 1992 when China supplied Pakistan with 34 short-range ballistic M–11 missiles." [9] Beijing also assisted Pakistan with the development of the solid-fueled Shaheen-1 ballistic missile and the construction of a ballistic-missile manufacturing facility in northeastern Pakistan.[10] Between 2003 and 2007, China's weapons sales to Pakistan included JF–17 aircraft and production facilities, F–22P frigates with helicopters, K–8 jet trainers, T–85 tanks, F–7 aircraft, small arms, and ammunition.[11]

Sino-Pakistani nuclear cooperation began in the early 1980s. This cooperation has included both civil and military nuclear agreements. In 1983, US intelligence agencies reported that China had transferred to Pakistan a complete nuclear weapon design and enough weapons-grade uranium for two nuclear weapons. In 1986, Beijing and Islamabad penned a comprehensive nuclear cooperation agreement, and China began assisting with Pakistan's uranium enrichment programme.[12] Despite Pakistan's poor track record for preventing proliferation of nuclear materials and technology,* China continues to support Islamabad's nuclear development.[13] Beijing recently agreed to assist with the construction of two new nuclear plants in Pakistan in addition to the three that China already has helped to build.[14]

Similar to its ties with Pakistan, China's relationship with Afghanistan derives from China's anti-Soviet stance during the Cold War. Following the 1979 Soviet invasion of Afghanistan, China worked with the United States to support the mujahideen and provide weapons to Afghan fighters.[15] Although China broke off diplomatic relations with Afghanistan in 1993 as the country fell into factional fighting and civil war, it resumed those relations in 1996.[16] Beijing adopted a policy of engagement with the Taliban in order to ensure the safety of its borders and engaged in low-level economic and technical cooperation.[17] However, after the terrorist attacks on the United States in 2001 and the subsequent US invasion in Afghanistan, China, as well as much of the rest of the world, considerably changed its relationship with both Pakistan and Afghanistan.

China's Current Interests in the Region

China's interests in Pakistan and Afghanistan are vast. While Beijing is concerned with the presence of major powers in the region, it is also interested in the security of its shared border with Afghanistan and Pakistan and ensuring that Islamic extremists do not penetrate into Chinese territory. In addition, having a stable Afghanistan and Pakistan enhances the security of Chinese economic interests in the region. By expanding its economic ties with the two countries, China is able to support its own domestic economic development and stability while helping to increase stability in the region as well.

Balancing Traditional Powers in the Region

One of the fundamental interests China has in strengthening relations with Pakistan and Afghanistan is balancing traditional powers in the region, such as India and the United States. Despite the warming of ties between India and China in recent years, China still remains concerned about India's rise and maintains a close military relationship with Pakistan in order to contain the perceived threat.[18] Since 9/11, India has become more closely allied with Afghanistan in delivering aid and providing military support to the war-torn country.[19] Given India's increasing presence and influence in Afghanistan, China wishes to strike a balance and ensure that India does not gain a preponderance of influence. Beyond India, China's

* During the 1980s, Abdul Qadeer Khan, well-known as the founder of Pakistan's nuclear programme, created a network of nuclear suppliers in order to develop the country's nuclear capabilities. Dr. Khan began to use this network to sell nuclear knowhow, technology, and materials to other countries seeking a nuclear weapons capability. Among these countries were Iran, Libya, and North Korea. Many nuclear proliferation experts assert that Dr. Khan had significant support from elements of the Pakistani military and civilian nuclear establishment. Richard P. Cronin, "Pakistan's Nuclear Proliferation Activities and the Recommendations of the 9/ 11 Commission: US Policy Constraints and Options," Congressional Research Service (*CRS*) Report to Congress (Washington, DC: January 25, 2005).

geopolitical strategy in Pakistan and Afghanistan involves countering the presence of the United States.[20] Since 2001, the war in Afghanistan and the growth of anti-terrorism cooperation have increased the US presence in continental Asia. In addition to stationing tens of thousands of US troops in Afghanistan, the United States has provided Pakistan with billions of dollars in aid and proclaimed the country as a key ally in the US's fight against terrorism.[21] President Obama's March 2009 white paper regarding Washington's new Afghanistan/Pakistan strategy recommended further increasing the US presence in both of the countries.[22] According to Michael Schiffer, deputy assistant secretary of Defence for East Asia, China is concerned that the US presence in the two countries may lead to a long-term military encampment on China's borders.[23] Chinese researchers have echoed this sentiment. Li Li, a researcher with the China Institutes of Contemporary International Relations (a think tank affiliated with the Ministry of State Security), wrote in a *China Daily* * opinion piece that

> *[t]he real intention of the [United States] in Afghanistan is widely doubted. The [United States] moves its anti-terror focus eastward. Whether it really aims to facilitate the war against terror, or is this just to veil its ambition of seeking hegemony [sic]?* [24]

Regional Security

Another one of Beijing's priorities in Pakistan and Afghanistan is establishing security along China's borders. Both countries are located on China's periphery and share with China a combined 371-mile border. Beijing is concerned deeply about maintaining stability on this border and ensuring that the region, specifically nuclear armed Pakistan, is not overrun by Islamic extremists. Walid Phares, director of Washington, DC's, Future Terrorism Project, testified to the Commission that

> *[i]f the Taliban comes back to Afghanistan, there are 76 kilometers between Afghanistan and China that border [the northwestern region], leading to potential cross-border attacks between jihadists based in Afghanistan and in China. If Pakistan's northern areas are controlled by the Taliban or if the government falls into the hands of the Taliban, the* problem is even greater for the national security of China.[25]

Not only would this situation be a threat to China's physical security, but also it would jeopardize China's increased investments in the energy and commercial sectors.[26] Instability in the region already has led to greater risks for Chinese investors. In 2007, Islamic militants kidnapped six Chinese women working in Islamabad.[27] In August 2008, Islamist extremists abducted two Chinese engineers in Pakistan's Swat Valley. The Pakistani Army recovered one of the engineers in October 2008, while the other was released by the militants in February 2009 after vehement protests to Islamabad from the Chinese government.[28]

While security within Pakistan and Afghanistan is a primary concern for the Chinese government, even more essential for Beijing is maintaining stability within China's borders. Pakistan and Afghanistan are located along China's Xinjiang

---

* China Daily is a government-owned newspaper and is widely regarded as the mouthpiece of the Chinese Communist Party.

Province—an area with a history of separatist movements and ethnic conflict between Uighurs, a Turkic-speaking Muslim people, and Han, the largest ethnic group in China.* The ethnic tensions and instability in the region were highlighted in July 2009 when protests by Uighurs in Xinjiang led to severe ethnic clashes, leaving at least 197 people dead and more than 1,600 injured. During past social upheavals in Xinjiang, local opposition movements were able to recruit additional members from the province and carry out operations against the Chinese.[29] Indeed, three months after the unrest in October 2009, one of Al Qaeda's top leaders, Abu Yahya al-Libi, called upon Xinjiang's Uighurs to prepare for a holy war against "oppressive" China.[30]

Walid Phares illustrated the extremist threat in his testimony to the Commission in May 2008:

> The separatist claim in [Xinjiang] is a classical ethnic conflict, but in the last few years a Jihadist movement has made inroads inside the Muslim communities, indoctrinating and recruiting a significant number of Jihadi militants. Many 'Chinese Jihadists' have been recruited by Al Qaeda and have fought in Afghanistan. Some are now fighting in the ranks of the Taliban in Pakistan.[31]

The most prominent separatist threat in Xinjiang is the East Turkestan Islamic Movement. This group has been labeled a terrorist organization by the governments of China, Kazakhstan, Pakistan, and the United States, as well as the United Nations. The US State Department also has linked the group to Al Qaeda.[32] Beijing has blamed the group for car bombings in Xinjiang and the murder of a Chinese diplomat in Kyrgyzstan. In 2008, Chinese authorities arrested members of the East Turkestan Islamic Movement for planning to execute terrorist attacks during the Beijing Olympics.[33] If Islamic extremists were to gain a stronger presence along China's border with Pakistan and Afghanistan, it could empower terrorist networks already in Xinjiang and threaten the economic and political stability of China. While the US Department of Defence's Joint Intelligence Task Force—Combating Terrorism has found that the threat of an ideology-based global jihad to China is "relatively low," China still presumably wants to continue to avoid attracting the attention of Islamic extremist groups.**

---

* In Xinjiang, Uighurs make up 45 percent of the population, whereas Han make up 40 percent of the population. However, Han comprise 92 percent of the total population of China, whereas Uighurs comprise only 0.6 percent of the total. Preeti Bhattacharji, "Uighurs and China's Xinjiang Region," Council on Foreign Relations (New York: July 6, 2009). http://www.cfr.org/publication/16870/#5.

**In the 1990s, China experienced a string of bombings and assassination attempts in Xinjiang. Chinese police subsequently arrested hundreds of Uighurs believed to be associated with the terrorist attacks. Martin I. Wayne, "Five Lessons from China's War on Terror," National Defence University, *Joint Force Quarterly* 47 (4th Quarter 2007): 42. *http://www.ndu.edu/ inss/Press/jfq/pages/editions/i47/09.pdf.* See also US-China Economic and Security Review Commission, *Hearing on the Impact of China's Economic and Security Interests in Continental Asia on the United States*, written testimony of Michael Schiffer, May 20, 2009.

Another major regional security concern that could affect China's internal stability is drug trafficking. The transit of heroin and opium from Afghanistan via Pakistan poses a significant problem for China's western provinces. In 2008, local police in Xinjiang prosecuted 1,563 drug-related cases, arresting nearly 2,000 suspects and seizing 144 kilograms of heroin transported from Pakistan and Afghanistan.[34] Proceeds from the drug trade have been linked to the funding of Central Asian Islamic militant groups.[35] In addition, the drug trade into Xinjiang has contributed to rising HIV/AIDS rates. Figures from the Chinese Center for Disease Control and Prevention show that by September 2008, Xinjiang had reported 24,818 HIV-infection cases (up from 11,303 in 2005), ranking fourth among all provinces, municipalities, and autonomous regions in the country. Xinjiang has the highest infection rate in the country.[36] According to Chinese media, increased instability in Pakistan and Afghanistan has exacerbated the drug problem.[37]

In order to counter these nontraditional security threats, Beijing has supported a number of measures to fight what it has labeled the "three evils": terrorism, separatism, and extremism.[38] Among these measures, in 2006, China and Afghanistan signed an agreement of cooperation to support Afghanistan's efforts in "combating terrorism and safeguarding national stability." [39] In April 2009, China announced that it would donate $75 million in aid to Afghanistan in order to increase the capacity of its military to combat terrorism.[40]

China has supported Pakistan's economic development through bilateral aid agreements. China offered a $500 million loan for budgetary support to Pakistan and pledged $1 million in cash in May 2009 for emergency humanitarian relief. In June 2009, Beijing agreed to provide an additional $8.8 million.[41] In addition, China also is part of the "Friends of Democratic Pakistan," a 13-member group formed in September 2008 aimed at promoting economic development in Pakistan and preventing the Pakistani government from being overthrown by Taliban militants.† The group collectively has pledged more than $5.28 billion to help secure the region.[42] In addition, because China is Pakistan's biggest defence supplier, it is likely that Chinese arms are being used in Pakistan's offensive against the Taliban.[43]

During the Commission's May 2009 trip to China, representatives from the China Institutes of Contemporary International Relations stated that China is interested in engaging in counterterrorism cooperation with the United States to prevent the Taliban from gaining inroads in Xinjiang. However, they made it clear that China is not interested in sending military troops either to Afghanistan or Pakistan.

---

† The members of the Friends of Democratic Pakistan are Australia, China, the European Union, France, Germany, Great Britain, Italy, Japan, Saudi Arabia, Turkey, the United Arab Emirates, the United States, the European Union, and the United Nations. While this group has provided a forum for the member nations to discuss aid projects to promote stability and capacity building in Pakistan, most of the pledges made by members have been bilateral agreements between Pakistan and the donor country or agency.

Economic Interests in the Region

The Chinese have been involved heavily in commercial and energy investments in both Pakistan and Afghanistan, including the building of key infrastructure that has, in addition to its primary purpose of providing access to resources in the region, helped to support US and NATO security efforts. This involvement helps to augment China's economic growth, foster business opportunities for Chinese firms, and create a bridge to further investment in the Middle East. These investments also lead to increased economic development for Pakistan and Afghanistan, which can be a force for stability in the region.

Walid Phares testified before the Commission that one of the reasons China has developed its economic relationship with Pakistan is because the relationship serves as a "testing ground of influence"into the wider Muslim world.[44] It is significant for China to establish a working relationship with the greater Middle East in order to ensure China's energy security and increase its economic and political opportunities. Abraham M. Denmark of the Center for a New American Security stated in the Commission's May hearing that "China seeks to cultivate positive relations with Muslim-majority countries for their natural resources and their votes in multilateral fora." [45] Beijing's cooperation with Islamabad creates an opportunity to forge these relationships.

China has utilized its close relations with the region in order to obtain natural resources for its burgeoning domestic needs. In 2007, China signed a memorandum of understanding to enter into a joint venture for oil and gas exploration in Pakistan. The deal gave China Zhenhua Oil Co., Ltd., a wholly owned unit of China North Industries Corp. (NORINCO), production-sharing contracts to explore two oil and gas blocks in the country.[46]

In Afghanistan, in 2007, the state-owned China Metallurgical Group Corporation invested $3.5 billion to develop the Aynak copper deposit in Logar Province, located south of Kabul. The contract is the largest investment in Afghanistan's history. The China Metallurgical Group Corporation has agreed to build schools, clinics, markets, and mosques in exchange for a deal that may yield up to $88 billion of copper ore.[47] The mine originally was estimated to sell for less than $2 billion, but the Chinese firm far outbid four major Russian, British, Canadian, and US competitors.[48] During the tender process, the China Metallurgical Group Corporation also agreed to the construction of an electrical plant and a railway from Tajikistan to Pakistan to support exploration and mining. The development of the mine is expected to provide the Afghan government with $400 million annually—more than half of its current annual state budget—and employ between 6,000 and 10,000 Afghans.[49] Because the mine is considered to be critical infrastructure for Afghanistan, it is under the protection of US and NATO forces.*

---

* While the Aynak copper mine is being protected by US and NATO forces in Afghanistan, there is no specific agreement between China and the United States or NATO to protect the mine. The protection is part of a larger strategy of securing key and critical infrastructure to help foster economic development. US and NATO forces are also protecting investments by other countries as well. US-China Economic and Security Review Commission, *Hearing on the Impact of China's Economic and Security Interests in Continental Asia on the United States*, testimony of Michael Schiffer, May 20, 2009.

A report by James R. Yeager, a former consultant to the Afghan Ministry of Mines and Industry in 2007, raises serious questions about the Aynak copper tender process. Among other problems, in his report, Mr. Yeager noted that the China Metallurgical Group Corporation, as a state-owned company, included infrastructure development in the bid package relying on funding support it received from the Chinese government. According to Mr. Yeager, this effectively gave the company a competitive advantage over western private firms.[50]

While China's natural resource investments are significant, a lack of adequate infrastructure in the embattled region has made further projects difficult.[51] For this reason, China has invested heavily in infrastructure construction as well. In 2008, Chinese companies had 33 infrastructure projects, valued at $580 million, under way in Afghanistan. Many of these investments include roads through Afghanistan's mountainous regions that secondarily provide easier access to Kabul for US and NATO forces.[52] Also in Afghanistan, China has participated in water supply projects in Parwar Province, as well as in the reconstruction of public hospitals in Kabul and Kandahar.[53]

In 2008, China and Pakistan entered into an agreement to upgrade and expand the Karakorum Highway, which was built by the two countries during the 1960s and 1970s and connects Pakistan with Xinjiang. With the goal of enhancing tourism and trade between the two countries, the Export-Import Bank of China provided a $327 million credit line to finance the project's construction. Chinese state-owned China Road and Bridge Corporation and Pakistan's National Highway Authority jointly are undertaking the project.[54]

One of the Chinese infrastructure investments that has gained the most media attention is the Gwadar Port on the Arabian Sea in southwestern Pakistan's Balochistan Province.[55] The construction of the Gwadar Port began in March 2002 and consisted of two phases. The Chinese government provided $198 million of the $248 million needed for the first phase, which was completed in November 2005. The second phase, which concluded in 2007, cost approximately $600 million and was funded primarily by China.[56] Stateowned China Harbor Engineering Company was the principal contractor involved in the project, and in February 2007 the Port Authority of Singapore won a 40-year contract for the management of the port.[57] The Gwadar Port became fully functional in December 2008.[58]

Several analysts have expressed concern that China may turn its investment in the port into access for its warships and potentially project its power in the Indian Ocean.[59] In his testimony to the Commission, Deputy Assistant Secretary of Defence Schiffer noted that

> *China's construction of a major port facility at Gwadar could serve to promote economic development in the region. On the other hand, China may view the port as an anchor for naval expansion into the West Indian Ocean, a development that may prove to be very destabilizing. It is in the interest of all parties active in South Asia, including the US, that China be open and transparent regarding its intentions for Gwadar.*[60]

China has been able to build upon its investment in the Gwadar Port in order to develop other business opportunities in Gwadar. For example, in 2006, China and Pakistan signed a memorandum of understanding for China's Great United Petroleum Holding Company to build a Chinese-funded $12.5 billion refinery in the port city.[61]

However, due to the global financial crisis, the project has been shelved until 2010.[62] Chinese construction companies are active in several other prominent projects there, including construction of a $70 million international airport. According to a report by the South Asia Analysis Group, a think tank based in India consisting of former government officials and academics, the airport and its construction will be overseen by the Pakistani military as opposed to the Civil Aviation Authority, which controls other commercial airports in the country. The same report states that "Pakistani authorities have agreed to allow the Chinese Air Force to use this airport in an emergency."[63]

Chinese companies have made inroads in the region's telecommunications sector as well. In Pakistan, Chinese state-owned China Mobile acquired PakTel, a major telecommunications provider in Pakistan, for $460 million in 2007.[64] Additionally, plans have been made for a Chinese company, China Great Wall Industry Corporation, to launch a telecommunications satellite for Pakistan. The satellite will be launched from Sichuan Province in 2011 and will have a lifespan of 15 years.[65] In Afghanistan, in August 2003, Chinese state-owned companies ZTE and Huawei partnered with the Afghan Ministry of Communications to implement digital telephone switches, providing roughly 200,000 subscriber lines.[66]

China and Pakistan also have become involved in each others' banking and financial services sectors. In July 2007, Pakistan's Ministry of Finance and the China Development Bank launched the $200 million Pak-China Investment Company Ltd.[67] According to Pakistan's Ministry of Finance, the joint venture currently is investing in commercial banking in Pakistan and in specialized services such as asset management, housing finance, and investment banking.[68]

Limitations to Chinese Involvement in the Region

While China has taken several measures to improve the security of its investments in the region, several analysts have openly criticized China for "free-riding" upon US and NATO security forces to protect its economic interests and secure its borders from attacks.[69] Although China has made contributions to developing the economies of Pakistan and Afghanistan, Lisa Curtis told the Commission that China wants the United States "to do the heavy lifting."[70] While China is wary of the United States having a permanent presence in the region, Beijing has not opposed US forces in Pakistan and Afghanistan in large part because they are indirectly protecting China's border security and economic interests. Deputy Assistant Secretary of Defence Schiffer said that "China recognizes that the US-led efforts are the primary force preventing Afghanistan from slipping into greater anarchy, and given its interests in secure and stable borders and concerns about extremist terrorists, does not want [the United States] to fail."[71]

China is not interested in dedicating military support toward maintaining stability in the region, for several reasons. First and foremost, Beijing claims that a fundamental principle of its foreign policy is the respect for sovereignty and territorial integrity.* This underlying tenet would be contradicted if Beijing were to intervene

* While China claims that a fundamental principle of its foreign policy is the respect for sovereignty, in recent years China's foreign policy has begun to evolve so that it no longer is as strictly adherent to the "noninterference policy." For example, China provided peacekeeping forces to the United Nations-African Union hybrid force in Darfur. For more information, please see the Commission's 2008 Annual Report to Congress, chapter 4, section 1.

militarily in Pakistan and Afghanistan.[72] Some analysts also have argued that the reason China is not pledging more resources to enhance regional security is because China has yet to experience a significant terrorist threat or strike against Chinese mainland and urban zones.[73] Another explanation for China's reluctance is Beijing's unwillingness to provoke anger from the Muslim world and Islamic extremists, preferring rather that that sentiment be targeted at the United States. Lisa Curtis testified that while China benefits from stability in the region, animosity toward military forces in Afghanistan is directed at the United States.[74] The importance of not upsetting the Muslim world became pronounced in the wake of Chinese authorities' crackdown on ethnic violence in Xinjiang in July. In trying to appeal for understanding, Foreign Ministry spokesman Qin Gang stated,

> *We hope that the Islamic countries and our Muslim brothers could see the truth of July 5 incident in Urumqi . . . China and the Islamic countries have long been respecting and supporting each other, and the Chinese Government and people always firmly support the just cause of the Islamic countries to pursue national independence and safeguard* state sovereignty.[75]

Despite these pleas, anger among Muslims sparked protests in Turkey, Indonesia, and Kazakhstan.[76] Several prominent clerics and media outlets in Iran also denounced China for its crackdown in Xinjiang.†

China's unease about upsetting the Muslim world extends to Xinjiang's domestic Muslim community as well. Andrew Small of the German Marshall Fund of the United States argued that

> *[t]here is an abiding belief [among the Chinese leadership] that China should stay away from the front line [in Afghanistan and Pakistan] if it wants to avoid inflaming further unrest among its own Muslim population or becoming a more serious target of international terrorism. Chinese analysts acknowledge that they fall into the category of 'enemy number two' for transnational terrorism but that for now, the West—and particularly the United States—is 'enemy number one.'*[77]

China's Interests in Central Asia

Aside from its growing relationship with Pakistan and Afghanistan, China has been involved heavily in Central Asia as well. While China's interests in each of the Central Asian countries differ, there are several overlapping themes that permeate China's foreign policy in the region. Along its borders, China has developed a strategy to ensure regional stability and security by creating political alliances with its neighbours and investing in economic development. Not only does Beijing have

† While Iranian Foreign Minister Manucher Mottacki voiced concern about the Chinese government's actions in the days following the unrest, the widely read centrist newspaper *Tabnak* highly criticized the Iranian government for downplaying the murders of Muslims by Chinese officials. Senior clerics joined in criticizing the Chinese government for committing murders and the Iranian government for not confronting China. Among these clerics were Ayatollah Jafar Sohani, Ayatollah Naser Makarem-Shirazi, Ayatollah Hossein Nuri-Hamedani, and Ayatollah Yousef Saanei.

an interest in increasing trade and investment throughout Central Asia, but there is also a desire to diversify and secure energy interests and provide an alternate route for trade to the risky sea lanes in the Indian Ocean.

Regional Security

China has forged relationships with a number of Central Asian countries in order to maintain stability along its borders and limit the growth of what China characterizes as the "three evils." In order to check separatist factions of Muslim Turkic-speaking Uighurs in Xinjiang, China has developed a two-pronged approach: (1) encourage non-Muslim Han migration into Xinjiang so that Han become the majority, and (2) maintain positive relations with the countries bordering Xinjiang in order to seek assurances from them that they will not support separatist movements or Muslim extremism by Uighurs in their respective countries. The second approach has been used as an important reason for forging relationships with Central Asia.

One of the main vehicles China has used to combat security threats along its borders has been involvement in the Shanghai Cooperation Organization. In 1996, China signed a protocol with the presidents of Russia, Kazakhstan, Kyrgyzstan, and Tajikistan establishing the "Shanghai Five." The leaders agreed to reduce military forces within a 100-kilometer zone along each side of the border and to exchange information on military personnel and equipment.[78] The protocol was reaffirmed in 1999 when the member countries committed to respecting border security and suppressing terrorism, drug smuggling, and separatism. Later in June 2001, Uzbekistan was added to the group, and the name was changed to the Shanghai Cooperation Organization. The addition of Uzbekistan signaled that the organization was no longer limited to border issues but now included ensuring national security and domestic stability.[79] The organization also has four observer states: Iran, India, Mongolia, and Pakistan.[80] The Shanghai Cooperation Organization has since collaborated on a number of military exercises, including an April 2009 antiterrorism exercise in Tajikistan.[81] Despite these exercises, numerous analysts have argued that the Shanghai Cooperation Organization is merely a forum for discussion and does not lead to actual enhanced multilateral security measures. Martha Olcott, senior associate at the Carnegie Endowment for International Peace, says that "[w]hile members of the [Shanghai Cooperation Organization] will continue to hold bilateral military exercises with China and could organize multilateral military exercises involving the entire membership, these are likely to be more symbolic than a demonstration of a shared capacity to meet common threats." [82] Deputy Assistant Secretary of Defence Schiffer expressed a similar sentiment to the Commission:

> *I think the Chinese haven't yet managed to figure out what they can actually do with the [Shanghai Cooperation Organization]. . . . It's hard to draw a line between [Shanghai Cooperation Organization] meetings and actual policy outputs or influence, but I think they see it as an organization that may be able to develop into something that as Chinese power and influence grows, they may be able to use it more effectively to shape multilateral diplomacy in the region.*[83]

One of the reasons the Shanghai Cooperation Organization has been such a weak institution is because tensions and mistrust exist between Russia and China within the organization. Both Russian and Chinese military staff are wary about divulging sensitive information concerning new technologies and the nuclear sector. On several occasions, Russia has refused to participate in military exercises in which China has been involved.[84] Rather than share intelligence with China through the Shanghai Cooperation Organization, Moscow has been more willing to give priority to the Collective Security Treaty Organization, a Russian-dominated Central Asian security organization of which China is not a member.[85] In addition, the two countries have differed in the economic domain. Because of the divergence between China's dynamic economic growth and that of the Central Asian states, Russia is fearful of Central Asian states becoming Chinese protectorates. For this reason, Moscow has opposed China's proposal of a free-trade zone among the Shanghai Cooperation Organization states.[86] These fundamental differences between the group's two most prominent members cause the Shanghai Cooperation Organization to be relatively ineffective in creating a genuine security alliance in the region.

Nevertheless, China has used the Shanghai Cooperation Organization as a forum to negotiate bilateral deals on the sidelines of meetings and thus forge relationships with Central Asian governments, particularly to develop economic and energy ties. Daniel Twining, a senior fellow for Asia at the German Marshall Fund, told the Commission that the Shanghai Cooperation Organization also has allowed Beijing to pursue economic agreements that privilege its trade and investment interests in Central Asia, allowing Chinese companies to gain entry into the region.[87]

Energy Interests

Another reason why China has become more involved in Central Asia is to obtain energy resources and diversify its energy suppliers. China's tremendous foreign reserves have allowed it to challenge Russian hegemony in the Central Asian oil and gas sectors. Traditionally, Russia has been the principal player in the region's energy sector. Julia Nanay, senior director of PFC Energy, a consulting firm for energy companies and governments in the region, told the Commission that

> *[p]rior to the breakup of the Soviet Union, everything was oriented from South to North. Everything went to Russia, and that created a monopoly hold on the energy sector in [the Central Asian countries], and it is the Chinese that have helped to create optionality.*[88]

The energy partnership between China and Central Asia not only satisfies Central Asia's desire to diversify energy export partners but also meets China's stated interest in diversifying its own oil suppliers and finding alternative supply routes. Currently, approximately 45 percent of China's crude oil imports originate in the Middle East.[89] This oil must be shipped to the People's Republic of China (PRC) through the Malacca Strait, which separates Singapore and Malaysia from Indonesia. In November 2003, Chinese President Hu Jintao highlighted what became dubbed the "Malacca Dilemma," noting that if "certain major powers" were bent on controlling the strait, there would be little that China could do.[90] (For further discussion of the Malacca Dilemma, see chap. 2, sec. 4, of this Report, "China's Naval Modernization and Strategy.") Stephen Blank, research professor of National Security Affairs at the Strategic Studies Institute, told the Commission that he believes PRC leaders fear that in the event of a conflict in the Middle East or in the Indian Ocean, the United States or India could close the Malacca Strait to Chinese maritime transport. In that case, China would have no independent source of energy except for what it could get over land.[91]

To help address this dilemma, China is tapping into resource rich Central Asia. The amount that China currently receives in oil imports from Central Asia—about 10 percent of the total—is on the rise as China participates in the building of pipelines,* negotiates long-term supply gas and petroleum-for-finance contracts, and invests in assets deemed less desirable to western oil companies.[92] China has played a major role in the construction of two Central Asian oil and gas pipelines. China's first major oil pipeline project in Central Asia was the Kazakhstan-China pipeline, which stretches 3,000 kilometers from the Caspian Sea in western Kazakhstan to Xinjiang in China. The project is being undertaken by China National Petroleum Corporation and Kazakhstan's largest state-owned oil and gas company, KazMunaiGaz, at a cost of about $3 billion.[93] In addition, in August 2007, China began construction of a natural gas pipeline that would start in Turkmenistan and pass through Uzbekistan and Kazakhstan en route to China. The $7.3 billion project is scheduled to start operations in December 2009 and be fully operational by 2011.[94]

Figure 2: Kazakh-China Oil Pipeline *

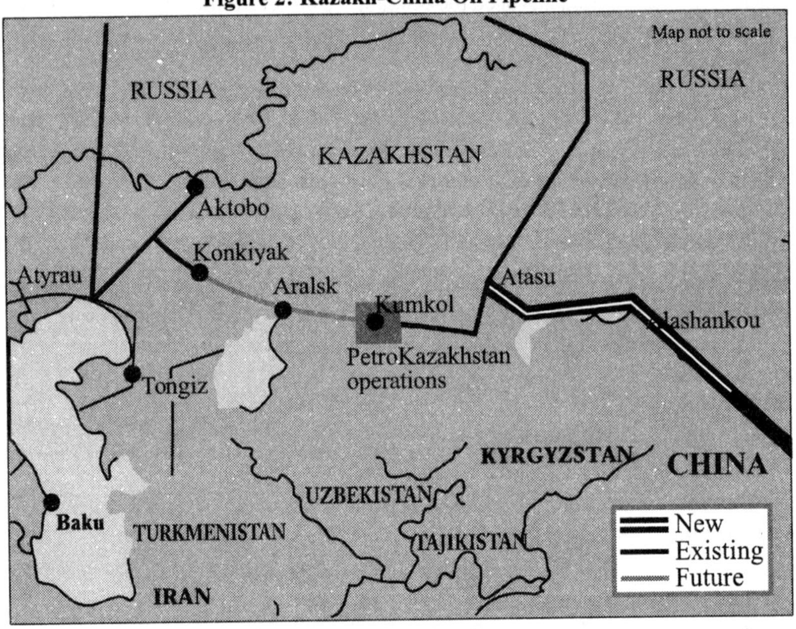

Source: Energy Information Administration, "Country Analysis Briefs: China" (Washington, DC: Department of Energy, July 2009). *http://www.eia.doe.gov*.

* China's strategy of building pipelines over land in order to avoid shipping through the Malacca Strait is not only limited to Central Asia. In Russia, the China National Petroleum Corporation soon will start building a pipeline from its terminal in northeastern China to the Russian border, called the East Siberia-Pacific Ocean pipeline. When completed in 2014, the pipeline is estimated to deliver up to 1.6 million barrels per day from Russia to the Pacific coast. In Burma, Sinopec and the China National Petroleum Corporation have signed contracts for the construction of oil and gas pipelines from Burma to southern China. While agreements between the two countries' leadership have been signed, the status of the oil and natural gas pipelines is unclear because of conflicting reports from Chinese and English-language media. For more information on China's interests in land-based energy investment projects in Asia, please see chapter 3, section 1, of the Commission's 2008 Annual Report to Congress.

Figure 3: Turkmenistan-China Gas Pipeline *

Source: Stratfor, "China: Buying Friends in Turkmenistan," June 25, 2009. *http://www. strat for.com/analysis /20090625l chinalbuyinglfriendsl turkmenistan.*

Chinese companies also have sought long-term petroleum and natural gas supply contracts to complement their investments in Central Asia's pipeline network. For example, in 2007, the China National Petroleum Corporation signed a production-

* The first stage of the Kazakh-China oil pipeline was completed in May 2006, connecting Atasu in central Kazakhstan with Alashankou on the Chinese border in Xinjiang. Both Kazakh and Russian oil is being delivered through the new pipeline. The pipeline's final leg from Kenkiyak to Atasu is set to be finished by 2011 by the China National Petroleum Corporation. When this stage is completed, it will double capacity to 400,000 barrels of crude per day. A contract signed between KazMunaiGaz and the China National Petroleum Corporation has given the corporation equity in the upstream oil in return for loans financing downstream infrastructure projects, including the Kenkiyak to Atasu section. The pipeline will also connect to existing Russian pipelines to obtain Russian crude from western Siberia. Energy Information Administration, "Country Analysis Briefs: China" (Washington, DC: Department of Energy, July 2009). *http://www.eia.doe.gov.*
The Turkmenistan-China gas pipeline, also known as the Central Asian Gas Pipeline, will stretch across 1,130 miles to Turkmenistan when it is completed in 2011. The proposed line will cross Kazakhstan and Uzbekistan and into Turkmenistan. Both countries are likely to contribute some of the natural gas exports to the pipeline. The China National Petroleum Corporation has signed a production-sharing agreement for the development of natural gas resources at Turkmenistan's South Yolotan gas fields alongside the pipeline. Energy Information Administration, "Country Analysis Briefs: China" (Washington, DC: July 2009). *http://www.eia.doe.gov.*

sharing agreement for 30 billion cubic meters of natural gas annually from Turkmenistan for 30 years that will be delivered through the pipeline currently under construction.[95]

China has sealed a number of oil and gas-for-finance deals in Kazakhstan that have established it as China's most important energy partner in Central Asia. In April 2009, the Export-Import Bank of China loaned the Kazakhstan Development Bank $5 billion, and the China National Petroleum Corporation lent Kazakhstan's national oil company, KazMunaiGaz, another $5 billion. As a result of this deal, the China National Petroleum Corporation will control about 15 percent of Kazakhstan's total oil production. [96]

In addition to oil and gas, China also seeks to increase its imports of uranium from Kazakhstan, which holds almost 20 percent of the world's uranium reserves.[97] The National Nuclear Company of Kazakhstan (KazAtomProm) and the China Guangdong Nuclear Power Company are building the Irkol uranium mine in Kazakhstan that is expected to produce 250 tons of uranium per year once it reaches full capacity in 2010.[98]

Because China is a late comer to energy exploitation in Central Asia and Russia, Chinese companies have sought fields that western oil companies consider to be less desirable or off-limits because of political restrictions. For example, China entered into a $600 million oil deal with Uzbekistan's state-owned oil company, Uzbekneftegaz, in 2005 at a time when the regime faced a broad range of sanctions and international criticism for human rights violations. [99] In addition, in Kazakhstan, China has invested in isolated oil fields that are only valuable to Chinese firms because they are adjacent to the pipeline built by the China National Petroleum Corporation and KazMunaiGaz.[100] Because of this, these new oil deals do not pose an immediate competitive threat to international oil companies in the region. Western companies, as well as Russian oil and gas companies, still have significant access to Central Asian resources.[101]

Chinese Energy Investments in Central Asia

Kazakhstan	China National Petroleum Corporation (CNPC) and Kazakhstan's largest state-owned oil company, KazMunaiGaz, are constructing a $3 billion, 3,000 kilometer (km) pipeline from the Caspian Sea to Xinjiang. It will have a capacity of more than 200,000 barrels per day when it is completed in October 2009.[102]
	CNPC owns major stakes in several large Kazakh energy companies, including the Aktobemunaigaz Company, Petro Kazakhstan, and Mangystau MunayGaz. As these deals were negotiated, the Export-Import Bank of China agreed to loan Kazakhstan Development Bank $5 billion, and CNPC agreed to lend Kaz MunaiGaz $5 billion.[103]
	In April 2009, a joint venture established by National Nuclear Company of Kazakhstan and China Guangdong Nuclear Power Company launched the operation of a new Kazakh uranium mine. It is expected to produce 250 tons of uranium per year once it reaches full capacity in 2010. All uranium produced in the mine will supply the Chinese market. The joint venture will finance $664,000 per year in social projects in the region.[104]

Turkmenistan	CNPC is building a $7.3 billion, 7,000 km natural gas pipeline that would begin in Turkmenistan and pass through Uzbekistan and Kazakhstan en route to China, called the Central Asia Gas Pipeline. The pipeline is estimated to be completed in 2010 and will produce 40 billion cubic meters per year for 30 years.[105]
	In June 2009, China agreed to loan Turkmenistan $4 billion to develop its South Yolotan natural gas field. The field likely holds 6 trillion cubic meters of gas, making it one of the five largest deposits in the world.[106]
Uzbekistan	CNPC and Uzbekistan's national oil company, Uzbekneftegaz, signed an agreement in October 2008 to develop the Mingulak oil field in the Namangan region of Uzbekistan.[107]
	In December 2006, a CNPC subsidiary, CNPC Silk Road, was created for exploration in Uzbek oil and gas regions. It is licensed to explore five blocks within the Ustyurt, Bukhara- Khiva, and Fergana oil and gas regions. Under the agreement, CNPC Silk Road will invest $208.5 million in exploration in Uzbekistan.[108]

Economic Interests

In addition to Chinese energy interests, China has established other economic ties with the Central Asian states. Chinese companies have found business opportunities through furthering trade, developing infrastructure, and providing preferential loans in the region.

Trade between China and Central Asia has expanded significantly, going from about $1 billion in 2002 to $18 billion in 2007. Finished goods comprise more than 85 percent of China's exports to the former Soviet republics in Central Asia. These exports consist of consumer products, machinery and parts, processed foodstuff, textiles, electronics, and pharmaceutical products.[109] Conversely, more than 85 percent of Central Asian states' exports to China are raw materials or commodities.[110] This is a pattern similar to China's trade relationship with Africa and Latin America.[111] Increased trade and investment in Central Asia also have led to an influx of Chinese workers living in the region. For example, according to one report, there are currently 30,000 Chinese nationals living and working on various infrastructure projects in Tajikistan, worth roughly $720 million.[112] Many of these numbers, however, are difficult to measure, because labour migration laws in Central Asian states are relatively weak.[113] For example, in 2008, there were only 6,000 legal work permits issued in Kyrgyzstan, but reportedly there are approximately 30,000 Chinese migrants currently living in the country.[114]

One area of significant economic involvement by Chinese companies has been in the building of large-scale infrastructure projects. For example, China and the governments of Afghanistan, Azerbaijan, Kazakhstan, Kyrgyzstan, Mongolia, Tajikistan, and Uzbekistan have agreed to an $18 billion "New Silk Road" project across Central Asia. The project will include six highway corridors that will facilitate traffic from Europe to East Asia, including roads from Siberia to Iran, Siberia to China, Pakistan to China through Afghanistan and Tajikistan, and northwestern Kazakhstan to Xinjiang.[115]

Key Chinese Infrastructure Investments in Central Asia

Power transmission lines: In 2006, the Export-Import Bank of China provided more than $300 million in loans for the construction of power transmission lines in Tajikistan to be completed by China Theban Electric Apparatus Stock and Tajikistan's national electric power company.[116]

Highway construction: In Kyrgyzstan, Beijing has financed part of the reconstruction of the country's Irkeshtam-Osh highway, an 80-kilometer section of which will be completed by the China Road and Bridge Corporation at a cost of $15 million.[117]

Railway development: Kazakhstan's state-owned national railway company has purchased passenger carriages from Chinese locomotive manufacturers. The deal was financed by loans from the Kazakhstan Development Bank and the Export-Import Bank of China for $60 million.[118] In June 2009, President Hu Jintao agreed to the construction of a $2 billion railway in return for control of a lucrative coal mine in Kyrgyzstan. The proposed railway would connect Kashgar in China to Andijan in Uzbekistan via Kyrgyzstan.[119] President Hu and Kyrgyz Prime Minister Igor Chudinov have agreed to set up a working group to determine the details of the agreement.[120]

In addition to Chinese companies' building infrastructure in the region, Chinese state-owned financial institutions, including the Export-Import Bank of China, also have issued numerous preferential loans to enhance economic development. The Chinese government has granted multiple loans and export credit lines to Uzbekistan, including $300 million in export credit to the government. [121] Moreover, the Chinese government has given Uzbekistan a $12 million interest-free loan and a $36.3 million low-interest loan to pay for a number of social projects.[122] In January 2007, two Chinese firms won a bid in Turkmenistan for the construction of a glass factory which, when operational in late 2009, will be the largest in Central Asia. The $67 million cost of the project was financed by a loan from the Export-Import Bank of China to the Turkmen authorities.[123]

Increasing Influence

Several western observers have argued that China's growing investments in Central Asia are based on a strategic design that may lead to increased influence in the region. Because many Central Asian states have been hit particularly hard during the global economic crisis, China has been able to provide aid for the ailing economies. For example, in Kazakhstan, foreign investment from other countries has fallen by half since 2008.[124] Russia, once the dominant investor in Central Asia, also experienced a 10.9 percent contraction in gross domestic product (GDP) in the second quarter of 2009 due to declining oil and gas prices. As Russia's economy continues to decline, Russia is severely dampening its investments in Central Asia.[125] In contrast, China has increased its economic support to the region. On the sidelines of the June 2009 Shanghai Cooperation Organization meeting in Yekaterinburg, Russia, President Hu Jintao pledged $10 billion in credit support for the Central Asian members of the organization in order to deal with the global financial crisis.[126] Stephen Blank testified to the Commission that

> *China is able to leverage its superior economic power vis-a-vis these states in order to induce them to change their previous policy preferences on key questions relating to the sale and distribution of their energy. This suggests that in broader terms, China is beginning to be able to leverage its economic power in order to induce Asian states into a pattern of accommodation with China's preferences. . . . China is able to influence their policies in a direction that suits China more than it might have suited those states in other* times.[127]

While this influence is nearly impossible to measure concretely, it is clear that China has effectively broken the Russian monopoly on oil and gas shipments from Central Asia, thus decreasing Russian control of the energy market.[128]

Additionally, China's new role in the region may offset US influence. "US leverage for various goals, whether democratization, human rights, or commercial concerns, will diminish," predicted Julia Nanay.[129] China may have utilized this leverage in 2005 when the Shanghai Cooperation Organization called for the removal of all US military bases in Central Asia, leading to the closure of a US staging base in Uzbekistan. In February 2009, Kyrgyzstan, too, called for the eviction of US forces from the Manas military base, one of the closest US bases to China's western border.[130] However, in July 2009, Kyrgyzstan agreed to allow the United States to maintain its air base in the country.[131]

While China's entry into Central Asia is growing, there are still large problems that thwart Beijing's ability to gain substantial influence in the region. Martin Spechler, professor of economics at Indiana University-Purdue University, cautioned not to view Central Asian countries as entirely dependent on China:

> *[Central Asian countries], especially Uzbekistan and Kazakhstan, have become much more independent, self-confident, and aware of their possibilities and their interests over the last 20 years. To talk about Central Asian countries as if they're some kind of pawns to be sacrificed on a big chessboard is simply wrong.*[132]

Over the past several years, Sebastien Peyrouse, senior research fellow with the Central Asia and Caucasus Institute, conducted a survey of all Central Asian think tank publications focusing on China. Mr. Peyrouse found that many of their experts are extremely distrustful of Beijing. This mistrust has limited military cooperation and intelligence-gathering in the countries' antiterrorism campaigns. Fears of "invasion" and imperialism are still pervasive among policy analysts in the region.[133]

In terms of trade, while many Central Asian elites have welcomed increased business with China, many are concerned that Central Asian economies have been restricted to the role of producers and exporters of natural resources. Central Asian think tanks have espoused views that China's investments are undermining local production and are creating increased, unwanted competition for light industry, construction, processing, and agribusiness. [134]

Culture barriers also serve as a large impediment to developing significant bilateral and regional relationships. Historic Soviet propaganda casting China as an enemy still lingers in the writings of many Central Asian experts. Deep-seated sinophobia has cast a negative light on increasing Chinese migration. Tensions caused by a strong Muslim population in Central Asia, Russo-Soviet acculturation, and views by some Chinese of the Central Asians as "barbarians" have precluded China from gaining deeper clout in the region. [135] Because of historic Sino-Soviet tensions and deep cultural and religious differences, China has been limited in its ability to influence Central Asia through its business relationships.[136]

Russia, too, has provided challenges for Chinese entry into Central Asia. Because of distrust and sinophobia, Moscow remains the intellectual, economic, and business capital for many Central Asians. In addition to Moscow, other Russian cities draw millions of Central Asian students, merchants, and workers.[137] Thus far, it does not seem as if China has developed a similar bond with the region. Further, as Professor Spechler pointed out, "[Central Asian] countries have become increasingly self-confident and independent, conducting a multivectoral foreign policy."[138] This growing confidence is allowing the countries to play Russia and China off one another in negotiating energy and commercial agreements, making it difficult for China simply to establish deals on its own terms.

Conclusion

- Beijing's primary interests in Afghanistan, Pakistan, and Central Asia concern isolating Chinese Muslim separatist groups from fundamentalist influences in Central Asia, maintaining stability along China's borders, diversifying its energy supplies, and increasing economic investments in the region.
- China continues to exercise a great deal of influence over Pakistan, stemming from the historic military and political ties between the two countries and their mutual desire to balance India's power.
- In Afghanistan, China also is increasing its influence due to its ability to offer economic aid and invest in large-scale infrastructure projects. However, China's influence in Afghanistan is still less than that of the United States.
- While China has not provided any direct military support to US and coalition forces in Afghanistan, Chinese investments in Afghanistan and Pakistan are contributing to those countries' economic development. China contributes no forces of its own, relying on US and NATO forces to protect these investments.
- China is increasing its economic, security, and political influence in Central Asia, possibly to the detriment of the United States. However, China's influence over the region is still limited because of historical mistrust, cultural barriers, and traditional Russian influence.
- The Shanghai Cooperation Organization has provided a forum for China to negotiate bilateral trade and energy deals with Central Asian states. It is not yet a genuine security alliance.
- In the wake of the June 2009 riots in Xinjiang, China will likely devote even more attention to developing political, security, and economic ties with Central Asia in order to ensure the security of its border and bolster stability in Xinjiang Province.
- China's energy investments in Central Asia are large. As Beijing seeks a means of importing oil and gas over land to ensure its 1energy security, Chinese investments in the Central Asian energy sector will continue to expand.

SECTION 2

Taiwan

> ". . . the United States-China Economic and Security Review Commission . . . shall investigate and report exclusively on—
>
> "Regional Economic and Security Impacts—The triangular economic and security relationship among the United States, Taipei and the People's Republic of China (including the military modernization and force deployments of the People's Republic of China aimed at Taipei), the national budget of the People's Republic of China, and the fiscal strength of the People's Republic of China in relation to internal instability in the People's Republic of China and the likelihood of the externalization of problems arising from such internal instability. . . ."

Introduction

Since Ma Ying-jeou was inaugurated as president of Taiwan in May 2008, many developments have occurred in the relationship between Taiwan and the People's Republic of China (PRC). Almost immediately after President Ma took office, official meetings between Taiwan and the mainland began, including high-level interactions. During these meetings, the two sides signed several agreements—primarily economic in nature—and made progress toward a free trade agreement. These political and economic improvements in the relationship were summed up in a speech President Ma gave on January 1, 2009:

> *In the past year, cross-Strait relations also underwent a historic transition. Upon coming into office, my administration not only swiftly reactivated the mechanism for institutionalized talks between [Taiwan] and [China], but we also entered an era of comprehensive, normalized economic relations.* [139]

However, despite the apparent progress in cross-Strait relations on some fronts, the PRC has shown no signs of abating its buildup of military capacities vis-a-vis Taiwan, increasing the disparity between China and Taiwan's respective military capabilities. This section of the Commission's Annual Report will address developments in the cross-Strait relationship since President Ma's inauguration. It will look at recent meetings the two sides have held and agreements they have signed. In addition, it will provide an overview of changes in the cross-Strait military balance.

Developments in the Cross-Strait Relationship

Official Signs of Warming from Beijing

Since President Ma's May 2008 inauguration, Beijing has repeatedly signaled that it is willing to work with the Ma Administration in an attempt to promote cross-Strait relations. Beijing's signaling has come in three official government forms: statements, documents, and actions.

Over the past year, Chinese government officials have made several statements professing a willingness to work with Taiwan on some issues. For example, on December 31, 2008, China's President Hu Jintao gave a major address on the issue of cross-Strait relations. During this speech, President Hu laid out six proposals for how the mainland envisioned making progress on cross-Strait reconciliation. Hu proposed that both sides adhere firmly to the "One China" principle; strengthen commercial ties, including negotiating an economic cooperation agreement; promote personnel exchanges; stress common cultural links between the two sides; allow Taiwan's "reasonable" participation in global organizations; and negotiate a peace agreement.[140] In addition to these six proposals, President Hu also floated the idea of military exchanges as a confidence building measure. In December 2008, President Hu said, "The two sides can engage in . . . contacts and communications on military issues when appropriate, and discussions on building a trust mechanism for military safety." [141] A few months later, Premier Wen Jiabao reiterated President Hu's statements during his March 2009 address to the PRC's National People's Congress, saying, "[w]e are also ready to hold talks on cross-Straits political and military issues and create conditions for ending the state of hostility and concluding a peace agreement between the two sides of the Taiwan Straits." [142]

Official Chinese government documents released recently further signify Beijing's desire to improve relations with Taiwan. For example, the PRC's 2008 defence white paper (released in January 2009) presented a significantly less bellicose assessment of the cross-Strait scenario than the 2006 version.* According to the 2008 version:

> *The attempts of the separatist forces for 'Taiwan independence' to seek de jure Taiwan independence' have been thwarted, and the situation across the Taiwan Straits has taken a significantly positive turn. The two sides have resumed and made progress in consultations on the common political basis of the '1992 Consensus,' and consequently cross-Straits relations have improved.*[143]

This view of the relationship contrasts sharply with the view that the 2006 version presented:

> *The struggle to oppose and contain the separatist forces for 'Taiwan independence' and their activities remains a hard one. By pursuing a radical policy for 'Taiwan independence,' the Taiwan authorities aim at creating 'de jure Taiwan independence' through 'constitutional reform,' thus still posing a grave threat to China's sovereignty and territorial integrity, as well as to peace and stability across the Taiwan Straits and in the Asia-Pacific region as a whole.*[144]

Finally, Beijing has also made several symbolic gestures toward Taiwan as actions to improve the relationship. In what President Ma called a "goodwill gesture," Beijing acquiesced to Taiwan participating in the World Health Organization's (WHO) ruling body, the World Health Assembly, in April 2009—

---

* Chinese defence white papers are authoritative documents published every two years since 1998 and should be taken to represent the official views of the Chinese government.

albeit under the name of "Chinese Taipei." Although officially only an observer without voting rights, Taiwan has made its first appearance at the WHO since 1971, when it lost its seat to the PRC.[145] More recently, during the Dalai Lama's August 2009 visit to Taiwan, Beijing's official response was much more low key than during previous visits, suggesting that the mainland wanted to prevent the event from derailing recent progress on cross-Strait relations. Rather than rebuking President Ma or jeopardizing recently signed agreements with Taiwan, Beijing directed its criticism toward the Democratic Progressive Party, characterizing the visit as a political ploy by the party to detract from warming ties with Beijing. In addition, China only retaliated symbolically by canceling or postponing several low-level events.[146]

Cross-Strait Meetings

Since President Ma's inauguration, numerous high-level meetings between the PRC and Taiwan have occurred. Some of the more important meetings are discussed here, while a more complete list is presented in the table overleaf. After a 10-year hiatus, Taiwan accepted a PRC invitation to resume quasi-official, cross- Strait dialogues between Taiwan's Straits Exchange Forum and China's Association for Relations Across the Taiwan Strait in May 2008.* Since then, these two organizations have met three times, with a fourth meeting tentatively planned for late 2009.[147] Another high-level meeting occurred in November 2008, when former Taiwanese Vice President and Premier Lien Chan met with PRC President Hu Jintao during an Asia-Pacific Economic Cooperation meeting in Peru—the "highest-level meeting between the two sides in an international forum since 1949." [148] In May 2009, Wu Pohhsiung, then chairman of Taiwan's ruling Chinese Nationalist Party, met with President Hu to discuss cross-Strait economic issues.[149] To support these various initiatives, on July 27, 2009, President Hu sent a telegram congratulating President Ma on his election as chairman of the Chinese Nationalist Party, the first time the leaders of the PRC and Taiwan had directly communicated with each other since the founding of the PRC in 1949.[150] Some analysts have speculated that this direct contact could facilitate the event ual meeting between the two individual leaders, ostensibly as head of their respective parties.[151] Meetings with Chinese officials were not limited just to Chinese Nationalist Party members. In May 2009, Chen Chu, Democratic Progressive Party member and mayor of Kaoshiung, Taiwan, visited mainland China to lobby for PRC promotion of the July 2009 World Games, which her district was hosting.[152]

---

* It is worth noting that, technically, Taipei and Beijing do not negotiate directly. According to Kerry Dumbaugh, a specialist in Asian affairs at the Congressional Research Srvice, Taiwan's Straits Exchange Foundation is not an official government entity but rather "a nominally non-government organization authorized to handle [cross-Strait] exchanges." China's Association for Relations Across the Taiwan Strait, however, is subordinate to the Taiwan Affairs Office of the State Council. Kerry Dumbaugh, *Taiwan-US Relations: Developments and Policy Implications* (Washington, D.C.: Congressional Research Service, August 2009), p. 24; and Web site ofthe Taiwan Affairs Office of the State Council. *http://www.gwytb.gov.cn: 8088/.*

Figure 1: Cross-Strait Actions since May 2008 *

Date	Taiwan Individual/ Organization	PRC Individual/ Organization	Location/Event
May 2008	Wu Poh-hsiung, Chinese Nationalist Party chairman	CCP General Secretary Hu Jintao	Beijing, China: highest-level cross-Strait meeting
June 2008	Straits Exchange Foundation	Association for Relations Across the Taiwan Strait	First round of cross-Strait talks in a decade
Nov. 2008	Lien Chan, former vice president and premier	PRC President Hu Jintao	Asia-Pacific Economic Cooperation meeting, Lima, Peru
Nov. 2008	Straits Exchange Foundation	Association for Relations Across the Taiwan Strait	Second round of cross-Strait talks
Dec. 2008	Wu Poh-hsiung, Chinese Nationalist Party chairman; and Lien Chan, former vice president and premier	Jia Qinglin, chairman of the National Committee of the Chinese People's Political Consultative Conference	Fourth Cross Straits Economic,Trade and Cultural Forum
Jan. 2009	Chiang Pin-kung, chairman of Straits Exchange Foundation	Various	Tour of four mainland cities
Apr. 2009	Fredrick Chien, Control Yuan president	Premier Wen Jiaobao	2009 Boao Forum for Asia meeting, Hainan Island, PRC
Apr. 2009	Straits Exchange Foundation	Association for Relations Across the Taiwan Strait	Third round of cross-Strait talks
May 2009	Chen Chu, mayor of Kaohsiung	Taiwan Affairs Office, State Council	Beijing and Shanghai, China
May 2009	Wu Poh-hsiung, Chinese Nationalist Party chairman	CCP General Secretary Hu Jintao	Beijing, China
June 2009	Hsu Tain-tsair, Tainan City mayor	Various	Xiamen, China
July 2009	Wu Poh-hsiung, KMT chairman; Hsu Jung-shu then DPP legislator; Fan Chen-tsung, former minister of agriculture	Jia Qinglin, chairman of the National Committee of the Chinese People's Political Consultative Conference	The fifth Cross Straits Economic, Trade and Cultural Forum, Changsha, China.

* This list begins with May 2008, since this is the date of President Ma's inauguration.

Date	Taiwan Individual/ Organization	PRC Individual/ Organization	Location/Event
July 2009	Taiwanese journalists, academics, and media executives	Chinese journalists, academics, and media executives, led by the director of the Information Department, Taiwan Affairs Office, Yang Yi	Taiwan
July 2009	President Ma Ying-jeou	President Hu Jintao	Direct telegram from President Hu to President Ma
Late 2009 (tentative)	Straits Exchange Foundation	Association for Relations Across the Taiwan Strait	Fourth round of talks

Source: US-China Economic and Security Review Commission staff based upon various sources.

Cross-Strait Agreements

As a result of many of these actions, Beijing and Taipei have proposed or signed several agreements, including the following:

- *The "Three Direct Links"*—A major milestone in recent cross-Strait relations are the various agreements to resume direct shipping, commercial airline flights, and mail service across the Taiwan Strait, officially banned by Taiwan since 1949. Direct transportation between the mainland and Taiwan officially resumed on December 15, 2008, after a series of steps over the past decade.[153] In 2000, for example, China and Taiwan agreed to allow trade and passenger traffic between the Taiwanese islands of Quemoy and Matsu and the mainland, referred to as the "Three Mini-Links."[154] With the 2008 resumption of direct links, Taiwan opened 11 seaports for direct shipping—including its two largest, Kaohsiung and Keelung *—while the PRC opened up 63.† Using previous steps such as the 2005 resumption of direct flights during holidays and the July 2008 agreement for weekend direct charter flights, a limited number of daily direct charter flights began in December 2008.[155] Originally capped at 108 direct flights a week, the number increased to 270 in August 2009 (see *Supplementary Agreement on Cross-Strait Air Transport* below). In addition to the daily chartered flights, regularly scheduled cargo flights across the Taiwan Strait also began in August 2009.[156] The final direct link is postal service,

* The other nine ports are Wuchi, Hualien, Putai,and Mailiao, as well as several ports on the Taiwanese islands of Penghu, Jimen, and Mazu. *China Post,* "Direct Cross-Strait Links in Place," December 15, 2008. *http://www.chinapost.com .tw/taiwan/china-taiwan-relations/2008/12/ 15/187643/Direct-across-strait.htm.*

†A sampling of these ports includes Dairen, Fuzhou, Guangzhou, Nanjing, Qingdao, Quanzhou, Shanghai, Shantou, Tianjin, Wuhan, and Xiamen.

allowing mail and cargo to travel directly from the mainland to Taiwan. The resumption of direct links between Taiwan and the mainland could benefit Taiwan's economy. Flight and maritime shipping costs could be reduced by $90 million a year, and postage costs could shrink by a third.[157] In addition, as the Commission learned on a May 2009 trip to Xiamen, China, the closest point opposite Taiwan, a greater number of people are traveling, and more containers are being shipped directly between Taiwan and the mainland. The deputy director of Xiamen City's Taiwan Affairs Office said that the number of passengers traveling by ferry between the mainland and Taiwan had grown from 677,000 in 2007 to 910,000 in 2008 and had already surpassed 400,000 at the time of the Commission's trip.[158] The Taiwanese Minister of Transportation and Communications, Mao Chih-kuo, substantiated this, stating that the number of mainland visits to Taiwan in the first six months of the year had increased 260 percent from the same period in 2008. By the end of 2009, the total number of visits to the island could reach 900,000, with revenues from these visits possibly reaching $1 billion.[159]

- *The Financial Cooperation Agreement*—Signed during the third round of the Straits Exchange Foundation-Association for Relations Across the Taiwan Strait cross-Strait dialogue in April 2009, the Financial Cooperation Agreement established a cooperative financial regulatory mechanism to evaluate whether the banking, securities, futures, and insurance sectors on both sides would be conducive to further financial cooperation. This cooperation could include currency management and exchanges of commercial banking branches.[160] Under this financial cooperation agreement, regulators on both sides will evaluate the cross-Strait financial sector in order to help Chinese and Taiwanese commercial and financial institutions establish agencies across the Taiwan Strait and to begin currency exchanges. [161] After the agreement was signed, the Bank of China applied to be the first mainland bank to set up a branch in Taiwan after financial regulators finish pending their initial evaluation.[162]
- *The Cross-Strait Food Safety Agreement*—Partially driven by poisonings from melamine-tainted milk powder the mainland sold to Taiwan, the Straits Exchange Foundation and the Association for Relations Across the Taiwan Strait signed an agreement concerning food safety on November 4, 2008. According to Taiwan's official entity responsible for handling cross-Strait affairs, the Mainland Affairs Council,* the main content of the cross-Strait Food Safety Agreement involves the prompt notification of major incidents concerning trade food safety, the establishment of a coordination mechanism to handle major food safety incidents, and the creation of a system of institutionalized meetings and visits of experts from both sides.[163] This agreement went into effect in mid-November 2008.[164]

---

* The Mainland Affairs Council was established in 1991 to deal with burgeoning Cross-Strait relations and is the "authorized agency directly under the Executive Yuan responsible for handling China affairs." Mainland Affairs Council, "Mainland Affairs Council—An Introduction," August 2005. *http://www.mac.gov. tw/english/english/orafunc/ora01.pdf.*

- *The Agreement on Joint Cross-Strait Crime-fighting and Mutual Judicial Assistance*—Signed during the third Straits Exchange Foundation-Association for Relations Across the Taiwan Strait meeting in April 2009, this agreement established "an institutionalized cooperation platform for joint cross-Strait crime prevention" to exchange information and cooperate on crime prevention activities.[165] This was the first formal agreement on law enforcement cooperation between Taipei and Beijing. [166]
- *The Supplementary Agreement on Cross-Strait Air Transport*— Also signed during the third Straits Exchange Foundation-Association for Relations Across the Taiwan Strait meeting (April 2009), this agreement significantly expanded cross-Strait air travel options. In particular, both sides agreed to the addition of two new flight routes, an increase in the number of airports involved in direct flights on both sides of the Strait, an expansion in the number of weekly chartered flights from 108 to 270, and a doubling of the weekly cargo flights from 14 to 28.[167] The effects of direct air travel are beginning to show—according to Taiwan's Mainland Affairs Council, the number of mainland visitors to Taiwan in the month of June 2009 increased 218 percent over June 2008.[168]
- *The Tourism Promotion Agreement*—In July 2009, representatives from the Taiwan Strait Tourism Association and the mainland's Cross-Strait Tourism Exchange Association agreed to set up offices on both sides of the Taiwan Strait.[169] The offices are aimed at promoting tourism through the distribution of information and services. However, they are separate from the official offices that handle cross-Strait tourism links and visa distribution.[170]

Growing Cross-Strait Informal Ties

During the Commission's May 2009 trip to China, the Commission learned about the growing informal ties between Taiwan and China.[171] In a meeting with the Commission, the deputy director of Xiamen City's Taiwan Affairs Office described how Taiwan and China were increasingly linked by more than just official agreements. For example:

- Taiwan investment into Xiamen has surpassed $9 billion.
- Xiamen-Taiwan two-way trade totals $3.8 billion.
- There are more than 3,000 Taiwanese businesses in Xiamen City.
- Roughly 80,000 Taiwanese live or conduct business in Xiamen City.
- 10,000 Taiwanese own apartments in the area.
- 1,300 Taiwanese children attend school in Xiamen City.
- Frequent municipality-sponsored conventions and expos occur with participants from both sides of the Taiwan Strait.
- Reciprocal visits occur between mainland and Taiwanese think tanks.

In addition to the above agreements, progress also has been made toward a cross-Strait free trade agreement. In February 2009, the Ma Administration first raised the idea of a free trade agreement for economic cooperation between Taiwan and the mainland, entitled the Economic Cooperation Framework Agreement. Originally the administration called it the Comprehensive Economic Cooperation

Agreement but changed it for political reasons.* If finalized, it will allow for "the free flow of goods, services and capital across the Taiwan Strait."[172] Specific issues contained within the proposal include tariffs, nontariff measures, investment protection, intellectual property rights, and a mechanism for dispute mediation.[173] According to President Ma, the intention of the proposal is to prevent the marginalization of Taiwan's regional economic ties, promote normalization of cross-Strait economic relations, and increase Taiwan's international economic relations.[174] The proposal enjoys only mixed support within Taiwan.

Proponents, spearheaded by the Ma Administration and major industry associations, argue that signing this proposal with China represents Taiwan's best near-term option for revitalizing its economy after the effects of the global economic crisis.[175] Because of its reliance on exports, Taiwan has been hit particularly hard during the global financial crisis. According to official Taiwan government calculations, Taiwan's economy is projected to shrink 3.75 percent in 2009, primarily as a result of the drop in exports. Taiwan's first and second quarter 2009 exports declined by 36.7 and 32 percent, respectively (year on year).[176] In addition, unemployment on the island rose to a record 6 percent in August 2009.[177] In a study commissioned by the Taiwanese Ministry of Economic Affairs to assess the economic impact of this financial agreement, the Chung-Hua Institution for Economic Research predicted that the agreement could increase Taiwan's gross domestic product (GDP) by 1.65–1.72 percent; raise mainland foreign direct investment into Taiwan by $8.9 billion over seven years; create more than 230,000 jobs in Taiwan; and benefit domestic industries, such as plastics, petrochemicals, petroleum, textiles, coal, and steel.[178]

There is widespread opposition to the plan on Taiwan, however. Some opponents of the plan, led by the Democratic Progressive Party, charge that a free trade agreement would "sell out" Taiwan. Skeptics also maintain that it would be tantamount to a "one- China market" and, eventually, political reunification with the mainland.[179] Tsai Ing-wen, Democratic Progressive Party chairperson, said that the Economic Cooperation Framework Agreement was not just an economic issue but rather "a security issue that involved the cross-Strait political agenda and economic interaction."[180] Other commentators maintain that signing the agreement

* The name was changed by the Ma Administration because its acronym (CECA) sounded too similar to the acronyms of the economic cooperation agreements signed between the mainland and the Hong Kong and Macao Special Administrative Regions, the Closer Economic Partnership Arrangement, or CEPA. According to the Macao CEPA, these agreements are "an FTA [free trade agreement]-like arrangement concluded between two separate customs territories of a single sovereign state." To avoid invoking the notion of China and Taiwan as one state, the name was changed to its current Economic Cooperation Framework Agreement. Terry Cooke, "Cross- Strait Matrix: The Economic Cooperation Framework Agreement," *China Brief* 9:11 (May 2009); Rupert Hammond-Chambers, "Taiwan and China Make Strides: Can America Respond?" (Washington, DC: The Brookings Institution, March 2009). *http://www.brookings.edu/opinions/2009/03/taiwan/china/hammondchambers.aspx*; and Economic Services Bureau, "Mainland and Macao Closer Economic Partnership Arrangement (CEPA)," (Macao SAR [Special Administrative Region]: October 2003). *http://www.economia.gov.mo/web/DSE/public?\nfpb=true&\page Label =Pg\EETR\CEPA\S&locale=en\US.*

with China would harm Taiwan's economy by "hollowing out" its manufacturing and electronics industries; crowding out trade with the United States, Japan, the European Union, and the Association of Southeast Asian Nations (ASEAN); and increasing Taiwan's economic dependency on China.[181]

President Ma also faces opposition over this proposal within his own party. Taiwan's Chinese Nationalist Party-controlled Legislative Yuan has expressed its concern that it has been left out of these cross-Strait economic negotiations. In February 2009, Legislative Speaker and Chinese Nationalist Party member Wang Jin Pyng called for a legislative review of the proposal before it is signed into effect.[182] In addition, on September 17, 2009, Taiwan's Legislative Yuan collectively released a report noting that it should be allowed to play a part in policy formation with regard to the Economic Cooperation Framework Agreement.[183] Further fueling uncertainty on Taiwan is the belief among many Taiwanese that they have had insufficient information about the proposal—according to one poll, upwards of 90 percent of those surveyed do not know what the proposal actually entails.[184] Although the Ma Administration originally intended to have a completed agreement by late 2009, domestic opposition to the plan has slowed the administration's timeline, and a date for signing the proposal has yet to be announced.[185]

Currently, the United States officially supports these attempts to improve cross-Strait relations. According to then director of the American Institute in Taiwan Stephen A. Young, Washington "fully supports and applauds Taiwan's efforts to enhance cooperation and lower tension in the cross-strait region."[186] Four months later, he again mentioned US support for attempts to improve Taiwan mainland relations, stating that strong US-Taiwan ties are not incompatible with the "recently warming links between Taiwan and China."[187]

As part of a new diplomatic strategy, President Ma has signaled that Taiwan is taking a moderated approach to its international space. For example, Taiwan's Ministry of Foreign Affairs stated in June 2009 that rather than seeking direct participation in the United Nations (UN) as it has in the past, it would take a more pragmatic stance by seeking entry to UN-affiliated activities and specialized agencies, as it did successfully with the World Health Assembly, mentioned above.[188]

Cross-Strait Military Balance Tilts Further in Beijing's Direction

Despite the above-mentioned improvements in the cross-Strait relationship, there has been no progress on the military side. In March 2009, then Deputy Assistant Secretary of Defence for East Asia David S. Sedney testified to the Commission that there is no evidence of the People's Liberation Army (PLA) reducing its military posture or capabilities across the Taiwan Strait.[189] According to the Department of Defence, "China's military build-up and the deployment of advanced capabilities opposite the island have not eased."[190] A report that the Science Applications International Corporation completed for the Commission on the cross-Strait military balance found that China's military had become a "clear and present threat" to Taiwan's autonomy due to significant improvements in its missile, air, and naval capabilities.[191] China's continued buildup of military capabilities opposite Taiwan "despite a thaw in the once-strained relations across the Taiwan Strait over the past year" led President Ma in September 2009 to call on Taiwanese defence forces to improve their combat capabilities.[192] The remainder of this section will discuss China's growing capabilities in these three areas as they relate to Taiwan.

Missile Capabilities

In the event of a military conflict between China and Taiwan, one possible option that the PLA could employ is a missile saturation campaign in order to soften the island's defences.[193] The table below demonstrates that the PLA has a large inventory of ballistic and cruise missiles, as well as antiradiation attack drones—used to knock out radar installations—at its disposal for such a campaign. China's 1,100+ short-range ballistic missiles targeting Taiwan are sufficiently accurate to pose a serious threat to a wide range of immobile targets on the island, such as command and control facilities, air defence nodes, air bases, naval bases, and political targets. [194] According to a 2009 RAND Corporation study, China's arsenal is more than sufficient to seriously affect Taiwan's defences; depending on missile accuracy, the PLA would only need between 90 and 240 short-range ballistic missiles to "cut every runway at Taiwan's half-dozen main fighter bases and destroy essentially all of the aircraft parked on ramps in the open at those installations." [195]

Figure 2: PRC Missiles Targeting Taiwan

Name	Type	Quantity
DF 11 (CSS–7)	Short-range ballistic missile	700–750
DF–15 (CSS–6)	Short-range ballistic missile	350–400
DH–10	Cruise missile	150–300
C–602	Cruise missile	unknown
As-17 (Kh-31)	Antiradiation cruise missile	unknown
Harpy	Antiradiation drone	unknown

Source: Eric C. Anderson and Jeffrey G. Engstrom, *Capabilities of* the Chinese People's Liberation Army to Carry Out Military Action in *the Event of a Regional Military Conflict* (McLean, VA: Science Applications International Corporation, May 2009), p.37.

The PLA would likely conduct missile saturation attacks along with land-attack cruise missiles and antiradiation attack drones.[196] The PLA's growing arsenal of land-attack cruise missiles (both ground and air launched) would target immobile, hard-to-strike, high-value assets and would pose a serious challenge to Taiwanese defenders. Antiradiation attack drones, such as China's Israeli-produced Harpy, would target hidden air defence radars. In the event of a successful attack, these drones could severely weaken Taiwan's air defence capabilities. The PLA also could use domestically produced cruise missiles, such as the air-launched AS–17 antiradiation cruise missile, to augment its Harpy drone attacks.[197]

Complicating matters for Taiwan are its limited missile defences. Currently, Taiwan's missile defence arsenal has only 330 missiles, consisting of the Patriot (PAC–2), Hawk, and Skybow/Tien Kung surface-to-air missile batteries.[198] In the event of a PLA missile saturation attack, these limited amounts would be incapable of providing sustained protection and would likely be exhausted quickly. [199]

Taipei does, however, have a limited missile counter-attack capability. Taiwanese cruise missiles could be used to strike mainland missile repositories, command and control facilities, and possibly even air bases or ports. In addition, Taiwanese aircraft are capable of attacking the mainland. However, the Taiwanese military is likely to conserve these for air defence purposes instead.[200]

Taiwan's 2009 Quadrennial Defence Review

In March 2009, Taiwan's Ministry of National Defence released its first-ever Quadrennial Defence Review in order to "describe the prospects and reform directions of [Taiwan's] Armed Forces in the face of challenges in an evolving strategic environment." Based on the central theme of "building a professional armed force and maintaining peace in the Taiwan Strait," the Quadrennial Defence Review is broken into four chapters:

- *Core Defence Challenges*—focuses primarily on PRC challenges to Taiwan's international space, the growing cross-Strait military imbalance, the influence of defence transformation, and the necessity for defence reform.
- *National Defence Strategic Guidance*—focuses on describing the "Hard ROC" [Republic of China] defence policy and how Taiwan's defence and military strategy conforms to this policy.*
- *Defence Transformation Planning*—focuses on transforming and modernizing Taiwan's military, to include organization, personnel, planning, command, and fiscal reforms. In addition, this section discusses Taiwan's goal of achieving an allvolunteer force by 2014.
- *Guidance for Joint Warfighting Capability Development*— focuses on the need to develop various capabilities required for joint operations.[201]

Air Capabilities

After initial attacks, the PLA could be expected to launch a campaign to seize air superiority.[202] The success of seizing air superiority is critical in determining the outcome of any large-scale use of force against Taiwan.[203] Over the years, Taiwan's air capabilities relative to China's have begun to shrink.[204] The table below shows a comparison between current PLA and Taiwanese aircraft.

Figure 3: Total Taiwan and PLA Fighters and Airborne Early Warning and Control (AEW&C) Aircraft †

Taiwan			PLA		
Name	*Type*	*QTY*	*Name*	*Type*	*QTY*
Mirage 2000	Fighter-Interceptor	57	Su-30MKK	Fighter-Multirole	127
F-16 A/B	Fighter-Multirole	144	Su-27SK/J–11B	Fighter-Multirole	132
F–CK–1 A/B	Fighter-Multirole	125	J–10	Fighter-Multirole	80
F–5E	Fighter-Multirole	50	J–8	Fighter-Interceptor	390

* According to the Taiwanese Ministry of Defence, the Hard ROC defence policy centers around three aspects: ensuring the survivability of Taiwan's warfighting capability and infrastructure, making maximum use of joint operations to destroy the enemy at sea or in the air (prior to landing on Taiwan), and improving defence mobilization activities. Ministry of National Defence, *Quadrennial Defence Review 2009* (Taipei: March, 2009), p. 65.

† This table represents the total number of aircraft available for each military. It does not account for the number of aircraft that would be held in reserve due to other missions, such as defending Beijing or providing border defence in other parts of China or held in reserve for later use.

E–2T	AEW&C	6	J–7 Q–5 JH–7A KJ–2000 Y–8J	Fighter-Multirole Fighter-Ground Attack Fighter-Ground Attack AEW&C AEW&C	579 235 70 5 2

Source: Eric C. Anderson and Jeffrey G. Engstrom,, *Capabilities of the Chinese People's Liberation Army to Carry Out Military Action in the Event of a Regional Military Conflict* (McLean, VA: Science Applications International Corporation, May 2009), p. 41.

In recent years, the PLA has taken three steps to improve its air capabilities. First, it is increasing the number of its advanced combat aircraft through domestic production or foreign acquisition. For example, the RAND Corporation projects that by 2013 there will be a significant increase in the number of all of the PLA Air Force's advanced combat aircraft—already significantly larger than Taiwan's. [205] Second, the PLA is improving its older aircraft, such as the J–8, by equipping them with updated avionics to enhance missile- launching capabilities.[206] Third, Beijing is strengthening its ability to coordinate air strikes by acquiring improved airborne early warning and control aircraft, such as the KJ–2000 and the Y–8J.[207]

In contrast to the growing size and quality of the PLA's fighter force, Taiwan has not substantially upgraded its fighter force in the past decade and may not do so in the near future.[208] Although Taiwan requested the sale of 66 F–16 C/D fighters from the United States, these aircraft were not part of the Bush Administration's October 2008 notification to Congress of US arms sales to Taiwan. Although these fighters are still desired by Taiwan, it is unclear whether the Obama Administration will agree to sell these, or other, modern aircraft to Taiwan.[209]

Naval Capabilities

As discussed in chapter 2, section 2, of this Report, Beijing expects the PLA Navy to prevent Taiwan's secession. The key focus of this mission is to seize maritime superiority around Taiwan, thus enabling an amphibious invasion or blockade of the island.[210] According to the Science Applications International Corporation's report, China holds "nearly a 29:1 advantage in attack submarines, a 7:1 advantage in destroyers, and an approximate 2:1 advantage in frigates and fast [attack] craft."[211] Furthermore, if China did achieve air superiority over the Strait, PLA air and surface attacks would likely overwhelm Taiwan's naval forces, rendering its antisubmarine assets unusable.[212] Although discussion of US support for a Taiwanese indigenous submarine programme has occurred for several years, a submarine design programme was not included in the 2008 arms deal.[213] The table below demonstrates the naval advantage China currently enjoys over Taiwan.

Figure 4: Comparison of PLA and Taiwan Naval Surface and Subsurface Fleets

Taiwan			***PLA***		
Name	*Type*	*QTY*	*Name*	*Type*	*QTY*
Keelung	Destroyer	4	*Luyang I, II* *Luzhou* *Sovremenny*	Destroyer Destroyer Destroyer	4 2 4

			Luhu	Destroyer	2
			Luda I, II	Destroyer	14
			Luhai	Destroyer	1
Cheng Kung	Frigate	8	*Jiangkai I*	Frigate	3
Kang Ding	Frigate	6	*Jianghu I–V*	Frigate	1
Knox	Frigate	8	*Jiangwei I, II*	Frigate	14
Hai Lung	Attack Submarine	2	*Han*	Attack Submarine	4
			Shang	Attack Submarine	1
			Yuan	Attack Submarine	1
			Song	Attack Submarine	13
			Kilo	Attack Submarinc	12
			Ming	Attack Submarine	19
			Romeo	Attack Submarine	7
N/A	Fast Attack Craft	50	N/A	Fast Attack Craft.	77

Source: Eric C. Anderson and Jeffrey G. Engstrom, *Capabilities of the Chinese People's Liberation Army to Carry Out Military Action in the Event of a Regional Military Conflict* (McLean, VA: Science Applications International Corporation, May 2009), p. 45.

Conclusion

- Since the May 2008 inauguration of President Ma Ying-jeou, cross-Strait relations between China and Taiwan have improved on some fronts. Although noticeable political and economic improvements in the relationship have occurred, these improvements are not matched in the military arena. Instead, the PLA's capabilities continue to grow, increasing the military threat confronting Taiwan.
- One area of improvement entails the resumption of semiregular, high-level meetings between the two sides. In particular, the cross-Strait dialogue between Taiwan's Straits Exchange Foundation and mainland China's Association for Relations Across the Taiwan Strait has occurred three times, with a fourth tentatively scheduled for late in 2009.
- As a result of improving cross-Strait relations, a growing number of agreements have been signed between Taiwan and China since May 2008. These agreements include the resumption of the Three Direct Links, the signing of a financial cooperation agreement, the commencement of cooperation on combating cross-Strait crime, and the establishment of a food safety agreement. In addition, there has been substantial progress toward the establishment of a free trade agreement.

SECTION 3

Hong Kong

> "... the United States-China Economic and Security Review Commission ... shall investigate and report exclusively on—
>
> "Regional Economic and Security Impacts—The triangular economic and security relationship among the United States, Taipei and the People's Republic of China (including the military modernization and force deployments of the People's Republic of China aimed at Taipei), the national budget of the People's Republic of China, and the fiscal strength of the People's Republic of China in relation to internal instability in the People's Republic of China and the likelihood of the externalization of problems arising from such internal instability. . . ."

Introduction

The Chinese central government in Beijing has continued to expand its influence over the government and economy of Hong Kong, despite formal denials of interference from Beijing and explicit safeguards in the 1984 Sino-British Joint Declaration setting the terms of the handover of Hong Kong from British to Chinese control.*

Beijing has moved decisively in several areas to exert increased influence over the Hong Kong Special Administrative Region's (SAR) government. Beijing has been strengthening its official liaison office in Hong Kong, the Central Government Liaison Office, even to the point of attempting to influence day-to-day affairs in Hong Kong. The central government in Beijing took an active role in limiting demonstrations in Hong Kong to mark the 20th anniversary of the Tiananmen Square massacre. The global financial crisis and Beijing's response have allowed the central government increased leverage over Hong Kong's much smaller economy, which is dependent on financial and trade ties to the mainland.

Beijing's Growing Political Influence over Hong Kong

A frequent theme during the Commission's May 2009 meetings in Hong Kong was the concern expressed by some residents and officials that the government in Beijing has been deliberately and steadily encroaching upon the autonomy of Hong Kong's

---

* In 1992, Congress passed the United States-Hong Kong Policy Act, in which the United States agreed to treat Hong Kong as an entity separate from mainland China as long as its political, economic, and trade systems remain autonomous. The act required the secretary of State to submit an annual report to Congress on the conditions of Hong Kong through the year 2000, and it was amended to extend the reporting requirement through 2006. Since 2007, no reporting requirement has been reestablished. *United States -Hong Kong Policy Act*, 102nd Cong., 2nd sess., 1992, Pub. L. 102–383, 106 Stat. 1448. *http://hongkong.usconsulate.gov/ushk/pa/1992.html.*

government. In particular, meeting participants said that the Chinese central government has been strengthening the Central Government Liaison Office in order to increase Beijing's oversight over the Hong Kong government. A 2008 article in a newspaper affiliated with the Chinese Communist Party's (CCP) Central Party School was frequently cited. This article stated that Beijing has the right to exert its influence over the Hong Kong SAR government in certain key areas.[214] This line of reasoning appears to contravene article 22 of Hong Kong's Basic Law, as explained later in this section.

Prodemocracy Hong Kong Legislative Council delegates expressed concern at a May 10, 2009, meeting with the Commission about the growing influence of the Central Government Liaison Office in Hong Kong's domestic affairs. According to the delegates present, the liaison office was taking on a more active role in the daily affairs of Hong Kong. Some complained that the office was orchestrating elections within the Hong Kong government, in part by requiring the office to review and approve all potential candidates, effectively operating as a "second government" in Hong Kong.[215] US consulate staff also noted that the Central Government Liaison Office was "taking a more active role in Hong Kong civil affairs." Consulate staff viewed the growing strength of the office as something that should be closely monitored, especially given that the US consulate had yet to make contact successfully with the liaison office by the time of the Commission's trip, despite repeated US attempts.[216]

According to the Central Government Liaison Office's Web site, as Beijing's representative office in Hong Kong, the office's official functions are the following:

1. "Integrate the Ministry of Foreign Affairs' Special Delegation Office in Hong Kong and the Hong Kong detachment of the Chinese People's Liberation Army.
2. Integrate and help the mainland's relevant departments to manage Chinese investment organizations.
3. Promote economic, educational, science and technology, cultural, and athletic exchanges and cooperation between Hong Kong and the mainland. Integrate with Hong Kong people from all levels of society, and advance the exchanges between the mainland and Hong Kong. Report on the Hong Kong residents' views toward the mainland.
4. Handle relevant issues that touch upon Taiwan.
5. Undertake other matters handed over from the central government."[217]

The Central Government Liaison Office's membership guarantees its loyalty to Beijing. For China's leaders, it is particularly important to have "loyalists" upon whom it can consistently rely to carry out Beijing's will.[218] Currently, the liaison office's senior leadership consists entirely of individuals who have previously held trusted positions within CCP organizations. For example, the current director of the liaison office, Peng Qinghua, was once secretary of the CCP's Central Organization Department, director of the Party Building Research Institute, and editor of the CCP journal, *Party Building Research.*[219] Li Gang, a deputy director of the Central Government Liaison Office, was previously a deputy director of the CCP's Office of Foreign Propaganda.[220]

In essence, this concern revolves around the interpretation of article 22 of the Basic Law, Hong Kong's de facto constitution. According to article 22, Beijing is not allowed to interfere in the Hong Kong government's local affairs.[221] However, the previously cited 2008 CCP newspaper article argued that Beijing does indeed have the right to exert its influence over Hong Kong on certain issues. The author, Cao Erbao, currently the director of the Central Government Liaison Office's Research Department, wrote that after Hong Kong reverted back to Chinese control on July 1, 1997, it went from being ruled by one entity to being ruled by two: the Hong Kong government and "a team of Central and Mainland authorities carrying out Hong Kong work." Mr. Cao stated that Beijing has responsibility for issues related to China's sovereignty and Beijing-Hong Kong relations, while the Hong Kong SAR government is responsible for internal issues.[222] Furthermore, Mr. Cao wrote that the central government representatives

> *exercise constitutional powers to govern the Special Administrative Region (including handling relationships between central and mainland authorities, and the Hong Kong Special Administrative Region, in accordance with our constitution and the Basic Law of the Hong Kong Special Administrative Region, without interfering in affairs within the scope of Special Administrative Region self-government.*[223]

Most importantly, Mr. Cao also wrote that the relationship between the central authorities and the Hong Kong SAR government is one of "authorizer and authorized," respectively.[224] According to Ching Cheong, a senior writer at the Singapore-based newspaper *The Straits Times,* Mr. Cao's article demonstrated that Beijing is taking "a very liberal interpretation" of the Basic Law. Furthermore, if Mr. Cao's views were to be implemented, it would result in "a very serious change to the Basic Law."[225]

Article 22 of Hong Kong's Basic Law

No department of the Central People's Government and no province, autonomous region, or municipality directly under the Central Government may interfere in the affairs which the Hong Kong Special Administrative Region administers on its own in accordance with this Law.

If there is a need for departments of the Central Government, or for provinces, autonomous regions, or municipalities directly under the Central Government to set up offices in the Hong Kong Special Administrative Region, they must obtain the consent of the government of the Region and the approval of the Central People's Government.

All offices set up in the Hong Kong Special Administrative Region by departments of the Central Government, or by provinces, autonomous regions, or municipalities directly under the Central Government and the personnel of these offices shall abide by the laws of the Region.

For entry into the Hong Kong Special Administrative Region, people from other parts of China must apply for approval. Among them, the number of persons who enter the Region for the purpose of settlement shall be determined by the competent authorities of the Central People's Government after consulting the government of the Region. The Hong Kong Special Administrative Region may establish an office in Beijing.[226]

One example of Beijing exerting its influence over Hong Kong was the Hong Kong SAR decision to deny visas for people seeking to enter Hong Kong to attend demonstrations commemorating the 20th anniversary of the Tiananmen Square massacre. According to news reports, several individuals—mostly participants in the original Tiananmen protest in 1989—were alternately denied visas or entry to Hong Kong. Tiananmen-era dissidents Xiang Xiaoji (a US citizen) and Yang Jianli (a US permanent resident) were denied entry to Hong Kong, while Wang Dan and Wang Juntao, both exiled Chinese citizens residing in the United States, were denied entry visas.[227] In addition to former Tiananmen protesters, Jens Galschiot, a Danish artist who created a sculpture depicting victims from the Tiananmen massacre, was also denied entry to Hong Kong.[228]

Transshipment of Controlled Technology of China, and the Particular Problem of Hong Kong

The transshipment of controlled technology through false endusers in other countries or regions is a significant means of illegal technology transfer from the United States to other nations.[229] Expert testimony presented to the Commission this year indicated a problem with Hong Kong serving as a way station for illegal dualuse technology exports into the People's Republic of China (PRC). Under US law, the Hong Kong Special Administrative Region and the PRC are treated as separate customs entities for purposes of export control. Hong Kong is treated more liberally as an export destination than is the PRC, and some items subject to the US government's Export Administration regulations that require an export license for exports to the PRC do not require such a license for exports to Hong Kong.[230]

There are instances in which this dual system has made Hong Kong an export destination for those wishing to do an end-run around US export control regulations, notwithstanding strict Hong Kong regulations.[231] As James Mulvenon, an expert on the Chinese military-industrial complex, testified to the Commission:

> *Hong Kong . . . was established as a separate customs entity during the handover [from Britain to China] for very . . . noble and pure reasons, but [it] has now become a very troubling transshipment point for Chinese economic espionage. . . . I would submit that it is a significant problem . . . [and] a large percentage of the export control cases that I have seen have involved Hong Kong transshipment.*[232]

This may present a particular problem in light of the long history of Hong Kong as a center for PRC intelligence operations.[233] Furthermore, well-connected relatives of high-level CCP cadres, known as "princelings," within the People's Liberation Army (PLA) hierarchy also have a long record of involvement with enterprises in Hong Kong,[234] including the alleged placement of agents in companies such as the Everbright Group and China Resources Holding Company.[235] However, the proliferation of "entrepreneurial espionage" carried out by private actors on behalf of the PRC means that virtually any firm willing to profit from service as a middleman could potentially act as a legally and geographically convenient transshipment point for controlled technology headed to an unauthorized end-user in the PRC. (For further discussion of "entrepreneurial espionage" and illicit technology transfers conducted on behalf of the PRC, see chap. 2, sec. 3 of this Report, "China's Human Espionage Activities that Target the United States, and the Resulting Impacts on US National Security.") The ease of transshipment from addresses in Hong Kong to the PRC represents a significant and exploitable weakness in US export control policy related to China.

Impact of the Global Economic Crisis, and Hong Kong's Growing Dependence on Mainland China

Hong Kong's economic success stems from its reliance on the rule of law, its open markets, its banking system, and from being one of the world's biggest ports and the financial gateway to Asia and mainland China in particular.* China is Hong Kong's biggest and most important trading partner, with bilateral trade in 2008 amounting to HK$2.7 trillion ($359 billion).[236] So it is little surprise that the global financial crisis, which has depressed demand for Chinese exports shipped through Hong Kong, triggered Hong Kong's biggest contraction since the Asian financial crisis in 1997. The year-on-year decline in Hong Kong's gross domestic product (GDP) narrowed from 7.8 percent in the first quarter to 3.8 percent in the second quarter.[237] Hong Kong's exports slid by the largest amount since 1954, dropping 13.9 percent in August 2009 over the year earlier, after shrinking 19.9 percent in July 2009 year-onyear.[238] The unemployment rate, which has been rising steadily since September 2008, climbed to 5.4 percent in August 2009.[239] Due in part to improved export performance and to the pickup in economic activity in China, in the second quarter of the year Hong Kong's economy actually grew by a seasonally adjusted 3.3 percent, suggesting that the recession may be over in Hong Kong.[240] This was the first positive growth in Hong Kong's economy, following four consecutive quarters of decline.[241]

Costs for shipping goods have fallen in the past year, partly because retailers are paring orders due to weak consumer spending. Container lines have parked ships and delayed deliveries of new vessels to curb excess capacity. Shipping lines are also trying to delay deliveries of new vessels to ease a capacity glut.[242] Investors hope, however, that a revival of the Chinese economy may help Hong Kong recover as well. Despite the downturn, K.C. Chan, Hong Kong secretary for Financial Services and the Treasury, told the Commission during its 2009 trip to Hong Kong that Hong Kong's banking system is very healthy and less leveraged, unlike that in the West, so there is much less worry over the financial crisis, despite short-term volatility in the stock market.

To help increase its exports, Hong Kong has rolled out HK$87.6 billion ($11.2 billion) of stimulus measures, including increased transportation infrastructure spending and various tax cuts.[243] Hong Kong's economic distress also has provided an opportunity for the central government in Beijing to come to the rescue and, in doing so, to forge closer economic and political ties. In a December 2008 meeting with Hong Kong's Chief Executive Donald Tsang, Premier Wen Jiabao promised

---

* Since 1983, the Hong Kong dollar has been pegged to the US dollar at a rate of $1 to 7.8 Hong Kong dollars, and since 2005 the Hong Kong dollar has been allowed to trade up to five cents on either side of that level. The fixed exchange rate against the dollar has conferred several advantages on Hong Kong, including the ability to withstand speculative attacks (as was the case during the Asian financial crisis) and the indirect subsidization of its exports through undervaluation.

that Beijing would implement 14 measures to help Hong Kong deal with the financial crisis.[244] These include

- Strengthening cooperation on financial affairs between the mainland and Hong Kong, including allowing companies to settle trade in renminbi (RMB) with Hong Kong. The People's Bank of China and the Hong Kong monetary authority entered into a currency swap agreement with the Hong Kong Monetary Authority on January 20, 2009, providing liquidity support of up to HK$227 billion or 200 billion RMB ($29 billion).[245]
- Launching measures to help small- and medium-sized enterprises, including increasing tax rebates on exports and assisting trade and providing guarantees to help small- and medium-sized enterprises get capital.
- Expanding the individual travelers' programme, allowing mainlanders living in Shenzhen to apply for 12-month, multientry visas to travel to Hong Kong.[246]
- Opening up the mainland's service industry to Hong Kong companies.
- Speeding up infrastructure projects, such as the Hong Kong-Zhuhai-Macao Bridge, and ensuring a stable supply of food, water, electricity, and natural gas.
- Strengthening economic cooperation between Hong Kong and the Pearl River Delta region.
- Encouraging Hong Kong firms to participate in the construction of the Shenzhen railway.

The initial plan for individual travelers' programme would have extended it to some eight million other mainlanders living in Shenzhen although not registered in Guangdong Province, but Beijing suspended the project in May 2009 without any definitive timetable for implementation.[247] Hong Kong Secretary for Commerce and Economic Development Rita Lau Ng Wai-lan said she anticipates that the new multientry visas would significantly increase tourism, which would benefit the hospitality, retail, and entertainment sectors battered by the economic crisis and assuage fears relating to the H1N1 ("swine flu") influenza.[248]

On May 9, 2009, Hong Kong and mainland China also signed a sixth round of the Closer Economic Partnership Agreement, originally launched in 2003 in the midst of the SARS epidemic.[249] Under the new supplement, which came into effect on October 1, 2009, qualified mainland securities firms will be able to set up subsidiaries in Hong Kong upon approval by regulatory authorities, while Hong Kong banks will be able to open branches in Guangdong more easily. Also, securities firms in the mainland and Hong Kong will be allowed to set up joint-venture advisory companies in Guangdong.[250] In addition, China eliminated import tariffs on 28 goods from Hong Kong, including food, medicine, and textiles, starting July 1, 2009.[251] The Closer Economic Partnership Agreement also eased visa rules, allowing mainland tourist groups to visit Taiwan and Hong Kong using a single visa.[252]

The introduction of the pilot programme on April 8, 2009, to use RMB to settle cross-border trade with Hong Kong is a particularly important step. Following calls by the People's Bank of China to replace the US dollar as the global reserve currency, China has been promoting greater use of the RMB in international trade, including 650 billion RMB ($95 billion) in swap agreements with Hong Kong, Argentina, Indonesia, South Korea, Malaysia, and Belarus (see chap. 1, sec. 1, for more details).[253] The new cross-border trade programme with Hong Kong, however, will be a first true test for the use of the RMB outside of mainland China. The programme would allow Shanghai and four cities in the Pearl River Delta—Shenzhen, Guanzhou, Zhuhai, and Dongguan—to settle international trade in RMB. The Bank of China, China's largest foreign exchange bank, announced on July 6, 2009, that it had transacted the first cross-border RMB trade settlement deal.[254] Hong Kong Chief Executive Donald Tsang said the programme will further the city's bid to become a regional RMB clearing center and help shield companies doing business with the mainland from exchange-rate risk.[255]

During the Commission's May trip to China and Hong Kong, Hong Kong democratic activists expressed concern that China plans to marginalize and eventually absorb Hong Kong. According to the activists, following the July 1, 2003, protests to oppose the antisubversion Hong Kong Basic Law article 23, the Chinese government started using its vast financial resources to penetrate Hong Kong's political and economic establishment. Hong Kong's growing economic dependence on the mainland is seen by some as a weakness, making Hong Kong's political development subject to China's financial clout.

At the same time, China is trying to reduce its dependency on Hong Kong by developing Shanghai into a major global financial center and shipping hub by 2020.[256] For many years, Hong Kong has profited from its status as the gateway to trade and investment in mainland China as well as from its rule of law, open business environment, taxation policy, and more rigorous regulatory regime. As China positions Shanghai as a major financial center, the various pilot programmes that the central government is running in the Pearl River Delta are challenging Hong Kong's role. Hong Kong's competitive edge is its independence, financial freedom, and rule of law. This transition will be a gradual process, however, because the RMB is still not convertible, and China's institutions and the rule of law do not provide the protection of Hong Kong's. If the RMB were to become convertible, Shanghai would have a much broader appeal, especially for companies trying to get access to RMB business, leading to a possible flight of capital and a relocation of business from Hong Kong to the mainland.

Politicians on both the mainland and in Hong Kong have consistently played down the rivalry between Hong Kong and Shanghai, underscoring their complementary natures.[257] Hong Kong has international standing, while Shanghai has advantages in China's domestic markets, including the large number of state-owned enterprises that are listed on Shanghai's stock exchange.

Speaking about Hong Kong's economic cooperation with the central government during the Commission's trip to China, Secretary K.C. Chan stressed that Hong Kong is very independent and sets its own economic policy. Secretary Chan said that there is a very clear understanding, however, that future economic growth in the region will depend on China. According to Mr. Chan, Hong Kong does its own lobbying in Beijing, but Hong Kong's access to the central government is not as good as that of the mainland provinces, such as Guangdong Province.

Media Control in Hong Kong

There are signs of "creeping repression" for journalists in Hong Kong. Journalists from Hong Kong have expressed concerns that China's increasing economic influence in their territories could undermine local press freedom.[258] For example, Hong Kong-based reporter Daisy Chu was fired from her position at the Hong

Kong edition of *Esquire* magazine when she reported on her blog that the magazine's editors withdrew her story on the 20th anniversary of the Tiananmen massacre.[259] Journalists from Hong Kong are now required to obtain a press pass from the central government and the consent of interviewees in order to travel to the mainland to report.[260] When reporting in the mainland, Hong Kong journalists' operations have been subject to a disproportionate amount of violence and harassment.[261] For example, on September 4, 2009, three reporters from Hong Kong were "kicked, punched, shoved to the ground, handcuffed by police and detained for about three hours" as they were trying to escape tear gas fired to disperse crowds in Urumqi.[262]

On February 25, 2009, Macao's legislative assembly enacted a national security law that included the same vaguely worded "state secrets" provisions that are used on the mainland to intimidate, detain, and punish dissidents.[263] This is significant for Hong Kong as well, because the government of Hong Kong tried to introduce similar legislation in 2003 but backed down in the face of strong public opposition.[264] Now, concerns are mounting that this move could pressure Hong Kong authorities to follow and that Macao's legislation could act as a template.[265] According to the Hong Kong Journalists Association, "Media freedoms remain largely intact [but] the scope for expressing dissenting views—in particular on subjects that are sensitive to Beijing—is narrowing."[266]

Conclusion

- The influence of China's central government in Hong Kong is increasing, including in the political and economic spheres.
- As a very export-dependent economy, Hong Kong has been severely impacted by the current economic crisis, both in its own right and as result of a fall in demand for Chinese exports.
- Beijing has been very active in offering economic support to Hong Kong, but democratic activists are worried about Hong Kong's growing economic dependence on the mainland, which they see as undermining Hong Kong's autonomy and international competitive edge.
- Beijing appears to be increasing its influence over the Hong Kong SAR government by strengthening the position of its official representative organization, the Central Government Liaison Office, and promoting pro-Beijing political parties within the Hong Kong Legislative Committee.
- A crucial component of Beijing's strategy of reining in Hong Kong appears to be its policy of chipping away incrementally at the legal support for Hong Kong's autonomy in domestic affairs. Evidence exists that Beijing already may be interfering in Hong Kong's domestic issues.
- Due to its geographic convenience as a transshipment point, as well as the long-standing presence of Chinese government-affiliated intelligence and commercial interests, Hong Kong could emerge as a significant transshipment point for transfers of export controlled technologies into China in violation of US law.

RECOMMENDATIONS

China in Afghanistan, Pakistan, and Central Asia

- The Commission recommends that Congress encourage the administration to continue to work with China to utilize its influence with Islamabad to bolster Pakistan's stability and prevent the Taliban from gaining control of the region.
- The Commission recommends that Congress encourage the administration to examine carefully development programmes and investment opportunities in Afghanistan and work with US private businesses interested in investing there to ensure that they are able to compete effectively with Chinese state-owned companies.

Taiwan

- The Commission recommends that Congress urge the administration to support recent improvements in the cross-Strait relationship. . The Commission recommends that Congress urge the administration to take additional steps to encourage the People's Republic of China (PRC) to demonstrate the sincerity of its desire for improved cross-Strait relations by drawing down the number of forces, including missiles, opposite Taiwan.
- The Commission recommends that Congress encourage the administration to identify opportunities to strengthen bilateral economic relations between the United States and Taiwan.
- The Commission recommends that Congress encourage the administration to continue to work with Taiwan to modernize its armed forces, with particular emphasis on its air defence needs.

Hong Kong

- The Commission recommends that Members of Congress, when visiting mainland China, also visit Hong Kong and that Congress encourage senior administration officials, including the secretary of State, to make visits to Hong Kong part of their travel. The Commission also recommends that Members of Congress seek dialogue with members of the Legislative Council of Hong Kong.
- The Commission recommends that Congress encourage its Members to raise the issue of preserving Hong Kong's special status when meeting with members of China's National People's Congress.
- The Commission recommends that Congress reenact the United States-Hong Kong Policy Act of 1992, which expired in 2007.
- The Commission recommends that Congress examine and assess the adequacy of US export control policy for dual-use technology as it relates to the treatment of Hong Kong and the PRC as separate customs entities. The Commission further recommends that Congress urge the administration to consider ways to collaborate more closely with the authorities in Hong Kong in order to prevent the transshipment of controlled technologies from Hong Kong into the PRC.

ENDNOTES

1. Ministry of Foreign Affairs for the People's Republic of China, "China and Afghanistan," August 25, 2003. *http://www.mfa.gov.cn/eng/wjb/zzjg/yzs/gjlb/2676/ t15822.htm;* Ministry of Foreign Affairs for the People's Republic of China, "China and Pakistan," October 23, 2003. *http://www.fmprc.gov.cn/eng/wjb/zzjg/yzs/gjlb/2757/.*
2. Asif Ali Zardari, "Sino-Pakistan relations higher than the Himalayas," *China Daily*, February 23, 2009. *http://www.chinadaily.cn/opinion/2009–02/23/content_ 7501699.htm.*
3. Ziad Haider, "Sino-Pakistan relations and Xinjiang's Uighurs: Politics, Trade, and Islam along the Karakoram Highway," *Asian Survey* 45:4 (July/August 2005): 530.
4. US-China Economic and Security Review Commission, *Hearing on the Impact of China's Economic and Security Interests in Continental Asia on the United States*, written testimony of Lisa Curtis, May 20, 2009.
5. US-China Economic and Security Review Commission, *Hearing on the Impact of China's Economic and Security Interests in Continental Asia on the United States*, written testimony of Lisa Curtis, May 20, 2009.
6. Reuters, "Main events in Chinese-Pakistani relations," November, 24, 2006. *http:// www.reuters.com/article/worldNews/idUSISL9262520061124.*
7. Eric Arnett, *Military Capacity and the Risk of War: China, India, Pakistan and Iran* (Stockholm, Sweden: Stockholm International Peace Research Institute [SIPRI], 1997), pp. 157–158.
8. Ahmad Faruqui, "The Complex Dynamics of Pakistan's Relationship with China," *Islamabad Policy Research Institute* (Summer 2001).
9. US-China Economic and Security Review Commission, *Hearing on the Impact of China's Economic and Security Interests in Continental Asia on the United States*, written testimony of Lisa Curtis, May 20, 2009.
10. US-China Economic and Security Review Commission, *Hearing on the Impact of China's Economic and Security Interests in Continental Asia on the United States*, written testimony of Lisa Curtis, May 20, 2009.
11. US-China Economic and Security Review Commission, *Hearing on the Impact of China's Economic and Security Interests in Continental Asia on the United States*, written testimony of Lisa Curtis, May 20, 2009; Office of the Secretary of Defence, *Annual Report to Congress: Military Power of the People's Republic of China, 2009* (Washington, DC: US Department of Defence, 2009), p. 57.
12. *Nuclear Threat Initiative*, "China's Nuclear Exports and Assistance to Pakistan," November 14, 2003.
13. Agence France-Presse, "China to help Pakistan build two more nuclear plants," October 18, 2008.
14. Mohan Malik, "The China Factor in the India-Pakistan Conflict," *Parameters* (Spring 2003); Agence France-Presse, "China to help Pakistan build two more nuclear plants," October 18, 2008.
15. Ziad Haider, "Sino-Pakistan relations and Xinjiang's Uighurs: Politics, Trade, and Islam along the Karakoram Highway," *Asian Survey* 45:4 (July/August 2005): 530; George Crile, *Charlie Wilson's War* (New York, NY: First Grove Press,2003).

16. Ministry of Foreign Affairs of the People's Republic of China, "China and Afghanistan," August 25, 2008. *http://www.mfa.gov.cn/eng/wjb/zzjg/yzs/gjlb/2676/t15822 .htm.*
17. US-China Economic and Security Review Commission, *Hearing on the Impact of China's Economic and Security Interests in Continental Asia on the United States*, testimony of Walid Phares, May 20, 2009.
18. US-China Economic and Security Review Commission, *Hearing on the Impact of China's Economic and Security Interests in Continental Asia on the United States*, written testimony of Abraham M. Denmark, May 20, 2009.
19. Jayshree Bajoria, "India-Afghanistan Relations," Council on Foreign Relations Backgrounder (New York: October 23, 2008). *http://www.cfr.org/publication/ 17474/.*
20. US-China Economic and Security Review Commission, *Hearing on the Impact of China's Economic and Security Interests in Continental Asia on the United States*, testimony of Michael Schiffer, May 20, 2009.
21. US Department of State, "Background Note: Pakistan" (Washington, DC: March 2009). *http://www.state.gov/r/pa/ei/bgn/3453.htm.* See also BBC News, "Bush names Pakistan 'major ally,' " June 17, 2004.
22. White House Press Office, "What's New in the Strategy for Afghanistan and Pakistan" (Washington, DC: March 27, 2009). *http://www.whitehouse.gov/the/press_office/Whats-New-in-the-Strategy-for-Afghanistan-and-Pakistan/.*
23. US-China Economic and Security Review Commission, *Hearing on the Impact of China's Economic and Security Interests in Continental Asia on the United States*, testimony of Michael Schiffer, May 20, 2009.
24. Li Li, "China Daily: The Many Sides of Global Efforts in Afghanistan," *China Daily Online*, April 29, 2009. OSC ID: CPP20090429968045.
25. US-China Economic and Security Review Commission, *Hearing on the Impact of China's Economic and Security Interests in Continental Asia on the United States*, written testimony of Walid Phares, May 20, 2009.
26. US-China Economic and Security Review Commission, *Hearing on the Impact of China's Economic and Security Interests in Continental Asia on the United States*, written testimony of Abraham M. Denmark, May 20, 2009.
27. Associated Press, "Attack on convoy of Chinese workers kills 4 Pakistani police guards," July 19, 2007. *http://w3.nexis.com/new/.*
28. US-China Economic and Security Review Commission, *Hearing on the Impact of China's Economic and Security Interests in Continental Asia on the United States*, testimony of Lisa Curtis, May 20, 2009.
29. *Stratfor Today*, "China: Unusually Lethal Unrest," July 6, 2009.
30. Inal Erson, "Prepare to fight China, al Qaeda figure tells Uighurs," Reuters, October 7, 2009.
31. US-China Economic and Security Review Commission, *Hearing on the Impact of China's Economic and Security Interests in Continental Asia on the United States*, written testimony of Walid Phares, May 20, 2009.
32. US Department of State, *Country Reports on Terrorism 2008*, "Chapter 2: Country Reports: East Asia and Pacific Overview" (Washington, DC: April 30, 2009). *http://www.state.gov/s/ct/rls/crt/2008/122413.htm.*
33. US-China Economic and Security Review Commission, *Hearing on the Impact of China's Economic and Security Interests in Continental Asia on the United States*, written testimony of Walid Phares, May 20, 2009.

34. Lei Xiaoxun and Zhu Zhe, "Xinjiang Targets Drug Trafficking," *China Daily*, March 10, 2009. *http://www.chinadaily.com.cn/china/2009–03/10/content_7557566.htm.*
35. Ziad Haider, "Sino-Pakistan Relations and Xinjiang's Uighurs: Politics, Trade, and Islam along the Karakoram Highway," *Asian Survey* 45:4 (July/August 2005): 533.
36. "*Guojia renkou he jihua shengyu weiyuanhui*" (National Population and Family Planning Commission of China), "*Xinjiang: Luxing chengnuo, zhenghe ziyuan, zhendui liudong ren kou deng renqun kaizhan aizibing yufang*" (Xinjiang: Launching prevention of AIDS to fulfill a promise, integrate resources, and focus on the floating population), March 6, 2009. *http://www.npfpc.gov.cn/cn/file/aids/AIDS–XJ.pdf.* For more information, see Joint United Nations Programme on HIV/AIDS, "China 2008 Country Progress Report," 2008. *http://data.unaids.org/pub/Report/2008/china_2008_country|progress_report_en.pdf.*
37. Lei Xiaoxun and Zhu Zhe, "Xinjiang Targets Drug Trafficking," *China Daily*, March 10, 2009. *http://www.chinadaily.com.cn/china/2009–03/10/content_7557566.htm.* See also Sarah McDowall, "China to Boost Security Along Borders to Curb Terrorism and Drug Trafficking," *Global Insight*, March 10, 2009.
38. *People's Daily Online*, "SCO joint drill to crack down on 'three evil forces,' " August 12, 2007. *http://english.people.com.cn/90001/90777/6237431.html.*
39. US-China Economic and Security Review Commission, *Hearing on the Impact of China's Economic and Security Interests in Continental Asia on the United States*, written testimony of Walid Phares, May 20, 2009.
40. Xinhua, "China pledges $75 m in aid for Afghanistan," April 1, 2009. *http://www.chinadaily.com.cn/china/2009–04/01/content_7638635.htm.*
41. *China Daily*, "China offers aid to Pakistan, Hu meets C. Asian leaders," June 6, 2009.
42. Asma Razaq, "Government does not feel additional IMF aid necessary," *Business Recorder*, April 23, 2009. *http://w3.nexis.com/new/.*
43. US-China Economic and Security Review Commission, *Hearing on the Impact of China's Economic and Security Interests in Continental Asia on the United States*, written testimony of Lisa Curtis, May 20, 2009.
44. US-China Economic and Security Review Commission, *Hearing on the Impact of China's Economic and Security Interests in Continental Asia on the United States*, written testimony of Walid Phares, May 20, 2009.
45. US-China Economic and Security Review Commission, *Hearing on the Impact of China's Economic and Security Interests in Continental Asia on the United States*, written testimony of Abraham M. Denmark, May 20, 2009.
46. Xinhua Financial Network, "China's Zhenhua Oil wins oil and gas exploration rights in Pakistan," March 30, 2007.
47. Michael M. Phillips, "US and China Work Together to Rebuild Afghanistan," *Wall Street Journal*, June 20, 2009.
48. Ron Synovitz, "Afghanistan: China's Winning Bid for Copper Rights Includes Power Plant, Railroad," Radio Free Europe Radio Liberty, November 24, 2007.
49. Nicholas Norling, "The Emerging China-Afghanistan Relationship," *Central Asia-Caucasus Analyst* (May 14, 2008).
50. James R. Yeager, *The Aynak Copper Tender: Implications for Afghanistan and the West* (Tuscon, Arizona: Skyline Laboratories and Assayers, October 2009).
51. Jon Boone, "Copper project tests Afghanistan's resources," *Financial Times*, January 8, 2008. *http://www.ft.com/cms/s/0/0fddbc1e-bd74–11dc-b7e6–0000779fd2ac.html?nclick_check=1.*

52. Michael M. Phillips, "US and China Work Together to Rebuild Afghanistan," *Wall Street Journal*, June 20, 2009.
53. The Economic and Commercial Counselor's Office of the Embassy of the People's Republic of China in Afghanistan, "Vice President Zeng Qinghong Holds Talks with Afghan Vice President Nimartullah Shaharani," November 28, 2004.
54. The News International, "Accord on KKH upgradation signed," January 22, 2008.
55. Ziad Haider, "Baluchis, Beijing, and Pakistan's Gwadar Port," *Politics & Diplomacy* (Winter/Spring 2005).
56. Ziad Haider, "Baluchis, Beijing, and Pakistan's Gwadar Port," *Politics & Diplomacy* (Winter/Spring 2005): 95–103.
57. Syed Fazel-e-Haider, "Singapore takes over Pakistani port," *Asia Times*, March 26, 2009.
58. *Gwadar News*, "Gwadar port becomes fully functional," December 21, 2008.
59. US-China Economic and Security Review Commission, *Hearing on the Impact of China's Economic and Security Interests in Continental Asia on the United States*, testimony of Lisa Curtis, May 20, 2009.
60. US-China Economic and Security Review Commission, *Hearing on the Impact of China's Economic and Security Interests in Continental Asia on the United States*, written testimony of Michael Schiffer, May 20, 2009.
61. Syed Fazel-e-Haider, "Chinese interests caught in drone threat," *Asia Times*, March 26, 2009.
62. Syed Fazl-e-Haider, "China calls halt to Gwadar refinery," *Asia Times*, August 14, 2009.
63. B. Raman, "Chinese to Construct Civil-Military Airport at Gwadar," South Asia Analysis Group Paper No. 2131, November 2, 2007.
64. *Asia Media*, "PAKISTAN: China Mobile competition to benefit cell phone users," January 23, 2007.
65. *People's Daily*, "China to deliver telecom satellite to Pakistan," October 16, 2008.
66. Interfax, "Chinese Companies Win Contracts in Postwar Afghanistan," August 27, 2003.
67. *Pakistan Newswire*, "$200 m Pak-China Investment Company launched," December 17, 2007.
68. Sohail Sarfraz, "Finance Releases Data of Joint Investment Companies," *Business Recorder*, March 18, 2009. *http://www.brecorder.com/index.php?id=7412*.
69. US-China Economic and Security Review Commission, *Hearing on the Impact of China's Economic and Security Interests in Continental Asia on the United States*, testimony of Lisa Curtis, May 20, 2009.
70. US-China Economic and Security Review Commission, *Hearing on the Impact of China's Economic and Security Interests in Continental Asia on the United States*, testimony of Lisa Curtis, May 20, 2009.
71. US-China Economic and Security Review Commission, *Hearing on the Impact of China's Economic and Security Interests in Continental Asia on the United States*, written testimony of Michael Schiffer, May 20, 2009.
72. Embassy of the People's Republic of China in the United Kingdom of Great Britain and Northern Ireland, "Five Principles of Peaceful Coexistence," October 10, 2003. *www.chinese-embassy.org.uk/eng/wjzc/t27084.htm*.
73. US-China Economic and Security Review Commission, *Hearing on the Impact of China's Economic and Security Interests in Continental Asia on the United States*, testimony of Walid Phares, May 20, 2009.

74. US-China Economic and Security Review Commission, *Hearing on the Impact of China's Economic and Security Interests in Continental Asia on the United States*, testimony of Lisa Curtis, May 20, 2009.
75. Qin Gang, "Foreign Ministry Spokesperson Qin Gang's Regular Press Conference," Beijing, China, July 14, 2009. *http://www.china-embassy.org/eng/fyrth/ t573182.htm.*
76. Open Source Center, "Tehran Faces Criticism Over Response to China Unrest," *OSC Feature*, July 20, 2009. OSC ID: FEA20090720871485. *http://www.open source.gov.*
77. Andrew Small, "China's Af-Pak Moment," German Marshall Fund of the United States Policy Brief, May 20, 2009.
78. Yitchak Shichor, "The Great Wall of Steel: Military and Strategy in Xinjiang," in *Xinjiang: China's Muslim Borderland* (Armonk, NY: Central Asia Caucasus Institute, 2004), p. 154.
79. Dru C. Gladney, "Chinese Programme of Development and Control, 1978–2001," in *Xinjiang: China's Muslim Borderland* (Armonk, NY: Central Asia Caucasus Institute, 2004), p. 109.
80. Shanghai Cooperation Organization, "Member States." *http://www.sectsco .org/EN/#.*
81. BBC Monitoring Central Asia Unit, "Shanghai bloc's anti-terror drills to be held in Tajikistan," April 2, 2009.
82. US Helsinki Commission, *Hearing on the Shanghai Cooperation Organization: Changing the Playing Field in Central Asia*, written testimony of Martha Brill Olcott, September 27, 2006.
83. US-China Economic and Security Review Commission, *Hearing on the Impact of China's Economic and Security Interests in Continental Asia on the United States*, testimony of Michael Schiffer, May 20, 2009.
84. Marlene Laruelle and Sebastien Peyrouse, *China as a Neighbor: Central Asian Perspectives and Strategies* (Washington, DC: Central Asia-Caucasus Institute Silk Road Studies Programme, 2009), pp. 35–36.
85. Alyson J.K. Bailes et al., "The Shanghai Cooperation Organization," *SIPRI* [Stockholm International Peace Research Institute] *Policy Paper* no. 7 (May 2007): 10. *http://books.sipri.org/files/PP/SIPRIPP17.pdf.*
86. Marlene Laruelle and Sebastien Peyrouse, *China as a Neighbor: Central Asian Perspectives and Strategies* (Washington, DC: Central Asia-Caucasus Institute Silk Road Studies Programme, 2009), pp. 35–36.
87. US-China Economic and Security Review Commission, *Hearing on the Impact of China's Economic and Security Interests in Continental Asia on the United States*, testimony of Daniel Twining, May 20, 2009.
88. US-China Economic and Security Review Commission, *Hearing on the Impact of China's Economic and Security Interests in Continental Asia on the United States*, testimony of Julia Nanay, May 20, 2009.
89. US-China Economic and Security Review Commission, *Hearing on the Impact of China's Economic and Security Interests in Continental Asia on the United States*, written testimony of Julia Nanay, May 20, 2009.
90. Ian Storey, "China's 'Malacca Dilemma,' " *The Jamestown Foundation: China Brief* 6:8 (April 12, 2006).
91. US-China Economic and Security Review Commission, *Hearing on the Impact of China's Economic and Security Interests in Continental Asia on the United States*, testimony of Stephen Blank, May 20, 2009.

92. Sebastien Peyrouse, "Economic Aspects of the Chinese-Central Asia Rapprochement," *Silk Road Paper* (September 2007): p. 50.
93. *Shenzhen Daily*, "Sino-Kazakh Oil Pipeline Construction Starts," September 29, 2004.
94. *EurasiaNet*, "Turkmenistan-China Pipeline on Target for 2009," *Eurasia Net News Briefs*, March 30, 2009. See also Agence France-Presse, "Natural Gas Pipeline From Turkmenistan to PRC To Start Operations in Dec 09," September 16, 2009.
95. Radio Free Europe Radio Liberty, "China, Turkmenistan Sign Natural-Gas Deal," July 18, 2007.
96. US-China Economic and Security Review Commission, *Hearing on the Impact of China's Economic and Security Interests in Continental Asia on the United States*, written testimony of Stephen Blank, May 20, 2009.
97. Institution of Chemical Engineers, "China to boost Kazakhstan uranium," *TCE Today*, May 11, 2009.
98. Marston-Nicholson, "New uranium mine opens in Kazakhstan," *Kazakhstan Live*, April 29, 2009.
99. Arthur Bright, "US undecided in sanctions against Uzbekistan for human rights abuses," *Christian Science Monitor*, October 28, 2005.
100. Sebastien Peyrouse, "China's Recent Advances in Central Asia," *Central Asia—Caucasus Institute Analyst* 10:24 (December 10, 2008): 6–9. *http://www.caci analyst.org/files/081210Analyst.pdf.*
101. US-China Economic and Security Review Commission, *Hearing on the Impact of China's Economic and Security Interests in Continental Asia on the United States*, testimony of Julia Nanay, May 20, 2009.
102. *Shenzhen Daily*, "Sino-Kazakh Oil Pipeline Construction Starts," September 29, 2004.
103. Sebastien Peyrouse, "Economic Aspects of China's Rapprochement with Central Asia," *Silk Road Paper* (September 2007); BBC News, "CNPC secures PetroKazakhstan bid," October 26, 2005; *Silk Road Engineer*, "CNPC and KMG to pay $3.3 billion for MangistauMunaiGas" (April 27, 2009).
104. Marston-Nicholson, "New uranium mine opens in Kazakhstan," *Kazakhstan Live*, April 29, 2009.
105. Trend Capital News Agency, "Work continues on schedule in Turkmenistan- China gas pipeline: CNPC," January 7, 2009; News Central Asia, "CNPC Starts Building Turkmenistan-China Gas Pipeline," August 30, 2007.
106. Radio Free Europe Radio Liberty, "China, Turkmenistan Sign Natural-Gas Deal," July 18, 2007.
107. *Forbes*, "China's CNPC signs oil exploration deal with Uzbekneftegaz," October 19, 2008.
108. *Alexander's Oil & Gas Connections*, "CNPC to expand in Uzbekistan," March 25, 2009.
109. Hsiu-Ling Wu and Chien-Hsun Chen, "The Prospects for Regional Economic Integration Between China and the Five Central Asian Countries," *Europe-Asia Studies* 56:7 (2004): 1059–1080.
110. Sebastien Peyrouse, "Economic Aspects of China's Rapprochement with Central Asia," *Silk Road Paper* (September 2007): 14.
111. Tamara Trinh, "China's Commodity Hunger: Implications for Africa and Latin America," Deutsche Bank Research, June 13, 2006. *http://www.dbresearch.com/PROD/DBR_INTERNET_DE-PROD/PROD0000000000199956.pdf.*

112. David Trilling, "Tajikistan: A Chinese Road in the Future," *Eurasia Insight*, August 1, 2007. *http://www.eurasianet.org/departments/insight/articles/eav080107a.shtml.*

113. *Kazakhstan General Newswire*, "Problems of Chinese migration to Kazakhstan shall be settled through unification of the regulatory framework, says expert," June 10, 2008. *http://w3.nexis.com/new/.*

114. US-China Economic and Security Review Commission, *Hearing on the Impact of China's Economic and Security Interests in Continental Asia on the United States*, testimony of Martin Spechler, May 20, 2009.

115. Manmohan Parkash, *Connecting Central Asia: A Road Map for Regional Development* (Philippines: Asian Development Bank, 2006).

116. US-China Economic and Security Review Commission, *Hearing on the Impact of China's Economic and Security Interests in Continental Asia on the United States*, written testimony of Martin Spechler, May 20, 2009.

117. *Times of Central Asia*, "Kyrgyzstan and China signed agreement on technical and economic cooperation," March 4. 2009. *http://w3.nexis.com/new/.*

118. BBC Monitoring Central Asia Unit, "Kazakhstan to buy 152 carriages from Chinese company," November 21, 2006. *http://w3.nexis.com/new/.*

119. *EurasiaNet*, "Kyrgyzstan: China Considers Building $2 Billion Railway in Exchange for Coalmine," April 21, 2009. *http://www.eurasianet.org/departments/ news/articles/ eav042109i.shtml.*

120. AKI News Agency, "Kyrgyzstan offers China to finance construction of China-Kyrgyzstan-Uzbekistan railway in exchange for resources," June 11, 2009. *http:// w3.nexis.com/new/.*

121. Alexei Matveyev, "Beijing Moves into Central Asia: China is becoming Russia's rival as well as partner," *Voenno-Promyshlennyi Kurier* 47 (December 6, 2007): 2. *http://w3.nexis.com/new/.*

122. Nationwide International News, "Uzbek-Chinese relations stepping up in line with principles of strategic partnership," July 10, 2007.

123. Sebastien Peyrouse, "The Economic Aspects of China's Rapprochement with Central Asia," *Silk Road Paper* (September 2007): 34.

124. US-China Economic and Security Review Commission, *Hearing on the Impact of China's Economic and Security Interests in Continental Asia on the United States*, testimony of Stephen Blank, May 20, 2009.

125. Polya Lesova, "Oil-rich Russia battles the global economic crisis," *Market Watch*, June 12, 2009. *http://www.marketwatch.com/story/oil-rich-russia-battles-theglobal-economic-crisis?pagenumber=1.*

126. *Stratfor Today*, "China: Preserving Influence in the SCO," June 16, 2009.

127. US-China Economic and Security Review Commission, *Hearing on the Impact of China's Economic and Security Interests in Continental Asia on the United States*, testimony of Stephen Blank, May 20, 2009.

128. Douglas Birch and Mansur Mirovalev, "China, Russia competing for Central Asia's abundant energy resources," Associated Press, December 17, 2007.

129. US-China Economic and Security Review Commission, *Hearing on the Impact of China's Economic and Security Interests in Continental Asia on the United States*, written testimony of Julia Nanay, May 20, 2009.

130. Vladimir Isachenkov, "Russia, China, Central Asian Nations Hold Summit," Associated Press, June 15, 2009.

131. *Washington Times*, "President Signs US Base Deal," July 8, 2009.

132. US-China Economic and Security Review Commission, *Hearing on the Impact of China's Economic and Security Interests in Continental Asia on the United States*, testimony of Martin Spechler, May 20, 2009. See also Marlene Laruelle and Sebastien Peyrouse, *China as a Neighbor: Central Asian Perspectives and Strategies* (Washington, DC: Central Asia-Caucasus Institute Silk Road Studies Programme, 2009).

133. Sebastien Peyrouse, "Sinophilia and Sinophobia in Central Asia" (Central Asia-Caucasus Institute Silk Road Studies Programme conference on "Sino-Russian Relations: Old Patterns, New Realities," Washington, DC, May 6–7, 2009), pp. 1–4.

134. Sebastien Peyrouse, "Sinophilia and Sinophobia in Central Asia" (Central Asia-Caucasus Institute Silk Road Studies Programme conference on "Sino-Russian Relations: Old Patterns, New Realities," Washington, DC, May 6–7, 2009), pp. 1–4.

135. Sebastien Peyrouse, "Sinophilia and Sinophobia in Central Asia" (Central Asia-Caucasus Institute Silk Road Studies Programme conference on "Sino-Russian Relations: Old Patterns, New Realities," Washington, DC, May 6–7, 2009), pp. 1–4.

136. US-China Economic and Security Review Commission, *Hearing on the Impact of China's Economic and Security Interests in Continental Asia on the United States*, written testimony of Martin Spechler, May 20, 2009.

137. Douglas Birch and Mansur Mirovalev, "China, Russia competing for Central Asia's abundant energy resources," Associated Press, December 17, 2007.

138. US-China Economic and Security Review Commission, *Hearing on the Impact of China's Economic and Security Interests in Continental Asia on the United States*, testimony of Martin Spechler, May 20, 2009.

139. Ma Ying-jeou, "New Year's Day Celebratory Message," Office of the President, (Taipei, Taiwan: January 1, 2009). *http://www.president.gov.tw/en/prog/news_release/print.php?id=1105499867.*

140. Agence France-Press, "Taiwan Calls for New Ties," *Straits Times* (Singapore), January 2, 2009. *http://www.straitstimes.com/Breaking%2BNews/Asia/Story/ STIStory_321046.html.*

141. BBC, "China Suggests Talks with Taiwan," December 31, 2008. *http://news.bbc.co.uk/2/low/asia-pacific/7805773.stm.*

142. Xinhua, "Premier Wen Calls for Normalization of Cross-Strait Economic Relations," March 5, 2009. *http://news.xinhuanet.com/english/2009–03/05/content_310945758.htm.*

143. Information Office of the State Council, *China's National Defence in 2008* (Beijing: January 2009).

144. Information Office of the State Council, *China's National Defence in 2006* (Beijing: December 2006).

145. Jason Dean, "Taiwan to Participate as Observer at WHO Meeting," *Wall Street Journal*, April 29, 2009. *http://online.wsj.com/*. One reason Beijing dropped its original objections was to prevent the recurrence of past criticism when Beijing blocked the WHO from assisting Taiwan during the 2003 outbreak of SARS, or Severe Acute Respiratory Syndrome. See Keith Bradsher, "Taiwan Takes Step Forward at U.N. Health Agency," *New York Times*, April 30, 2009. *http://www. nytimes.com/2009/04/30/world/asia/30taiwan.html?_r=1&ref=global-home&page wante.*

146. Open Source Center, "OSC Analysis: PRC, Taiwan Officials Seek To Limit Impact of Dalai Lama Visit," September 4, 2009. OSC ID: CPF20090904565001. *http://www.opensource.gov.*

147. Kerry Dumbaugh, *Taiwan-US Relations: Developments and Policy Implications* (Washington, D.C.: Congressional Research Service, August 2009), p. 24.

148. Kerry Dumbaugh, "Taiwan-US Relations: Developments and Policy Implications" (Washington, D.C.: Congressional Research Service, August 2009), p. 24. This was the third time that Lien Chan and Hu Jintao met. Previous meetings between the two included Lien Chan's April 29, 2005, and May 2008 trips to the mainland. The April 2005 meeting was the first ever high-level meeting between the two sides since 1949. See Patricia O'Connell, "Taiwan's 'Step-by-Step Process,' " *BusinessWeek* (May 9, 2005). *http://www.businessweek.com/bwdaily/dnflash/may2005/nf2005 0591461 6\db053.htm*; and Xinhua, "Hu Jintao meets KMT Honorary Chairman Lien Chan in Beijing," April 29, 2008. *http://www.china-embassy.org/eng/zt/twwt/ t430227.htm.*

149. Michael Wines, "Chinese President Meets Leader of Taiwanese Party," *New York Times*, May 26, 2009. *http://www.nytimes.com/2009/05/27/world/asia/27taiwan.html?_r=2&ref=world.* Chairman Wu again visited the mainland in July for the fifth meeting of the Cross-Strait Economic, Trade, and Culture Forum, during which time he met with Jia Qinglin, chairman of the National Committee of the Chinese People's Political Consultative Conference. Xinhua, "Cross-Straits Forum Presents Proposal to Promote Cultural Exchanges," July 12, 2009. *http://news. xinhuanet.com/english/2009–07/12/content_11695970.htm.*

150. Weiyi Lim, "China's Hu Congratulates Taiwan's Ma on Party Post," Bloomberg, July 27, 2009. *http://www.bloomberg.com/apps/news?pid=20601080 & sid=aNQ. dUPMBSv0.*

151. Tania Branigan, "Taiwanese and Chinese Presidents Exchange First Message in 60 Years," *Guardian*, July 27, 2009. *http://www.guardian.co.uk/world/2009/jul/27/china-taiwan-presidents-contact.*

152. David Young, "Mayor of Kaohsiung Chen Chu in Beijing," *China Post*, May 22, 2009. *http://www.chinapost.com.tw/taiwan/china-taiwan-relations/2009/05/22/209126/Mayor-of.htm.* A month later, fellow Democratic Progressive Party member and mayor of Tainan Hsu Tain-tsair traveled to Xiamen, China, to attend the opening ceremony of the First Strait Cup Sailing Event. *China Post*, "Another Opposition DPP Mayor to Visit China," June 4, 2009. *http:/ www. china post. com.tw/taiwan/china-taiwan-relations/2009/06/04/210785/Another-opposition.htm.*

153. *China Post*, "Direct Cross-Strait Links in Place," December 15, 2008. *http://www.chinapost.com.tw / taiwan / china-taiwan-relations / 2008/12/15/187643/Directacross-strait.htm.* The agreement officially permitting the Three Direct Links was signed on November 4, 2008, between the Straits Exchange Foundation and China's Association for Relations Across the Taiwan Strait. See James Peng and Yu-huay Sun, "China, Taiwan Agree on Direct Flight, Shipping, Mail," Bloomberg, November 4, 2009. *http://www.bloomberg.com/apps/news?pid =20601110 &sid =aQvle GFjAaz U#.*

154. John Pomfret, "China Accepts Taiwan Offer to Open Islands; Goods and Passengers to Flow," *Washington Post*, December 29, 2000. *http://w3.nexis.com.*

155. Philip P. Pan and Tim Culpan, "China, Taiwan Agree to Direct Flights," *Washington Post*, January 16, 2005. *http://www.washingtonpost.com/wp-dyn/articles/A12524–2005Jan15.html.*

156. Xinhua, "Chinese Mainland, Taiwan Increase Regular Direct Flights," August 31, 2009. *http://news.xinhuanet.com/english/2009–08/31/content\11970811 .htm.*

157. *China Post*, "Direct Cross-Strait Links in Place," December 15, 2008. *http://www.chinapost.com.tw / taiwan / china-taiwan-relations / 2008/12/15/187643/Directacross- strait.htm.*

158. Representative from Xiamen City's Taiwan Affairs Office, meeting with US- China Economic and Security Review Commission, Xiamen, China, May 7, 2009.

159. Staff Reporter, "Chinese Have Made 660,000 Visits to Taiwan in Past Year," *Taipei Times*, July 19, 2009, *http://www.taipeitimes.com/News/taiwan/archives/2009/07/19/2003449018.*

160. Xinhua, "Mainland, Taiwan Clinch Financial Regulatory Mechanism amid Global Crisis," April 26, 2009. *http://news.xinhuanet.com/english/2009–04/26/content_11261192.htm.* See also *China Post*, "Green Light given on more Cross-Strait Financial Exchanges," April 27, 2009. *http://w3.nexis.com/new/.*

161. Ho Ai Li, "China, Taiwan Ink Financial Alliance Pact," *Straits Times* (Singapore), April 27, 2009. *http://w3.nexis.com/new/.*

162. *CCTV International, "Bank of China Strives to Become First Mainland Bank to set up Taiwan Branch," April 29, 2009. http://www.cctv.com/english/special/ C22025/20090429/102511.shtml.*

163. Mainland Affairs Council, "Explanation Concerning the Cross-Strait Food Safety Agreement," November 4, 2008. *http://www.mac.gov.tw/english/english/cc2/ ag04b.pdf.*

164. *China Post*, "Direct Cross-Strait Links in Place," December 15, 2008. *http://www.chinapost.com.tw/taiwan/china-taiwan-relations/2008/12/15/187643/Directacross-strait.htm.*

165. Mainland Affairs Council, "Third Chiang-Chen Talks Proceeds Smoothly and Produces Fruitful Results," April 26, 2009. *http://www.mac.gov.tw/english/english/news/09426.htm.*

166. *Jane's Intelligence Weekly*, "Strait and Narrow—China and Taiwan's Criminal Crackdown," August 27, 2009. *http://www.janes.com/news/security/jir/jir090827_1_n.shtml.*

167. Mainland Affairs Council, "Third Chiang-Chen Talks Proceeds Smoothly and Produces Fruitful Results," April 26, 2009. *http://www.mac.gov.tw/english/english/news/09426.htm*

168. Mainland Affairs Council, "Preliminary Statistics of Cross-Strait Economic Relations," September 1, 2009. *http://www.mac.gov.tw/english/english/csexchan/economic/9806e.pdf.*

169. Agence France-Presse, "Taiwan, China to open tourist liaison offices: official," Channel NewsAsia, July 20, 2009. *http://www.channelnewsasia.com/stories/afp_asiapacific/view/443664/1/.html.*

170. Y. F. Low, "Exchanging Tourism Offices with China Necessary: Taiwanese Official," Central News Agency, July 21, 2009. *http://www.chinapost.com.tw/taiwan/china-taiwan-relations/2009/07/21/217195/Exchanging-tourism.htm.*

171. Representative from Xiamen City's Taiwan Affairs Office, meeting with US- China Economic and Security Review Commission, Xiamen, China, May 7, 2009.

172. Ariana Eunjung Cha, "Taiwan, China Negotiating a Landmark Free-Trade Agreement," *Washington Post*, February 21, 2009, p. A09. *http://www.washington post.com/wp-dyn/content/article/2009/02/20/AR2009022003388.html.*

173. Zhao Hong and Sarah Y. Tong, "Taiwan-Mainland Economic Cooperation Framework Agreement (ECFA): Implications for Cross-Strait Relations," East Asia Institute, Background Brief 452 (Singapore: May 21, 2009).

174. Erika Wang, "ECFA Won't Boost China Imports: Ma," *China Post,* March 6, 2009. *http://www.chinapost.com.tw/taiwan/2009/03/06/198915/ECFA-won't.htm.*

175. Terry Cooke, "Cross-Strait Matrix: The Economic Cooperation Framework Agreement," *China Brief* 9:11 (May 2009). *http://www.jamestown.org/single/?no_cache=1&tx_ttnews%5Btt_news%5D=35041&tx|ttnews%5BbackPid%5D=7&cHash=f0b872132a.*

176. Associated Press, "Taiwan Sees Shallower Recession This Year," in *Business Week*, August 20, 2009. *www.businessweek.com/ap/financialnews/D9A6IB PG0.htm.*

177. *Forbes,* "Taiwan sees Shallower Recession this Year," August 20, 2009. *http://www.forbes.com/feeds/ap/2009/08/20/business-as-taiwan-economy 1 679 7880 .html*; and Bloomberg, "Taiwan's Export Orders Fall the Least in Nine Months," August 24, 2009. *http://www.bloomberg.com/apps/news?pid=news archive &sid =aql acEW7H87k.*

178. *Taiwan News,* "MOEA [Ministry of Economic Affairs] Denies ECFA Will Harm Taiwan's Electronic Sector," July 28, 2009. *http://www.etaiwannews.com/etn/news_content.php?id=1015074&lang=eng_news*; and *Economist*, "Reunification by Trade?" August 6, 2009. *http://www.economist.com/world/asia/Printer Friendly.cfm?story_id=14191252.*

179. Rich Chang, "Forum Slams Proposed ECFA," *Taipei Times*, March 2009. *http://www.bilaterals.org/article.php3?id_article=14549.*

180. *Taipei Times,* "Chiu DeniesCECASells Out Taiwan," February 24, 2009, p. 3.

181. Zhao Hong and Sarah Y. Hong, "Taiwan-Mainland Economic Cooperation Framework Agreement (ECFA): Implications for Cross-Strait Relations," East Asia Institute, Background Brief 452 (Singapore: May 21, 2009), p. 7; and *Taiwan Today News*, "Forum Attendees Say 'Chinese FTA' Better Than ECFA," August 4, 2009. *http://www.taiwantodaynews.com / index.php / forum-attendees-say-chinese-fta-betterthan- ecfa.*

182. Flora Wang and Jenny W. Hsu, "Wang Opposes CECA Without Review," *Taipei Times*, February 27, 2009, p. 1. *http://www.taipeitimes.com/News/front/archives / 2009/02/27/2003437143.*

183. Central News Agency, "Legislature should be represented in ECFA talks: report," September 17, 2009. *http://www.etaiwannews.com/etn/news_content.php?id =1059645&lang=eng_news.*

184. Loa Lok-sin, "Survey Shows Knowledge Gap on ECFA," *Taipei Times,* August 3, 2009. *http://www.taipeitimes.com/News/front/archives/2009/08/03/2003 450215.*

185. Rupert Hammond-Chambers, "Taiwan and China Make Strides: Can America Respond?" (Washington, DC: The Brookings Institution, March 2009). *http://www.brookings.edu/opinions/2009/03_ taiwan_china_hammondchambers.aspx.* Originally the fourth round of Straits Exchange Foundation-Association for Relations Across the Taiwan Strait talks to be held in late 2009 were to include the Economic Cooperation Framework Agreement on the agenda. However, Straits Exchange Foundation Vice Chairman Kao Koong-lian denied this on September 15, 2009. Agence France-Presse, "Taiwan to resume trade talks with China 'soon,' September 10, 2009. *http://www.google.com/hostednews/afp/article/ALeqM5hc5-WgU dJ7xYzLX2-CgKJ0MfJXiQ*; and Elizabeth Hsu, "Next Round of Cross-Strait Talks will not Include ECFA: Official," Central News Agency, September 15, 2009. *http://english.cna.com.tw/ReadNews/Eng_Top News.aspx?ID=200909150010.*

186. Jenny W. Hsu, "Ma, Young Speak on Cross-Strait Efforts," *Taipei Times*, March 6, 2009. *http://www.taipeitimes.com/News/taiwan/archives/2009/03/06/ 2003437735.*

187. *China Post*, "Ties not Competing with Cross-Strait Relations: Outgoing AIT Chief," July 3, 2009. *http://www.chinapost.com.tw/taiwan/local/taipei/2009/07/03/214686/Taiwan-US-ties.htm.*

188. Deborah Kuo, "Taiwan to Focus on Joining UN Agencies: Foreign Ministry," Central News Agency, June 7, 2009. *http://www.etaiwannews.com/etn/news_content.php?id=970059&lang=eng_news.*

189. US-China Economic and Security Review Commission, *Hearing on China's Military and Security Activities Abroad,* testimony of David S. Sedney, March 4, 2009.

190. Office of the Secretary of Defence, *Military Report of the People's Republic of China: 2009* (Washington, D.C.: Department of Defence, 2009), p. 51.
191. Eric C. Anderson and Jeffrey G. Engstrom, *Capabilities of the Chinese People's Liberation Army to Carry Out Military Action in the Event of a Regional Military Conflict* (McLean, VA: Science Applications International Corporation, May 2009), p. 36.
192. Sofia Wu, "President calls for Continued Combat Preparedness," *Taiwan News*, September 24, 2009. *http://www.etaiwannews.com/etn/news_content.php?id=1065382&lang=eng_news&cate_img=83.jpg&cate_rss=news_Politics_TAIWAN.*
193. Eric C. Anderson and Jeffrey G. Engstrom, *Capabilities of the Chinese People's Liberation Army to Carry Out Military Action in the Event of a Regional Military Conflict* (McLean, VA: Science Applications International Corporation, May 2009), p. 36.
194. Eric C. Anderson and Jeffrey G. Engstrom, *Capabilities of the Chinese People's Liberation Army to Carry Out Military Action in the Event of a Regional Military Conflict* (McLean, VA: Science Applications International Corporation, May 2009), p. 37. See also David A. Shlapak et al., *A Question of Balance: Political Context and Military Aspects of the China-Taiwan Dispute* (Arlington, VA: RAND Corporation, 2009), p. xv.
195. David A. Shlapak et al., *A Question of Balance: Political Context and Military Aspects of the China-Taiwan Dispute* (Alexandria, VA: RAND Corporation, 2009), p. xv.
196. Eric C. Anderson and Jeffrey G. Engstrom, *Capabilities of the Chinese People's Liberation Army to Carry Out Military Action in the Event of a Regional Military Conflict* (McLean, VA: Science Applications International Corporation, May 2009), pp. 36–38.
197. Eric C. Anderson and Jeffrey G. Engstrom, *Capabilities of the Chinese People's Liberation Army to Carry Out Military Action in the Event of a Regional Military Conflict* (McLean, VA: Science Applications International Corporation, May 2009), pp. 38–39.
198. Eric C. Anderson and Jeffrey G. Engstrom, *Capabilities of the Chinese People's Liberation Army to Carry Out Military Action in the Event of a Regional Military Conflict* (McLean, VA: Science Applications International Corporation, May 2009), p. 38.
199. Eric C. Anderson and Jeffrey G. Engstrom, *Capabilities of the Chinese People's Liberation Army to Carry Out Military Action in the Event of a Regional Military Conflict* (McLean, VA: Science Applications International Corporation, May 2009), p. 39.
200. Eric C. Anderson and Jeffrey G. Engstrom, *Capabilities of the Chinese People's Liberation Army to Carry Out Military Action in the Event of a Regional Military Conflict* (McLean, VA: Science Applications International Corporation, May 2009), pp. 42–43.
201. Ministry of National Defence, *Quadrennial Defence Review 2009* (Taipei: March, 2009).
202. Eric C. Anderson and Jeffrey G. Engstrom, *Capabilities of the Chinese People's Liberation Army to Carry Out Military Action in the Event of a Regional Military Conflict* (McLean, VA: Science Applications International Corporation, May 2009), p. 40.
203. David A. Shlapak et al., *A Question of Balance: Political Context and Military Aspects of the China-Taiwan Dispute* (Alexandria, VA: RAND Corporation, 2009), p. 53.
204. Eric C. Anderson and Jeffrey G. Engstrom, *Capabilities of the Chinese People's Liberation Army to Carry Out Military Action in the Event of a Regional Military Conflict* (McLean, VA: Science Applications International Corporation, May 2009), p. 42.
205. David A. Shlapak et al., *A Question of Balance: Political Context and Military Aspects of the China-Taiwan Dispute* (Alexandria, VA: RAND Corporation, 2009), pp. 53, 54.

206. David A. Shlapak et al., *A Question of Balance: Political Context and Military Aspects of the China-Taiwan Dispute* (Alexandria, VA: RAND Corporation, 2009), p. 53.
207. Eric C. Anderson and Jeffrey G. Engstrom, *Capabilities of the Chinese People's Liberation Army to Carry Out Military Action in the Event of a Regional Military Conflict* (McLean, VA: Science Applications International Corporation, May 2009), p. 41.
208. David A. Shlapak et al., *A Question of Balance: Political Context and Military Aspects of the China-Taiwan Dispute* (Alexandria, VA: RAND Corporation, 2009), p. 55.
209. Jim Wolf, "Taiwan Renews Push for Modern US F–16 Fighters," Reuters (March 15, 2009). *http://www.reuters.com/article/reutersEdge/idUSTRE52E1 C820090315?pageNumber=2&virtualBrandChannel=0.*
210. Eric C. Anderson and Jeffrey G. Engstrom, *Capabilities of the Chinese People's Liberation Army to Carry Out Military Action in the Event of a Regional Military Conflict* (McLean, VA: Science Applications International Corporation, May 2009), p. 44.
211. Eric C. Anderson and Jeffrey G. Engstrom, *Capabilities of the Chinese People's Liberation Army to Carry Out Military Action in the Event of a Regional Military Conflict* (McLean, VA: Science Applications International Corporation, May 2009), pp. 44–45.
212. Eric C. Anderson and Jeffrey G. Engstrom, *Capabilities of the Chinese People's Liberation Army to Carry Out Military Action in the Event of a Regional Military Conflict* (McLean, VA: Science Applications International Corporation, May 2009), pp. 44–45.
213. Shirley A. Kan, *Taiwan: Major US Arms Sales Since 1990* (Washington, DC: Congressional Research Service, February 2009), pp. 11–12.
214. Cao Erbao, " '*Yiguo Liangzhi*' *Tiaojianxia Xianggang de Guanzhi Liliang*" (Governing Force in Hong Kong under the Condition of "One Country, Two Systems"), *Xuexi Shibao*, January 28, 2008.
215. Hong Kong Democratic delegates to the Legislative Council, meeting with the Commission, May 10, 2009.
216. US consulate (Hong Kong) staff, meeting with the Commission, May 11, 2009.
217. Central Government Liaison Web site, "*Zhuyao Zhineng*" (Main Functions). *http://www.locpg.gov.cn/jgjj/zyzn.*
218. Hong Kong Democratic delegates to the Legislative Council, meeting with the Commission, May 10, 2009.
219. Central Government Liaison Web site, "*Peng Qinghua Jianli*" (Curriculum Vitae of Peng Qinghua). *http://www.locpg.gov.cn/jgjj/zygy/200612/t20061218_896.asp.*
220. Central Government Liaison Web site, "*Li Gang Jianli*" (Curriculum Vitae of Li Gang). *http://www.locpg.gov.cn/jgjj/zygy/200612/t20061218_894.asp.*
221. National People's Congress, *The Basic Law of the Hong Kong Special Administrative Region of the People's Republic of China: Chapter II: Relationship between the Central Authorities and the Hong Kong Special Administrative Region* (Beijing: April 4, 1990). *http://www.basiclaw.gov.hk/en/basiclawtext/images/Basic_Law.pdf.*
222. Cao Erbao, " '*Yiguo Liangzhi*' *Tiaojianxia Xianggang de Guanzhi Liliang*" (Governing Force in Hong Kong under the Condition of "One Country, Two Systems"), *Xuexi Shibao*, January 28, 2008.
223. Cao Erbao, " '*Yiguo Liangzhi*' *Tiaojianxia Xianggang de Guanzhi Liliang*" (Governing Force in Hong Kong under the Condition of "One Country, Two Systems"), *Xuexi Shibao*, January 28, 2008.

224. Cao Erbao, " '*Yiguo Liangzhi' Tiaojianxia Xianggang de Guanzhi Liliang*" (Governing Force in Hong Kong under the Condition of "One Country, Two Systems"), *Xuexi Shibao*, January 28, 2008.

225. Ching Cheong, " 'One City, Two Stoves' and its Implications for 'One Country, Two Systems' " (speech at the Hong Kong Democratic Foundation, May 11, 2009).

226. National People's Congress of the People's Republic of China, *The Basic Law of the Hong Kong Special Administrative Region of the People's Republic of China*, April 4, 1990. *http://www.basiclaw.gov.hk/en/basiclawtext/images/Basic_Law.pdf.*

227. Sharon LaFrantiere, "Police Swarm Tiananmen Square to Bar Protests," *New York Times*, June 5, 2009; Sophie Leung and Theresa Tang, "Hong Kong's Tiananmen Vigil May Draw Double Turnout (Update1)," Bloomberg, June 4, 2009. *http://www.bloomberg.com/apps/news?sid= ad7iX4 wxrho U&pid = 20601087*; and "Hong Kong Denies Entry to Tiananmen Dissidents," *Taipei Times*, May 26, 2009. *http://www.taipeitimes.com/News/world/archives/2009/05/26/2003444519.*

228. Peter Foster and Malcolm Moore, "Police flood Tiananmen Square ahead of anniversary," *Telegraph* (London), June 3, 2009. *http://www.telegraph.co.uk/news/worldnews/asia/china/5436835/Police-flood-Tiananmen-Square-ahead-of-anniversary .html.*

229. For a discussion of how this problem relates both to the People's Republic of China (PRC) and to other countries, see House Committee on Energy and Commerce, Subcommittee on Oversight and Investigations, *Military and Dual-Use Technology: Covert Testing Shows Continuing Vulnerabilities of Domestic Sales for Illegal Export*, testimony of Gregory D. Kutz, managing director for Forensic Audits and Special Investigations, Government Accountability Office, 111th Cong., 1st sess., June 4, 2009.

230. Bureau of Industry and Security, "Hong Kong Frequently Asked Questions" (Washington, DC: US Department of Commerce). *http://www.bis.doc.gov/licensing/hkongfaqs.htm.*

231. One example is the case of Chitron Electronics and Shenzhen Chitron Electronics, which were charged with conspiring to violate US export laws for shipping weapons and parts to the Chinese military through a Hong Kong front company. See "3 Chinese, 2 firms Face Export Charges in Boston," Associated Press, October 5, 2009. *http://www.google.com/hostednews/ap/article/ALeqM5jz5RbPOBb3vf_R_T5LffWsRzeDsgD9B59S980*; Thomas Grillo, "3 Accused of Selling Weapons to Chinese Military," *Boston Herald*, October 6, 2009. *http://www. bostonher ald.com/business/ general/view/200910063_accused_of_selling_weapons_to_chinese_military\feds_charge_waltham_co/*; "Local Firm Charged with Illegal Export of Defence Items," *Wicked Local Waltham* (GateHouse Media New England), October 6, 2009. *http://www.wickedlocal.com/waltham/news/x1699615499/Local-firmcharged-with-illegal-export-of-defence-items.*

232. US-China Economic and Security Review Commission, *Hearing on China's Propaganda and Influence Operations, Its Intelligence Activities that Target the United States, and the Resulting Impacts on US National Security*, testimony of James Mulvenon, April 30, 2009.

233. Howard DeVore, *China's Intelligence and Internal Security Forces* (London, United Kingdom: Jane's Information Group, 1999), pp. 31, 47.

234. Report of the Select Committee of the US House of Representatives, *US National Security and Military/Commercial Concerns with the People's Republic of China* (declassified version, May 25, 1999), chapter 1. *http://www.house.gov/coxreport /chapfs/ch1.html.*

235. Howard DeVore, *China's Intelligence and Internal Security Forces* (London, United Kingdom: Jane's Information Group, 1999), p. 43.

236. Census and Statistics Department, "Table 060: External Merchandise Trade by Ten Main Countries/Territories—Total Trade with Ten Main Countries/Territories" (Government of Hong Kong Special Administrative Region: August 25, 2009). *http://www.censtatd.gov.hk/hong_kong_statistics/statistical_tables/index.jsp?subjectID=3&tableID=060.*

237. Economic Analysis and Business Facilitation Unit, "Economic Situation in the Second Quarter of 2009 and Latest GDP and Price Forecasts for 2009" (Office of the Financial Secretary of the Government of Hong Kong Special Administrative Region: August 14, 2009). *http://www.info.gov.hk/gia/general/200908/14/P20090814 0234.htm.*

238. Census and Statistics Department, "External Merchandise Trade Statistics for August 2009" (Government of Hong Kong Special Administrative Region: September 24, 2009). *http://www.censtatd.gov.hk/press_release/press_releases_on_ statistics/index.jsp?sID=2411&sSUBID=14624&displayMode=D*; Sophie Leung, "Hong Kong's Export Decline Slows as Demand Recovers," Bloomberg, July 27, 2009.

239. Census and Statistics Department, "Unemployment and Underemployment Statistics for June-August 2009" (Government of Hong Kong Special Administrative Region: September 17, 2009). *http://www.censtatd.gov.hk/press_release/press_releases_on_statistics/index.jsp?sID=2400&s SUBID =14478 &displayMode=D*; Sophie Leung, "Hong Kong's Export Decline Slows as Demand Recovers," Bloomberg, July 27, 2009; Sophie Leung, "Hong Kong Jobless Rate Rises to Highest Since 2005," Bloomberg, July 20, 2009.

240. Bettina Wassener, "Hong Kong Joins Asia's Rapid Climb Out of Recession," Bloomberg, August 15, 2009.

241. "Hong Kong Emerges from Recession," BBC News, August 14, 2009.

242. Wendy Leung, "China Shipping to Almost Double Asia-Europe Rates," Bloomberg, June 26, 2009.

243. Theresa Tang and Kevin Hamlin, "Hong Kong Adds HK$16.8 Billion to Relief Amid Slump," Bloomberg, May 26, 2009.

244. *China Daily*, "Hu Offers Full Support to Hong Kong, Macao," December 20, 2008.

245. Li Yanping and Belinda Cao, "China, Hong Kong Central Banks Agree on Currency Swap," Bloomberg, January 20, 2009. *http://www.bloomberg.com/apps/news?pid=newsarchive&sid=aXbZz.03FfNk*; and Kwong Man-ki, "Hong Kong Chosen for Yuan Settlement Pilot," *China Daily*, March 11, 2009. *http://www.chinadaily.com.cn/cndy/2009–03/11/content_7565816.htm.*

246. He Huifeng and Paggie Leung, "Multi-Entry Visas a Hit in Shenzhen," *South China Morning Post*, April 2, 2009.

247. Fiona Tam, "Plan for Multi-Visits from Shenzhen Suspended," *South China Morning Post*, May 7, 2009.

248. He Huifeng and Paggie Leung, "Multi-Entry Visas a Hit in Shenzhen," *South China Morning Post*, April 2, 2009.

249. James Peng, "Hong Kong-China Deal Eases Investments, Hong Kong-Taiwan Travel," Bloomberg, May 9, 2009.

250. *China Daily*, "Financial Services to Expand," May 11, 2009.

251. BBC Monitoring Asia-Pacific, "China to Exempt Tariffs on Some Hong Kong, Macao Products," June 24, 2009.

252. James Peng, "Hong Kong-China Deal Eases Investments, Hong Kong-Taiwan Travel," Bloomberg, May 9, 2009.

253. Judy Chen, "China to Start Yuan Trade Settlements in Shanghai," Bloomberg, April 8, 2009.

254. Xinhua, "Bank of China Transacts First Cross-Border Yuan Settlement," July 6, 2009. *http://news.xinhuanet.com/english/2009–07/06/content_11660027.htm.*

255. Dennis Eng and Maria Chan, "Decision on Renminbi Transactions Welcomed; Tsang Sees HK as Region's Yuan Clearing Hub," *South China Morning Post*, April 10, 2009.

256. "State Council: Making Shanghai a New Global Financial Center," *People's Daily Online*, March 26, 2009. *http://english.peopledaily.com.cn/90001/90778/90857/90862/6623230.html.*

257. Cary Huang and Daniel Ren, "Shanghai No Threat to Hong Kong: Party Chief; Cities Will 'Always be Brothers,' " *South China Morning Post*, June 19, 2009.

258. US-China Economic and Security Review Commission, *Hearing on China's Media and Information Controls*, written testimony of Madeline Earp, September 10, 2009.

259. US-China Economic and Security Review Commission, *Hearing on China's Media and Information Controls*, written testimony of Madeline Earp, September 10, 2009.

260. US-China Economic and Security Review Commission, *Hearing on China's Media and Information Controls*, written testimony of Madeline Earp, September 10, 2009.

261. US-China Economic and Security Review Commission, *Hearing on China's Media and Information Controls*, testimony of Phelim Kine, September 10, 2009.

262. International Freedom of Expression Exchange, "Journalists protest savage attacks on colleagues," September 16, 2009. *http://www.ifex.org/china/hong_kong/2009/09/16/journalists/protest_assaulted/.*

263. For Sam Zarifi, "Open letter to the Chief Executive of the Macao Special Administrative Region of the People's Republic of China," Amnesty International, January 20, 2009.

264. Hong Kong Journalists Association, *2009 Annual Report: Macau Takes the Lead—Dangers for freedom of expression in Hong Kong* (Hong Kong: July 2009) p. 5. *http://www.hkja.org.hk/site/Host/hkja/UserFiles/File/annualreport/annual_report_2009_lowres.pdf.*

265. Hong Kong Journalists Association, *2009 Annual Report: Macau Takes the Lead—Dangers for freedom of expression in Hong Kong* (Hong Kong: July 2009) p. 5. *http://www.hkja.org.hk/site/Host/hkja/UserFiles/File/annualreport/annual_report_2009_lowres.pdf.*

266. Hong Kong Journalists Association, *2009 Annual Report: Macau Takes the Lead—Dangers for freedom of expression in Hong Kong* (Hong Kong: July 2009) p. 3. *http://www.hkja.org.hk/site/Host/hkja/UserFiles/File/annualreport/annual_report_2009_lowres.pdf.*

CHAPTER 4

China's Media and Information Controls—the impact in China and the United States

SECTION 1

Freedom of Expression in China

> "The Commission shall investigate and report exclusively on—
>
> "FREEDOM OF EXPRESSION—The implications of restrictions on speech and access to information in the People's Republic of China or its relations with the United States in the areas of economic and security policy. . . ."

Introduction

In the run-up to the 2008 Beijing Olympic Games, both international pressure and a concern for China's image prompted the Chinese government to announce a set of reforms that relaxed some restrictions for foreign journalists. Some journalists and civil society organizations have asserted that these reforms amounted only to the illusion of media liberalization, [1] as the Chinese government has employed new techniques for controlling or "guiding" flows of publicly available information. And when propaganda authorities and Chinese government officials deem an issue to be "sensitive," [2] the reforms are substantively ignored.

Although the Internet has provided a venue for discussion of sensitive issues, the Chinese government maintains the world's most sophisticated system for controlling Web content. Recently, increased government concerns about the Internet's potential to enable mass protests, or to embarrass government officials through revelations of malfeasance, have prompted the government to employ controversial new methods for Internet control. These methods have included the introduction of the "Green Dam Youth Escort" filtering software in May 2009. The reversal of the government's original decision to mandate the installment of this software reveals that the government's media policies may, to a limited degree, be affected by public opinion.

Public health emergencies that became international problems as a result of China's media and information control practices illustrate how such policies may have a direct and detrimental impact on US-China relations. Finally, the involvement of US companies in Chinese Internet censorship has been an issue of concern and controversy in the United States during the past several years, and legislative initiatives and a voluntary industry code of ethics have both been proposed to address this situation. This section will discuss the means that China uses to restrict foreign and Chinese journalists, the controls that China places on promulgating "sensitive" news stories, the Internet's challenges to these restrictions and controls, China's system for managing the use of the Internet, and the role of US companies in handling China's information control efforts.

The Impact of Recent Media Reforms on Reporting Conditions for International Journalists in China

In January 2007, amid increased international scrutiny and pressure for greater media freedom in the run-up to the 2008 Summer Olympic Games in Beijing, the Chinese Ministry of Foreign Affairs announced a series of media reforms.[3] These reforms, which were initially intended to be temporary, lifted restrictions on the ability of foreign journalists to travel throughout China and to interview Chinese citizens without official permission.[4] After the conclusion of the Olympic Games, there was a period of uncertainty as to whether these policies would continue; however, during a hastily organized press conference convened 15 minutes before the regulations originally were set to expire at midnight on October 17, 2008, the Chinese Ministry of Foreign Affairs announced that the reforms would be made permanent.[5]

These reforms have resulted in modest improvements in the reporting climate for foreign journalists in China, but the Chinese government's selective implementation of these policies and use of alternative means for impeding the work of foreign journalists have significantly reduced their potential benefits.[6] Phelim Kine, Asia research associate at Human Rights Watch, testified that "the Chinese government is giving something on paper with regards to a new freedom while undermining the ability of journalists to really be able to take advantage of those freedoms." [7]

For example, the central government has restricted journalists' travel to certain regions in an attempt to reduce coverage of specific "sensitive" issues.[8] In fact, a Foreign Correspondents' Club of China's survey of 57 of its members revealed 100 instances of journalists restricted from entering public places in the year following the 2008 Summer Olympic Games in Beijing.[9] This was the case in the lead-up to the one-year anniversary of the May 12, 2008, earthquake in Sichuan Province, when numerous journalists reported that they were detained, harassed, and intimidated as they attempted to report from the earthquake zone.[10]

More recently, in August 2009, provincial officials from Shaanxi Province harassed and turned away a BBC correspondent, stating that "the central government has its rules, and we have ours." [11] Officials at some levels of the Chinese government have simply ignored the January 2007 media reforms when they could be politically damaging.

Assaults against foreign journalists remain a problem. For example, on September 18, 2009, authorities stormed the Beijing hotel room of three correspondents from Japan's Kyodo News Agency who were covering a rehearsal for the October 1 National Day Parade, attacked the reporters, and damaged their equipment.[12] Other foreign journalists have reported experiencing a less violent form of harassment from Chinese officials.[13] For example, on the 20th anniversary of the June 4, 1989, Tiananmen Square massacre, plainclothes police used umbrellas to obstruct the cameras of foreign reporters from CNN, BBC, and Agence France-Presse reporting from Tiananmen Square.[14] Although this type of harassment is not as physically threatening to the journalist, it has been a successful means of impeding effective reporting.[15]

Pressure on Chinese News Assistants and Interviewees

The Chinese government has undermined journalists' ability to report by pressuring and influencing the Chinese news assistants and sources who contribute to foreign journalists' work on sensitive issues.[16] On February 13, 2009, the Chinese government issued a code of conduct for foreign correspondents' Chinese news assistants that forbids the news assistants and translators from engaging in "independent reporting" and obliges them to spread "positive information."[17] One Chinese news assistant told Human Rights Watch, "I won't do stories about forced evictions anymore because there is a chance that there will be thugs there and I will be beaten. I will be the Chinese guy [with a foreign reporter], so I'll be a target." [18] Authorities often directly contact Chinese news assistants and translators to warn them not to publicize news before it appears in state media.[19] Phelim Kine of Human Rights Watch said, "That intensified pressure appears designed to maintain a veneer of freedom for foreign journalists while seriously undermining their capacity to report effectively." [20]

Foreign journalists are finding that Chinese citizens may be less willing to cooperate than in the past. According to Madeline Earp, Asia research associate at the Committee to Protect Journalists, there is a rising sense of antiwestern nationalism and a widely shared perception—reinforced by messages in the People's Republic of China's (PRC) media—that foreign journalists have an "anti-China" bias. This perception has prompted many Chinese citizens to greet foreign journalists with suspicion or hostility.[21] In some instances, Chinese citizens may abstain from participating in interviews because they fear punitive action by the Chinese government, particularly when "sensitive" issues are involved. For example, the *Christian Science Monitor* has reported that Uighurs in Urumqi are "too terrified of the government to say anything" to foreign journalists about the riots that occurred there in July 2009.[22] Thus, while promises to permit foreign journalists greater latitude in conducting interviews with ordinary citizens may sound like a significant advance in press freedoms, the absence of an environment in which citizens are willing to speak openly to journalists has limited the potential improvements in the actual quality of information available about social conditions in China.

The Environment for Chinese Journalists

Tight Restrictions Remain on the Chinese Media

The Chinese government's promises of greater press freedom did not extend to China's own journalists, and China maintains one of the world's most controlled media systems. According to 2009 rankings of press freedom compiled by Freedom House, China ranks 181 out of 195 countries evaluated.[23] Furthermore, according to the Committee to Protect Journalists, China's 28 reporters jailed as of December 1, 2008, represent the largest number for any single country.[24]

The Chinese Communist Party's (CCP) Central Propaganda Department

The Chinese Communist Party's propaganda and information control efforts are aimed at minimizing the public's exposure to information deemed harmful to the ruling position of the CCP and proactively engaging the public with positive propaganda in order to "guide" public opinion.[25] The principal organization managing this endeavour is the Chinese Communist Party's Central Propaganda Department (hereafter "Propaganda Department"), a secretive organization that maintains a presence at the national, provincial, and local levels of China's government and media institutions.[26]

The Propaganda Department wields power through its guiding role in promulgating the overall ideological direction of Communist Party institutions; in establishing authority over personnel appointments; in having the ability to suppress information and establish official narratives through directives to media officials; and in its power to allocate and terminate licenses and contracts for media outlets.[27] Propaganda officials use these channels of influence to communicate the latest CCP policies; update news agencies with the "correct" vocabulary and terminology to use with regard to certain issues; inform editors about which stories to promote and which to avoid; and guide news agencies' coverage of sensitive issues and crises.[28] Reporters and editors who stray too far from the norms established by the Propaganda Department do so at the risk of being demoted, fired, or imprisoned.[29]

The reporting climate in China is especially hazardous for journalists who report on "sensitive" political issues or investigate allegations of corruption at the local level.[30] Several Chinese journalists reported that their cars were smashed by people using iron bars and hammers while the journalists were attempting to report on the July 2009 riots in Xinjiang.[31] On September 1, 2009, *Guangzhou Daily* reported that a reporter was thrown to the ground and beaten for 10 minutes by security guards when he attempted to take photos of a crime scene in Guangdong, the province's third attack on the press in two months.[32] Chinese investigative reporters who seek to expose official corruption face "a climate of impunity for local officials who attack journalists." [33]

Limited Improvements in Chinese Media Freedom

While the overall picture for press freedom in China is not good, certain areas have improved, partly as a result of the commercialization of China's media sector over the past several decades. Editors' selection of stories on the basis of what will sell has resulted in an increased number of reports about topics that appeal to their target audiences.[34] Media commercialization also has led to a "new ethos of professionalism" among Chinese journalists, and publications such as the *Southern Metropolitan News, Southern Weekend,* and *Caijing* magazine have encouraged reporters to test the boundaries of the central government.[35]

Judy Polumbaum, professor of communications at the University of Iowa, testified to the Commission that this new professionalism has increased the extent and quality of investigative reporting on social problems such as corruption. She also noted that the foreign press now closely watches Chinese media for important stories, stating that much of the "best foreign reporting [now] hinges on the best domestic Chinese reporting."[36] Several investigative stories have had a major impact in China, such as the reports about the poor construction of school buildings in Sichuan Province that contributed to the deaths of scores of children during the 2008 earthquake.[37] However, the subsequent clampdown on reporting about the school construction problem[38] has demonstrated the Chinese government's willingness and capability to monopolize discussion on sensitive issues or to silence discussion of certain topics entirely when it feels that they pose a threat to Communist Party rule.

"State Secrets" in China

The Chinese government has employed vaguely defined state secrets laws to detain and imprison dissident journalists and activists.[39] The definition of a "state secret" is both ambiguous and highly elastic. State secrets can include common economic and sociological data, such as the numbers of workers laid off from state enterprises, or statistics regarding prisoners in "reeducation through labour" facilities. "State secrets" can also encompass arbitrary and retroactive classification of nearly anything that portrays the government in a negative light.[40] Evidence in state secrets cases can be treated as classified information, the proceedings are held behind closed doors, and journalists can be detained for extended pretrial periods.[41] A revised draft state secrets law was unveiled in July 2009 by China's National People's Congress, but the new law would do little to clarify the vague and expansive definitions of what may be classified as a "state secret."[42] Instead, the new law focuses on "strengthening rules for protecting secrets and supervising their use within government institutions . . . there is no attempt to narrow the expansive scope of state secrets." The revised law still allows for "classification of information that if leaked would negatively impact one of several vague national interests, such as ethnic unity and social stability . . . [Chinese courts have also endorsed] prosecutions where the accused 'should have known' that an unlabelled document sent abroad would have an impact on state interests."[43]

"State Secrets" in China—Continued

The arbitrary and politicized invocation of "state secrets" was observable in the June 2009 arrests in Gansu Province of antinuclear campaigner Sun Xiaodi and his daughter, who were detained on charges of "divulging state secrets abroad" for publicizing information about radioactive contamination at a uranium mine. Mr. Sun and his daughter were both sentenced to "reeducation through labour" at a prison camp.[44]

The arbitrary and politicized handling of "state secrets" may also affect the business world, as seen in the July 2009 arrests in Shanghai of Stern Hu, a senior representative of the Australian mining company Rio Tinto and a naturalized Australian citizen of Chinese origin, and three local Chinese employees of Rio Tinto. Chinese officials initially stated that the Rio Tinto employees had "stolen state secrets which [have] greatly damaged China's economic security."[45] Chinese press outlets subsequently claimed that Rio Tinto company computers were found to contain information regarding the status of individual steel mills in China, such as production schedules, projected sales and purchases, and raw material stocks.[46] Amid international criticism, the Chinese government backed away from initial indications that the Rio Tinto employees would be charged with espionage and violation of China's vaguely defined "state secrets" law. The Chinese government charged the four on August 11 with commercial bribery and trade secrets infringement.[47] As of the writing of this Report, the case has yet to be adjudicated.

Control of Information Regarding "Sensitive" News Stories in China

Economic Propaganda in China

The Chinese government considers the economy to be an extremely sensitive issue, because the Communist Party bases much of its legitimacy on the ability to maintain robust levels of economic growth. The central government uses official media outlets to propagate narratives of national macrolevel economic success as well as to present stories of common citizens who have benefited greatly from economic reform. Such examples include profiles of workers laid off from state-owned enterprises who subsequently found good paying jobs in other fields of work.[48] State-owned media outlets proactively report and publish in support of government positions and seek to refute any criticism of the government's economic policies.[49] The official media also actively promotes the government's official economic statistics on matters such as unemployment levels, retail sales, and gross domestic product (GDP) growth, even though journalists are restricted from investigating the reliability of such information.[50]

The PRC's economic propaganda messages for foreign audiences emphasize China's attractiveness as a destination for investment and also seek to restrict information about social problems that might raise concerns among foreign investors. (For more on this topic, see chap. 4, sec. 2, of this Report, "China's External Propaganda and Influence Operations.") However, according to testimony provided to the Commission by Victor Shih, professor of political science at Northwestern University, the Chinese government also understands investors' crucial need for accurate international economic and financial news and has relaxed information controls in that realm to a limited degree.[51] Business media in China, such as *Caijing, 21st Century Business Herald,* and *Economic Observer,* now publish financial and economic news from more objective perspectives. [52] In one example cited by Dr. Shih, these media have published articles that expressed major skepticism when the central government claimed that urban wages in China had increased significantly.[53] Additionally, these media sometimes publish the opinions of, and interviews with, foreign economists and government officials, even if their views contradict Chinese official policy. [54] These media generally maintain a stance that is sympathetic to the Chinese government, but the opposing perspective is still reported.[55]

It remains to be seen whether China's bolder print publications will be able to maintain their more independent reporting on economic and political issues. The magazine *Caijing* has been frequently cited by many experts on the Chinese media as one of the publications most willing to tackle sensitive issues such as corruption or to question certain aspects of government policy. However, in October 2009 *Caijing's* general manager Wu Chuanhui, along with 60 to 70 of the magazine's staff, resigned as a result of a struggle over editorial control of the magazine. The magazine's publisher reportedly asked that it "focus more on finance and the economy, and leave politics more on the side."[56]

China's media coverage of the current global financial crisis has primarily been aimed at promoting a narrative of the government's ability to guide the country smoothly through the crisis and to refute arguments that China has a partial role in its origins.[57] Chinese media outlets have been extremely critical of the failings of US and U.K. (United Kingdom) government regulation and overly relaxed monetary policies.[58] Chinese state media have also focused attention on the US government's budget deficit and on refuting claims that China's exchange rate policies may have exacerbated global economic imbalances and might therefore be partially responsible for the global economic recession.[59] (For further discussion of China's role in these matters, see chap.1, sec. 2, of this Report, "China's Role in the Origins of the Global Financial Crisis, and China's Response.").

"Sensitive" Anniversaries in 2009

Anniversaries of protest movements, as well as any events that allow for large public gatherings, have always been viewed with concern by the CCP. In 2009, the Chinese government sought to control media coverage on these "sensitive" dates.[60] While foreign journalists were obstructed in reporting from Tiananmen Square on June 4, many Chinese journalists considered the anniversary of the Tiananmen Square massacre to be an unofficial "vacation" and refrained from reporting anything negative until the anniversary passed, even on stories unrelated to the 1989 crack down.[61] Foreign reporters were barred from Tibet during the weeks surrounding the one-year anniversary of the March 2008 riots in the region.[62] In preparation for the 60th anniversary of the PRC's founding on October 1, the Chinese government prohibited journalists from reporting on military parade rehearsals, conducting interviews, or taking photographs in Tiananmen Square prior to the event.[63]

The July 2009 Riots in Xinjiang, and "Flooding the Zone"

China's media strategy in the aftermath of the July 2009 riots in Xinjiang Province marked a drastic departure from its handling of the March 2008 riots in Tibet.[64] Many Chinese officials now appear to believe that shutting journalists out in a postcrisis situation may make that action a large part of the story in and of itself. Therefore, China has begun to employ new controls over the flow of information.[65] In contrast to its actions after the riots in Tibet, in July 2009 the Chinese government welcomed journalists to Urumqi following the crisis, set up press centers, and inundated journalists with information to "keep journalists busy with good information so that they would not get busy with rumours," according to Stephen Dong Guanpeng, director of the Global Journalism Institute at Tsinghua University and a media advisor to China's State Council.[66] Chinese security forces also protected foreign correspondents in Xinjiang rather than harassing them, as they did just over a year earlier in Tibet.[67] The government organized official tours to propagate the official narrative that the riots were incited by separatist terrorists.[68] According to one witness who testified before the Commission in April, such measures are part of a new effort to "flood the zone" with information sympathetic to the government's point of view.[69]

Obtaining objective information remained difficult for several reasons: First, the majority of the city's residents were afraid to talk to journalists; [70] and second, the Chinese government was quick to shut down the Internet, block Twitter, and cleanse Internet search engines of unofficial accounts of the violence, thereby cutting journalists off from tools that are essential for modern reporting. [71] The official response to the crisis illustrated that the Chinese government is placing a higher priority on conveying its message in a timely manner and demonstrated a strategy of providing foreign journalists with perceived increased access while restricting their ability to take advantage of it.[72]

Public Health Emergency Cover-ups: The San Lu Tainted Milk Scandal

The San Lu tainted milk scandal demonstrates how Chinese government attempts to cover up official corruption or corporate malfeasance can have dangerous consequences and potentially exacerbate public health emergencies. The scandal occurred as a result of two seemingly unrelated government policies in the run-up to the 2008 Beijing Olympic Games: First, the Central Propaganda Department instructed Chinese media to refrain from reporting on "sensitive" issues, specifically including food safety issues; and second, the Chinese government pressured producers of staple food products and other basic commodities to avoid price increases that might threaten "social stability" during such a sensitive time period.[73] In order to maximize profits, some dairy farmers and food distributers began to add melamine, a toxic industrial chemical that produces artificially high protein readings in product testing, to their dairy products in order to conceal the widespread dilution of milk products as a cost-cutting, or profit-increasing, measure.

Melamine contamination in milk products reached harmful, even deadly, levels by the end of 2007. The products of San Lu, one of China's largest dairy companies, were particularly affected, and by December 2007 the company was receiving complaints about its products causing children to become sick. Customers were offered money and boxes of formula to keep quiet.[74] The local government in Shijiazhuang, Hebei Province, where San Lu is headquartered, forbade media discussion of the complaints. The local government also failed to inform provincial or central health authorities and allowed those implicated to continue production of melamine-contaminated products through August 2008.[75] In June 2008, the PRC Ministry of Health was alerted to large numbers of babies suffering from kidney problems after drinking San Lu milk but did nothing.

In August 2008, Fonterra, a New Zealand company that formerly owned 43 percent of San Lu, [76] was notified about the melamine contamination, and a trade recall of San Lu products was conducted privately, with distributors being told to take San Lu products off shelves and replace them with new shipments, with little or no explanation.[77] Children continued to become ill, and when the story finally broke into the public domain in September 2008, propaganda directives were issued instructing media not to criticize the government's role in the handling of the scandal and to follow the Xinhua version of the story. San Lu offered 3 million renminbi (RMB) (approximately $439,000) in "public relations" payments to Chinese Web portals to screen or black out negative information on the company.[78]

As per official Chinese figures, more than 279,000 infants were affected with problems such as kidney stones, and six infants died. However, these figures were likely kept artificially low for political reasons, and many more families came forward saying their children had died from drinking San Lu baby formula.[79] San Lu Chief Executive Officer Tian Wenhua and four directors were arrested and sentenced in a one-day, closed trial for selling "fake or shoddy products." [80] No one else involved with San Lu milk production or the Ministry of Health was held accountable.

Citizen Initiatives for Political Reform: The Case of Charter 08

Charter 08 is a citizens' manifesto that was introduced in China on December 9, 2008, the eve of the 60th anniversary of the United Nations' (UN) introduction of the Universal Declaration of Human Rights. Charter 08, drafted by several dozen Chinese intellectuals and signed by nearly 10,000 supporters throughout the country, called for sweeping political reforms, including "constitutional democracy, human rights, rule of law, and a republican government that observes the tri-partite separation of powers." [81] Inspired by the example of Charter 77, a 1977 manifesto on political reform issued by dissident intellectuals in Czechoslovakia, Charter 08 is a strong public statement seeking an end to one-party rule.[82]

The ruling CCP views calls for democratic reform as a fundamental threat to its ruling position and to the security and cohesion of China itself. The CCP treated Charter 08 as an attempt to diminish its control over both the Chinese government and the People's Liberation Army—and, therefore, a direct challenge to the PRC's authoritarian political system and the CCP's hold on power. The Chinese government's immediate response to the release of Charter 08 was therefore predictable: to identify, interrogate, and detain the charter's 303 original signatories. Chinese officials raided the homes of numerous organizers, confiscating books, computers, bank information, notebooks, and papers. According to Charter 08's organizers, Chinese police met with all of the charter's 303 original signers for "chats" in order to uncover information about the charter's organization and to attempt to dissuade its followers from engaging in similar activities in the future. Liu Xiaobo, one of the more famous signatories of Charter 08, was physically detained by police on December 8, 2008, and held at an undisclosed location until June 23, 2009, when he was charged with "inciting subversion of state power." According to Perry Link, professor of Comparative Literature and Foreign Languages, University of California-Riverside, the detention of Mr. Liu was a clear attempt to intimidate anyone else who has signed, or is considering signing, Charter 08.[83]

Around the world, Charter 08 received significant attention from news agencies, but inside China the topic has been banned from the state-controlled press and purged from the Internet.[84] According to Professor Link, a *Google.cn* search for "Charter 08" yielded several hundred thousand results in early January but came up empty following the purge.[85] There has been virtually no mention of Charter 08 in China's print media. The few publications that could be construed as references to the charter are indirect, do not mention Charter 08 by name, and have not been widely publicized. According to Professor Link, "We know that the media silence is not mere oversight or indifference, because there is powerful evidence that Charter 08 has drawn the attention of China's rulers, who have taken measures to repress it." [86]

According to Professor Link, there are two probable reasons why the Chinese government withheld comment about Charter 08. First, the central government understands that the ideas expressed in the manifesto are attractive to many Chinese citizens and difficult to refute. The Chinese government also understands from past experience that attempts to refute movements in support of human rights and democracy easily can backfire. The second factor inhibiting the Chinese government's ability to refute Charter 08 is Beijing's insistence that it has a meaningful constitution and that it is, in fact, already a "people's democracy." As Professor Link stated, "Even as the Chinese government criticizes [calls for democratic reform], it needs to pretend that it is, in fact, democratic." [87]

Sensitive International Political Events: The June 2009 Iranian Elections

Since the fall of the Soviet Union and continuing through the course of nonviolent "people power" protests that have challenged authoritarian post-Soviet regimes—the "Orange Revolution" in Ukraine, the "Rose Revolution" in Georgia, and the "Tulip Revolution" in Kyrgyzstan—the CCP has maintained a deep sense of anxiety regarding these "color revolutions." [88] Some Chinese bloggers drew comparisons between the demonstrations in Tehran with China's own large-scale protests in 1989.[89] As a result of such factors, the disputed July 2009 elections in Iran and the large-scale protests that followed in their wake attracted considerable attention from Chinese propaganda authorities.

After a week of relatively open reporting on the elections and protests, the Chinese government began to clamp down on media coverage of, and Internet discussion about, Iran.[90] The *Washington Post* reported that tens of thousands of comments about Iran were deleted from Chinese online discussion boards.[91] China's propaganda authorities issued a directive banning news editors and columnists from "criticizing or commenting on the Iranian government's latest measures to control the disorder" and prohibiting any news agency other than Xinhua and *People's Daily* from publishing reports on the elections.[92]

Official media began to publish editorials supporting Iranian President Mahmoud Ahmadinejad's victory and criticizing the reactions of western governments.[93] The editorials claimed that western governments were using social-networking applications, such as Twitter, to interfere in Iran's "internal affairs" and further claimed that news services such as BBC and Voice of America are merely "Western government mouthpieces." [94] Additionally, the Chinese press portrayed Twitter in a negative light, claiming that it was "undemocratic" and used to spread false information.[95]

The Chinese state media also sympathetically echoed statements from the Iranian government and slanted coverage to make assertions that the unrest in Iran was supported by western intelligence agencies intent on covertly subverting the Iranian government. As stated in one paper run by the Central Propaganda Department,

> *[the western forces] arranged for intelligence agents and anti-government organizations to 'cause trouble and disorder'. . . .Those arrested have already admitted that they were trained at camps in Iraq run by the American military, tasked with sowing chaos after the elections in Iran. Meanwhile, in Britain, there are still . . . command centers which control their movements. . . .While these nations have denied 'meddling' in Iran's election, it is a widely known secret that Western intelligence agents have long participated in activities to subvert the Iranian regime. [The West] has used its media and the Internet to foment unrest . . . In recent news reports on the Iranian elections, Voice of America and the British Broadcasting Corporation [took] on the role of mouthpieces for the United States and Britain, and command centers for inciting unrest in Iran with the objective of fostering divisions amongst the Iranian* people.[96] *The reaction of the PRC state media to the Iranian unrest illustrates the Chinese government's perception—and/or desire to perpetuate the perception—that western media outlets are tools of their national governments and are used to spread hostile propaganda against other countries.*

The Internet's Challenges to China's Information Control Regime

The Chinese government insists its Internet filtering efforts are used primarily to limit the spread of phenomena such as pornography and gambling. However, Chinese Internet users can access such information much more easily than politically sensitive content, such as information related to human rights violations or political and religious groups.[97] In practice, the goal of China's Internet censorship is the same as its efforts to control traditional media: to keep the Chinese Communist Party in power. As with the Chinese government's efforts to control traditional news media, the central government seeks to filter content that challenges the CCP's legitimacy or contradicts the party line on sensitive issues.[98] Information technology-enabled protests and reform movements, and the use of the Internet to scrutinize individualpublic officials, have motivated the Chinese government to tighten its control over the Internet.[99] The Chinese government also seeks to embrace the Internet as a tool for disseminating proactive propaganda and "guiding" public opinion.[100]

Internet-enabled Protests and Campaigns

The "viral" nature of the dissemination of information on the Internet has caused major concern among Chinese propaganda officials, who place a particular emphasis on preventing the mass distribution of information that may lead to further collective action such as organized public protests and signature campaigns.[101] In China, the Internet provides a forum for discussion that is freer than traditional media, enabling new forms of protests and campaigns that deeply concern the Chinese government.[102] The reaction to Charter 08 and the "Twitter Revolution" in Iran, as well as the decision to shut down Twitter, Facebook, and other social networking sites following the Xinjiang riots, illustrates the depth of the government's concern over the Internet's potential as a channel for organizing dissent.[103]

Scrutiny of Individual Public Officials on the Internet

The use of the Internet to expose personal information about the private lives of individuals has become a cause for concern among Chinese government officials.[104] Chinese "cyber-vigilantes" use the power of the Internet to harass or embarrass targeted individuals by uncovering and publishing information about their private lives on the Web—a phenomenon known in China as the "human flesh search engine." Chinese netizens have used the "human flesh search engine" to target and humiliate individuals ranging from unfaithful spouses to corrupt public officials.[105] Stephen Dong Guanpeng, who advises the State Council on publicity and crisis communication issues, stated in August 2009 that "the Internet has become a major concern for [local and provincial] officials, who are increasingly being scrutinized by the general public." [106] During the past year, numerous government officials have been fined, fired, or imprisoned as a result of corrupt practices or illegal activities exposed on the Internet. In response to this phenomenon, one local propaganda official told a Chinese journalist "it was so much better when there was no Internet." [107]

Examples of Government Corruption and Malfeasance Exposed on the Internet in China

Date	Location	Description
March 2007	Zhaoqing, Guangdong	Thirteen officials from haoqing used public funds totaling 450,000 renminbi ($65,800) to pay for a "study trip" to the Middle East and Africa. After a 17-minute video of the trip portraying the officials as being on vacation was posted on the Internet, the local deputy Communist Party secretary was sacked.
October 2008	Shenzhen, Guangdong	Lin Jiaxiang, a party secretary of the Shenzhen Maritime Administration, was accused of grabbing an 11-year-

		old girl by the neck and attempting to force her into the men's room of a Shenzhen restaurant after asking her to show him its location.
Dec. 2008	Luoyang, Henan	Dan Shuqin was relieved of his official post after netizens disclosed that villas were being built dangerously close to the Longmen Grottoes, a Buddhist World Heritage site. Nine other supervisory officials involved in the construction were punished for serious breach of duty.
Dec. 2008	Nanjing, Jiangsu	Zhou Jiugeng, a director of the Real Estate Management Bureau of Jiangjing District, lost his job because photos surfaced on the Internet showing him smoking very expensive cigarettes and wearing a $15,000 Swiss watch. Outrage from netizens forced local officials to investigate his misuse of public funds and dismiss him from his position.
March 2009	Maoming, Guangdong	A prison chief and his senior staff were fired for corruption after a former inmate leaked information on the Internet that the chief allowed prisoners to deal drugs, sold the best prison jobs to inmates, and accepted illegal cash payments for reduced sentences.The chief and his deputy made more than 10 million renminbi ($1.46 million) each year from prisoners.
May 2009	Enshi, Hubei	Netizens helped a waitress, Deng Yujiao, avoid punishment after she stabbed a Hubei official to death when he attempted to sexually assault her.

Source: Compiled by Commission staff from multiple sources.

The Internet's Potential as a Propaganda Tool

Although the Chinese government sees many challenges that the Internet poses to its regime of information control, it also views the Internet as an extremely effective tool for propaganda and "thought work." [108] The government has come to realize the Internet's effectiveness as a means for publicizing its version of a story before alternative versions appear elsewhere.[109] Moreover, the largest segment of Internet users consists of young, educated urbanites, the social group considered a priority by China's propaganda authorities. Instead of just attempting to control the content already on the Internet, the Chinese propaganda authorities seek to create content that conveys the Communist Party's message and is attractive to a large audience of Internet users.[110] For example, in July 2000, propaganda authorities supported the development of three computer games in which the sole objective was to attack and ridicule then Taiwanese President Lee Tung-hui.[111]

China's System for Controlling the Internet

The Chinese government allegedly maintains a large workforce of Internet police to monitor Web content. Although there are no publicly available official figures on its size, some estimate that the Chinese government employs upwards of 30,000 cyberpolice.[112] PRC authorities also sponsor large, loosely organized groups of Internet monitors—sometimes called the "Fifty Cent Party" or "commentator teams"—to screen Web sites for objectionable material and to "guide public opinion" by interjecting progovernment political commentary.[113]

The Chinese government's physical system of controlling the Internet through the use of software has sometimes been referred to as the "Golden Shield" or the "Great Firewall" [114] and is one of the most technologically sophisticated in the world. The primary infrastructural limitation on open access to the Internet in China is the arrangement by which the country's Internet connections are controlled by "six to eight state-run operators that maintain advanced international gateways in Beijing, Shanghai, and Guangzhou." [115] Additionally, the Chinese government has begun to exploit the system of "automated packet filtering." [116] Under this system, "packets" of electronic information pass through the Chinese government-controlled international Internet routers, and those containing politically sensitive or controversial keywords are detected. Internet users attempting to access information deemed inappropriate by the Chinese propaganda authorities often are redirected to Web sites deemed "safe" or "politically neutral." [117]

China's Great Firewall is largely successful in restricting the majority of China's Internet users from accessing foreign sources of information deemed undesirable. However, technologically advanced netizens in China are able to bypass the firewall.[118] Additionally, this system is not an absolute means of controlling information and has produced some unintended consequences for the Chinese government and Internet users: In particular, the system of requiring all information to travel through a small number of control points has proven costly for the Chinese government and has drastically reduced Internet connection speeds. This problem was one of the main reasons that prompted the Chinese government to attempt to modify the control system to incorporate client-side filtering software, effectively offloading the burden of sorting through content to individual computers connected to the network.[119]

The Controversy Surrounding "Green Dam Youth Escort"

On May 19, 2009, the Ministry of Industry and Information Technology notified computer manufacturers that it would require the preinstallation of "Green Dam Youth Escort" (hereafter "Green Dam"), a filtering software, on all new personal computers sold in China.[120] Although the software's purported function was to filter "unhealthy and vulgar" material from the Internet, Green Dam's primary purpose appears to be political in nature. Green Dam uses keyword filtering and image processing to block a wide range of Web sites, including pornography, gaming, gay content, religious, and political sites. In practice, content censored by Green

Dam's filter has been unpredictable and seemingly arbitrary, ranging from material related to the 1989 prodemocracy protests in Tiananmen Square to images of Garfield, a popular American cartoon character. [121] The widespread use of this type of software system would allow for a "much more intrusive and comprehensive filtering system than the more centralized [Internet Service Provider]-level filtering schemes." [122]

In addition to its filtering functions, with its automated update feature Green Dam is capable of actively monitoring personal communications and Internet browsing behavior.[123] The software is capable of shutting down applications like Microsoft Word if blacklisted terms are entered.[124] An investigation undertaken by scholars at the University of Michigan found that Green Dam software "contains serious security vulnerabilities due to programming errors" and that "[o]nce Green Dam is installed, any web site the user visits can exploit these problems to take control of the computer." [125]

The introduction of Green Dam was met with swift and diverse criticism from both Chinese netizens and international observers. Chinese citizens complained about the security risks, the potential waste of taxpayers' money, the lack of due diligence, and the violation of China's antimonopoly law.[126] Netizens also posted a number of mocking cartoons depicting a character named "Green Dam Youth Girl."[127] At least one school system in Wuhan, Hubei Province, announced in September 2009 that it was uninstalling Green Dam from its computers due to the programme's blocking of access to software programmes necessary for normal school administrative functions. [128]

Additionally, a coalition of technology and business associations, including the US Chamber of Commerce and the European-American Business Council, presented a letter to Chinese Premier Wen Jiabao requesting that the Green Dam requirement be lifted.[129] US Trade Representative Ron Kirk and Secretary of Commerce Gary Locke wrote a letter to the Chinese government urging Beijing to repeal the installation requirement for Green Dam, hinting that this might warrant a World Trade Organization challenge on the grounds that a portion of the software may have been illegally sourced from a US company called Solid Oak Software.

As a result of this widespread criticism of Green Dam, the Chinese government postponed its requirement to preinstall the software on computers manufactured in China.[130] As of mid-September 2009, Hewlett-Packard and Dell had not shipped the software with their computers sold in China; Sony and Acer initially shipped laptops with Green Dam but have since stopped doing so; and Lenovo, a Chinese computer manufacturer, includes a Green Dam disc with its computers.[131] Although efforts to install Green Dam have been postponed, many analysts believe that the Chinese government's quest to install filtering software on computers in China is "far from over." [132] The Chinese government may make a more subtle attempt to have similar software installed in the future once it has addressed some of Green Dam's technical problems.[133] Nonetheless, the case of Green Dam provides an example of how the Internet provided a forum for the mobilization of successful opposition to government policy. This opposition, combined with a challenge to the state's economic interests, forced a temporary change in government policy.[134] Moreover, it demonstrated that the Chinese government's Internet and media policies are not immune to criticism and that in some limited circumstances propaganda authorities may respond to popular reaction.[135]

Encouraging Self-censorship Online

The Chinese government encourages online self-censorship by restricting anonymity and by placing the primary burden for content censorship on Internet Service Providers, Internet Content Providers, and cybercafe´ owners. These entities are responsible for any patron who violates the government's "stringent but ambiguous" Internet regulations.[136] The Propaganda Department's power to allocate or terminate licenses and lucrative contracts to state and commercial organizations in the media sector provides a strong incentive for service providers to censor content.[137] As a result, Internet Content Providers have begun to regulate and censor chat rooms and bulletin boards to avoid potentially serious financial and legal repercussions.[138]

Additionally, increased momentum over the past years for realname registration systems threatens the ability of netizens to use the Internet anonymously. In March 2005, the Communist Party ordered that all university online bulletin board systems must block off-campus users and require users to register personal identifying information when going online.[139] In January 2009, Beijing Mobile announced that it would require customers to show identification when purchasing prepaid celi phone SIM cards; [140] and in May 2009 the city of Hangzhou attempted to become the first city in China to require real-name registration in order to participate in local chat rooms or online forums, but this plan has since been placed in abeyance.[141] However, according to a government official in Nanjing, the State Council Information Office issued a notice on July 27, 2009, mandating that domestic news Web sites require users to register with their real names and identity numbers prior to publishing any comments online.[142] Furthermore, the central government requires Internet Service Providers to retain users' personal information—such as the user's identity, Web sites visited, length of visit, and the content of electronic communications— and must turn this information over to authorities upon request.[143] These restrictions on Chinese netizens' anonymity will likely result in increased self-censorship, because Internet users will have greater reason to fear punitive action for their online activities.

Examples of Individuals Punished for Activities on the Internet in 2009

Date	Location	Description
February 2009	Beijing	Blogger-lawyer Liu Xiaoyuan was harassed by authorities because he supported a direct election of the Beijing Lawyers Association. The Haidain District Bureau of Justice forced his law firm to shut down for six months and required the firm to turn in all of its lawyers' licences.
April 2009	Ordos, Inner Mongolia	Netizen Wu Baoquan was forced to serve a two-year sentence for defaming the government, because he posted information that peasants were being forced to sell their land to the

		government at extremely low prices. The government then auctioned off the land for a healthy profit. Government officials' cottages were built on the requisitioned land.
July 2009	Beijing	Ilham Tohti, professor at Minzu University and founder of *Uighurbiz.cn* was detained from July 7 until August 23 for posting a statement on his blog that the Shaoguang factory fight preceding the Xinjiang riots should be discussed and that he was ready to go to trial to defend his rights.
July 2009	Fuzhou, Fujian	Twitterer Guo Baofeng and five other netizens were arrested for posting the story of Yan Xioaling, a woman who was allegedly gangraped and killed by Mongolia authorities in Fujian Province.
August 2009	Hangzhou, Zhejiang	Xiong Zhongjun, an influential blogger, was arrested and held for 10 days after questioning the identity of a person who appeared in court as Hu Bin, a member of a wealthy family who was accused of vehicular manslaughter in May 2009.

Source: Compiled by Commission staff from multiple sources.

The Role of US Companies in China's Information Control Efforts

US high-tech companies operating in China are faced with the sometimes difficult decision of either complying with directives from PRC officials or risking the loss of access to the Chinese market. Nart Villeneuve, a fellow with the Citizen Lab at the University of Toronto, described the predicament of US companies as follows:

> *A failure to comply with China's censorship policies can result in the wholesale blocking of a company's entire service or significant levels of interference due to China's filtering system. Companies that have a physical presence in China face the challenge of obtaining proper licensing, and their Chinese employees may face legal threats for the foreign company's failure to comply with China's censorship policies.*[144]

As a result, many US companies have been involved in China's Internet censorship regime. Indeed, most of China's Internet surveillance technology is sourced from western companies, [145] including Cisco's sale of the switches and routers that served as the hardware foundation for the "Golden Shield." [146] US-based Internet Service Providers and Internet Content Providers, such as Yahoo! and Google, have complied with China's demands to filter undesirable material and have also faced pressure to provide the Chinese government with personally identifiable user information on individual Chinese citizens.[147] In particular, Yahoo! came under heavy public criticism after admitting to providing information to the Chinese government that led to the arrest and imprisonment of at least two Chinese online dissidents.[148]

US Policy Options for dealing with Internet Censorship

Developing a response to these challenges has focused on two different policy approaches. The first policy approach is the "Global Network Initiative," a voluntary industry code of ethics and best practices announced in late 2008. The second policy approach under consideration in the United States is the Global Online Freedom Act of 2009 (H.R. 2271), legislation that would regulate the activities of US high-tech companies operating in authoritarian states.[149]

Google, Microsoft, and Yahoo! are members of the Global Network Initiative, as are several human rights organizations and media watchdog organizations. The stated purpose of the Global Network Initiative is "to provide guidance to the [information & communication technology] industry and its stakeholders on how to protect and advance the human rights of freedom of expression and privacy when faced with pressures from governments to take actions that infringe upon these rights."[150] According to Robert Faris, research director at the Berkman Center for Internet and Society, Harvard University, "after three years of collective negotiations, the GNI [Global Network Initiative] is showing promise," but "it's too soon to evaluate the ultimate effectiveness of the organization and the approach."[151]

Other observers of the Global Network Initiative's progress have been more critical of the pace of the organization's development and the prospects for its effectiveness. Robert Guerra, project director for Internet Freedom at Freedom House, has stated that "GNI [Global Network Initiative] has not advanced at an acceptable pace" and, as a result, key players have been left out of, or have chosen not to participate in, the discussions about its development, including many of the major "Web 2.0" companies such as Facebook and Twitter, which are leading players in the rapidly changing field of Internet usage.[152] However, Professor Faris noted that "planning is underway for outreach and public events designed to expand membership of the Initiative to include additional technology companies and human rights groups."[153]

The second policy approach under consideration in the United States is the Global Online Freedom Act of 2009.[154] Among the provisions of the act, it would create an "Office of Global Internet Freedom" within the Department of State and direct the Secretary of State annually to designate Internet-restricting countries; prohibit US businesses that provide or host Internet services from locating any personally identifiable user information in Internet-restricting countries; and require any US businesses that collect or obtain personally identifiable information through the Internet to notify the Office of Global Internet Freedom and the attorney general before responding to a disclosure request from an Internet-restricting country. In addition, the attorney general would have the authority to prohibit a business from complying with the request except for legitimate foreign law enforcement purposes.[155]

Some claim that the Global Online Freedom Act would place US companies at a competitive disadvantage.[156] Professor Faris has stated that the legislation might have the unintended consequence of shutting US companies out of the Chinese market, an outcome that is "unlikely to have a positive impact on the human rights situations there . . . [leaving] consumers with fewer and worse choices and the West with a reduced understanding of government activities and opportunities to engage."[157] Expressing the opposing view, Daniel Calingaert, deputy director of Programmes at Freedom House, has stated that "rather than put US companies at a competitive disadvantage, GOFA [the Global Online Freedom Act] is likely to raise international standards for business to protect and advance Internet freedom, much as the Foreign Corrupt Practices Act led to the OECD [Organization for Economic Co-operation and Development] Convention on Combating Bribery of Foreign Public Officials in International Business Transactions." [158] On May 6, 2009, H.R. 2271 was referred to the House Foreign Affairs Committee and the House Energy and Commerce Committee.[159]

Conclusion

- The January 2007 media reforms instituted in response to international pressure leading up to the Summer Olympics Games in Beijing and extended indefinitely in October 2008 have resulted in modest improvements in the working conditions for foreign journalists in China, but their effect has been limited because of the Chinese government's selective implementation and adoption of new strategies for restricting the flow of information.
- The January 2007 reforms have not improved working conditions for Chinese journalists, who remain subject to intimidation, harassment, violence, and imprisonment, often on vaguely defined "state secrets" charges.
- The Chinese government is employing a diverse array of strategies for silencing or guiding discussion about issues it considers politically sensitive.
- The Internet has emerged as a contested space in China. It provides a venue for discussion that is more open than traditional media but is also subject to the world's most sophisticated Web filtering system. The Chinese government's insecurity about Internet-enabled protests and the increased scrutiny of government officials on the Web has prompted the government to add additional elements to its already advanced Internet control system.
- The case of Green Dam demonstrates that even if the Chinese government had the technological capability to assert complete control over the Internet, it would not necessarily have the political clout to achieve this end. Furthermore, the case of Green Dam demonstrates that the Chinese government is not immune to pressure on information control issues from the international community.

SECTION 2

China's external propaganda and influence operations, and the resulting impacts in the United States

> "The Commission shall investigate and report exclusively on—
>
> "Regional Economic And Security Impacts—The triangular economic and security relationship among the United States, Taipei and the People's Republic of China (including the military modernization and force deployments of the People's Republic of China aimed at Taipei), the national budget of the People's Republic of China, and the fiscal strength of the People's Republic of China in relation to internal instability in the People's Republic of China and the likelihood of the externalization of problems arising from such internal instability.
>
> "Freedom of Expression—The implications of restrictions on speech and access to information in the People's Republic of China for its relations with the United States in the areas of economic and security policy. . . ."

Introduction

The Chinese government makes a considerable effort to shape international perceptions of China through the extensive use of propaganda and the dissemination of selective information. The coordinated messages of the party and the government emphasize China's economic growth and attractiveness as a destination for investment, the government's stated desire for a peaceful international system, and China's "stability" and "harmony" under party leadership. The effort serves two goals: the continued survival and growth in influence of the Communist Party within China and the enhancement of China's reputation and influence abroad.

The Chinese government views foreign propaganda as an essential tool of state power and maintains an extensive bureaucracy dedicated to this purpose. It also seeks to deploy its state-controlled media in the service of China's foreign policy goals. Motivated by a pervasive belief that western governments manipulate the press to unfairly portray China in a negative light, the Chinese government is increasing resources devoted to China's state-sponsored foreign language media outlets. In addition to the expansion of media directly controlled by the government, China is expanding the creation of facade "independent" news outlets in which the Chinese government or Chinese state-owned firms exercise influence behind the scenes.

In recent years, Beijing has also increasingly sought out the assistance of western public relations and lobbying firms to help improve its international image as well as to advocate for its preferred policies. The advice of these firms has helped to shape the messages that the Chinese government presents to international audiences.

Additionally, the Chinese government seeks to shape opinion in elite policy-making circles by influencing the commentary about China and US-China relations that emerges from US academics and think tanks. This effort includes giving rewards to "friendly" scholars, such as preferred access to career-enhancing interviews and documents, as well as taking punitive actions, such as visa denials, for academics who anger the authorities. These rewards and punishments offer the Chinese government leverage over the careers of foreign scholars and thereby encourage a culture of academic self-censorship. By influencing scholars, these actions also shape analysis and public understanding of China.

Foreign Propaganda of the People's Republic of China in the wake of the Tiananmen Square Massacre

The events of 1989 proved to be a watershed in the relations between China's Communist government and the rest of the world. The Tiananmen Square massacre was followed by a lurch back to an authoritarian hardline and a period of diplomatic isolation from much of the rest of the world. While much of this temporary isolation was imposed by foreign governments and foreign public opinion, it was also engendered from within by declarations from senior leaders that blamed the 1989 protests on the instigation of western governments.[160] Chinese propaganda campaigns declared China to be under siege from foreign "hostile forces" intent on overthrowing the government and making China into a weak, vassal state.[161] This official post-Tiananmen narrative has shaped the Chinese Communist Party's (CCP) outlook on the western world in general and the United States in particular.

Post-June 1989, the CCP leadership also recognized the need to revive China's image in the rest of the world. A primary focus was placed on emphasizing three broad themes: first, maintaining China's social and economic stability, under the leadership of the CCP; second, continuing the policies of "reform and opening up;" and, third, promoting foreign trade and investment. Chinese leaders also placed a renewed emphasis on attracting the support of influential foreigners "friendly to China," with a particular stress on cultivating business leaders and political figures.[162]

China's Institutions for conducting Foreign Propaganda

Prior to the June 1989 Tiananmen Square Massacre, the bodies responsible for the CCP's internal and external propaganda were concentrated in the Central Propaganda Department. Internal and external propaganda contained many of the same messages, and the information relayed to outsiders was not especially refined, frequently taking the form of rhetoric directly translated from domestic Chinese propaganda.

In the wake of Tiananmen and its impact on the People's Republic of China's (PRC) reputation, the government's external propaganda efforts became more controlled, and the CCP tightened media and message management in an effort to better shape China's outwardly projected image. In 1990, the CCP revived the Central Committee Foreign Propaganda Group to function as the most senior bureaucratic entity overseeing the field of foreign propaganda. [163] The group plays the leading role in guiding the messages that are promoted by subordinate and provincial propaganda organs. These themes touch upon foreign trade; tourism; overseas Chinese affairs; radio and television; print media; and cultural, educational, and sporting institutions.[164]

In 1991, primary responsibility for external propaganda work was taken out of the Central Propaganda Department and moved to its own department under the names of both the Office of Foreign Propaganda and the State Council Information Office. Its role is to develop China's foreign publicity activities and to monitor and censor all activities that the CCP sees as belonging to the foreign propaganda domain, including policing the activities of foreign journalists, monitoring foreign social science research on China, and controlling the Internet.[165] The Central Propaganda Department and the dual bureaucracy of the Office of Foreign Propaganda/State Council Information Office remain closely coordinated.[166] Provinces and localities in China also have their own foreign propaganda units that mirror those higher in the state/party apparatus, focusing on more localized issues.

The CCP's Motivations and Ideology in conducting Foreign Propaganda

The Need for a positive International Image to build the Economy

The CCP believes that projecting a positive international image for China is necessary to attract foreign investment and to boost China's economic and technological development. Much of the discourse within CCP circles on foreign-directed propaganda stresses economic goals. The party guidance on these matters emphasizes the need to accentuate positive messages—such as the value of China as a destination for investment—while restricting information that might raise doubts among foreign investors.[167]

One example is seen in the excerpts below, taken from an address delivered at a 2007 conference on foreign propaganda held in Suixi County, Anhui Province. In the speech, a local CCP official lectures on the trends to follow in communicating with a foreign audience:

> *At present our country is in the grand development and opening up period . . . development tasks require us to work hard to eliminate noise and interference to ensure the big picture of development without any negative impact . . . The current mission of external propaganda is to effectively promote each region, each sector to the outside world, in order to attract outside investors' attention and build up outside investors' confidence. We can safely say that the purpose of doing external propaganda work is to attract outside investment and undertake commercial projects.*
>
> *The Information Center of the county government must strengthen the Internet news management, and do a good job in selecting, filtering and transmitting information from different work units. It must quickly block, divert and respond to bad public opinion and information online . . . In the meantime, it must strengthen positive online propaganda, using mainstream, positive opinion to influence and* guide netizens. [168]

As revealed in such messages, CCP internal discussions on information control approach it from a strict view of its utilitarian value to the authorities. In this case, whatever message is of value for attracting foreign investment to Suixi County must be promoted; whatever is contrary to this political and economic goal must be suppressed.

The Need for a Great Power to have Great Propaganda

Nicholas Cull, a professor of communications at the University of Southern California, testified to the Commission that PRC officials emphasize effective "public diplomacy"—which he defined as "the process by which an international actor conducts foreign policy by engaging a foreign public"—as a primary component of national power.[169] Li Changchun—a member of the Standing Committee of the Politburo, the most senior policy-making body in the Chinese government—is the official in overall charge of the government's ideology and propaganda system.[170] During a November 2008 visit to the state television channel China Central Television, Mr. Li extolled the role of the television channel in "guiding public opinion" and "actively publicizing the ideology, line, principles and policy of the Party." Mr. Li also addressed the proper role of the media in the "going out' of Chinese culture" as follows:

> *Communication capacity determines influence. In the modern age, whichever nation's communication methods are most advanced, whichever nation's communication capacity is strongest, it is that nation whose culture and core values are able to spread far and wide, and that nation that has the most power to influence the world . . . Enhancing our communication capacity domestically and internationally is of direct consequence to our nation's international influence and international position, of direct consequence to the raising of our nation's cultural soft power, and of direct consequence to the function and role of our nation's media within the international public opinion structure.* [171]

These and other comments indicate that the CCP views "communication capacity" as both a critical element of national power and a competition in which China has fallen behind. China intends to catch up by sponsoring media that promote Beijing's points of view.

The Need for Propaganda to "Break the Siege"

Another striking aspect of the CCP's discourse on internationally directed propaganda is the frequent use of militaristic language to describe public relations efforts, with language evoking struggle and warfare used to describe the party's need to promote its messages to the world. CCP leaders have come to see themselves as more and more engaged in a "global war for public opinion." [172]

One February 2009 article, which appeared in a media outlet managed by a special branch of Xinhua that prepares information and analysis for CCP cadres,[173] is titled "A Careful Analysis of China's Public Relations Map." The article stated that "[i]t is obvious that the West still has the upper hand while the East remains weak. . . . Whenever there is an agenda dispute, international public opinion will form a force that involves the West's besieging the East." In response, the article called for "national public relations weapons," defined as "dialogues between nations or between a country and relevant stakeholders against the backdrop of competition over power and interest." [174]

Language from the article compared international public relations with combat in even starker terms and advocated more active foreign propaganda work:

> *China's public relations drive is . . . a long-running battle [that] involve[s] three stages: defence, confrontation, and counterattack. From the strategic level of national public relations, the defence stage comprises passive defence and active defence. We divide the confrontation period into two parts: confrontation resulting from both sides being well matched in strength, and [then] dialogue brought about by a balance of power. The counterattack stage involves attacking and conquering. . . . While we should not demonstrate toughness characteristic of the confrontation stage and the counterattack stage, we cannot continue making the kind of unprincipled compromises or maintaining the unrestrained modesty that marks the passive defence* stage.[175]

Using Foreign Propaganda to conduct Domestic Propaganda

Perhaps the most important motivation for the Chinese government's efforts at foreign propaganda actually relates back to China's own domestic politics. As the CCP worked to rebuild its tattered legitimacy in the wake of June 1989, a cornerstone of its efforts was the construction of a nationalist narrative of restored Chinese historical greatness. One component of this effort is presenting to China's own citizens a message that foreigners now greatly admire China due to its recent achievements under CCP leadership. Dr. Cull testified that this is a matter of "conducting domestic propaganda by conducting foreign propaganda." [176]

This process includes emphasizing to a domestic audience the expanding number of foreigners studying the Chinese language and the similarly expanded level of Chinese-language news media now available within US cities. It also includes spectacles such as the lavish opening ceremonies surrounding the August 2008 Beijing Olympics. As Dr. Cull stated, this is about "display[ing] the kudos that come to the Communist Party by saying, 'Look, behold, we give you the gift of the admiration of the world.' " [177]

China's International Media Outlets

In January 2009, media reports indicated that the Chinese government plans to expand its current external propaganda efforts by investing 45 billion renminbi (RMB) (approximately $6.6 billion) to expand its foreign language news coverage. Included in these plans are a 24-hour English-language, news-based television network intended to be modeled after CNN or Al Jazeera.[178] When the plan was announced, Li Changchun, China's top propaganda official, stated that China needed to take its "key central media and make them into first-rate international media with a global influence." [179]

Witnesses before the Commission this year indicated that these plans for media expansion are motivated by a genuine sense of frustration that news about China is distorted by foreign media outlets. As described by Anne-Marie Brady, professor of political science at the University of Canterbury, Christchurch, New Zealand,

> *Those in propaganda work feel, and the population [as well] are in great sympathy with this idea that the West is continually distorting news about China . . . [China] feels very hard done by the western media and western media companies. So they think it's worth putting a lot of money in on all sorts of levels so that people will hear what they have to say and their perspective on world events.*[180]

Judy Polumbaum, a professor of communications at the University of Iowa, testified that other issues could also be in play in China's plans for expanded support of its foreign language media. Many propaganda officials may hold a genuine but mistaken belief that the market in the United States for Chinese media is greater than it actually is. Dr. Polumbaum also stated that these expansions of media organizations could represent a certain amount of bureaucratic "empire building" by actors within the state media system.[181]

This intent to increase the reach of the Chinese foreign language media has been clearly displayed in the expanded scope of China Central Television, the official television news network of the PRC. In 2002, China Central Television started a 24-hour English language service called CCTV–9. The channel is available on a number of cable and satellite providers in the United States, in the United Kingdom, and throughout Asia. Since 2004, China Central Television has also broadcast in Spanish and French,[182] and an Arabic language China Central Television channel went on the air in July 2009.[183] There are also reported plans to start a Russian language channel by December 2009.[184]

The example of CCTV–9 provides an insight into some of the problems inherent in China's efforts to compete in the realm of international media. An inherent tension exists between the need to make stories compelling and convincing to a foreign audience and the restrictions imposed by Chinese government censors. CCTV–9 is widely viewed as a mouthpiece for the Chinese government's perspective on international affairs,[185] and its reporters may be sanctioned for deviating too far from the preferred script. In one illustrative example presented to the Commission this year, in 2005 CCTV–9 journalists reported factually on a series of coalmining disasters in China. This was followed by a complaint from the Ministry of Foreign Affairs that such reporting hurt China's image, resulting in disciplinary actions against the editorial staff and reporters.[186]

China Daily, the country's most widely published English language newspaper, serves a function similar to that of CCTV–9 as an official mouthpiece of the Chinese government. The Office of Foreign Propaganda/Information Office of the State Council conducts regular meetings with editors and journalists at the newspaper in order to provide "guidance" and updates on what they should and should not print. According to figures from its own Web site, *China Daily* has an average daily circulation of 300,000 in about 150 and regions. The newspaper's Web site claims that it receives more than 12 million daily hits, two-thirds of which are from overseas.[187] The Chinese government sponsors the publication of *China Daily* within the United States and has paid an approximate average of $726,000 per year between 2003 and 2008 for printing and distribution services.[188]

The Chinese government also operates a radio news service called China Radio International, which is self-identified as one of "three central media organizations in China," alongside China National Radio and China Central Television.[189] According to information from China Radio International itself, the radio network has emerged as "one of the major broadcasting networks in the world," broadcasting in 53 languages to listeners in 161 different "countries and regions" throughout the world.[190]

Dr. Brady testified that another significant model could be emerging for the future operations of Chinese state-affiliated media outlets. Phoenix Television, based in Hong Kong, is nominally independent; however, its founder has close ties to the Chinese state propaganda system, and its largest shareholder (with approximately 20 percent of stock) is the state-owned enterprise, China Mobile. She further argued that its outward image as an independent entity lends Phoenix's news coverage an air of greater objectivity relative to directly state-controlled outlets such as CCTV–9; however, Phoenix Television takes a strongly pro-Chinese government stance in its news coverage and is viewed by CCP propaganda officials as "more loyal than CCTV." The Chinese government reportedly has plans to support the establishment of another television station, possibly operating out of Singapore or Thailand, which would similarly cover world news from a point of view friendly to Beijing.[191]

Most witnesses who testified before the Commission this year heard a view that the expansion of the English language coverage by the Chinese state media is not a cause for alarm. The real issue to be addressed, in Dr. Cull's view, is not that China's efforts in this realm are so active but rather that parallel US efforts in recent years have been comparatively anemic and ineffective. He warned that the United States risks losing influence in the international realm if it does not increase its own efforts in public diplomacy. [192]

Media Directed Toward Overseas Chinese

Witness testimony and research also indicated to the Commission that the Chinese government has invested considerable attention to shaping the messages received by ethnic Chinese outside of China. In the aftermath of Tiananmen, the CCP found itself concerned about the extent of support for the prodemocracy movement among ethnic Chinese communities abroad. The Chinese government therefore became directly engaged in an effort to perform public relations, lobbying, and mobilization work among overseas Chinese communities in order to "turn them into propaganda bases for China," in the words of Dr. Brady.[193]

The Chinese government operates multiple media outlets aimed primarily at ethnic Chinese outside the borders of the PRC. The PRC's China News Service is a state-run international news service aimed at Hong Kong, Macao, Taiwan, and ethnic Chinese living in other countries. While its central office is located in Beijing, the network has offices in nine different countries, including four branches located in the United States: New York, Washington, Los Angeles, and San Francisco.[194] China News Service feeds many of its stories to CCTV–4, China Central Television's international television broadcast in Mandarin Chinese that is directed at Chinese living outside the country. CCTV–4 tends to take a more political line than CCTV–9 and is meant to compete with Taiwan television stations broadcasting abroad. On the east and west coasts of the United States, the channel is broadcast for free on the Fox and Time Warner networks.[195]

There are also a number of Chinese language newspapers that are printed and distributed in the United States.[196] In the past, Chinese language newspapers and other media outlets in the United States relied heavily on news services in Hong Kong and Taiwan. However, in more recent years, the PRC has worked actively to supplant these outlets by providing overseas Chinese media with free material derived from mainland sources. From 2003 to 2008, the Chinese government paid an average of more than $2 million per year for the printing and distribution of Chinese language newspapers within the United States, although the actual figure is likely higher.[197] PRC embassy and consular officials are also directly engaged in the Chinese language broadcast media, seeking to ensure that pro-Chinese government views are the predominant message received by ethnic Chinese citizens of other countries.[198]

The most important form of media for the Chinese government in its recent efforts to influence overseas Chinese perceptions has been the Internet. Web sites based in mainland China have emerged as the leading source of Chinese language news for ethnic Chinese audiences overseas, providing the Chinese government with a highly effective means of "guiding" opinion within this target audience and a means of organizing and mobilizing these communities to act on its behalf.[199] (For examples of the Chinese government's effort to mobilize some Chinese-American civic groups to act on its behalf, see chap. 2, sec. 3, of this report, "China's Human Espionage Activities that Target the United States, and the Resulting Impacts on US National Security.")

Is the PRC Deceptive in its Foreign Propaganda?

While all governments seek to present their policies in the best possible light, the Chinese government frequently conceals negative information about itself or Chinese society and sometimes actively propagates false information. This is practiced when the CCP is in a reactive mode responding to an unexpected crisis or criticism; during "sensitive" periods such as the anniversaries of major political events; or when the CCP is otherwise seeking to suppress, in the name of "social stability," information deemed damaging to the party's image and authority.

An example of deceptive messages during a "sensitive" time period occurred in the lead-up to the August 2008 Olympics, when the Chinese government announced to both the domestic and foreign press that three parks would be designated as legal "protest zones" for citizens to air their grievances. However, those actually seeking to demonstrate were either warned away by police or arrested, leading to suspicions that the "protest parks" were either an empty public relations gesture or a ruse designed to draw out potential troublemakers.[200]

A recent example of suppressing information deemed harmful to "social stability" was seen in the San Lu tainted milk scandal of 2008, in which a variety of dairy products produced by the San Lu company were revealed to be contaminated with the toxic industrial chemical melamine. PRC government officials were aware of the contamination problem for months before the story became public but suppressed information about the affair in part to comply with central government directives to suppress bad news stories and maintain "social stability" in the lead-up to the Beijing Olympics. (For a fuller account of the San Lu scandal, see chap. 4, sec. 1, of this Report, "Freedom of Expression in China.")

Explanations for such behavior may be found within the institutional culture and accustomed practices of the Chinese Communist Party. The CCP has a deeply ingrained tendency toward secretiveness and a long history of proactively using information to promote the party's objectives while suppressing information deemed harmful to its interests.[201] Concentric circles of truth and partial truth surround the leadership of the CCP: While information in the public domain remains subject to control, party leaders receive classified reporting on both domestic and international news prepared by the security services and the Xinhua state news agency.[202] These restricted reports are made available in multiple versions to CCP officials, with classification levels and distribution both growing more restricted at higher levels of authority. These documents include information on events such as outbreaks of social unrest that party leaders may wish to know about but do not want discussed in public.[203]

The dual practices of secrecy and the manipulation of information are so ingrained in CCP institutional culture and discourse that the propaganda system will promote whatever message is deemed to be most advantageous to the authorities, without regard to whether or not it is objectively "true." The leadership of the CCP is unlikely to regard such actions as being in any way unusual, as it assumes that governments in other countries naturally control information in the same way.[204]

China's Efforts to Influence US Institutions and Public Opinion

This year, the Commission also examined alleged efforts by the Chinese government to influence both public and elite opinion as it relates to China policy. The CCP employs a range of both carrots and sticks to ensure that those able to shape US public opinion and government policies advance positions that are in alignment with Beijing's interests. This has included efforts to influence commentary emerging from the US academic and think tank community, encouraging US-based corporations to advocate policies that are in Beijing's interests, and sponsoring lobbying and public relations activities by US firms.

Efforts to Influence US Academics and Think Tanks

Testimony received and interviews conducted by the Commission this year demonstrated that the Chinese government employs both positive inducements and coercive pressure to draw favourable commentary from scholars in US universities and think tanks. This influence can take the form of giving career rewards for favoured authors, such as providing greater access to officials and documents for research, as well as the harsher hand of meeting out penalties for scholars who publish materials critical of the Chinese government. As stated by one academic economist, "Academics who study China . . . habitually please the Chinese Communist Party, sometimes consciously, and often unconsciously . . . the incentives for academics all go one way: one does not upset the Party." [205]

One of the punitive tools that the Chinese government may employ to intimidate foreign academics is the denial of visas to enter China to conduct research. Although the PRC will not officially acknowledge doing so, elements within the Chinese government have clearly placed a number of foreign academics on a visa denial "blacklist" due to their publishing on topics that hit a nerve with Beijing. One example may be seen in the case of several authors who contributed to a 2004 collection of articles about Xinjiang and subsequently found themselves denied visas to enter China. As described by one of the affected authors, no official explanation was given, other than, "You are not welcome in China. You should know why." [206]

To be denied access to China for research purposes can seriously damage scholarly careers, particularly for younger academics still seeking tenure or hoping to become established in their fields.[207] The resulting fear of visa denial throws a shadow of self-censorship over sociological and political science research on China, but this phenomenon has not been widely discussed in public—most likely because those not blacklisted fear bringing attention to the issue, and many of those who have been blacklisted may hope to be "forgiven" if they keep silent. Out of six allegedly blacklisted academics contacted by Commission staff this year, only two were willing and available to speak publicly on the record about the issue.[208]

Such control over access—along with the positive rewards granted to academics deemed "friendly" [209]—can give the Chinese government real influence over the ways in which academic opinion makers address issues related to China. Perry Link, professor of comparative literature at the University of California–Riverside—and himself denied visas to enter China since 1996 [210]— has described this phenomenon as an "anaconda in the chandelier" that hangs silently over scholars who deal with China. He has stated that "[t]he problem is most salient . . . for political scientists who study the Chinese government and need to nurture their contacts among Chinese officials. The effects are hard to measure, because people are reluctant to speak about them [and] no scholar likes to acknowledge self-censorship." [211]

Another prominent Sinologist, Orville Schell, has described the process of self-censorship as follows:

> *I try to say, 'Okay, here is what I think, what I understand, what I think I see, have learned and read.' Then, I try and think through what the Chinese government's reaction will be. . . . And then I try to be as truthful as I can in a way that is respectful and unprovocative but that is not pandering. China has a tremendously highly evolved capacity to create panderers both among its own people and foreigners who become involved with them.*[212]

One academic who was willing to speak in public about this issue was Ross Terrill, a professor of modern Chinese history and currently a fellow in research at Harvard University's John K. Fairbank Center for Chinese Studies. Dr. Terrill put the matter this way:

> *Self-censorship, which is a daily necessity for journalists in China, also occurs in diluted form among American editors, academics, and others dealing with China. Folk worry about their next visa, their access to a sensitive area like Xinjiang for research, or take a Beijing point of view because of the largesse available for their projects from the Chinese side.*[213]

Dr. Link, who testified before the Commission this year, stated that both academics and government officials are also encouraged to self-censor by the opportunities available for profitable consulting work outside of the channels of academia and government. He expressed concern that the US government might not always receive the best or most objective advice on US-China policy as a result of the "subterranean economic interests that are at play." [214] Dr. Victor Shih, professor of political science at Northwestern University, echoed some of these concerns. He testified to the Commission that

> *[a] problem is [that] Western academics and government officials. . . are self-censoring themselves . . . For example . . . People who do research in Xinjiang in a very serious way are barred from going to China. So many of us avoid that topic . . . and then there [are] the economic interests*

which face both academics and government officials. They don't want to offend the Chinese government and . . . close the doors to future opportunities to make money.[215]

Others among the handful of academics willing to discuss this issue in public have further described a "radiation effect," in which the negative example of those penalized by the Chinese government deters other scholars from researching or writing on "sensitive" issues that might offend the CCP.[216] As summed up by another academic sinologist, "There is a tendency not to do anything that will threaten your ability to get access." [217]

The resulting power either to foster or to hobble academic careers has given the Chinese government significant authority to shape the formation of public knowledge and opinion regarding China. In response, Dr. Terrill recommended to the Commission that the government of the United States should "resist China's picking of winners and losers among Americans dealing with cultural and intellectual exchanges with the PRC." [218]

Exchanges between US and Chinese Think Tanks and Academic Institutions

In recent years, exchanges have continued to expand between academic and think tank institutions in the United States and their counterparts in China. However, despite many potential benefits of academic dialogue, these are not exchanges between groups of objective scholars: Chinese academics working in the social sciences at prominent institutions are selected in part based on their loyalty to the CCP.[219] Chinese think tanks do have limited leeway to engage in debates on public policy; however, they operate as adjunct institutions of the party-state, with no independent status.[220] Chinese think tanks are also actively engaged in the process of formulating government policy, a role that has been increasing in importance in recent years.[221] Notwithstanding a tendency by many foreign academics to treat Chinese institutions as if they operate in a parallel fashion to their western counterparts,[222] the status of Chinese think tanks as government institutions inherently means that they serve as a channel for propagating the preferred messages of the Chinese Communist Party.

One of China's most prominent think tanks is the China Institutes for Contemporary International Relations (CICIR) in Beijing, which also functions as a bureau of one of China's leading foreign intelligence agencies, the Ministry of State Security. (For further information on the ministry and other Chinese intelligence services, see chap. 2, sec. 3, of this Report, "China's Human Espionage Activities that Target the United States, and the Resulting Impacts on US National Security.") CICIR is one of the largest foreign policy think tanks in China, employing approximately 150 research analysts and 220 support staff. [223] According to information from the institute's Web site, CICIR participated in 119 different visits or exchanges with scholars from US think tanks and universities from January 2007 through June 2009.[224] Members of this Commission have also held discussions with representatives of CICIR in the course of fact-finding trips to China, including meetings in March 2008 and May 2009.[225] While such visits offer a genuine opportunity for exchanges of scholarly views—as well as a potentially productive pathway for "Track Two" dialogue—they also offer the PRC a channel for controlled and coordinated efforts at perception management. CICIR's expanding international contacts allow it greater opportunities to shape international perceptions of China: As one such example, a workshop held at CICIR contributed to the deliberations of the US National Intelligence Council in producing its 2008 report, *Global Trends 2025: A Transformed World.*[226]

The Employment of Public Relations and Lobbying Firms

Public Relations Firms

In addition to revamping its foreign propaganda messages, in recent years the Chinese government also has sought out the assistance of western public relations firms in an effort to improve its image abroad. Hill & Knowlton is one of the largest international firms in the field of "communications consultancy," with 80 offices in 43 different countries.[227] The New York-based firm has operated in China since 1984 [228] and became one of the first companies involved in public relations work on behalf of the Chinese government in the aftermath of the Tiananmen Square massacre.[229] Such support dates to June 1991, when Hill & Knowlton signed a contract with the PRC embassy in Washington, DC, to offer services including

> *[a]dvis[ing the] Client on public relations/public affairs aspects of China's policies and problems . . . Build[ing] public relations support to avoid negative effects on China-US relations by all means permitted by laws of the United States . . . Respond[ing] to urgent criticism about [the] situation in China . . . [and] Identify[ing], recruit[ing] and organiz[ing] third party allies on bilateral issues between China and the United States.*[230]

Among the more recent public relations support provided by Hill & Knowlton was sponsorship of a 2007 study titled *Brand China,* which laid out recommendations as to how the Chinese government might seek to improve its image in western countries.[231] The author of the study, Joshua Cooper Ramo, a partner and managing director with the consulting firm Kissinger & Associates, [232] was the same person appointed to act as the English-language commentator for the National Broadcasting Corporation's coverage of the 2008 Olympics opening ceremonies.[233] Hill & Knowlton was also under contract with the Beijing Olympic Organizing Committee throughout 2007 and 2008 to provide public relations support for the 2008 Beijing Summer Olympic Games.[234]

Other firms also have been involved in providing public relations advice to the Chinese government. After the 1993 failure of China's bid for the 2000 Olympics—led by Chen Xitong, the hard-line mayor of Beijing in 1989 and a leading figure in the Tiananmen massacre—the much smoother bid for the 2008 Olympics was advised by the US firm Weber Shandwick Worldwide and the United Kingdom (UK) firm Bell Pottinger. The firms both provided public relations advice and lobbied the International Olympic Committee on China's behalf. A central message promoted in the course of the bid was that hosting the Olympics would improve human rights conditions in China—a theme promoted to foreign audiences but not widely disseminated within China itself. [235] The firm Saatchi & Saatchi also provided recommendations to the Chinese government in the late 1990s that it should promote "brand values" emphasizing China's ancient cultural achievements, its "mystery" and "harmony," and its social and economic dynamism. Many of these ideas emerged as central themes symbolically displayed in the ceremonies of the 2008 Olympics.[236]

Lobbying by US Corporate Interests

In past years, the Chinese government had only limited involvement with directly hiring lobbying firms in Washington, DC, to advocate for their preferred policies. Chinese officials preferred instead to cultivate close personal relationships with influential US political figures.[237] Where lobbying was involved, the Chinese government preferred to encourage US corporations and US business associations with a common interest in trade issues to act on its behalf. As one US business executive said, "We used to get calls from the [Chinese] embassy almost every time there was some kind of anti-China measure on Capitol Hill. . . . It was like we had to put out fires for them." [238] However, whatever China's preferred policies may be, it is worth noting that US corporations and trade associations engaged in such lobbying activity are acting in the pursuit of their own interests, which on many trade issues run parallel to the interests of China.

Pressure on US Businessmen and China's Bid for the Olympics

One of the clearest public examples of lobbying activity on behalf of the PRC by US businessmen was revealed in the course of court proceedings in 2008, in which billionaire Las Vegas gaming executive Sheldon Adelson described meetings in Beijing in early July 2001 with Qian Qichen, the PRC vice premier, and Liu Qi, the mayor of Beijing. These meetings took place in the context of Mr. Adelson's "not leaving any friendship stone unturned" in hopes of ultimately obtaining licenses from the Chinese government to open casinos in Macao, [239] and also took place immediately prior to the International Olympics Committee's selection of the host city for the 2008 Olympics Games. According to the account provided by Mr. Adelson, these PRC officials asked him to exercise his influence with Members of Congress to help defeat a draft House resolution sponsored by the late Representative Tom Lantos (D–CA). This draft resolution, H.Con.Res.73, would have "[e]xpress[ed] the sense of Congress that the 2008 Olympic Games should not be held in Beijing unless the Government of the People's Republic of China releases all political prisoners, ratifies the International Covenant on Civil and Political Rights, and observes internationally recognized human rights." [240] Mr. Adelson stated that in response to these requests from PRC officials, he called "four or five"

Members of Congress and requested information from them regarding the status of the resolution.[241] The draft resolution had been reported (amended) by the House Committee on International Relations and placed on the House calendar in April 2001 but was never brought to the floor for a vote.[242]

Washington-based business associations, such as the Business Roundtable and the US-China Business Council, have in the past generally taken the lead in opposing legislation before Congress intended to force the Chinese government to change its policies on trade and currency valuations.[243] Other US trade associations, such as the National Association of Manufacturers, have found themselves divided: Smaller member firms of the association have advocated tougher trade stances vis-a'-vis China, while larger member firms with interests in China have tended to support more conciliatory positions.[244]

However, some US corporate leaders and trade associations have recently displayed a greater willingness to voice measured complaints about the trade policies of the Chinese government. For example, in testimony presented in early October 2009 to the US government's interagency Trade Policy Staff Committee, the president of the US-China Business Council presented a generally upbeat picture of US-China trade ties but did express concerns regarding the state of China's compliance with trade commitments in areas such as intellectual property rights pertaining to pharmaceuticals; restrictions on market access for many US goods, such as agricultural products; and barriers to foreign providers of services such as insurance, transportation, and financial services.[245] (For a fuller discussion of the status of the US-China trade relationship, see chap. 1, sec. 1, of this Report, "The US-China Trade and Economic Relationship's Current Status and Significant Changes During 2009.")

Direct Lobbying on Behalf of the Chinese Government and Chinese State-owned Firms

In recent years, the Chinese central government—as well as provincial governments and large Chinese corporations and stateowned enterprises—have become more directly involved in retaining US lobbying firms to act on their behalf. Part of this change may be due to a relative weakening in the determination of some US corporations and trade groups to press issues on behalf of China—spurred in part by splits between larger and smaller firms regarding the outsourcing of production to China and by a continuing lack of adequate intellectual property protection.[246] However, some Chinese actors and investors also may feel an increasing need for lobbying and public relations assistance to overcome US concerns regarding the security implications of certain Chinese state-backed investments.

A watershed event appears to have been the controversy surrounding the abortive 2005 attempt by the state-owned China National Off-Shore Oil Corporation (CNOOC) to purchase the California- based energy conglomerate Unocal. Officials of CNOOC and the Chinese government were surprised by the negative reaction to the deal within the United States, and CNOOC hired several lobbying and public relations firms—Akin Gump Strauss Hauer & Feld, BKSH & Associates, the Brunswick Group, and Public Strategies— in pursuit of the deal.247 As part of a full-court press on the deal, employees of Akin Gump Strauss Hauer & Feld made contacts with federal and state officials 250 times in a single one month period as the sale was under consideration.[248] Chevron Corporation, CNOOC's rival bidder in the purchase of Unocal, hired its own lobbyists and public relations companies to oppose the CNOOC purchase before Congress. Citing political pressures, CNOOC eventually dropped out of the bidding, and Chevron purchased Unocal for about $18 billion.[249]

In terms of US lobbying activity directly funded by the Chinese central government—to exclude lobbying activities performed by Chinese state-owned firms—there has been a significant increase in such activity from 2006 to 2008. (Full data for 2009 were not yet available as of the writing of this Report.) According to data from the US Department of Justice's database for disclosure filings under the Foreign Agents Registration Act, US-based lobbying and public relations firms performing work on contracts directly for the government of the PRC earned at least $432,000 in 2006; $587,920 in 2007; and $1,230,932 in 2008.[250] The full, actual figures will be higher, as not all payments to these firms are required to be reported. These activities included media and public relations work to improve China's image in the United States, lobbying with Members of Congress and staff regarding trade issues of interest to the PRC, and providing counsel to the Chinese government regarding the US government's policy-making process (see box below).

Selected Examples of Lobbying Activity Performed on behalf of the Chinese government, 2005–2008

2005

The PRC Ministry of Commerce hires McDermott Will & Emery for legal services and to lobby against proposed restrictions on the imports of textile products from China. The firm is paid $514,940 for the six-month period ending November 30, 2005.[251]

The Chinese government hires the firm Patton Boggs to perform undisclosed lobbying services, primarily directed at Members of the Senate Foreign Relations and the Senate Armed Services committees. The firm has 116 reported contacts with lawmakers or aides from July to December 2005 and is paid $22,000 per month for this period.[252]

2006

The Beijing Organizing Committee for the Games of the XXIX Olympiad contracts with Hill & Knowlton throughout 2006 for "public relations communications and public relations counsel" related to the 2008 Olympics. (Amount of remuneration not disclosed.)[253]

Patton Boggs continues lobbying work on behalf of the PRC embassy, earning $264,000 for the year.[254]

Hogan & Hartson provides counsel related to World Trade Organization (WTO) issues and performs lobbying services on behalf of the Chinese government. The firm also represents the Liaoning provincial government in litigation. (Amount of remuneration not fully disclosed.)[255]

The firm Jones Day performs lobbying work on behalf of the Chinese embassy and advises the client on the status of draft legislation (related to tariff and intellectual property issues, human rights, Tibet, and Taiwan) that might affect US-China relations. The firm earns $168,000 for the year.[256]

2007

Hill & Knowlton continues work with the Beijing Olympics Committee for public relations work related to the 2008 Olympics. (Amount of remuneration not disclosed.) [257]

Patton Boggs performs lobbying work on behalf of the PRC embassy. The firm lobbies with the legislative branch, including holding discussions of "US-China bilateral issues" and "trade and currency legislation." The firm earns $198,000 in the first half of the year and $66,000 in the second half. [258]

Hogan & Hartson performs lobbying work on behalf of the central government of the PRC, providing "strategic advice and counsel" related to "the World Trade Organization's negotiations and related matters." The firm earns $143,920 for the first half of the year and an additional $273,947 for a six-month period ending in February 2008.[259]

2008

Patton Boggs continues lobbying work on behalf of the PRC embassy, contacting US government officials and Congressional staffers on issues affecting US-China relations. The firm earns a reported total of $418,000 for the year.[260]

Hogan & Hartson continues lobbying work on behalf of the PRC central government on trade and other issues. The firm reports earnings of $389,985 for the six-month period ending in August 2008.[261]

Selected Examples of Lobbying Activity Performed on behalf of Chinese State-owned and State-affiliated Firms, 2005–2008

2005

The state-owned enterprise CNOOC hires several firms (Akin Gump Strauss Hauer & Feld; BKSH & Associates; the Brunswick Group; and Public Strategies) in an unsuccessful attempt to purchase Unocal.[262] Two of the most active are Public Strategies and Akin Gump Strauss Hauer & Feld, paid $669,909 and $3,159,166, respectively, for the six-month period ending December 31, 2005.[263]

2006

The Bank of China pays the firm Public Strategies $285,000 for public relations work on its behalf, including "implementing a media plan . . . in conjunction with an initial public offering." The firm is paid $255,687 for the second half of the year; remuneration for the first half of the year not disclosed.[264]

Lenovo Group, Ltd., spends $429,000 in the first half of 2006 for lobbying efforts on its own behalf. A company lobbyist contacts Members of Congress and multiple agencies of the executive branch in regards to multiple legislative initiatives involving US-China trade issues.[265]

2007

Hogan & Hartson registers as a lobbyist performing work on behalf of the Hangzhou Zhongce Rubber Company, a tire and rubber company in which the largest shareholder is the Hangzhou Provincial Government. Specific services provided, and the amount of remuneration, are not publicly disclosed.[266] Vinson & Elkins LLP provides legal advice and briefing materials, and makes contacts with US government officials on behalf of the China Chamber of Commerce of Metals, Minerals and Chemicals Importers and Exporters, earning $40,000 for the year.[267]

2008

International Government Relations Group registers as a lobbyist for Huawei Technologies Company, Ltd., to perform lobbying on trade and tax issues. (Amount of remuneration not disclosed.) [268]

However, despite such a significant increase in recent years, the Chinese government's direct sponsorship of lobbying activities remains relatively modest in contrast with the efforts of many other foreign governments. By way of comparison, Barbour Griffiths & Rogers, one of 12 US firms retained by Taiwan, received payments of $1.5 million for services on behalf of Taiwan's government in 2006.[269] In all, Taiwan's government paid US firms $2,993,230 for lobbying services in 2007 and $2,550,457 in 2008.[270] In 2008, some of the biggest lobbying sponsors spent amounts that significantly eclipsed those of either the PRC or Taiwan: The United Arab Emirates spent $11 million, the United Kingdom spent $6 million, and Japan and Turkey each spent $4 million.[271]

Figure 1: Lobbying Efforts on behalf of the PRC Government by US Firms, 1995–2008

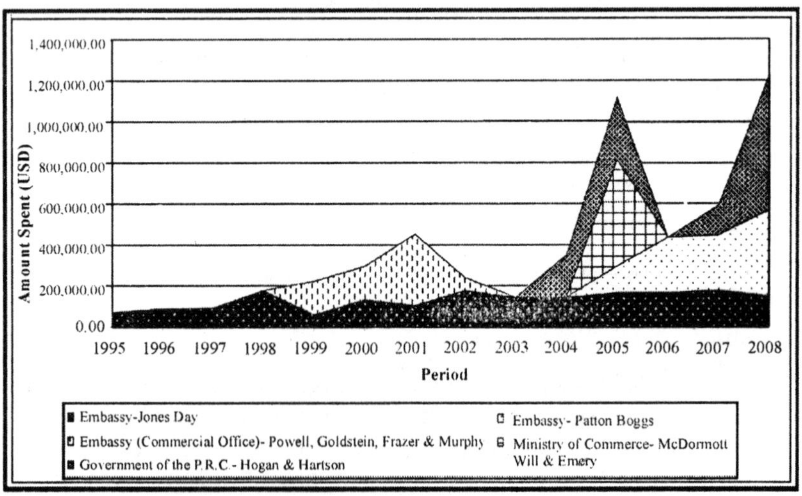

Note: Significant spike in lobbying activity in 2005 assessed to be related primarily to the abortive effort by the PRC state-owned firm China National Offshore Oil Company to purchase the US energy firm Unocal 76.

Source: Data compiled by Commission staff from *Reports of the Attorney General to the Congress* of the United States on the Administration of the Foreign Agents Registration Act of 1938 (Washington, DC: 1995–2008).

Conclusions

- The Chinese government is directly engaged in promoting its preferred propaganda narratives to foreign audiences and has an extensive bureaucracy dedicated to work in this area. The international propaganda messages of the government are similar in most respects to those for a Chinese audience—emphasizing China's economic growth, China's desire for a peaceful international system, and China's "stability" under CCP leadership.
- To its domestic audience, the Chinese government promotes the message that China is under attack from hostile forces abroad. Many figures within both the Chinese government and the public express a sense of frustration that the western media presents unfair portrayals of China and state that China therefore needs more effective international communication tools to counter such "attacks."
- The Chinese government views effective foreign propaganda as an essential tool of state power and is significantly increasing the level of effort and resources devoted to China's state-sponsored foreign language media outlets. Some of these efforts may also assume the form of nominally "independent" news outlets in which the Chinese government or Chinese state-owned firms exercise considerable influence behind the scenes.
- The Chinese government actively seeks to influence the commentary about China and US-China relations that comes from US academics and think tanks. This takes the form of providing both positive rewards to "friendly" scholars—such as preferred access to interviews and documents—as well as taking punitive actions such as denying visas for academics who anger Beijing. These rewards and punishments offer the Chinese government leverage over the careers of foreign scholars and thereby encourage a culture of academic self-censorship.
- In recent years, US public relations and lobbying firms have played a more prominent role in Beijing's efforts to improve its image and advocate for its preferred policies. The advice of western public relations firms has helped to shape the messages that the Chinese government presents to international audiences. However, China's use of direct lobbying in the United States is still limited in scale compared to the efforts of many other countries.

RECOMMENDATIONS

Freedom of Expression in China

- The Commission recommends that Members of Congress in their interparliamentary exchanges continue to raise concerns regarding freedom of expression in China in their dialogues with officials of the Chinese government.
- The Commission recommends that Congress continue to monitor and assess the development and progress of industry and other efforts to create and implement an effective code of ethics and best practices related to the operations of US high-tech firms in China and other authoritarian countries where Internet content and activity are controlled and monitored by the government.
- The Commission recommends that Congress continue to monitor and assess the Chinese government's efforts to implement an end-user Internet control system. The Commission further recommends that Congress assess whether such efforts are compliant with China's commitments as a signatory to the World Trade Organization.

China's External Propaganda and Influence Operations' and the Resulting Impacts on the United States

- The Commission recommends that Congress urge the administration to have the US Department of State raise with its counterparts in the PRC Foreign Ministry concerns related to the denial of visas to US academics who require travel to China in order to engage in substantive research.

ENDNOTES

1. Madeline Earp (Asia research associate with the Committee to Protect Journalists), telephone interview with Commission staff, August 14, 2009; US-China Economic and Security Review Commission, *Hearing on China's Media and Information Controls,* testimony of Phelim Kine, September 10, 2009.
2. For a discussion of the handling of issues deemed to be politically "sensitive," see Human Rights Watch, *China's Forbidden Zones: Shutting the Media Out of Tibet and Other 'Sensitive' Stories"* (New York, NY: July 2008).
3. US-China Economic and Security Review Commission, *Hearing on China's Media and Information Controls,* written testimony of Madeline Earp, September 10, 2009.
4. US-China Economic and Security Review Commission, *Hearing on China's Media and Information Controls,* written testimony of Madeline Earp, September 10, 2009.
5. US-China Economic and Security Review Commission, *Hearing on China's Media and Information Controls,* written testimony of Madeline Earp, September 10, 2009.
6. US-China Economic and Security Review Commission, *Hearing on China's Media and Information Controls,* testimony of Phelim Kine, September 10, 2009.
7. US-China Economic and Security Review Commission, *Hearing on China's Media and Information Controls,* testimony of Phelim Kine, September 10, 2009.
8. US-China Economic and Security Review Commission, *Hearing on China's Media and Information Controls,* testimony of Phelim Kine, September 10, 2009.
9. Foreign Correspondents Club of China, "Results of July Membership Survey," August 6, 2009. *http://www.fccchina.org/2009/08/06/results-of-july-membershipsurvey/.*

10. US-China Economic and Security Review Commission, *Hearing on China's Media and Information Controls,* testimony of Phelim Kine, September 10, 2009.
11. US-China Economic and Security Review Commission, *Hearing on China's Media and Information Controls,* testimony of Madeline Earp, September 10, 2009.
12. Foreign Correspondents Club of China, "Assault On Kyodo Reporters Is Reprehensible," September 10. 2009. *http://www.fccchina.org/2009/09/19/assault-onkyodo- reporters-is-reprehensible/.*
13. Congressional-Executive Commission on China, *Roundtable Discussion on Reporting the News in China: First-Hand Accounts and Current Trends,* testimony of Kathleen McLaughlin (Washington, DC: July 31, 2009).
14. US-China Economic and Security Review Commission, *Hearing on China's Media and Information Controls,* written testimony of Madeline Earp, September 10, 2009.
15. Congressional-Executive Commission on China, *Roundtable Discussion on Reporting the News in China: First-Hand Accounts and Current Trends,* testimony of Kathleen McLaughlin (Washington, DC: July 31, 2009).
16. US-China Economic and Security Review Commission, *Hearing on China's Media and Information Controls,* written testimony of Madeline Earp, September 10, 2009.
17. US-China Economic and Security Review Commission, *Hearing on China's Media and Information Controls,* written testimony of Madeline Earp. September 10, 2009.\
18. Human Rights Watch, *You Will Be Harassed and Detained* (New York, NY: 2008). p.38.
19. US-China Economic and Security Review Commission, *Hearing on China's Media and Information Controls,* written testimony of Madeline Earp, September 10, 2009.
20. US-China Economic and Security Review Commission, *Hearing on China's Media and Information Controls,* written testimony of Phelim Kine, September 10, 2009.
21. US-China Economic and Security Review Commission, *Hearing on China's Media and Information Controls,* testimony of Madeline Earp, September 10. 2009.
22. Peter Ford, "Sources in Urumqi? They're (very) hard to come by," *Christian Science Monitor,* July 6, 2009. *http://features.csmonitor.com/globalnews/2009/07/06/ sources-in-urumqi-theyre-very-hard-to-come-by/.*
23. Freedom House, "Freedom of the Press 2009: Table of Global Press Freedom Rankings" (Washington, D.C.: May 2009). *http://www.freedomhouse.org/uploads/fop/2009/ Freedom of the Press2009__tables.pdf.*
24. Committee to Protect Journalists, "CPJ's 2008 prison census: Online and in jail," *CPJ Special Report,* (New York, NY: December 4, 2008).
25. See David Shambaugh, "China's Propaganda System: Institutions, Processes and Efficacy," *The China Journal* 57 (January 2007); Anne-Marie Brady, *Marketing Dictatorship: Propaganda and Thought Work in Contemporary China* (New York: Rowman & Littlefield, 2008).
26. David Shambaugh, "China's Propaganda System: Institutions, Processes and Efficacy,"*The China Journal* 57 (January 2007); Anne-Marie Brady, *Marketing Dictatorship: Propaganda and Thought Work in Contemporary China* (New York: Rowman & Littlefield, 2008) pp. 9–33.
27. Ashley Esarey, "Speak No Evil: Mass Media Control in Contemporary China," Freedom House Special Report (Washington, DC: February 2006).
28. Anne-Marie Brady, *Marketing Dictatorship: Propaganda and Thought Work in Contemporary China* (New York: Rowman & Littlefield, 2008) pp. 19, 95–104.
29. For further discussion of the roles and practices of the Central Propaganda Department, see U.S–China Economic and Security Review Commission, *2008 Annual Report to*

Congress (Washington, DC: November 2008), Chapter 5: "China's Media and information Controls: The Impact in China and the United States," pp. 291–310.

30. US-China Economic and Security Review Commission, *Hearing on China's Media and Information Controls,* written testimony of Madeline Earp, September 10, 2009.
31. International Freedom of Expression Exchange. "Journalists attacked while reporting on riots," Alert, July 9, 2009.
32. US-China Economic and Security Review Commission, *Hearing on China's Media and Information Controls,* written testimony of Madeline Earp, September 10, 2009.
33. US-China Economic and Security Review Commission, *Hearing on China's Media and Information Controls,* written testimony of Madeline Earp, September 10, 2009.
34. Susan L. Shirk, *China: Fragile Superpower* (New York: Oxford University Press, 2007) p. 84.
35. Congressional-Executive Commission on China, *Roundtable Discussion on Reporting the News in China: First-Hand Accounts and Current Trends,* testimony of Ashley Esarey (Washington, DC: July 31, 2009).
36. US-China Economic and Security Review Commission, *Hearing on China's Propaganda and Influence Operations, its Intelligence Activities that Target the United States, and the Resulting Impacts on US National Security,* testimony of Judy Polumbaum, April 30, 2009.
37. Congressional-Executive Commission on China, *Roundtable Discussion on Reporting the News in China: First-Hand Accounts and Current Trends,* testimony of Ashley Esarey (Washington, DC: July 31, 2009).
38. As one example, see Tom Mitchell, "Beijing Orders Media to Rein In Quake Coverage, "*Financial Times,* June 2, 2008.
39. US-China Economic and Security Review Commission, *Hearing on China's Media and Information Controls,* testimony of Phelim Kine, September 10, 2009.
40. Human Rights in China, *State Secrets: China's Legal Labyrinth* (New York, NY: June 2007).
41. US-China Economic and Security Review Commission, *Hearing on China's Media and Information Controls,* written testimony of Madeline Earp, September 10, 2009.
42. Jerome Cohen and Jeremy Daum, "State of Secrecy," *South China Morning Post OnLine,* August 6, 2009. OSC ID: CPP20090806715008. See also "Rio Tinto and China's 'State Secret' Debate," *Caijing Online,* July 24, 2009. OSC ID: CPP20090724968130. *http://www.opensource.gov.*
43. Jerome Cohen and Jeremy Daum, "State of Secrecy," *South China Morning Post onLine,* August 6, 2009. OSC ID: CPP20090806715008. Also available at *http://www.usasialaw.org/wp-content/uploads/2009/08/08062009scmp.pdf.*
44. Reporters Without Borders, "The Dangers for Journalists Who Expose Environmental Issues," September 2009. *http://www.rsf.org/IMG/rapport _en_md.pdf*
45. Stephen McDonnell, "China Claims Proof Rio Execs Spied," Australian Broadcasting Corporation, July 9, 2009.
46. Strategic Forecasting, Inc. (STRATFOR), "China, Australia: The Espionage Case Continues" (Austin, TX: July 14, 2009).
47. David Barboza, "China Charges 4 Rio Tinto Employees; Spying Allegations Are Dropped," *New York Times,* August 12, 2009.
48. Anne-Marie Brady, briefing to the US-China Economic and Security Review Commission, Washington, D.C., September 24, 2009.
49. US-China Economic and Security Review Commission, *Hearing on China's Media and Information Controls,* written testimony of Victor Shih, September 10,2009.

50. See Jordan Calinoff, "How China Cooks its Books," *Foreign Policy OnLine*, September 3,2009. *http://www.foreignpolicy.com/articles/2009/09/03/how_china_cooks_its_books?page=0,1*; and Anne-Marie Brady and He Yong, "Talking Up the Market: Economic Propaganda in Contemporary China," forthcoming chapter in *Thought Management: China's Modernised Propaganda Work* (publisher information forthcoming).
51. US-China Economic and Security Review Commission, *Hearing on China's Media and Information Controls*, written testimony of Victor Shih, September 10, 2009.
52. US-China Economic and Security Review Commission, *Hearing on China's Media and Information Controls*, written testimony of Victor Shih, September 10, 2009.
53. US-China Economic and Security Review Commission, *Hearing on China's Media and Information Controls*, written testimony of Victor Shih, September 10, 2009.
54. US-China Economic and Security Review Commission, *Hearing on China's Media and Information Controls*, written testimony of Victor Shih, September 10, 2009.
55. US-China Economic and Security Review Commission, *Hearing on China's Media and Information Controls*, written testimony of Victor Shih, September 10, 2009.
56. Agence France-Presse, "AFP Told: Turmoil at China's Influential Caijing Magazine as Executives Quit," October 13, 2009.
57. US-China Economic and Security Review Commission, *Hearing on China's Media and Information Controls*, written testimony of Victor Shih, September 10, 2009.
58. US-China Economic and Security Review Commission, *Hearing on China's Media and Information Controls*, written testimony of Victor Shih, September 10, 2009.
59. US-China Economic and Security Review Commission, *Hearing on China's Media and Information Controls*, written testimony of Victor Shih, September 10, 2009.
60. US-China Economic and Security Review Commission, *Hearing on China's Media and Information Controls*, written testimony of Madeline Earp. September 10, 2009.
61. US-China Economic and Security Review Commission, *Hearing on China's Media and Information Controls*, written testimony of Madeline Earp, September 10, 2009.
62. US-China Economic and Security Review Commission, *Hearing on China's Media and Information Controls*, written testimony of Madeline Earp, September 10, 2009.
63. Foreign Correspondents Club of China, "09/18/09 Beijing Authorities Beat Kyodo Journalists," Incident Reports, September 19, 2009.
64. Congressional-Executive Commission on China, *Roundtable Discussion on Reporting the News in China: First-Hand Accounts and Current Trends*, testimony of Kathleen McLaughlin (Washington, DC: July 31, 2009).
65. US-China Economic and Security Review Commission, *Hearing on China's Media and Information Controls*, testimony of Phelim Kine, September 10, 2009.
66. Steven Dong Guanpeng, quoted in *Malaysian Observer*, "China opens up with new media strategy," August 11, 2009.
67. US-China Economic and Security Review Commission, *Hearing on China's Media and Information Controls*, written testimony of Madeline Earp, September 10, 2009.
68. US-China Economic and Security Review Commission, *Hearing on China's Media and Information Controls*, written testimony of Madeline Earp, September 10, 2009.
69. US-China Economic and Security Review Commission, *Hearing on China's Propaganda and Influence Operations, Its Intelligence Activities that Target the United States, and the Resulting Impacts on US National Security*, written testimony of Jacqueline Newmyer, April 30, 2009.
70. Congressional-Executive Commission on China, *Roundtable Discussion on Reporting the News in China: First-Hand Accounts and Current Trends*, testimony of Kathleen McLaughlin (Washington, DC: July 31, 2009).

71. Michael Wines, "In Latest Upheaval, China Applies New Strategies to Control Flow of Information," *New York Times,* July 7, 2009; US-China Economic and Security Review Commission, *Hearing on China's Media and Information Controls,* testimony of Phelim Kine, September 10, 2009.

72. US-China Economic and Security Review Commission, *Hearing on China's Media and Information Controls,* testimony of Phelim Kine, September 10, 2009.

73. Anne-Marie Brady and He Yong, "Talking Up the Market: Economic Propaganda in Contemporary China," forthcoming chapter in *Thought Management: China's Modernised Propaganda Work* (publisher information forthcoming); and Anita Chang, "Parents' Dilemma: Which Food Company Can we Trust not to Poison our Babies?" *Honolulu Adviser*, September 20, 2008

74. Anne-Marie Brady and He Yong, "Talking Up the Market: Economic Propaganda in Contemporary China," forthcoming chapter in *Thought Management: China's Modernised Propaganda Work* (publisher information forthcoming); Mary-Anne Toy, "Milk of Human Blindness," *The Age* (Melbourne, Australia), September 27, 2008.

75. Anne-Marie Brady and He Yong, "Talking Up the Market: Economic Propaganda in Contemporary China," forthcoming chapter in *Thought Management: China's Modernised Propaganda Work* (publisher information forthcoming).

76. Following the exposure of the scandal, Fonterra reportedly divested itself of itsinvestments in San Lu. See Fran O'Sullivan, "So long, Sanlu," *New Zealand Herald,* May 2, 2009. *http://www.nzherald.co.nz/fonterras-chinese-milk-scandal/news/article.cfm?c_id=1502761&objectid=10569769.*

77. Trini Tran, "China Tainted Milk Scandal Widens," Associated Press Financial Wire,September 19, 2008.

78. Anne-Marie Brady and He Yong, "Talking Up the Market: Economic Propaganda in Contemporary China," forthcoming chapter in *Thought Management: China's Modernised Propaganda Work* (publisher information forthcoming).

79. Anne-Marie Brady and He Yong, "Talking Up the Market: Economic Propaganda in Contemporary China," forthcoming chapter in *Thought Management: China's Modernised Propaganda Work* (publisher information forthcoming).\

80. Anne-Marie Brady and He Yong, "Talking Up the Market: Economic Propaganda in Contemporary China," forthcoming chapter in *Thought Management: China's Modernised Propaganda Work* (publisher information forthcoming).

81. US-China Economic and Security Review Commission, *Hearing on China's Media and Information Controls,* written testimony of Perry Link, September 10, 2009.

82. US-China Economic and Security Review Commission, *Hearing on China's Media and Information Controls,* written testimony of Perry Link, September 10, 2009.

83. US-China Economic and Security Review Commission, *Hearing on China's Media and Information Controls,* written testimony of Perry Link, September 10, 2009.

84. US-China Economic and Security Review Commission, *Hearing on China's Media and Information Controls,* written testimony of Perry Link, September 10, 2009.

85. US-China Economic and Security Review Commission, *Hearing on China's Media and Information Controls,* written testimony of Perry Link, September 10, 2009.\

86. US-China Economic and Security Review Commission, *Hearing on China's Media and Information Controls,* written testimony of Perry Link, September 10, 2009.

87. US-China Economic and Security Review Commission, *Hearing on China's Media and Information Controls,* written testimony of Perry Link, September 10, 2009.

88. US-China Economic and Security Review Commission, *Annual Report to Congress 2008* (Washington, D.C.: November 2008), pp. 294–295.

89. Ariana Eunjung Cha, "Authoritarian Regimes Censor News from Iran," *Washington Post,* June 27, 2009. *http://www.washingtonpost.com/wp-dyn/content/article/ 2009/ 06/26/AR200906 2604343_2.html? hpid=topnews &sid=ST2009 062504596.*
90. US-China Economic and Security Review Commission, *Hearing on China's Media and Information Controls,* written testimony of Lawrence Liu, September 10,2009.
91. Ariana Eunjung Cha, "Authoritarian Regimes Censor News from Iran," *Washington Post,* June 27, 2009. *http://www.washingtonpost.com/wp-dyn/content/article/ 2009/ 06/26/AR200906 2604343_2.html? hpid= topnews &sid =ST2009 062504596.*
92. Congressional-Executive Commission on China "China Human Rights and Rule of Law Update" (Washington, DC: August, 6, 2009). *http://www.cecc.gov/pages/ virtualAcad/newsletterListing.phpd?NLdate=20090730&show=PRESS.*
93. US-China Economic and Security Review Commission, *Hearing on China's Media and Information Controls,* written testimony of Lawrence Liu, September 10, 2009.
94. US-China Economic and Security Review Commission, *Hearing on China's Media and Information Controls,* written testimony of Lawrence Liu, September 10,2009.
95. US-China Economic and Security Review Commission, *Hearing on China's Media and Information Controls,* written testimony of Lawrence Liu, September 10, 2009.
96. *"Yi Lang Xuanju Weiji Houbei de 'Xifang Yinsu"*(The "Western Factor" Behind Iran's Election Crisis), *Guangming Daily,* June 24, 2009. *http://www.gmw.cn/ content/2009-06/24/content_*939341.htm. Translation performed by Commission staff and by David Bandurski, "Guangming Daily: Western 'Hostile Forces' at Work in Iran," China Media Project, June 25, 2009. *http://cmp.hku.hk/2009/06/25/1670.*
97. Freedom House, "Freedom on the Net" (Washington, DC: March 30, 2009). *http:// www.freedomhouse.org/template.cfm?page=383&report=79.*
98. Xiao Qiang, "The Rise of Online Public Opinion and Its Political Implications" (paper presented to the China Internet Research Conference at the Journalism and Media Studies Centre of the University of Hong Kong, June 13–14, 2008).
99. Willy Lam, "The Net Revolution: Chinese Netizens vs. Green Dam," *China Brief* 9:14 (July 9, 2009); and Xiao Qiang, "The Rise of Online Public Opinion and Its Political Implications" (paper presented to the China Internet Research Conference\ at the Journalism and Media Studies Centre of the University of Hong Kong, June 13–14, 2008).
100. Anne-Marie Brady, *Marketing Dictatorship: Propaganda and Thought Work in Contemporary China* (New York; Rowman & Littlefield), pp. 137–139.
101. Xiao Qiang, "The Rise of Online Public Opinion and Its Political Implications" (paper presented to the China Internet Research Conference at the Journalism and Media Studies Centre of the University of Hong Kong, June 13–14, 2008).
102. US-China Economic and Security Review Commission, *Hearing on China's Media and Information Controls,* written testimony of Victor Shih, September 10, 2009; and Willy Lam, "The Net Revolution: Chinese Netizens vs. Green Dam," *China Brief* 9:14 (July 9, 2009).
103. See Willy Lam, "The Net Revolution: Chinese Netizens vs. Green Dam," *China Brief* 9:14 (July 9, 2009); and Michael Wines, "In Latest Upheaval, China Applies New Strategies to Control Flow of Information," *New York Times,* July 7, 2009.
104. Chris O'Brien, "The Human Flesh Search Engine," *Forbes.com,* November 21, 2008. *http://www.forbes.com/2008/11/21/human-flesh-search-tech-identity08-cx_ cb_1121obrien.html.*
105. Chris O'Brien, "The Human Flesh Search Engine," *Forbes.com,* November 21, 2008. *http://www.forbes.com/2008/11/21/human-flesh-search-tech-identity08-cx_* cb_*1121obrien.html.*

106. Agence France-Presse, "China's Internet a major concern to officials," August 10, 2009.
107. Zheng Tingxing, quoted in Lye Liang Fook and Yang Yi, "The Chinese Leadership and the Internet," *East Asia Policy* (2009): 32–41.
108. Anne-Marie Brady, *Marketing Dictatorship: Propaganda and Thought Work in Contemporary China* (New York; Rowman & Little field), pp. 137–139.
109. Qian Gang, "Central party media 'grab the megaphone'," China Media Project, August 17, 2009. *http://cmp.hku.hk/2009/08/21/1709/.*
110. Anne-Marie Brady, *Marketing Dictatorship: Propaganda and Thought Work in Contemporary China* (New York: Rowman & Little field, 2008) p. 137.
111. Anne-Marie Brady, *Marketing Dictatorship: Propaganda and Thought Work in Contemporary China* (New York; Rowman & Littlefield), p. 138.
112. Jonathan Watts, "China's Secret Internet Police Targets Critics with Web of Propaganda," *Guardian,* June 14, 2005. *http://www.guardian.co.uk/technology/2005/jun/14/newmedia.china.*
113. See David Bandurski, "China's Guerrilla War for the Web," *Far Eastern Economic Review* (July 2008); and Open Source Center, "PRC Organizations Seek Internet Monitors, Commentators," OSC ID: CPP20090918565001. *http://www.opensource.gov.*
114. James Fallows, "The Connection Has Been Reset," *The Atlantic,* March 2008. *http://www.theatlantic.com/doc/200803/chinese-firewall.* For a more detailed description of the physical infrastructure and censorship regime of China's Internet, see US-China Economic and Security Review Commission, *Annual Report to Congress 2008* (Washington, D.C.: November 2008), pp. 297–302.
115. Freedom House, "Freedom on the Net" (Washington, DC: March 30, 2009) *http://www.freedomhouse.org/template.cfm?page=383&report=79.*
116. Chin-fu Hung, "The Politics of Governing the Information and Communications Technologies in East Asian Authoritarian States: Case Study of China," in Francesco Amoretti, *Electronic Constitution: Social Cultural, and Political Implications* (New York: Information Science Reference, 2009), p. 140.
117. Chin-fu Hung, "The Politics of Governing the Information and Communications Technologies in East Asian Authoritarian States: Case Study of China," in Francesco Amoretti, *Electronic Constitution: Social Cultural, and Political Implications* (New York: Information Science Reference, 2009), pp. 140–141.
118. Anne-Marie Brady, *Marketing Dictatorship: Propaganda and Thought Work in Contemporary China* (New York: Rowman & Littlefield, 2008), p. 131.
119. OpenNet Initiative, "China's Green Dam: The Implications of Government Control Encroaching on the Home PC," *OpenNet Initiative Bulletin,* June 11, 2009, pp. 16–17.
120. Open Net Initiative, "China's Green Dam: The Implications of Government Control Encroaching on the Home PC," *Open Net Initiative Bulletin,* June 11, 2009, p. 4.
121. Tom Lantos Human Rights Commission, *Hearing on Current Threats to Internet reedom,* testimony of Daniel Calingaert (Washington, DC: June 18, 2009); "China's Green Dam: The Implications of Government Control Encroaching on the Home PC," *OpenNet Initiative Bulletin,* June 11, 2009. p. 1.
122. OpenNet Initiative, "China's Green Dam: The Implications of Government Control Encroaching on the Home PC," *OpenNet Initiative Bulletin,* June 11, 2009, pp. 16–17.
123. OpenNet Initiative, "China's Green Dam: The Implications of Government Control Encroaching on the Home PC," *OpenNet Initiative Bulletin,* June 11, 2009.p. 2.

124. Tom Lantos Human Rights Commission, *Hearing on Current Threats to Internet reedom,* testimony of Daniel Calingaert (Washington, DC: June 18, 2009).
125. Scott Wolchok, Randy Yao, and J. Alex Halderman, "Analysis of the Green Dam Censorware System," Computer Science and Engineering Division of the University of Michigan, Revision 2.41 (Ann Arbor, MI: July 11, 2009).
126. US-China Economic and Security Review Commission, *Hearing on China's Media and Information Controls,* written testimony of Robert Guerra, September 10, 2009; and OpenNet Initiative, "China's Green Dam: The Implications of Government Control Encroaching on the Home PC," *OpenNet Initiative Bulletin,* June 11, 2009, p. 19.
127. "Technical, Legal, and Political Blunders: Ingredients of the Green Dam Debacle," *China Digital Times,* June 14, 2009. *http://chinadigitaltimes.net/2009/06/technical-*legal-and-political-blunders-ingredients-of-the-green-dam-debacle.\
128. Loretta Chao, "Schools Defy Beijing, Remove Web Filter," *Wall Street Journal,* September 17, 2009.
129. US-China Economic and Security Review Commission, *Hearing on China's Media and Information Controls,* written testimony of Robert Guerra, September 10,2009.
130. Phelim Kine, "Leaning on the Dragon," *New York Times,* July 7, 2009.
131. Loretta Chao, "Schools Defy Beijing, Remove Web Filter," *Wall Street Journal,* September 17, 2009.
132. Phelim Kine, "Leaning on the Dragon," *New York Times,* July 7, 2009.
133. Willy Lam, "The Net Revolution: Chinese Netizens vs. Green Dam," *China Brief* 9:14 (July 9, 2009).
134. Phelim Kine, "Leaning on the Dragon," *New York Times,* July 7, 2009.
135. US-China Economic and Security Review Commission, *Hearing on China's Media and Information Controls,* written testimony of Robert Guerra, September 10, 2009.
136. Chin-fu Hung, "The Politics of Governing the Information and Communications Technologies in East Asian Authoritarian States: Case Study of China," in Francesco Amoretti, *Electronic Constitution: Social Cultural, and Political Implications* (New York: Information Science Reference, 2009) p. 144
137. Anne-Marie Brady, *Marketing Dictatorship: Propaganda and Thought Work in Contemporary China* (New York: Rowman & Littlefield, 2008) p. 126.
138. Chin-fu Hung, "The Politics of Governing the Information and Communications Technologies in East Asian Authoritarian States: Case Study of China," in Francesco Amoretti, *Electronic Constitution: Social Cultural, and Political Implications* (New York: Information Science Reference, 2009) p. 144.
139. OpenNet Initiative, "Internet Filtering in China," *OpenNet Initiative Bulletin,* June 11, 2009, p. 36.
140. OpenNet Initiative, "Internet Filtering in China," *OpenNet Initiative Bulletin,* June 11, 2009, p. 36.
141. OpenNet Initiative, "Internet Filtering in China," *OpenNet Initiative Bulletin,* June 11, 2009, p. 15.
142. Ta Kung Pao, "State Council Information Office: Real Name Registration to Be Required for All Domestic News Sites," August 2009 [translated by the Center for Democracy and Technology, Washington, DC].
143. OpenNet Initiative, "Internet Filtering in China," *OpenNet Initiative Bulletin,* June 11, 2009, p. 36.
144. Nart Villeneuve, "Search Monitor: Toward a Measure of Transparency," Citizen Lab Occasional Paper, June 18, 2008. *http://www.nartv.org/2008/06/18/searchmonitor-toward-a-measure-of-transparency.*

145. Thomas Lum, "Internet Development and Information Control in the People's Republic of China," Congressional Research Service Report (Washington, DC: 2006).

146. US Senate Judiciary Committee, Subcommittee on Human Rights and the Law, *Hearing on Global Internet Freedom: Corporate Responsibility and the Rule of Law,* 110th Cong., 2nd sess., May 20, 2008.

147. Amnesty International, *Undermining Freedom of Expression in China: The Role of Yahoo!, Microsoft, and Google* (London, United Kingdom: 2006). *http://www.amnestyusa.org/business/Undermining_Freedom_of_Expression_in_China.pdf.*

148. Amnesty International, *Undermining Freedom of Expression in China: The Role of Yahoo!, Microsoft, and Google* (London, United Kingdom: 2006). *http://www.amnestyusa.org/business/Undermining_Freedom_of_Expression_in_China.pdf.*

149. Text of H.R. 2271, *Global Online Freedom Act of 2009,* introduced May 6, 2009. *http://thomas.loc.gov/cgi-bin/bdquery/D?d111:1:./temp/¡-bdlpj Z:@ @@ L&summ2=m&|/bss/111search.html/.*

150. US-China Economic and Security Review Commission, *Hearing on China's Media and Information Controls,* testimony of Robert Faris, September 10, 2009; Robert Faris et al., "Censorship 2.0," *Innovations* 3:2 (Spring 2008).

151. US-China Economic and Security Review Commission, *Hearing on China's Media and Information Controls,* testimony of Robert Faris, September 10, 2009.

152. US-China Economic and Security Review Commission, *Hearing on China's Media and Information Controls,* written testimony of Robert Guerra, September 10, 2009

153. US-China Economic and Security Review Commission, *Hearing on China's Media and Information Controls,* testimony of Robert Faris, September 10, 2009.

154. Text of H.R. 2271, *Global Online Freedom Act of 2009,* introduced May 6, 2009. *http://thomas. loc.gov/cgi-bin /bdquery /D?d111:1 :./temp/¡-bdlpjZ: @@@ L& summ2=m&|/bss/111search.html|.*

155. Text of H.R. 2271, *Global Online Freedom Act of 2009,* introduced May 6, 2009. *http://thomas. loc.gov /cgi-bin /bdquery /D?d111 :1:./temp/bdlpjZ: @@@ L& summ2 = m&|/bss/111 search.html|*. Also on May 6, 2009, the Global Online Freedom Act was referred to the House Foreign Affairs Committee and the House Energy and Commerce Committee. See "Global Online Freedom Act of 2009: All Actions." *http://thomas.loc.gov/cgi-bin/bdquery/D?d111:1:./temp/¡-bdlpjZ:@@@L&summ2=m&/.bss/111search.html|*3Bmajor%20actions.

156. US-China Economic and Security Review Commission, *Hearing on China's Media and Information Controls,* written testimony of Robert Faris, September 10,2009.

157. US-China Economic and Security Review Commission. *Hearing on China's Media and Information Controls,* testimony of Robert Faris, September 10, 2009.

158. Tom Lantos Human Rights Commission, *Hearing on Current Threats to Internet Freedom,* testimony of Daniel Calingaert (Washington, DC: June 18, 2009).
159. Text of H.R. 2271, *Global Online Freedom Act of 2009,* introduced May 6, 2009. *http:/ /thomas.loc.gov /cgi-bin /bdquery /D?d111: 1:./temp/¡-bdlpj Z:@@ @L& summ2= m&|/bss/111search.html|.*

160. Deng Xiaoping, "We Are Confident that We Can Handle China's Affairs Well" (excerpted from a speech given in Beijing, September 16, 1989). *http:/english.peopledaily.com.cn/dengxp/vol3/text/d1040.html.*

161. Anne-Marie Brady, *Marketing Dictatorship: Propaganda and Thought Work in Contemporary China* (Lanham, MD: Rowman and Littlefield, 2008), pp. 154–155.

162. US-China Economic and Security Review Commission, *Hearing on China's Propaganda and Influence Operations, Its Intelligence Activities that Target the United States, and the Resulting Impacts on US National Security,* testimony of Anne-Marie Brady, April 30, 2009.
163. Anne-Marie Brady, *Marketing Dictatorship: Propaganda and Thought Work in Contemporary China* (Lanham, MD: Rowman and Littlefield, 2008), p. 156.
164. Anne-Marie Brady, *Marketing Dictatorship: Propaganda and Thought Work in Contemporary China* (Lanham, MD: Rowman and Littlefield, 2008), p. 157.
165. Anne-Marie Brady, *Marketing Dictatorship: Propaganda and Thought Work in Contemporary China* (Lanham, MD: Rowman and Littlefield, 2008), p. 156.
166. US-China Economic and Security Review Commission, *Hearing on China's Propaganda and Influence Operations, Its Intelligence Activities that Target the United States, and the Resulting Impacts on US National Security,* testimony of Anne-Marie Brady, April 30, 2009.
167. Anne-Marie Brady and He Yong, "Talking up the Market: Economic Propaganda in Contemporary China," chapter forthcoming in Anne-Marie Brady and He Yong, *Thought Management: China's Modernised Propaganda Work* (publishing information forthcoming).
168. Li Changchun, speech delivered at the Suixi County Conference on Foreign Propaganda (September 21, 2007). *China Digital Times,* "How to do Propaganda Work for a Foreign Audience." *http://chinadigitaltimes.net/2007/11/how-to-do-propaganda-work-for-a-foreign-audience.*
169. US-China Economic and Security Review Commission, *Hearing on China's Propaganda and Influence Operations, Its Intelligence Activities that Target the United States, and the Resulting Impacts on US National Security,* testimony of Nicholas J. Cull, April 30, 2009.
170. Anne-Marie Brady, "Guiding Hand: The Role of the CCP Central Propaganda Department in the Current Era," *Westminster Papers in Communication and Culture* (London: University of Westminster, 2006).
171. Li Changchun, speech made on the occasion of the 50th anniversary of China Central Television. See David Bandurski, "Li Changchun on the Media and China's 'Global Influence'," China Media Project. *http://cmp.hku.hk/2009/01/19/1457.*
172. David Bandurski, "Li Changchun on the Media and China's 'Global Influence'," China Media Project, *http://cmp.hku.hk/2009/01/19/1457.*
173. US-China Economic and Security Review Commission, *Hearing on China's Propaganda and Influence Operations, Its Intelligence Activities that Target the United States, and the Resulting Impacts on US National Security,* testimony of Jacqueline Newmyer, April 30, 2009.
174. Hu Baijing, "A Careful Analysis of China's Public Relations Map," *Guoji Xianqu Daobao* "(International Herald Leader On-Line), February 3, 2009. Available as "PRC Scholar Draws Road Map for China's Public Relations Campaign," February 3, 2009. OSC ID: CPP20090210671006. *http://www.opensource.gov.* The article is cited in US-China Economic and Security Review Commission, *Hearing on China's* Propaganda and Influence Operations, Its Intelligence Activities that Target the *United States, and the Resulting Impacts on US National Security,* testimony of Jacqueline Newmyer, April 30, 2009.
175. Hu Baijing, "A Careful Analysis of China's Public Relations Map," *Guoji Xianqu Daobao* (International Herald Leader On-Line), February 3, 2009. Available as "PRC

Scholar Draws Road Map for China's Public Relations Campaign," February 3, 2009. OSC ID: CPP20090210671006. *http://www.opensource.gov.* The article is cited in US-ChinaEconomic and Security Review Commission, *Hearing on China's* Propaganda and Influence Operations, Its Intelligence Activities that Target the *United States, and the Resulting Impacts on US National Security,* testimony of Jacqueline Newmyer, April 30, 2009.

176. US-China Economic and Security Review Commission, *Hearing on China's* Propaganda and Influence Operations, Its Intelligence Activities that Target the *United States, and the Resulting Impacts on US National Security,* testimony of Nicholas J. Cull, April 30, 2009.

177. US-China Economic and Security Review Commission, *Hearing on China's Propaganda and Influence Operations, Its Intelligence Activities that Target the United States, and the Resulting Impacts on US National Security,* testimony of Nicholas J. Cull, April 30, 2009.

178. Nicholas Bequelin, "China's New Propaganda Machine," *Wall Street Journal,* January 29, 2009.

179. Li Changchun, speech made on the occasion of the 50th anniversary of China Central Television. See David Bandurski, "Li Changchun on the Media and China's 'Global Influence'," China Media Project. *http://cmp.hku.hk/2009/01/19/1457.*

180. US-China Economic and Security Review Commission, *Hearing on China's Propaganda and Influence Operations, Its Intelligence Activities that Target the United States, and the Resulting Impacts on US National Security,* testimony of Anne-Marie Brady, April 30, 2009.

181. US-China Economic and Security Review Commission, *Hearing on China's Propaganda and Influence Operations, Its Intelligence Activities that Target the United States, and the Resulting Impacts on US National Security,* testimony of Judy Polumbaum, April 30, 2009.

182. China Central Television International Web site, "Profile of CCTV.com." *http://ww.cctv.com/english/20090123/107205.shtml.*

183. Agence France-Presse, "China Launches Arabic International TV Channel," July 25, 2009.

184. China Central Television International Web site, "Profile of CCTV.com." *http://www.cctv.com/english/20090123/107205.shtml.*

185. Anne-Marie Brady, *Marketing Dictatorship: Propaganda and Thought Work in Contemporary China* (Lanham, MD: Rowman and Littlefield, 2008), p. 167.

186. US-China Economic and Security Review Commission, *Hearing on China's Propaganda and Influence Operations, Its Intelligence Activities that Target the United States, and the Resulting Impacts on US National Security,* testimony of Anne-Marie Brady, April 30, 2009.

187. *China Daily* Web site, "About China Daily." *http://www.chinadaily.com.cn/cd/* introduction.html.

188. As per calculation by Commission staff, an average yearly expenditure of $726,387.27 per year between 2003 and 2008 was paid to the China Daily Distribution Corporation, based in New York, NY. Based on data obtained from the US Department of Justice, *Report of the Attorney General to the Congress of the United* States on the Administration of the Foreign Agents Registration Act of 1938, as *Amended, for the Six Months Ending June 30, 2003* (Washington, DC: February 2004); *for the Six Months Ending December 31, 2003* (November 2004); *for the Six Months Ending June 30, 2004* (February 2006);

for the Six Months Ending December 31, 2004 (February 2006); *for the Six Months Ending June 30, 2005* (March 2006); *for the Six Months Ending December 31, 2005* (November 2006); *for the Six MonthsEnding June 30, 2006* (June 2007); *for the Six Months Ending December 31, 2006* (November 2007); *for the Six Months Ending June 30, 2007* (February 2008); *for the Six Months Ending December 31, 2007* (October 2008); *for the Six Months Ending June 30, 2008* (February 2009); *and for the Six Months Ending December 31, 2008* (July 2009).

189. *China Radio International English Service On-Line,* "Who We Are." *http://english.cri.cn/about_us/who-we-are.htm.*

190. *China Radio International On-Line, "Zhongguo Guoji Guangbo Diantai"* (China RadioInternational). Translation by Commission staff. *http://gb.cri.cn/21344/ 2007/09/29/1885@1788521.htm.*

191. US-China Economic and Security Review Commission, *Hearing on China's Propaganda and Influence Operations, Its Intelligence Activities that Target the United States, and the Resulting Impacts on US National Security,* testimony of Anne-Marie Brady, April 30, 2009.

192. US-China Economic and Security Review Commission, *Hearing on China's Propaganda and Influence Operations, Its Intelligence Activities that Target the United States, and the Resulting Impacts on US National Security,* testimony of Nicholas J. Cull, April 30, 2009.

193. US-China Economic and Security Review Commission, *Hearing on China's Propaganda and Influence Operations, Its Intelligence Activities that Target the United States, and the Resulting Impacts on US National Security,* testimony of Anne-Marie Brady, April 30, 2009.

194. China News Service Web site, "China News Service English Introduction." *http://www.chinanews.com.cn/common/footer/aboutus.shtml.*

195. Mei Duzhe, "How China's Government is Attempting to Control Chinese Media in America," *China Brief* 1:10 (November 21, 2001); see also Anne-Marie Brady, *Marketing Dictatorship: Propaganda and Thought Work in Contemporary China* (Lanham, MD: Rowman and Littlefield, 2008), p. 167.

196. Examples of Chinese language newspapers published in the United States include the overseas edition of the *Renmin Ribao* (People's Daily); *Qiao Bao* (Overseas Chinese Times); *Shijie Ribao* (World Times); and *Sing Tao Ribao* (Star Island Daily), the US edition of major Hong Kong newspaper.

197. Per calculation by Commission staff, a total average yearly expenditure of $2,133,782.69 between 2003 and 2008 was paid to Hai Tian Development USA (Flushing, NY) for distribution of the overseas edition of *People's Daily;* and to Xin Min International (Alhambra, CA) for distribution of *Xin Min Wan Bao* (New People's Evening News). A third company, KMC Trading (Oakland, CA) also performed services during at least part of this period (2003 to 2005) for distribution of the overseas version of *People's Daily* as well as other periodicals but did not disclose its remuneration for these services. Calculations based on data obtained from the US Department of Justice, *Report of the Attorney General to the Congress of the United* States on the Administration of the Foreign Agents Registration Act of 1938, as *Amended, for the Six Months Ending June 30, 2003* (Washington, DC: February 2004); *for the Six Months Ending December 31, 2003* (November 2004):, *for the Six Months Ending June 30, 2004* (February 2006); *for the Six Months Ending December 31, 2004* (February 2006; *for the Six Months Ending June 30, 2005* (March 2006): *for the Six Months Ending December 31, 2005* (November 2006); *for the Six Months Ending June 30, 2006* (June 2007); *for the Six*

Months Ending December 31, 2006 (November 2007); *for the Six Months Ending* 1. Madeline Earp (Asia research associate with the Committee to Protect Journalists), telephone interview with Commission staff, August 14, 2009; U.S.-China *June 30, 2007* (February 2008);, *for the Six Months Ending December 31, 2007* (October 2008): *for the Six Months Ending June 30, 2008* (February 2009); and *for the Six Months Ending December 31, 2008* (July 2009).

198. US-China Economic and Security Review Commission, *Hearing on China's* Propaganda and Influence Operations, Its Intelligence Activities that Target the *United States, and the Resulting Impacts on US National Security,* testimony of Anne-Marie Brady, April 30, 2009; see also "On the Subject of Misinformation," China Brief 1:11 (December 10, 2001).

199. US-China Economic and Security Review Commission, *Hearing on China's Propaganda and Influence Operations, Its Intelligence Activities that Target the United States, and the Resulting Impacts on US National Security,* testimony of Anne-Marie Brady, April 30, 2009.

200. "Protests Still Unwelcome in Beijing," BBC News, August 14, 2008. *http://news.bbc.co.uk/2/hi/asia-pacific/7559217.stm.*

201. On the employment of "proactive" propaganda, see David Shambaugh, "China's Propaganda System: Institutions, Processes and Efficacy," *China Journal* no. 57 (January 2007). For discussion of the suppression of negative news, see Ashley Esarey, "Speak No Evil: Mass Media Control in Contemporary China," Freedom House Special Report (Washington, DC: February 2006). *http:// www. freedom house. org/uploads/special_report/33.pdf.*

202. Andrew Nathan and Perry Link, eds., *The Tiananmen Papers* (New York: Public Affairs Books, 2001), pp. 120, 453.

203. He Qinglian, *The Fog of Censorship: Media Control in China* (New York: Human Rights in China, 2008), pp. 71–75.

204. For comments regarding Chinese official assumptions that the US media is under government control, see US-China Economic and Security Review Commission, Hearing on China's Propaganda and Influence Operations, Its Intelligence Activities that Target the United States, and the Resulting Impacts on US National Security, testimony of Ross Terrill, April 30, 2009. For discussion of the PRC government's concept of "information sovereignty," see US-China Economic and Security Review Commission, *2008 Annual Report to Congress* (Washington, DC: November 2008), pp. 293–295.

205. Carsten Holz, "Have China Scholars All Been Bought?" *Far Eastern Economic Review* (April 2007).

206. Elizabeth Redden, "The Blacklist Academic Leaders Ignore," *Inside Higher Education* (July 14, 2008).

207. Elizabeth Redden, "The Blacklist Academic Leaders Ignore," *Inside Higher Education* (July 14, 2008).

208. Communications between Commission staff and multiple academics (individual names withheld), 2009.

209. Paul Mooney, "Want Access? Go Easy on China," *The National* (UAE), June 21, 2008.

210. Perry Link, "Turned Back at China's Door," *Princeton Alumni Weekly,* February 9,2005.

211. Perry Link, "The Anaconda in the Chandelier: Chinese Censorship Today," *New York Review of Books,* 49, no. 6 (April 11, 2002).

212. Orville Schell interview, *Media Studies Journal* 13:1 (Winter 1999), p. 72. The quote is cited in US-China Economic and Security Review Commission, *Hearing on China's Propaganda and Influence Operations, Its Intelligence Activities that Target the United States, and the Resulting Impacts on US National Security,* testimony of Jacqueline Newmyer, April 30, 2009.
213. US-China Economic and Security Review Commission, *Hearing on China's Propaganda and Influence Operations, Its Intelligence Activities that Target the United States, and the Resulting Impacts on US National Security,* testimony of Ross Terrill, April 30, 2009.
214. US-China Economic and Security Review Commission, *Hearing on China's Media and Information Controls: The Impact in China and the United States,* testimony of Perry Link, September 10, 2009.
215. US-China Economic and Security Review Commission, *Hearing on China's Media and Information Controls: The Impact in China and the United States,* testimony of Victor Shih, September 10, 2009.
216. Perry Link, as cited in Elizabeth Redden, "The Blacklist Academic Leaders Ignore," *Inside Higher Education* (July 14, 2008).
217. Edward Friedman, as cited in Paul Mooney, "Want Access? Go Easy on China," *The National* (UAE), June 21, 2008.
218. US-China Economic and Security Review Commission, *Hearing on China's Propaganda and Influence Operations, Its Intelligence Activities that Target the United States, and the Resulting Impacts on US National Security,* testimony of Ross Terrill, April 30, 2009.
219. US-China Economic and Security Review Commission, *Annual Report to Congress 2008* (Washington, DC: November 2008), p. 292.
220. Michael Pillsbury, "China's Research Institutes" (contracted research paper for the US-China Economic and Security Review Commission, October 2001). *http://www.uscc.gov/researchpapers/2000_2003/pdfs/cri.pdf*
221. Cheng Li, "China's New Think Tanks: Where Officials, Entrepreneurs, and Scholars Interact," *China Leadership Monitor* 29 (Summer 2009).
222. Carsten A. Holz, "Have China Scholars All Been Bought?" *Far Eastern Economic Review (*April 2007).
223. China Institutes for Contemporary International Relations, "*Ben Yuan Jieshao*" (Introduction to this Institute). *http://www.cicir.ac.cn/tbscms/html/byjj.asp.*
224. Calculation by Commission staff based on listings of academic exchanges on the CICIR Web site. See China Institutes for Contemporary International Relations, "Academic Exchange." *http://www.cicir.ac.cn/tbscms/html/xsjl_en.asp?rid= xsjl_en.*
225. Representatives of the China Institutes for Contemporary International Relations, discussions with Commissioners of the US-China Economic and Security Review Commission, Beijing, China, March 31, 2008, and May 4, 2009.
226. US National Intelligence Council, *Global Trends 2025: A Transformed World* (Washington, DC: November 2008), p. 6. *http://www.dni.gov/nic/PDF_2025/2025_Global_Trends_Final_Report.pdf.*
227. Hill & Knowlton home page, "About Hill & Knowlton." *http://www.hillandknowlton.com/about.*
228. Hill & Knowlton press release, "Hill & Knowlton Launches 'Global Communications' Services for Chinese Companies 'Going Global'," December 12, 2008. *http: //www.wpp.com/NR/rdonlyres/4763D621-1207-49B0-99E6-96DF5D778B66/29244/hill*

knowlton /press release_comms_ china_ dec08_ guid8c.pdf?pageContent_PressRelease.

229. US-China Economic and Security Review Commission, *Hearing on China's Propaganda and Influence Operations, Its Intelligence Activities that Target the United States, and the Resulting Impacts on US National Security,* testimony of Nicholas J. Cull, April 30, 2009.

230. Contract between Hill & Knowlton and the Embassy of the People's Republic of China, dated June 26, 1991, obtained by Commission staff from the Foreign Agents Registration Act library of the US Department of Justice (Washington, DC: July 2009).

231. Joshua Cooper Ramo, "Brand China" (London, UK: Foreign Policy Centre, February 2007). *http://joshuaramo.com/_files/pdf/Brand-China.pdf.* The study was published by the Foreign Policy Centre, a U.K. think tank, which lists Hill & Knowlton as one of its corporate sponsors. See Foreign Policy Centre, "Our Partners." *http://fpc.org.uk/membership.* The study itself states in its acknowledgements on page 3 that "[t]he Foreign Policy Centre would also like to thank Hill & Knowlton for their support of this project"—the only corporate sponsor so identified. Hill & Knowlton also has a promotional statement at the end of the report on page 49.

232. Professional Web page of Joshua Cooper-Ramo, "Bio + Book Speeches." *http://joshuaramo.com/contact-bio/index.php.*

233. Notes taken by Commission staff from the National Broadcasting Corporation's broadcast coverage of the opening ceremonies of the 2008 Beijing Olympic Games, August 8, 2008. See also "Joshua Cooper Ramo: Who Is NBC's China Analyst during the Olympics?" *Huffington Post,* August 13, 2008. *http:// www.huffingtonpost.com/2008/08/11/joshua-cooper-ramo-who-is_n_118225.html.*

234. US Department of Justice, *Report of the Attorney General to the Congress of the United States on the Administration of the Foreign Agents Registration Act of 1938, as Amended, for the Six Months Ending June 30, 2007* (Washington, DC: February 2008); *for the Six Months Ending December 31, 2007* (October 2008); and *for the Six Months Ending June 30, 2008* (February 2009).

235. Anne-Marie Brady, "A Campaign of Mass Distraction," *China Quarterly* (March 2009).

236. Anne-Marie Brady, "A Campaign of Mass Distraction," *China Quarterly* (March 2009).

237. US-China Economic and Security Review Commission, *Hearing on China's Propaganda and Influence Operations, Its Intelligence Activities that Target the United States, and the Resulting Impacts on US National Security,* testimony of Anne-Marie Brady, April 30, 2009.

238. *Economist Intelligence Unit,* "China Joins a Favourite Washington Game," June 11, 2007.

239. Richard Suen and Round Square Company, Ltd., Stephens Medial, LLC vs. Sheldon Adelson et al., William P. Weidner, Las Vegas Sands, Inc., case #A493744 of the District Court of Clark County, Nevada, 2008, testimony of Sheldon Adelson, presented April 17, 2008.

240. Text of H.Con.Res.73, 107th Cong., 1st sess., introduced March 21, 2001. *http://thomas.loc.gov/cgi-bin/bdquery/D?d107:1:./temp/¡-bdJBxq::*

241. See Howard Stutz, "Adelson Fights Lawsuit," *Las Vegas Review-Journal* (April 18, 2008); and Connie Bruck, "The Brass Ring," *The New Yorker,* June 30, 2008. *http: // www.newyorker.com/reporting/2008/06/30/080630fa_lfact_*bruck? currentPage=all.

242. "Major Congressional Actions," H.Con.Res.73, 107th Cong., 1st sess., introduced March 21, 2001. *http://thomas.loc.gov/cgi-bin/bdquery/z?d107:HC00073: @@@R.*

243. As examples, see Erin Ennis, "All Quiet on the Potomac?" *China Business Review* (July-August 2006); and US-China Business Council press release, "US-China Business Council Statement on China Currency Legislation Delay," *PR Newswire US,* June 30, 005.
244. Neil King Jr., "Beijing on the Potomac," *Washingtonian,* January 2007.
245. Trade Policy Staff Committee (acting in support of the US-China Trade Representative), *Hearing Concerning China's Compliance with WTO Commitments,* written testimony of US-China Business Council President John Frisbie (Washington, DC, October 2, 2009). *http://www.uschina.org/public/documents/2009/10/ wto_testimony.pdf.*
246. Bara Vaida, "Red Star Rising on K Street," *National Journal,* July 23, 2005; and *Economist Intelligence Unit,* "China Joins a Favourite Washington Game," June 11, 2007.
247. Bara Vaida, "Red Star Rising on K Street," *National Journal,* July 23, 2005.
248. *Economist Intelligence Unit,* "China Joins a Favourite Washington Game," June 11, 2007.
249. Justin Blum, "Shareholders Vote in Favour of Unocal Acquisition," *Washington Post. http://www.washingtonpost.com/wp-dyn/content/article/2005/08/10/* AR2005081000986.html.
250. Calculations by Commission staff based on data obtained from the US Department of Justice, *Report of the Attorney General to the Congress of the United* States *on the Administration of the Foreign Agents Registration Act of 1938, as Amended, for the Six Months Ending June 30, 2006* (Washington, DC: June 2007); *for the Six Months Ending December 31, 2006* (November 2007); *for the Six Months Ending June 30, 2007* (February 2008); *for the Six Months Ending December 31, 2007* (October 2008); *for the Six Months Ending June 30, 2008* (February 2009); and *for the Six Months Ending December 31, 2008* (July 2009).
251. US Department of Justice, *Report of the Attorney General to the Congress of the United States on the Administration of the Foreign Agents Registration Act of 1938, as Amended, for the Six Months Ending June 30, 2005* (Washington, DC: Marc0h 2006); and *for the Six Months Ending December 31, 2005* (November 2006). \
252. Michael Forsythe. "China Plays the Lobbying Game," *International Herald Tribune,* April 19, 2006.
253. US Department of Justice, *Report of the Attorney General to the Congress of the United States on the Administration of the Foreign Agents Registration Act of 1938, as Amended, for the Six Months Ending June 30, 2006* (Washington, DC: June 2007); and *for the Six Months Ending December 31, 2006* (November 2007)..
254. US Department of Justice, *Report of the Attorney General to the Congress of the United States on the Administration of the Foreign Agents Registration Act of 1938, as Amended, for the Six Months Ending June 30, 2006* (Washington, DC: June 2007); and *for the Six Months Ending December 31, 2006* (November 2007).
255. US Department of Justice, *Report of the Attorney General to the Congress of the United States on the Administration of the Foreign Agents Registration Act of 1938, as Amended, for the Six Months Ending June 30, 2006* (Washington, DC: June 2007); and *for the Six Months Ending December 31, 2006* (November 2007).
256. US Department of Justice, *Report of the Attorney General to the Congress of the United States on the Administration of the Foreign Agents Registration Act of 1938, as Amended, for the Six Months Ending June 30, 2006* (Washington, DC: June 2007); and *for the Six Months Ending December 31, 2006* (November 2007).
257. US Department of Justice, *Report of the Attorney General to the Congress of the United States on the Administration of the Foreign Agents Registration Act of 1938, as*

Amended, for the Six Months Ending June 30, 2007 (Washington, DC: February 2008); and *for the Six Months Ending December 31, 2007* (October 2008).

258. US Department of Justice, *Report of the Attorney General to the Congress of the United States on the Administration of the Foreign Agents Registration Act of 1938, as Amended, for the Six Months Ending June 30, 2007* (Washington, DC: February 2008); and *for the Six Months Ending December 31, 2007* (October 2008).
259. US Department of Justice, *Report of the Attorney General to the Congressof the United States on the Administration of the Foreign Agents Registration Act of 1938, as Amended, for the Six Months Ending June 30, 2007* (Washington, DC:February 2008); and *for the Six Months Ending December 31, 2007* (October 2008);US Department of Justice, *Report of the Attorney General to the Congress of theUnited States on the Administration of the Foreign Agents Registration Act of 1938, as Amended, for the Six Months Ending June 30, 2008* (Washington, DC: February2009).
260. US Department of Justice, *Report of the Attorney General to the Congress of the United States on the Administration of the Foreign Agents Registration Act of 1938, as Amended, for the Six Months Ending June 30, 2008* (Washington, DC: February 2009); and *for the Six Months Ending December 31, 2008* (July 2009).
261. US Department of Justice, *Report of the Attorney General to the Congress of the United States on the Administration of the Foreign Agents Registration Act of 1938, as Amended, for the Six Months Ending December 31, 2008* (July 2009).
262. Bara Vaida, "Red Star Rising on K Street," *National Journal,* July 23, 2005.
263. US Department of Justice, *Report of the Attorney General to the Congress of the United States on the Administration of the Foreign Agents Registration Act of 1938, as Amended, for the Six Months Ending December 31, 2005* (Washington, DC: November 2006).
264. *Economist Intelligence Unit,* "China Joins a Favourite Washington Game," June 11, 2007. *See also US Department of Justice, Report of the Attorney General to the Congress of the United States on the Administration of the Foreign Agents Registration Act of 1938, as Amended, for the Six Months Ending June 30, 2006* (Washington, DC: June 2007); and *for the Six Months Ending December 31, 2006* (November 2007).
265. Lenovo Group, Ltd., disclosure under Lobbying Disclosure Act, dated August 10, 2006. Accessed via the US Senate Lobbying Disclosure Act database. *http:/ www.senate.gov/legislative/Public_Disclosure/LDA_reports.htm.*
266. Hogan & Hartson disclosure under the Lobbying Disclosure Act (US Senate Identification Number 18422--1004011), dated August 30, 2007. Accessed via the US Senate Lobbying Disclosure Act database. *http://www.senate.gov/legislative/Public_Disclosure/LDA_reports.htm.*
267. US Department of Justice, *Report of the Attorney General to the Congress of the United States on the Administration of the Foreign Agents Registration Act of 1938, as Amended, for the Six Months Ending June 30, 2007* (Washington, DC: February 2008); and *for the Six Months Ending December 31, 2007* (October 2008).
268. International Government Relations Group disclosure under the Lobbying Disclosure Act, dated November 30, 2008. Accessed via the US Senate Lobbying Disclosure Act database. *http://www.senate.gov/legislative/Public_Disclosure/LDA_ reports.htm.*
269. Michael Forsythe, "China Plays the Lobbying Game," *International Herald Tribune,* April 19, 2006; and "China Joins a Favourite Washington Game," *Economist Intelligence Unit,* June 11, 2007.

Comprehensive List of the Commission's Recommendations

Chapter 1

The US-China Trade and Economic Relationship

Section 1: *The US-China Trade and Economic Relationship's Current Status and Significant Changes During 2009*

1. The Commission recommends that Congress urge the administration to employ more aggressively all trade remedies authorized by World Trade Organization (WTO) rules to counteract the Chinese government's practices. The Commission further recommends that Congress urge the administration to ensure that US trade remedy laws are preserved and effectively implemented to respond to China's unfair or predatory trade activities.
2. The Commission recommends that Congress urge the United States Trade Representative (USTR) to strengthen its oversight of China's compliance with the rulings of the WTO's dispute settlement panels.
3. The Commission recommends that Congress urge the USTR, as part of its annual National Trade Estimates report, to identify and prioritize for elimination barriers in China limiting the export of US goods and services.
4. The Commission recommends that Congress undertake oversight of the Strategic and Economic Dialogue to ensure that the talks benefit American farmers, workers, and businesses.
5. The Commission recommends that Congress direct the US Department of the Treasury to report annually on the status of the US dollar as the world's reserve currency. This report should highlight actions, if any, taken during the reporting period by China and other nations that may contribute to the erosion of this status.

Section 2: *China's Role in the Origins of the Global Financial Crisis and China's Response*

6. The Commission recommends that Congress urge the administration to press China to allow the renminbi (RMB) to become flexible and responsive to market forces, thereby contributing to the correction of global economic imbalances. The Commission further recommends that Congress consider legislation that has the effect of offsetting the impact on the US economy of China's currency manipulation.
7. The Commission recommends that Congress pass legislation urging the administration to report specifically on information regarding Chinese-sourced products and services used in US federally funded stimulus programmes and make this information available to the public on a periodic basis.

Section 3: *China's Industrial Policy and its Impact on US Companies, Workers, and the American Economy*

8. The Commission recommends that Congress urge the administration to employ more aggressively trade remedies to counteract the Chinese government's

subsidies to favoured industries. The Commission further recommends that Congress assess the adequacy of the resources of the US Department of Commerce to investigate such subsidies.

9. The Commission recommends that Congress urge the National Science Foundation to study and recommend to Congress ways to enhance the effectiveness of basic and applied research programmes in the United States, with particular emphasis on advancing the competitiveness of key domestic production sectors.
10. The Commission recommends that Congress urge the US Department of Commerce to prepare an annual report on productive capacity in China in major industrial sectors. The report should identify what steps, if any, China has taken to develop, expand, retract, or change the utilization of capacity in these sectors over the previous years.
11. The Commission recommends that Congress urge the US Department of Commerce to develop rules and procedures for the collection and evaluation of information on the activities of US companies in terms of their sourcing arrangements with producers (whether independent, joint venture, subsidiary, or other relationship) in China, to the extent authorized by law. The US Department of Commerce shall prepare an annual report, based on this information, identifying changing sourcing patterns and key areas of interest and concern. This information should be subject to business proprietary confidentiality and only utilized in the report, to the extent practicable, on an aggregate basis.
12. The Commission recommends that Congress urge the United States Trade Representative to evaluate the use of selective value added tax rebates by China and their trade-distorting effect and determine what steps, if any, should be taken to address the issue.

Section 4: *China's Industrial Policy and its Impact on Upstate New York*

13. The Commission recommends that Congress explore the economic benefits to local communities of a national innovation strategy to meet the challenges of China's industrial policy.
14. The Commission recommends that Congress request the National Academy of Sciences to conduct a study on the impact of outsourcing of manufacturing on US domestic research, development, and innovation.
15. The Commission recommends that Congress urge the Department of Energy, in consultation with other appropriate agencies, to report to Congress on the impact of Chinese subsidies and other elements of China's industrial policy on US-based companies manufacturing clean energy products.

CHAPTER 2

CHINA'S ACTIVITIES DIRECTLY AFFECTING US SECURITY INTERESTS

Section 1: *China's Military and Security Activities Abroad*

16. The Commission recommends that Congress make freedom of navigation a priority issue in its US-China interparliamentary exchanges.

17. The Commission recommends Congress urge the administration to encourage further People's Liberation Army (PLA) participation in United Nations (UN) multinational security operations.
18. To emphasize continued US commitments to and interests in the region, the Commission recommends that Congress encourage the US Department of Defence to maintain and strengthen military diplomacy with nations throughout East Asia.

Section 2: *China's Naval Modernization*

19. The Commission recommends that Congress assess the adequacy of planning and resourcing of US Department of Defence programmes that would limit China's anti-access capabilities. In particular, Congress should focus on antisubmarine warfare and ballistic missile defence programmes. Congress should also assess the adequacy of funding and resources for the US Department of Defence's Pacific Command.
20. The Commission recommends that Members of Congress in their interparliamentary exchanges encourage Beijing to increase the transparency of its naval modernization efforts. Of particular interest are China's aircraft carrier, antiship ballistic missile, and ballistic missile submarine programmes, as well as its naval expansion and modernization efforts.
21. The Commission recommends that Congress urge the US Department of Defence to continue to interact actively with US allies and friends in Asia to reassure them of the US's commitment to the region.
22. The Commission recommends that Congress encourage the administration to continue to push for more engagement between the US Navy and the PLA Navy as a confidence-building measure.
23. The Commission recommends that Congress encourage the administration to consider establishing a formal mechanism for preventing and managing maritime incidents between the US and Chinese navies.

Section 3: *China's Human Espionage Activities that Target the United States, and the Resulting Impacts on US National Security*

24. The Commission recommends that Congress assess the adequacy of resources available for intelligence, counterintelligence, and export control enforcement programmes to ensure that US government agencies are able to meet the rising challenge of Chinese human intelligence and illicit technology collection.
25. The Commission recommends that Congress assess the adequacy of resources available for China-oriented counterintelligence awareness and law enforcement programmes throughout the US government and contractor community.
26. The Commission recommends that Members of Congress in their interparliamentary exchanges raise US concerns regarding the monitoring and harassment of US citizens and legal permanent residents by agents of the Chinese government.

Section 4: *China's Cyber Activities that Target the United States, and the Resulting Impacts on US National Security*

27. The Commission recommends that Congress assess the effectiveness of and resourcing for law enforcement, defence, and intelligence community initiatives

that aim to develop effective and reliable attribution techniques for computer exploitation and computer attacks.

28. The Commission recommends that Congress urge the administration to develop measures to deter malicious Chinese cyber activity that is directed at critical US infrastructure and US government information systems.

Chapter 3

China in Asia

Section 1: *China in Afghanistan, Pakistan, and Central Asia*

29. The Commission recommends that Congress encourage the administration to continue to work with China to utilize its influence with Islamabad to bolster Pakistan's stability and prevent the Taliban from gaining control of the region.
30. The Commission recommends that Congress encourage the administration to examine carefully development programmes and investment opportunities in Afghanistan and work with US private businesses interested in investing there to ensure that they are able to compete effectively with Chinese state-owned companies.

Section 2: *Taiwan*

31. The Commission recommends that Congress urge the administration to support recent improvements in the cross-Strait relationship.
32. The Commission recommends that Congress urge the administration to take additional steps to encourage the People's Republic of China (PRC) to demonstrate the sincerity of its desire for improved cross-Strait relations by drawing down the number of forces, including missiles, opposite Taiwan.
33. The Commission recommends that Congress encourage the administration to identify opportunities to strengthen bilateral economic relations between the United States and Taiwan.
34. The Commission recommends that Congress encourage the administration to continue to work with Taiwan to modernize its armed forces, with particular emphasis on air defence needs.

Section 3: *Hong Kong*

35. The Commission recommends that Members of Congress, when visiting mainland China, also visit Hong Kong and that Congress encourage senior administration officials, including the secretary of State, to make visits to Hong Kong part of their travel. The Commission also recommends that Members of Congress seek dialogue with members of the Legislative Council of Hong Kong.
36. The Commission recommends that Congress encourage its Members to raise the issue of preserving Hong Kong's special status when meeting with members of China's National People's Congress.
37. The Commission recommends that Congress reenact the United States-Hong Kong Policy Act of 1992, which expired in 2007.
38. The Commission recommends that Congress examine and assess the adequacy of US export control policy for dual-use technology as it relates to the treatment

of Hong Kong and the PRC as separate customs entities. The Commission further recommends that Congress urge the administration to consider ways to collaborate more closely with the authorities in Hong Kong in order to prevent the transshipment of controlled technologies from Hong Kong into the PRC.

Chapter 4

China's Media and Information Controls —The Impact in China and the United States

Section 1: *Freedom of Expression in China*

39. The Commission recommends that Members of Congress in their interparliamentary exchanges continue to raise concerns regarding freedom of expression in China in their dialogues with officials of the Chinese government.
40. The Commission recommends that Congress continue to monitor and assess the development and progress of industry and other efforts to create and implement an effective code of ethics and best practices related to the operations of US high-tech firms in China and other authoritarian countries where Internet content and activity are controlled and monitored by the government.
41. The Commission recommends that Congress continue to monitor and assess the Chinese government's efforts to implement an end-user Internet control system. The Commission further recommends that Congress assess whether such efforts are compliant with China's commitments as a signatory to the World Trade Organization.

Section 2: *China's External Propaganda and Influence Operations, and the Resulting Impacts on the United States*

42. The Commission recommends that Congress urge the administration to have the US Department of State raise with its counterparts in the PRC Foreign Ministry concerns related to the denial of visas to US academics who require travel to China in order to engage in substantive research.

Additional Views of Commissioner

Patrick A. Mulloy

The Commission in this Report has attempted to elucidate the nature of the industrial policies and mercantilist trade practices that China has followed for 30 years to grow its economy at nearly a 10 percent annual rate. That unprecedented economic growth underpins the dramatic increase of China's military power and global political and financial influence that the Report also discusses.

It is important that our political leaders and citizens understand that these developments, with their enormous geopolitical implications, are not simply the outgrowth of free market forces and free trade. China's impressive economic growth stems from sophisticated economic policies adopted by that nation to restore its great power status. To help understand the context of what is happening, it is useful to review a little Chinese history.

China was for thousands of years the dominant power and civilization in Asia. The Chinese considered their Emperor the supreme political authority and themselves the geopolitical center of the world. China's Qing Dynasty (1644–1911) at its high point around 1760, was cultured and wealthy, held sway over a vast territory, and received tributes from neighboring states.

When the Western powers, whose strength was being fueled by industrialization and scientific advances, arrived in Asia in the 17th and 18th centuries, they sought to trade with the prosperous Chinese Empire. The Chinese viewed the new arrivals as barbarians, who offered little that China needed, and opened only the city of Canton as a port and then only on a part-time basis. In time the British found they could trade opium grown in India to the Chinese for the tea and porcelains the British wanted. In time the Chinese imperial authorities, disturbed by the harmful economic and social consequences of opium addiction, tried to shut off the opium imports. The British launched the first Opium War (1839–1843) in the name of free trade, and the Chinese were shocked to discover their opponent's superior military technologies and capabilities. Over the next 30 years, after a series of other conflicts between China and Western powers, the great Chinese Empire was reduced to a semi-colony. Only the so-called "Open Door" policy championed by the US government saved China from total dismemberment and formal colonization. The Chinese Empire and its once proud people were totally humiliated, and by 1911 the last Emperor fell and China experienced a period of civil wars, famine, and foreign invasion. The Chinese struggled to find a way to restore their lost great power status and standard of living.

The Communist Party, led by Mao Tse Tung, eventually triumphed over the Nationalists after a long civil war. On October 1, 1949, Mao announced the founding of the People's Republic of China (PRC) and proclaimed that "China has stood up." In short order he drove foreign influences, including foreign missionaries, out of China. The trauma suffered by China during its "century of humiliation" still drives China's policies. China's President Hu Jintao in an October 1, 2009, speech marking the founding of the PRC stated:

> *Sixty years ago today, the Chinese people after more than 100 years of bloody struggle, finally scored the great victory of the Chinese revolution. Sixty years ago, Chairman Mao solemnly proclaimed to the world the establishment of the People's Republic of China, and stated that the Chinese people had stood up. The Chinese nation, with some 5,000 years of civilization and history, thus entered a new historic era of development and progress.*

From 1949 to his death in 1976, Mao and his government attempted, without success, to restore China's great power status and rebuild its economy through a domestic-based, centrally planned economy. In the struggle for power after Mao's death, Deng Xiaoping emerged as China's new ruler. He promptly advocated in 1978 the development of a new economic programme which could help build what the Chinese call their "comprehensive national power." That new economic strategy was built on the concept of enticing foreigners to help China grow its economy by attracting their capital, technology, know-how, and markets. Since 1978 China has grown increasingly sophisticated in its use of investment incentives such as subsidies, an underpriced currency, and import barriers. The goal is to induce foreign companies, including US-based multinationals, to increase their profits by transferring production facilities, advanced technologies, and increasingly even research and development to China, where goods could be made and sold in China and also exported to America and other markets.

Since 1979, when America established official diplomatic relations with the PRC and granted it annual most-favoured-nation (MFN) trading status, our country has run approximately $2 trillion worth of trade deficits with China. Since 2001 alone, when China joined the WTO and thereby locked permanent MFN (with its low tariffs) into place, outsourcing by US and other foreign companies of production to China has increased dramatically, and our China trade deficits have totaled approximately $1.5 trillion since then. Sixty per cent of China's exports are produced by foreign-invested companies.

I would have no objection to China's growth if it was not being achieved at the expense of our own country's productive capacities and the future standard of living of our citizens and with the assistance of mercantilist trade practices that violate China's WTO and IMF treaty obligations. The shift of wealth and power from America to China that is described is this Report is not good for our nation.

After experiencing a century of decline, China developed a strategy to grow its comprehensive national power. Now our nation needs to develop a coordinated, comprehensive national policy and strategy to maintain our own manufacturing and technological base. That strategy should include modernizing our infrastructure, improving our educational system, reforming our health care system, and investing to develop new technologies. Even doing that will not be enough. We must also develop trade policies that will balance our trade account and tax policies that will incentivize American-based producers to keep good-paying jobs in this country.

Additional Views of Commissioner

William A. Reinsch and Robin Cleveland

We join our colleagues in endorsing this report. Commissioner Reinsch has in past years been critical of a number of the recommendations in previous reports, but this year's edition largely abandons suggestions that would disrupt our bilateral relationship if implemented.

The Commission continues its record of thorough, balanced hearings with expert witnesses from the government and the private sector. That body of work provides an in-depth set of studies on topics important to the bilateral relationship, and the hearing records contain significant amounts of data and other information of use to scholars and policymakers. In addition, now that its research contracting process has been established, the Commission has begun to fund more innovative research that will contribute significantly to our understanding of China. In the future, this is where the Commission's value added will lie. The hearings, while enlightening, risk becoming repetitive. There are only so many times one can review Chinese exchange rate policy, for example, and still learn something new. As the global economy recovers and visible irritants in the relationship are hopefully resolved, it makes more sense for the Commission to focus on research that examines some of the complex, underlying trends in China that may not make headlines today but that will challenge the relationship tomorrow.

This year's report, as usual, is critical of China on many points. Some are well-taken, but they are too often made out of fear rather than out of confidence. While blame is tempting in global policy debates—and often well placed—it is our destiny we control, not China's. Faulting Beijing for doing things in their own interest may be politically expedient but ultimately an empty gesture. Our leaders serve our people best when they act in our interests and when they persuade the Chinese to work with us in pursuit of common interests.

One such area of growing importance is climate change, a global commons issue where our interests are aligned. There, in many ways, the Chinese have quietly made progress, which is admittedly easier for them since they do not have an independent legislative process with which to contend. However, they still have not taken the lead in the developing world by stepping up with clear public commitments on reducing their emissions. The report does not review this important issue nor discuss the progress made. We hope China's policies on climate change and environmental degradation will be a matter for consideration in hearings early next year.

An additional area of growing concern is the disturbing trend away from the evolution toward a market system. When Jiang Zemin and Zhu Rongji led the government, there was an uneven but nonetheless consistent march in the direction of a market economy. Hu Jintao and Wen Jiabao, on the other hand, have halted that trend and in some areas reversed it. Instead of concentrating on meeting its WTO obligations, welcoming foreign investment, and encouraging private sector activity, the current government has turned to selecting national champions, increasing subsidies and selective tax benefits, creating new standards barriers, and discouraging joint ventures. These actions will make China's economic relations with the rest of the world more acrimonious, as already can be seen in the growing number of unfair trade complaints being filed against China by many countries.

In the short term, this is a problem for the United States and the other victims of their practices; in the long run, it will be a problem for China as it will magnify distortions in its economy and create unsustainable bubbles. The United States has the unenviable challenge of trying to persuade China to change policies that appear to be quite successful for it in the short run by arguing that they make things worse for everybody in the long run.

As Commissioner Reinsch reflected in previous Reports, for China to become a responsible stakeholder does not simply mean that it must agree with us on all important issues. Each subsequent Report has reflected greater understanding of this point and the reality that we do best with China when we can explain to its leaders why a particular action is good for it rather than why that action is good for us. America's challenge is patience and perspective. Progress will inevitably be two steps forward and one step backward, and, most recently, the reverse. The Commission could perform a real service to Congress by making that point from time to time and recommending to Congress a degree of patience at the same time as we urge China to move more rapidly.

China, in turn, if it wishes to assume a global role commensurate with its size, potential, and aspirations, must understand and be prepared to assume the obligations of leadership, which often requires a degree of self-abnegation. China's leaders have demonstrated that they have a clear understanding of what is in their immediate interest. Their challenge will be to demonstrate they also understand what is in the larger interest of the global system of which they are a part, that the health of that system is inextricably tied with their own, and that they are prepared to act responsibly on that understanding.

APPENDIX - I

LIST OF RESEARCH MATERIAL

Funded Research Projects, 2009 *

> * The research projects listed below were funded in 2009. Upon acceptance by the Commission, the research material will be posted to the Commission's Web site *www.uscc.gov* in fiscal year 2010.

- Economist Intelligence Unit, *Report Examining Issues Surrounding a Potential Bilateral Investment Treaty Between the United States and the People's Republic of China*
- Defence Group, Inc., *Report Examining Reforms in the Defence Industry of the People's Republic of China. NSD Biogroup, LLC, Report Examining Potential Health & Safety Impacts of the Use of Chinese-Produced Raw Ingredients in the Manufacture of US Pharmaceutical Products*
- Northrop Grumman Corp., *Report Examining Capabilities of the People's Republic of China to Conduct Cyber Warfare and Computer Network Exploitation*
- Reperi, LLC, *Report Examining Potential National Security Implications of Chinese Investments in the Communications Industry*

* The material noted below is available online at *www.uscc.gov*.

> All of the Commissioned research projects listed below were prepared at the request of the Commission to support its deliberations and is intended to promote greater public understanding of the issues addressed by the Commission. Inclusion in the Report does not imply an endorsement by the Commission or any individual Commissioner of views expressed in the material.

*Completed and Released Research Studies by the Commission Awarded in 2008**

- Capital Trade, Inc.: *"An Assessment of China's Subsidies to Strategic and Heavyweight Industries"*
- MBG Information Services: *"China's Soaring Commercial and Financial Power: How it is Affecting the US and the World"*
- NSD BioGroup, LLC: *"Research Report on Chinese High- Tech Industries"*
- Science Applications International Corporation: *"Capabilities of the Chinese People's Liberation Army to Carry Out Military Action in the Event of a Regional Conflict"*

APPENDIX - II

ABBREVIATIONS AND ACRONYMS

AEW&C	Airborne Early Warning & Control Aircraft
ASEAN	Association of Southeast Asian Nations
AVIC	China Aviation Industry Corporation
C4ISR	Command, control, communications, computers, intelligence, surveillance, and reconnaissance
CCP	Chinese Communist Party
CCTV	China Central Television
Chinalco	China Aluminium Company
CIA	Central Intelligence Agency
CICIR	China Institutes for Contemporary International Relations
CIISS	China Institute of International Strategic Studies
CNOOC	China National Off-Shore Oil Corporation
DHS	Department of Homeland Security
DoD	Department of Defence
EU	European Union
FBI	Federal Bureau of Investigation
GATT	General Agreement on Tariffs and Trade
GDP	Gross domestic product
IMF	International Monetary Fund
NATO	North Atlantic Treaty Organization
NORINCO	China North Industries Corp.
NSA	National Security Agency
PLA	People's Liberation Army
PRC	People's Republic of China
RAT	Remote Administration Tool
RMB	Renminbi
SAR	Special Administrative Region
SARS	Severe Acute Respiratory Syndrome
3G	Third generation (wireless standard)
UN	United Nations
USDA	US Department of Agriculture
USTR	US Trade Representative
VAT	Value Added Tax
WAPI	Wireless Application Protocol Standard
WHO	World Health Organization
WTO	World Trade Organization